LEFT LEGALISM / LEFT CRITIQUE

Left Legalism / Left Critique

EDITED BY WENDY BROWN AND JANET HALLEY

DUKE UNIVERSITY PRESS / DURHAM & LONDON 2002

© 2002 Duke University Press   All rights reserved
Printed in the United States of America on acid-free paper ∞
Designed by Rebecca M. Gimenez   Typeset in Sabon by
Keystone Typesetting, Inc.   Library of Congress Cataloging-in-
Publication Data appear on the last printed page of this book.

CONTENTS

Acknowledgments / vii

Wendy Brown and Janet Halley
Introduction / 1

Richard T. Ford
Beyond "Difference": A Reluctant Critique of Legal Identity Politics / 38

Janet Halley
Sexuality Harassment / 80

Lauren Berlant
The Subject of True Feeling: Pain, Privacy, and Politics / 105

Mark Kelman and Gillian Lester
Ideology and Entitlement / 134

Duncan Kennedy
The Critique of Rights in Critical Legal Studies / 178

Judith Butler
Is Kinship Always Already Heterosexual? / 229

Michael Warner
Beyond Gay Marriage / 259

Katherine M. Franke
Putting Sex to Work / 290

Drucilla Cornell
Dismembered Selves and Wandering Wombs / 337

David Kennedy
When Renewal Repeats: Thinking against the Box / 373

Wendy Brown
Suffering the Paradoxes of Rights / 420

Contributors / 435

Index / 439

ACKNOWLEDGMENTS

The making of an anthology, and particularly one that involves the collaborative authorship of an introduction, is a more labor-intensive and socially extended process than appearances might suggest. We have been fortunate to have superb assistance in this work. For their critical readings of early drafts of the introduction, we are grateful to Judith Butler, Gail Hershatter, David Kennedy, and Duncan Kennedy. We benefited from thoughtful engagement with the text at the Jurisdictions Conference at Ohio State University in May 2000 and at Cornell University Law School in March 2001. In addition, anonymous readers for the manuscript at Duke University Press offered valuable suggestions for improvement.

We are grateful for the research and technical assistance offered by Anne Marie Calareso, Robyn Marasco, and Deeni Stevens. Robyn Marasco also prepared the index. Financial support of the project was generously provided by the Dorothy Redwine Estate, Richard W. Weiland, the Robert E. Paradise Faculty Scholarship for Excellence in Research and Teaching (all of Stanford University), the Harvard Law School, and the Academic Senate Committee on Research of the University of California, Berkeley.

For their permission to reprint previously published material, we acknowledge the following. Lauren Berlant, "The Subject of True Feeling: Pain, Privacy, and Politics" appeared in a longer version in *Cultural Pluralism, Identity Politics, and the Law* (Ann Arbor: University of Michigan Press, 1996). Mark Kelman and Gillian Lester, "Ideology and Entitlement," was originally published in *Jumping the Queue: An Inquiry into the Legal Treatment of Students with Learning Disabilities* (Cambridge, MA:

Harvard University Press. Copyright © 1997 by the President and Fellows of Harvard College). Duncan Kennedy, "The Critique of Rights in Critical Legal Studies," is drawn from material that originally appeared in *A Critique of Adjudication (fin de siècle)* (Cambridge, MA: Harvard University Press. Copyright © 1997 by the President and Fellows of Harvard College). Michael Warner, "Beyond Gay Marriage," appeared in a longer version in *The Trouble with Normal: Sex, Politics, and the Ethics of Queer Life* (New York: Simon and Schuster, 1999). Katherine M. Franke, "Putting Sex to Work," was originally published in the *Denver University Law Review* 75 (1998). Drucilla Cornell, "Dismembered Selves and Wandering Wombs," appeared in a longer version in *The Imaginary Domain: Abortion, Pornography, and Sexual Harassment* (New York: Routledge, 1995). David Kennedy, "When Renewal Repeats: Thinking against the Box," appeared in a different version in the *New York University Journal of International Law and Politics* 32 (2000). Wendy Brown, "Suffering the Paradoxes of Rights," originally appeared in *Constellations* 7.2 (2000). Judith Butler, "Is Kinship Always Already Heterosexual?" originally appeared in *differences: a journal of feminist cultural studies* 13, no. 1 (spring 2002).

WENDY BROWN AND JANET HALLEY

Introduction

A colleague of ours was giving a paper on the vexed problem of veiling among contemporary Islamic women and Western feminist responses to it.[1] From the audience, an American woman of South Asian descent challenged our colleague, a feminist Arab secularist, for intervening in a domain properly belonging to religious Arab women: "What right have you to be saying such things?" "Right?" our colleague responded. "I have no right—I have a critique!"

This collection emerges from conversations enjoyed and endured by the coeditors as we explored the intersection of certain progressive political projects we care about and certain intellectual undertakings we were pursuing. We were both veterans of various feminist, antiracist, multicultural, sexual liberationist, and antihomophobic efforts. We were both engaged, in different ways, in teaching, thinking, and writing about nationalism. We were both convinced that contemporary traditions of social, political, and literary theory offer rich hypotheses that can be vital ways of testing our own political situations and desires. And we shared an absorption with the many ways that the political projects in which we are involved depicted various elements in the legal system as "the problem" to which they address themselves and framed strategies for social change—indeed, models sometimes of justice itself—that turned in some crucial way on law reform.

Our intellectual and political concerns were thickly intertwined: if we could help identify effective ways to loosen the grip of gender strictures at work, in sex, at home; beat back even by an inch the effects of racism on the educational environments in which we work and social environments in which we live; slow down even by a moment the ranking and reranking of new immigrant groups in an ever more elaborate racial paradigm; pry apart even by a millimeter sexual shame from sexual desire; revive even slightly a practical critical recognition of the way a capitalist political economy shapes the parameters of freedom and equality in our time — we would think we'd really accomplished something.

But we were increasingly frustrated with ourselves and with the intellectual and political environment we were operating in. It seemed to us less and less an environment in which the question of what the left should be "for" and what kinds of concrete projects could embody and activate those visions was eagerly asked and openly debated. It also seemed to us less and less an environment in which left-allied critical assessments of any putatively progressive political or legal project were welcome. We reviewed, in this regard, all the times that we had let the following sentences — uttered by students, embedded in the work of valued colleagues, lobbed at academic progressives from allies "in the trenches" — slow down our thinking and persuade us to mince words:

- My injury is real; you are just theorizing.
- Why, just now, when women (blacks, Latinos, homosexuals) are finally gaining subjectivity, must we engage in a critique of the subject?
- Writing that's difficult to understand is elitist (and hence bad).
- Writing that's difficult to understand can't be politically effective; anyone who teaches, uses, or produces writing that's difficult to understand must not care about politically inflicted suffering.
- Difficult writing can't be understood by the masses, so it can't possibly be useful to political mobilization.
- Postmodern social and critical theory is an indulgence of "tenured radicals" and has nothing to say about how power really works.
- What can all these abstractions *do* for a woman living in a fifth-floor cold water walkup?
- It's easy to criticize; what do you have to offer that's better?
- You couldn't possibly understand, not being [fill in here the name of any congealed, subordinated identity], and therefore lack authority to speak about the needs of people bearing that identity.
- You couldn't possibly understand, not having had the experience of [fill in here the name of any politically inflicted suffering], and therefore lack authority to speak about how it feels or how to stop it.

- The dignity of my group depends on [fill in the name of any law re-form effort undertaken to address group-based stigma]; questioning the premises of that law reform effort reinflicts the stigma.
- The safety and survival of my group depend on [fill in the name of any law reform effort undertaken to protect a subordinated group]; questioning the premises of that law reform effort endorses our sub-ordination.
- Questioning the premises of [fill in the name of any law reform effort currently understood to be "left"] gives aid and comfort to "the right." [Then pick one of the following normative denunciations:]

    The questioner is naïve.

    The questioner is covertly, perhaps subconsciously, on "the right."

    Avoiding co-optation by "the right" is categorically, or perhaps merely *obviously*, more important than reexamining the current com-mitments or project of "the left."
- Questioning the premises of [fill in the name of any rights-claiming effort currently understood to be "left"] is pointless; after all, we are talking here about human, or civil, or fundamental *rights*. QED.
- Your critique is so far removed from the language of the courtroom or everyday politics that it can't possibly be of practical value.
- Your critique is a luxury we can't afford; what we need right now is solidarity and consensus, not deconstruction.
- I'm offended.
- It's unacceptable.

We were dismayed to find ourselves ceding to these precepts not only because the "common sense" they represented was, upon close examina-tion, almost always intellectually incoherent, but because their invocation in political and intellectual debate bestowed sacred cow status on certain law reform projects whose problematics worried us and which we yearned to understand. Affirmative action, sex harassment, the immersion of the ideal of equality in rights claiming, the displacement of distributive con-cerns by equality, the central place given to injured subjectivity and ideas of personal dignity in hate speech efforts and sexual liberation projects, the merger of racial justice into the language of essentialized identity and cul-tural preservation, the deployment of identity-based claims in the form of rights supposedly trumping all competing normative claims: Would these various legal undertakings seem liberatory — would they seem *left* — if the prohibitive dicta listed above were suspended and the acid of critical theory had a chance to work on them?

And so we set out to write, and to find, work that upended or ignored these precepts and that illuminated what could happen in our understanding of what the left could do with (or without) the law if their prohibitive power were suspended. The essays collected here reflect what we discovered: the state of the art of "left internal critique" focused on law reform. With this volume, we are attempting to reinvigorate and revalue the tradition of critique as vital to what the intellectual left has to offer, and, perhaps, to the very existence and health of the left itself. The book is thus intended as a case for the worth of critique on interconstitutive intellectual, political, and hedonic grounds.

We have gathered essays that examine the tensions between state-centered left legalism, on the one hand, and left theoretical critiques of the state, the law, and identity, on the other. Together, they function as exercises in left critique of certain contemporary left legal and political conventions. They do not advocate a unified political position on the value of left legal reform, nor do they agree about appropriate strategies for such reform. Instead, these essays vary widely — and the differences arise just as much from the specific "real world" problem to which each author is attending as from differences in the kind of justice-seeking project by which each author is guided. Yet, in their different ways, each asks: What are the limits, paradoxes, and perils attending contemporary practices of left legalism? What can we learn from studying these effects? What politics might be refashioned from the critiques?

Between concern with being politically "relevant," usually understood as being "practical," and concern with holding the fort (and hence not criticizing what the fort holds), critique has come to be cast increasingly as an unaffordable luxury, or as simply to one side of the action of political life. We propose instead that theoretical critique is a crucial practice for understanding how legalism can transform and attenuate the values and aims that leftists bring to it. How might left legalism convert into liberal legalism? How or when does legalism sap the political substance from a highly politicized issue or event? How do desires to transform identity unwittingly become projects that instantiate identity? When do strategies of redress become techniques of domination? We do not argue, nor do any of our authors, that legalism or liberalism is irredeemable or that left projects oriented to the state, and more specifically to law, can or should be foresworn. But we do believe that the left's current absorption with legal strategies means that liberal legalism persistently threatens to defang the left we want to inhabit, saturating it with anti-intellectualism, limiting its normative aspirations, turning its attention away from the regulatory norms it ought to be upending, and hammering its swords into boomerangs.

The Left/Liberal Distinction

What is the difference between left legalism and liberal legalism? These, of course, are terms without fixed meaning and, in part, the essays collected here plumb, negotiate, and even aim to invent anew their possible meanings and relations. Indeed, it would be hubristic as well as contrary to our political impulses to offer, for example, a definitive account of what counts as "the left" here. It is not possible to circumscribe that project at this point in history, nor would we want to engage in the kind of gatekeeping and policing that such a definition would entail. However, given our desire to drive a distinction between liberal legalism and left critique, indeed, between liberal and left legalism, neither can we forgo some venture into this terrain. So we offer the following as partial, provisional, and contestable — a conversational gambit rather than a definitive account.

What has conventionally distinguished the left from liberalism is not merely a matter of attitude or precept, but turns on the objects of affirmation and negation that each takes as central to justice. Attempting to map this distinction returns us to the classical meaning of liberalism — not a political position opposite to conservatism but a political order that replaces Tudor monarchy rooted in explicit class privilege with modern democratic constitutionalism rooted in abstract individualism. It is the liberal political order, and not simply an ideological position, that leftists conventionally challenge as inadequate to the production of substantive freedom and equality. Thus leftists often refer to liberalism without making distinctions between "liberals" and "conservatives" or between "liberals" and "communitarians" — all of whom, in a left analysis, inhabit comfortably the liberalism that the analysis seeks to question. However, in what follows, we also try to mark a few of the ideological differences within liberal formulations of justice; to that end, we distinguish between a liberal political order and a "liberal" political position by putting the latter in quotation marks.

Liberalism presumes the legitimacy of a state in which we are guaranteed equality before the law and in which individual liberty is paramount. It presumes as well a rough equation of freedom with individual rights. Liberal justice is an order in which this equality and this freedom are maximized to the point where they would begin to cancel one another. Within the liberal order, "free market" and "libertarian" conservatives usually draw the line closer to freedom (as distinct from "moral conservatives," who argue for strong limits on both equality and freedom), and "liberals" usually draw it closer to equality (and thus differ from "civil libertarians," whose primary desideratum is liberty). But these are differences of degree; almost no one in contemporary political life disaffirms one in favor of the other.

Law and the state are ordinarily figured as technically neutral within liberalism, even if "liberals" recognize that these institutions have been historically beholden to socially dominant powers, and even if "conservatives" sometimes regard the state as an inappropriate intruder into the domain of personal and economic freedom. The challenge for "liberal" reformers is to wield the state on behalf of those on the lower end of various social hierarchies or at the losing end of various maldistributions; "conservatives" generally aim to wield it for purposes of consolidating the moral and political order, or to release putatively autonomous individuals or market forces from inappropriate constraints.

Left analysis takes its bearings from what it conceives the liberal formulation of justice to elide, as well as from a different vision of justice itself. Thus, a left political orientation begins with a critique — not necessarily a rejection — of liberalism itself as well as an explicit focus on the *social powers* producing and stratifying subjects that liberalism largely ignores. Of these, capital, male dominance, racial formations, and regimes of sexuality have been of persistent importance, but there are, of course, others. Liberalism's dearest treasure, equality before the law, though preferred to inequality before the law, is regarded by leftists as too abstract to produce substantive egalitarianism without transformation of the social powers that produce inequality. Equal access to rights and opportunities is seen as a false bouquet to those who, consequent to a range of possible constraints issuing from these social powers, cannot make equal use of them. Rights within liberalism are thus conceived as equal only at the formal level, and in concrete terms are seen as differentially deployed by differently situated subjects in a complexly stratified society. To the extent that rights themselves are powers, this differential itself constitutes both an index and a reinforcement of social inequality. This does not mean that leftists *necessarily* oppose rights, but rather that they are wary of liberalism's generally more sanguine equations between rights and liberty, equal rights and equality.

Leftists conceive of the liberal state as a site and potential instrument of dominance insofar as it masks unequal and unfree conditions with an ideology of freedom and liberty that entrenches or extends the powers of the already advantaged. Traditionally, leftists have focused on the domination and stratification inherent in capitalism and have focused most of their critical and political attention on the effects of the depoliticized status of political economy in liberal orders. More recently, influenced by a range of poststructuralist thinkers, many leftists have added the problem of norms and regulation to their analysis. Here, powers of subordination and inequality are no longer seen as simply achieved through the structure of class society, or through the state-society relationship that secures the interests of capital and class dominance, but as located in norms regulating a great variety of social relations, including but not limited to class, gender, sexuality, and race. From this angle, law and the state are seen neither as neutral nor as merely prohibitive, but as importantly productive of identity and subjectivity. Identity, in turn, is conceived as a crucial site of regulation, and not simply (as it is for many "liberals") a basis of equality or emancipation claims or (as it is for many "conservatives") at best a largely personal or subjective matter irrelevant to justice claims. Whereas liberalism tends to cast identity as arising from a source other than norms, institutions, and social powers, these are the wellsprings and regulatory sites of identity for this strand of left thinking. Whereas "liberals" treat identities as mechanisms for voicing injustice that the state must be made to recognize and repair, from this left perspective, identities are double-edged: they can be crucial sites of cultural belonging and political mobilization, but they can also be important vehicles of domination through regulation. Indeed, to the extent that liberalism bribes the left to frame its justice projects in terms of identity, cultural belonging and political mobilization become problematically regulatory. Grappling with such difficult paradoxes is one goal of this book.

The Left Turn to Legalism

We want to scrutinize projects of the left that invoke the liberal state's promise to make justice happen by means of law. Our concern is with a strong turn toward law by the left in recent decades, and especially with the implications of this turn both for left political aims and for left internal critique.

To argue that the left has lately become more heavily implicated in liberal legalism is not to suggest that there was a past in which the left did not engage with the law or the liberal state. In pursuit of racial justice by means of civil rights, the American left entered into a deep collaboration with a liberal legalistic project. The Montgomery bus boycott (seeking to establish blacks' right to use public accommodations on an equal basis with whites); Freedom Summer (seeking to establish blacks' equal voting rights); the 1964 March on Washington (seeking to pressure President Johnson and Congress to pass federal civil rights legislation) — these are classics in American legalism: they pointedly and directly tie broad-based, locally and culturally rich "movement" politics to demands for state-enforced rights. People whose political posture was decidedly left engaged in all these efforts, thus infusing their leftism with legalism and producing something that could be called left legalism. This was never an unproblematic undertaking for them. Liberal goals such as race universalism and national integrationism contended with left goals such as radical transformation of the racial economy. And legalistic engagements were challenged by participants acting under left motives. Moreover, the civil rights movement was persistently both roiled and energized by nonlegalistic initiatives and constituencies; recall the agonized struggle within the Student Nonviolent Coordinating Committee (SNCC) over the decision to sacrifice lives for ("mere"?) voting rights, black nationalists' efforts in the direction of community self-help, and Martin Luther King's turn in the last years of his life from race to poverty, from rights to redistribution.

Many of these tensions have subsided and must be actively recalled to memory. As a language and strategy for seeking justice for the historically subordinated, the civil rights discourse coined for racial justice has become almost hegemonic. More recent emancipatory and egalitarian efforts model themselves explicitly and seemingly inevitably on the black civil rights movement remembered only in its liberal and legalistic modalities: the women's movement, the disabled movement, even transsexual and transgendered activists have turned to the vocabulary of civil rights as to an ineluctable fund of justice claims. The classic status of the black civil rights effort has made it seem natural, inevitable to think that rights are central, exemplary, paradigmatic in any understanding of the justice-seeking legal resources of the liberal state.

But rights are not the only form in which the left has sought to mobilize the implicit promise of the liberal state that it will attempt to make justice happen by means of law. In the early part of the twentieth century what put the left on the political map in the United States was, surely, pursuit of collective bargaining. As Duncan Kennedy reminds us in his contribution to this volume, this effort involved an *attack* on rights in the form of freedom of contract and strong property entitlements; when the core left project was collective bargaining, employers' monopoly over rights — and thus rights — were viewed as *the problem*. Moreover, those involved in the project sought face-to-face relations between employee and employer under conditions of equalized bargaining power and in pursuit of improved wages and working conditions; neither the procedure nor the remedy was centrally legalistic or liberal. Eventually, more legalistic rights to unionize, to strike, and to fair representation took shape as the National Labor Relations Act and within various related legal regimes. But certain characteristic themes of liberalism — proceduralism, or justice as rights, etc. — however crucial they may be at any particular juncture, are typically *instrumental* to players working the labor side of that piece of governance.

Clearly, "the left" has no "natural" relationship to the legalism of rights. One reason for this is that rights cannot be fully saturated with the aims that animate their deployment. For all the content they may be given by their location in liberal orders, they retain a certain formality and emptiness which allow them to be deployed and redeployed by different political contestants. A right to be free from state-sponsored race discrimination can be asserted not only by black schoolchildren assigned to racially segregated schools, but also by Alan Bakke in his 1975 challenge to affirmative action and by Ward Connerly in his more far-reaching 1998 Civil Rights Initiative. And the Janus-faced character of rights can precipitate realignments of the left aims to which they might, until that moment, seem fixedly attached. For instance, the legal realist critique of rights corresponded well with a left attack on constitutional protection of freedom of contract but had to be backgrounded in the course of civil rights activism. And thus one reason for the complex and contingent relationship between "the left" and legalism is that "the left" situates itself as such in part by engaging and disengaging various legalisms. Within left labor politics, for example, the legal effort to secure the power to bargain collectively gives way at another moment to intra-union legal and political struggles to democratize the structure of unions or to force gender equity issues onto union agendas; as economic, political, and institutional conditions change, and left aims contest with one another, the value of and engagement with various legalisms will vary as well.

Civil rights, however dominant as a form of contemporary left legalism, does not exhaust the ways the left engages legalism. Consider those justice projects in which the left attempts to capture or at least influence some fragment of the state's administrative apparatus. For our purposes, such projects could be arrayed under the rubric *governance legalism*. We do not mean to imply a relationship of mutual exclusivity between rights legalism and governance legalism; certainly there are overlaps. But when antipornography activists turned to zoning restrictions, attempting to map pornography out; when left multiculturalists weighed in with francophone nationalists and sought to justify the secession of Quebec from Canada, attempting to map minority culture in; when ACT-UP staged its rage on the steps of the Food and Drug Administration's Washington, D.C. headquarters, attempting to secure a place at the bureaucratic table where the speed of drug approval would be decided—when the left has engaged in these projects, it has engaged with elements of the state that have little or nothing to do with rights, that are sometimes even illiberal, but are perhaps even more legalistic than a rights project. This kind of left legalism seeks to involve the left directly in governance: once you win, you *are* the state.

The mutability we have detected in rights legalism can emerge in governance legalism as well. Consider the aim of left multiculturalists in Quebec: to achieve francophone sovereignty by the secession of Quebec from Canada and its establishment as a new nation-state. Left multiculturalists sought to tie themselves to the state in this way because of their concern for a minority population, in this case, the French-speaking Québecois. But if they had attained their goal, their governance project would have been running an ethnic state in which French-speaking Québecois enjoyed dominant status with respect to a new set of subordinates. As francophone Québecois had been to Quebec before secession, anglophone Quebecers would have been to Quebec after it (although each is positioned differently vis-à-vis Canada as a whole and in the political economic order). In addition, a new chapter in the history of colonialization for First Nations peoples would have been inaugurated; the hard-won deal they had cemented with Canada would have been reopened under a new sovereign. However distinct the locations of First Nations and anglophone Quebecers (they would have been indexed differently to dispositions of power outside Quebec), the problem of ethnically and linguistically ordered dominance and subordination inside Quebec would not have been solved, but merely rearranged. And in the course of that rearrangement, a left preoccupation with francophone cultural survival would have been supplanted by new minoritizing projects ready to disavow the initial left impulse to run a state.

The Regulatory Capacities of Legalism

We have suggested thus far that left projects in liberal democratic orders can rarely avoid rights and governance legalism; nor can they avoid the problematics of these modes of legalism. We want to go further now, to suggest that legalism has regulatory capacities which have been particularly dangerous for left projects because they remain so unstudied, so unavowed.

Perhaps the practice of forgetting the regulatory capacities of legalism is animated by an idea that the production of regulated subjects and disciplined populations belongs to "culture" or "society" rather than "the state." Although this is not the argument of Michel Foucault, it seems he is sometimes read this way. His genealogy of the rise of biopower in modernity — of power in its microphysical, disciplinary, and regulatory form — combined with his insistence that we must "cut off the king's head in political theory" (i.e., redirect our attention from the state and law to culture and society as the domain of power in society) are taken together to imply that law has been historically superseded by nonlegal forms of power. But this is a poor reading of a thinker who, if anything, has taught us to be alert to the imbrication of juridical and disciplinary discourses, an imbrication that can range from the overt to the very subtle. Indeed, law has a penchant for hiding itself in background rules so minute that they facilitate or activate regulatory regimes that seem immune from legalistic effects.

This appearance can be quite convincing. Take the invention of standardized clothing sizes and the diffusion of the practice of sized clothing throughout the apparel market. Standardized clothing sizes standardize the bodies that wear clothes: they make possible an imagined community of "size 10s," rendering it both a form of consumer rhetoric and a form of subjectivity. "What size *are you*?" we ask, acknowledging that this marketing device constitutes us with precision and intimacy. Indeed, if it doesn't constitute us, consequences emerge in the kind of selfhood we experience and present. If the slippage takes a dysphoric form, we become nonstandard, deviant, possessed of a wrong body that could not have been imagined as wrong in quite this way before sized clothing became the market standard. If the slippage takes a more euphoric form — as it does, for instance, when young black and Latino men wear clothes carefully selected to be "too large" or when women seeking to produce one kind of sexy effect wear clothes carefully selected to be "too small" — we achieve a kind of ironic play on the idea of standardization. However it plays out, sized clothing regulates diet, exercise, healthiness, posture; it interpellates us into gender, sex, and class; it normalizes along all these dimensions and more without once touching on the implicit promise of the liberal state: that it will attempt to make justice happen by means of law.

We are not claiming that a "free market in sized clothing" could exist without all the requisite state apparatuses — contract enforcement, capital accumulation in the corporate form, tax-subsidized interstate commerce — that make mass markets possible. The so-called free market is surely subtended by the state in myriad ways. But the particular thing that happened in the marketing of clothing — the standardizing of size — seems to be perfectly intelligible without reference to those legal supports, and certainly without reference to the idea that legal technologies are distinctively associated with our yearning for justice. And so legalism as we are framing it for this book appears to have a jurisdictional edge: it can have little or no bearing upon some modes of regulation that are nonetheless quite potent in producing and organizing subjects.

But recall now our caution that legalism has ways of hiding its presence, of providing background rules so backgrounded that we can forget they are there. Perhaps we have committed this very error in our sized clothing example. Consider that there is no legally enforceable warranty that a pair of size 10 jeans will actually have dimensions similar to any other pair of size 10 jeans sold by another manufacturer, or indeed the same one, last year or yesterday. The regime of sized clothing includes, then, an implicit "right" of manufacturers to change the parameters of clothing sizes. They can exercise this "right" unilaterally, without affording consumers notice and an opportunity to be heard on the matter, without even letting consumers know what they're doing. Perhaps this "right" contributes to the strange mixture of anxiety and excitement, dread and relief, with which we greet sized clothing; clothing sizes are always midpoint in a narrative of our embodiment, one that mysteriously alters the meaning of any answer to the question "What size *are you*?" and thus one that can intimately *re*shape the kind of selfhood we experience and present. The legal rule that clothing sizes are not subject to an implied warranty of rigid standardization may have an important role in what at first appears to be a "purely" cultural form of regulation.

Because law can take the shape of permissions rather than prohibitions, it can invisibly capacitate social and cultural actors to do particular kinds of social and cultural work. Suddenly seeing legalism operating as the background rules of culture, whence it is supposed to be absent, should defeat, at least for the case at hand, the presumption that culture is profoundly distinct from law. And once we have a firm grip on this hypothesis (of course, it is merely that; in any particular situation the point may be utterly unimportant) we can assign a number of possible conceptual consequences to it. First, the left yearning (like the right one) to live "outside of law" may be unattainable; we may think we've gotten free of law only to realize that it creates the conditions for who we are or what we do, and that realization can profoundly alter our normative assessment of our situation. And second, the effects of law can be complex, multiple, and contingent in the same way that cultural powers like sized clothing are complex, multiple, and contingent. Left legalism will imagine its own effects much more adequately if it is ready to see them not as monolithic installations of "justice" but as mutable, contestable entries into complex discursive and distributive systems.

Although Foucault helpfully drew our attention to ways that powers of regulation operate and regulate in extralegal or legal domains, he may have underestimated the degree to which the modern liberal state itself can operate *as* micropower. It seems clear to us that "the law" exceeds the figure, supposed by Foucault to define it, of the prohibiting, death-wielding sovereign, and has *incorporated* the managerial, normativizing, regularizing, biopoweristic forms that he proposed were distinguishable from the juridical form, even if historically entwined with it. "The law" in our world takes not only the form of the sovereign who kills in the name of the rule "Thou shalt not kill," but also the form of the Department of Youth Services worker who inspects your personal life in minute detail to decide whether you are a fit person to adopt your lover's child. This underpaid and overworked functionary, laden with forms that standardize good parenting, has his or her effects on you and on parenting more broadly not through rules about it but through mobile, shifting, highly momentary assessments — discretionary *standards* that are nevertheless intrinsic to the design of adoption *law*.

To be sure, state-sponsored regulation of good parenting can operate in culture much as temple-, synagogue-, and church-sponsored normalization of good parenting does. Indeed, there may ultimately be no interesting difference between the cultural effectivities generated when the state, on one hand, and *Rugrats,* on the other, regulate good parenting. That may suggest that the state is not more culturally powerful than other cultural players, but it also suggests that law is capable of intensely intimate effects.

Left legalism has been repeatedly willing to seek these effects. Every time the left seeks to achieve its aims by increasing state "services," every time it seeks to enlist the state in endorsing the personhoods and the values that it thinks deserve recognition and respect, every time it calls upon judges or legislatures to substitute rigid legal rules with flexible discretionary standards it commits itself to normativizing deployments of state power of this kind. To take but one example: the feminist critique of legal rules as insufficiently attentive to circumstance and perspective has led feminists to advocate a shift to standards such as "the reasonable person" or indeed "the reasonable woman." The introduction of these standards should, we think, be seen as a normatively saturated and deeply interpellating legalistic gesture.

Moreover, while left legalism has often been willing to produce normalizations, it has less often been willing to subject them to close scrutiny. It presumes, for example, that cultural preservation for racial minorities merely liberates racially marked subjects to express their racial selves, without exploring how cultural preservation will *produce* racial selves. It presumes that changing the Department of Youth Services' standards of good parenting to include rather than exclude the goodness of same-sex couples as parents will liberate same-sex couples to become parents, setting to one side the question of how it may *induce* them to imagine themselves as couples of a very particular sort and as parents within very particularized parameters of parenthood.

The problem here is not just one of unintended regulatory effects. There is also the problem of intended but unavowed ones. We take an example from our own engagement with a project in which both of us are invested and each of us understands to be deeply connected to her left aspirations:

fostering intimate attachments between adults and between adults and children that can't be found on the nuclear family menu. As part of this project, we have endorsed lesbian and gay male coparent adoption because it would secure the relationships between nonbiological parents and the children in whose conception, gestation, birth, and/or upbringing they have participated. Nor are we alone: the feminist and queer left loves these liberal family law projects because they signify the possibility of a more open texture of kinship, beyond the specific families they are consecrating and in the hope of disabling a certain privilege that otherwise devolves on biological and/or heterosocial parentage.

So left, feminist, queer, and liberal constituencies together have celebrated these reforms as a way for the law to recognize brave, exploratory "families we choose" as they evolve into ever new forms of intimate attachment. But our loose, fluid normativity stiffens when, in the aftermath of a breakup between lesbian coparents who had not secured a second-parent adoption, the biological mother asserts a unique status as parent to deny her legally unprotected lover access to the(ir) child. Let us confess it now: we furiously want those women to be married, or to be tied to one another by a coparent adoption decree, so that they enter the custody struggle as formal equals. Now we are willing to deploy "best interests of the child" rhetoric even though our political rage attaches not to the child's welfare but to the way the biological mother has turned the state against a lesbian for *being* a lesbian, and tightened the epistemological and social grip of an official representation — posited by our feminism to be subordinating — of maternity as biological rather than social. It would seem that we want to interpellate lesbians through new family law structures so that it *doesn't even occur to them* to deny their former partner full parental status.

Acknowledging the rawness and fury of this will to power, and the contradiction between it and our sunny confidence that intimate attachments should evolve under conditions of the maximum deregulation, pries us loose from both. We are startled: suddenly we can ask whether mobility or stability, invention or fixity, liberation or regulation is what we want in our discourses and practices of intimacy. This moment of disorientation can happen — we offer this book as an affirmation that it *should* happen — within a variety of left legalistic projects. Consider what it would do in the context of cultural preservation projects. The aim of these projects seems to be unequivocally desirable when we imagine them as a counter to cultural extinction or erasure. But once we note the will to power involved in a left project of keeping certain cultures alive, we can also suddenly see them as problematically related to our left commitments to cultural transformability, cosmopolitanism, ethnic hybridity, feminism, anti-racism, and the liberation of children from the exclusive dominion of their families. And suddenly, again, we are disoriented, and again we can seize the moment for a reexamination of our political desires and commitments. Forming a new sense of purposive aims won't be easy; surely the production of racial subjects may be good, bad, or indifferent depending on the normativities and distributive circuits that those subjects will inhabit. Deciding these matters is delicate work, provisional work almost always. But it cannot even be undertaken unless we acknowledge the deep cultural productivity of left legalism.

Left Legalism in a Liberal Political Order

As we've indicated, the range of yearnings and objections that we're designating "left" is relatively, sometimes acutely, inconsistent with that of liberalism. And yet legalism in the United States is largely *liberal* legalism.

Submitting left projects to the terms of liberal legalism translates the former into the terms of the latter, a translation which will necessarily introduce tensions with, and sometimes outright cancellations of, the originating aims that animate left legalism in the first place. When liberal legalism frames the problem of racial stratification as a problem in the register of "rights," for instance, and then frames rights as either "special" (and thus normatively suspect) or "universal" (and thus oblivious to racial particularities), anyone making a race-based justice claim can reap the benefits of universalism only at the cost of paving the way for judicial protection of white people, and can reap the benefits of a particularized focus on the distinctive injury suffered by a racially subordinated group only by conceding that it is special (not universal) and needs protection (not equality).[2]

Or consider affirmative action, a project to which the left has become adamantly committed the more it has been attacked by the right. Surely affirmative action has accumulated effects that are precisely what the left could not have intended when it joined liberals on this path to racial justice. It could not have intended that a mere remedy would take the place, conceptually and politically, of antidiscrimination tout court, nor could it have intended that all race-based equality jurisprudence would be the target of the same backlash ostensibly aimed only at affirmative action. It could not have intended the startling effect, subjected to critique in these pages by Richard T. Ford, that, once legitimated by the Supreme Court only to the extent that it promoted "diversity," affirmative action as practiced in educational institutions would effectively *require* its beneficiaries to affirm rather than disaffirm, to consolidate rather than mobilize identities produced by racially organized power.

Indeed, the entanglements of left legalism with the liberalism scribed into so many dimensions of legalism can be deeply normalizing. Here we propose that legalism often deploys liberalism as a normativizing, regulatory form of power: when liberalism posits that we are individuals primordially, that human selfhood is given, not constituted, that choosing is the preeminent human deed, it bids to constitute us as individuals and choosers. To the extent that this set of liberal entailments interpellates us in this way, liberalism has its subjections. And to the extent that left legalism engages liberalism, it can be directly responsible for these regulatory effects.

One way of exploring the dangers here is to ask how the act of making justice claims in the language of liberal legalism shapes us as justice-worthy subjects. How, for example, did we become people for whom domestic, economically interdependent, long-term, coupled and monogamous intimacy is *the* paradigm of adult intimacy itself, if not, at least in part, through the centrality guaranteed for marriage by the unique and preeminent place it enjoys in the law governing personal relationships? Given that, what are the interpellations risked by the gay-centrist project of gaining legal recognition for same-sex marriage? Though this effort purports to reflect a natural desire for the institution of marriage, it actually draws upon and endorses the state's deep involvement in shaping our ideas of human intimacy and connection, in guiding our desires, and in persuading us to assume status-like relations with respect to one another.[3] Yet the same-sex marriage project glides along, obdurately oblivious of the productive, regulatory forces that course through state-sanctioned marriage; if it succeeds, the reach of the state into certain intimacies can only deepen and the normative ordering of sexual objects according to their willingness to be so regulated can only intensify. Thus Michael Warner worries that gay marriage achieved in the name of equality will actually regulate sexuality and order sexual subjects in ways that will dramatically reshape queer political and social life; he predicts that many who have been gathered under that sign will be repatriated to its edges by this move.

This volume features other examples of left-endorsed liberal legalist projects that generate troubling social subjects and subjectivities. Mark Kelman and Gillian Lester argue that the very articulation of the identity "learning disabled" probably owes its genesis to a liberal legalist idea affirmed by the left: the decision to provide education in a particular way to particular people not on the basis of some model of distributive justice, but on a civil rights model. Kelman and Lester ask: Can we imagine a distribution of educational benefits better than the resulting one, in which those with learning disabilities "jump the queue" filled with garden-variety slow learners? And we would add: How deep does the sense of "being learning disabled" run for those bearing this new identity? How liberatory *is* this new personhood? Lauren Berlant asks whether the persistent left aspiration to ensure remedies for injured feelings might not also interpellate us into a sentimental affectivity that is fundamentally reactionary. And Richard Ford warns that rights to cultural preservation may end up strengthening the hand of the most conservative and constraining elements in the cultural life of subordinated groups. If cultural preservation projects have this tendency (a tendency that would seem to reside in the very grammar of "preservation"), should the left antiracist enterprise embrace them uncritically?

Each of these examples tracks effects of legalism that, though imbricated in liberalism and mediated by the liberal state, cannot be captured by liberal categories or an orthodox left analytics of power. And this is no mere disability: liberalism in particular is frequently then heard to announce the nonexistence of what it cannot see. Recall that liberalism credits itself with crisp institutional limits and formal aridity, while leaking into social and cultural life at every orifice. When liberal legalism frames rights as empty, formal, procedurally rather than substantively bestowed and bestowing — when it insists that rights merely protect the potential choices of the autonomous selves we are and always have been — it nevertheless produces and orders subjectivities while according these grave rearrangements of social life the importance, on a scale of one to ten, of approximately zero.

Left legalistic projects, entwined as they are with the regulatory tugs of liberalism and legalism, are going to produce unintended consequences. We want a critical theoretical engagement with left legalism in part because we want to apprehend these side effects. To see and to evaluate them, we need to step back from our legalism, to open up the space for *politics* that can put legalism under a viewfinder, and to examine both politics and legalism with the attitude of *critique*.

Legalism's Political Outside

Is there such a thing as nonlegalistic political practice, a politics even a few degrees outside legalism, especially if legalism is not defined simply in reference to the state and law, but to less institutionally codified practices and effects? So saturated by legalism is contemporary political life that it is often difficult to imagine alternative ways of deliberating about and pursuing justice. Yet the legal realist point that law is politics by other means should not commit us to its converse: that all endeavors to shape and order collective life are legalistic.

Legalism not only carries a politics (and liberal legalism carries a very specific politics) but also incessantly translates wide-ranging political questions into more narrowly framed legal questions. Thus politics conceived and practiced legalistically bears a certain hostility to discursively open-ended, multigenre, and polyvocal political conversations about how we should live, what we should value and what we should prohibit, and what is possible in collective life. The preemptive conversion of political questions into legal questions can displace open-ended discursive contestation: adversarial and yes/no structures can quash exploration; expert and specialized languages can preclude democratic participation; a pretense that deontological grounds can and must always be found masks the historical embeddedness of many political questions; the covertness of norms and political power within legal spaces repeatedly divests political questions of their most crucial concerns. When the available range of legal remedies preempts exploration of the deep constitutive causes of an injury (think hate speech and the racial order that makes it sting), when the question of which rights pertain overrides attention to what occasions the urgently felt need for the right (think abortion and the way reproductive work is organized, valued and [un]remunerated in male-dominant orders), we sacrifice our chance to be deliberative, inventive political beings who create our collective life form. Legalism that draws its parameters of justice from liberalism imposes its own standards of fairness when we might need a public argument about what constitutes fairness; its formulas for equality when we may need to reconsider all the powers that must be negotiated in the making of an egalitarian order; its definitions of liberty at the price of an exploratory argument about the constituent elements of freedom.

As we incessantly refer our political life to the law, we not only sacrifice opportunities to take our inherited political condition into our own hands, we sacrifice as well the chance to address at a more fundamental or at least far-reaching level various troubling conditions which appear to require redress. Consider: What if some of the disturbing aspects of contemporary sex harassment doctrine, in which redress of gender subordination has been increasingly usurped by greater sexual regulation, can be traced to a certain failure on the part of second-wave feminism actually to effect a significant transformation in the social construction of women and men, a project that was once deeply constitutive of that political and cultural enterprise? And what if the tendency toward ever more intensive legal regulation of gender and sexuality is a compensatory response to that failure, a response that effectively gives up on the project of transforming gender in favor of pro-tecting a historically subordinated group from some of the most severe effects of that subordination, even as it tacitly defines women through those effects? If feminism once aimed to make women the sexual equals of men, this aim entails the complex social, psychological, and political project of making gender differently, and not simply the legal one of protecting (his-torically and culturally produced) vulnerable women from (historically and culturally produced) rapacious men. Indeed, the legal project, in its in-stantiation of sexuality as subordinating, especially of women, may be substantially at odds with the political project of fashioning women as men's substantive equals, that is, as people who cannot be "reduced to their gender" through an unwanted sexualizing gesture or word.

This is not to argue that there is some pure left political space indepen-dent of legalism, nor that left political projects implicated in legalism inev-itably sacrifice their aims and values. Rather, it is to assert the possibility of political life and political projects not fully saturated by legalistic con-straints and aims. It is to recover radically democratic political aims from legalism's grip in order to cultivate collective political and cultural delibera-tion about governing values and practices.

We remember a mode of activism among antipornography feminists that was more political than legalistic. Women walked into porn shops and trashed the pornography, shamed the customers, and mock-shamed them-selves. They also led tours through the porn districts, offering feminist interpretations of pornographic representations and marketing of women, interpretations which others could and sometimes did argue with. The antiporn activists worked in the name of feminism, and though all feminists did not condone the stance toward porn and the depiction of women that this activism represented, our dissension itself was not monolithic or fully codified. This mode of antiporn activism thus provoked argument and reflection among and across feminists and nonfeminists alike.

This political mode presupposed an interlocutory relationship between those who valued pornography and those who condemned it, indeed between porn and its consumers or audiences. In that interlocutory relationship, many women encountered and studied pornography for the first time. As this occurred, women found themselves having all kinds of responses to porn that could not simply be classified as for or against: some were distressed by it but grasped their distress as an index of the sexual shame their gender construction entailed; others were drawn to it and flatly delighted to be let into a sexual order previously designated for men; others were more ambivalent, liking the idea of porn or liking bits of it but troubled or turned off by the misogynistic (or racist or colonial) strains in it (some were confusingly turned on by these very same strains); still others were inspired to try to make good porn for women. What was the political cache of this rich array of responses? It produced a wave of new feminist work on sexuality: new questions, new theories, new domains of research, new practices, new arguments, new positions in every sense of the word. Hence followed as well new possibilities of alliances with gay men as well as new forms of alliance across a presumed heterosexual-homosexual divide, the possibility of queer thought, and the invention of new sexual subjectivities and identities through a proliferation of cultural discourses of and cultural struggles over sexuality. "Feminism" so constituted was a field of widely divergent values, beliefs, and practices, all of which had to contest with one another over the question of "the good" for women.

Compare this marvelously fertile political contestation and intellectual exploration with the social and ideological concomitants of antipornography activists' turn to the state. Antipornography activism took a legalistic turn with the invention of a tort claim for damages arising from the injury to women's sexual status supposedly inflicted by pornography (rights legalism) and the deployment of zoning ordinances to shut down the public space devoted to sex commerce (governance legalism). Wherever feminists took this turn, the politics of sexuality in feminism and feminist communities, and the form of feminist internal critique, changed dramatically.

Defining porn narrowly (and badly) as "the graphic sexual subordination of women," the legalists promulgated local ordinances establishing porn as a violation of women's civil rights. This move brought into play local governments and judges as authoritative decision makers. And the arguments that could then be addressed to those decision makers were as flat and impoverished as the arguments characteristic of the political struggle were multidimensional and rich: to participate in the legalistic moment, feminists had to declare themselves for or against porn, and even for or against sex, as they took a position on the ordinances.[4] The debate about porn became framed by the terms of free speech, censorship, and privacy rights. In short, it became consolidated by a narrow rights framework: Should your right not to be violated/offended trump my right to consume what I want? Does Larry Flynt's free speech silence Catharine MacKinnon's? In this consolidation, all the complexities of sexual representation, of the imbrication of sexuality and gender, of the relation of fantasy to reality, and above all, of the extraordinary and detailed range in the sexual construction and desires of women and men were eclipsed. The adversarial structure of rights legalism as deployed by all the parties meant that the stakes were now "winner takes all." In that context neither side could risk nuance, internal dissension, or differentiation of positions along a continuum. Hence the debates produced a new form of internal silencing of each side's constituents; solidarity and a united front became mandatory. Above all, neither side could afford to break with liberalism (a notoriously impoverished discourse on the subject of sexuality) in its arguments: the terms of the new debate were set not only by established definitions of equality, civil rights, and free speech, but by flat and monolithic conceptions of gender, women, sexuality, and representation. And this debate, dessicated because it adopted rather than contested the terms of liberal legalism, was the form in which the feminist question about pornography hit the mainstream.

To be sure, the porn wars in their political mode had their brutal and punitive dimensions; open-ended political contestation in unbounded spaces and unregulated by settled rules of engagement can be an arena for raw aggressions and un-self-knowing posturing of the most grandiose sort. Thus, in the political struggle, women accused each other of false consciousness, mocked each other's sexual desires, set themselves up as sexually righteous, and denounced each other viciously for their positions in these battles. But the political mode had several virtues that the legalistic mode distinctively lacked: it was open-ended in the questioning and conversations it incited; it was accessible to a wide variety of participants (and was probably the most interracial, cross-class, and intersexual political moment second-wave feminism had); and it occurred in a range of different idioms, from analytic position papers to poetry to biography. Perhaps most important, because the arguments were about sex, gender, and representation rather than free speech, censorship, and civil rights, the political mode incited a substantial body of rich new political, cultural, and psychological inquiry and political understandings that were both valuable in themselves and gave new life to the social movements that bred them.

If we are right about the legalistic usurpation of many left political projects, then what we are calling left legalism has sometimes turned left projects against themselves. Yet left legalistic discourse has at least three arguments that admit that legalism may be eccentric to left aims but that deny its capacity to translate and usurp them. We hear, first, that the rights sought in left legalistic projects are mere legal placeholders that will be occupied, if at all, only by people who want to occupy them; thus, the argument concludes, no broadly sweeping rearrangement of the social field or of movement aims is intended or risked. This is the gravamen of MacKinnon's claim that her private right of action against pornography will merely vindicate those women who are actually injured by pornography; it is the rationale for making hate speech a "mere" tort or a "mere" basis for sentence enhancement rather than a crime; it is the rationale for procuring a right to marriage that is presumed to have no effect on those who do not wish to marry. But a private right of action against pornography would deter its production and distribution; a tort claim for hate speech would radically alter the utterability of some parts of the racial vocabulary; and an extension of marriage rights to new couple forms would reconfigure, perhaps strengthen, the normalizing power of marriage.

Second, we hear that left legalistic moves are merely incremental, that they merely seek to take down the beasts of sexism and racism with BBs because more effective weaponry is currently inaccessible. For example, sexual harassment is portrayed by some feminists as a small fragment of a seamless wrong, "women's sexual subordination," so that making it actionable addresses a paradigmatic piece of the totality of women's subordination, a classic incrementalizing move. But such a formulation of the feminist endorsement of sex harassment regulation ignores a profound disgreement among feminists about what subordinates women and about whether protecting women from sex protects them from harm or inflicts it. Here and, we think, elsewhere, a left legalistic project has not deferred or incrementalized the left's engagement with racism, sexism, and heterosexism: but has transformed it into something else, infused left politics with its own discursive forms, and substituted left with legalistic debate.

Third, left legalism often borrows from liberalism certain representations of law that purport to empty it of substantive elements that impede left aims. In these representations, law is depicted as a mere instrument rather than a politics, as a tool deployed for goals external to it. We are thus asked to understand law to have no content of its own and also to be independent of the extralegal discourses that endlessly supply and supplement its content. To review but one recent example: For a time, pro-gay litigators argued that homosexuality was an "immutable characteristic" and thus more deserving of judicial solicitude than, say, age; they even put "gay gene" geneticists on the stand to prove their point. Challenged by bisexual, gender-transitive, and queer constituencies to account for this intervention in a hotly contested politics of knowledge about sexuality, they invariably replied that the immutability argument would have effects only on the judges to whom it was pitched, not elsewhere, and that if it helped a gay plaintiff win a favorable ruling it could then fade without a trace from the culture it had made more egalitarian. But the argument from immutability, particularly in its "gay gene" form, was far from empty in this way; instead, it helped to produce the very science on which it then relied — a dynamic that made it richly productive and substantive. This episode counsels that both rights and governance legalism should be hypothesized as rife with normative categories, indeed as powerfully productive discourses that draw their normativity from widely dispersed sites in the culture, economy, and polity. We should not be surprised, then, by the phenomenon in which you go to the state with your sexual injury and come out as a Woman, or in which you go to the state for legitimation of your gay relationship and come out as an embodiment of the idea that sexuality is subject to a stable set of regulatory norms, or in which you go to the state with your fury about a racial epithet and come out as a member of a permanently hateable racial minority. Once again, this apology for left legalism fails to account for the *capture* and transformation of its political aims. It is this capture and transformation of a left critical project engaged with legalism that calls for the scrutinizing practice called critique.

Critique

The most common complaint from liberal and left activists about left critique is that it is a "negative" practice that fails to offer clear avenues for progressive change. This complaint comes with diverse accent marks. Critique is variously charged with being academic, impractical, merely critical, unattuned to the political exigencies at hand, intellectually indulgent, easier than fixing things or saying what is to be done — in short, either ultraleftist or ultratheoretical but in either case without purchase on or in something called the Real World. Critique is thus characterized as an abandonment of politics, insofar as it is an abandonment of the terms and constraints of real political life, a flight to an elsewhere, politically and theoretically.

The fact that the nineteenth-century tradition of critique is beset by such an impoverished understanding and has fallen into such disrepute signifies more than can be said here about the condition of contemporary intellectual life, political life, and their relation. Critique, as it emerges in the German philosophical tradition starting with Kant and continuing through Hegel, Marx, and the Frankfurt School, represents a genre of theoretical work that neither presumes a specific political outcome nor forsakes the political world for the purely intellectual one. Critique derives from the ancient Greek *crisis,* a term that connotes "the art and tools of making distinctions, deciding, and judging."[5] Interestingly for the purposes of this book, for the ancient Athenians, *crisis* was a jurisprudential term and was especially important in expressing the function of the Athenian court in judging: "separating, distinguishing, discerning, and so with deciding what (or who) properly fell under the categories articulated by the indictment. . . . It therefore had little if anything to do with criticism in the general sense of fault-finding and censure."[6] Heidegger maintains proximity to the Greek meaning in his own formulation of critique: "Because critique is a separation and lifting out of the special, the uncommon, and at the same time, decisive, therefore, and only as a consequence, it is also a rejection of the commonplace and unsuitable."[7]

Critique in Enlightenment hands is inflected with the conviction that only that which can withstand the press of reason deserves intellectual or political fealty. Thus, for Kant and his successors, critique expressed the recognition that no formulation — political or intellectual, empirical or theoretical, institutional or philosophical — is unpremised, and that only a critical reckoning with premises will yield an understanding of the terms by which we live. There are, of course, many varieties of critique that emerge in the eighteenth and nineteenth centuries — for example, those that call themselves immanent and presume only to be working the elements of a particular formulation against itself (the tradition of Hegelian-Marxist critique from which both early Frankfurt School theory and Derridean deconstruction are derived) and those that work more expressly against the grain of a text in order to bring forth the unspoken or suppressed constituents of its existence. Foucault is a contemporary heir of this latter strain of the tradition of critique, a strain that might be seen as drawing more from Nietzsche's formulation of genealogy than from the philosophic exercises of German idealism. There are also a variety of objects of critique; in addition to the philosophical critique that inaugurates the modern tradition, there is ideology critique, culture critique, critique of political economy, and more.

Although critique has at times presumed that a truth could be arrived at with regard to the constitutive nature and meaning of the premises of a given work or doctrine, it does not inevitably entail this particular Enlightenment conceit. Critique is not weakened by admitting its investments — consider Kant in *The Critique of Pure Reason,* or Marx in his *Critique of Hegel's Philosophy of Right* or "On the Jewish Question" — because the aim of critique is to reveal subterranean structures or aspects of a particular discourse, not necessarily to reveal the truth of or about that discourse. What critique promises is not objectivity but perspective; indeed, critique is part of the arsenal of intellectual movements of the past two centuries that shatters the plausibility of objectivity claims once and for all. In the insistence on the availability of all human productions to critique, that is, to the possibility of being rethought through an examination of constitutive premises, the work of critique is potentially without boundary or end.

So what is the value of critique, and why should the left in particular cherish it both intellectually and politically? Critique offers possibilities of analyzing existing discourses of power to understand how subjects are fabricated or positioned by them, what powers they secure (and disguise or veil), what assumptions they naturalize, what privileges they fix, what norms they mobilize, and what or whom these norms exclude. Critique is thus a practice that allows us to scrutinize the form, content, and possible reworking of our apparent political choices; we no longer have to take them as givens. Critique focuses on the workings of ideology and power in the production of existing political and legal possibilities. It facilitates discernment of how the very problem we want to solve is itself produced, and thus may help us avoid entrenching or reproducing the problem in our solutions. It aims to distinguish between symptoms and sources, as well as between effects of power and origins of power. It invites us to analyze our most amorphous and inchoate discontents and worries, indeed to let these discontents and worries themselves spirit the critique. And it invites us to dissect our most established maxims and shibboleths, not only for scholastic purposes, but also for the deeply political ones of renewing perspective and opening new possibility.

Let us admit forthrightly, however, that critique does not guarantee political outcomes, let alone political resolutions. Yet, rather than apologize for this aspect of critique, why not affirm it? For part of what it means to dissect the discursive practices that organize our lives is to embark on an inquiry whose outcome is unknown, and the process of which will be radically disorienting at times. To probe for its constituent elements discontent about a particular political aim or strategy is not to know immediately what might reform or replace that aim. Indeed, one of our worries about legalism pertains to its impulse to call the question too peremptorily. Marx's early critiques of left Hegelianism worked closely with the texts and political formulations that he found dissatisfying, but they were not expressly organized by a clear alternative. It was *through* the process of subjecting political and philosophical idealism to critique that Marx found his way to dialectical materialism and political economy, but a careful reading of this early work makes clear that Marx did not know *in advance* where his critiques would take him, and that premature closure on the question would have stymied both the critique and the productive disorientation it achieved for him about left Hegelianism. Surely we should not disavow a left critique of the tensions and contradictions in affirmative action simply because that critique does not deliver in advance a blueprint or set of strategies for achieving racial, gender, or class justice in America.

Not knowing what a critique will yield is not the same as suspending all political values while engaged in critique. It is possible to care passionately about offering richer educational opportunities to those historically excluded from them while subjecting to ruthless critique the institutional and discursive practices that have thus far organized that aim. It is possible to sustain a deep commitment to the vision of equality for sexual minorities in a heterosexual culture while subjecting to critique a range of techniques — from the campaign for gay marriage to the constitution of queers as genetically predetermined — advanced in the name of such equality. And even if critique reveals problematics that shake those commitments — for instance, by revealing maldistributions in education that lack the historical pedigree of racially marked ones but that strike us as urgently unjust, or by revealing that the idea of "sexual minorities" is at once so incoherent and so interpellative that it may belong under the heading "the problem" rather than the heading "the solution" — the resulting disorientation remains deeply *political*. And so, although political commitments may constitute both the incitement to critique and the sustaining impulse of it, these commitments themselves will almost inevitably change their shape in the course of its undertaking. Critique is worth nothing if it does not bring the very terms of such commitments under scrutiny, if it does not transform its content and the discourse in which it is advanced. In this volume, Judith Butler argues for just such a transformation when she warns that to remain within the existing terms of the gay kinship debates is to accept "an epistemological field structured by a fundamental loss, one that we can no longer name enough even to grieve."

So critique is risky. It can be a disruptive, disorienting, and at times destructive enterprise of knowledge. It can be vertiginous knowledge, knowledge that produces bouts of political inarticulateness and uncertainty, knowledge that bears no immediate policy outcomes or table of tactics. And it can include on its casualty list a number of losses — discarded ways of thinking and operating — with no clear replacements. But critique is risky in another sense as well, what might be called an affirmative sense. For critique hazards the opening of new modalities of thought and political possibility, and potentially affords as well the possibility of enormous pleasure — political, intellectual, and ethical.

One of the preeminent pleasures of critique is its relief effect. Rather than suppressing or banishing our political anxieties or discontents, critique invites us to take them seriously and attend to them. Rather than wait out mutely a political campaign to which we feel we in some way ought to belong but whose terms are faintly or overtly untenable to us, critique allows us a form of engagement. Critique, in short, gives us something to do other than go home when the current aims and strategies of a constituency to which we feel some degree of belonging have choked us into silence. If, as Janet Halley argues, sex harassment law, which we as feminists once heralded as offering a crucial name and source of redress to one site of women's subordination, now appears to be on a doctrinal path of hetero-normativity and sexual moralism, critique enables interlocution with sex harassment regulation. If the recently passed federal Defense of Marriage Act and state versions such as the Knight Initiative in California, which prohibits recognition of out-of-state gay marriages, strikes some feminists, leftists, and queers as having been incited by a wrongheaded ambition on the part of gays to obtain access to an institution subject to critique from many angles, critique affords us something to do besides voting for "neither of the above." Critique, in other words, offers relief from political double binds that may paralyze both action and speech, and this by itself can be an enormous source of pleasure. Indeed, there can be a kind of euphoria in being released to think critically about something that one experiences as constraining, limited, or gagging. Rather than simply live the double binds, we are enabled through critique to articulate them and, then, to begin to rework them.

But there is more than relief at stake in the relationship of critique to double binds. For even as critique brings out the tensions, problems, or binds in a particular political formation, it also has the capacity to recon-nect us to our aims and hopes, as it helps us to disengage from the twisted version of those aims and hopes in particular political or legal formations. If we care deeply about the struggle for racial justice in the United States, but have grown wary of the exhaustive identification of that struggle with uninterrogated and tension-ridden affirmative action policies under siege, critique allows us to recover the kindling spirit of what has become a cynical or disingenuous relationship to those policies—the spirit that at-tached itself to racial justice in the first place. Here, we ask our fellow teachers: How many times have you grimaced with irony when your pas-sionate desire to bring racial diversity to your institution got you assigned to make recruitment phone calls to the ten African American students admitted by your program (and by the counterparts to your program at every institution yours competes with)? How may times have you read an admissions file and wondered: Where did this student learn the diversity dance ("When my grandmother came to America, she never dreamed that I would be writing this essay"), and how is it hiding her real trajectory? How many times have you pondered whether the students of color you are admitting under the rubric of affirmative action are the ones most unfairly deprived of educational opportunity till now, or the ones whose lives would be most improved if they had a creamier slice of the higher-education pie? How many times have you watched an implicit requirement that your program admit the "right" number of blacks with respect to Latinos with respect to Native Americans displace the questions: Which of these students can benefit most from being here? Which have intellectual appetites that will most readily gain energy from the particular education we offer? How did this chilly, technocratic exercise in achieving "mix" become the object of our protracted labor to abrade the whiteness of our institutions and repair the injustice of race-based exclusions? And how many times, while reading with pain the work of a student of color who has radically disappointed your expectations, have you asked yourself: Sure, the stigma of being an "affirmative action baby" has been deployed by conservatives to delegitimate affirmative action, but what if we stopped denouncing the stigma as wholly illusory and dealt forthrightly with the demoralization — and alienated performance — it can produce?

Critique begins by allowing such torments, worries, and questions — those surfacing from practice, from engagement, from experience, as well as from theoretical quandaries — to shape its pursuit. Katherine Franke's anxiety about the overreach of sexuality as an analytical category of power and Wendy Brown's distress about the regulatory dimensions of many feminist rights claims are examples of just such beginnings. The gesture can relieve these worries of their shadowy, traitorous, and often suppressed status as it crafts them into a project that insists on understanding by precisely what paths, mechanisms, and contingencies we have come to a particular troubling pass. It embodies a will to knowledge, *it really wants to know* how things work and why, not just what principle we are supposed to uphold, what line we are supposed to toe, what side we are supposed to cheer. And in this work, it can free us from our all too frequently cynical or despairing relationships to our most deeply held values and rekindle the animating spirit of those values. Thus Brown details the contradictions that seemingly beset feminist identity-based rights claiming in order to argue that they are not double binds that should constrain feminist justice seeking, but rather paradoxes that can extend its diagnostic and utopian reach if we read and navigate them carefully. Drucilla Cornell offers a ruthless critique of liberal legalist bases for abortion access in order to arrive at politically more satisfying if in some ways also riskier arguments for abortion rights. As Halley and Ford seek to peel away cultural regulatory projects imported into the antidiscrimination regime when we made hostile environment, sexual harassment, and discrimination against "racial cultures" actionable, they aim in part to return priority to sex and race antidiscrimination. And David Kennedy shows how international law systematically captures renewal efforts so that he can illuminate the political stakes of a breakaway effort that engaged scholars and practitioners in agonized and ecstatic social practices of critique and professional engagement.

Critique offers another source of pleasure related to this one. It can interrupt the isolation of those silenced or excluded by the binds of current legal or political strategies; indeed, it can produce conversation in which alternative political formations might be forged. Far from being the isolated reproach of a malcontent, critique can conjure intellectual community where there was none, where the hegemonic terms of political discourse only set one for or against a particular issue or campaign but did not permit of alternatives. The relief effect, in other words, can be contagious, releasing from political and intellectual constraints not only the authors of critique but an audience interpellated by it. To consider this in terms of the concrete project of this book: if part of the reason the left feels so small and beleaguered today pertains to the fact that legalism has nearly saturated the entire political culture, thus making left projects nearly indistinguishable from more mainstream liberal ones, then critique of the sort this book features enables the possibility of discerning and reclaiming left projects within liberalism, thereby connecting with one another those who have a common concern with certain kinds of political problems, constraints, and ideals. In this light, critique bids to operate as the basis of the resuscitation of left communities; it can be formative and potentially connective, an image which stands in sharp contrast to the now conventional view of critique as either destructive or irrelevant.

This discovery of others who share one's worries and discontents with existing political practices or reform strategies, this opening of conversation outside the lines of existing practices also sketches a sensibility that itself might be worth cultivating both politically and intellectually. This is a sensibility extralegal in character, one that presses against limits in part to understand their binding force, one that is irreverent toward identity categories and other governing norms, and above all, one that is unattached to the intellectual suffering that attends intellectual isolation. It wants to recover the pleasure of connection in intellectual and political work; indeed, it casts pleasure as that which makes such work both rich and compelling.

Of course, there are those who would render this very valuation of pleasure an objection to the work we are attempting to cultivate and promulgate, who would treat attention to suffering rather than pleasure as an index of the value of all intellectual and political work. There are those who not only cast progressive politics as necessarily bound to the relief of suffering but regard any pleasure taken in intellectual or political work with suspicion, as a sign that the work is not serious in its range or reach, that it is not committed to the downtrodden, that it does not depict the world from their point of view. In this hydraulic model of suffering and pleasure in politics, in which the presence of each signifies the absence of the other, pleasure is presumed to be indifferent to or to erase suffering. The sign of true political commitment is unstinting, self-effacing devotion to a cause of misery, and where there is misery, no pleasure can be had.

But what if pleasure is itself a crucial source of political motivation? The desire and energy to make a better world, one in which one really wants to live, cannot be easily generated from an ethos that casts pleasure as a luxury. Moreover, what if pleasure and the relief of suffering are not opposites? What if they can be intermixed in complex and productive ways? And what if the relief of suffering is not the sole basis of worthy political work? Some emancipatory and egalitarian visions may require more of us than the present demands. Some might even induce a certain suffering, for example, more intense involvement in the making of collective life, more responsibility for others, more limitations on wealth or in the use of the earth's resources. Similarly, some of these projects may have little to do with what ordinarily qualifies as suffering but may pertain instead to challenging regimes of domination in which palpable suffering is largely imperceptible. Let us suppose for a moment that most people actually enjoy life under capitalism, that most women do not experience the unequal sexual division of labor as a source of pain, that most slaves were happy most of the time: Would that disable a left critique of capitalist regimes for the domination, alienation, inequality, and wasteful production that they entail? Would that preclude feminists from seeking to restructure a gendered political economy? Would that foreclose systematic critiques of sheer domination?

We wish to challenge yet another constraint on critique issued by the suffer-mongerers. In the insistence that all political intellectual work must be directly addressed to suffering and its potential redress, there is a radical foreclosure of the very intellectual range and reach that we have been arguing for as that which is opened and pursued by critique. An intrepid inquiry into the discourses that organize suffering and political life more generally, or the genealogical, deconstructive, historical, or discourse analytical exercises that allow us to rethink the constitutive terms of particular political problems — this kind of work is often ruled out by presuppositions about what constitutes political work, what suffering is, and what its mandates are. So it is not simply that we wish to demote suffering from its pride of place as an organizing value for political intellectual work, not simply that we refuse the antinomy between suffering and pleasure, not simply that we want to recuperate the value and practice of pleasure in intellectual and political life, not simply that we want political thinking to be unrestricted by moralistic mandates unselfconscious about their own origins and energies. The cultivation of critique also upends the semiotic and political fixity and stability of suffering itself.

If it seems we are simultaneously arguing *for* the politically enriching dimensions of critique and *against* the direct subordination of critique to politics — against a construction of the intellectual as a political service worker — then we have achieved precisely the tension we want. Critique potentially reinvigorates politics by describing problems and constraints anew, by attending to what is hidden, disavowed, or implicit, and by discerning or inventing new possibilities within it. But critique can do this only to the extent that it is unbridled from the terms of the political problem that animate it. Similarly, while political life requires responses according to its own contingencies and temporalities, critique cannot bear fruit if it is unilaterally submitted to that urgency, if seamless reconciliation of political and intellectual life is demanded, if we bestow the power of foreclosure on the questions Where is all this going? What are the political implications? What is to be done?[8] Not only will the intellectual reach of critique be dramatically foreshortened by such demands, but both its political inventiveness and the richness of intellectual pleasure that it offers will be curtailed as well. In short, we want to affirm and articulate the important relation between critique and political work without identifying or collapsing the two projects.

The Essays

The work gathered here indicates that left internal critique is alive and well, if dispersed and perhaps undervalued. It also suggests that current left critiques of left legalism are both wide-ranging and felicitously free of a univocal line or approach. Duncan Kennedy offers a relentless exposé of rights as double-bound by the same contradictions that plague adjudication; he is sustained in this destructive work by a vision of a vital left undertaking that resists rather than acquiesces in these traps. Compare with this Drucilla Cornell's effort to wrestle from conventional rights discourse a new set of possibilities for women's equality, her effort to simultaneously feature subjectivity, semiotic indeterminacy, linguistic power, and individual experience in a discourse that, Duncan Kennedy might say, *must* elide these things. Wendy Brown and David Kennedy are cartographers: both map the discursive forms that drive the articulable in two vastly different legal domains (identity-bound rights for Brown, international law for Kennedy). But Brown's argument that paradox is the inherent condition of left-oriented rights work contrasts with David Kennedy's opening dare — let's think "*against* the box" — and his concluding promise to dance across a field of double binds if someone will just start the music.

Or consider the shared commitment of Mark Kelman and Gillian Lester on one hand and Lauren Berlant on the other to revive rights critique. Both projects expose to withering criticism recent productions of identity founded on injury (Kelman and Lester the idea that "the learning disabled" are "discriminated against"; Berlant the personhood defined by trauma). But these essays diverge acutely in the academic locales they inhabit, the disciplinarity they make use of, and in the degree of normativity they avow in their own projects: Berlant is most concerned to criticize the normativity at work in legal discourses of injury, while Kelman and Lester regard norms as inescapable in determining school expenditures for different kinds of learners. Richard T. Ford and Katherine Franke both explore how certain categories intended to classify and represent a subordination — in the one case "racial culture," in the other "sexuality" — actually serve as what Foucault called "dense transfer points for power." Thus, although racial culture and sexuality may depict a congealed, hierarchical subordination, they may obscure other and more mobile relations of power coursing through them. Ford and Franke both examine how these reifications gain ominous force when installed in legalism. Yet their ends vary as much as their objects of study: Franke returns to a legalistic project of affirming a reform in international human rights, and Ford's aim is to invoke a self-critical attitude in critical race theory and, with it, a skepticism about current reform projects. Now compare Michael Warner and Janet Halley. Warner's critique of the gay-centrist arguments for same-sex marriage and Halley's critique of sex harassment regulation emerge from very similar engagements with queer thought: both chart the dangers of assimilating queers into legal regimes saturated with heterosexual and conventionally gendered norms; both seek to minimize legal regimes that threaten mobile sexualities with fixity. But whereas Warner grounds his critique in a strong queer normativity that has propositional content and an authoritative origin in Stonewall sexual liberation, Halley attempts to launch hers from a critique of the very practice of knowing sexuality and its normativities.

Finally, many of the essays collected here reflect on the social practices of left legalism and on the affiliative life of critique. Warner sheds his academic robes to denounce the political and intellectual project of gay centrists seeking same-sex marriage — a direct engagement in a current political question and an explicit effort both to invoke a certain gay public and to persuade it to heed certain gay norms. Butler, engaging the same political question, is also concerned that queer politics not regulate affiliative desires. But Butler seeks to suture a cold critical assessment of the state-centered gay marriage project with a commitment to recognizing the yearnings for visibility, intelligibility, and legitimacy that give rise to this project. Duncan Kennedy delicately introduces the idea that a "loss of faith in rights" is a fatality to which critique has exposed him, one which cannot be undone any more than a loss of faith in God can be undone, and one which raises a series of problems — problems which should be named, not hidden, he implies — in his relations with left allies who have not, or who refuse to, undergo a similar critical turn. David Kennedy situates in a critical sociology of the field of international law the comico-tragical story of a left intellectual collectivity, the NAIL (New Approaches to International Law), a story full of celebratory energy and intense mourning, which he tells "to make known the dark side of the box."

Certainly these are not easy or easily met bids for new affiliations and affinities. Nor do they converge perfectly with one another. We propose that these diverse demands for difficulty do not fragment what remains of the left; instead, they can reawaken our desire to dodge the constraining orthodoxies often locked into left thinking. There is no new school to be formed here, no set of included and excluded objects, no party line about the right level of risk to be run with legalism, no correct or valorized audience. There is neither a demand that there must be a solution for every critique advanced, nor a conceit that solutions are mere practical things having no place in scholarly work. What unites these projects is a yearning for justice that exceeds the imagination of liberal legalism, a critical and self-critical intellectual orientation, and a certain courage to open the door of political and legal thought as if the wolves were not there.

Notes

1. Lama Abu-Odeh, "Post-Colonial Feminism and the Veil: Considering the Differences," *New England Law Review* 26 (1992): 1527.

2. See Karen Engle, "What's So Special about Special Rights?" *Denver University Law Review* 75 (1998):1265, for an excellent discussion of this double bind in equality discourse.

3. We use "status" here in the classic sense, as "a legal personal relationship, not temporary in its nature nor terminable at the mere will of the parties, with which third persons and the state are concerned." *Black's Law Dictionary,* 5th ed. (St. Paul, MN: West Publishing, 1979). Think king, serf, felon, wife.

4. Catharine A. MacKinnon often challenged audiences: If you are for women, you are against pornography. The analysis behind this challenge appears in her book *Feminism Unmodified: Discourses on Life and Law* (Cambridge, MA: Harvard University Press, 1987): "Gender is sexual. Pornography constitutes the meaning of that sexuality. Men treat women as whom they see women as being. Pornography constructs who that is. Men's power over women means that the way men see women defines who women can be. Pornography is that way. . . . The feminist critique of pornography . . . proceeds from women's point of view, meaning the standpoint of the subordination of women to men" (197). "Pornography turns a woman into a thing to be acquired and used" (199). "In a feminist perspective, pornography is the essence of a sexist social order, its quintessential social act" (204).

5. Tim Walters, *Critique* (Ph.D. diss., University of California, Berkeley, in progress).

6. Ibid.

7. Martin Heidegger, *What Is a Thing?* trans. W. B. Barton Jr. and Vera Deutsch (Chicago: H. Regenery, 1967): 119–20.

8. There is a moment in Plato's *Crito,* after Socrates has been sentenced to death but before he has drunk the hemlock, in which a group of Socrates' friends visit him in prison with an escape plan. To decide whether to go with them, Socrates insists on thinking through both his obligation to Athens and especially to its laws (which he would be breaking if he escaped) and the nature of death (which he would be deferring if he escaped). As Socrates begins to frame the importance of deliberating about the rights and wrongs of escaping, Crito responds impatiently: "I agree with what you say, Socrates; but I wish you would consider what we ought to *do*" (48d; emphasis added). The implication is that the question of what action to take is so urgent that the basis for the action cannot be examined. The implication is also that thinking, questioning, and theorizing are orders of activity different from action, and without bearing on it. Crito's attitude, supplemented by a certain moralism, has gained an ascendency in contemporary American political life, where too often it precludes the deep questioning that Socrates stubbornly insisted on.

RICHARD T. FORD

Beyond "Difference": A Reluctant Critique of Legal Identity Politics

The Discourse of Difference

Plaintiff is a black woman who seeks $10,000 damages, injunctive, and declaratory relief against enforcement of a grooming policy of the defendant American Airlines that prohibits employees in certain employment categories from wearing an all-braided hairstyle. Plaintiff has been an American Airlines employee for approximately eleven years, and has been an airport operations agent for over one year. Her duties involve extensive passenger contact, including greeting passengers, issuing boarding passes, and checking luggage. She alleges that the policy violates her rights under the Thirteenth Amendment of the United States Constitution, under Title VII of the Civil Rights Act, 42 *U.S.C.* § *2000e* et seq. (1976), and under 42 *U.S.C.* § *1981* (1976), in that it discriminates against her as a woman, and more specifically as a black woman. . . .

[Plaintiff asserts] that the "corn row" style has a special significance for black women. She contends that it "has been, historically, a fashion and style adopted by Black American women, reflective of cultural, historical essence of the Black women in American society." "The style was 'popularized' so to speak, within the larger society, when Cicely Tyson adopted the same for an appearance on nationally viewed Academy Awards presentation several years ago. . . . It was and is analogous to the public statement by the late Malcolm X regarding the Afro hair style. . . . At the bottom line, the completely braided hair style, sometimes referred to as corn rows, has been and continues to be part of the cultural and historical essence of Black American women.[1]

This has long been an easy case for the ideological left. A large, impersonal, capitalist, mainstream, uptight, and possibly even racist corporation versus a proletarian underdog whose deeply personal mode of self-expression is also the quite literal embodiment of the soul of a subject people. Milquetoast versus multiculturalism; bureaucracy versus braids: we know what side we're on.

But isn't the argument as Rogers advanced it at least as disquieting? Cornrows are "the cultural and historical essence of Black American women"? Leaving aside the volumes of critique of racial essentialism as a conceptual matter, as a matter of historical fact, this statement is false: Rogers's own pleadings assert that the style was popularized *in the 1970s* by a Hollywood actress.

And there are larger problems that concern the theory of racial discrimination and civil rights that Rogers's claim assumes. Rogers cites Malcolm X in support of the importance of the cornrow hairstyle. But it is far from clear that Title VII protects or should protect politically controversial if racially salient behavior even if advanced through the vehicle of physical grooming. Suppose some black women employed by American Airlines wished to wear cornrows and advance the political message they ostensibly embody, and others thought cornrows damaged the interests of black women in particular and reflected badly on the race as a whole. (Given the cultural politics of black America in the mid- to late 1970s there almost certainly were such black women employed by American Airlines, and even more certainly were there such black women among its customers.) Suppose further that the management of American Airlines, either formally or informally, sought out and considered the opinions of its employees as well as its customers and made its grooming policies based at least in part on such information. (There's nothing in the record that contradicts this narrative; it's at least possible.) Now Rogers's claim is no longer plausibly described as a claim on behalf of black women. Instead, it is a claim on behalf of some black women over the possible objections of other black women.

Rogers and her supporters might object: What business is it of other black women whether *we* wear braids—no one will be forced to wear them. But this individualistic account of the stakes of the case flatly contradicts the proffered rationale for conceiving of the hairstyle as a legal right: that cornrows are the "cultural essence" not of one black woman but of black *women*. If this essentialist claim is to be taken seriously, then cornrows cannot be the cultural essence of only those black women who choose to wear them—they must be the cultural essence of *all* black women. And in this case, *all* black women have a stake in the rights claim and the message about them that it will necessarily send—not only those who support the political and cultural statement conveyed by cornrows but also those who oppose that statement.

We'd need a fairly detailed account of the cultural and political stakes of cornrows to have a real sense of the normative dimensions of this legal conflict. Does the wearing of cornrows track social class (it's not clear whether most cornrow wearers are working-class "authentics" or bourgeois trendies) or ideological (nationalist versus integrationist?) splits within the black community? Do cornrows reflect a sophisticated racial politics in which the essentialist message is subordinate, ambiguous, or even insincere, or is an extremely crude essentialism a central or indispensable part of the politics of cornrows? Is the symbolism of cornrows widely shared and understood at least within some subset of American society, or is it ambiguous and over- or underdetermined? What is clear is that the assertion that cornrows are the cultural essence of black women cannot be taken as conclusive evidence that a "right to cornrows" is an unadulterated good thing for blacks or black women.

Even if we take it on faith that cornrows represent black nationalist pride as against the integrationist and assimilationist coiffure of chemically straightened hair, it is clear that a right to cornrows would be an intervention in a long-standing debate *among* African Americans about empowerment strategies and norms of identity and identification. It is by no means clear that an argument that presumes that blacks or black women have a cultural *essence as blacks or as black women* is a vehicle of racial empowerment.

With the *Rogers* case available for comparison and contrast, consider another case in which an employer makes policy that implicates a theory of racial culture:

> TPG is a telephone marketing corporation, often hired to perform work for political candidates. The conduct at issue in this case involves TPG's work making "get-out-the-vote" calls for various political candi-

dates. . . . Approximately 10% of such calling is race-matched, such that black voters are called by black TPG employees who use the "black" script, while white voters are called by white TPG employees who use a different "white" script. . . . TPG employees doing the race matched calling in 1994 were assigned separate calling areas and separate scripts according to race. . . . TPG also physically segregated employees who worked at race matched calling. Black callers were segregated into one room, and white callers segregated into another.[2]

Is TPG's practice, as the court held, racially discriminatory, is it "based on a racial stereotype that blacks would respond to blacks and . . . that [Shirley] Ferrill's race was directly related to her ability to do the job"? Or is the employment practice the natural outgrowth of the recognition of cultural differences between the races — and therefore justifiable, perhaps even laudable? If Rogers's cultural essence as a black woman entails the right to wear cornrows, mightn't even a good faith employer conclude that her cultural essence would also enable her to better persuade other blacks and disable her from connecting with whites?

This essay focuses on an *approach* to racial justice — an often obsessive insistence on racial *difference* — and the set of beliefs and discourse that that approach entails in the attempt to expand civil rights by protecting "cultural difference" and "racially linked traits." It is in part directed at the proposals that would advance cultural rights as a logical (even logically required) extension of traditional civil rights protections for racial minorities, but only as a salient instance of the larger approach. Examples of this approach have expanded, both in number and in comprehensiveness, since Rogers lost her lawsuit almost twenty years ago. For instance, in recent years Barbara Flagg suggests that Title VII should prohibit discrimination on the basis of "personal characteristics that . . . intersect seamlessly with [one's racial] self-definition."[3] Juan Perea proposes that Title VII should prohibit discrimination based, not on ethnicity, but on "ethnic traits." William Bratton and Drucilla Cornell propose that Title VII prohibit employers from requiring that bilingual Spanish- and English-speaking employees speak only English while on the job, not because all people should have a right to speak their first language but *because of the centrality of Spanish to Latino identity*.[4]

The race-conscious left has been largely focused, at least since the early 1980s, on a specific approach to racial justice: that of the assertion of racial difference. It is important to briefly trace the genealogy of this approach. The "difference approach" to racial justice was a reaction to a mainstream civil rights discourse that, over time, came to be obsessively preoccupied with racial integration and assimilation. The American mainstream considered integration and assimilation to be both effective strategies for racial justice considered in terms of economic and political empowerment, and laudable ends in and of themselves. The utopian dream of racial integration and assimilation was captured in the figure of the color-blind society, a society in which race had no normative significance, in which it was scarcely noticeable at all. Indeed, many imagined that racial difference would literally be eliminated through intermarriage and miscegenation; the painter Ed Ruscha, for instance, opined, only half in jest, that one day we will be a society of tall, attractive people, clad in khaki, with complexions of a ruddy beige.

It is important to emphasize that color blindness was not simply an ideal that a white mainstream forced on people of color. Some of the most passionate advocates of color blindness, strong racial integration, and even assimilation were people of color who truly believed in the moral justice and pragmatic necessity of these ideals. These advocates of color blindness were not neoconservative sellouts. In the 1960s and early 1970s color blindness was a truly radical idea. Programmatic racial desegregation of schools had only recently begun in earnest. Many workplaces and public accommodations had explicitly excluded people of color a few years earlier. Interracial marriages were not legally recognized in many states until 1967: the Supreme Court decision in *Loving v. Virginia* changed the black-letter law but not black-baiting public attitudes. In this context integration and even assimilation — born of a universalist humanism — were the ideas of a courageous left-wing avant-garde. Opposition to these in the name of tradition and racial difference, though a competing position of the left, was most notably the position of the racist right.

Integration and especially color blindness and assimilation became the ideas of the mainstream in the late 1970s and 1980s. To a real extent this must be considered a decisive victory for the radicals. But these ideas were cynically redeployed to stymie progress: color blindness was deployed against affirmative action, integration was used to undermine any form of racial solidarity, assimilation became a bludgeon to discipline any practice that made the milquetoast mainstream uncomfortable. This story is familiar.

At the same time it must be acknowledged that the tug of war over integration, color blindness, and assimilation reflected real substantive disagreements even among those unequivocally committed to racial justice and even among the ideological left. For instance, the civil rights movement never really resolved within the black community the conflict between integration and separatism. Despite the victory of integration in mainstream civil rights, separatism survived as a "loyal opposition" to integrationist civil rights. Some people accepted integration only as a means to an end—green follows white—whereas others embraced it as a goal. Some thought integration should naturally lead to assimilation and a color-blind utopia; others thought it would lead to a Du Boisian ideal of separate nations living together. These conflicts came to the surface when the initial battles for formal equality were won (and the victories proved inadequate): the question What now? was as much a philosophical question as a strategic one.

To a real extent, the contemporary frustration with mainstream civil rights reflects, not its failure to produce results, but this latent, unresolved conflict over ultimate ends. Resistance to what may seem to some a natural extension of civil rights may reflect retrenchment, but may also reflect honest disagreement about what racial justice entails. This normative disagreement is not well described as a failure of will, a lack of commitment, or a mistake about the facts.

The "politics of difference" that has emerged as the dominant approach of the race-conscious left must be understood as a widespread reaction to the hegemony of integration and assimilation and to their cynical redeployment as limits on racial justice. It was a necessary corrective to the hegemony of universalist humanism—an important development for everyone concerned with racial justice. But it should also be seen as a partial victory of one wing of the racial justice left over another. For those who wished to save the ideals of universalist humanism from their cynical highjackers, the rise of the politics of difference is a hard blow.

So this essay is inspired by the following question: What if the politics of difference threatens to become another hegemonic discourse, no less total, no less obsessive, no less myopic than the universalist ideal that preceded it? Suppose the race-conscious left has become blinded by the obsession with a singular approach to racial justice. Are we certain that integration, even its strong and somewhat coercive variant, is *never* the right approach to racial justice? Is it beyond question that cultural difference is always preferable to cultural melding and the common creation of common cultural practices and artifacts — what many would deride as assimilation? Is it a matter of fact, or an article of faith, that such cultural melding must result in the elimination of the minority culture, in cultural genocide?

Faust in Blackface: Multicultural "Difference" as Corrupt Detente

In the 1980s something called multiculturalism made a big splash in the academy and later in political and popular conversation. At first many believed (hoped) that multiculturalism was a fad that would sweep through the ivied halls of higher learning for a time and then fade into obscurity, like designer jeans or mopeds. They were half right: multiculturalism was like designer jeans. The astute reader will note that designer jeans did not exactly fade into obscurity; instead, they morphed into designer chinos, designer T-shirts, designer windbreakers, designer polo neck shirts, and, let's not forget, more designer jeans. Similarly, although the heady days of the canon wars and Western Civ skirmishes are behind us, multiculturalism's durability is marked by its new ubiquitous anonymity. Multiculturalism is no longer notable because it is everywhere. As with designer jeans, many who will not admit being fans of multiculturalism still put it on every morning, and many more of us will resort to it when we don't have anything else to wear.

The conviction that informs this section is that liberal multiculturalism, at least in the form it generally greets us today, is often an analytically deficient and normatively impoverished approach to the issues — racial justice, cultural pluralism, and group identity politics — that it purports to inform. When it is analytically deficient, it conflates issues that are most usefully considered separately. When it is normatively impoverished, its aspirations are both anemic and unattainable.

So why is multiculturalism so popular, commitment to it so apparently fierce and consistent, and alternative approaches to the issues it addresses almost nonexistent? My hypothesis is that liberal multiculturalism is best understood as the terms of a sort of Faustian detente that much of the left, especially the race-conscious left, was effectively, if not intentionally, maneuvered into.

To be sure, multiculturalism vindicates long-standing and strongly held commitments among many members of socially subordinated groups. But the dominant liberal form in which the discourse of multiculturalism presents itself today, especially its particular emphasis on the *preservation* of difference, was not, I submit, either the inevitable outgrowth of historically held political commitments or the product of considered and thoughtful strategic or normative analysis. Instead, the development of multicultural-ist discourse in its peculiar liberal form was largely reactive and defensive, and the commitment to it the function of a plausible but, I contend, mis-guided tactical pragmatism that has become confused with ultimate ends.

ALAN BAKKE: MULTICULTURALIST?

One of the most important figures in the development of liberal legal multi-culturalism in the United States was neither a lawyer nor a person of color, yet his ideas profoundly changed modern civil rights. He was a white male and an aspiring medical student named Alan Bakke. For those few readers not familiar with the notorious case *Regents of University of California v. Bakke,* decided in 1978, a brief summary will suffice. Alan Bakke applied for admission to the University of California at Davis medical school and was denied admission. Bakke discovered that racial minorities with lower grades and test scores than his were admitted under an affirmative action program that essentially established separate admission tracks for various racial groups. Bakke sued the university, asserting that his Fourteenth Amendment right to equal protection had been violated. Bakke prevailed.

Justice Powell, the author of what is widely considered the controlling opinion, did not find that all affirmative action was unconstitutional. In-stead, the Court applied strict scrutiny to the university's program, under which the racial classification would have to serve a compelling govern-mental interest and be narrowly tailored to the furtherance of that interest. The Court then found that rigid numerical quotas could never be suffi-ciently narrowly tailored and that the governmental purpose of remedying past discrimination was sufficiently compelling only if the university could identify specific discriminatory practices in which it had engaged but not to remedy societal discrimination in general.

This was, of course, a bad day for the race-conscious left. But all was not lost. The Powell opinion left one door tantalizingly ajar: a non-quota-based affirmative action plan served a compelling interest (and thereby could overcome strict scrutiny) if it was designed to promote "diversity." Colleges and universities could continue to consider the race of applicants as a factor in admissions provided that their purpose was to attain a student body enriched by diverse perspectives arising from the racial backgrounds of its members.

The diversity rationale embraced in the Powell opinion silently analogized racial diversity to ethnic diversity: both the Powell opinion and the amici curiae brief submitted by Columbia, Harvard, Stanford, and the University of Pennsylvania on which Powell relied use the terms "racial" and "ethnic" almost interchangeably. The Powell opinion silently institutionalized an ethnicity model of race that emphasizes cultural difference over status hierarchy. In the ethnicity paradigm, the position of blacks is analogous to that of, say, Italian Americans: both have distinctive cultural backgrounds and therefore may contribute a unique perspective to the university environment. What is explicitly excluded by this paradigm is any acknowledgment that a very recent history of state-sponsored and institutional subordination distinguishes the two groups and may make differential treatment appropriate. The result is that the *cultural* identity of a racial minority group is foregrounded at the expense of the history of racism.

The diversity rationale is benign when understood as one of many possible reasons a university might care about the racial demographics of its student body. But it is dangerous when codified as the only reason race is significant. *Bakke*'s codification of the diversity rationale required institutions that wished to engage in affirmative action *and* minority groups themselves to *emphasize* cultural difference. Only by highlighting stark differences in perspectives and experiences marked by race could universities justify affirmative action post-*Bakke*. And a more subtle and much more pernicious implication hovered over post-*Bakke* university life: *only* by highlighting their own distinctiveness could minority students justify their presence in the universities that admitted them.

Bakke was widely understood to mark a movement to the ideological right, assuming that the right wished to de-emphasize race while the left insisted on its salience. Powell's opinion was "difference splitting" at its liberal best and worst: limit affirmative action without eliminating it. But the opinion did not simply affect the *scope* of affirmative action; it also altered its *character*. And with this came an unintended side effect: by altering the character of the institutional treatment of race, it also altered the incentives surrounding racial identity and thereby altered performance of racial identity, at least among those directly affected by the institutions. And because those so affected were disproportionately wealthy, socially elite, and culturally influential (the applicants, students, and faculty of selective universities), they in turn profoundly influenced the meaning of racial identity in society as a whole.

We can't know what the racial landscape at America's elite universities and in the nation as a whole would look like had *Bakke* come out the other way. But it's safe to say it would look different. Subtle and overt pressures for social integration and at times assimilation might have encouraged a different performance of racial identity had *Bakke* not counterbalanced them by explicitly encouraging the emphasis on cultural diversity. The resulting racial identities would not have been less or more authentic than those we have today, but they would have been different, and quite likely in ways that both left and right would have preferred: more overtly focused on the politics of antisubordination, less concerned with cultural differences and the corresponding production of racial affect.

Thus my working hypothesis (which contains an irony that would be funny if it were not so tragic): the "conservative victory" in *Bakke* in no small part encouraged the development and popularity of that bête noire of American conservatives, contemporary race-conscious multiculturalism. I suggest that the development of the study of racism and race relations as "ethnic" studies, the enduring popularity of nationalism and racial separatism, and the socialization of students of color into a multiculturalist identity can all be attributed in some part to the *Bakke* opinion.

Without *Bakke* it is likely that affirmative action programs would have continued to use race as one factor among many to serve a number of goals, including both promoting diversity and helping to remedy societal discrimination. Free of *Bakke*'s requirement of specific findings of identifiable discrimination, universities may have used (and admitted using) racial preferences as a means of correcting for the societal racial bias that certainly affects the grades and test scores of many individual applicants. Indeed, the Court could have eliminated quotas without limiting universities to the diversity rationale, and there is no reason that affirmative action based on these criteria should have been any more expansive or severe than that based only on diversity. Given the cultural and social investment elite institutions have in maintaining a white plurality, if not majority, it is unlikely that affirmative action would have expanded at any greater rate regardless of the proffered rationale; the effect on white applicants would most likely have been the same.

But the effect on the character of student life and on the intellectual and cultural development of ideas about race would not, I submit, have been the same. A race-conscious policy that focused on the need to undo the legacy of racial subordination and to correct for its contemporary manifestations might have made a greater number of racial "scripts" available and encouraged a richer and more nuanced understanding of racial identity.[5] This understanding would not have focused exclusively on diversity (which later hardened into a quite specific idea of *cultural* diversity, as I discuss below), with its implicit requirement that people of color stand out in specific and prescribed ways to justify their presence. Instead, it might have acknowledged that the history of American racial hierarchy creates a mix of racial identities that are based on a complex relationship to mainstream American culture and institutions — a relationship of cooperation and subversion, of sincere admiration, deep-seeded contempt, and ironic detachment, of a desire for acceptance and an insistence on distance. These identities are indeed unique and will contribute to a diverse institution. But the contribution can be fully appreciated only in the context of a society thoroughly shaped by racial status and racial hierarchy. In this context, racial difference marks the difference in experience and perspective developed because of one's position in a racial hierarchy, not necessarily *cultural* difference (and certainly not intrinsic or inherited cultural difference) in the sense of different norms, traditions, epistemologies, or standards of aesthetic evaluation.

Such an understanding of race may well have pleased both the color-blind right and the color-conscious left more than contemporary racial multiculturalism. To the happiness of the right, racial identity would have been understood not as monolithic, nor would racial justice have seemed to necessarily require rejection of mainstream norms. Instead, racial identity would have been understood as fluid and kaleidoscopic, and racial justice as potentially consistent with a range of identities and relationships to mainstream America, including the embrace of majority norms and assimilation to existing institutions. To the benefit of the left, racial identity would not have entailed an essentially conservative project of cultural preservation and a fetishism of pedigree and tradition, as it increasingly does under the rubric of liberal multiculturalism. Instead, racial identity would have been ripe with the potential eruption of new cultural forms and new ways of being, the liberation of the human spirit, and the creativity of the avant-garde.

Multiculturalism might not have seemed a logical extension of antiracism in this alternative reality. Instead, it might have seemed what for the most part it is: a separate project with different normative stakes, different factual assumptions, and animated by different ideological commitments.

Of course, even without *Bakke* we may not have developed such an understanding of racial identity; plenty of other forces contributed to the development of identity politics in its current form. But *Bakke* gave the diversity conception of race the imprimatur of the Supreme Court and underwrote it with the force of law. The significance of this intervention should not be underestimated.

"Recognition" of Difference as Social Control

At the very same time that the universalist ideologues were preaching the merits of Westernization or "assimilation," they were also (or others were also) preaching the eternal existence and virtue of difference. Thus a universalist message of cultural multiplicity could serve as a justification of educating various groups in their separate "cultures" and hence preparing them for different tasks in the single economy. The extreme version of this . . . is *apartheid*. But lesser versions . . . have been widespread. . . . Furthermore, we can enlist the dominated groups in their own oppression. Insofar as they cultivate their separateness as "cultural" groups . . . they socialize their members into cultural expressions which distinguish them . . . [and valorize] some at least of the values attributed to them by racist and sexist theories. And they do this, in a seeming paradox, on the grounds of the universal principle of the equal validity of all cultural expressions. — Immanuel Wallerstein, *Geopolitics and Geoculture: Essays on the Changing World-System*

RACIAL CULTURE AS COMMON KNOWLEDGE

Although Rogers lost in court, the theory of racial identity and cultural membership entailed by her Title VII claim is widely accepted, not only among left/liberals and communities of color, but by mainstream American society. The idea that racial identity is defined by a set of *objective characteristics* shared by members of the race — a racial culture — is so widespread and accepted an idea that it is taken for granted. Racial culture is a matter of common knowledge.

This assertion may strike some readers as surprising. It is a fantasy of multiculturalists that the American mainstream is hell-bent on destroying cultural difference, that the new face of racial hegemony speaks the false gospel of assimilation. Alex Johnson's discussion of the role of the card games Bid Whist and Tonk in African American culture provides an articulate expression of a typical liberal multiculturalist view:

Bid Whist and Tonk, like many other African-American institutions, are maintained because they are ours: they provide us with a *safe harbor* for the preservation of the idiopathic rules, customs, and norms that developed in our community while we were kept separate from whites by law. This safe harbor also allows those who choose not to fully embrace the norms of white society to retain a place in an African-American *community in which confrontation between African-American norms and conflicting white norms never takes place.* Moreover, this safe harbor protects African-American culture, because *when the assimilationist version of integration occurs African-American culture is typically not merged into majoritarian culture but obliterated by it* — leaving no trace of what was once a unique cultural vehicle.[6]

In this account, the social practices belong to a particular group and provide safety from a hostile majority with inconsistent practices that threaten to obliterate the practices of the minority group. In fact, more than inconsistent practices are at stake, according to the account: here, a "culture" includes not only practices but distinctive norms, ideologies, cognitive maps, and epistemologies (at one point, Johnson describes the African American culture as a distinct "nomos" following the work of Robert Cover).

In Johnson's account the conflict is between the (monolithic? universally held within the group?) norms of blacks and the inconsistent norms of mainstream or white society. And confrontation with conflicting norms is assumed to lead, almost inevitably, to the obliteration of the minority group's norms and culture. Informed by the image of a society divided into distinct racial groups, each of which has its own culture that all or at least most members share, Johnson argues that "a white cultural perspective or norm . . . has the effect of stifling or *eradicating the consciousness* of African-American[s]."[7]

In this narrative, assimilation is thought to be the conjoined twin of color blindness, the discourse that would bury the legacy of state-sponsored racism and its contemporary institutionalization in a deafening and disingenuous chorus of "People are people." This narrative imagines the threat of assimilation to be its comprehensiveness and inescapability, its character as a moral imperative and a legal injunction that gives no quarter and brooks no compromise. This reading is both devastating and perversely attractive: because the enemy is monolithic and implacable, the multiculturalists can fancy themselves as a heroic *resistance,* keeping the flame of liberty alive against all odds as they await the coming of the good society.

But the discourse of assimilation is Janus-faced, is both compulsory and unavailable. Even as certain formal rules, official proclamations, and cultural narratives insist on the moral necessity of assimilation to a common norm and identity, others reinforce the inevitability and natural character of difference. The nonassimilated minority is to blame for her disadvantage, while the assimilated minority is to be apprehended with suspicion: she is a mutant, warped and unnatural like a leopard that changed its spots, but also deceptive, like a wolf in sheep's attire.

The truth of racial culture is retold (as a story one already knows) in countless and diverse forms: the racist humor of the blackface minstrel, Steppinfetchit, Amos n' Andy, Uncle Remus, Uncle Tom, Sanford and Son, Chino and the Man, but also the Moynihan Report on the pathology of black urban culture. In contemporary popular culture, racial culture is the dominant figure in a host of "odd couple/buddy" films (the prototype is the now classic *Silver Streak* starring Richard Pryor and Gene Wilder; perhaps the most popular are *48 Hours* and *Beverly Hills Cop,* both starring Eddie Murphy) in which two protagonists of difference races are forced together by circumstances and overcome treacherous and comic obstacles (at least one of which must involve racial passing or racial displacement: a white guy in the ghetto or a black guy in a redneck bar) and ultimately, *despite their severe cultural differences, manage to see that people are people after all.*

These racial buddy films illustrate the Janus-faced nature of contemporary racial ideology. They advance a color-blind ideology while reinforcing the idea of distinctive and unassimilable, if not opaque, racial cultures. Issues of racial subordination are absent from these films — racism is reduced to one or two "incidents" that are relatively easily and comically overcome — whereas racial cultural difference is portrayed as natural and inevitable: the natural place for Eddie Murphy's character in *Beverly Hills Cop* is Detroit, not Beverly Hills, and after gaining the respect and admiration of the Beverly Hills police force *despite his distinctive racial culture,* he goes back to where he belongs. So the ideal racial minority is one who retains his distinctive racial culture, functions effectively in the mainstream despite it, and, because of his racial culture, both knows his place and wants to stay there.

Popular, academic, and governmental discourse alike reproduce this Janus-faced ideology of compulsory assimilation and the inevitability of cultural difference. Multiculturalists have been right to identify the discourse of assimilation and to insist that this discourse is a mechanism of oppression. But they have largely failed to see that this discourse *contains and relies on its opposite* — the discourse of cultural difference — and therefore cannot be resisted by simple opposition. The attempt to run from compulsory assimilation toward recognition of difference in fact delivers us all the more firmly into the grasp of a racism that always includes both.

RECOGNITION AND THE INTERNALIZATION OF STEREOTYPES

As a *Black lesbian feminist* comfortable with the many different ingredients of my identity . . . I find I am constantly being encouraged to pluck out some one aspect of myself and present this as the meaningful whole, eclipsing or denying the other parts of self. But . . . my fullest concentration of energy is available to me only when I integrate all the parts of who I am . . . *without the restrictions of externally imposed definition.* — Audre Lorde, "Age, Race, Class and Sex: Redefining Difference" (emphasis added)

Is it possible to comprehend, much less embrace or be "comfortable with," identity categories such as black, lesbian, or feminist "without the restrictions of externally imposed definition"? Or are these identity categories (as opposed to their supposed referents: dark skin, female same-sex eroticism, a commitment to a certain practice of gender) the *product* of those restrictions? This is a crucial and unanswered question for the politics of difference.

The politics of difference and proposals for rights to difference are described in the writings and ideas of philosopher Charles Taylor and what he calls the "politics of recognition." Taylor's definition of the politics of recognition is illuminating:

The demand for recognition . . . is given urgency by the supposed links between recognition and identity, where this latter term designates something like a person's understanding of who they are, of their fundamental defining characteristics as a human being. The thesis is that our identity is partly shaped by recognition or its absence. . . . Nonrecognition or misrecognition can inflict harm, can be a form of oppression, imprisoning someone in a false, distorted, and reduced mode of being. Thus some feminists have argued that women . . . have been induced to adopt a depreciatory image of themselves. They have internalized a picture of their own inferiority, so that even when some of the objective obstacles to their advancement fall away, they may be incapable of taking advantage of the new opportunities. . . . An analogous point has been made in relation to blacks: that white society has for generations projected a demeaning image of them, which some of them have been unable to resist adopting. Their own self-depreciation has been, on this view, one of the most potent instruments of their own oppression.[8]

The politics of recognition is full of valuable insights. Foremost among them are the idea that identity is dialogical, that it depends on a social interaction in which the understanding and esteem of others plays a crucial role, and the related idea that the internalization of negative stereotypes is a significant source of harm with tangible consequences in term of physical health, political empowerment, and material wealth.

But something happens when these ideas are translated into a political platform that includes proposals for governmental policy. First, the concern about *non*recognition is elevated in importance while the concern about *mis*recognition recedes from view. Contemporary multiculturalism worries a lot about "silence," "absence," and "exclusion" but very little about "speaking for others," "conscription," and "compelled performance." If misrecognition is a serious harm then we must be concerned that legal recognition may go wrong, misrecognizing already subordinated groups and codifying that misrecognition with the force of law and the intractability of stare decisis. We'd better be pretty sure that the traits the law recognizes are the right ones.

But how sure can we be? When advocates of cultural rights argue for legal recognition, they typically offer very broad and vague definitions of the traits that should be protected and very thin arguments for *why* the traits should be defined as "fundamental" to a person's (and by necessary extension, a group's) identity. A common approach is to offer a list that begins with traits that can be objectively identified as familiar objects of antidiscrimination law and end with vague or more controversial traits. The argument can then cite the more familiar traits when defending the proposal, adding the more controversial or problematic traits when defining it. For instance, Juan Perea, in arguing that federal antidiscrimination law should be amended to prohibit discrimination against ethnic traits, defines ethnicity to include "race, national origin, ancestry, language, religion, shared history, traditions, values and symbols . . . which contribute to a sense of distinctiveness among members of the group." Later in the article he proposes specific language for a statutory amendment, there defining ethnic traits to include but not be limited to "language, accent, surname, and ethnic appearance." He then defines ethnic appearance, tautologically, as "expressions of ethnic identity."[9]

Notice that, in both cases, the list includes elements that are relatively uncontroversial and easily defined and elements that are quite controversial and ambiguous. For instance, race, national origin, ancestry, and religion all currently enjoy protection under federal statutory and constitutional law. Discrimination on the basis of a surname is a transparent proxy for prohibited discrimination on the basis of race and national origin. Discrimination on the basis of an accent is more problematic (there are almost certainly some cases in which an accent makes the speaker objectively more difficult to understand and in which ease of comprehension is quite important: a waiter at a restaurant is one example, a taxi dispatcher a better one, an air traffic controller an even better one). Discrimination on the basis of language is quite ambiguous; for instance, at times Perea writes of discrimination against bilingualism,[10] but the cases he cites do not, precisely speaking, involve such discrimination. Instead, they involve rules that require employees to speak English while on the job or while performing certain tasks, a requirement that bilingual employees are perfectly capable of complying with. There may be good reasons for such rules in some cases (employees who must communicate with the public or with other, nonbilingual employees), tough judgment calls in others (does non-English speaking contribute to a fracturing of the workplace and the formation of cliques, intergroup tensions among employees?), and in some cases rules will be inexplicable accept by reference to racial animus. But by describing the discrimination as against "bilingual speakers," Perea tacitly assumes that all such rules are a form of *status* discrimination, whereas there are good reasons in at least some cases to consider them behavioral regulations.

In the absence of any clear metric by which to distinguish status from behavior, the proponents of cultural/style rights often default to the subjective determination of the individual litigant. For instance, Barbara Flagg argues for Title VII protection for traits that "intersect seamlessly with [the plaintiff's] *self-definition*." Perea, somewhat less specific, seems to vacillate between an assumption that the determination of ethnicity can be ascertained as a matter of sociology (he cites sociological literature extensively and writes of discrimination on the basis of "ethnicity" or "ethnic traits," as if these terms were subject to objective meaning) and an assumption, similar to Flagg's, that any trait that an individual subjectively determines is ethnic should be considered so for legal purposes.[11]

Because the proposals implicitly assume either that group-based cultural or ethnic traits have a reasonably determinate meaning or that the individual definition of these terms offered by the plaintiff should be definitive, the proponents do not consider the possibility that plaintiffs will make insincere claims for strategic or simply self-serving reasons. But anyone familiar with politically charged litigation knows that the docket can be scripted by organized groups who seek out ideal plaintiffs with standing to bring the types of cases the groups wish to bring. This strategy has been successfully used by both left/liberal and conservative groups who use the legal system to advance their own ideological agenda. There's nothing wrong with such a use of the legal system; some of the twentieth century's greatest legal advances were secured by groups doing just this. But it does disprove the assumption that litigation is driven exclusively by the initiative of sincere individual plaintiffs with pressing grievances. Given the vast number of potential plaintiffs with standing to raise cultural rights claims, one can expect that virtually any conceivable claim — some that will horrify us — will eventually make its way to a courtroom.

Similarly, the assumption that one's subjective belief about one's identity is definitive is flatly contradicted by the premises of the politics of recognition itself. The harm of misrecognition is that members of the misrecognized group may internalize the depreciating stereotypes of others. Such individuals, then, may not always appropriately determine what is fundamental to their identity, or better put, what *should* be fundamental to their identity. If misrecognition can lead people to fail to take advantage of opportunities even after "objective obstacles to their advancement fall away," then misrecognition might also lead those same people to push for rights to self-detrimental traits and adopt misconceived legal strategies in the name of safeguarding an identity that was shaped by the misrecognition of others.

CULTURAL RECOGNITION AS SOCIAL INVALIDATION

It may be objected that individuals are the best, if not the perfect, judges of what is and should be fundamental to their identity. But even if this is so, individual litigants pressing group recognition claims do not decide only for themselves what is fundamental to their identity; they decide for all members of the group what is to be deemed fundamental to the identity of the group.

During the Clarence Thomas confirmation hearing, sociologist Orlando Patterson wrote in a newspaper Op Ed that Anita Hill's reaction to Thomas's alleged sexual overtures was "unfair and disingenuous" because although the comments were "completely out of the *cultural* frame of his white, upper-middle-class work world" they were "immediately recognizable to Hill and most women of southern working-class backgrounds, white or black, especially the latter," and "Hill perfectly understood the psycho-cultural context in which Thomas allegedly regaled her with his Rabelaisian humor . . . as a way of affirming their common origins."[12]

The point here is that the discourse of racial difference can take on a life quite independent of the good intentions of those advancing cultural identity rights. The nature of rights discourse is that anyone can assert a right and have it tested in court. But the ill effects of the codification of bad definitions of group culture and identity will not be limited to the litigant asserting the right: they will instead be deployed to regulate all members of the group.

Note that I'm concerned not only about women in general who might have to endure Justice Thomas's "Rabelaisian" bon mots. I'm particularly concerned about blacks, especially black women who are implicated in the description of black culture (Patterson explicitly implicates "nearly all African Americans" in his description of black culture). Clarence Thomas's claim to racial culture necessarily discredits Anita Hill (and any other black person who objects to or disclaims his behavior). Not only is Hill told that she must forebear Thomas's behavior because it is *his* culture, she is also told she must embrace it because it is *her* culture as well. Not only is she told that she *should* embrace the raunchy esprit de corps that Thomas offers, she is told that she *does* in fact embrace it, that she "perfectly understands" it, and that her objections to it and disclaimers of it are therefore "disingenuous."

Of course, a newspaper editorial is not the same as a published judicial opinion and a social commentator does not write with the authority of a judge. But the Op Ed page of a mainstream American newspaper is a fairly good barometer of middlebrow to elite public opinion: if Patterson's ideas about black culture got onto the Op Ed page, they would almost certainly convince at least some judges.

It's not hard to imagine attorney Patterson's successful litigation on behalf of defendant Thomas in a sex harassment suit. The resulting legal articulation of a racial cultural right would have affected not only Thomas, it would also have implicated Anita Hill, black women, indeed "nearly all African Americans." We cannot be at all confident that individual litigants will press only, or even predominantly, positive narratives of identity. Yet every time such a claim is pressed, it will be pressed not only for the individual litigant but for everyone else in the group to which he or she belongs. Ask not for whom the gavel strikes — it strikes for thee.

THE TWO FACES OF CRYSTAL

The two-faced aspect of difference discourse produces a double bind for identity politics. On the one hand, we want to assert our distinctive identity and have others recognize it as distinctive. On the other hand, we want to avoid those forms of recognition that we experience as demeaning or simply inaccurate. To make sense of identity politics, one must be able to make valid generalizations about social groups. But one also wishes to avoid demeaning stereotypes.

It can be difficult to tell the difference. Consider Professor Regina Austin's discussion of *Chambers v. Omaha Girls Club*. This case involved a young black woman employed as an instructor in a charitable club for girls in which 90 percent of the participants were black. Crystal Chambers was dismissed when she became pregnant outside of wedlock, a violation of the club's "negative role model rule." Chambers sued, claiming that the club's "rule would have a disparate impact on black women because of their significantly higher fertility rate."[13]

Austin argues against the club's assertion that "to permit single pregnant staff members to work with the girls would convey the impression that the Girls Club condoned pregnancy for the girls . . . it serves" and the implicit aspiration that "its members could be influenced by committed counselors who, by example, would prove that life offers more attractive alternatives than early pregnancy." She points out that Crystal Chambers's pregnancy is unattractive in part because employers, like the Girls Club itself, condemn single pregnant women and deny them respect and the opportunity to earn a livelihood: "The club managed to replicate the very economic hardships and social biases that, according to the district court, made the role model rule necessary in the first place."[14]

To defend Chambers and condemn the court's verdict for the defendants, Austin must embrace Chambers's generalization about black women's fertility rates. Indeed, she not only accepts the generalization as a statistical matter but embraces it as a potentially important element of black female identity. Austin complains that "implicit in the *Chambers* decision is an assumption that the *actual cultural practices* and articulated moral positions of the black females who know the struggles of early and single motherhood firsthand are both misguided and destructive. . . . Yet, for some of us, their portrayal in the *Chambers* opinions is more flattering than the authors intended." So for Austin, early single pregnancy is the by-product of the *actual cultural practices* of (at least some salient group of) black females. The "epidemic" of single black female pregnancy is not a stereotype and more than a statistical fact: it is an effect of black culture.[15]

But at the same time Austin wishes to condemn the stereotype of the oversexed, pregnant single black female. She condemns the image of Jezebel, "the wanton, libidinous black woman . . . [who] was 'free of the social constraints that surrounded the sexuality of white women,'" and insists that "black women who attempt to express their sexuality and control their reproduction should not have to travel through a minefield of stereotypes, clichés and material hardships."[16]

Austin's account reveals the other face of racial recognition: Crystal Chambers finds herself unemployed not because her employer was unwilling to acknowledge her distinctive racial culture, but because it *did* acknowledge it. According to Austin, the Girls Club believed that Chambers would function "as an icon, a reminder of a powerful culture from which the club members had to be rescued." Of course, for Austin the club did not see Chambers's real culture but a distorted stereotype: the Jezebel. However, it is not only the Girls Club but also Austin herself who finds this distinction hard to make. For instance, when Austin criticizes the judicial attitude toward Chambers she decries the court's disdain for the "actual cultural practices" (not mistaken stereotypes) of black women like Chambers. And even in her condemnation of unquestionably demeaning stereotypes, she equivocates, saying that the Mammy and Jezebel images are "not totally divorced from reality."[17]

Austin's ultimate position — that Chambers and indeed all black women should embrace (their) cultural difference — forbids her to reject racial stereotypes in convincing terms. An ethic that, as she describes it, "declares as wily, audacious, and good *all* conduct that offends the white, male, and middle-class establishments" requires her to embrace precisely those negative stereotypes that racists deploy to delegitimate people of color.

But do people of color who behave as racist stereotypes would depict them really "attempt to break out of the rigid economic, social, and political categories that a racist, sexist, and class-stratified society would impose upon them"? Can we be certain, as Austin seems to be, that the goal of racism, sexism, and class stratification is to erase social differences between groups and force, for example, women of color into the same set of social constraints that regulate the lives of white women? Isn't it more likely that a racist and sexist social order wants different constraints for different groups? Is Chambers really less constrained as an unemployed single mother than she was as an employee of the Girls Club, even taking as given Austin's description of the club's rules as part of a "repress and replace" mission?[18]

Against what Austin knows will be the widespread inclination to lament, if not condemn, Chambers's pregnancy as the consequence of poor decisions, she defaults to liberal individualism: "Some of the black women who are not married yet have babies may be young and wise; others may be poor and brave; and yet a third group may be rich and selfish. Whether they confirm or confound the stereotypes, all of them deserve a measure of freedom with regard to their sexuality that the dominant culture withholds."[19]

Even if we were to accept Austin's rhetorical vehicle of liberal "free choice" as a general matter, this seems a particularly awkward place for it to come to rest. *Chambers* (especially in Austin's account of the case) is not a simple employment discrimination case; it is also about the acculturation of minors, who, regardless of race, class, or gender, society feels are not competent to exercise their own unassisted judgment in matters of reproduction. If Austin is right (I think she is) to imply that *Chambers* is a case about constructing the meaning of racial and gender identity then it's simply no good to evoke "free choice" as if the meaning of that term were not contingent on the meaning of the social identities that are at the center of the controversy.

Austin's account of Crystal Chambers as a rebellious heroine exercising authentic free will is only barely plausible. It relies on a host of unstated assumptions about the nature of racism, of mainstream institutions, and of black culture. Most strikingly, Austin assumes that Chambers's "decision" to become and remain pregnant is the reflection of an authentic choice, the manifestation of a culture that is her birthright and of an identity that emanates from within. The stereotype becomes an authentic persona; a youthful indiscretion is elevated to a "cultural practice." We know the difference because Chambers as an autonomous rights-bearing individual, has *chosen*, because the identity she articulates comes from within (whereas the stereotype of Jezebel and the disciplinary ideal of Mammy are imposed from without).

It can't be this simple. As Charles Taylor points out, identity is produced through dialogue and recognition, not by internal and autonomous choices. Indeed, Austin's argument depends on this idea. How can we understand identification with a culture "that declares as wily, audacious, and good all conduct that offends the white, male, and middle-class establishment" without a dialogical account of identity formation? And if we embrace the dialogical account, as we must, then the attempt to distinguish stereotype from authentic identity by reference to the autonomous choice of the individual is unavailable.

In the absence of the choice=authentic persona/coercion=stereotype equation, Austin's account of the *Chambers* case is at best an optimistic postulate that we are free to question or reject. I'm afraid there is another account of *Chambers,* in which a young woman plays the victim of racism, not by *failing* to conform to what the "racist mainstream" wants of her, but by her absolute complicity with a racist stereotype. Coerced by the imperative to "stay true" to a distorted image of her cultural roots, influenced by the subtle and overt racism of the mainstream media, and pressured by members of her community who internalized the stereotypes of the racist society of which they are a part (and perhaps those who cynically used the language of solidarity to have their way with her), this Crystal Chambers looked at a caricature and mistook it for a mirror. In doing so she remade herself to conform to the caricature, her "free choices" verbatim lines in a long-running tragedy. In this narrative there are no heroines and no innocents, only degrees of guilt, complicity, and frustrated struggle.

Cultural Rights as Protective Custody

Let's suppose the image of minority cultures and identities as the helpless victims of thuggery and genocide by the mainstream were accurate. (As I have argued above, I think this is at most a small part of the story, overshadowed in importance by its less overt but more oppressive photo negative, the production and compelled performance of difference.) Even so, the *best* one can say for rights to identity and culture is that they would have the merits of protective custody. Like a person compelled to testify against a mob boss, the identity minority who wishes (or is compelled) to bear witness to her cultural difference fears for her life. The state (interested in securing the testimony) offers a bribe Dr. Faust would understand: a witness protection program, protective custody.

Cultural or identity rights are a form of protective custody: the witness gets protection, sure. The violent accused is thwarted in his plot to silence the witness or exact revenge. But the price of protection is incarceration: one's movement is scripted and controlled, the state implements round-the-clock surveillance, a cop sits in one's kitchen or parks across the street. Worst of all, the trial never ends, the watch cannot be lifted: protective custody is a permanent condition, an ongoing public policy. Tempted to take your chances on the outside?

Of course, no one is proposing culture or identity police who tell us what to do. So how are rights themselves a form of protective custody? This section makes the case.

RIGHTS AS SOCIAL CONTROL

Perhaps the most serious risk of rights to difference is not that they will fail and take other, more established rights down with them, but that they will succeed and in so doing become a significant new source of governmental regulation over the lives of people of color.

This may seem counterintuitive: mainstream liberal discourse teaches us that rights protect us from governmental regulation, that rights are a limit on state action, not a source of it. But this way of understanding rights is quite wrong. Legal rights are a form of public policy and therefore regulation: they are a limit on personal freedom, not on the power of the state.

This, of course, doesn't mean we should abolish rights. Against total critiques of legal rights, scholars such as Patricia Williams and Kimberlé Crenshaw have argued, convincingly I believe, that many legal rights are valuable and necessary in contemporary society. Indeed, one of the reasons I question proposals for cultural rights is that I fear such new rights will undermine other civil rights that I believe are vital for social justice.

But we should admit that legal rights are, functionally speaking, a form of public policy that controls social relationships. Rights may be especially symbolically powerful, especially difficult to change or rescind, and/or more often developed and administered by a different set of institutions than most public policy (courts as opposed to the executive or the legislature). But they are still policy. Indeed, some of the most important legal rights enjoyed by Americans, for instance, the Civil Rights Acts of 1965 and 1968, were Acts of Congress, formally as well as functionally indistinguishable from any other policy of the federal legislature.

Legal entitlements in general and especially rights do not simply protect people from outside interference; they also channel energies and shape perceptions about what is important, necessary, and good in life. Rights have a tutelary function: they send a message about what society values.

It is difficult to see how rights impose specific and controversial substantive norms in this way because we have been taught in the liberal tradition to believe that rights safeguard freedom in an ideologically neutral fashion. Moreover, the process is one that covers its tracks: because people internalize the norms advanced by the discourse in question, those norms are experienced as chosen, intuitive, and organic rather than imposed, contrived, and, to some extent, state-made.

Perhaps an example will illustrate the point. Any first-year law student knows that the First Amendment protects religion and freedom of speech from governmental regulation based on content. It forbids government from discriminating against either the content of expression or the teachings of a religion. Therefore, liberal constitutionalism concludes, First Amendment rights are ideologically neutral and enhance the freedom of the individual. But this conclusion rests on a questionable framing decision: the rights can be presented as ideologically neutral only by limiting the frame of analysis to the question of distinctions within a sphere (speech or religion) and assuming the ideology that underlies the choice and definition of that sphere. Broaden the frame and we can see that the First Amendment codifies a very specific ideology, one that asserts that expression is either more important or less dangerous than other forms of activity, one that assumes a particular definition of expression and excludes many expressive activities from rights protection, one that generates a practice of "free" expression heavily conditioned by the existence of the right. In short, one could argue that First Amendment rights serve to channel social activity, protest, and unrest in a prescribed way, to institutionalize particular forms of expression (leafletting, marches and demonstrations, political advertising) at the expense of others (situationist pranks, civil disobedience, transgressive performances, shock art, obscene gestures). We could say something similar about the religion clauses, pointing out that spirituality is protected at the expense of philosophy and politics — Catholicism but not Thoreau — and therefore individuals and groups are encouraged, both by law and by the set of practices that law supports, to join a house of worship and to present their ideas in a religious form.

This is not necessarily bad. Whether it's bad depends on what you think of the practices that are institutionalized as opposed to those that are not. But what's clear is that the rights don't simply give people "more freedom" by providing an option; they also channel activity and energies. They encourage and institutionalize certain practices; indeed, they are an institution themselves, they are a productive public policy. Legal rights are a *form* of state action, not a limit on state action.

Our analysis of legal rights should then be no different from our analysis of any public policy: we should look to the likely effects of the right in question to determine whether it is good policy or bad. If we adopt such a realist approach to rights it becomes obvious that rights in no way limit the authority of the state; to the contrary, they are an instance of that authority. Even in the context of rights that an individual can assert against the government (say, the Fifth Amendment's right to just compensation for governmental taking of property), what is at issue is not a *limit* on the authority of "the state" but an *exercise of that authority* by one institution of the state as opposed to another.

This conceptual distinction has important ideological stakes. The conception of rights as *limits* on state power occludes the way rights are a *form* of state power. Under the influence of the former conception, when we analyze rights we do so with one eye closed, blind to the possibility that the right in question itself produces a new type of social control that we may not want to submit to in the long run.

Against Vulgar Legal Realism. Of course, the risks I discuss below are not limited to the assertion of culture through legal rights or other governmental policies or discourses. All of the concerns I have are potentially equally applicable to private actors: private action as much as state action can be an exercise of potentially oppressive social power. So why all of this emphasis on the state? Suppose everything I've argued is true. Nevertheless, if the state doesn't enforce the rights (with the inevitable side effect of state regulation of cultural practices), we will not have *freedom from* regulation, just different regulation. Without cultural rights private institutions will regulate cultural practices and enforce *their* cultural norms.

One could argue that private institutions, as much as those of the state, will reward particular cultural styles at the expense of others and therefore the cultural discipline of private institutional practice will be at least as great as that of the state. But the state occupies a privileged position in this regard, not because its *formal* powers are distinct from those of private institutions (although they arguably are in the context of antidiscrimination rights), but because in matters of the secular in the developed mass democracies of the West the state is understood to have the exclusive ability to grant an *imprimatur*. This is true despite widespread popular dissatisfaction with the institutions of the modern state and the popularity of libertarian or antistatist political agendas. In the United States, despite antistatist rhetoric, both of the major political parties and both the ideological left and right in general rely on and actively seek official state approval of their ideological agenda.

Moreover, the people who would seek to promulgate and enforce cultural rights are likely to be the most susceptible to the allure of the state's imprimatur. The desire for cultural rights is intimately tied up with the politics of recognition: the desire for official acknowledgment of the value of one's distinctive identity and cultural heritage.

Private institutions, in marked contrast to the state, with a very few exceptions, do not even attempt to provide such authoritative censorship and approval. When and if they do, they usually are met with equally legitimate competitors who censor and approve of different things. For instance, if Yale's requirement of coeducational residences threatens to affix the imprimatur of the academic and social elite on an attitude of liberal indulgence in sexual promiscuity and experimentation, Georgetown and Notre Dame can serve as a counterbalance by promoting sexual restraint (and segregation) and U.C. Berkeley and Columbia can offer yet another alternative of residential laissez faire. Similarly, if Spelman College encourages a particular set of ideas about African American identity, Morehouse can promote others, and Harvard still others.

The well-worn critique of the public/private distinction (developed by the American legal realists) allows for no *formal* or *universal* distinction between public and private, but it does not rule out a context-specific, pragmatic distinction between them. We must not assume that a formal distinction necessarily mirrors a practical one, but we also must not ignore obvious differences between state and private actors as they are presently institutionalized.

To be sure, there is nothing in the *formal* nature of state institutions that makes them more authoritative or more univocal than private ones. Therefore, we could, *in theory*, have a multiplicity of state actors with different rules about protected culture (as local governments and states have varying standards of obscenity) and one highly influential private institution could establish a hegemonic cultural norm (as the Education Testing Service has done in the context of standardized testing for university admissions). But it is unlikely that such a hegemonic private cultural institution will emerge. By contrast, the state is *already* hegemonic with respect to definitions of illicit discrimination in employment and public accommodations. And the *theoretical* possibility of multiple state actors with different norms of racial culture is not at issue because such an arrangement is not what the advocates of cultural rights have proposed. In fact, such an arrangement is flatly inconsistent, both with the spirit and underlying arguments of these proposals and with their explicit recommendations, which are in every case to establish comprehensive federal law on the subject through amendments to the Civil Rights Act or reinterpretation of constitutional doctrine. I am justified in positing a univocal and exclusively authoritative state, despite the theoretical possibility of a multivocal state that shares authority, because the former is the type of state actor that the proponents of racial cultural rights envision.

Finally, I focus on rights assertion because so few commentators have analyzed *rights* as a form of state power — as public policy — whereas analogous actions by private institutions have been the target of fairly intensive scrutiny. I believe that the cause of this disparity is that the discourse of rights hides many of the consequences of rights assertion by presenting rights as a *limit* on state power rather than an exercise of it.

THE DEAD HAND OF THE PAST: LEGAL RECOGNITION OF DIFFERENCE AS CONSERVATIVE TRADITIONALISM

Many cultural rights claims have conservative implications for those bringing them, for their contemporaries, and for future generations. Consider, for instance, Juan Perea's defense of Title VII protection for "ethnic traits" against the common argument offered by defendants and many courts that such traits are mutable, within the control of the individual, and therefore do not merit civil rights protection: "Mutability should not be relevant in fundamental matters of individual identity, such as ethnicity. We do not deem mutability relevant in protecting against discrimination because of religion, an aspect of ethnicity which is easily and sometimes actually changed. The possibility or actuality of religious transformation does not dampen the sincerity of religious belief nor dilute its fundamentality to a person's identity. The aspects of our identities *with which we are born, or that develop as a result of our families*, do not become less important because we choose to, or must, maintain them. Nor are aspects of our identities less important because we have chosen them, if we have ability to choose."[20] Perea's use of the word "fundamental" suggests that only those cultural styles and expressions that are the authentic expression of the identity of a recognized protected group would receive protection. For instance, he emphasizes "the aspects of our identities with which we are born, or that develop as a result of our families."

But there is no reason to imagine that inherited social practices are more benign or more valuable — more fundamental — than those that are learned and developed later in life. This notion is deeply conservative in its premises and implications: it implies that individuals should not challenge and at times reject the norms of their family and ethnic community. It ignores or rejects without argument the idea that individuals *should* at times be exposed to new ideas and pushed to consider them.

To be encouraged or pressed to change in response to new circumstances is not *necessarily* an assault on one's dignity; it can be a recognition of one's dignity, a mark of respect for one's mettle, as well as a learning experience. Consider in this regard the concept of false consciousness. This concept has come under a great deal of attack from the ideological right as failing to respect the autonomy of the individual. But the left has insisted on some version of false consciousness to explain the many ways individuals are conditioned to accept, embrace, and eroticize conditions of domination. For the feminist who argues that women eroticize their own domination due to years of conditioning by a patriarchal culture, it is vital that women be exposed, at times against their will, to ideas and conditions that will allow them to shed the distorting lens of patriarchal false consciousness. I don't wish to engage the difficult debate about false consciousness here, but only to point out that if we allow for *any* possibility of false consciousness we must allow for institutions and practices that encourage individuals to question and reject their inherited norms and beliefs. Yet if legal rights to culture are premised on the idea that inherited norms and practices are to be protected simply because they are part of an identifiable ethnic culture, what room is there for institutional practices that explicitly seek to challenge those norms?

Perea is not alone in his conception of identity and culture as inherited. The philosopher Anthony Appiah argues that such a conception (indeed, an even stronger conception, as we shall see) of identity and culture is inherent in the very idea of cultural survival that underlies political multiculturalism:

> The desire for survival is not simply the desire that the culture that gives meaning to the lives of currently existing individuals should continue for them, but requires the continued existence of the culture through indefinite future generations. . . . Let me stress first that the indefinite future generations in question should be the descendants of the current population. The desire for the survival of . . . identity is not the desire that there should always be people somewhere who speak that . . . language and practice those . . . practices. . . . A proposal to solve the problems . . . by paying a group of unrelated people to carry on [the] culture on some island in the South Pacific simply would not meet the need. This matters because it seems to me not at all clear that this aim is one that we can acknowledge while respecting the autonomy of future individuals.[21]

In this light Perea's emphasis on "the aspects of our identities we are born with or develop as a result of our families" takes on an ominous undertone. Whereas Perea wishes us to focus on the individual who has already developed the aspects of identity that he argues should be legally reinforced, Appiah focuses our attention on the "future individuals," whose relationship to any cultural trait or identity is entirely contingent. The policy question at issue in rights to culture and identity is not well understood in terms of the autonomy of the individuals pressing recognition claims. Instead, it involves the socialization of future generations and the relationship of future generations to existing ones. In this sense the analogous area of legal inquiry is family law and educational policy, and the analogous questions are: To what extent should the state enforce the will of parents over children and for how long? Should the state reinforce the already extremely broad control of parents over children in those contexts where the children might be exposed to opposing influences and competing views? Should the state do so long after the children have reached maturity by offering legal remediation *only* for those practices and traits that are inherited? Should it add to that formal reinforcement the unstated but nonetheless necessary disciplinary message that adherence to inherited practices and norms is fundamental to the child's identity (and therefore the child who rejects or modifies such practices is self-destructive or self-denying)?

Privileging inherited social practices codifies a narrow and questionable norm of the appropriate relationship among family members. The necessary premise is that the identity modeled on familial norms and social practices is more important, more deserving of protection, than the identity based on social norms outside the family or the identity based on a rejection of familial norms. To be sure, such a rights proposal arguably empowers the litigant who can put his or her grievance in terms of family and pedigree. But by making the family the author of culture such a proposal must also reinforce problematic and often oppressive family relations. The individual who wishes to escape the suffocating conformity and oppressive social norms of the family and ethnic community will be blessed by the intermeddling state with a "right" to retain them forever.

Rights to Cultural Diversity: Why Not

My critique thus far will provoke a predictable retort, similar but not identical to the (vulgar) legal realist objection to my emphasis on the role of the state: the absence of explicit legal regulation of culture and identity do not leave them unregulated; without cultural rights the regulation of culture and identity will take place in the form of background norms and rules; the absence of explicit cultural regulation does not make the law culturally neutral; the law and other social practices that rights might regulate and temper have a culture and that culture is often incompatible with the cultures of cultural minorities.

Although I would question the assumption that "the law" is a monolith with *a* culture — courts, legislatures, and the laws they pass undoubtedly reflect a number of different local legal cultures as well as a set of compromises among multiple cultural influences — this retort is more or less on the mark. *Of course* legal institutions and law "have" a culture. They are not culturally neutral. And of course this means that law will weigh more heavily on those whose cultural norms most sharply diverge from those of the laws and institutions under whose authority they must live.

But this is not a critique of law, it is a truism about it. Law is an authoritative intervention in the (cultural) life of its subjects; it encourages certain (cultural) practices and tries to crush others. Law discriminates on the basis of culture.

Cultural rights are premised on the idea that the cultural bias of the law is an unfortunate side effect. In the absence of culturally neutral law, the argument goes, the law (and analogous private regulations) may legitimately coerce only those who share "its" culture. But if we substitute the word "norms" or "ideology" for "culture" we can see how wrong this idea is. From the perspective of the authors of a given law it is most crucial that the law coerce precisely those people whom the rights proposal would exempt: those who do not accept the norms that law wishes to insist on. It makes little sense to enact regulation only for those people who would conform their behavior to the prescribed norms voluntarily. The tragic flaw of cultural rights is that law (and the civil regulation of culture it entails) is of necessity directed at those people who will suffer the most if forced to conform to it and who will therefore resist it most. But this is obvious if one considers the matter unburdened by the mystifications of cultural discourse. One passes a law in order to press a norm on people who would not otherwise accept it. The speed limit is designed to control lead-footed speed demons, public intoxication laws target barflies, statutory rape laws are written with pedophiles in mind. It is not an unfortunate side effect of these laws that they unequally burden these groups — it is a central objective of the laws.

Similarly, when laws are informed by a particular set of norms (as they always are) it is possible and indeed quite right to describe such laws as a reflection of the norms and practices of a particular *culture*. And because any law or rule will indeed be more burdensome for those people who do not share the norms informing it than for those who do, if a distinctive national, ethnic, or social group does not share the norms underlying a law or rule that group often will experience the law as especially, if not singularly, oppressive to them.

Now, for the most part, the laws and rules that upset cultural rights proponents do not unambiguously target a social group; instead, they are aimed at a practice and unequally burden a social group or certain members of that group. But even in the extreme case where a law or rule directly targets the group, that fact alone cannot discredit the law or rule. This is true due to precisely the insight that multiculturalism urges on us: different social groups do in fact have different norms and different practices.

Suppose social group x has a number of distinctive social practices, including ritual animal sacrifice that involves slow torture of the animal for several days. This group establishes a presence in a particular town and begins, among other practices, this ritual. The town council (which does not share group x's culture) responds with an ordinance outlawing animal sacrifice. To be sure, the ordinance is directed at the group. But it does not necessarily reflect prejudice or bias against the group or its members; after all, the group is *actually doing something* that the majority of the town disapproves of and would disapprove of no matter who did it. To be sure, the reason for the conflict is cultural difference. But to point this out tells us nothing about how the conflict should be resolved.[22]

CULTURE VERSUS IDENTITY

Cultural rights analysis tries to resolve such conflicts by collapsing cultural difference and status difference. By analogizing and collapsing cultural difference with difference based on purely ascriptive statuses (such as race) the cultural rights advocate seeks to make cases of cultural discrimination as easily resolved as cases of discrimination based on ascribed status. To be sure, status discrimination cases are "easily resolved" only in their most "pure" form (blatant and intentional discrimination for no reason other than animus) and even then only because we have developed a consensus about them through years of struggle. But this limited consensus is nevertheless a powerful social, political, and legal force. Cultural rights analysis seeks to capitalize on this consensus, arguing either that cultural discrimination is analogous to racial discrimination or that it is identical to it.

This conflation of culture and identity is difficult to avoid: many social identities are believed to be the manifestation of some underlying culture (the identity of a "cultural minority") and others are thought to be generative of cultural difference ("gay culture," for instance). Nevertheless, a working distinction between culture and identity is necessary for at least two reasons. First, some social groups have a distinctive identity without significant cultural difference from the mainstream (many homosexuals fall into this category), and likewise, some groups may have cultural differences but not a distinctive social identity. Second, even for those groups for whom identity and culture converge, we may think that each raises distinctive normative issues that demand different treatment as a policy matter. We generally think that law should not discriminate based on ascribed identities, but as I have argued above, it is inevitable that law discriminates on the basis of culture.

Two examples will clarify the distinction. As to identity without cultural difference, consider the perhaps hypothetical ideal case of race as status. Suppose two social groups are identical in every respect except that one group has some striking phenotypical feature — say, a star-shaped birthmark on the abdomen — and the other does not. Further, suppose that the star-bellied group of individuals begin to believe, for a host of socially and historically contingent reasons that need not concern us here, that they are superior to those without the star-shaped birthmark. Further, suppose that the star-endowed individuals, again by means that need not concern us, succeed in perpetuating the ideology of star-bellied superiority to such an extent that the entire society in which they live is organized around the principle of star-bellied superiority and privilege. Yet in every other respect, the two groups are indistinguishable. In such a scenario, we have identity without cultural (indeed, without any morally relevant) difference.[23]

As to cultural difference without identity, let's imagine two groups of German immigrants who settle in Northern Wisconsin, one group from Northern Germany and one from Southern Germany. In many respects we would expect these two groups to exhibit cultural difference: some would recall with fondness the streets of Hamburg, others would dream of the metropolis of Munich; some would consider lederhosen a national costume, others would consider it foreign; one group would be Protestant, the other Catholic; one group would eat pickled herring, the other sauerbraten and spaetzle; the two groups would speak with strikingly different accents — indeed, they would likely speak what linguists would consider different dialects of the German tongue. Let's also suppose that immigrants from Northern Germany outnumber those from Southern Germany and that the Northerners control most of the resources in the region in which both groups reside. To the non-German, their cultural differences would be invisible, their identity would be defined in terms of national origin. Nevertheless, the groups retain their distinctive cultural differences, and in overt and subtle ways the Northern Germans impose their ways on the less powerful Southern Germans: workplaces are organized around Northern German norms of precision, formality, and rule adherence as opposed to the more relaxed, Gallic tendencies familiar to Southern Germans; Northern German accents are a mark of status and Northern German dialect is tolerated while that of Southern Germany is frowned upon; the canteens at many businesses serve Northern German but not Southern German specialties. But, aside from the occasional comment about cultural practices ("In Hamburg people are so formal"), the two groups quickly come to think of each other as "fellow Germans" in a milieu populated by Anglos and Swedes, and Southern Germans who assimilate to Northern German customs (now thought of as simply "German" customs) succeed as easily as Northern Germans born with such customs. In this case, our two groups of German Americans would be, in terms of *identity,* just that: German Americans and not Northern German and Southern German Americans. But to an anthropologist, the cultural differences between the Northern and Southern German immigrants would be as significant as those dividing Germans generally from the Dutch or the French.

It should be obvious that we might think of the status distinction between the star-bellied and plain-bellied Sneetches in terms entirely different from the cultural distinction between the Northern and Southern Germans. We might believe it necessary to pass legislation outlawing discrimination on the basis of plain-bellied-ness, but it does not follow from that commitment that we would be compelled to prohibit discrimination on the basis of any of the cultural characteristics (let's put the issue of religion aside for purely doctrinal reasons) that distinguish immigrants from Northern Germany from those from Southern Germany. Discrimination on the basis of star-bellied-ness is without normative justification. Moreover, star-bellied-ness is a characteristic outside the control of the individual (or at least "natural" star-bellied-ness is). Star-bellied-ness is both normatively irrelevant and immutable: it is an ideal form of a status distinction.

Discrimination on the basis of various cultural traits raises much more complicated issues. Unlike pure status differences, cultural differences *are* normatively relevant; this fact is central to the moral position of those who would protect them with legal rights. But if this is so, there may be good reasons to discriminate on the basis of various cultural traits. Some cultural traits may be "better suited" than others to certain tasks or institutions, some may be less valuable in general than others, and some may be downright destructive of a society or enterprise. This rather harsh conclusion is unavoidable if we think that cultural traits matter.

By conflating issues of culture with those of ascriptive identities, advocates of cultural rights have it both ways. The trait in question is important to the person who has it (it is "culture") but irrelevant to the person who "discriminates" against it (it is "status").

Of course, at times this may be true. But we cannot assume that it is true in every case. In at least some cases, the trait in question is either relatively trivial to both the putative rights asserter and the "discriminator" (and then why have legal intervention at all: *de minimis non curat lex*) or, and this is where the strap bites into the flesh, is important to both the rights asserter and the "discriminator."

In these latter cases, the cases of true cultural difference, the "simple discrimination" analysis that cultural rights discourse suggests is inadequate. Instead, we must confront issues of culture, cultural difference, cultural assimilation, and cultural solidarity on their own merits, as questions of policy that involve conflicting goals, the allocation of social costs, and inevitable trade-offs. Rights analysis, which insists that protecting the right in question is an absolute side constraint on public policy, is simply too crude to deal with the complex policy questions generated by cultural pluralism.

For instance, assuming that a central goal of antidiscrimination law is to promote the social and economic integration of stigmatized groups (though admittedly this is an assumption some would question) then cultural rights proposals raise thorny factual and normative questions. In the face of social and economic pressure to assimilate, when will cultural minorities do so, when will they retreat to isolated enclaves, and when will they suffer the cost of retaining difference in mainstream institutions? Is cultural diversity desirable in and of itself, or only as a means to the end of social integration that might otherwise be difficult to achieve? How should the costs of accommodating insular cultural minorities or of achieving a more unified culture be borne? If cultural assimilation could be achieved at some significant emotional and psychological cost to one generation of cultural minorities, but at dramatically and constantly lessening costs to each successive generation until "full assimilation" is achieved (and future costs are zero), would such a policy be morally acceptable? Would it affect our evaluation of such a "tough assimilation" policy if we knew that the alternative was intractable social fragmentation with high and consistent costs for both cultural minorities and the majority? To be clear, I think these are very difficult questions. But it seems to me that they are the kinds of questions any proposal regarding cultural differences raises. The rights approaches I have examined tend to assume such questions have answers we can take as given. This is a serious deficiency.

Postscript

The cultural rights approach I have critiqued might help *some* people of color with serious grievances (although most likely at the expense of others). Sometimes discrimination against "identity-correlated" cultural practices will be a prosthetic for forbidden status discrimination based on animus. Rights to culture would capture some discrimination that traditional antidiscrimination law misses because the plaintiffs can't prove their case under existing law. But if the problem cultural rights proposals seek to address is status discrimination by proxy, a better solution (and one at least as politically feasible) is one that civil rights advocates have wanted for decades: relax the burden of proof on civil rights plaintiffs generally and admit additional evidence of intentional racial discrimination.

Moreover, my argument doesn't categorically oppose legal rights to protect, say, the person sporting a cornrow hairstyle (or a Mohawk or multiple body piercings). My own impulse is one of sympathy for people who wish — for reasons of sincere belief in an authentic cultural identity, self-fashioned biography, newly minted persona, or adventurous aesthetic taste — to assert themselves in a nonmainstream style. But the African American's claim to her cornrows is arguably more like the claim of her white male counterpart to long hair and a beard, or like the claim of her male counterpart to wear earrings; in all these cases we confront a mainstream distaste for a counter-cultural personal style. If so, it is a mistake to conceive of and argue for these claims in the uniquely charged language of race.

At this point the cultural rights advocate might object that the relationship between identity and culture is more complex than I've allowed for. Ascriptive identity is in a hermeneutic relationship with culture: the reason racists dislike the race is because of (what they take to be) its culture, but the reason they dislike (what they take to be) the culture is because of *its* race. Thus discrimination against the cultural style is almost indistinguishable from actionable discrimination against the race. First, there's almost no avoiding the discrimination by changing one's behavior because *any* behavior that is associated with the race becomes, *for that very reason*, disfavored and stigmatized. The only way out would be to scrupulously avoid any behavior that most members of one's race engage in: to practice a studied policy of alienation from one's race. Thus antidiscrimination law that fails to protect culture effectively punishes (or allows others to punish) members of racial minority groups for developing *any common cultural traits or styles at all*—or at least from exhibiting them in a host of public places. Not only traditional cultural practices, but the hybrid, politically attuned affiliations of race consciousness would all be freely punished by racist or racially paranoid employers and institutional actors.

This is a real dilemma, and perhaps it's the strongest case for the kind of legal remedies I've critiqued. In a sense, it is precisely the dilemma that introduced this essay. Racist discourse is Janus-faced: it articulates difference with one mouth and condemns it with the other. My critique doesn't offer a solution to this double bind; it only insists that it is a *double* bind and therefore cannot be effectively resisted by an approach that grabs only one side of the pincers. I believe critique is necessary because so much of contemporary discourse is obsessed with the repression of difference and blind to the more subtle *production* of social difference.

■

This has been a critique. It is a proposal that we avoid or at least be cautious of something. It is not a proposal that we replace that something with something else. Of course, I could try to develop a comprehensive new approach to antidiscrimination law that would negotiate the tightrope of production and punishment of difference more effectively than either contemporary antidiscrimination law or cultural rights type proposals do. Perhaps that's for another essay. But no matter how successfully I carried it off it would do only that: *negotiate* the contradiction. I don't think law is capable of resolving or banishing this contradiction. In that sense law is incapable of guaranteeing social justice. Social justice for people of color and for other stigmatized minorities will require a revolutionary cultural transformation, one more sweeping and more penetrating perhaps than any we've seen. Perhaps one more profound than any society can achieve while remaining the same society.

Some of the revolutionaries of the civil rights movement remarked that racial justice can never be secured as long as American society continues to exist. The conviction that inspires this essay is that in a profound sense they were right: America without racism, without sexism, without homophobia would be a society none of us alive today would recognize. And—this is the truly thrilling and terrifying part—it would be a society that could not produce or sustain people like us. It may be that the price of providing our descendants with a world free of the social stigma and oppression of identities such as race, a world we could be proud to call more just, is that they would not share our identities, that they would be our heirs but *not* our descendants.

Suppose you could make a deal with the angel that Faust never got to meet. The angel offers you this: a world free of racism, of sexism, of homophobia, of all of the illegitimate hierarchies and oppressive aspects of ascriptive identities. And no, this is not a world of sterile color blindness or lockstep uniformity; instead, it is world of diversity without stigma, of social justice that reaches every corner of the globe and nourishes every human heart. But there's a catch: you can't go there. You're too far gone, too fallen, too conflicted, too invested in the conditions that make your own wretched world so far from the world the angel has descibed. For you, this just world would be a kind of hell in which you could never find a comfortable place. The angel offers a ticket for your unborn children, or perhaps their children; this is a pass good for all and only those still supple enough to adapt to the good society. Moreover, it's a one-way ticket: if your children or grandchildren and descendants-to-be take this ticket, they can't come back to you. It is not an arbitrary restriction, the angel explains; it's inherent in the nature of the journey they will have to make. If they go, they will be just as alienated from this world as you would be from the good society. And—here's the rub—they will also be as alienated from you. Of course, they will love and respect you, but they will also fear and pity you. They will be repelled by the petty bigotries you harbor, the dangerous little myths you cling to, your alibis, your shortcuts past Truth, the golden calves you worship when you think Moses and God are not watching. Train's leaving, all aboard who's coming aboard. Would you let them go?

Notes

1. *Renee Rogers, et al. v. American Airlines, Inc.,* 527 F. Supp. 229 (1981).

2. *Ferrill v. The Parker Group, Inc.,* 168 F.3d 468 (1999).

3. See Barbara J. Flagg, "Fashioning a Title VII Remedy for Transparently White Subjective Decisionmaking," *Yale Law Journal* 104 (1995): 2009, 2012.

4. Juan F. Perea, "Ethnicity and Prejudice: Reevaluating 'National Origin' Discrimination under Title VII," *William and Mary Law Review* 35 (1994): 805, 866–67; Drucilla Cornell and William W. Bratton, "Deadweight Costs and Intrinsic Wrongs of Nativism: Economics, Freedom, and Legal Suppression of Spanish," *Cornell Law Review* 84 (1999): 595.

5. See Anthony Appiah, "Race, Culture, Identity: Misunderstood Connections," in *Color Conscious: The Political Morality of Race* (Princeton, NJ: Princeton University Press, 1996), 99.

6. Alex M. Johnson Jr., "Bid Whist, Tonk, and *United States v. Fordice:* Why Integrationism Fails African-Americans Again," *California Law Review* 81 (1993): 1401, 1450 (all emphases added).

7. Ibid. 1456.

8. Charles Taylor, "The Politics of Recognition" in *Multiculturalism: Examining the Politics of Recognition,* ed. Amy Gutmann (Princeton: Princeton University Press, 1994): 25–26.

9. Perea, 833, 861, 862.

10. Ibid., 835–36, 852, 858–59.

11. Perea criticizes an approach that would limit antidiscrimination protection to those cases where "ethnic traits . . . function as [statistical] proxies for national origin or race" (851). Both prohibited bases for discrimination under existing law as insufficiently inclusive. He worries that a requirement of statistical correlation will leave plaintiffs vulnerable to a judicial determination of the degree of statistical correlation required to establish that a given trait is a proxy for prohibited classification (851–53). But in the absence of such an objective criterion, what would serve to establish the ethnicity of a trait? Perea seems to think that ethnicity has a sufficiently self-evident meaning to overcome this problem, hence his proposal to expand federal antidiscrimination statutes to include "ethnicity and ethnic traits" (860–61).

12. Orlando Patterson, "Thomas Hearings Can Help Us Reassess Views of Race and Sex," *St. Petersburg Times* 22 Oct. 1991, 11A.

13. Regina Austin, "Sapphire Bound!" In *Critical Race Theory: The Key Writings That Formed the Movement,* ed. Kimberlé Crenshaw et al. (New York: New Press, 1995), 426, 428.

14. Ibid., 429.

15. Ibid., 429 (emphasis added).

16. Ibid., 432, 433, quoting Elizabeth Fox-Genovese, *Within the Plantation Household: Black and White Women of the Old South* (1988), 292.

17. Ibid., 430, 432.

18. Ibid., 430. Austin would object that the constraints of single motherhood are socially and politically contingent, but most constraints are. (We could argue, for instance, that the constraints facing an illiterate person are socially contingent; if we lived in a society that did not value and assume literacy, the illiterate person would have more options.) And not all of the constraints of single motherhood are well understood as socially contingent: children require a good deal of care that must be supplied by parents and there may be natural biological bonds between parents and their biological offspring, making the dedication of substantial time to caregiving a biological—not social— imperative. We need an account of the social dynamics of single pregnancy and motherhood and a theory of illegitimate and justified constraints and incentives to conclude that the constraints facing Chambers were unjust. (Are single mothers limited because of bigotry or because of the objective demands of single motherhood?)

19. Ibid., 433.

20. Perea, 866–67 (emphases added).

21. K. Anthony Appiah, "Identity, Authenticity, Survival," in *Multiculturalism: Examining the Politics of Recognition,* ed. Amy Gutmann (Princeton: Princeton University Press, 1994), 157.

22. At this point I expect that the cultural rights proponent will seek common cause with the gay rights advocate by making the following argument: "You could just as easily justify homophobic legislation, say, the outcome in *Bowers v. Hardwick,* by arguing that consenting adults engaged in homosexual sodomy are 'in fact doing something that the majority disapproves of and would disapprove no matter who did it.' We cannot so easily separate acts from statuses; in the case of culture, just as in the case of sexuality, they are one and the same." I submit that this approach to the status/conduct problem reproduces precisely the *Bowers* Court's mistake. In *Bowers* the Court began considering a sodomy statute that presumably applied to heterosexual and homosexual couples alike, but very quickly the case became one about homosexuality. *Bowers* was famously *not* decided on status-neutral grounds; instead, the case was from beginning to end an attack on (perhaps I should say "a production of") homosexual *status.* And the opposite (and I believe correct) outcome in the case did not depend on a recognition of homosexual status but instead on the recognition of a status-neutral privacy right protecting any consensual sexual activity between adults from state regulation.

Indeed, politically speaking, the oppressive result in *Bowers* depended on producing a distinction between the homosexual couple and the heterosexual couple who also claimed to be victims of the sodomy statute and whom the Court chose not to address. Only by ignoring the heterosexual couple with whom many people could easily identify could the *Bowers* Court successfully depict the case as one about deviant sexuality rather than one about the autonomy of adults to engage in consensual sex free of state surveillance and intrusion.

I derive this analysis from Janet Halley, who makes a similar point with devastating clarity in her analysis of the military's "don't ask, don't tell" regulations. See generally Janet Halley, *Don't: A Reader's Guide to the Military's Anti-Gay Policy* (Durham: Duke University Press, 1999). Although "don't ask, don't tell" may at first glance appear to be a perfect example of a policy that harms a minority by refusing recognition and punishing the assertion of difference (don't tell), in fact the policy worked its most oppressive consequences through exactly the type of interrogation and the production of identities that I have attacked in this article. Halley painstakingly demonstrates that in practice the policy operates through a little discussed (but formally codified) regulation that made "conduct manifesting a propensity" to engage in homosexual acts a basis for administrative inquiries under the "don't tell" prohibition. The regulation required military decision makers to decide whether certain conduct "manifested a propensity" and offered guidelines based on questionable stereotypes and popular fantasies about homosexuals. Enlisted men and women who had not, and presumably had no interest in, "telling" of their sexual proclivities were then interrogated (colloquially, one might say "asked") on the basis of suspicions that arose from their "conduct manifesting a propensity." What is crucial for our purposes is that many of the soldiers who suffered under "don't ask, don't tell" suffered not because their identity was repressed — not because they told and were punished or because they wanted to tell but couldn't — but because their identity was *produced* by the "conduct manifesting a propensity" regulation. The regulations did their dirty work not by refusing to recognize homosexual identity but by insisting on it, and by ascribing it to individuals who preferred and in some cases pleaded for anonymity.

23. Apologies to Dr. Seuss. *The Sneetches and Other Stories* (New York: Random House, 1989).

JANET HALLEY

Sexuality Harassment

The Supreme Court has held that same-sex harassment may be sex discrimination within the ambit of Title VII. Its opinion in *Oncale v. Sundowner Offshore Services, Inc.*[1] tells us that same-sex harassing conduct that meets other criteria in the doctrinal scheme is conclusively sex discrimination when it is motivated by erotic attraction. Thus the Court indicates that same-sex erotic overtures at work can be sex discrimination, and invites lower courts to test for erotic content by inquiring into the sexual orientation of the individual defendant. Where the defendant in a same-sex sex harassment case is not homosexual, the Court says that the "social context" will indicate whether harassing conduct is sex-based and thus sex discriminatory. The purportedly clarifying example is the (presumptively heterosexual) coach of a professional football team. This person is not engaging in actionable harassment when he "smacks" a player on the butt out on the field (the Court seems not to notice its own salacious double entendre), but he may come within the reach of Title VII if he commits the same act upon a secretary (male or female) back in the office. Apparently, we know that the former leaves men on the football team *in statu quo ante* as men and as employees, while the latter, if deemed objectively severe, could make the office a hostile environment for members of the secretary's sex. If this strikes you as a bit mysterious, do not be concerned. Justice Scalia ends the opinion with a reassurance that courts and juries will use *common sense* to distinguish "simple teasing and roughhousing among members of the same sex" from actionable sex discrimination.

Common sense is precisely what I am afraid judges and juries *will* use.

After all, homophobia and homosexual panic are common sense. To be sure, a gay-friendly analysis has to welcome the Court's decision that same-sex sex harassment is actionable sex discrimination: without it, federal antidiscrimination law would have explicitly declared open season on gay men and lesbians, leaving us unprotected from sexual interference that can threaten our very ability to work and learn. But with it, federal antidiscrimination law may *implicitly* declare open season on gay men and lesbians, leaving us unprotected from lawsuits that threaten our very ability to work and learn.

Moreover, the new legitimacy of same-sex cases presents us with a miner's canary, capable of revealing aspects of sex harassment enforcement that seem quite innocuous until you imagine how they would work when driven by the energies of homophobia. When the canary dies, it's time to ask whether the space is good for anyone.

Feminist, Pro-Gay, and Queer Readings of Same-Sex Sexual Harassment

Women's subordination feminism posits that women are subordinated to men. Some women's subordination feminisms claim that this is a structural feature of human life (MacKinnon; cultural feminism in its "patriarchy" mode); others think that subordination is more episodic (historicist Marxist feminism; cultural feminism in its "social meanings" mode). Some object to women's subordination as an unjust effect of power (MacKinnon); others detect in it an error in values (cultural feminism). And whereas some locate the primary or paradigm site of women's subordination in the market/family complex (Marxist and socialist feminisms), others locate it in reproduction and women's experience of care (cultural feminism), while still others locate it in sexuality (MacKinnon; cultural feminism focused on sexuality rather than maternity). I call the last of these *sexual subordination feminism*.

One basic thing that went wrong in the left project of remedying women's subordination at work is that sexual subordination feminism — MacKinnon's feminism in an alliance with cultural feminism — came to subtend the legal and regulatory project and to locate its contours, all at the expense of socialist feminism. I argue that it is time for a return to a socialist feminist understanding of this piece of left legalism. This is in part because socialist feminism provides the more germane insights into women's working lives. Because this project is already well articulated in a pathbreaking article by

Vicki Schultz, I will not concentrate on it here.[2] Instead I want to concentrate on another reason for such a shift, one emerging from gay identity and queer interests and thinking. By a gay identity project, I mean one that supposes that there are and should be gay men and lesbians, that they are subordinated unjustly, and that justice projects should focus on their equality. By a queer project, I mean one that emphasizes the fictional status of sex, gender, and sexual orientation identity, and that affirms rather than abhors sexuality, "dark side" and all. From the perspective of these projects, we can notice that sexual subordination feminism makes policy choices that put gay and queer constituencies in the line of regulatory fire, and that it depends on feminist models of gender and sexuality from which pro-gay and queer thought diverge.

Confronting this, moreover, requires us to be able to notice as well that gay and queer thought and aims diverge. Each seeks the welfare of a different kind of sexual subject. A gay-identity approach posits that some people are homosexual and that the stigma attached to this kind of person should be removed. By contrast, a queer approach regards the homosexual/heterosexual distinction with skepticism and even resentment, arguing that it is historically contingent and is itself oppressive. This divergence, as that between gay identity and queer projects on one hand and sexual-subordination feminism on the other, is of course only crudely indicated by this sketch. I hope some of the nuances will emerge in the following analysis of real interpretive and policy choices they are all are faced with in sex harassment law.

In the following pages I spell out the terms of MacKinnon's theory, the differences between it and cultural feminism, and the differences between them and gay identity and queer thinking, and deploy all of them to produce divergent readings of *Oncale*. My goal is to make clear the inadequacy of sexual subordination feminism to assess certain effects and defects of its own law reform project, to suggest an overall need to alter the left attitude toward sexual harassment law. Sexual harassment law has become, I argue, sexuality harassment, and it is time to build left resistance to it.

SEXUAL SUBORDINATION FEMINISM

The Structural Male/Female Model. In the book that did more than anything else to provide the theoretic basis for sex harassment law, *Sexual Harassment of Working Women,* published in 1979, Catharine A. MacKinnon set out a theory of sex, gender, sexuality, and power that explains why male/female sexual overtures at work are sex discrimination. Here's MacKinnon's male/female model: "Analysis of sexuality must not be severed and abstracted from analysis of gender. What the current interpretations of rape [as an exercise of power, not of sexuality] fail to grasp . . . is the argument most conducive to conceiving sexual harassment as sex discrimination: a crime of sex *is* a crime of power. Sexual harassment (and rape) have everything to do with sexuality. Gender *is* a power division and sexuality is one sphere of its expression. One thing wrong with sexual harassment (and with rape) is that it eroticizes women's subordination. It acts out and deepens the powerlessness of women as a gender, *as women*."[3] This paragraph uses a number of ambiguous terms, but it gives them very stable, intelligible meanings. Sex appears here both as the difference between men and women (I call this sex1, to indicate bodily dimorphism, the purportedly stable difference between male and female bodies) and as erotic appeal, genital eroticism, and everything that makes "fucking" a central focus of attention (I call this sex2). Sexuality is the structural rather than interpersonal dimension of sex2 (it appears that MacKinnon was not thinking here about sexual orientation at all).

The crucial term, however, is gender. Rape and sex harassment are homologous crimes of sex1 because they use sex2 to generate gender. Gender renders men as men (that is, superordinate) and women as women (that is, subordinate). Women *as women* are powerless. Their *gender* is this subordination.

In the important theoretical article that MacKinnon published in the feminist journal *Signs* in 1982 but had written well before the publication of *Sexual Harassment of Working Women*[4] she restated this point and elaborated it: "Sexuality, then, is a form of power. Gender, as socially constructed, embodies it, not the reverse. Women and men are divided by gender, made into the sexes as we know them, by the social requirements of heterosexuality, which institutionalizes male sexual dominance and female sexual submission. If this is true, sexuality is the linchpin of gender inequality."[5] As MacKinnon suggested in 1979 and as she explicitly states here, gender renders sex hierarchy as what men and women *are;* it produces rather than reflects sex1. This is one of the most radical elements of MacKinnon's theory of sex2. The reality of sex1, and the consciousness in which that reality seems real, natural, and inevitable, are *effects* of power. As MacKinnon put it in her subsequent 1983 *Signs* article, sex hierarchy is ontologically and epistemologically "nearly perfect":[6] by producing both its own reality and our every mode of apprehending that reality (with the sole exception of feminist method as MacKinnon defines it), it almost completely occupies the horizon of possibility.

I call this the male/female model. It is a neat, tight system; indeed, for all its constructedness and contingency, it is total, structural, complete.[7] Purportedly operating on the ground of sex1 but actually producing it, men use sex2 to make themselves superordinate, and that is their gender; and to make women subordinate, and that is our gender. They win, we lose.

Of course, this is not inevitable; rather, it is a historical catastrophe. Almost luckily, rape and sex harassment are especially concentrated forms of sex2. Just like myriad other rituals of heterosexual interaction, but with particular force and clarity, rape and sex harassment give men and women gender (that is, makes them men and women), which, for MacKinnon, means their relative place in a male/female hierarchy. And here is where MacKinnon places her Archimedes' lever. According to MacKinnon's theory of legal remediation, the law of rape and of sex harassment, when they provide a remedy for the injury of sex2 *based on a woman's claim to women's point of view,* provide ways of exposing this terrible mistake, interrupting the ontological and epistemological seamlessness of sex2, and enlisting the energies of the state in the project of justice.

Now, the claim of any one woman to "women's point of view" is necessarily problematic. Not only do women disagree, but their epistemic powers are, MacKinnon insists, fundamentally constructed by the eroticization of male dominance. In 1982 MacKinnon urged feminism to address, not resolve, this problematic, by dedicating itself not to the assertion of women's point of view but to the search for it.[8] In 1982, the essence of feminism to MacKinnon was not the male/female model but a methodological commitment to consciousness raising. But by 1983 she began to claim that CR had revealed women's point of view, and revealed it to be nothing other than the social truth of the male/female model. By 2000 she could make the following claim:

> Gender . . . was what was *found there, by women, in women's lives.* Piece by bloody piece, in *articulating direct experiences*, in resisting the disclosed particulars, in trying to make women's status be different than it was, a theory of the status of women was forged, and with it a theory of the method that could be adequate to it: *how we had to know in order to know this.*

. . . In and from the experience of woman after woman emerged a systematic, systemic, organized, structured, newly coherent picture of the relations between women and men that discernibly extended from intimacy throughout the social order and the state. Our minds *could know it was real* because our bodies, collectively, lived through it. . . .

My own work provides just one illustration of how this philosophical approach of theory from-the-ground-up has been productive in practice. . . .

Feminism made a bold claim in Western philosophy: *women can access our own reality because we live it;* slightly more broadly, that living a subordinated status can give one access to its reality. . . . We . . . claimed *the reality of women's experience as a ground to stand on and move from,* as a basis for conscious political action. . . . Women turned the realities of powerlessness into a form of power: credibility. And reality supported us. *What we said was credible because it was real.*[9]

Between 1982 and 2000, then, MacKinnon made a transition from critique to Enlightenment knowing, one that helps to explain how, originally the radical feminist par excellence, she has been able to make an almost complete reconciliation with liberal feminism.

A second change was also necessary. In 1983 MacKinnon offered the bold proposal that the state, its law, and the rule of law are male. She "propose[d] that the state is male in the feminist sense" not only because it pursued and protected men's interests in sexual control over women by adopting particular rules (which presumably could be rewritten), but because "formally, the state is male in that objectivity is its norm." The very "rule form . . . institutionalizes the objective stance as jurisprudence," which, in liberalism, is "the law of law."[10] Asking the law, rather than women, to speak the meaning of sexuality from women's point of view would be a hopelessly contradictory undertaking. And so rewriting the rules of rape adjudication to make women's subjective experience decisive would merely reinscribe the terms of male dominance into the feminist project: "Even though the rape law oscillates between subjective tests and more objective standards invoking social reasonableness, it uniformly presumes a single underlying reality, not a reality split by divergent meanings, such as those inequality produces. . . . One-sidedly erasing women's violation or dissolving the presumptions into the subjectivity *of either side* are alternatives dictated by the terms of the object/subject split respectively.

These are alternatives that will only retrace that split until its terms are confronted as gendered to the ground."[11] This at least suggests what the *Signs* articles repeatedly affirm: that women's subjective experience, no less than men's, is part of the epistemological dilemma posed by male dominance. To move "toward a feminist jurisprudence," for the MacKinnon of 1983, was to engage in critique by exposing that dilemma in all its stringency, as an opening for a feminist consciousness currently unattainable in its terms. And so, just after affirming, in the passage quoted above, that "what is wrong with rape is that it is an act of the subordination of women to men," MacKinnon turned from law and rape to the system of meaning in which they are embedded: "the issue is not so much what rape 'is' as the way its social conception is shaped to interpret particular encounters."[12] It seems quite fitting, then, that the second *Signs* article ends in the mode of critique. Its last section warns that "making and enforcing certain acts as illegal reinforces a structure of subordination," catalogues the dilemmas posed for her feminist project by liberal and left jurisprudence, insists in its last line that "justice" would require something quite "new" — and avoids any effort to reconcile the idea of a charge of rape or cause of action for sex harassment by a particular woman with the problematic relationship that may obtain between her understanding and "women's point of view."[13]

But by 1989 MacKinnon was able to say that there can be "feminist law": "Abstract rights authoritize [*sic*] the male experience of the world. Substantive rights for women would not. Their authority would be the currently unthinkable: nondominant authority, the authority of excluded truth, the voice of silence."[14] An individual woman who suffers sex harassment at work thereby exemplifies, in her sexual injury, women's gender. As long as her legal cause of action for sex harassment performs the perspective produced by *women's point of view,* it will allow her to interrupt the ontological seamlessness joining male superordination with the law, enabling her to make not only her injury but the injury of all women visible, audible, and interruptable.

The idea that the legal claim of one woman flawlessly reveals the injury that male superordination and female subordination inflict on all women seems quite foreign to the radicalism and the critical stance of MacKinnon's *Signs* articles, but nevertheless pervades her practice of legal remediation. The MacKinnon/Dworkin antipornography ordinance would have allowed an individual woman, acting "as a woman acting against the subordination of women," to obtain an injunction against "trafficking" in "pornography." Though MacKinnon and others frequently defended the ordinance on the grounds that an individual woman would have to "prove injury,"[15] that is precisely what women complainants seeking to enjoin "trafficking" in pornography were *not* required to do. Instead, it would have allowed one woman to act for all women, without any showing of actual harm to herself or anyone else, by enjoining the production, sale, exhibition, and distribution of a wide array of "pornography," even against defendants who thought in good faith that the materials were not subordinating to women.[16] Nor was MacKinnon's aim providing recompense to injured individuals or securing a locale in which those seeking to avoid pornography could do so; at least in the Minneapolis phase of their activism, MacKinnon and Dworkin urged the municipal Zoning and Planning Commission to reject a zoning approach and to adopt the private right of action not because the latter would recognize harm to individual women but because any pornography anywhere is sex discrimination. As MacKinnon told the Commission, "I do not admit that pornography has to exist."[17] Similarly, MacKinnon would remove any requirement that an individual woman prove that her employer fired her with actual illegal intent; "statistical proofs of disparity would be conclusive" because harm to an individual woman is the 100 percent pure distillate of the harm suffered by all women.[18] Clearly, the private lawsuit is an opportunity to remedy the injury sex2 imposes on all women. Of course, if some women think pornography helps them, or if a woman has been fired not because she is a woman but because she has committed a series of safety infractions on the shop floor, giving her claim this priority will hurt, not liberate, (some) women.

The Moralistic Male/Female Model. For two reasons I am going to sketch cultural feminism rather than exemplify it in one of its exponents' work. First, it has so many exponents in feminist legal theory that selecting one would seem arbitrary. Second, although it has generated many different "takes" on same-sex harassment, all of them bear such a strong family resemblance that a general rather than particular description should suffice for my purposes here.

Cultural feminism holds that women have a distinct consciousness and/or culture. In some versions, this distinctiveness derives from their biological situation; in others, it emerges from their historical oppression by men. Some versions emphasize women's reproductive experience; others focus on their situation in sexuality. What makes a feminism *cultural* feminist is not its position on the essentialist/social constructivist divide, but its dedication to the propositions that women's feminine attributes amount to a consciousness or culture, that their consciousness or culture is improperly devalued, and that the reform goal is to revalue it upwards, until it has cultural status equal to or perhaps superior to the culture of men and maleness.

How does cultural feminism differ from and repeat the male/female model as MacKinnon deploys it? It's not a structural theory. Male domination is not perfect; women escape dominance much or some of the time, have agency, are authentic, and so on. Indeed, women have more of every kind of virtue than men, including the epistemological and ontological ones of knowledge and existence. And while MacKinnon's theory attributes sex inequality to *power* — male domination, for her, is "not a moral issue"[19] — cultural feminism is intensely moralistic. Women's subordination is a moral error, and it has produced women's moral superiority to men.

These two differences produce very different takes on sex2 and on law. Sex2 first. Whereas MacKinnon's theory makes it impossible to know the difference between normal heterosexual intercourse and rape, cultural feminism (when it is about sexuality, not maternity) knows a lot about what good sex2 between men and women looks like. It has the virtues that have been, at least since the late nineteenth century in the West, associated with women. Good sex is intersubjective, caring, respectful, alert to human dignity, human values, human sensibilities, human sensitivities. Good sex involves taking one's pleasure in the pleasure of the other, or at least only on the condition of the pleasure of the other. Good sex is expressive; it respects, reflects, and/or constitutes personhood. In the name of these ideals, good sex, to be good, must depress masculinity in either partner and promote femininity in both.

And the differences between the male/female model and cultural feminism produce a very different relation to liberal feminism and a different approach to legal reform. Unlike MacKinnon's theory, cultural feminism has a firm grasp on the categorical imperative in sex2. It can speak to liberalism about human dignity in a way MacKinnon cannot. There are people on the planet — women — who are doing life right; we can all model ourselves on them. This is why cultural feminism (though it has its apocalyptic moments) basically has a sunny disposition. If we could let women run things, or convert men to femininity, things would be better. Women's oppression is episodic; there is almost always light at the end of the tunnel. Cultural feminism thus fits into liberal feminism without all the angst that attends MacKinnon's relation to it. It has permeated feminist *legal* theory, I think, because it is good at designing incremental reforms and maintaining faith in them, and because liberal feminism is hospitable about half of the time to its search for special treatment.

For all that, though, cultural feminism shares a lot with the male/female model. When it is about sexuality, not maternity, it is a sexual dominance theory. That is, it holds that sexuality is central to women's subordination and that women's subordination is the central fact in sexuality; that masculinity is dominance and objectification; that femininity is its opposite; that masculinity belongs to men and femininity to women; that this formula states the relevant alternatives so exclusively that, if a man is sexually subordinated, he must be understood to be feminized;[20] and that whenever in sexuality we find dominance it is masculine and morally erroneous.

And the moralism of cultural feminism makes it just as radical as MacKinnon's early theory, though in a very different way. MacKinnon would like to get them by the balls because she doesn't believe their minds and hearts *can* follow; whereas cultural feminism has detailed plans for their hearts and minds. It is a fighting faith seeking the moral conversion of a little less than half the human race. The emphasis on values in cultural feminism has led it to have reform aspirations that are at once minute and diffuse; it knows things like "Lesbians should not wear strap-ons" and "People having sex should be required to ask permission for every new intimate touch," and "A husband who introduces his penis into the vagina of his sleeping wife has raped her and should be prosecuted." It can't stand to listen to Randy Newman's "You Can Leave Your Hat On." It thinks that a man who would joke to a female subordinate at work about pubic hairs appearing on his Coke can has shown himself unfit for high office. It's easily offended; it is schoolmarmish, judgmental, self-righteous. And here it begins to look not like a species of liberal feminism but like an alien infiltrator in it: we have seen it seeking to clear the airwaves of all endorsements of values it thinks are bad; we have seen it thinking that *referring* to a value is *endorsing* it.[21] It can insist that people not only do the right thing, but do it with the right spirit. In short, cultural feminist moralism can trend toward totalitarian regulatory projects. Opposing it makes one sound like a libertarian.

READINGS OF *ONCALE*

By the Structural Male/Female Model. Almost twenty years after publishing *Sexual Harassment of Working Women,* MacKinnon wrote a brief in the *Oncale* case for a group of amici committed to stopping violence by and against men.[22] It shows concisely how MacKinnon's male/female model works when it incorporates three new elements of sex harassment: men's subordination *of a man, male/male* sex2, and thus *sexuality* reconstrued as the social dimension not of male/female sex2 but of sex2 more generally.

The facts alleged by Joseph Oncale are disturbing. Working on an oil rig in an all-male workforce, he was repeatedly threatened and assaulted by his supervisor and two coworkers. They threatened to rape him; twice they held him down while placing their penises up against his body; once they grabbed him in the shower and did something (one cannot be sure quite what) with a piece of soap. His complaints were ignored, and he quit under protest.

In the male/female model as the MacKinnon brief elaborates it, Oncale suffered sex discrimination because he was injured *as a man.* He and other male victims of male sexual aggression are "victimized through their masculinity, violated in their minds and bodies as individual members of their gender" (7). This happens because they are given not only the *worse* gender, but the *wrong* one: "They are feminized: made to serve the function and play the role customarily assigned to women as men's social inferiors. . . . For a man to be sexually attacked, by placing him in a woman's role, demeans his masculinity; he loses it, so to speak. This cannot be done to a woman. What he loses, he loses through gender, as a man" (10). What is utterly remarkable about this formulation is the endorsement it offers to a rigid, monolithic association of male bodies with male gender with superordination, and of female bodies with female gender and subordination. This endorsement is even normative to the extent that it maintains MacKinnon's project of articulating "the authority of excluded truth, the voice of silence." Adopting the perspective of male victims of male sexual violence requires us to recognize that they are persecuted by other men because they fail to represent dominant masculinity seamlessly. Here the brief seems to detach sex1 from gender, to recognize a political project of loosening the stringencies of masculinty. But the brief's articulation of the wrong suffered by Oncale also requires us to acknowledge that his primary, definitional injury is the loss of masculine superordination. How can this be a compensable loss in a feminist theory of injury?

The answer lies in the structural character — the totalism, if you will — of the male/female model. Like MacKinnon's articles and books analyzed in the prior section, the MacKinnon brief formulates the male/female model not as natural — it is, au contraire, a historical contingency which the law can resist (11) — but as total. This is unequivocally clear for women: a woman has no masculinity to lose. Men, however, can endure gender downward mobility. Though the brief is careful to flag the socially constructed quality of male gender, it is equally insistent that a man who loses masculinity is necessarily feminized: *there is nowhere else for him to go.* Thus men who lose their masculinity do so in "their gender, as gender is socially defined" (7), but there is nothing socially negotiable about their fate "as men": because of the harassment they "*are* feminized." Similarly, the brief posits that the attacks on Oncale "violat[ed] (what is conventionally considered) his manhood" (25). This would be a nice recognition of the social negotiability of that outcome except for the parentheses, which give us the option of reading the violation as real: the attacks "violat[ed] . . . his manhood." Whether it's conventional or not, his manhood is all Joseph Oncale has got that is properly his. Take it away, and he is wronged.

The MacKinnon brief again reveals the structural ambitions, the totalism, of the male/female model when it insists that homoeroticism and homosexuality have no independence of its terms. The latter are *subsumed* into the former. The MacKinnon brief achieves this by arguing that the question of homosexuality is both irrelevant to the question of sex discrimination and fundamentally the same as it. It is irrelevant because a homosexual harassing a person of his or her own sex is acting *just like* a heterosexual harassing a member of what the brief calls "the opposite sex" (1, 24), and because victims of sex harassment are victims whether they are straight or gay (25). Harassment is harassment no matter who does it to whom; it always reproduces the paradigm of male/female harassment, and thus we need not take into account anything distinctive about the same-sex-ness of the parties. But at the same time homosexuality is really fundamentally male/female gender all over again: the sex of one's sexual object choice is a "powerful constituent" of one's gender, and antigay discrimination fundamentally disadvantages people for deviating from gender expectations (26–27). As MacKinnon wrote on her own behalf in 1989, "Since sexuality largely defines gender, discrimination based on sexuality *is* discrimination based on gender."

The MacKinnon brief thus maintains the ontological supremacy of the male/female model by simultaneously evacuating sexual orientation of any distinct components and flooding it with gender understood as male super-ordination and female subordination. This is, I think, a big mistake.

Why? Two points. First, this formulation causes the brief to argue that the homosexual orientation of the "perpetrator" (not the "defendant") may be relevant because it would make a male-male harassment case homolo-gous to a male-female case. This would be a good thing for the plaintiff, the brief acknowledges, because the court would then be in a position to say that the defendant would not have selected a woman as his target (24). This is a quick and easy route to a legal finding of sex discrimination, one that the Supreme Court explicitly opened up in its decision in *Oncale*. Gay rights organizations have fought to close this route off ever since circuit courts first opened it, however, because it is also a quick and easy route to homophobia, via the inference that because the defendant is homosexual, he probably has done this bad sexual thing. In a male-male case the in-ference is even richer, borrowing as it does from the male/female model: because the defendant is a *male* homosexual, he is a sexual dominator.

To be sure, the brief counsels that courts may be institutionally unable to make findings of parties' sexual orientations, and it also indicates that courts allowing evidence of the parties' sexual orientations must prevent "homophobic attacks" (24). But it entirely misses the commonsense status of the virulent inference from defendant's homosexuality to his character as a sexual wrongdoer. Indeed, the brief virtually invites the Supreme Court to indulge in them by dropping an entirely unnecessary footnote quoting from Joseph Oncale's deposition testimony: "I feel that they made homosexual advances toward me," Oncale opined, according to the brief. "I feel they are homosexuals" (23 n.7).

And so second: neither lower-court opinion in *Oncale*, and none of the briefs submitted to the Supreme Court, brought this detail in the record to the Justices' attention. And the Justices did not ask for it: the questions they certified for their review made no mention of homosexuality. *Oncale* made its way up the appellate ladder as an "Animal House" case: the plaintiff's allegations of cruel, repeated, and unwelcome sexual assaults were per-sistently read as male-male homosocial highjinks gone awry — in Justice Scalia's terms, "simple teasing or roughhousing among members of the same sex" that is aberrational only in that it has become "objectively se-vere." Alternatively, of course, Oncale's deposition testimony could sup-port a reading of the scene as homosexual predation. It is difficult to escape the conclusion that the MacKinnon brief aimed to induce the Court to adopt just such a reading.

By the Moralistic Male/Female Model. Cultural feminism sees the facts alleged by Oncale to constitute a classic moral struggle between a virtuous feminine or at least not masculine (and in either case, a feminized) Oncale and his morally defective, testosterone-poisoned coworkers. Oncale on this reading is a surrogate woman: the harassment he suffered would have been targeted at a woman had she been there, and serves to masculinize oil rig work, to warn women that the oil rig is a province for male privilege. The masculinity of the rig, consolidated by Oncale's ejection, not only limits women's employment opportunities, but also confirms that sexuality is a, if not the, crucial vehicle for women's subordination.

Cultural feminism wants Oncale to be able to sue for sex discrimination to vindicate his feminine/feminized persona. It wants to borrow the authority of a federal court to make an official statement about gender virtue and gender vice. It also wants to feminize or, faut de mieux, degender the oil rig. That too would send a good moral message; it would push male-dominant values out of this form of public life, and it would clear the way for women to work there and to bring femininity with them. And it wants to desexualize the workplace, either because it shares MacKinnon's structuralism, and so thinks that sex always carries male dominance and female subordination, or because it thinks morally good sex — intersubjective, caring, respectful, alert to human dignity, human values, human sensibilities, human sensitivities — just can't happen between people as lightly connected as coworkers (only domestic monogamy is up to the challenge).

Finally, cultural feminism shares MacKinnon's suspicion of male/male eroticism: unless redeemed by the femininity of one partner, or a thoroughgoing display of categorical imperative respect, etc., what men do with men strikes cultural feminism as morally risky. It would suspect Oncale was right that his assailants were homosexuals, and would regard their sexual aggression as a textbook case of morally defective masculine eroticism.

By Gay Identity and Queer Understandings of Sexuality. There are two other ways to imagine the case — neither of them antigay — and none of the facts published in the various court decisions in the case preclude either one. I want to be very clear about what I am about to do. I am not saying anything about the human being Joseph Oncale, or making any truth claims about what actually happened on the oil rig. Instead, I want to show how his factual allegations can be read. I am going to put his allegation of unwantedness aside, as a mere allegation, and then connect the remaining dots. And because that heuristic produces the equivalent of a court's knowledge of a same-sex harassment case of this type up to and beyond summary judgment, the patterns I draw will become predictions about two alarming classes of cases that will make it to trial under *Oncale*.

In the first of these alternative readings, we can posit, at least for purposes of contemplating what sex harassment law after *Oncale* might authorize, that a plaintiff with these facts willingly engaged in erotic conduct of precisely the kinds described in Oncale's complaint (or that he engaged in some of that conduct and fantasized the rest; or even that he fantasized all of it), and then was struck with a profound desire to refuse the homosexual potential those experiences revealed in him.

That is to say, *Oncale* might have been a homosexual panic case. It would be easy enough to generate this reading of the case out of entirely gay identity presuppositions; in that event, Oncale is actually a gay or bisexual man, but a shame-ridden one, who reacted to his own (identity-appropriate) sexual behavior and/or desires and fantasies with remorse and a lawyer. Oncale's many television appearances in which he (I am told) affirmed his horrified heterosexuality would merely be taken, on this reading, as a closet drama, a project in deep bad faith; my insistence on the possibility of this other reading of the case would be, then, a gesture in the direction of an outing (though note that my reading is of the record, not the human being). On this, first rereading of the case, we would have to understand Oncale as the aggressor, the other men on the oil rig as the victims, and the lawsuit (not any sexual encounter on the oil rig) as the wrong.

But a more thoroughgoing queer approach would make the case outright undecidable. Recall that I posited that a queer approach would detach male bodies from masculinity and superordination, and female bodies from feminity and subordination; it wants to undermine, historicize, celebrate every current supercession of, and generally "get beyond" discrete homo- and heterosexual identities; and it wants to notice that sexual super- *and* subordination can *both* be complex objects of desire, whether they are inflected by any particular configuration of bodies, genders, or homo/hetero identifications, or go bare of all of that.

Once you try, it's perfectly easy to read the facts in *Oncale* in a number of ways that perform many of these detachments. We can imagine that the oil rig has a culture with rules, and that these rules draw not on the male/female model or a gay identity script, but on the ways in which masculine and feminine performances and gay-identified and gay-disidentified performances can diverge and converge to make the power relationships in sex expressly problematic. The rules allow Oncale to indicate a willingness to be mastered, indeed to demand that he is sexually accessible only on the stipulation that those approaching him take on the task of mastery; they submit by taking control; and something happens with a piece of soap. There's not enough in the record to say much more about how it could have been, but (assuming we are going to take Oncale's allegations about unwelcomeness as merely that: allegations) nothing I've said so far is ruled out by the record. From this starting point, the possibilities, in terms of masculinity and femininity and in terms of gay and straight, are probably endless. Mix, match, and omit as you will:[23]

> 1. Oncale performs a feminine man to signal his willingness to be mastered; it's the *discrepancy* between his male body and his gender that gets things going; the other guys comply with a big display of masculinity; and it's the *discrepancy* between their mere bodily selves and the grand controlling personae they assume that keeps things going; so "man fucks woman" but with a twist that undoes the capacity of the male/female model to underwrite Oncale as a victim.
>
> 2. Oncale performs a perfectly masculine man but only one kind of masculine man; it's the discrepancy between his masculinity and that performed by the other men involved that gets things going. Femininity is not important in this version — it's just absent; the men are differentiating themselves within some diacritics in masculinity. The terms of differentiation could sound in sentiment, age, refinement, race, moodiness, or simply (this is important; convergence is not mandated) masculinity itself. So, "it's a guy thing" that creates the space for a dominance/submission sexual interaction. So, "man fucks man": maleness and masculinity are important products of the interaction, but with a twist that undoes the capacity of the male/female model to underwrite Oncale as a victim.
>
> 3. The other men perform a kind of femininity associated with power; for example, they become bitchy. There is no necessary gender correlate for Oncale. He could be the heterosexual partner of the bitch and thus masculinized, but that doesn't tell us whether he's henpecked or intensely

phallic. He could be their lesbian partner, but that doesn't tell us whether she's butch or femme. Or he could merely play the bottom to the power on display: no gender at all. So "man or woman fucks man or woman," or perhaps "man or woman fucks," always with a twist that undoes the capacity of the male/female model to underwrite Oncale as a victim.

4. Possibly more than one of these is happening at the same time, or rather, perhaps they shift in and out of focus as the scene unfolds. Or it could be that the sheer bodily homosexuality of the scene is so dominantly *what it is about* that any effort to attribute to it legible gender signification is simply doomed to defeat. In either case we would have a power/submission relay, but with a twist that undoes the capacity of the male/female model to underwrite Oncale as a victim.

None of the above involves homosexual panic. Indeed, a person could pass through most of the scenes I've described without a sexual orientation identity; you could even do some of them "as" heterosexual. More likely, homosexual and heterosexual desire would — each — be, at every moment, complexly achieved, defeated, and deferred. To that extent the object of desire for any of the players would be some *relationship* to sexual orientation. Similarly, where gender is of any moment, it reads not as a property or determinant of the bodily self but as a performative language, as a means of transmitting desire. Certainly we can say that, when gender matters at all, the object of desire is not a gendered object, but a *relationship* to a gender or perhaps to gender more generally.

But I've made the assumption that the lead theme in the scene is power and submission. And here's the rub. The mix-and-match volatilities of gender and sexual orientation work to make the question of who is submitting to whom extremely difficult to answer. Indeed, the chief theme would have to be that the desire of the parties to any of these scenes has as its object a *mise-en-problème* of desire itself. To the extent that the decision in *Oncale* allows one participant in scenes like these to have a panic about it afterward and sue, it sets courts and juries administering Title VII a deeply problematic function.

Let me reapproach that last point from the perspective of the male/female model. The rereadability of the facts in *Oncale,* rather than confirming the male/female model, shows what's wrong with it. It is just too complete and too settled. Men are over there with masculinity and superordination; women are over here with femininity and subordination. Sex and sexuality are never good; they are always tools by which women are as-signed subordination and men either assign or suffer it. Sexual orientation both matters and doesn't matter precisely and only to the extent that it confirms this mapping. Everything is accounted for; there is nothing left over. The model produces great certainty: Oncale transparently represents all men injured by this totalized gender system because the system frames all options for understanding his injury. But if the model doesn't apply, if homosexual panic or more complex "problematicness" panic is what the "case is about," that certainty will evaporate.

The resulting uncertainty intensifies, moreover, as we move from the homosexual panic hypothesis to the problematicness panic hypothesis. Things are bad enough under the former. Surely, on that reading of the facts, Joseph Oncale's hesitant sense that his attackers "are homosexuals" is volatile in a way that disables the male/female model. Does his "feeling" about his attackers tell us that they are homosexuals or that he might be? That they attacked him on the oil rig or that he attacked them by invoking the remarkable powers of the federal court to restore his social position as heterosexual? If we could know the answer to these questions, at least we'd know how to judge the case: we know we're against assault, and we know we're against homosexual panic. But how, in an actual case, *would* we know? Surely we would not want Justice Scalia's "common sense" to be our guide: as I've posited, homosexual panic *is* common sense.

Still less do I relish the idea of Sundowner Offshore Services deciding whether to put Pat Califia on the stand in an effort to persuade juries out of their commonsense intuition that no one could want to be mastered sex-ually, or could take control by demanding to be mastered. But the problem in the problematicness panic rereading of the *Oncale* facts runs much deeper than that. On that reading, it was precisely the loss of certainty about wantedness that the players were seeking. That *was* their desire. It's a risky desire: acting on it places one in the way of having some unwanted sex. Things can go wrong; we need to keep one eye on the cause of action for assault. But more profoundly, if things go right, the wantedness of the sex that happens will be *undecidable*.

On the way to confronting that, there are four more conventional rea-sons not to want this case ever to be tried as a sex harassment claim. First, this Oncale contradicts his own past decision when he claims access now to a less problematic set of norms about wantedness. We can and should estop him from claiming now that then he didn't want to put wantedness *en abysme.* Second, if we don't estop him, we set up a one-way cultural ratchet: Title VII (and the background norms we will have further confirmed when we decide to use it in this way) will always turn the normative screw in the direction of less problematic sex. The male/female model is not a transparent translation of suppressed consciousness into the law; it's a trumping move. Third, to the extent that that changes the culture of the oil rig and the culture generally, that would be a huge loss. I may not be able to convince you of it, but I think the problematic of wantedness isn't just tolerable; it's beautiful. It's brave. It's complicated and fleeting and elaborate and human.

Fourth, suppressing performances that make the problematic of wantedness explicit would not make it go away; the regulatory project would only make the problematic of wantedness more covert; indeed, regulation might intensify by narrowing the vocabularies that subversion has to mobilize. After all, it's not just the perverts who engage in scenes like those I've just affirmed as good who seek incoherent experiences in sex: I think most of us experience sex (when it's not routinized) as an alarming mix of desire and fear, delight and disgust, power and surrender, surrender and power, attachment and alienation, ecstasy in the root sense of the word and enmired embodiedness. Essential elements of the third Oncale scenario are enacted, I imagine, in many more sexual relationships than you would guess just by looking around the boardroom or seminar room, and the edgy experience of unwantedness in sex is probably cherished by more people than are willing to say so. Suppressing performances like my third Oncale scenario might make sex on Sunday afternoon, with your spouse, in the sacred precincts of the marital bedroom, more banal or more weird—it's hard to tell which, in a domain of experience so routinely enriched by prohibition. The queer project carries a brief for the weirdness of sex wherever it appears; it is (or should be) agnostic about where, when, and among or between whom the intensities of sex are possible. But (and this is probably the queerest reason to protect the problematic of unwantedness from regulation as sex harassment) it would resist the redistribution of sexual intensities achieved under color of women's equality or moral virtue.

Some Doctrinal and Political Consequences

Homosexual panic—the experience of terror that some people feel when they think that someone of their own sex finds them sexually attractive—

can be extremely dysphoric. Some people might even say that having a homosexual panic experience at work was unwelcome and sufficiently severe to alter the conditions of their employment and create an abusive working environment. Under *Oncale,* they can sue for that. And because juries might well think that a single same-sex erotic overture was more obviously unwanted, and more "severe," than a single cross-sex one, these suits could place gay men and lesbians in the workplace (especially the "known" ones) under tighter surveillance than their obviously heterosexual counterparts.

Both gay identity and queer thinking are thus in tension with feminist projects of maintaining a copious definition of a "hostile work environment" here. From a gay identity perspective, *Oncale* should be read as a direct, disproportionate threat to the constituent group. And there is more to it than that if we move in a queer direction. The idea there is to regard homosexual panic with the utmost suspicion. It's not just that the experience appears from this perspective to be silly; it's deemed to be *in bad faith.* The idea is that no one would *panic* over the possibility of a homosexual engagement unless he or she both didn't *and did* want it. Homosexual panic, when it produces an attack on a gay man or lesbian, is thought to be a way of punishing someone else for desires that are properly one's own. A queer approach would question whether the homosexual panic plaintiff is making credible assertions about what the supposed perpetrator did to initiate his or her dysphoria, and whether the plaintiff's reaction is objectively reasonable. It would want the doctrinal machinery applied at these points to be skeptical, resistant to the plaintiff.

And so a gay-friendly or queer approach would be unhappy about achievements that feminists have sought and gained to make these bits of the doctrinal machinery more plaintiff-friendly. For instance, they would be worried about a recent change in the Rules of Evidence, sought and hailed by feminists, barring admission of evidence of plaintiff's sexual history in civil cases involving "sexual assault" or attempted sexual assault. (Sexual assault includes any unwanted sexual touching, so a lot of sex harassment cases are governed by this new rule.) The new rule could make it difficult to undermine the credibility of a homosexual panic complainant. And a queer approach would worry about reforms sought and, when achieved, hailed by most feminists, that tailor the reasonableness inquiry to match the "perspective" or "social knowledge" attributed to the plaintiff's demography. Both gay identity and queer projects would worry, for example, about the Ninth Circuit's holding that the socially sensitive judgments in cases involving women's complaints about the behavior of men be subjected to a "reasonable *woman*" test. What's next? Are we going to refer these elements in male/male cases to the "reasonable (thus presumably the heterosexual) man"? I hope not. Feminism focused on sexuality as the central mechanism of women's subordination and gay-affirmative thought show trajectories across these bits of doctrinal turf that are veering into collision.

And there is even more to the problem than that. Unlike a gay identity approach, a queer approach tends to minimize rather than maximize the differences between same-sex eroticism and cross-sex eroticism. There are many reasons for this, but I suggest that the chief one is a sense that gender and power circulate far more complexly and with far more contingency than is thought in feminisms focused on woman's sexual subordination. The phenomenon of lesbians wearing dildos (big news fifteen years ago) leads to heterosexual women wearing dildos (not news yet, but it's happening). What's the difference, asks queer theory? Or take a footnote from Jessica Benjamin's book, *The Bonds of Love*. There she tells us, "A woman who had once been involved in a sadomasochistic relationship complained of her partner that "he was bumbling, he never hurt me where or how *I wanted* to be hurt.' Indeed," Benjamin continues, "a good sadist is hard to find: he has to intuit his victim's hidden desires, protect *the illusion* of oneness and mastery that stem from *his knowing what she wants*."[24] Feminism focused on the badness of women's sexual pain at the hands of men and committed to the idea that women's sexual subordination is the core reason for women's social subordination has trouble liking a sentence like that. But gay and queer thinking have no problem with it; indeed, they exult over how it rearranges conventional associations of the feminine with subordination and the masculine with power.

This tendency in queer thinking creates a deep tension between it and what may be *the* central goal of women's-sexual-subordination-feminist law reform in the area of sexuality. If the queer project reacts with so much skepticism to claims of same-sex sexual injury, and if the reason for that lies not only in its understanding of the historical fate of same-sex love but in its understanding of the complexities and ambivalences of eroticism, then the queer project undermines our reasons for believing women who assert that they are sexually injured by men. If same-sex sexual injury can be phantasmatic and based as much on desire as its opposite, why not also its cross-sex counterpart? Indeed, *feminist* queer thinking might even say that we insult women by attributing to them such milquetoast psyches that they must be assumed incapable of fomenting powerful phantasmatic cathexes on abjection. And so we have queer and *feminist* queer projects of asking whether, when a woman claims that a male coworker or supervisor or teacher injures her by desiring her sexually, we should believe her, or think her claim of injury is reasonable. And here we are near the heart of the women's-sexual-subordination-feminist sexual regulatory project, which has been to change things so that women are believed when they claim sexual injury.

Near the heart. *At* the heart is the claim that the sexual—male/female or masculine/feminine sex2 and, in more structural versions, sexuality tout court—is subordinating for women. The astonishing cultural success of this defining idea of sexual subordination feminism can be traced in the intuition of women we know, and perhaps the women we are, that we are more injured when a male supervisor asks to sleep with us than when he forgets to sign us up for a reskilling conference or power lunch. And in the assumption that we are more injured when he asks than he is when we say no (or, for that matter, yes).

As we have seen, the idea that his overture is *sex discrimination* depends on an assumption that it is heterosexual: he would not have issued the same invitation to a man, say Catharine MacKinnon and Justice Scalia. And as we have seen, gay identity thinking seeks to cut that link in its concern that the logic in same-sex cases will be anything but benign for known or suspected gay and lesbian "perpetrators" and for homosexuality generally. More to the point, perhaps, queer thinking questions the very idea that there *are* homosexuals and heterosexuals, and objects to this element in sex harassment law because it promises to authorize and produce the narrowly conceived erotic personhoods it supposedly merely proves.

That is to say, gay identity and queer thinking *disagree* with sexual subordination feminism over the idea that sex2 and sexuality are consistently structured as top-down male/female power, and thus *disagree* with the idea that eroticism at work is presumptively sex discrimination that subordinates women. To be sure, they are or should be ready to recognize that sexuality can be deployed in cruel ways, and that erotic conduct can be prosthetic to a sex discrimination project that harms women. But I think their current political goals must be to dethrone feminism as the sole authoritative source for left understandings of the sexual normativity, and to look to socialist feminism for left understandings of sex discrimination. At the very least, gay identity and queer thinking would sever the doctrinal link making sexual harassment a first-order species of sex discrimination, sending the former out of the discrimination paradigm and reducing allegations of sexual cruelties at work to the status of mere evidence, no different in legal value from evidence that someone threw a stapler across the room.

To say so is to violate a left-multicultural norm favoring left/liberal feminist/socialist/gay/sex-positive/queer convergence — intersectionality, coalition formation, conflation, what you will. Left social theory has been conducted on an assumption that a really successful analysis would show that feminism, socialism, gay affirmativity, sex positivity, and queer thought would discover that, in theory and in the real world, their findings and aspirations converge. The waters have been muddied by a general left/liberal desire always to reconcile its various ideas, commitments, constituencies, and projects, and the resulting confusion has protected sexual subordination feminism from critique and smoothed the way for its regulatory successes — many of which must seem like costs, not benefits, once a splitting becomes articulate. It seems timely to urge feminists to learn to suspend feminism, to interrupt it, to sustain its displacement by inconsistent hypotheses about power, hierarchy, and progressive struggle.

That is not to say that sexual subordination feminism might not ultimately be the best choice for a vocabulary in which to conduct a sex discrimination regime. Certainly it seemed necessary when women first entered the workforce in the United States. Whatever the benefits of sex harassment regulation when it was introduced, and even now, I argue here, not that it is instrinsically mistaken but that it has costs that have not been counted and that, if you take a socialist feminist, sex-positive feminist, pro-gay, or queer approach to life, you think some of those costs now outweigh many of the corresponding benefits. Revealing and balancing those costs and those benefits — and doing so under the weight of the uncertainty brought to the table by the possibility of problematicness panic and all that it suggests about the dark side of power and knowledge in sexual interaction — would return sex harassment to political contestation understood as an indeterminate, decisionistic enterprise:

> One might say that a decision is "political" when and to the extent that it is made under conditions of ambiguity and with knowledge of consequences. A political decision is one which the decision maker had room

to make, within or against the terms of his role and expertise [and, I would add, favorite social theory], in various ways, and which was understood to have consequences—making some things more likely, some less, some people better off, some [worse], and so forth. The point is not *which* interests are advanced and which retarded, nor the ideological associations we can associate with the decision once the determinacy of the experts' identity and vocabulary run out, but the human experience of deciding knowing there will *be* consequences, and that one *can* decide in various ways.[25]

Even more pleasurable than loosening the feminist grip on sex harassment, and even more surprising than seeing how sex harassment law has become a mechanism for sexuality harassment, is the pleasurable surprise that politics could happen in a contestatory engagement of various feminisms with their gay identity and queer critiques.

Notes

1. 118 S. Ct. 998 (1998).

2. Vicki Schultz, "Reconceptualizing Sexual Harassment," *Yale Law Journal* 107 (1998): 1683.

3. Catharine A. MacKinnon. *Sexual Harassment of Working Women* (New Haven: Yale University Press, 1986), 220–21.

4. Catharine A. MacKinnon, *Toward a Feminist Theory of the State* (Cambridge, MA: Harvard University Press, 1989), xiv.

5. Catharine A. MacKinnon, "Feminism, Marxism, Method and the State: An Agenda for Theory," *Signs* 7.3 (1982): 515, 533; hereafter, "An Agenda for Theory."

6. Catharine A. MacKinnon, "Feminism, Marxism, Method and the State: Toward Feminist Jurisprudence," *Signs* 8.4 (1983): 635, 638; hereafter, "Toward Feminist Jurisprudence."

7. Male dominance, MacKinnon concluded, is "total on the one side and a delusion on the other" ("Agenda for Theory," 542). The inequality of women is structural: "The inequality approach . . . sees women's situation as a structural problem of enforced interiority that needs to be radically altered" (MacKinnon, *Sexual Harassment of Working Women*, 4–5).

8. MacKinnon, "Toward Feminist Jurisprudence," 637–38 n. 5.

9. Catharine A. MacKinnon, "Points against Postmodernism," *Chicago-Kent Law Review* 75 (2000): 687, 688–89, 691, 692–93; emphasis added.

10. MacKinnon, "Toward Feminist Jurisprudence," 644–45.

11. Ibid., 652, 654–55; emphasis added.

12. Ibid., 652.

13. Ibid., 655–58.

14. MacKinnon, *Toward*, 248–49.

15. For example: "In 1982, Andrea Dworkin and I advanced our equality approach to pornography through our ordinance allowing civil suits for sex discrimination *by those who can prove harm through pornography*." Catharine A. MacKinnon and Ronald Dworkin, "Pornography: An Exchange," *New York Review of Books* 3 Mar. 1994, 47–48; rpt. in Drucilla Cornell, *Feminism and Pornography* (Oxford: Oxford University Press, 2000), 121.

16. I rely on the ordinance as reprinted in *American Booksellers Ass'n v. Hudnut*, 598 F.2d 323 (7th Cir. 1985), *aff'g on other grounds* 598 F. Supp. 1316 (S.D.Ind. 1984), *aff'd* 106 S.Ct. 1172 (1986) (mem.) and in Andrea Dworkin and Catharine A. MacKinnon, eds., *Harm's Way: The Pornography Civil Rights Hearing* (Cambridge, MA: Harvard University Press, 1997), 438–57. See also Catharine A. MacKinnon, "Pornography, Civil Rights, and Speech," *Harvard Civil Rights–Civil Liberties Law Review* 20 (1985): 1, 60 ("The hearings establish the harm. The definition sets the standard"); and Catharine A. MacKinnon, "The Roar on the Other Side of Silence," in *In Harm's Way*, 3–24, for a general defense of the assertion that the hearings were conclusive on this point.

17. Quoted in Paul Brest and Ann Vandenberg, "Politics, Feminism, and the Constitution: The Anti-Pornography Movement in Minneapolis," *Stanford Law Review* 39 (1987): 607, 613.

18. MacKinnon, *Toward*, 248.

19. Thus pornography poses a question not of morality but of power. See Catharine A. MacKinnon, "Not a Moral Issue," *Yale Law and Policy Review* 2 (1984): 321; see also MacKinnon, "Toward Feminist Jurisprudence," 654 n. 41 ("In feminist analysis, a rape is not an isolated or individual or moral transgression but a terrorist act within a systematic context of group subjection, like lynching").

20. Though there is a subdifference here: MacKinnon sees the feminization of a man as an injury, while cultural feminism sees it as an instance of moral uplift.

21. For a rich description and canny critique of this move, see Amy Adler, "What's Left? Hate Speech, Pornography, and the Problem for Artistic Expression," *California Law Review* 84 (1996): 1499.

22. Brief of National Organization on Male Victimization, Inc., et al. In *Oncale*, No. 96-568 (U.S.S.C.) (11 Aug. 1997); rpt. at *U.C.L.A. Women's Law Journal* 8 (1997): 9.

23. A memorial moment for David Charny, who opened this avenue for me.

24. Jessica Benjamin, *The Bonds of Love: Psychoanalysis, Feminism, and the Problem of Domination* (New York: Pantheon, 1998), 64.

25. David Kennedy, *Global Governance and the Politics of the Professions*, draft of 26 Sept. 2001, p. 16.

LAUREN BERLANT

The Subject of True Feeling:
Pain, Privacy, and Politics

Liberty finds no refuge in a jurisprudence of doubt. — *Planned Parenthood of South-eastern Pennsylvania v. Casey,* 112 S.Ct. 2791 (1992)

Pain

Ravaged wages and ravaged bodies saturate the global marketplace in which the United States seeks desperately to compete "competitively," as the euphemism goes, signifying a race that will be won by the nations whose labor conditions are most optimal for profit.[1] In the United States the media of the political public sphere regularly register new scandals of the proliferating sweatshop networks "at home" and "abroad," which has to be a good thing, because it produces *feeling* and with it something at least akin to *consciousness* that can lead to *action*.[2] Yet, even as the image of the traumatized worker proliferates, even as evidence of exploitation is found under every rock or commodity, it competes with a normative/utopian image of the U.S. citizen who remains unmarked, framed, and protected by the private trajectory of his life project, which is sanctified at the juncture where the unconscious meets history: the American Dream.[3] In that story one's identity is not born of suffering, mental, physical, or economic. If the U.S. worker is lucky enough to live at an economic moment that sustains the Dream, he gets to appear at his *least* national when he is working and at his most national at leisure, with his family or in semipublic worlds of other men producing surplus manliness (e.g., via sports). In the American dreamscape his identity is private property, a zone in which

structural obstacles and cultural differences fade into an ether of prolonged, deferred, and individuating enjoyment that he has earned and that
the nation has helped him to earn. Meanwhile, exploitation appears only as
a scandalous nugget in the sieve of memory when it can be condensed into
an exotic thing of momentary fascination, a squalor of the bottom too
horrible to be read in its own actual banality.

The exposed traumas of workers in ongoing extreme conditions do not
generally induce more than mourning on the part of the state and the public
culture to whose feeling-based opinions the state is said to respond. Mourning is what happens when a grounding object is lost, is dead, or no longer
living (to you). Mourning is an experience of irreducible boundedness: I am
here, I am living, he is dead, I am mourning. It is a beautiful, not sublime,
experience of emancipation: mourning supplies the subject the definitional
perfection of a being no longer in flux. It takes place over a distance: even if
the object who induces the feeling of loss and helplessness is neither dead
nor at any great distance from where you are.[4] In other words, mourning
can also be an act of aggression, of social deathmaking: it can perform the
evacuation of significance from actually existing subjects. Even when liberals do it, one might say, "others" are ghosted for a good cause.[5] The
sorrow songs of scandal that sing of the exploitation that is always "elsewhere" (even a few blocks away) are in this sense aggressively songs of
mourning. Play them backward, and the military march of capitalist triumphalism (*The Trans-Nationale*) can be heard. Its lyric, currently crooned
by every organ of record in the United States, is about necessity. It exhorts
citizens to understand that the "bottom line"[6] of national life is neither
utopia nor freedom but survival, which can be achieved only by a citizenry
that eats its anger, makes no unreasonable claims on resources or control
over value, and uses its most creative energy to cultivate intimate spheres
while scraping together a life flexibly in response to the market world's
caprice.[7]

In this particular moment of expanding class unconsciousness that looks
like consciousness emerges a peculiar, though not unprecedented, hero: the
exploited child. If a worker can be infantilized, pictured as young, as small,
as feminine or feminized, as starving, as bleeding and diseased, and as a
(virtual) slave, the righteous indignation around procuring his survival re-
sounds everywhere. The child must not be sacrificed to states or to prof-
iteering. His wounded image speaks a truth that subordinates narrative: he
has not "freely" chosen his exploitation; the optimism and play that are

putatively the right of childhood have been stolen from him. Yet only "voluntary" steps are ever taken to try to control this visible sign of what is ordinary and systemic amid the chaos of capitalism, to make its localized nightmares seem uninevitable. Privatize the atrocity, delete the visible sign, make it seem *foreign*. Return the child to the family, replace the children with adults who can look dignified while being paid virtually the same revolting wage. The problem that organizes so much feeling then regains livable proportions, and the uncomfortable pressure of feeling dissipates, like so much gas.

Meanwhile, the pressure of feeling the shock of being uncomfortably political produces a cry for a double therapy — to the victim and the viewer. But before "we" appear too complacently different from the privileged citizens who desire to caption the mute image of exotic suffering with an aversively fascinated mourning (a desire for the image to be *dead*, a ghost), we must note that this feeling culture crosses over into other domains, the domains of what we call identity politics, where the wronged take up voice and agency to produce transformative testimony, which depends on an analogous conviction about the *self-evidence* and therefore the *objectivity* of painful feeling.

The central concern of this essay is to address the place of painful feeling in the making of political worlds. In particular, I mean to challenge a powerful popular belief in the positive workings of something I call national sentimentality, a rhetoric of promise that a nation can be built across fields of social difference through channels of affective identification and empathy. Sentimental politics generally promotes and maintains the hegemony of the national identity form, no mean feat in the face of continued widespread intercultural antagonism and economic cleavage. But national sentimentality is more than a current of feeling that circulates in a political field: the phrase describes a long-standing contest between two models of U.S. citizenship. In one, the classic model, each citizen's value is secured by an equation between abstractness and emancipation: a cell of national identity provides juridically protected personhood for citizens regardless of anything specific about them. In the second model, which was initially organized around labor, feminist, and antiracist struggles of the nineteenth-century United States, another version of the nation is imagined as the index of collective life. This nation is peopled by suffering citizens and noncitizens whose structural exclusion from the utopian-American dreamscape exposes the state's claim of legitimacy and virtue to an acid wash of truth telling that makes hegemonic disavowal virtually impossible at certain moments of political intensity.

Sentimentality has long been the means by which mass subaltern pain is advanced, in the dominant public sphere, as the true core of national collectivity. It operates when the pain of intimate others burns into the conscience of classically privileged national subjects, such that they feel the pain of flawed or denied citizenship as their pain. Theoretically, to eradicate the pain those with power will do whatever is necessary to return the nation once more to its legitimately utopian odor. Identification with pain, a universal true feeling, then leads to structural social change. In return, subalterns scarred by the pain of failed democracy will reauthorize universalist notions of citizenship in the national utopia, which involves believing in a redemptive notion of law as the guardian of public good. The object of the nation and the law in this light is to eradicate systemic social pain, the absence of which becomes the definition of freedom.

Yet, because these very sources of protection — the state, the law, patriotic ideology — have traditionally buttressed traditional matrices of cultural hierarchy, and because their historic job has been to protect universal subject-citizens from feeling their cultural and corporeal specificity as a political vulnerability, the imagined capacity of these institutions to assimilate to the affective tactics of subaltern counterpolitics suggests some weaknesses, or misrecognitions, in these tactics. For one thing, it may be that the sharp specificity of the traumatic model of pain implicitly mischaracterizes what a person is as what a person becomes in the experience of social negation; this model also falsely promises a sharp picture of structural violence's source and scope, in turn promoting a dubious optimism that law and other visible sources of inequality, for example, can provide the best remedies for their own taxonomizing harms. It is also possible that counterhegemonic deployments of pain as the measure of structural injustice actually sustain the utopian image of a homogeneous national metaculture, which can look like a healed or healthy body in contrast to the scarred and exhausted ones. Finally, it might be that the tactical use of trauma to describe the effects of social inequality so overidentifies the eradication of pain with the achievement of justice that it enables various confusions: for instance, the equation of pleasure with freedom or the sense that changes in feeling, even on a mass scale, amount to substantial social change. Sentimental politics makes these confusions credible and these violences bearable, as its cultural power confirms the centrality of interpersonal identification and empathy to the vitality and viability of collective life. This gives citizens something to do in response to overwhelming structural violence. Meanwhile, by equating mass society with that thing called "national culture," these important transpersonal linkages and intimacies all too frequently serve as proleptic shields, as ethically uncontestable legitimating devices for sustaining the hegemonic field.[8]

Our first example, the child laborer, a ghost of the nineteenth century, taps into a current vogue to reflect in the premature exposure of children to capitalist publicity and adult depravity the nation's moral and economic decline, citing it as a scandal of citizenship, something shocking and un-American. Elsewhere I have described the ways the infantile citizen has been exploited, in the United States, to become both the inspiring sign of the painless good life and the evacuating optimistic cipher of contemporary national identity.[9] During the 1980s a desperate search to protect the United States from what seemed to be an imminently powerful alliance of parties on the bottom of so many traditional hierarchies — the poor, people of color, women, gays and lesbians — provoked a counterinsurgent fantasy on behalf of "traditional American values." The nation imagined in this reactive rhetoric is dedicated not to the survival or emancipation of traumatized marginal subjects but, rather, to freedom for the American innocent: the adult without sin, the abducted and neglected child, and, above all, and most effectively, the fetus. Although it had first appeared as a technological miracle of photographic biopower in the mid-1960s, in the post-*Roe* era the fetus became consolidated as a political commodity, a supernatural sign of national iconicity. What constituted this national iconicity was an image of an American, perhaps the last living American, not yet bruised by history: not yet caught up in the excitement of mass consumption or ethnic, racial, or sexual mixing, not yet tainted by knowledge, by money, or by war. This fetus was an American to identify with, to aspire to make a world for: it organized a kind of beautiful citizenship politics of good intention and virtuous fantasy that could not be said to be dirty, or whose dirt was attributed to the sexually or politically immoral.

By *citizenship* I refer here both to the legal sense in which persons are juridically subject to the law's privileges and protections by virtue of national identity status but also the experiential, vernacular context in which people customarily understand their relation to state power and social membership. It is to bridge these two axes of political identity and identification that Bernard Nathanson, founder of the National Abortion Rights

Action League (NARAL) and now a pro-life activist, makes political films starring the traumatically posticonic fetal body. His aim is to solicit *aversive identifications* with the fetus, ones that strike deeply the empathetic imaginary of people's best selves while creating pressure for the erasure of empathy's scene. First, he shows graphic images of abortion, captioned by pornographic descriptions of the procedures by which the total body is visibly turned into hideous fragmented flesh. He then calls on the national conscience to delete what he has created, an "unmistakable trademark of the irrational violence that has pervaded the twentieth century."[10] The trademark to which he refers is abortion. He exhorts the public to abort the fetal trademark so as to save the fetus itself and, by extension, the national identity form and its future history. In this sense the fetus's sanctified national identity is the opposite of any multicultural, sexual, or classed identity: the fetus is a blinding light that, triumphant as the modal citizen form, would white out the marks of hierarchy, taxonomy, and violence that seem now so central to the public struggle over who should possess the material and cultural resources of contemporary national life.

It will be clear by now how the struggle over child labor takes on the same form as fetal rights discourse: revelations of trauma, incitements to rescue, the reprivatization of victims as the ground of hope, and, above all, the notion that the feeling self is the true self, the self that must be protected from pain or from history, that scene of unwelcome changing. The infantile citizen then enfigures the adult's true self, his inner child in all its undistorted or untraumatized possibility. But to say this is to show how the fetal/infantile icon is a fetish of citizenship with a double social function. As an object of fascination and disavowal, it stands in for (while remanding to social obscurity) the traumatized virtuous private citizen around whom history ought to be organized, for whom there is not a good-enough world. (This currently includes the formerly tacit, or "normal," citizen and the sexually and racially subordinated ones.) In addition to its life as a figure for the injured adult, the fetus has another life as a utopian sign of a just and pleasant socius, both in pro-life, pro-family values rhetoric and in advertisements and Hollywood films about the state of white reproductive heterosexuality in the United States during an era of great cultural, economic, and technological upheaval. Its two scenes of citizenship can be spatialized: one takes place in a traumatized public and the other in a pain-free intimate zone. These zones mirror each other perfectly, and so betray the fetish form of sentimental citizenship, the wish it expresses to signify a political world beyond contradiction.[11]

I have elaborated these basic Freudian dicta about mourning, the theory of infantile citizenship, and this account of U.S. political culture to make a context for four claims: that this is an age of sentimental politics in which policy and law and public experiences of personhood in everyday life are conveyed through rhetorics of utopian/traumatized feeling; that national-popular struggle is now expressed in fetishes of utopian/traumatic affect that overorganize and overorganicize social antagonism; that utopian/traumatized subjectivity has replaced rational subjectivity as the essential index of value for personhood and thus for society; and that, while on all sides of the political spectrum political rhetoric generates a high degree of cynicism and boredom,[12] those same sides manifest, simultaneously, a sanctifying respect for sentiment. Thus, in the sentimental national contract antagonistic class positions mirror each other in their mutual conviction about the *self-evidence* and *objectivity* of painful feeling, and about the nation's duty to eradicate it. In the conjuncture "utopian/traumatized" I mean to convey a logic of fantasy reparation involved in the therapeutic conversion of the scene of pain and its eradication to the scene of the political itself. Questions of social inequity and social value are now adjudicated in the register not of power but of sincere surplus feeling: worry about whether public figures seem "caring" subordinates analyses of their visions of injustice; subalternized groups attempt to forge alliances on behalf of radical social transformation through testimonial rhetorics of true pain;[13] people believe that they know what they feel when they feel it, can locate its origin, measure its effects.

The traffic in affect of these political struggles finds validity in those seemingly superpolitical moments when a "clear" wrong—say, the spectacle of children violently exploited—produces a "universal" response. Feeling politics takes all kinds: it is a politics of protection, reparation, rescue. It claims a hardwired truth, a core of common sense. It is beyond ideology, beyond mediation, beyond contestation. It seems to dissolve contradiction and dissent into pools of basic and also higher truth. It seems strong and clear, as opposed to confused or ambivalent (thus: the unconscious has left the ballpark). It seems the inevitable or desperately only core material of community.

What does it mean for the struggle to shape collective life when a politics of true feeling organizes analysis, discussion, fantasy, and policy? When feeling, the most subjective thing, the thing that makes persons public and marks their location, takes the temperature of power; mediates person-hood, experience, and history; takes over the space of ethics and truth? When the shock of pain is said only to produce *clarity* when shock can as powerfully be said to produce panic, misrecognition, the shakiness of per-ception's ground? Finally, what happens to questions of managing alterity or difference or resources in collective life when feeling *bad* becomes evi-dence for a structural condition of injustice? What does it mean for the theory and practice of social transformation when feeling *good* becomes evidence of justice's triumph? As many historians and theorists of "rights talk" have shown, the beautiful and simple categories of legitimation in liberal society can bestow on the phenomenal form of proper personhood the status of normative value, which is expressed in feeling terms as "com-fort";[14] meanwhile, political arguments that challenge the claim of painful feeling's analytical clarity are frequently characterized as causing further violence to already damaged persons and the world of their desires.

This essay raises uncomfortable questions about what the evidence of trauma is: its desire is to exhort serious critical, but not cynical, attention to the fetish of true feeling in which social antagonism is, frequently, being worked without being worked through. My larger aim is to bring into being as an object of critique the all too explicit "commonsense" feeling culture of national life, evident in the law, identity politics, and mass society generally: it is about the problem of trying juridically and culturally to administer society as a space ideally void of struggle and ambivalence, a place made on the model of fetal simplicity. I am not trying to posit feeling as the bad opposite of something good called thinking: as we will see in the cases that follow, politicized feeling is a kind of thinking that too often assumes the obviousness of the thought it has, which stymies the produc-tion of the thought it might become.

Privacy

It would not be too strong to say that where regulating sexuality is con-cerned the law has a special sentimental relation to banality. But to say this is not to accuse the law of irrelevance or shallowness. In contrast to the primary sense of banality as a condition of reiterated ordinary conventionality, banality can also mark the experience of deeply felt emotion, as in the case of "I love you," "Did you come?" or "O' Say, Can You See?"[15] But for an occasion of banality to be both utopian and sublime its ordinariness must be thrust into a zone of overwhelming disavowal. This act of optimistic forgetting is neither simple nor easy: it takes the legitimating force of institutions — for example, the nation form or heterosexuality — to establish the virtue of forgetting banality's banality. Take a classic instance of this process, an entirely forgettable moment in *The Wizard of Oz* that precedes an unforgettable one. Auntie Em says to Dorothy, who has been interfering with the work on the farm (no child labor there: Dorothy carries *books*): "Find yourself a place where you won't get into any trouble." Dorothy, in a trance, seems to repeat the phrase but misrepeats it, sighing, "a place where there isn't any trouble," which leads her then to fantasize "somewhere over the Rainbow." Between the phrase's first and second incarnations the agency of the subject disappears and is transferred to the place: the magic of will and intention has been made a property of property.

The unenumerated relation between *the* place where *you* won't get into trouble and *a* place where, definitionally, *there is no trouble* expresses the foggy fantasy of happiness pronounced in the constitutional concept of privacy, whose emergence in sexuality law during the 1960s brought heterosexual intimacy explicitly into the antagonistic field of U.S. citizenship. Privacy is the Oz of America. Based on a notion of safe space, a hybrid space of home and law in which people will act legally and lovingly toward one another, free from the determinations of history or the coercions of pain, the constitutional theorization of sexual privacy is drawn from a lexicon of romantic sentiment, a longing for a space where there is no trouble, a place whose constitution in law would be so powerful that desire would meet moral discipline there, making real the dreamy rule. In this dream the zone of privacy is a paradigmatic national space too, where freedom and desire meet up in their full suprapolitical expression, a site of embodiment that also leaves unchallenged fundamental dicta about the universality or abstractness of the modal citizen.

Much has been written on the general status of privacy doctrine in constitutional history, a "broad and ambiguous concept which can easily be shrunken in meaning but which can also, on the other hand, easily be interpreted as a constitutional ban against many things other than searches and seizures."[16] Privacy was first conceived as a constitutionally mandated but unenumerated right of sexual citizenship in *Griswold v. Connecticut* (381 U.S. 479 [1965]). The case is about the use of birth control in marriage: a nineteenth-century Connecticut law made it illegal for married couples to use contraceptives for birth control (oral arguments suggest that the "rhythm method" was not illegal in that state);[17] they were allowed prophylaxis only to prevent disease. To challenge this law Esther Griswold, director of Planned Parenthood in Connecticut, and Lee Buxton, the chief physician there, were arrested, by arrangement with the district attorney, for giving "information, instruction, and medical advice to *married persons* as to the means of preventing conception."[18]

The arguments made in *Griswold* stress the Due Process clause of the Fourteenth Amendment, because denying the sale of contraceptives "constitutes a deprivation of right against invasion of privacy."[19] This kind of privacy is allotted only to married couples: Justice Goldberg quotes approvingly a previous opinion of Justice Harlan (*Poe v. Ullman,* 367 U.S. 497, at 533), which states that "adultery, homosexuality, and the like are sexual intimacy which the State forbids . . . but the intimacy of husband and wife is necessarily an essential and accepted feature of the institution of marriage, an institution which the State not only must allow, but which always and in every age it has fostered and protected."[20]

We can see in Harlan's phrasing and Goldberg's citation of it the sentimental complexities of making constitutional law about sexual practice in the modern United States. The logic of equivalence between adultery and homosexuality in the previous passage locates these antithetical sexual acts/practices in an unprotected public space that allows and even compels *zoning* in the form of continual state discipline (e.g., laws):[21] in contrast, marital privacy is drawn up here in a zone elsewhere to the law and takes its authority from tradition, which means that the law simultaneously protects it and turns away its active disciplinary gaze. At this juncture of space, time, legitimacy, and the law Gayatri Spivak's distinction between *Time* and *timing* will also clarify the stakes of privacy law's optimistic apartheid where sexuality is concerned. Spivak argues that the difference between hegemonic and "colonized" conceptions of imperial legal authority can be tracked by graphing Time as that property of transcendental continuity that locates state power to sustain worlds in the capacity to enunciate master concepts such as liberty and legitimacy in a zone of monumental time, a seemingly postpolitical space of abstraction from the everyday. In contrast, timing marks the always processual, drowning-in-the-present quality of subaltern survival in the face of the law's scrutiny and subject-making pedagogy.[22] Mapped onto sexuality law here, in privacy's early and most happy conceptualization, we see that nonmarital and therefore non-private sex exists in the antagonistic performance of the law's present tense, whereas the marital is virtually antinomian, Time above fallen timing. It is not only superior to the juropolitical but also, apparently, its boss and taskmaster.

The banality of intimacy's sentimental standing in and above the law is most beautifully and enduringly articulated in the majority opinion in *Griswold,* written by Justice William O. Douglas. Douglas argues that a combination of precedents derived from the First, Fourth, Fifth, Ninth, and Fourteenth Amendments[23] supports his designation of a heretofore un-enumerated constitutional right for married persons to inhabit a zone of privacy, a zone free from police access or the "pure [state] power" for which Connecticut was arguing as the doctrinal foundation of its right to discipline immorality in its citizens.[24] The language Douglas uses both to make this space visible and to enunciate the law's relation to it shuttles between the application of stare decisis (the rule of common law that binds judicial authority to judicial precedent) and the traditional conventionalities of heteronormative Hallmark-style sentimentality:

> The present case, then, concerns a relationship lying within the zone of privacy created by several fundamental constitutional guarantees. And it concerns a law which, in forbidding the *use* of contraceptives rather than regulating their manufacture or sale, seeks to achieve its goals by means having a maximum destructive impact upon that relationship. Such a law cannot stand in light of the familiar principle, so often applied by this Court, that a "governmental purpose to control or prevent activities constitutionally subject to state regulation may not be achieved by means which sweep unnecessarily broadly and thereby invade the area of protected freedoms" [*NAACP v. Alabama,* 377 U.S. 288, at 307]. Would we allow the police to search the sacred precincts of marital bedrooms for telltale signs of the use of contraceptives? The very idea is repulsive to the notions of privacy surrounding the marriage relationship. We deal with a right of privacy older than the Bill of Rights — older than our political parties, older than our school system. Marriage is a coming together for better or for worse, hopefully enduring, and intimate to the degree of being sacred. It is an association that promotes

a way of life, not causes; a harmony in living, not political faiths; a bilateral loyalty, not commercial or social projects. Yet it is an association for as noble a purpose as any involved in our prior decisions.[25]

Douglas bases his view that sexuality in marriage must be constitutionally protected — being above the law, prior to it, and beyond its proper gaze — on a sense that "specific guarantees in the Bill of Rights have penumbras, formed by emanations from those guarantees that help give them life and substance."[26] A penumbra is generally a "partial shadow between regions of complete shadow and complete illumination," but I believe the sense in which Douglas uses this dreamy concept is more proper to its application in the science of astronomy: "the partly darkened ridge around a sunspot." In other words, privacy protections around even marital sexuality are the dark emanations from the sunspot of explicit constitutional enumeration, and the zone of privacy in which marital sexuality thrives is the shadowland of the "noble" institution of marriage, with its sacred obligational emanations of social stability and continuity, intimate noninstrumentality, and superiority to the dividedness that otherwise characterizes the social. To back him up Justices Harlan's and Goldberg's opinions invoke the state and the Court's propriety in pedagogically bolstering the institutions of traditional American morality and values: after all, the theater of marital intimacy is "older than our political parties, older than our schools."

Justice Hugo Black's dissent in *Griswold* blasts Justices Douglas, Goldberg, Harlan, and White for the unethical emotionality of what he calls the "natural law due process formula [used] to strike down all state laws which [the Justices] think are unwise, dangerous, or irrational." He feels that it introduces into constitutional jurisprudence justifications for measuring "constitutionality by our belief that legislation is arbitrary, capricious or unreasonable, or accomplishes no justifiable purpose, or is offensive to our own notions of civilized standards of conduct. Such an appraisal of the wisdom of legislation is an attribute of the power to make laws, not of the power to interpret them." He finds precedent in this critique in a Learned Hand essay on the Bill of Rights that reviles judges' tendency to "wrap up their veto in a protective veil of adjectives such as 'arbitrary,' 'artificial,' 'normal,' 'reasonable,' 'inherent,' 'fundamental,' or 'essential' whose office usually, though quite innocently, is to disguise what they are doing and impute to it a derivation far more impressive than their personal preferences, which are all that in fact lie behind the decision."[27] In this view, whenever judges enter the zone of constitutional penumbra, they manufacture euphemisms that disguise the relation between proper law and personal inclination. Patricia Williams has suggested that this charge (and the countercharge that at the heights of feeling it is no different from reason) is at the heart of the fiction of stare decisis that produces post facto justifications from judicial or social tradition for judges who inevitably impose their will on problems of law but who must, for legitimacy's sake, disavow admission of the uninevitability of their claim. The virtually genetic image legal judgment has of itself in history veils not only the personal instabilities of judges but also the madness of the law itself, its instability and fictive stability, its articulation at the place where interpretive will and desire mix up to produce someone's image of a right/just/proper world.[28]

After sexual privacy was donated to the U.S. heterosexual couple in *Griswold* by way of the sentimental reason the Court adopts — through the spatialization of intimacy in a bell jar of frozen history — a judicial and political nightmare over the property of sexual privacy ensued, whose mad struggle between state privilege and private liberty is too long to enumerate here. We can conclude that the romantic banality that sanctions certain forms of intimacy as nationally privileged remains hardwired into the practice of sex privacy law in the United States. Almost twenty years later, however, *Planned Parenthood of Southeastern Pennsylvania v. Casey* (112 S. Ct. 2791 [1992]) recasts the force of its machinery remarkably, replacing the monumentality of sexual privacy that *Roe* had established as a fundamental condition of women's liberty with the monumentality of *Roe* itself as evidence of the Court's very authority.

In her opinion for the majority, Justice O'Connor recognizes the sovereignty of the zone of privacy as a model for freedom or liberty, returning explicitly to the method of penumbral enumeration and stare decisis introduced in *Griswold*. But the real originality of *Planned Parenthood v. Casey* is in the extent to which it supplants *entirely* the utopia of heterosexual intimacy on which sexual privacy law was based in the first place, putting *women's pain* in heterosexual culture at the center of the story of privacy and legal protections. In this sense the legitimating force of deep juridical feelings about the sacred pleasures of marital intimacy are here inverted and displaced onto the woman, whose sexual and political trauma is now the index of the meaning and value of her privacy and her citizenship.

Briefly, *Eisenstadt v. Baird* (405 U.S. 438 [1972]) extended *Griswold* to unmarried women through the equal protection clause, transforming sexual privacy from its initial scene — the two-as-one utopia of coupled intimacy — into a property of individual liberty. This muted the concretely spatial aspects of the "zone of privacy," dismantling the original homology between the marital/sexual bedroom and the citizen's sense of self-sovereignty. It placed the focus on the space of the woman's body, which includes her capacities, passions, and intentions. But the shift from reframing contraception to adjudicating abortion required the discovery of more emanations from constitutional penumbra: in *Roe v. Wade* (410 U.S. 113 [1973]) the right of privacy remains the *woman's* right but here one that has internal limits at the juncture where state interest over potential "life" and social self-continuity overtake the woman's interest in controlling her sexual and reproductive existence. Gone from that decision is *Griswold*'s rhetoric of the Court's moral pedagogy or its chivalry toward sexually sacred precincts: indeed, Justice Blackmun writes that, because of the "sensitive and emotional nature of the abortion controversy," he wants to adhere to "constitutional measurement, free of emotion and predilection."[29] (There is not a sexuality/privacy case in which such a caveat against emotion is not passionately uttered.) *Roe* attempts to achieve its postemotionality by deploying knowledge, plumbing the juridical and historical archive on abortion: its emphasis is on expanding liberty not by thinking through the contexts of its practice but, rather, by massaging precedent and tradition.

Planned Parenthood v. Casey was widely seen as an opportunity for a new set of Justices to overturn *Roe*. The Pennsylvania Abortion Control Act of 1982 (amended in 1988–1989) did not abolish abortion in the state but intensified the discursive contexts in which it happened, seeking to create around abortion a state-sanctioned, morally pedagogical *zone of publicity*. Provisions included a twenty-four-hour waiting period, minor notification of parents and wife notification of husband, and intensified standards of "informed consent" (including a state-authored brochure condemning abortion). The O'Connor opinion has two explicit aims: to affirm the fundamental holdings of *Roe* on behalf of the sovereignty of women's citizenship, the unity of national culture, and the status of the Court's authority; and to enumerate what it felt was underenumerated in *Roe*, the conditions of the state's sovereignty over the contexts of reproduction. In other words, as Justice Scalia's dissent argues, the leading opinion by Justice O'Connor seeks to affirm *Roe* while also significantly dismantling it. Its technical mechanism for achieving this impossible feat is the substitution of an "undue burden" rule for a whole set of other protections that *Roe* provides: especially by dismantling the trimester framework that determined the woman's sovereignty over reproduction in a pregnancy's first six months and substituting for it a rule that favors the state's right to place restrictions on the woman's reproductive practice (restrictions that can then be weighed by courts that will determine whether a given law mounts egregiously burdensome obstacles to the woman's exercise of her constitutional right to abortion).

Scalia claims that the majority pulls off this impossible feat (in its claim to refuse a "jurisprudence of doubt" while making equivocal legal judgments) by disguising its own muddy impulses in a sentimental and "empty" rhetoric of intimacy:

> The best that the Court can do to explain how it is that the word "liberty" *must* be thought to include the right to destroy human fetuses is to rattle off a collection of adjectives that simply decorate a value judgement and conceal a political choice. The right to abort, we are told, inheres in "liberty" because it is among "a person's most basic decisions," . . . it involves a "most intimate and personal choic[e]," . . . it is "central to personal dignity and autonomy," . . . it "originate[s] within the zone of conscience and belief," . . . it is "too intimate and personal" for state interference, . . . it reflects "intimate views" of a "deep, personal character," . . . it involves "intimate relationships," and "notions of personal autonomy and bodily integrity."[30]

Correctly, Scalia goes on to point out that these very same qualities meant nothing to the Justices when they heard *Bowers v. Hardwick* (478 U.S. 186 [1986]), "because, like abortion, they are forms of conduct that have long been criminalized in American society. Those adjectives might be applied, for example, to homosexual sodomy, polygamy, adult incest, and suicide, all of which are equally 'intimate.' "[31]

But Scalia's critique is trivial, in the sense that the majority opinion does not seek to rethink sexual privacy or intimacy in any serious way. The rhetoric of intimacy in the case is part of its argument from stare decisis,[32] but the majority Justices' originality is located in their representation of the specificity, what they call the "uniqueness," of the material conditions of citizenship for women in the United States. Because the right to sexual privacy has been individuated by *Roe,* privacy no longer takes place in a concrete zone but, rather, a "zone of conscience" — the place where, as Nietzsche tells us, the law is painfully and portably inscribed in subjects.[33] The Justices refer to women's "anxieties," "physical constraints," and "sacrifices [that] have since the beginning of the human race been endured by woman with a pride that ennobles her": they contend that a woman's "suffering is too intimate and personal for the State to insist . . . upon its own vision of the woman's role." Therefore, abortion definitively grounds and sustains women's political legitimacy: their "ability to participate equally in the economic and social life of the Nation has been facilitated by their ability to control their reproductive lives."[34]

The Justices here concede that femininity in the United States is virtually and generically an undue burden, however ennobling it might be. The deutopianization of sexual privacy established in *Griswold* and the installation of female citizenship at the juncture of law and suffering is further reinforced by the one part of the Pennsylvania law that the majority finds unconstitutional: the clause that commands women to notify their husbands of their intention to abort. The segment in which this happens exposes women's suffering in the zone of privacy, where, it turns out, men beat their wives. They cite evidence, supported by the American Medical Association, that men are raping their wives, terrorizing them (especially when pregnant), *forcing* them to inhabit a zone of privacy that keeps secreted men's abuse of women. In short, the "gruesome and torturous" conditions of marital domesticity in battering households requires the Court *not to protect privacy* for the couple but to keep the couple from becoming the unit of modal citizenship where privacy law is concerned.[35]

Catharine MacKinnon deems privacy law a tool of patriarchal supremacy:

> Women in everyday life have no privacy in private. In private, women are objects of male subjectivity and male power. The private is that place where men can do whatever they want because women reside there. The consent that supposedly demarcates this private surrounds women and follows us everywhere we go. Men [in contrast], reside in public, where laws against harm exist. . . . As a legal doctrine, privacy has become the affirmative triumph of the state's abdication of women.[36]

MacKinnon's arguments in these essays — which purport to be about "women" and "men" but which to my ear are more profoundly about heterosexuality as a virtual institution and a way of life — derive from

Court practice through the late 1980s and do not consider the work that jurists such as O'Connor have done to deprivatize privacy. But it should be no surprise that the citizen imagined by even moderates these days is no longer a complex subject with rights, needs, reciprocal obligations to the state and society, conflicting self-interests, or prospects for happiness in realms beyond the juridical: the citizen now is a trauma effect who requires protection and political reparation, whether or not that citizen can be fully described by the terms in which historically subordinated classes circulate in the United States. The majority in *Casey* answers the dissenters' argument — which asserts that so few women are battered in the United States that the husband notification principle stands within constitutional norms — by arguing that "the analysis does not end with the one percent of women upon whom the statute operates: it begins there."[37] Here their jurisprudence is not so far from Mari Matsuda's when she claims that "looking to the bottom" of social hierarchy and making reparative law from there is the only politically ethical thing to do.[38]

In the twenty years between *Roe* and *Planned Parenthood v. Casey* the general scene of public citizenship in the United States has become suffused with a practice of making pain count politically. The law of sexual privacy has followed this change, registering with symptomatic incoherence a more general struggle to maintain the contradictory rights and privileges of women, heterosexuality, the family, the state, and patriarchalized sexual privilege. The sheer ineloquence of this jumble of categories should say something about the cramped space of analysis and praxis to which the rhetoric and jurisprudence of sexual privacy has brought us — a place where there *is* much trouble: a utopia of law.

Politics

In *Griswold,* I have argued, we see codified the assurance of some jurists that the intimate feelings of married sexual partners represent that zone of privacy and personhood beyond the scrutiny of the law whose value is so absolute that the law must protect its sovereignty. Between *Griswold* and *Roe* these intimate feelings and their relation to liberty were still assumed as the sovereign materials of the law of sexual privacy. Now, however, many of the political and juridical contexts have dissolved that once sustained the fantasy of a core national culture, threatening the capacity of sentimental politics to create feeling cultures of consensus that distract from the lived

violences and fractures of everyday life in the polis. The class, racial, economic, and sexual fragmentation of U.S. society has emerged into the vision of the law and the public not as an exception to a utopian norm but as
a new governing rule of the present. The legal struggles over affirmative
action, welfare, abortion, and immigration the courts currently worry are
also about whether the utopian or the traumatic story of national life will
govern jurisprudence and the world it seeks to confirm. Trauma is winning.

Central to the legal emergence of the politics of trauma against the scene
of liberal-patriotic disavowal has been a group of activists from within
(mainly academic) legal studies who speak from feminist, gay and lesbian,
antiracist, and anticapitalist movements. They take their different but generally painful experiences of social hierarchy in the United States to require
a radical rhetorical and conceptual transformation of legal scholarship that
embraces "subjectivity of perspective," asserts the collective nature of subject formation (around stereotypical social identities), and refuses traditional liberal notions that organize the social optimism of law around
relatively unimpeded individuality, privacy, property, and conventional
values.[39] At stake in this transformation of law is the importance of antinor-
mativity to counterhegemonic critical theory and practice: because liberal
law has long recognized a particular and traditionally sanctioned form of
universal personhood as that around which society, theory, forms of discipline, and aspirational pedagogies should be organized, antiliberal activism
has had strategically to *ground* law in experience (in all senses of the pun)
and particular identities.

In this sense critical legal praxis is the opposite of national sentimentality, which pursues collective cohesion by circulating a universalist cur-
rency of distress. At the same time, the structure of reparation central to
radical legal politics suggests an unevenness in this general tactic of making
legal notions of subjectivity historically and corporeally specific. Subaltern
pain is not considered *universal* (the privileged do not experience it, they do
not live expecting that at any moment their ordinarily loose selves might be
codified into a single humiliated atom of subpersonhood). But subaltern
pain is deemed, in this context, universally *intelligible,* constituting objective evidence of trauma reparable by the law and the law's more privileged
subjects. In other words, the universal value is here no longer a property of
political personhood but, instead, a property of a rhetoric that claims to
represent not the universal but the true self. But, if historical contexts are
incomparable across fields of simple and complex distinction, how can

someone's pain or traumatized identity produce such perfect knowledge? And if the pedagogies of politics were necessary to reframe a set of experiences, knowledges, and feelings as the kind of pain that exposes injustice, what is "true" about it, exactly?

In this political model of identity trauma stands as truth. We can't use happiness as a guide to the aspirations for social change, because the feeling of it might well be false consciousness, nor boredom, which might be depression, illness, or merely a spreading malaise. Pain, in contrast, is something quick and sharp that simultaneously specifies you and makes you generic: it is something that happens to you before you "know" it, and it is intensely individuating, for surviving its shock lets you know it is your general survival at stake. Yet, if the pain is at the juncture of you and the stereotype that represents you, you know that you are hurt not because of your relation to history but because of *someone else's* relation to it, a type of someone whose privilege or comfort depends on the pain that diminishes you, locks you into identity, covers you with shame, and sentences you to a hell of constant potential exposure to the banality of derision.

Pain thus organizes your specific experience of the world, separating you from others and connecting you with others similarly shocked (but not surprised) by the strategies of violence that constantly regenerate the bottom of the hierarchies of social value you inhabit. In this sense subaltern pain is a public form because its outcome is to make you readable, for others. This is, perhaps, why activists from identity politics generally assume pain as the only sign readable across hierarchies of social life: the subaltern is the surrogate form of cultural intelligibility generally, and negated identities are pain effects. Know me, know my pain — you caused it: in this context paranoia would seem adaptive and would make understandable a desire for law to be both the origin *and* end of my experience of injustice. It might even make my wish to see even subaltern suffering as something more mediated seem, perhaps, cold or an effect of the leisure of privilege. Who has time, after all, to query violence between shock and the moment it becomes true meaning?

These dicta ground much current countertraditional legal argument. Take, for example, an original and impassioned work such as Robin West's *Narrative, Authority, and Law,* which sees as its task the production of moral criticism and transformation of the law from the point of view of its and a society's victims. West wields narratives powerfully throughout the book that reveal the law's fundamental immorality (and therefore its fundamentally immoralizing effect on the subjects who are educated to its standards) where women's lives are concerned, and her powerful feminist arguments for the need to deprivatize women's structurally induced pain testify to the radical changes in the law and other institutions of intimacy that would have to happen if women are to attain legitimacy as social subjects. But West assumes that women's pain is already available as knowledge. To her it *is* meaning and the material for radical pedagogy. To think otherwise is to be either misogynist or guilty of shallow and overacademic postmodernism. Empathy is an ethical rule. Not surprisingly, as it happens, one example of pain's pure force that she uses to summarize her argument comes from a child: "We must be able to say, to quote my two-year-old, 'don't do that — you're hurting me,' and we must be able to hear that utterance as an ethical mandate to change course."[40]

Not all radical legal theorists so simplify pain as to make the emblem of true wisdom about injustice and its eradication something as sentimental and fictive (to adults) as a child's consciousness:[41] yet the desire expressed in its seeming extreme clarity signals a lost opportunity for rethinking the relation of critique and culture building at this juncture of identity politics and legal theory. Would the child build a just world from the knowledge he gleans from being hurt? What would the child need to know for that to happen? How could this child learn to think beyond trauma, to make a context for it? It seems hard for this group of legal theorists to imagine the value of such questions, for a few reasons. One may be due to the centrality of "pain and suffering" to tort law, which endorses a construction of the true subject as a feeling subject whose suffering disables a person's ability to live at his full capacities, as he has been doing, and thus requires reparations from the agents who wielded the force. A great deal has been and will be written on this general area, for feminist antipornography and antiracist hate speech litigation borrows much of its legitimation from this hoary jurisprudential domain:[42] their tactic here is to challenge local purveyors of structural violence in order to make racism and misogyny *less profitable,* even symbolically, and meanwhile to use the law to debanalize violence by making illegal that which has been ordinary practice, on the model, say, of sexual harassment law or even more extremely, using the constitutional model of "cruel and unusual punishment" to revoke legitimation from social relations of violence traditionally authorized by the state and the law.

Kendall Thomas has made this latter point in an essay on privacy after *Bowers.*[43] He takes up Elaine Scarry's model of torture as a vehicle for the legitimating fiction of state power and claims that the cruel and unusual punishment clause of the Eighth Amendment should be applied to state discrimination against gays and lesbians. The strength and clarity of his vision and the sense that his suggestion seems to make brings us to the second reason it seems hard for theorists who equate subjectivity in general with legal subjectivity to work beyond the rule of traumatic pain in imagining the conditions for progressive social change. Thomas's model works only if the agent of violence is the state or the law; it works only if the domain of law is deemed interchangeable with the entire field of injury and reparation, and if the subject of law is fully described by the taxonomies that law recognizes. This position would look awkward if it were rephrased: subjects are always citizens. But the fact is that the notion of reparation for identity-based subordination assumes that the law describes what a person is, and that social violence can be located the way physical injury can be tracked. The law's typical practice is to recognize kinds of subjects, acts, and identities: it is to taxonomize. What is the relation between the (seemingly inevitable) authoritarianism of juridical categorization and the other, looser spaces of social life and personhood that do not congeal in categories of power, cause, and effect the way the law does? Is the "cruel and unusual punishment" tactic merely a reversal in extremis that points to the sublime banality of state cruelty, or is it a policy aspiration seeking a specific reparation for the specific violation/creation of gay and lesbian identities? Would the homeopathy of law against its own toxins in this domain of state cruelty work for women or the poor African Americans, Hispanics, and immigrants who are currently being economically disenfranchised from the resources that state capitalism manages?

Without making a ridiculous argument that the state is merely a mirage or a fetish that represents networks of inchoate forces that control, without constituting, the realm of society, it should be possible to say that radical counterpolitics needs to contend with notions of personhood and power that do not attain the clarity of state and juridical taxonomy, even across fields of practice and stigma. The desire to find an origin for trauma, and to rework culture at the violating origin, effectively imagines subjects only within that zone, reducing the social to that zone (in this case, the state and the laws that legislate nonnormative sex) and covertly reauthorizing the hegemony of the national. The desire to use trauma as the model for the pain of subordination that gets congealed into identities forgets the difference between trauma and adversity: trauma takes you out of your life shockingly and places you into another one, whereas structural subordination is not a surprise to the subjects who experience it, and the pain of subordination *is* ordinary life.

■

I have not meant to argue that identity politics has become a mode of "victim politics" too reductive to see the world clearly or to have positive effects. In its most tawdry version this accusation reads that a politics organized around publicizing pain constitutes a further degradation of subaltern selves into a species of subcivilized nonagency. The people who make this argument usually recognize structural social inequality and the devastating impacts it has on persons but continue to believe that the United States operates meritocratically, for worthy individuals. In contrast, Wendy Brown's deconstruction of contemporary U.S. identity rhetorics places skepticism about traumatic identity in the context of imagining a more radical politics. Brown sees people who claim their pain and build collective struggles around it as potentially overidentifying with their pain, then identifying with it, becoming passive to it, becoming addicted to seeing themselves as virtuous in the face of bad, unethical power. She follows Nietzsche's dictum against a passive-aggressive politics of *ressentiment*:

> Politicized identity thus enunciates itself, makes claims for itself, only by retrenching, restating, dramatizing, and inscribing its pain in politics, and can hold out no future — for itself or others — which triumphs over this pain. The loss of historical direction, and with it the loss of futurity characteristic of the late-modern age, is thus homologically refigured in the structure of desire of the dominant political expression of the age — identity politics. . . . What if we sought to supplant the language of "I am" — with its defensive closure on identity, its insistence on the fixity of position, its equation of social with moral positioning — with the language of "I want"?[44]

The critical clarity of a subordinate population's politicized pain has provided crucially destabilizing material that disaffirms the organization of liberal national culture around a utopian form of personhood that lives in zones of privacy and abstraction beyond pain, and, as a counterhegemonic *tactic*, this logic of radical juridicality affirms more powerfully than anything the fragile and violent disavowals that bolster hegemonic worlds of reason and the law.

But to say that the traumatized self is the true self is to say that a particular facet of subjective experience is where the truth of history lies: it is to suggest that the clarity of pain marks a political map for achieving the good life, if only we would read it. It is also to imply that in the good life there will be no pain. Brown suggests that a replacement of traumatic identity with a subjectivity articulated utopianly, via the agency of imagined demand, will take from pain the energy for social transformation beyond the field of its sensual experience. For this to happen *psychic pain experienced by subordinated populations must be treated as ideology,* not as prelapsarian knowledge or a condensed comprehensive social theory. It is more like a capital letter at the beginning of an old bad sentence that needs rewriting. To think otherwise is to assert that pain is merely banal, a story always already told. It is to think that the moment of its gestation is, indeed, life itself.

■

The world I have tried to telegraph here, in this story about privacy's fall from the utopia of normal intimacy, finds the law articulating its subjects as public and American through their position within a hegemonic regime of heterosexuality, which involves coordination with many other normative social positions that are racially and economically coded toward privilege. I have argued that the split between the patriotic context of national metaculture and the practical fragmentations and hierarchies of everyday life has become powerfully mediated by a discourse of trauma, which imagines "relief" through juridicalized national remedies because, in fighting against the false utopia of privacy, it imagines subjects wholly created by law.

Too often, and almost always in the work of legal radicals, the nation remains sanctified as a political "zone of privacy" in *Griswold*'s sense: it holds out a promise that it can relieve specific subjects of the pain of their specificity, even as the very project of nation formation virtually requires the public exposure to those who do not structurally assimilate to the national norm (so, if population x is relieved of the obstacles to its juridical and cultural citizenship, a given population y will almost inevitably come to bear the burden of surrogacy that expresses citizenship's status as *privilege*). Fighting for justice under the law in the face of these normative strategies is crucial, a tactic of necessity. If it means telling half-truths (that an experience of painful identity shocks a minoritized subject) to change juridical norms about that kind of subject, it still must be a good thing. But thinking that the good life will be achieved when there is no more pain but only (your) happiness does nothing to alter the hegemonic structures of normativity and mourning whose saturation of the diminished expectations for liberty in national life I have sketched out in this essay. The reparation of pain does not bring into being a just life.

Notes

1. See, for example, George DeMartino and Stephen Cullenberg, "Beyond the Competitiveness Debate: An Internationalist Agenda," *Social Text* 41 (1994): 11–39.

2. Take the case of the talk show host Kathie Lee Gifford, whose clothing line at the U.S. low-price megastore Wal-Mart generated for her $10 million of profit in its first year. During May and June 1996 Gifford was exposed by Charles Kernaghan, of the National Labor Education Fund in Support of Worker and Human Rights in Central America, for allowing her clothes to be made by tragically underpaid and mistreated young Honduran children, mostly girls. A Lexis/Nexus search under the keywords *Kathie Lee Gifford/Child Labor* nets close to two hundred stories, from all over the world, reporting on this event. A few main plots emerge from these stories: it is cast as a revenge story against privilege from the ranks of the less well-off, which strips from Gifford the protection of her perky, populist, and intimate persona to reveal the entrepreneurial profiteer beneath; it implicates an entire culture of celebrity-centered consumerism (Jaclyn Smith, K-Mart; Spike Lee, The Gap; Michael Jordan, Nike) that is organized around a "virtuous" role modelesque public figure or label that seems to certify healthy conscientious social membership for consumers; it becomes an exemplum of the banality of sweatshop labor in the United States and around the world and a call to belated conscience. Through Gifford's apparent intimacy with her devoted audience a "public" outraged by child exploitation seemed instantly to emerge, which led in turn to a kind of state action, involving an intensified federal push for voluntary covenants against child labor and subminimum wages (measured by "local," not U.S., standards of remuneration). It also eventuated in the development of a new label, No Sweat, to be put on any clothes produced by adequately paid workers — a sad substitute for the union labels of years past. This issue has quickly joined child abuse as an ongoing zone of fascination and (mainly) impotent concern in the political public sphere. See, for a relatively unjaded extended example, Sidney Schamberg, "Six Cents an Hour," *Life* (June 1996): 38–48. For a more general view of the political/media exploitation of the exploited child figure, see McKenzie Wark, "Fresh Maimed Babies: The Uses of Innocence," *Transition* 65 (spring 1995): 36–47.

3. For more exposition on the ways political cultures that value abstract or universal personhood produce privileged bodies and identities that travel unmarked, unremarkable, and free of structural humiliation, see Lauren Berlant, "National Brands/National Bodies: *Imitation of Life*," in *The Phantom Public Sphere,* ed. Bruce Robbins (Minneapolis: University of Minnesota Press, 1993), 173–208, and *The Queen of America Goes to Washington City: Essays on Sex and Citizenship* (Durham, NC: Duke University Press, 1997); Richard Dyer, "White," in *The Matter of Images* (New York: Routledge,

1993), 141–63; and Peggy Phelan, *Unmarked: The Politics of Performance* (New York: Routledge, 1993).

4. The essay of Sigmund Freud's summarized here is "Mourning and Melancholia," in *General Psychological Theory,* intro. Philip Rieff (New York: Collier Books, 1963), 164–79.

5. The best work on the civilized barbarism of mourning has been done on AIDS discourse in U.S. culture: see Douglas Crimp, "Mourning and Militancy," in *Out There: Marginalization and Contemporary Cultures,* ed. Russell Ferguson, Martha Gever, Trinh T. Min-ha, and Cornell West (Cambridge, MA: MIT Press, 1990), 233–45; and virtually every essay in Douglas Crimp, ed., *AIDS: Cultural Analysis/Cultural Activism* (Cambridge, MA: MIT Press, 1988). Crimp is especially astute on the necessary articulation of sentimentality and politics: because processes of legitimation cannot do without the production of consent, and empathetic misrecognition is one tactic for creating it. The question is how, and at what cost, different kinds of subjects and contexts of empathy are imagined in the struggle for radical social transformation. See also Jeff Nunokowa, "AIDS and the Age of Mourning," *Yale Journal of Criticism* 4.2 (spring 1991): 1–12. Judith Butler's work has also been a crucial intertext here, notably its representation of heterosexual melancholia (the disavowed experience of loss heterosexuals endure as a consequence of having to divert ongoing same-sex love/identification/attachments), a condition that expresses itself through gender normativity, heterosexual hegemony, misogyny, homophobia, and other forms of disciplinary order. This opened a space for thinking about the social function of mourning in similar contexts of normative hierarchy in which intimacies appear to have to be constructed, not suppressed. See *Gender Trouble: Feminism and the Subversion of Identity* (New York: Routledge, 1990), and *Bodies That Matter: On the Discursive Limits of Sex* (New York: Routledge, 1993).

6. On the "bottom line" as a site of political articulation and struggle, see Elizabeth Alexander, " 'Can You Be BLACK and Look at This?': Reading the Rodney King Video(s)," in *The Black Public Sphere,* ed. Black Public Sphere Collective (Chicago: University of Chicago Press, 1995), 81–98.

7. On the structures and rhetorics of coercive flexibility in transnational times, see David Harvey, *The Condition of Postmodernity* (London: Basil Blackwell, 1989); Roger Rouse, "Thinking through Transnationalism: Notes on the Cultural Politics of Class Relations in the Contemporary United States," *Public Culture* 7 (winter 1995): 353–402; and Emily Martin, *Flexible Bodies: Tracking Immunity in American Culture — From the Days of Polio to the Age of AIDS* (Boston: Beacon Press, 1994).

8. One critic who has not underestimated the hegemonic capacities of state deployments of pain is Elaine Scarry, *The Body in Pain: The Making and Unmaking of the World* (New York: Oxford University Press, 1985). This book remains a stunning description of the ways control over actual physical and rhetorical pain provides the state and the law with control over what constitutes collective reality, the conjuncture of beliefs, and the material world. See especially part 2, on pain and imagining. Like the legal theorists and jurists whose writing this essay engages, Scarry works with a fully state- (or institutionally) saturated concept of the subject, a relation more specific and nonuniversal than it frequently seems to be in her representation of it.

9. See Berlant, *Queen of America*. The following paragraphs revise and repeat some arguments from this book. For an essay specifically on scandalized childhood in the contemporary United States, see Marilyn Ivy, "Recovering the Inner Child in Late Twentieth Century America," *Social Text* 37 (1993): 227–52.

10. Nathanson speaks this line in the film *The Silent Scream* (1984).

11. This intensification of national-popular patriotic familialism has taken place at a time when another kind of privatization — the disinvestment of the state economically and culturally in promoting public life — characterizes almost all the activity of the political public sphere. The economic defederalization of citizenship downsizes the public so drastically that it begins to look like "the private," its nineteenth-century antithesis (only this time mass-mediated and thus publicly sutured in a more classic Habermasean sense). Yet all too frequently the analysis of the institutions of intimacy is kept separate from the considerations of the material conditions of citizenship.

12. On cynicism and citizenship, see Slavoj Žižek, *The Sublime Object of Ideology* (London: Verso, 1989), 11–53.

13. On pain's place in forming the political imagination of subjects during the epoch of U.S. identity politics, see Wendy Brown's powerful essay "Wounded Attachments: Late Modern Oppositional Political Formations," in *The Identity in Question,* ed. John Rajchman (New York: Routledge, 1995), 199–227.

14. On rights talk and normativity, see the volume *Identities, Politics, and Rights,* ed. Austin Sarat and Thomas R. Kearns (Ann Arbor: University of Michigan Press, 1995). See especially Wendy Brown's contribution, an indispensable discussion of the ways "rights talk" enables the production of traumatized political identities: "Rights and Identity in Late Modernity: Revisiting the 'Jewish Question,' " 85–130.

15. Jean Baudrillard posits banality as the affective dominant of postmodern life: see *In the Shadow of the Silent Majorities . . . Or the End of the Social and Other Essays,* trans. Paul Foss, Paul Patton, and John Johnston (New York: Semiotext[e], 1983), and "From the System to the Destiny of Objects," in *The Ecstacy of Communication,* ed. Sylvere Lotringer (New York: Semiotext[e], 1987), 77–96. See also Achille Mbembe, "Prosaics of Servitude and Authoritarian Civilities," *Public Culture* 5 (fall 1992): 123–48; Achille Mbembe and Janet Roitman, "Figures of the Subject in Times of Crisis," *Public Culture* 7 (winter 1995): 323–52; and Meaghan Morris, "Banality in Cultural Studies," in *Logics of Television: Essays in Cultural Criticism,* ed. Patricia Mellencamp (Bloomington: Indiana University Press, 1990), 14–43.

16. Justice Hugo Black, dissenting, *Griswold v. Connecticut* 381 U.S. 479 (1965), at 509.

17. Stephanie Guitton and Peter Irons, eds., *May It Please the Court: Arguments on Abortion* (New York: New Press, 1995), 4.

18. Justice William O. Douglas, Opinion of the Court, *Griswold v. Connecticut,* at 480.

19. Ibid., 5.

20. Justice Arthur Goldberg, concurring, *Griswold v. Connecticut,* at 499.

21. I borrow this rhetoric of zoning, and specifically its relation to the production of normative sexuality, from Lauren Berlant and Michael Warner, "Sex in Public," *Critical Inquiry* 24 (winter 1998): 547–66.

22. Gayatri Chakravorty Spivak, "Time and Timing: Law and History," in *Chronotypes: The Construction of Time,* ed. John Bender and David E. Wellbery (Stanford: Stanford University Press, 1991), 99–117.

23. Douglas writes: "Various guarantees create zones of privacy. The right of association contained in the penumbra of the First Amendment is one, as we have seen. The Third Amendment in its prohibition against the quartering of soldiers 'in any house' in time of peace without the consent of the owner is another facet of that privacy. The Fourth Amendment explicitly affirms the 'right of the people to be secure in their persons, houses, papers, and effects, against unreasonable searches and seizures.' The Fifth Amendment in its Self-Incrimination Clause enables the citizen to create a zone of privacy which government may not force him to surrender to his detriment. The Ninth Amendment provides: "The enumeration in the Constitution, of certain rights, shall not be construed to deny or disparage others retained by the people' " (*Griswold v. Connecticut,* at 484). Justice Goldberg's concurring opinion, while mainly running a legal clinic on the Founders' relation to unenumerated rights, adds the due process clause of the Fourteenth Amendment to this constitutional congeries (488).

24. Guitton and Irons, *May It Please the Court,* 7.

25. Justice William O. Douglas, Opinion of the Court, *Griswold v. Connecticut,* at 485, 486.

26. Ibid., 484.

27. Ibid., 517 n.10.

28. Patricia J. Williams, *The Alchemy of Race and Rights* (Cambridge, MA: Harvard University Press, 1991), 7–8, 134–35.

29. Justice Blackmun, Opinion of the Court, *Roe v. Wade* 410 U.S. 113 (1973), at 708.

30. Justice Scalia, dissent, *Planned Parenthood v. Casey* 112 S.Ct. 2791 (1992), at 2876–77.

31. Ibid. Scalia also blasts Justice Blackmun (2876 n.2) for using the same intimate rhetoric that means nothing, constitutionally, at least to Scalia.

32. A passionate and creative argument about what cases constitute precedent for *Roe* takes place between Justices O'Connor, Kennedy, Souter (ibid., 2808–16), and Scalia (2860–67).

33. Friedrich Nietzsche, *On the Genealogy of Morals,* ed. Walter Kaufmann (New York: Vintage, 1967), 57–96. On the ways Nietzsche reproduces the individuating limits of pain-centered politics, see Brown, "Wounded Attachments."

34. Justices O'Connor, Kennedy, and Souter, Opinion of the Court, *Planned Parenthood v. Casey,* at 2807, 2809.

35. Ibid., 2827.

36. Catharine A. MacKinnon, "Reflections on Law in the Everyday Life of Women," in *Law in Everyday Life,* ed. Austin Sarat and Thomas R. Kearns (Ann Arbor: University of Michigan Press, 1995), 117–18. See also MacKinnon, *Toward a Feminist Theory of the State* (Cambridge, MA: Harvard University Press, 1989), 184–94.

37. *Planned Parenthood v. Casey,* at 2829.

38. Mari J. Matsuda, "Looking to the Bottom: Critical Legal Studies and Reparations," in *Critical Race Theory: The Key Writings That Formed the Movement,* ed. Kimberlé Crenshaw, Neil Gotanda, Gary Peller, and Kendall Thomas (New York: New Press, 1995), 63–80.

39. Critical legal studies, critical race theory, radical feminist legal theory, and an emergent body of work in gay and lesbian culture, power, and the law encompass a huge bibliography. Rather than dump a stupidly big omnibus footnote here, let me metonymically signal the archive via a few recent helpful anthologies or extended works: Mary Becker, Cynthia Grant Bowman, and Morrison Torrey, *Cases and Materials on Feminist Jurisprudence: Taking Women Seriously* (St. Paul, MN: West Publishing, 1994); Dan Danielsen and Karen Engle, *After Identity: A Reader in Law and Culture* (New York: Routledge, 1995); Lisa Duggan and Nan D. Hunter, *Sex Wars: Sexual Dissent and Political Culture* (New York: Routledge, 1995); Mari J. Matsuda, Charles R. Lawrence III, Richard Delgado, and Kimberlé Williams Crenshaw, *Words That Wound: Critical Race Theory, Assaultive Speech, and the First Amendment* (Boulder, CO: Westview Press, 1993), 1–15; Crenshaw, Gotanda, Peller, and Thomas, *Critical Race Theory;* Richard Delgado, *Critical Race Theory: The Cutting Edge* (Philadelphia: Temple University Press, 1995); Patricia Smith, ed., *Feminist Jurisprudence* (New York: Oxford University Press, 1993); Patricia J. Williams, *The Alchemy of Race and Rights: Diary of a Law Professor* (Cambridge, MA: Harvard University Press, 1991), and *The Rooster's Egg* (Cambridge, MA: Harvard University Press, 1995).

40. Robin West, *Narrative, Authority, and Law* (Ann Arbor: University of Michigan Press, 1993), 19–20. Much the same kind of respect and critique can be given to Catharine MacKinnon's promotion of juridical reparation on behalf of women's pain under patriarchy: in her work the inner little girl of every woman stands as the true abused self who is denied full citizenship in the United States. For an analysis of antipornography rhetoric's depiction of pain's place in women's citizenship, see Berlant, "Live Sex Acts," in *Queen of America.*

41. Another instance in which a generic child's nonideological relation to justice is held as the proper index of adult aspiration is found in Williams, *Alchemy of Race and Rights.* This brilliant book is fully dedicated to understanding the multiple contexts in which (Williams's) legal subjectivity inherits, inhabits, and reproduces the law's most insidious violences: its commitment to syncretic modes of storytelling about these conjunctures leaves open some questions about the relation between what she represents as the madness of inhabiting legal allegories of the self in everyday life and certain scenes of hyperclarity in which children know the true scale of justice and the true measure of pain (in contrast to adults, with their brains twisted by liberal ideologies of property and contract; e.g., 12, 27). Perhaps this is because, as she says, "Contract law reduces life to fairy tale" (224).

42. See Lucinda M. Finley, "A Break in the Silence: Including Women's Issues in a Torts Course," *Yale Journal of Law and Feminism* 1 (1989): 41–73. See also Scarry, *The Body in Pain;* Williams, *The Alchemy of Race and Rights;* MacKinnon, *Toward a Feminist Theory;* Matsuda, "Looking to the Bottom"; West, *Narrative, Authority, and Law.*

43. Kendall Thomas, "Beyond the Privacy Principle," in Danielsen and Engle, *After Identity,* 277–93.

44. Brown, "Wounded Attachments," 220, 221.

MARK KELMAN AND GILLIAN LESTER

Ideology and Entitlement

Students are said to have a learning disability or be learning disabled (LD) when there is a gap between their performance in some academic field (typically reading) and their "potential" (typically measured by their score on an IQ test) that is not explained by sociocultural disadvantage or limited English proficiency. Students diagnosed as having LDs are entitled under federal law to resources in the form of "special education" services. Not all students whose achievement is poor receive special education services, however. Only those whose achievement is below "intelligence"-based "expectations"—LD students, as opposed to ordinary "slow learners"— receive such services.

There are three significant consequences to being labeled LD. First, all students with disabilities (including those with LDs) receive an Individualized Educational Plan (IEP) under the requirements of the governing federal statute, the Individuals with Disabilities Education Act (IDEA). The goal (if not the inevitable result) of such a plan is to pick educational inputs and settings tailored to the particular child's circumstances that will help him attain higher levels of educational achievement than he would if he simply followed the standard regimen. In effect, the IEP is a claim on costly educational services (most typically, tutors, classroom aides, and smaller classes). The question of whether all such costly services are clearly to the student's benefit is controversial. For example, students with LDs who are pulled out of mainstream classes into full-time special day classes, populated only by students with disabilities, may receive an *expensive* education—student-teacher ratios are low in such classes—but a strong case can be made that such classes are often detrimental to the performance of the child. In theory, IDEA dictates that a separate class setting should be used only when placement in a less restrictive — more "mainstreamed" — setting would be less beneficial to the disabled student. In practice, though, students with disabilities are doubtless often pulled out of mainstream classes when it is seen to be in the interests of their classmates, not the disabled students themselves.

Second, students with disabilities are entitled to accommodations on exams. Most often, students with LDs receive extra time to complete exams and/or get to take exams in less distracting environments. Presumably, such accommodations permit students with LDs to receive higher grades than they would without the accommodations. It is a contested empirical issue whether non-LD students would benefit from receiving the sorts of accommodations students with LDs typically receive, but substantial evidence suggests that many tests (e.g., the SAT college entrance exam) are "speeded" even for non-LD pupils; that is, their raw scores would improve if they had more time.

Finally, to a significant degree, students with disabilities may enjoy immunity from severe discipline (expulsion or long-term suspension), at least for nonweapon and nondrug offenses. So long as students can demonstrate that the proscribed behavior (for which nondisabled students might be severely disciplined) is a manifestation of their disability, the district cannot impose the most serious disciplinary sanctions (though the district may achieve essentially the same purpose simply by moving the disabled student to a more restrictive educational placement).

This regime might be seen, analytically and ideologically, as consistent with two radically distinct sets of political presuppositions.[1] On the one hand, existing policy toward students with LDs draws heavily on a long-standing theme in conservative conceptions of the appropriate boundaries of the welfare state: that we are duty bound to treat the "deserving" poor considerably more favorably than the "undeserving" poor.[2] Children with LDs are, in this view, entitled to egalitarian interventions that other poor performers are not: their grades are (at least mildly) inflated, their claims for incremental social resources (largely) met, their immunity to the discipline system (partly) granted because they are subsumed in a morally favored category of those who fare poorly in the absence of self-conscious egalitarian interventions, the category of people with disabilities. They have become the moral equivalent, in nonlibertarian conservative thought, of the unfortunate, utterly blameless blind man, implicitly contrasted with the undeserving, "parasitic" never-married "welfare mother." It is surely the case that conservative support for programs that benefit the disabled, rather than other needy constituencies, has been high over the past two decades: federal legislative support for the disabled intensified during an era of pronounced welfare state retrenchment.[3] It is an interesting task, but not our task, to explore both why certain groups are deemed deserving by conservative moralists and whether traditional arguments for differentiating the claims of the worthy and unworthy poor were invoked in differentiating the claims of pupils with LDs and others seeking expanded levels of federal support.

At the same time, policy toward those with LDs draws at least as heavily on what we call "left-wing multiculturalism," and it is this ideological influence we examine in detail. From a social policy perspective, this is a political/ideological movement that attempts to defend egalitarian interventions largely on two bases.[4] First, it claims that existing patterns and levels of inequality of reward are problematic mainly because they are based on irrational and biased mischaracterization of the productive ability of the members of oppressed subgroups. Second, it appears to limit its normative egalitarian claims to individuals falling within cognizable groups, rather than extending it to individuals lacking such affiliation.

Both of these cornerstones of the left multiculturalist position are problematic. The first element slights what ought to be, in our view, compelling *moral* claims of need and equally compelling calls for increased solidarity among citizens with different productive potentials. Instead, the chief critique of existing inequality is grounded in an unpersuasive positivist description of irrationality rather than normative moralism. The claim is that (even? especially?) capitalist institutions frequently treat differences among individuals, especially when these differences are pronounced among more or less loosely defined "groups," including those with LDs, as relevant to successful performance of socially meaningful tasks when they are not. Those atop cultural hierarchies (white, straight, able-bodied males) control the firms that make hiring, promotion, and pay decisions, and they impose false, self-serving ideas about requisite job performance.[5] The basic problem those with LDs face, in this view, is the irrational overvaluation of the skills they cannot acquire by people who happen to have those skills.[6]

The tendency of left multiculturalist theory to locate distributive claims in group membership is similarly troubling. Distributive claims based on need, for instance, are hard to articulate unless the "needy" can be (re)defined as a "group": left multiculturalists thus often try to redefine the "needy" as victims of "classism" (the irrational devaluation of the contributions of a group of people on the basis of socioeconomic status/style).[7] The coherent *normative* basis of LD students' claims for resources may well be, when scrutinized, that they are a readily identifiable subset of pupils who would especially benefit from more help. But the broader "group" of "students who can particularly benefit from the infusion of incremental educational resources"—poor learners who are not identified as LD—cannot make typical left multiculturalist claims to resources, simply because they have no obvious cultural commonality. Pupils with LDs alone are *entitled* because they alone have been constructed as a politically plausible oppressed group, a subclass (albeit one of recent social—and legal—construction) of a larger oppressed group, people with disabilities, some of whom have surely been victims of both aversive prejudice and stereotyping.

Left Multiculturalism

We attempt in this section to describe in more detail both the general legal-political manifestations of left multiculturalism and its more specific ideological impact on policy toward the learning disabled. This requires first understanding, in some detail, the relationship among different political conceptions of the appropriate role of the state in combating "discrimination." Such conceptions are grounded both in competing notions of what illicit "discrimination" really is and on distinct beliefs about the capacity of the state to correct unwanted social practices. In our view, it is not surprising to find a wide political spectrum of opinions about the appropriate state role, or to find that the spectrum of views corresponds quite closely to the "left-right" political spectrum historically observed on standard economistic issues.

ECONOMISTIC POLITICAL THEORY

The traditional, economistic political spectrum can perhaps most readily be understood as the set of competing theories about the desirability of market allocations of goods and market distributions of economic wherewithal.

Those on the political right divided, historically, into two camps. On the one hand, traditional (nineteenth-century) liberals[8] (associated in the law school world with Chicago School law and economics) believed that both the distribution of income and the allocation of goods that resulted from spontaneous exchanges among legally unconstrained adults with different tastes and different endowments to satisfy one another's preferences were optimal and just. Self-conscious political action (especially by those with state authority) to constrain free choices (for example, on the basis of paternalistic motives or the belief that exchanges in which clear force or fraud were absent were nonetheless often likely to be tainted by subtler coercion or cognitive manipulation) was especially dangerous. Redistribution from those favorably endowed to satisfy market demands to those less able to do so was also problematic. Some derived this antiredistributive position from a libertarian, entitlement-centered perspective, which emphasized natural ownership rights and "freedom" to trade and contract.[9] Others derived fairly parallel policy prescriptions from a more openly utilitarian outlook, emphasizing the disincentive effects of redistributive measures[10] and our incapacity to discern "utility-enhancing" choices for others.[11]

Others on the political right (Burkeans, broadly construed) saw at least some conflict between market morality and the need to maintain traditional hierarchy, believing that, at least at the margin, traditional authority ought to be bolstered even at the cost of sacrificing the absolute primacy of unfettered market exchange. Reasonably strong redistributive obligations could grow out of traditional privilege or the need to mollify and pacify those who might otherwise feel politically dispossessed.[12] Free choice might govern the exchange of "routine" commodities, but liberty must be curtailed to ensure that antisocial, destructive wants were properly channeled or sublimated[13] (thus, for instance, for such conservatives, fixed-status marriage would take precedence over contractual partnership between cohabitants; prostitution and private consumption of pornography could be banned).

Political "centrists" historically tended to be more wary than the right-wing "traditional liberals" of numerous non-self-correcting market failures that precluded "free choosers" from reaching optimal positions. While still firmly antipaternalistic, at least when announcing self-conscious, general ideological views,[14] they were far more prone to see ubiquitous market failures:[15] misinformed choices,[16] public goods problems,[17] goods misallocated because of unaccounted-for externalities,[18] non-cost-justified monopolies that both misallocated and misdistributed,[19] and undue "macroeconomic" cyclicity that precluded labor markets from clearing and thus prevented the disadvantaged from working their way out of poverty, even given a reasonable level of skill and willingness to work.[20] Their distributive views were prone to be "pragmatic egalitarian": that is, they had no "principled" opposition to self-conscious redistribution. Quite to the contrary, they were prone, presumptively, to prefer greater levels of equality to lesser levels. Nonetheless, they believed that the "utilitarian" limits on redistribution were, though less extreme than the conservative utilitarians imagined, still far from trivial.[21]

Those on the political left typically were considerably more prone to be wary of "free choices." They perceived many preferences as, at best, "adaptive" to existing social practices (for example, people learn to value commodity acquisition over meaningful work when meaningful work is rarely provided)[22] and, at worst, coerced by those with social power (as working-class racism was thought to be largely engineered by capitalists seeking to rule the working class through "divide and conquer" tactics).[23] Although most leftists believed it would be unjust if even genuine differentials in productivity had pronounced material consequences,[24] they frequently argued that existing distributional patterns were largely a function not so much of differential productive endowments as differences in power. The hierarchical division of labor, for instance, was not primarily technologically determined, but instead dictated by the needs of those atop hierarchies to render themselves indispensable coordinators of laborers.[25]

CONTEMPORARY RIGHT AND CENTRIST
CONCEPTIONS OF ANTIDISCRIMINATION LAW

The political parallels in competing conceptions of antidiscrimination law and policy are remarkably strong. In illustrating this point, we draw primarily on examples from the area of employment discrimination law, where a good deal of modern antidiscrimination theory has developed. We subsequently analogize to the context of educational accommodations for pupils labeled LD.

The parallels between antidiscrimination law and economistic political thought have largely been suppressed, in significant part because the field is dominated by various centrist theories that radically *separate* "economistic" distributional issues from "rights-oriented" antidiscrimination issues. In these various (right, mainstream, and liberal) centrist conceptions, to which we will return, antidiscrimination law operates *prior* to redistributive efforts, both temporally and conceptually. In the mainstream centrist view, antidiscrimination law demands only that persons receive what they would receive in a "perfected" impersonal market, their "objective" factor share (marginal product).[26] But once antidiscrimination law does its (limited) job—to rid the world of the animus, false stereotyping, and perhaps rational statistical discrimination as well that block members of subordinated groups from receiving "marginal product" payments—we move on to a distinct redistributive realm.

In this realm of redistribution, all sorts of claims may be made. These include claims based on group rights (including claims to reparations)[27] and claims based on the desirability of encouraging cultural diversity by "overrewarding" (in market terms) activities in which members of distinct subordinated groups might more typically engage. However, centrists generally appear most comfortable entertaining redistributive claims based either (a) on the supposition that aggregate social welfare would increase if those with low income had access to funds that richer citizens initially controlled or that such poorer citizens have just claims on such resources;[28] (b) on the desire to minimize unequal opportunity by minimizing, though not eliminating, the environmental differences faced by children;[29] (c) on the perceived need to reward the "meritorious";[30] or (d) (especially in constitutional law circles) on the aspiration to make the capacity for political participation more nearly universal among individuals (and perhaps even equal).[31]

Libertarian views of appropriate antidiscrimination policy are not really "in play" in American politics at this point, though they were decidedly part of expressed opposition to the 1964 Civil Rights Act (along with states' rights arguments).[32] Even Richard Epstein, the most prominent legal academic libertarian, does not treat the 1964 Civil Rights Act as an impermissible taking of the (common law) right of owners of public accommodations to exclude unwanted patrons, though the omission to do so appears wholly tactical, rather than principled,[33] and Epstein certainly does treat Title VII as illegitimate (if not constitutionally suspect) except to the degree it helped dismantle formal state *bans* on integrating workplaces.[34] Nonetheless, it is fairly clear what the libertarian position on antidiscrimination has been: it is impermissible for the state to compel contracts between parties when all parties do not choose to contract voluntarily. Thus ordering employers to hire or retain someone they would not choose to hire is impermissible, even if their refusal to do so is motivated entirely by racist animus, as is requiring the owners of "public" accommodations to serve or deal with anyone they do not choose to.[35]

At the same time, libertarians emphasize that the state must not forbid voluntary contracts from being made; thus the role of antidiscrimination law and policy is solely to ensure that the state does not mandate racist and sexist practices. Descriptively, libertarians are prone to believe that discrimination (by race or gender) will survive only when the state mandates it; market pressures to maximize profits, they believe, typically will preclude entrepreneurs from acting on racist or sexist animus. Nor can those acting on false stereotypes survive as entities any better than entities laboring under any other sort of significant misinformation about the availability of "resources" or workers. As long as existing or potential competitors have profit opportunities created by their understanding that, say, African American and women workers are more capable than bigots wrongly believe them to be, the bigots will be at a distinct, and ultimately fatal, competitive disadvantage.[36]

Burkean social conservatives are somewhat more prone to distance themselves from both the libertarian tolerance for overt expressions of bigotry and the centrist's obsessive Enlightenment "rationalism." It is clear that social conservatives needn't tolerate overt racist or sexist language or direct slights (as libertarians do) as protected exercises of personal liberty. Conceptually, it is obvious that anyone (including the rare libertarian who doesn't make the familiar mistake of reifying common law entitlements as the unique set of "natural rights") *could* choose to treat such dignitary offenses as torts (parallel to the intentional infliction of emotional distress).[37] It is also clear that Burkeans might be predisposed to do so, both in the name of protecting civility against barbarian impulses and, more powerfully, to protect against the risk of social disintegration (alienation and "separatism" by minority group members). Racist "acts" — refusal to hire out of animus, refusal to provide public accommodations — are proscribed, in this view, dominantly because of their implicit speech content.[38]

At the same time, the centrists' Enlightenment hyperrationalism — in which the state *demands* impersonal, market-rational treatment of all job applicants and would-be customers, insisting that they be judged only as, respectively, productive assets and sources of spending — goes much too far for these social conservatives. *Griggs v. Duke Power Co.,*[39] the centerpiece of centrist Enlightenment social engineering, demands that employers use only technically validated screening devices (diplomas, tests, and so on) in selecting employees. Employers, says *Griggs*, ought to be concerned only with workers' output and cannot exclude minority group members if they are as productive as members of unprotected groups. This is so even though they may lack virtues the social conservative values, so long as these qualities do not correlate, systematically, with on-the-job performance. But the social conservative might be prone to think that even unvalidated tests of, say, reading skills, or Bloomian "cultural literacy," or school diplomas were all legitimate bases of privilege (hiring preference) because they are themselves signs of legitimate (relative) cultural authority and must be rewarded, both for intrinsic reasons and to encourage their preservation. (In a similar fashion, perhaps, recruitment through word of mouth, even though it could clearly disadvantage those now outside the world of privilege, might be legitimate for social conservatives because it bolsters stable communities.)

In fact, though, neither of these conservative positions on antidiscrimination law has much influence in American political life today. Instead, the chief politically viable conservative attack on the hyperrationalism of *Griggs* is pragmatic rather than "principled": the pragmatic "right centrist" opponents of the decision concede that the mainstream centrists are correct in their aspirations. It is indeed unjust if blacks and women do not receive rewards commensurate with their productivity, but the right centrists profoundly doubt the capacity of the state either to recognize or to correct genuine entrepreneurial irrationality. The problem with demanding that, say, tests or diplomas be validated—*proven* to correlate with on-the-job productivity—is twofold. First, the demand for validation overstates the observational skills of technocrats (the industrial psychologists asked to measure performance) and bureaucrats (the judges and EEOC hearing officers asked to decide whether those excluded in fact systematically perform worse on the job). Second, the demand for validation understates the rationality of entrepreneurs, who have powerful selfish material reasons to discard screening devices that exclude workers who could in fact do the work as well as those "screened in."[40]

Because the basic theme of "government failure," coupled with greater, if incomplete, faith in the self-correcting power of markets is *the* basic conceit of right centrist thought outside the domain of antidiscrimination law,[41] it ought not to be surprising that it will dominate some ideological understandings of appropriate antidiscrimination policy. Still, one must recall that the right centrists do not believe markets wipe out all social problems. They are more prone than libertarians, who oppose civil rights law far more thoroughly, to believe that discrimination based on animus or commonplace stereotypes can persist even in competitive markets. Thus, like the Burkean conservatives, they are certainly willing to proscribe expressions of animus and, perhaps to a lesser degree, decisions grounded in false stereotypes. But the motivation is different: they are not so much guarding against the social disintegration that might result from the toleration of racist "torts" as attempting to ensure "market rationality."

As an institutional matter, judges (or hearing officers) can, in this right centrist view, make reasonable factual findings only about hostile and (to a slightly lesser extent) stereotyped decisions, for example by "checking" the reactions of a landlord or employer to discrete individuals, one from the protected and one from the unprotected group,[42] identical along all legally relevant dimensions,[43] or by looking at paper trails of bigoted remarks. They are not, though, capable of judging the macrorationality of a process applied evenly to members of all groups.

Mainstream centrism normatively idealizes what it expects can in fact occur with the prodding of appropriate legal intervention: each member of a protected group must be treated as he or she would be in a thoroughly rational, impersonal market, that is, as a source of funds to a seller and, to an employer, as a factor of production paid his or her marginal product.[44]

The mainstream centrists note that this result need not occur spontaneously, even in competitive markets,[45] for a number of reasons. First, of course, individual employers or sellers may choose to indulge animus:[46] owners of public accommodations and employers may be willing to sacrifice financial opportunities to avoid or injure members of protected groups. Alternatively, there may be animus on the part of customers: an unbigoted profit-maximizing employer might refuse to hire those against whom customers are prejudiced. Some progressive commentators believe that the unambivalent and unambiguous refusal of courts to allow employers to raise customer preference defenses indicates that Title VII is unconcerned with enforcing the mainstream centrist version of "economic rationality." This argument would (and in our view should) not persuade the centrists: they might well argue that the courts are simply refusing to allow the employers to act as *agents* of the customers' economic irrationality. A customer is, conceptually, the worker's true employer in the sense that he or she is the source of the funds that provides the employee's pay: the (formal) employer merely acts as the customer's agent. Similarly, reliance on false stereotypes may preclude market-rational treatment: many owners simply do not realize that members of protected groups provide profit opportunities because of widespread social misimpressions of their qualities.[47] If false stereotypes are socially commonplace, particularly among those with the economic power to make hiring decisions, the capacity of markets to wipe out those acting on "wrong" beliefs diminishes.[48]

Similarly, centrists point out that if firms follow irrational customs whose impact adversely affects protected groups' members, the groups' members will not be treated market-rationally. Mainstream centrists are predisposed to believe that in addition to the most familiar sorts of "stereotypes" about groups of people (for example, "Women only work till they have kids"; "Jews are avaricious"), there is a narrow category of equally untrue "customary" beliefs about the universal dictates of work organization that don't arise out of such group prejudice (for example, "People with high school diplomas do better work than those without on all jobs"; "Police officers must always have a great deal of upper-body strength") but adversely affect members of subordinated groups. Recognizing the possibility that "custom" is irrational without regard to "prejudice" is almost surely the most politically radical aspect of *Griggs*. It echoes the leftists' more general accusation that markets may not eliminate wrongheaded beliefs about productive imperatives, but rather that those who command market institutions more typically overvalue "customary" practices that reward the conventionally culturally valued traits associated with higher levels of current social status.

The mainstream centrist accounts of entrepreneurial irrationalism are somewhat muted, though. Descriptively, the centrist view seems to be wary only of employers' demands for credentials, not their depictions of "good work" on the job. In terms of institutional competence concerns, the mainstream centrist position demands that judges or EEOC hearing officers interrogate only the form of customary prejudice that is simplest to evaluate: they simply demand proof of statistical correlation between the entrance criterion and job performance,[49] but measures of job performance remain defined by the employer. The centrists do not demand that the courts ascertain whether each organizational decision that puts protected group members at a disadvantage is adequately cost-effective to be sustained.[50]

Furthermore, the mainstream centrist position is that markets simply may not have the opportunity to function, even in the absence of state-mandated bigotry, the libertarians' bête noire, because there may be local, collective, nongovernmental pressures (ranging from violence to ostracism to implicit or explicit boycotts) to maintain the segregated caste system.[51]

Finally, if firms engage in rational statistical discrimination,[52] individual group members whose productivity is higher than that of most members of the group will be underpaid, though the impact on the group's compensation is more ambiguous.[53] If acting on generalizations is cheaper for an employer than gathering more particularized knowledge, it is economically rational for the employer to treat all group members as if they had the traits of typical group members. Members of protected groups who themselves don't possess unwanted traits commonplace in the group will lack opportunities, though.

It is clear that mainstream centrists seek to proscribe irrational business conduct (animus, false stereotypes, unvalidated predictors based on false suppositions about job requirements). It is likewise apparent that mainstream centrists seek to eliminate the most direct forms of statistical discrimination: for example, the refusal to administer strength tests to women when strength is a legitimate job requirement on the ground that most women are too weak to pass them and hence high administrative costs will be incurred in giving strength tests to all women when that will generate relatively few hires.[54] It bears emphasis, though, that the case for proscribing rational statistical discrimination is distinct from the cases against animus and stereotyping; instead of banning practices that ultimately waste resources (because they result in failures to consummate trades that would actually benefit all parties if made), it demands interventions that, at least in the short run, may increase net social expenditures. There is a twofold centrist case against permitting statistical discrimination, though: first, it is possible that such discrimination leads protected group members to underinvest in human capital acquisition (knowing that employers won't recognize that they have skills that are superior to most members of their ascriptive group even if they develop them).[55] Second, one might believe that individuals in protected groups, if not all citizens generally, are entitled to meritocratic treatment, even when more social resources must be expended identifying merit than are saved by ensuring that individuals are employed at as productive a position as they are capable of filling.[56]

The belief among more liberal centrists that firms ought not to be permitted to engage in rational statistical discrimination is buttressed by a more general *distributive* conviction that antidiscrimination law mandates that persons be rewarded commensurate with their gross output rather than their net output (that is, output net of the costs associated with hiring or employing them).[57] In our view, the case for rewarding gross rather than net output might well be strongest when input cost differentials between employees result essentially from distinct screening costs, that is, when the costs of identifying that worker A is as productive as worker B are higher for worker A. As we noted, this may be true in part because, we believe, it unduly discourages people from developing productive skills if they will be unable to demonstrate them. But it is clear that many liberal centrists believe that workers must be paid in accord with gross, not net, output, even when no claim could be made that social output will ultimately increase if they are so entitled. Thus the Americans with Disabilities Act (ADA), the clearest legal exemplar of this viewpoint, mandates that employers pay the costs of accommodating workers with disabilities without reducing their wages to account for the incremental costs of accommodation.[58] In the absence of such intervention, a profit-maximizing employer (or, for that matter, a central planner concerned only with reducing goods' production costs), when confronted with a worker requiring accommodations, would substitute an equally skilled worker who required no incremental accommodation costs for one who did.

This liberal centrist belief, when unpacked, is almost surely partly parasitic on the traditional conservative tendency we touched on earlier to distinguish the deserving and undeserving recipients of redistributive largesse. Thus, in the liberal centrist view, a blind lawyer cannot justly be economically penalized for his or her blindness (by having to pay an assistant or reader, or having the firm dock his or her pay to reflect the costs of hiring such an assistant). This view is difficult to reconcile with the equally characteristic liberal centrist belief that it is perfectly fair that that same lawyer is paid far more than that same assistant because he or she was born with (or educated to have) the capacity to handle the typical legal arguments he or she is required to make. One seemingly best maintains this cluster of convictions by treating the lawyer's disability as morally neutral or ennobling, and treating the assistant as affirmatively morally blameworthy (*unwilling* to develop cognitive capacity) or unworthy (because *cognitive* inability, unlike disability, is a shameful mark).

Although liberal centrists reject the mainstream centrist notion that members of subordinated groups can justly demand no more than "market rational" treatment, they also seek to maintain distance from the more radical left assertion that the "worth" of persons is purely "politically" determined by the decisions of those with social power, rather than market measured by the impersonal demands of consumers. The gross value added is still determined by the impersonal valuation of the goods the worker (helps to) produce: thus, the valuation of the blind lawyer's memos and briefs is a function in the liberal centrist view not of political/moralistic valuation of the worthiness or respectability of the work but of self-interested demand by the products' purchasers.

At the same time, the liberal centrist stance is that members of subordinated groups ought not to be rewarded less highly than workers *currently* more productive so long as the gap in productivity could be overcome by relatively simple, inexpensive shifts in the organization of the workplace. The liberal centrists, in this regard, view practices as illicitly "dynamically discriminatory" whenever easily avoided "static" distinctions in net output ground pay differentials. Thus, in this view, women guards might appear to be legitimately excluded from serving as guards at all-male prisons *unless* a court sympathetic to this view orders the prison authority to redesign work shifts so that not all guards must perform invasive strip searches (an order designed to eliminate what such a court sees as "dynamic" discrimination).[59]

LEFT MULTICULTURALIST ANTIDISCRIMINATION THEORY

Those on the ideological left go a significant step further than the liberal centrists in their desire to break the nexus between net value added and social rewards. As we have noted, left multiculturalism makes an egalitarian descriptive claim: that members of dominant social groups (defined by race, gender, physical ability, and sexual preference) control social institutions and misjudge the relative economic contributions of "outsiders" and members of their own group.[60] Thus, in this view, a self-conscious egalitarian intervention (mandating equal pay for those workers who entrepreneurs wrongly believe are differentially capable) will not have the adverse economic consequences that conventional centrist economists fear. Labor will not be misallocated; there will not be layoffs of those who must now receive higher nominal pay if hired at all; firms won't engage in covert and costly evasions of antidiscrimination regulations against nondiscriminatory hiring to avoid taking on employees who they believe will create net losses.[61]

In addition, though, left multiculturalism makes a strong, residual egalitarian normative claim: that even if there are real productivity differences among social groups, these differences ought to be without material consequences.[62] Even if women separate less readily from their children as a result of biological destiny or undominated choice (rather than illegitimate coercion and character-forming social pressure)[63] and even if this inability to separate compromises market productivity, it cannot justify lower pay.

As illustrated above, the liberal centrist use of antidiscrimination norms to squelch market tendencies to reward in accord with net, rather than gross, output is concretized and "legalized" largely in regard to people with physical disabilities, though, to a lesser degree, left liberal proposals to facilitate women's ability to work productively by adding (concededly) costly child care facilities that (by hypothesis) benefit women more than their male coworkers would resonate in the same tradition. Left multiculturalism has developed the argument for erasing the material consequences of real group differences in productivity largely in relationship to gender differences. This is true, most likely, because of political discomfort on the multiculturalist left with the possibility that groups defined in other ways — by, say, sexual orientation, ethnicity, or "handicap" — are "disabled" (or less productive) rather than "differently abled" (equally but differently productive) in performing market tasks.[64] The resistance to the rhetorical use of the term "handicap," and more recently "disability," rather than "different ability" seems to reflect this profound difficulty in confronting the possibility of differential market productivity between groups outside the gender context.

In the context of gender, it is reasonable to argue that even if women are less productive than men in performing "market work," they are "hyper-capable" in performing equally significant work in the historically demonetized sectors. Given this reasonable supposition, it is plausible to argue, first, that "overcompensating" women for their market work simply makes up for the morally indefensible nonmonetization and devaluation of their socially crucial nonmarket work (from child rearing to caring for extended family to nurturance of social relationships to community service). More critically, though, the recognition that the nonmarket work that has been dominated by women has been devalued permits left multiculturalists to acknowledge (or even embrace) group differences, whereas, for other groups, the "distinct" social contributions of the oppressed subgroup, even if just as real, are not so readily socially identified and accepted.

But the argument that empowered groups making valuation decisions misassess oppressed groups' genuine contributions almost surely fails (and in any event is not consistently maintained within left multiculturalism). And without it, the left multiculturalist position is revealed for what it really is: a normative claim that even if real productivity differences do exist between groups, they should not have any material impact. If "overcompensating" women in the traditional labor market were really an attempt to compensate women for performing (undervalued) household-based tasks, we would compensate those who performed household tasks equally (at least as long as they were equally productive in these tasks). To give higher compensation for household work to women who would have earned proportionately more in the market had they not labored at home — for example, to compensate an attorney who stays at home more highly than her secretary who stays at home, as we would do if we demanded that each woman's employer continue to pay her ordinary wages while she took extended maternity leave — would surely be problematic if our goal were to ensure appropriate respect for household work. The fact is that this is not a "rectification" principle that actually attempts to equalize pay for equal productive output by accounting fully for traditionally public and traditionally private output. Rather, it is an attempt to break the pay-product nexus entirely, at least when the nexus results in certain defined social groups being worse off than others.

If the left multiculturalist position really pressed us to reward true productivity, it would force us to ensure that some women achieve the social status the most successful men achieve by paying the "best mothers" salaries commensurate with, say, salaries paid high-priced lawyers and executives. But proposals to do so would serve largely to underscore the awkwardness of proposals to monetize the traditionally demonetized sectors. In this sense, the left multiculturalist position is even more difficult to administer, and conceptually more "state-ist" than the liberal centrist position that disdains market rationality to the extent that it demands that pay scales reflect gross, not net value added. The valuation of household labor, for instance, in this case, is entirely politicized, entirely a function of centralized group decision making on "moral merit," whereas the gross value added by the protected employee is judged in an impersonal market, in terms of the willingness of the purchasers of the producer's output to pay for that output. Confronted with these difficulties, left multiculturalists more commonly propose not to establish pay scales for historically unpaid domestic labor, but instead simply to ensure that places throughout the social hierarchy are more evenly allocated by group. If males receive a statistically disproportionate share of workplace privilege, there should be a presumption that it reflects discrimination that must be remediated. The difficulty with making this presumption is that the connection between either group or individual oppression, on the one hand, and nonrandom representation in the "pay elite," on the other, is not clearly explicated.

How, for example, can it be considered less moral for a less "productive" *group* to be paid less than a more productive *group* unless it is equally immoral to pay less productive individuals within a particular group less than more productive ones within the same group? Alternatively, why are policies designed to reduce inequality among groups less difficult to administer than programs designed to reduce inequality between individuals?

It is not that group consciousness cannot be justified in any way: it *can* readily be justified by, among other things, the fact that group members have atypically interdependent utility functions, that group members in historically disadvantaged communities require "role models," that social integration depends on some measure of group equality, and that members of groups that have been historically stigmatized require substantive improvements in economic outcomes not simply to increase their access to consumption goods but to signal that they are no longer held in disrepute by the dominant, mainstream culture.[65] We must recognize the degree to which individuals derive their identity in significant part from groups, which are not simple voluntary associations of presocial individuals but constitutive of individuality; as a result, high levels of group inequality will have negative impacts on individuals that unpatterned inequality would not.[66]

Individual equality claims may focus, unduly exclusively, on material deprivation — on the distribution of material goods — while much suffering may be experienced not so much as a longing for goods as some combination of a sense of powerlessness and suppressed self-esteem. But powerlessness and suppressed self-esteem may be mainly experienced by individuals as members of groups, groups that lack social power and groups that are subject to widespread social devaluation. Rectifying those problems may well require more attention to ensuring group participation in decision making and group access to meaning-giving cultural institutions, as well as attention to ensuring across-group representation in socially validated roles.

But none of these observations about the importance of accounting for "group" outcomes in assessing a distributive policy gives rise to anything as powerful as "group entitlement" trumping claims. In our view, they should give rise to something far more akin to contingent social engineering rules of thumb that *one* desideratum, *among many*, in designing social programs addressing the distribution of resources is that we reduce intergroup hierarchies.

Even more troublesome, in our view, is that the left multiculturalist position fails to confront adequately what seems to us the vitally important fact that the interventions required to mute group inequality are no less problematic than the interventions required by traditional socialists to mute "capitalist" inequality (the "devaluation" of those individuals, however socially identified, who are less market productive). Firms required to pay some employees more than market wages surely won't inevitably go out of business doing so (as conservative alarmists often claim): they will simply face a tax that they will, to some extent, pay and, to some extent, expend resources to evade (such a tax is easier to evade than an income tax because it can be ducked by refusing to hire protected workers or inducing those one must hire to quit). To the degree the tax is paid, it will have some adverse effects on productive incentives: the extent of these adverse incentives is a matter of empirical debate.[67] But the key fact is that this tax will have no more or fewer problems than radically redistributive social democratic taxes or the implicit taxes levied in controlled economies that mute permitted pay differentials. One cannot evade the responsibility to defend (or discard) certain sorts of centralized economic planning by renaming it antidiscrimination law.

While recognizing the burdens of defending the interventionist state, we must recall that even the most humane, legally developed capitalist economies may be radically underinclusive and impersonal, and the more laissez-faire versions are far worse. It is not enough to know, for instance, that markets, left to their own devices, will do a good job of putting pressure on people to leave communities to follow shifting job opportunities. One must also try to ascertain whether the mobility-based gains in productivity really outweigh the losses in social continuity. Neoconservative arguments that spontaneous private charity would attend to most genuine need if the state withdrew from the "welfare business" seem almost willfully perverse.[68] Many people have complicated problems, and their problems are rarely self-contained: perhaps these problems might best be handled by close-knit small communities in which there is a good deal of personalized oversight of troubled people, but we don't live in a world in which everyone lives in a tight-knit community. If the options are an imperfect "social work" state and a world filled with anomic, homeless labor market castoffs, we'll eagerly opt for inefficiently bloated, poorly managed social work budgets.

Capitalism remains a system filled with injustices, to individuals and to groups. But if the left multiculturalists are to persuade those on the left generally to move away from a focus on these injustices to a focus on the purported irrationality of capitalist institutions, they have a very tough task.

ANTIDISCRIMINATION CLAIMS ON
BEHALF OF THE LEARNING DISABLED

Naturally, the learning disabilities advocacy movement has not had to address these sorts of labor market issues explicitly. Advocates for students with LDs are far more inclined to concentrate on the distribution of educational opportunity than the distribution of social rewards.[69] The claim that students in one group — students with LDs — are more worthy than non-LD students to receive educational inputs that might help either group reach its potential is not easily shown to follow from the precepts of left multiculturalist antidiscrimination theory, but we think the connections are profoundly important. It is most illuminating, we believe, to look first at how the argument that students with LDs have especially powerful claims to material resources fares under the alternative conceptions of discrimination law that we have set out.

Full-blown libertarians typically deny the propriety of tax-funded education altogether, while acknowledging that differences in the status of children are somewhat problematic for libertarian theory generally.[70] Differentiated children's status is, of course, justified in libertarian theory as derivative of adults' (for example, parents') rights to dispose of their own just holdings as they see fit (and, correlatively, to refuse "coercive" demands to share with children with whom they do not freely choose to share).[71] But the political viability of libertarianism leans rather heavily on the commonplace instinct that rewards should be based on socially valued efforts, rather than on "ontological" claims to have "needs" or "wants" satisfied.[72] In this light, justifications for inequality among equally unproductive children are less socially resonant than justifications for adult inequality.

Libertarian-influenced legal scholars rely not only on the stricter natural rights–based position that the issue of the relative priority of students' claims for public resources never arises simply because *no* student can legitimately claim public resources. Many "quasi-libertarians" (especially those in the law schools)[73] emphasize as well the need to act "as if" there is a natural rights framework in order to avoid rent seeking by organized groups seeking unfair shares of state resources. In terms of "antidiscrimination" policy and the LD student, this quasi-libertarian position is that the state simply ought not to leave open the possibility that it might distinguish among the claims of different students. The state ought not to grant distinct privileges to distinct students, valuing some claims more than others or tempting citizens to devote their resources to making successful claims at the "public trough." This viewpoint would seem to mandate what Christopher Jencks has dubbed "democratic equality" (the principle that the state must distribute resources just as it distributes votes, with no person receiving more than any other). Federal antidiscrimination law might best simply bar local officials from refusing to grant pupils with LDs resources that are available to other students (because of the majority's aversive prejudice against students with LDs or because parents of children with LDs fail to mobilize adequately as an "interest group"), but it should also preclude students with LDs from making claims others cannot. The state cannot grant white children privileges it denies African Americans: illegitimate "racism" is simply the capture of the regulatory state by socially dominant groups to immunize themselves from market competition by "outsiders" or to capture undue subsidies for themselves as a result of majority status. Illegitimate prejudice against people with disabilities (including those with LDs) is, in a parallel fashion, nothing more or less than the attempt by the "able-bodied" to preclude the "disabled" from receiving subsidies made available to the socially dominant, majority group.

A Burkean social conservative would likely show initial sympathy for the quasi-libertarian position that precludes exclusion of any subgroup from the full range of available public benefits. The underlying motivation might differ, though: we suspect the Burkean would be more concerned than the quasi-libertarian that "favoritism" in social spending would compromise both social solidarity and the republican virtues of rulers. At the same time, we suspect Burkean conservatism more explicitly seeks to nurture the autonomy of local political institutions and "authoritative figures" (school boards, principals), institutions central to a stable social order, than would quasi-libertarianism, which is more willing to use central rights-creating authorities (preferably courts) to block even local majoritarian exercises in state favoritism.[74] Thus we suspect that a Burkean would be prone to show considerable deference to diverse local political decisions, unsure whether local authorities *are* unjustly dismissing the interests of "politically disfavored" outsiders in making the resource allocation judgments that advocates for pupils with LDs decry, or simply making distinct educational policy judgments about whether LDs are "real" or "effectively treatable" or whether students with LDs indeed have uniquely untapped potential.

A centrist, we imagine, would demand only that each student with a LD receive the resources she is entitled to in a "political market" allocating educational resources "fairly," that is, receiving inputs she would be expected to receive were she not a member of a group facing either aversive prejudice or false stereotypes. A right centrist, like a Burkean, would doubtless despair that "centralized activists" (in Congress, in special education institutes, in the courts) have any more capacity than locally elected bodies to distinguish a false stereotype about various students' potential from a proper educational judgment that certain disabilities are at least as recalcitrant as "general" academic problems or social disadvantage.

A mainstream centrist, worried about the possibility that local legislative judgments are clouded either by "first-degree prejudice" (discounting the welfare of the "outsider" group) or by unduly readily accepted false stereotypes about outsiders,[75] should be (but does not seem to be) as prone to worry that local boards will *overvalue* claims made by students with LDs as that they will undervalue them. If we are wondering whether a certain group of low-achieving students will be politically disadvantaged in the battle for incremental funds, it is not clear to us why we would believe that pupils with LDs — who are a more random set of poor achievers in class and race terms than poor achievers more generally — will fare worse than their classmates. Unless mainstream centrists believe the highly contestable proposition that students with LDs are victims of more general stereotypes about the incapacity of people with disabilities, in essence because they've got the word "disabled" as part of their label, they will not conclude that students with LDs need protection against especially poor local judgment about their ability to benefit from aid. We doubt that most mainstream centrists would, on reflection, accept the proposition that educators properly estimate the potential of all students they label "unintelligent" while uniquely underestimating the talents of students with LDs.

The movement advocating special protections for students with LDs to ensure that their rights against discrimination not be violated draws relatively heavily on two aspects of the "liberal centrist" viewpoint on what the antidiscrimination principle entails. Most significantly, it draws on the systematic tendency of left centrists to ignore the moral salience of "input costs" in evaluating distributive claims.

One can translate the claim of mainstream centrist opponents of both test accommodation *and* increased resource inputs for the subgroup of students with LDs as saying that those with LDs are not in fact as gifted as their proponents claim, because what it means to be gifted is not simply to be able to do work well when accommodated, whether on testing or with special tutoring, but to be able to do well when given "typical" inputs. In the "traditional" view, student A does not have the same reading potential as student B just because, with more effort, we can help him or her achieve as high a score on a reading comprehension test: A and B would have equal "talent" or "potential" only if they developed the same way given the same opportunities. Thus, in this view, even if we accepted the controversial empirical assumption made by the LD advocacy movement that LD pupils are uniquely capable of benefiting from intervention, it does not clearly follow that the school has breached an obligation to help each student meet his or her potential by failing to undertake unusual interventions. Potential is nothing more than realized output given certain inputs, just as productivity is net, not gross productivity. A worker is "better" than another worker if he or she produces more output given equal inputs; a worker is not better if he or she produces more output only when given dramatically greater inputs.

As we have noted, the basic liberal centrist claim in the labor market context is that differential input costs are irrelevant, at least as long as members of socially salient groups will be harmed if employers account for differential input costs. To treat workers equally (without illicit discrimination) is to ensure that their pay is in proportion to their ability to produce, without regard to the special inputs necessary to enable members of protected groups to produce equal amounts. In the context of framing policy toward pupils with LDs, we might well be seeing a parallel claim. To treat students equally is to permit each subgroup to reach as high a proportion of their potential as other students reach without regard to the relative costs of students meeting this proportion of potential, at least as long as the inputs provided to one group are of little or no benefit to those not so favored.

This of course meets a second aspect of the general liberal centrist program: the demand to eliminate "dynamic discrimination" (illicit treatment of people in accord with current, but not potential output). It does so, especially, if one defines "potential output" in gross rather than net output terms.

Ultimately, though, we suspect that existing LD policy draws even more heavily on left multiculturalism than liberal centrism, largely because we doubt that there is adequately widespread belief in the factual proposition that students with LDs are uniquely *aided* by interventions, rather than uniquely *entitled* to them. The "dictates" of left multiculturalist views of antidiscrimination law in this area are not obvious, but we will attempt to trace what we believe they might most plausibly be.

First, and foremost, the belief that the claims of pupils with LDs must have significant priority over the claims of other pupils in order to protect them against discrimination draws on the left multiculturalists' tendency to reject "needs-based" or solidarity-based claims. Thus children are not entitled to potential-maximizing resource infusions because the expenditures will make them function better as adults, or because they will not function above some minimalist baseline without the spending, but instead because they have been denied these resource infusions as a result of animus or irrational stereotypes. In this view, advocates for children with LDs would not seek "charity," or tell us that the children will suffer unless we help them. The task, instead, would be to expose the bigotry of society, to expose our unwillingness to see the true human potential of children with LDs because they are "different."[76] More important, because the claims to resources are not grounded in assertions of community or claims of need, they are not seen to compete with the claims made by others who believe they'd live happier, more productive lives if given incremental educational resources.

To make such "solidaristic" claims that the polity ought to alleviate suffering that we are capable of alleviating is to commit, albeit inadvertently, the paramount sin in left multiculturalist thought. Left multiculturalism most studiously avoids any hint of "blaming the victim,"[77] not in the traditional moral sense (in which we might hold a "victim" morally accountable if he or she chose to do something morally iniquitous), but in a descriptive sense (in which we believe we can best understand victims' problems by looking at their traits, rather than the traits of those who evaluate them or "treat" them in a particular way).

Second, left multiculturalism, distancing itself from both the class obsession of socialism and the "equal opportunity" obsession of liberal individualism, is prone to contend that irrationality arises from the hegemonic judgments made by those in privileged ascriptive groups. Given this predisposition, advocates for students with LDs, influenced by left multiculturalism more generally, tend to overlook the possibility that educators are no less likely to misjudge the true potential of a whole range of their poor students — whether their "stupid" students, their "antsy" students, or their "verbally inarticulate" students — than they are likely to misjudge the potential of their students with LDs.

In our view, the problem with this approach is not just the "internal" one — even if we assume "society" is generally more prone to devalue the competence and potential of many people with disabilities, are LDs really like other disabilities in this regard? — but a deeper moral one. The duties to students with LDs really ought not to depend, in any way, on educators' *misperceiving* how hard or easy it is to change their performance levels. If the duties arose solely in response to the problem of bigoted misperception, they ought to disappear when the misperception clears up. Thus if all educators learned, through years of implementing IDEA, that these children's achievement improved markedly if, but only if, they received substantially more resources than their non-LD classmates receive, then the duty to provide accommodations would end, because the problem of misperception would be solved.

Surely, the real task of the advocate for pupils with LDs is to persuade us that once the accommodation-dependent potential of students with LDs is recognized, we have the further moral obligation to actually make the additional expenditures. If we think the resource claims of students with LDs should defeat the administrators' potential argument, "We know perfectly well that they can do better if we spend much more educating them but we are unwilling to do so," it is because we believe as a policy matter that the incremental resources are well spent, not because the failure to spend bespeaks either ignorance of the abilities of children with LDs or dismissal of their interests.

Strong advocates for the primacy of obligations to pupils with LDs ultimately draw on some of the most contestable aspects of left multiculturalist employment law theory. For example, left multiculturalism tends to posit that centralized state actors can cleanly distinguish the ignorant prejudices of local dispersed powers (employers in the job context, local school boards and teachers in the LD one) from facts. But just as the claim that employers' bias systematically blinds them to the potential productivity improvements that radically restructured workplaces might bring is dubious in the employment context, the hard evidence for the proposition that local educators radically underestimate the positive impact of remedial efforts aimed at pupils with LDs (particularly relative to other competing interventions) turns out to be very slim.[78] There is plenty of reason to believe that correctly diagnosed students with LDs benefit rather little from special educational efforts.

In addition, left multiculturalism assumes that ignorant prejudices beset historically oppressed groups, but not individuals within the privileged mainstream: thus white working-class males are not subject to irrational devaluation of competence; students without labeled disabilities have no more "potential" than local administrators systematically attribute to them. Although we are wholly sympathetic to the claim that racism and sexism are unique and strong systemic sources of irrationality, the parallel claim, in this context, that there is a great deal of group-based irrational devaluation of people with LDs, is quite contestable.

Racist and sexist devaluation occurs in contexts in which decision makers make decisions about performance and potential knowing the ontological traits of the objects of their judgment; the same sort of devaluation could reasonably be said to occur when school officials or employers judge the capacity of students or workers with discernible physical disabilities. But supposedly "bigoted" administrator judging the potential of a student with an LD may not even know he is dealing with such a student. He does not misperceive potential because he undervalues people with disabilities; on the contrary, he does so for the very reason that he does *not* see that he is dealing with a disability. He is not averse to the individual because of his or her condition, nor does he move too hastily from recognition of a condition to ultimate judgment. The most plausible accusation, instead, is that he moves from a generally salient fact — the student's test scores are poor — to what is claimed to be a wrong conclusion: students with low achievement scores will persistently achieve poorly. But even if this conclusion is wrong, it would seem to be "bigoted" not against students with LDs, but against "poor test performers," whom the school officials falsely stereotype, or discriminate against statistically. "Poor achievers" is the group about whom the officials have (supposedly wrong) opinions: they make no suppositions about the (visually indistinguishable) subgroup who have LDs. Yet IDEA does not direct itself at protecting *all* poor students by mandating that districts develop IEPs for *all* such students to ensure that generalizations about their future capabilities be carefully tested. Unless IDEA's advocates are willing to make the strong supposition that we can correct false stereotypes about poor test performers simply by ensuring that students with LDs are precipitated out from that group, which *should* otherwise be treated as essentially homogeneous, IDEA is not, in any discernible way, even designed to correct false stereotypes.

Third, and most important perhaps, the strongest advocates for legal protection of students with LDs draw on the left multiculturalist rhetorical manipulation of the mainstream centrist conception of antidiscrimination law to "legalize" their claims, just as left multiculturalism does in the labor market context. This is most significant in the employment law context when we think of "cost defenses," which can be seen as attempts to "balance" the interest in eradicating "discrimination" with interests in pursuing other social projects.

In the mainstream centrist view, reflected in decisional law, it is fairly clear that employers cannot raise cost defenses once they have been found to discriminate. As we have noted, employers cannot act as agents of their customers' animus, for instance, so that the fact that profits might decrease if a company hires African American salespersons that a large group of customers won't as readily purchase from is of no legal moment.[79] Similarly, an employer might have designed a plant assuming it would never hire women: the fact that it is somewhat costly to remodel to account for the required presence of women will not be a defense.[80] The slogan "The cost of remedying discrimination is no bar to relief"[81] is a socially plausible slogan when one's *definition* of discrimination is as narrow as the centrist's definition: social resources must be expended to ensure that members of protected groups receive privileges commensurate with market product. Once more, the key rhetorical point is that if one's conception of antidiscrimination law is so narrow, legal claims arising under that body of law are *prior* to more general distributive claims. First we perfect the market, then "policy" claimants (arguing need, arguing subsidization of merit goods, such as subcultural preservation perhaps) tax some of the now justly earned funds and expend them appropriately.

Left multiculturalism "uses" that same "cost is no defense" slogan in a context where it is far less socially plausible, drawing on the rhetorical power of the centrist usage, but without being willing to adopt the whole centrist program. One can interpret employers' unwillingness to pay an unproductive protected group member what they pay a more productive unprotected worker as simply raising a cost defense: that is, it is true that it will indeed be costly to overpay the protected group worker, and that, from their selfish "defendant in this particular lawsuit" vantage point, that additional cost is in fact their primary concern. But the mainstream centrist simply would not accept the proposition that an employer in this case is raising a prohibited cost defense: rather, the centrist would surely argue that there is no discrimination against someone simply because he or she is paid according to productivity.

The left multiculturalist view blurs the "two stages" of public policy that the centrist so cleanly separates. A centrist is likely to believe one cannot consider making trade-offs between "Stage I" market purification goals and "Stage II" social redistributive goals, but that once we are into Stage II, various redistributive goals may compete with one another. The left multiculturalist is more likely to argue that the failure to do what the centrist calls "redistribution" — which the left multiculturalist calls either "overcoming misevaluation of the contributions of the socially marginalized" or "ensuring that genuine differences have no material consequences" — is discrimination and hence must be remedied without regard to competing uses of the funds expended to remedy it.

In the context of determining the appropriate scope for IDEA, this battle plays out in a structurally similar fashion. Centrists must ultimately be most prone to argue that pupils with LDs, in this culture, are simply making "policy" claims (claims that they are more worthy recipients of incremental resources than others), rather than genuine antidiscrimination claims (claims that their interests have been slighted because their interests are systematically undervalued by state administrators or misunderstood because of stereotypes about their capacities). If they are making such policy claims, though, their claims ought not to be so heavily "legalized," treated as having substantial aspects of "rights" claims, capable of trumping competing resource claims. (In practical terms, districts could compare the benefits of expending funds on students with LDs generally, as well as on particular LD students, with the benefits of other spending plans.)

Left multiculturalist–influenced advocates for those with LDs are prone to believe, once more, that pupils with LDs, a victimized group, are subject not to legitimate (even if wrongheaded) educational policy, whether that policy is democratic egalitarian, openly utilitarian, or corrective of prior resource disparities, but to discrimination. The definition of discrimination is even less clear in this context than in the employment context, where the *administrative,* if not the conceptual left multiculturalist, definition of discrimination is quite clear: any program with statistically adverse impact (unequal distribution of benefits to groups) is so strongly presumptively illicit that, for all intents and purposes, it cannot be defended.

In the IDEA context, the claim is a bit different, though it is animated by something of the same concern: if students with LDs don't end up performing as well as non-LD students in school, the schools must surely be duty bound to do much *more*, because acceptance by the local districts of anything shy of that end-point demonstrates an ongoing refusal to accommodate difference. The unstated (albeit unsupportable) supposition is that if differences were truly accommodated, performance gaps would end, just as the unstated supposition in the labor market context is that group inequality would be eradicated but for the persistence of intolerance of difference. As a discriminated-against group, pupils with LDs are then entitled, absolutely, to order that districts take all steps to end "discrimination" against them: what this has come to mean, practically, is that each student is entitled to the "standard" special ed regimen of treatment for his or her LD.

It is crucial to recall that the left multiculturalist–influenced advocate for pupils with LDs is not attacking what "centrists" would call discrimination, though the remedial requirement is largely premised on the supposition that such discrimination exists. It is not enough for the district to show that it has done far more to bring students with LDs closer to their "potential" than it has done for other students, nor is it enough to show that its policies manifest full awareness of and sensitivity to the importance of and the special needs of the "class" of pupils with LDs. In the left multiculturalist view, the district cannot argue that the advocates for increased spending on students with LDs have simply lost a fair pluralist battle over resource allocation, just as the employer cannot argue that "socially undervalued" women should take their case for socialized monetization of household tasks or subsidization of market-undervalued child-rearing tasks either to a policymaking legislature or to a court seeking to correct legislative sexism, rather than inventing a new and unworkable concept of market sexism.

Summary and Conclusions

Students with LDs receive incremental material benefits (resources, testing accommodation, and partial discipline immunity) that other students might well benefit from. It is possible that they do so in significant part because conservatives, believing this particular subgroup of troubled pupils more "deserving" than others, have not resisted relatively expansive support for them. More interesting, though, their claims appear frequently to trump those of other pupils who might benefit from similar interventions because the failure to give these benefits is deemed to arise from a form of discrimination.

The idea that students with LDs do not get all the benefits they seek because they are victims of discrimination is dependent on a certain vision of what discrimination means. In the traditional mainstream centrist view of the antidiscrimination norm in the labor market context, we demand no more than that employers treat protected group members impersonally, as factors of production, unaffected by false stereotypes or animus: demand for treatment *more* favorable than that may be legitimate, but is thought to raise distinct redistributive claims. In the parallel political context, the antidiscrimination norm forbids undervaluing the interests of a protected group (animus), misevaluating the impact of alternative policies on the group, or framing a policy that makes sense only given particular misconceptions of the group's qualities (stereotypes), but, once more, no treatment more favorable than that is owed as a matter of right.

Advocates for pupils with LDs cannot readily rely on this traditional centrist conception of discrimination, though, if they are to argue that students with LDs must be protected against discrimination. Instead, they must draw on aspects of both liberal centrist and left multiculturalist accounts of what the antidiscrimination norm entails.

Liberal centrism departs from mainstream centrism in demanding, first, that people receive market rewards not solely in terms of current productivity but in terms of the potential they would, over time, manifest under more ideal conditions (that is, it demands the state correct "dynamic discrimination") and, second, that they receive rewards commensurate with "gross" (accommodated), not "net" (unaccommodated), output when differences in input costs are a function of group membership. Advocates for pupils with LDs argue, in parallel fashion, that we are duty bound to ensure that students with LDs end up just like students without them if they are capable (dynamically) with resource infusions (gross, not net output) of performing like their non-LD classmates, and that to refuse to give such infusions is to discriminate because it will result in disparate outcomes that are unjust given equality of "gross" potential.

Left multiculturalism emphasizes the degree to which institutions most typically discriminate by misperceiving the skills and strengths of members of nondominant groups: "difference" is transformed into "incapacity" by the failure of the dominant institutions to appreciate and accommodate alternative styles of work in the employment setting, and of learning in the school setting. In this view, people with LDs, unlike other competing claimants, are victims of discrimination because their learning styles are systematically denigrated in the absence of federal protection. Moreover, left multiculturalism posits that groups can make distributive claims that individuals simply cannot: that group equality is the presumed goal of anti-discrimination law (in part because group inequality would result only from illegitimate undervaluation of subordinated groups' contributions) even though individual equality (within groups) is not so mandated. If one believes, then, that students with LDs form a social group and competing claimants do not, then LD students may be uniquely entitled to interventions that mute, even if they are incapable of eliminating, distinctions in the social rewards enjoyed by them and "mainstream" students.

The chief difficulties with the second claim are that the "redistributive" taxes needed to ensure group equality will prove at least as problematic in implementation as more traditional egalitarian social democratic taxes and that the argument overemphasizes the unique significance of attaining group equality, compared with other redistributive goals. In our view, though, it is the first multiculturalist claim that most drives advocates for pupils with LDs in seeking extra resources. The main difficulty with this first left multiculturalist view is that it turns our attention away from moralistic claims of need toward highly contestable claims that local actors (in markets and politics) are systematically far less rational than rights-creating centralized intervenors.

Pedagogic policy should ultimately come to dominate our treatment of students with LDs: if, say, "speeded tests" are outright pointless (or, more modestly, simply misassess skill levels for some class of students), then we should abandon them. If there are particular gains to certain expensive educational interventions that accrue to some, but not all, students, let those students receive the appropriate interventions.[82]

The very first time we interviewed a campus advocate for students with disabilities, she declared, with great confidence, that "treatment of the learning disabled is a civil rights matter." As long as that statement remains broadly socially plausible, it will remain quite hard to fashion good educational policy in this area. Many perfectly just claims—as well as any number of claims that are either intrinsically unworthy or must be balanced against competing concerns—are *not* civil rights claims, and claims to ensure that more students reach their educational potential, as well as claims that tests should measure genuine skills or that students not be disciplined when there are viable options that better serve their interests while protecting the interests of students around them, are among them. It will always be tempting to "jump the queue" by claiming that one's distributive interests take priority over the interests of another group: claim hopping on the (ideological) backs of instances of genuine victimization by racism, sexism, able-ism, and cultural stigmatization threatens the real battles against social caste at the same time that it threatens chaotic and irrational distributive politics.

Notes

1. For a general discussion broadly consistent with our framework, see Deborah Stone, *The Disabled State* (Philadelphia: Temple University Press, 1984).

2. The attempt to differentiate treatment of the "deserving" and "undeserving" poor has been a constant, critical theme in welfare administration, both in the United Kingdom and in the United States. "Liberal" welfare reformers (especially in the United Kingdom) have frequently sought to universalize benefits to avoid stigmatization of recipients who would otherwise have to "prove" their moral worthiness. Some of the standard historical discussions of the British experience can be found in Derek Fraser, *The Evolution of the British Welfare State* (Basingstoke, England: Macmillan, 1984); Maurice Bruce, *The Coming of the Welfare State: A History of Social Policy since the Industrial Revolution* (London: Batsford, 1966). See also Walter Trattner, *From Poor Law to Welfare State: A History of Social Welfare in America* (New York: Free Press, 1974). For a good, brief history focusing solely on the American experience, see Joel Handler and Ellen Jane Hollingsworth, *The "Deserving Poor": A Study of the Welfare Administration* (Chicago: Markham, 1971), 15–37. An interesting theoretical account of the stigmatic labeling of the "undeserving" pauper can be found in David Matza and Henry Miller, "Poverty and Disrepute," in *Contemporary Social Problems,* ed. R. Merton and R. Nisbet, 4th ed. (New York: Harcourt Brace Jovanovich, 1976), 601.

3. In fiscal year 1977, federal grants to the states under IDEA, Part B, were $251.7 million ($72/disabled child); they had risen to $1.543 billion by 1990 ($350/child) and $1.976 billion by the end of the first Bush administration in 1992 ($419/child). (In constant 1990 dollars, the change was from $599 million to $1.543 billion to $1.84 billion; the increase between 1977 and 1990 was 157 percent; from 1977 to 1992, 207 percent). Appropriations per child rose every year during the period. Rand studies indicate that, in real terms, special education expenditures by the states roughly doubled between 1977 and 1989. Moreover, the Rehabilitation Act of 1973 and the successor Americans with Disabilities Act of 1990, each proposed during Republican administrations, expanded both public and private obligations to those with disabilities during this period.

During the same era, Chapter One appropriations (to aid districts with high concentrations of children living in poverty) fluctuated widely, rather than exhibiting the sort of steady growth we see in appropriations under IDEA. In 1992–93 appropriations were, in real terms, only 16.8 percent higher than appropriations in the act's inaugural year (1965–66); appropriations from 1982–83 to 1989–90 were lower, in every year, in real terms, than they were in any year between 1965–66 and 1975–76.

Real poverty relief benefit levels dropped rather sharply as well during the period: in constant dollars, poor families received $5,355 in cash transfers in 1970; by 1979, the figure had dropped to $4,427, and by 1986, $3,910. AFDC recipients received $19,753 in constant dollar benefits in 1976; by 1989, this figure had dropped (by roughly 19 percent) to $15,952.

It is doubtless the case that these trends can be explained, at least in part, without reference to congressional or popular attitudes toward "deserving" and "undeserving" would-be recipients of governmental generosity. In each case, one could argue that Congress was most expansive only when it could readily impose an implicit, regulatory tax on private actors or local governments, rather than expend federal funds directly. The enactment of legislation in 1995 barring Congress from imposing "unfunded mandates" on state and local governments in excess of $50 million without explicitly analyzing the mandated costs reflects the fear that such implicit taxes have been unduly easy to enact.

4. We discuss "multiculturalism" as a theory of distributive justice, but do not attempt to survey the full range of academic commentary on multiculturalism more generally that has emerged in recent years in philosophy, sociology, constitutional law, and other fields. For more comprehensive accounts of multiculturalism as a social movement, see, e.g., Amy Gutmann, *Multiculturalism and the "The Politics of Recognition"* (Princeton: Princeton University Press, 1992); Kenneth Karst, *Belonging to America: Equal Citizenship and the Constitution* (New Haven: Yale University Press, 1989); Richard Abel, *Speech and Respect* (London: Sweet and Maxwell Stevens & Sons, 1994); Lawrence Foster and Patricia Herzog, *Contemporary Philosophical Perspectives on Pluralism and Multiculturalism: Defending Diversity* (London: Sweet and Maxwell Stevens & Sons, 1994); William Connolly, *Identity/Difference: Democratic Negotiations of Political Paradox* (Ithaca: Cornell University Press, 1991).

5. For rather "moderate" statements of this basic view, see, e.g., Lucinda Finley, "Transcending Equality Theory: A Way Out of the Maternity and the Workplace Debate," *Columbia Law Review* 86 (1986): 1118; Kathryn Abrams, "Gender Discrimination and the Transformation of Workplace Norms," *Vanderbilt Law Review* 42 (1989): 1183, 1189–92. See also Christine Littleton, "Reconstructing Sexual Equality," *California Law Review* 75 (1987): 1279, 1321–23; Diana Poole, "On Merit," *Law and Inequality* 1 (1983): 155. For a particularly vivid, nonacademic account of this viewpoint in the context of disabilities, see, e.g., Joseph Shapiro, *No Pity: People with Disabilities Forging a New Civil Rights Movement* (Times Books/Random House, 1993). "Our society automatically underestimates the capabilities of people with disabilities . . . a disability, of itself, is never as disabling as it first seems . . . the only thing that could have kept [a disabled reporter from working] would have been the paternalistic assumptions of his colleagues."

6. This position is distinct from the more politically moderate claims from the center and center left, which we discuss in some detail, that discriminatory stereotyping may result in individuals' being paid less than marginal product, or that current workplace organization needlessly prevents individuals from being able to manifest their true productivity. The left multiculturalists are, in ways we attempt to describe, far warier of claims that the traits those with power value are truly valuable traits; they do not simply believe that those with power fail to recognize that "outsiders" possess these virtues as often as they actually do.

7. For an example of this translation of the claims of the "needy" into claims of being victimized by "classism," see Brian Mikulak, "Classism and Equal Opportunity: A Proposal for Affirmative Action in Education Based on Social Class," *Howard Law Journal* 33 (1990): 113. Vicki Been criticizes the supposition that "classism," rather than inadequate income, leads to one particular form of suffering that the poor bear disproportionately (exposure to toxins and other environmental hazards). See Vicki Been, "Locally Undesirable Land Uses in Minority Neighborhoods: Disproportionate Siting or Market Dynamics?" *Yale Law Journal* 103 (1994): 1383.

8. For cogent summaries of such classical liberal views, see Milton Friedman, *Capitalism and Freedom* (Chicago: University of Chicago Press, 1962); Friedrich A. von Hayek, *The Constitution of Liberty* (Chicago: University of Chicago Press, 1960); Ludwig von Mises, *Liberalism: A Socio-Economic Exposition* (Kansas City: Sheed Andrews and McMeel, 1978). For representatives in the legal academic world of the nineteenth-century liberal perspective, see Richard Epstein, *Takings: Private Property and the Power of Eminent Domain* (Cambridge: Harvard University Press, 1985) and *Forbidden Grounds: The Case against Employment Discrimination Laws* (Cambridge: Harvard University Press, 1992); Bernard Siegan, *Economic Liberties and the Constitution* (Chicago: University of Chicago Press, 1980).

9. For the most persuasive version of the libertarian position, see Robert Nozick, *Anarchy, State, and Utopia*. Richard Epstein's *Takings* is dominated by natural rights language in the early goings, but it departs from it frequently as well in ways that stricter libertarians have noted, disapprovingly. For a discussion, see Mark Kelman, "Taking *Takings* Seriously: An Essay for Centrists," *California Law Review* 74 (1986): 1829, 1852–58.

10. See, e.g., Edgar Browning and William Johnson, "The Trade-Off between Equality and Efficiency," *Journal of Political Economy* 92 (1984): 175. In the legal academy, this sort of utilitarian antiredistributionism is best articulated by Richard Posner. See, e.g., Richard Posner, *Economic Analysis of Law* (4th ed., Little, Brown & Co., 1992).

11. Antipaternalist utilitarianism in the law schools is commonplace. For instances, see Posner, *Economic Analysis of Law,* 468–69; Richard Epstein, "In Defense of the Contract at Will," *University of Chicago Law Review* 51 (1984): 947. Obviously, it is commonplace outside the law schools as well. See, e.g., Francis Bator, "The Simple Analytics of Welfare Maximization," *American Economic Review* 47 (1957): 22, 25–31; James Buchanan, "What Kind of Redistribution Do We Want?" *Economica* 35 (1968): 185.

12. For an example of such Tory redistributive sentiments, based on the duty of the rich to care for their social inferiors, see, e.g., Anthony Ludovici, *A Defence of Aristocracy: A Text Book for Tories* (London: Constable, 1916), 44, 79–81, 101–102, 172–174.

13. See, e.g., Bruce Hafen, "The Constitutional Status of Marriage, Kinship, and Sexual Privacy: Balancing the Individual and Social Interests," *Michigan Law Review* 81 (1983): 463.

14. See, e.g., Melvin Eisenberg, "The Bargain Principle and Its Limits," *Harvard Law Review* 95 (1982): 741, 763–78 (attempting to establish coherent limits in enforcing contracts given this sort of presumptive antipaternalism).

15. Typical within the liberal centrist law school world in its members' belief in ubiquitous market failures are Bruce Ackerman, *Reconstructing American Law* (Cambridge: Harvard University Press, 1984), 56–58, 61–63; Richard Markovits, "The Distributive Impact, Allocative Efficiency, and Overall Desirability of Ideal Housing Codes: Some Theoretical Clarifications," *Harvard Law Review* 89 (1976): 1815.

16. See, e.g., Charles Stuart, "Consumer Protection in Markets with Informationally Weak Buyers," *Bell Journal of Economics* 12 (1981): 562; Michael Spence, "Consumer Misperceptions, Product Failure, and Producer Liability," *Review of Economic Studies* 44 (1977): 561; Dennis Epple and Artur Raviv, "Product Safety: Liability Rules, Market Structure, and Imperfect Information," *American Economic Review* 68 (1978): 80.

17. See, e.g., Richard Musgrave, *The Theory of Public Finance: A Study in Public Finance* (New York: McGraw-Hill, 1959), 43–44.

18. The classic statement was in A. C. Pigou, *The Economics of Welfare* (4th ed., London: MacMillan, 1932), 172–203. Obsession with unaccounted-for externalities dominated liberal torts scholarship in the postwar period. See, e.g., Fowler V. Harper and Fleming James, *The Law of Torts* (2d ed., Frederick, MD: Aspen, 1986). For an analysis of other "liberal" uses of externality analysis, see Duncan Kennedy, "Cost-Benefit Analysis of Entitlement Problems: A Critique," *Stanford Law Review* 33 (1981): 387, 398–400.

19. See, e.g., Ward Bowman Jr., "Toward Less Monopoly," *University of Pennsylvania Law Review* 101 (1953): 577.

20. Outside the legal academic world, the liberal centrist focus on involuntary unemployment has been pervasive. Typical centrist works in the "broad" Keynesian tradition include James Tobin, "Inflation and Unemployment," *American Economic Review* 67 (1972): 1; Arthur Okun, "Rational-Expectations-with-Misperceptions as a Theory of the Business Cycle," *Journal of Money, Credit, and Banking* 12 (1980): 817; George Akerlof, Andrew Rose, and Janet Yellen, "Job Switching and Job Satisfaction in the U.S. Labor Market," *Brookings Papers on Economic Activity* 2 (1988): 495. Few liberal centrist legal academics have paid much attention to the macroeconomy, though. For a discussion of the limited place of "macroeconomics" in the law school, see Mark Kelman, "Could Lawyers Stop Recessions? Speculations on Law and Macroeconomics," *Stanford Law Review* 45 (1993): 1215, 1216–27.

21. For especially lucid examples of the politically centrist views, see Arthur Okun,

Equality and Efficiency: The Big Trade-Off (Brookings Institute, 1975); Paul Krugman, *The Age of Diminished Expectations: U.S. Economic Policy in the 1990s* (New York: MIT Press, 1990): 19–25.

22. See, e.g., Herbert Gintis, "Consumer Behavior and the Concept of Sovereignty: Explanations of Social Decay," *American Economic Review (Papers and Proceedings)* 62 (1972): 261. Adaptive preferences are noted in the legal literature, in, e.g., Karl Klare, "Workplace Democracy and Market Reconstruction: An Agenda for Legal Reform," *Catholic University Law Review* 38 (1988): 1, and Mark Kelman, "Choice and Utility," *Wisconsin Law Review* (1979): 769.

23. See, e.g., Michael Reich, *Racial Inequality: A Political-Economic Analysis* (Princeton: Princeton University Press, 1981); David Gordon, Richard Edwards, and Michael Reich, *Segmented Work, Divided Workers: The Historical Transformation of Labor in the United States* (New York: Cambridge University Press, 1982).

24. Richard Tawney, *Equality* (4th ed., London: George Allen and Unwin, 1952); Allen Buchanan, *Marx and Justice: The Radical Critique of Liberalism* (London: Rowan and Littlefield, 1982). For examples in the legal academic world, see Sylvia Law, "Economic Justice," in *Our Endangered Rights,* ed. Normen Dorsen (New York: Pantheon, 1984); Peter Edelman, "The Next Century of Our Constitution: Rethinking Our Duty to the Poor," *Hastings Law Journal* 39 (1987): 1.

25. See, e.g., Stephen Marglin, "What Do Bosses Do? The Origins and Functions of Hierarchy in Capitalist Production," *Review of Radical Political Economy* (Summer 1974): 60; Paul Blumberg, *Industrial Democracy: The Sociology of Participation* (New York: Schocken, 1968).

26. For a fuller discussion of this aspect of centrist antidiscrimination ideology, see Mark Kelman, "Concepts of Discrimination in 'General Ability' Job Testing," *Harvard Law Review* 104 (1991): 1157, 1164–70. For a particularly clean statement of this traditional centrist view, see R. Marshall, C. Knapp, M. Liggett, and R. Glover, *Employment Discrimination: The Impact of Legal and Administrative Remedies* (New York: Praeger, 1978), where the authors indicate that "Institutional discrimination occurs when people are accorded different treatment because of attributes that are not associated with productivity," 1–2.

27. For good discussions of why groups might make valid claims on social resources as groups, see, e.g., Michael Piore, *Beyond Individualism* (Cambridge: Harvard University Press, 1995); Iris Young, *Justice and the Politics of Difference* (Princeton: Princeton University Press, 1990); Paul Brest and Miranda Oshige, "Affirmative Action for Whom?" *Stanford Law Review* 47 (1995): 855.

28. For an excellent discussion of welfarist theories of redistribution, see Joseph Bankman and Thomas Griffith, "Social Welfare and the Rate Structure: A New Look at Progressive Taxation," *California Law Review* 75 (1987): 1905, 1916–18, 1946–55. The most compelling entitlements-based claims for redistributing to poorer citizens are found in John Rawls, *A Theory of Justice* (Cambridge: Harvard University Press, 1971):

54, 108, 258–332. For arguments emphasizing the moral duties of societies to respond to need, and the requirements to reflect carefully on what others in fact do need, see Michael Ignatieff, *The Needs of Strangers* (New York: Penguin Books, 1984). For an excellent canvas of arguments about why societies might (and might not) be obliged to redistribute, see Robert Goodin, *Reasons for Welfare: The Political Theory of the Welfare State* (Princeton: Princeton University Press, 1988).

29. For a good discussion of the complex redistributive tasks that must be undertaken to make meaningful opportunity more nearly equal, see Jennifer Hochschild, "Race, Class, Power, and Equal Opportunity" in Norman Bowie, ed., *Equal Opportunity* (Boulder: Westview Press, 1988).

30. See, e.g., Wojciech Sadurski, *Giving Desert Its Due* (Dordrecht, Holland: D. Reidel, 1985): 116–57. But see Joel Feinberg's discussion of the substantial limitations on the commonplace instinct that economic income and desert, measured in a wide variety of ways, should be strongly connected. *Doing and Deserving*, 88–94.

31. See, e.g., Frank Michelman, "Welfare Rights in a Constitutional Democracy," *Washington University Law Quarterly* (1979): 659.

32. For a discussion of political opposition to the Civil Rights Act of 1964, particularly among Southern congressmen, see Robert Loevy, *To End All Segregation: The Politics of the Passage of the Civil Rights Act of 1964* (Lanham: University Press of America, 1990). As Loevy puts it, "When the bipartisan civil rights bill came before the Senate in March 1964, [Senator Richard] Russell [D-Georgia] and his Southern colleagues based most of their opposition on the idea that the bill was unconstitutional. The bill represented, they said, an unwarranted invasion by the United States Government of the property rights of those Americans who owned restaurants, motels, and swimming pools and who ought to be allowed to serve whomever they pleased. . . . There is a 'natural right to discriminate,' the Southerners concluded. . . . [Moreover], the bill . . . would create a 'Federal blackjack' under which U.S. Government officials could come into any community in the country and override the wishes of the local politicians and the local citizenry . . . giving the national government the power to dictate racial policies to the states violated . . . [the] territorial separation of powers and thus was unconstitutional." For other negative libertarian responses to the bill, see 22 Cong. Q.W. no. 26, 1274, June 26, 1964 (statements by Senators Hickenlooper [R-Iowa] and Ellender [D-Louisiana]: "I am compelled to conclude that the far-reaching authority given to the Attorney General . . . will establish the pattern by law for the erosion of those rights of personal decision and responsibilities essential to a private economy and a free system"; "It is not possible to force one, by law, to associate with another not of his choosing").

33. For a discussion of this point, see Kelman, "Concepts of Discrimination," 1170.

34. See Epstein, *Forbidden Grounds*.

35. See, e.g., Ellen Frankel-Paul, *Equity and Gender: The Comparable Worth Debate* (New Brunswick: Transaction Publishers, 1989). Frankel-Paul argues: "We ought not forget that in our headlong rush to create a discrimination free society — begun in the early 1960s with the Civil Rights Act . . . liberty is being squelched: liberty in the sense of freedom to associate, to hire whomever one chooses for whatever reason." See also Epstein, *Forbidden Grounds,* 496–97, 505.

36. See, e.g., Frankel-Paul, *Equity and Gender,* 44; Epstein, *Forbidden Grounds,* 91–115. Note, though, that libertarian theorists would expect that plantwide segregation, though not industrywide segregation, might survive in a competitive environment either if workers preferred to associate with members of their subculture or if members of subgroups preferred certain culturally specific public goods to be provided at their workplace. Epstein, *Forbidden Grounds,* 45–46.

37. But see Richard Epstein, "Standing Firm, on Forbidden Grounds," *San Diego Law Review* 31 (1994): 1, where Epstein denies that antidiscrimination law is needed to supplement traditional tort law protections against infliction of emotional distress because the psychological harms that victims of racism describe are not really distinguishable from the harms that majority males would suffer subjected to parallel slights.

38. In this sense, we think legal writers like Charles Lawrence are correct to point out the considerable continuity between "hate speech" codes, on the one hand, and traditional civil rights legislation and the constitutional mandates of *Brown v. Board of Education,* on the other, at least as concervative Burkeans might best conceive of such policies. See, e.g., Charles Lawrence, "If He Hollers Let Him Go: Regulating Racist Speech on Campus," *Duke Law Journal* (1990): 431, 436.

39. *Griggs v. Duke Power Co.,* 401 U.S. 424 (1971).

40. See Richard Posner, "The Efficiency and the Efficacy of Title VII," *University of Pennsylvania Law Review* 136 (1987): 513, 515, for the argument that government actors are unlikely to perceive an efficient mode of operation that market actors fail to perceive; Lino Graglia, "Title VII of the Civil Rights Act of 1964: From Prohibiting to Requiring Racial Discrimination in Employment," *Harvard Journal of Law and Public Policy* 14 (1991): 68, 71–76, for the argument that unjustified practices with adverse impact are indeed problematic but courts should treat traditional employment criteria as presumptively justified; and Stephen Coate and Glenn Loury, "Antidiscrimination Enforcement and the Problem of Patronization," *American Economic Review (Papers and Proceedings)* 83 (1993): 92 (for a nuanced position not objecting to rules requiring employers to treat protected workers "neutrally," by noting that use of neutral rules may be difficult to establish to the satisfaction of the court so that legal rules should allow firms to use bottom-line quotas instead).

41. Thus right centrists will note that an ideal zoning law might correct for low-level externalities that would not typically be corrected through high transaction cost negotiations among a multitude of "neighbors" but argue that *actual* zoning law will misfire. The reason, they argue, is because it relies excessively on unavailable technocratic "planning" expertise or understates the perverse political pressures that lead self-interested voter coalitions to capture the local legislative process and turn it to selfish advantage. At the same time, right centrists are likely to believe that the "market" remedies (nuisance suits, private contractual land-use plans, and, above all, developer-initiated systems of land-use planning for subdivisions whose units will be devalued if "imposed" land-use plans are suboptimal) work far more passably than we might at first imagine. For the classic discussion, see Robert C. Ellickson, "Alternatives to Zoning: Covenants, Nuisance Rules, and Fines as Land Use Controls," *University of Chicago Law Review* 40 (1977): 681.

42. For a good summary of the virtues of and problems with "audit pair" studies of discrimination, see James Heckman and Peter Siegelman, "The Urban Institute Audit Studies: Their Methods and Findings" in *Clear and Convincing Evidence: Measurement of Discrimination in America* (Washington, D.C.: Urban Institute Press, 1994): 165–216.

43. Such tests will be more easily performed when sellers of goods and services allegedly discriminate, because buyers have rather few relevant traits (solvency and mistreatment of seller facilities), than when employers allegedly discriminate, because tester pairs of job applicants can never be adequately matched along all relevant dimensions, and efforts to match them along some dimensions may only lead (as Heckman and Siegelman have noted) employers to overreact to remaining distinctions that would not generally be salient.

44. For a fuller discussion of this aspect of centrist antidiscrimination ideology, see Kelman, "Concepts of Discrimination," 1157, 1164–70.

45. For a careful empirical study demonstrating that blacks and women may pay more for new cars despite competition among dealers, see Ian Ayres and Peter Siegelman, "Race and Gender Discrimination in Bargaining for a New Car," *American Economic Review* 85 (1995): 304.

46. Traditionally, animus was (mis)understood as a desire on the part of the dominant group for separation or nonassociation. See, e.g., Gary Becker, *The Economics of Discrimination* (Chicago: University of Chicago Press, 1957; 2d ed. 1971): 14. For a more plausible conception, focusing on the desire by the socially dominant group to express and fortify its hierarchical position and to injure and stigmatize the victim group, see Richard McAdams, "Cooperation and Conflict: The Economics of Group Status Production and Race Discrimination," *Harvard Law Review* 108 (1995): 1003.

47. For a typical discussion of the prevalence of negative stereotyping, especially in the gender context, see Bernice Lott, "The Devaluation of Women's Competence," *Journal of Social Issues* 41.4 (1985): 43.

48. These views are consistent with the views we would ascribe to mainstream centrists generally, outside the discrimination context: such centrists are far more likely than those to their political right to emphasize the untoward effects of misinformation on consumer decisions and of nonmonitorable managerial slack and incompetence on firm performance. Centrists are much more prone than political conservatives to believe both in the frequency of persistent cognitive error and its significance.

49. For discussions of validation requirements, see Uniform Guidelines on Employee Selection Procedures, 29 C.F.R. §§1607.5(b), 1607.16(D)–(F) (1990); Mary Green Miner and John Miner, *Employee Selection within the Law* (Washington, D.C.: The Bureau of National Affairs, Inc., 1978).

50. Judicial inquiry into how work might be organized differently and whether organizational goals should shift has been very limited. See Kelman, "Concepts of Discrimination," 1177–83, 1187–90.

51. See James Heckman and John Donohue III, "Continuous versus Episodic Change: The Impact of Civil Rights Policy on the Economic Status of Blacks," *Journal of Economic Literature* 29 (1991): 1603, 1614–17, 1639–41; McAdams, "Cooperation and Conflict," 1003.

52. See Edmund Phelps, "The Statistical Theory of Racism and Sexism," *American Economic Review* 62 (1972): 659.

53. For a good summary of debates over whether statistical discrimination will adversely affect only atypically productive group members or adversely affect the group as a whole, see Dennis Aigner and Glen Cain, "Statistical Theories of Discrimination in Labor Markets," *Industrial and Labor Relations Review* 30 (1997): 175.

54. See, e.g., *Weeks v. Southern Bell Tel. & Tel. Co.* 408 F.2d 228, 235 n. 5 (5th Cir. 1969) (employers may use statistical rather than individualized screening devices only when "it is impossible or highly impractical to deal with women on an individualized basis").

55. See Stewart Schwab, "Is Statistical Discrimination Efficient?" *American Economic Review* 76 (1986): 228; Shelly Lundberg and Richard Startz, "Private Discrimination and Social Intervention in Competitive Labor Markets," *American Economic Review* 73 (1983): 340.

56. Rational statistical discrimination poses conceptual problems for political centrists for any number of reasons: first, the rational statistical discriminator is engaged in individually rational behavior, assessing probabilities in a world of costly information and testing hypotheses until beliefs correspond as closely as possible to reality, given that it is costly to make more precise judgments. This judgment process is just the sort most frequently glorified as the basic underpinning of liberal civil society. At the same time, though, the "object" of such rational statistical discrimination entirely loses her individuality, her capacity to be differentiated on the basis of her true self-created uniqueness; the possibility (or myth) of the self-created individual emerging out of an undifferentiated (status-based) mass is equally central to the ideology of liberal culture, and therein lies the paradox for centrists. Second, centrists cannot resolve questions about whether to focus on discrimination as a wrong perpetrated by morally compromised bigots, in which case the rational statistical discriminator must be *contrasted* with the bigot, or as an injury experienced by members of a historically subordinated community, in which case the injuries of statistical discrimination loom quite large.

Because the opposition to rational statistical discrimination is not based on attacking economic irrationality at the firm level, however, it is not wholly comfortably embraced by mainstream centrism. The mainstream centrist position on statistical discrimination most clearly strains when confronted with practices that do not overtly statistically discriminate on the basis of group membership as such, but that nevertheless preclude disproportionate numbers of capable members of historically oppressed groups from receiving rewards they would receive if it were costless to identify each individual's talents.

Imagine, say, a psychological test that weakly predicts an applicant's proclivity to stay in the workforce, which women fail in wildly disproportionate numbers: can the employer refuse to hire all those (men and women alike) who fail the test, knowing it has many false negatives (many who fail would, in fact, stay in the workforce) and that such false negatives are concentrated among women? Is such a test any more acceptable than a decision not to hire women if it is known that it is generally true that women are (very marginally) less likely to stay in the workforce? In the first instance, the screening is based on a psychological test, whereas in the second, stereotyping is applied to the group member qua group member, rather than the group member qua test failure. More realistically, can employers use relatively weakly predictive "general ability" job tests, knowing that African Americans fare far worse on the tests, and that false negatives are therefore disproportionately high among blacks?

57. For a discussion of the belief that people are entitled to be paid in accord with their gross output, rather than their output net of differential costs of employing them (so long as the unusually costly inputs used for one group of workers would not help other groups of workers produce more as well), see Kelman, "Concepts of Discrimination," 1198–204.

58. For a Rehabilitation Act case making this holding, which appears obvious (though not as yet specifically litigated) under the ADA as well, see *Nelson v. Thornburgh,* 567 F. Supp. 369 (E.D. Pa. 1983), aff'd 732 F.2d 146 (3d Cir. 1984), cert. denied 469 U.S. 1188 (1985). In fact, firms need not always pay the incremental costs of accommodation: state agencies or private charities often finance accommodations. Thus, for instance, employers alone funded the full cost of accommodating only fourteen of the initial forty-seven workers placed by Palo Alto's Sensory Aids Foundation. See J. Frierson, *Employer's Guide to the Americans with Disabilities Act* (Washington, D.C.: The Bureau of National Affairs, 1992): 1001.

59. For a fuller discussion of "dynamic discrimination," see Kelman, "Concepts of Discrimination," 1170–83.

60. See, e.g., Young, *Justice and the Politics of Difference,* 200–206. For an application to the special education context, see, e.g., Harlan Hahn, "The Politics of Special Education," in *Beyond Separate Education: Quality Education for All,* ed. D. Lipsky and A. Gartner (Baltimore: Paul H. Brookes Publishing Co., 1989): 225, 227, 228.

61. The various positions we have thus far reviewed might better be understood by considering alternative reactions to typical academic economists' findings that women are paid some significant chunk less than men who work equal hours, with equal experience, education, and skills.

It is not simply the case that the right centrist predisposition is to accept the lowest numerical estimates of how much variance between male and female wages remains unexplained once one accounts for "measurable" differences in worker quality. More interesting from our vantage point is the right centrist belief that such "unexplained" variance is far more likely to reflect the social scientist/market interventionist's inability to measure true distinctions in worker quality than it is to reflect actual discrimination against women. Thus, for instance, right centrists will typically argue that when women, as a group, have the same "years of schooling" as men, they will have learned fewer (technical, mathematical) skills relevant to job performance.

At the same time, the left multiculturalist position is that "wage decomposition" equations that attempt to predict women's and men's earning functions on the basis of measurable quality traits understate true discrimination just as the right centrist belief is that they overstate it. The argument is that many of the factors that statistically correlate with higher wages for both women and men are valued not because they actually increase productivity but because men, with cultural hegemonic power, typically possess them. Thus, for instance, job continuity or availability at all hours may be valued because male career patterns (which permit greater levels of such continuity and availability) are valorized without regard to their actual effect on output.

The liberal centrist view is not only that the existing unexplained gap is a result of the unwarranted static discrimination (grounded in animus and stereotypes) that mainstream centrists agree the state is duty bound to eliminate, but also that levels of gender inequality could be decreased still further if workplaces were reorganized to permit the greater flexibility in the market that women frequently require, given strong social conventions about the division of household labor. Thus the liberal centrist view in this regard is that current arrangements are "dynamically discriminatory," that is, they do not reward people in accord with the productivity they would manifest under more ideal conditions (assuming, for the moment only, that such "ideal" organizations are not perpetually more costly than current modes of organization). At the same time, the liberal centrist view might well be that women who could produce as much as men if, but only if, given certain *costly* inputs (e.g., on-site day care) are nonetheless entitled to pay based on gross, rather than lower net, output. The liberal centrist view, though, is distinct from the more politically radical position that given current work practices, the typical "male traits" are without genuine productive value (nor do the liberal centrists adopt the multiculturalist "distributive" claim we discuss that women deserve rewards from the firm for "socially valuable" activity of little benefit to the firm).

62. See Christine Littleton, "Reconstructing Sexual Equality," *California Law Review* 75 (1987): 1279.

63. For an argument that coercion and illicit character formation dominate women's experience of the workplace, see Vicki Schultz, "Telling Stories about Women and Work: Judicial Interpretations of Sex Segregation in the Workplace in Title VII Cases Raising the Lack of Interest Argument," *Harvard Law Review* 103 (1990): 1749.

64. Littleton, "Reconstructing Sexual Equality," 1287–91.

65. In our view, the last of these factors may well be the most important, especially, though by no means exclusively, in the context of disability rights. For a superb discussion of the degree to which identity groups seek resources to undo historical stigma, see Michael Piore, *Beyond Individualism*, 36–44.

66. Thus "white workers" in deindustrializing cities may focus not exclusively on the loss of convertible commodities (income, housing) but on their inability to influence the decisions that dramatically affect their lives; plant-closing legislation and antigentrification rent control statutes may reflect group-based political mobilization against group powerlessness, rather than loss of goods. Gays proudly reclaiming demeaning labels (Queer Nation, for instance) are not seeking to smooth their access to goods (by, for instance, forbidding economically irrational discrimination which would harm them in material terms), but rather struggling against social marginalization, hostility, and (the risk of) introjected lack of self-respect.

67. Obviously, conservatives are prone to believe that taxes and transfers have dramatic incentives effects, whereas politically progressive observers typically believe that incentive effects are more muted. One can see this contrast whether one is talking about income taxes on the wealthy, implicit taxes levied through the reduction of welfare benefits, or the choice between market work and benefits receipt when "welfare" eligibility loosens. For high (politically conservative) estimates of negative labor supply effects caused by taxation, see, e.g., Jerry Hausman, "Labor Supply" in *How Taxes Affect Economic Behavior,* ed. Henry Aaron and Joseph Pechman, 27 (Brookings Institute, 1981); for a high estimate of the impact of the availability of redistributive transfers on work decisions, see Charles Murray, *Losing Ground: American Social Policy, 1950–1980* (New York: Basic Books, 1984). For representative liberal responses, see, e.g., Barry Bosworth, *Tax Incentives and Economic Growth;* T. MaCurdy, D. Green, and H. Paarsch, "Assessing Empirical Approaches for Analyzing Taxes and Labor Supply," *Journal of Human Resources* 25 (1990): 415; David Ellwood and Lawrence Summers, "Poverty in America: Is Welfare the Answer or the Problem," in *Fighting Poverty: What Works and What Doesn't,* ed. Sheldon H. Danziger and Daniel H. Weinberg (Cambridge, MA: Harvard University Press, 1986).

68. See Epstein, *Takings,* 319–23. See also Russell Roberts, "A Positive Model of Private Charity and Public Transfers," *Journal of Political Economy* 92 (1984): 136.

69. To the degree that the advocacy movement is "outcome egalitarian" at all, it is only in the relatively trivial context of reforming the grading reward structure to dampen the inequalities that would result from ongoing use of unaccommodated exams.

70. See, e.g., Nozick, *Anarchy, State, and Utopia,* 238.

71. Ibid., 155–60.

72. Ibid., 158–60.

73. See Epstein, *Takings,* 344–46; Richard Epstein, "Toward a Revitalization of the Contract Clause," *University of Chicago Law Review* 51 (1984): 703; "Proceedings of the Conference on Takings of Property and the Constitution," *University of Miami Law Review* 41 (1986): 122–23, 177–78.

74. Compare Epstein's nondeferential attitudes toward state property law decisions that interfere with "natural rights" with the deferential attitudes of the more Burkean Justice Rehnquist, who places a much higher value on the capacity of local institutions (local leadership?) to mediate potential problems of social disorder. Compare, for instance, Justice Rehnquist's opinion in *PruneYard Shopping Center v. Robins,* 447 U.S. 74 (1980) with Epstein's condemnation of the opinion in *Takings* (65–66).

75. See John Hart Ely, *Democracy and Distrust: A Theory of Judicial Review* (Cambridge: Harvard University Press, 1980): 152–60.

76. The special educators we interviewed often differed in their beliefs about the degree to which LD children should generally expect to be able to do the same things (educationally and vocationally) as non-LD pupils with similar IQs, aspirations, and cultural advantages. These beliefs would affect, directly or indirectly, their views about the forms of counseling that are appropriate to older pupils. Two broad themes in this regard seemed to emerge in our interviews: some of our informants expressed the view that a learning disability is a genuine handicap that limits what the pupil is likely to be able to do, even in a world that accommodates appropriately to difference. The role of the counselor, in a sense, is (a) to help the pupil identify his strengths and weaknesses, to compensate as well as he can for his weaknesses, but then to "play to his strengths," and (b) to support the pupil's self-esteem by urging him to judge himself favorably while having a realistic sense that there are things that he does poorly, without disparaging these deficits as meaningless artifacts. One New York administrator told us:

> [We don't counsel much about how to cope in life given the learning problems] though we're concerned with the social and emotional problems that go with the learning disability. Many students are really relieved by the LD diagnosis [because it makes them feel] less stupid and more like they've got a very specific barrier to success which they can work around. . . .
>
> The trickiest issue is how to keep people motivated while still making them aware of realistic limits. Their teachers too often are passive ("They can't do anything, they've got an irremediable barrier") or angry ("They're just lazy and we're coddling them"), and they're ignoring that the *effect* of an LD varies tremendously with student effort. . . .
>
> We certainly don't tell dyslexics that they might be better off avoiding careers where they'll have to read a lot, but we think we help them realize that, so long as the decision they're making isn't too charged with negative self-esteem issues.

Other special educators expressed the view that pupils with LDs have difficulty performing certain tasks that are traditionally done in a certain way by the non-LD, but that the underlying ends can generally be met through some alternative mechanism. Thus even if pupils with LDs cannot be educated to do something the way mainstream classmates do, they can virtually always find a substitute that is perfectly satisfactory so long as institutions do not mindlessly force conformity with traditional work modes. A different New York administrator told us: "Junior high and high school are the only time these disabilities should really get in these kids' ways. College students record classes comfortably and don't bother to fail at taking notes; secretaries and computers cover up for them in adult life." Thus, in his district, there is no attempt to urge pupils to adjust their plans to their disability because, in his view, they really don't have to, as long as they are aware of accommodation strategies and their entitlements to accommodations.

77. Images of the horror of blaming the victim abound in left multiculturalist thought in the legal academic world: see, e.g., Robert Mison, "Homophobia in Manslaughter: The Homosexual Advance as Insufficient Provocation," *California Law Review* 80 (1992): 133, 170–74; Anthony Chase, "Toward a Legal Theory of Popular Culture," *Wisconsin Law Review* (1986): 527, 548–52; Timothy Lytton, "Responsibility for Human Suffering: Awareness, Participation, and the Frontiers of Tort Law," *Cornell Law Review* 78 (1993): 470, 482–83.

78. See Mark Kelman and Gillian Lester, *Jumping the Queue* (Cambridge: Harvard University Press, 1997), 138–52, for a review of evidence that efforts to improve the performance of pupils with LDs have been unsuccessful on the whole).

79. See, e.g,. *Fernandez v. Wynn Oil Co.*, 653 F.2d 1273 (9th Cir. 1981).

80. See Arthur Larson and Lee Larson, *Employment Discrimination* Vol. 1, § 11.02(4) (Matthew Bender, 1996).

81. One of the fullest and best defenses of the viewpoint embodied in the slogan is in Mark Brodin, "Costs, Profits, and Equal Employment Opportunity," *Notre Dame Law Review* 62 (1987): 318.

82. For an excellent argument consistent with the one we are making, in the context of reforming the ADA, see Jerry L. Mashaw, "Against First Principles," *San Diego Law Review* 31 (1994): 211.

DUNCAN KENNEDY

The Critique of Rights in Critical Legal Studies

This piece presents a critique, developed by a faction of the group that called itself critical legal studies, of rights as they figure in legal and general political discourse. This rights critique, like critical legal studies in general, operates at the uneasy juncture of two distinct, sometimes complementary and sometimes conflicting enterprises, which I call the left and the modernist/postmodernist projects.[1]

The goals of the left project are to change the existing system of social hierarchy, including its class, racial, and gender dimensions, in the direction of greater equality and greater participation in public and private government. The analytic part of the project includes a critique of the injustice and oppressiveness of current arrangements, a utopian part, and a positive theory of how things got so bad and why they stay that way.

Modernism/postmodernism (mpm), a no less contested concept, is a project with the goal of achieving transcendent aesthetic/emotional/intellectual experiences at the margins of or in the interstices of a disrupted rational grid. The practical activity of mpm centers on the artifact, something made or performed (could be high art, could be the most mundane object, could be the deconstruction of a text, could be the orchestration of dinner).[2]

The critique of rights I offer operates from within both of these projects (I call it left/mpm). It has three parts: an account of the role of rights in American legal consciousness (and, by indirection, in American political consciousness more generally); an account of how one might come to lose faith in the coherence of rights discourse; and a brief suggestion as to why one might make such a critique in spite of its unpleasantness.

Rights in American Legal Consciousness

Until World War II, there were two main left reconstructive projects in the United States. One was socialism, meaning public ownership of the means of production, or the more or less complete abolition of the markets for labor and products. The other was the "reform" program of reconstructing the market and also influencing it, by a combination of structural changes (e.g., empowering labor unions), fiscal policy (e.g., progressive taxation), welfare programs, and regulation of just about everything.

Groups favoring either of these approaches might have found ultimate justification in ideas like freedom or human rights, but they were strongly predisposed to understand outcomes for unfortunate people as the consequence of a *failure of planning*. That is, of a failure to properly understand the social totality and intervene to shape it from the center to make outcomes correspond to what *the collective* wanted, whether the collective was "the working class" or "the American people." (There were exceptions: the rights-of-labor versus the rights-of-capital rhetoric in labor disputes at the turn of the century; women's rights.) The counterprogram of the American right was usually cast in terms of the defense of individual rights against the collectivity (exceptions being protofascists; the Catholic right).

That is no longer the situation. This section describes the rise of a liberal rights-based version of reconstruction, the role of rights in American legal consciousness now that they are the basis of both liberal and conservative ideological projects, and the left/mpm phenomenon of loss of faith in rights.

THE ROLE OF RIGHTS IN LEFT LEGAL THOUGHT,
CIRCA 1975–1985
There are three liberal subdiscourses of rights that get deployed in and around legal reasoning. These are liberal constitutionalism, fancy reconstructive rights projects in legal philosophy, and the popular political language of rights that flow naturally or automatically from the assertion of "identity." The three discourses are partially autonomous, because each corresponds to a fraction of the liberal intelligentsia.

Liberal constitutionalism is part of the ideology of the milieu of activist liberal law professors, judges, and public interest lawyers mainly oriented to legal reform through the courts. Public interest lawyers include the American Civil Liberties Union, the Legal Defense Fund, and the dozens of newer institutions that have sprung up to litigate on behalf of women, Latinos, the environment, gays, and so on. This group also includes the post-1960s National Lawyers Guild and the Legal Services Corporation of the same era.

Liberal constitutionalists produce legal arguments in briefs and supporting law review articles for the legal recognition, development, or defense of liberal legal positions. The advocates argue that these positions are "required" by the correct legal interpretation of the constitutional law materials, particularly the provisions guaranteeing rights of various kinds. A recent addition to this family is international human rights activism, deploying legal arguments based on international legal materials that recognize rights.

Fancy theory (that, for example, of Ronald Dworkin, Bruce Ackerman, Frank Michelman, Martha Minow, Margaret Radin, Drucilla Cornell, and Patricia Williams) is the project of the milieu of elite legal academic intellectuals self-consciously concerned with universalizing the interests of various oppressed or disadvantaged groups. They support specific liberal positions that have gotten legal recognition, and are therefore already "represented" in legal discourse in (maybe only dissenting) judicial opinions, by linking them to the liberal political philosophy of the day (that of John Rawls, Richard Rorty, Carol Gilligan, Jürgen Habermas, Jacques Derrida, and others). In the 1980s, they were joined by Central European theorists of "limited revolution" under the banner of human rights. All show that philosophy, something at once higher than, more intellectually sophisticated than, and also more determinate than postrealist text-based constitutional argument, supports legalizing liberal rights claims.

Finally, the popular discourse of rights pervades not only the formal political culture but also just about every milieu where people argue about who should do what, including, for example, the family, the school, and the entertainment industry. The identity/rights rhetoric in particular is that of organizers, advocates, and spokespeople of subordinated groups (blacks, women, gays, the handicapped). They argue the existence of an identity, that given the identity there are rights, and that these rights should be recognized by the legal system.

Within legal academia, but virtually nowhere else either in the world of law or beyond it, there is a left/mpm critique, loosely identified with critical legal studies (cls), of the three versions of the liberal project.

The Effacement of Radicalism. The left intelligentsia has not always been organized this way. Although the current liberal project has its "origin" in the 1950s, during the 1960s the left intelligentsia grew exponentially and then split sharply and repeatedly over such questions as direct action versus legal strategies, revolutionary communism versus liberalism, black nationalism versus integrationism, separatist feminism versus "sleeping with the enemy." In each of these splits, one element was different attitudes toward rights and rights rhetoric, associated with different degrees of "radicalism," as we defined it then, meaning different beliefs about how great and possibly violent the changes would have to be before anything was "really" different.

The political radicals' critique of rights had little to do with the kind of internal critique of legal reasoning that absorbed first the legal realists and then the crits. Indeed, the 1960s radicals leaned toward external, economy-based, race-based, or gender-based theory (consider Shulamith Firestone and Eldridge Cleaver). The 1960s radicals also failed or were defeated or self-destructed, however you want to look at it. In the 1970s and 1980s, the left intelligentsia was much as it had been in the early 1960s, with a small radical fringe and a giant liberal mainstream always about to be devoured by neoconservatism, yuppieism, and lots of other things.

Perhaps the biggest change from the 1950s and early 1960s was that the white male working class no longer played a significant role in left thinking. White male left liberals and radicals saw themselves as deserted or betrayed by that class, had lost their faith in it, or had never identified with it. For most left political activists, the straight white male working class was, at worst, the core of the enemy camp and, at best, the necessary object of conversion.

From Class Politics to Identity Politics. The hopeful version of the situation of the new New Left is neatly put by Cornel West, who asserts the existence of an "inchoate, scattered yet gathering progressive movement that is emerging across the American landscape. This gathering now lacks both the vital moral vocabulary and the focused leadership that can constitute and sustain it. Yet it will be rooted ultimately in current activities by people of color, by labor and ecological groups, by women, by homosexuals."[3]

The different groups within the legal part of the liberal intelligentsia — liberal constitutionalists, fancy legal theorists, identity/rights-based organizers — have reorganized around or persisted in rights discourse and successfully *reinterpreted* what happened in the 1960s. They remember it as a triumph, in the civil rights, women's, and antiwar movements, of constitutional rights, representing the best instincts and true ideals of the American people, over an earlier regime representing a reactionary or morally torpid version of those instincts and ideals.

What happened, according to them, was the triumph of universalizing intellectuals (Martin Luther King, Gandhi), allied with civil rights lawyers and legal services lawyers, allied with community organizers. Together, they asserted, litigated, and then justified rights guaranteed in the Constitution against legislative and administrative regimes that denied those rights.

The rights were usually defined in terms of equality, but equality in a special sense. They did not involve the demand for equality in the distribution of income or wealth between social classes, regions, or communities, but rather "equal protection" for individual members of previously subordinated social groups. The rhetorical emphasis on identity and antidiscrimination was a complex new synthesis of the "nationalist" and "integrationist" strands in 1960s black and women's protest movements.[4]

By the 1970s and 1980s, there were no longer "popular movements" aggressively raising rights claims, there were no longer federal courts willing to invalidate legislation and regulations in the interests of oppressed groups, and there was no longer the sense of the undeniable moral/philosophical correctness and ineluctable coherence of left constitutional theory. From different places within the left intelligentsia, the causal links among these three failures looked different.

There were some advantages to the new situation, as well as obvious disadvantages. The remaining left intelligentsia was rid of the radicals who had made their lives miserable throughout the 1960s and freed of the worrisome problem of the white male working class. The left liberals were now *the left*. They could, sometimes, institutionalize themselves and develop all kinds of more or less oppositional or collaborative attitudes toward the mainstream, without worrying about the horrible dialectic of "taking up the gun" or "selling out." And the left intelligentsia did survive, with a good deal more in the way of numbers and resources and ideas than had been around in the 1950s and early 1960s.

New recruits, post-1960s children, continued to trickle in, particularly women and minority recruits to the law reform and theory intelligentsia fragments. For many of them, the 1960s seemed a Golden Age. They had personal memories of that time, often of formative events in their own lives. But their memories were filtered through childish consciousness, and there was little in them that might conflict with the rights-oriented reinterpretation of what had happened. Its nostalgic emphasis on the importance of popular movements, but suppression of intraleft division, seemed far more plausible than the mainstream story of the 1960s as the Dark Ages.

It is easy in retrospect to see the weakness of this project. But in 1981, say, the year Ronald Reagan took office, or even, just barely, in 1993, when Bill Clinton took office, it was plausible, even if the times were hard for the left. I think a lot of its strength, as an intelligentsia project, derived from the combination of political correctness (struggles of oppressed groups), legal correctness (the Constitution was law and authoritatively demanded massive liberal reform), and philosophical correctness (the fanciest moral philosophy supported left liberal law reform on behalf of oppressed groups). Wow.

The Critical Legal Studies Critique of Rights. Against this background, the cls critique of rights (Mark Tushnet, Peter Gabel, Frances Olsen, me)[5] was *perverse*. But it was *not* perverse for the reason asserted by the first-stage critics of cls, who saw only one of its originary strands, namely, Marx's critique of rights as individualist rather than communist, and specifically the Marcusian critique of "repressive tolerance." There is an undeniable genealogical connection between this critical strand and the communist practice of denying any legal enforcement of rights against the state, in the name of the revolutionary truth that "bourgeois civil liberties" were a reactionary or counterrevolutionary mystification.

The initial critics of cls on this front were veterans of the wars in the 1940s and 1950s and then again in the late 1960s and early 1970s between the communists (and other orthodox Marxists and third world Marxist-Leninist revolutionary types) and the liberals. For these anti-Marxists (Louis Schwartz), anti–New Leftists (Phil Johnson, the *New Republic*), and post- or ex-Marxists (Staughton Lynd, Edward Sparer, Michael Tigar), *any* critique of rights automatically smacked of Stalinism.[6]

But the crits were not the radical activists of 1965 to 1972 reemerging as Marxist academics to pursue the old war on a new front. Though they preserved the radicals' animus against mainstream liberalism, their critique was perverse not because it was Stalinist but because it was *modernist*. It developed, with many hesitations and false steps, the same kind of internal critique, leading to loss of faith, that the crits were then applying to legal reasoning.[7]

Feminists[8] and critical race theorists,[9] who took up the critique of the critique after the anti- and post-Marxists, saw this clearly. They objected not on the grounds of totalitarian tendency, but on the grounds that rights really did or should exist, or on the grounds that it was demoralizing to criticize them. This response was plausible because rights played more or less exactly the same role in their post-1960s political thinking that they played in American political thought in general.

RIGHTS IN AMERICAN POLITICAL DISCOURSE

Rights play a critical role in the American mode of political discourse. The role is intelligible only as part of the general structure of that particular discourse. It is a presupposition of the discourse that there is a crucial distinction between "value judgments" — which are a matter of preference, subjectivity, the arbitrary, the "philosophical" — and "factual judgments," or scientific, objective, or empirical judgments.

Rights Mediate between Factual and Value Judgments. Values are supposedly subjective, facts objective. It follows that the status of all kinds of normative assertion, including moral or utilitarian assertion, is uneasy. Claims that something is "right" or "wrong" or that a rule will "promote the general welfare" are *conventionally* understood to be on the subjective side of the divide, so much a matter of value judgment that they have to be arbitrary and are best settled by majority vote.

Although there are many ways to account for or understand the nature of rights, it seems to me that in American political discourse they all presuppose a basic distinction between rights argument and other kinds of normative argument. The point of an appeal to a right, the reason for making it, is that it *can't be reduced* to a mere "value judgment" that one outcome is better than another. Yet it is possible to make rights arguments about matters that fall outside the domain commonly understood as factual, that is, about political or policy questions of how the government ought to act. In other words, rights are mediators between the domain of pure value judgments and the domain of factual judgments.

The word "mediation" here means that reasoning from the right is understood to have properties from both sides of the divide: "value" as in value judgment, but "reasoning" as in "logic," with the possibility of correctness. Rights reasoning, in short, allows you to be right about your value judgments, rather than just stating "preferences," as in "I prefer chocolate to vanilla ice cream." The mediation is possible because rights are understood to have two crucial properties.

First, they are "universal" in the sense that they derive from needs or values or preferences that every person shares or ought to share. For this reason, everyone does or ought to agree that they are desirable. This is the first aspect of rights as mediators: they follow from values but are neither arbitrary nor subjective because they are universal.

Second, they are "factoid," in the sense that once you acknowledge the existence of the right, then you have to agree that its observance *requires x, y,* and *z.* Everyone recognizes that the statement "Be good" is too vague to help resolve concrete conflicts, even though it is universal. But once we have derived a *right* from universal needs or values, it is understood to be possible to have a relatively objective, rational, determinate discussion of how it ought to be instantiated in social or legal rules.

The two parts are equally important. It is no good to be a believer in universal human rights if you have to acknowledge that their application or definition in practice is no more a matter of "reason" as opposed to "values" than, say, the belief in Motherhood and Apple Pie. They have to be both universal and factoid, or they leave you in the domain of subjectivity.

The project of identifying and then working out the implications of rights is thus a part of the general project of social rationality. As such, the rights project is part of the same family as the project of identifying and working out in practice a judicial method based on interpretative fidelity rather than mere legislative preference. Moreover, because rights are conventionally understood to be entities in law and legal reasoning, as well as in popular discourse and political philosophy, the two projects are intermingled. But they are not the *same* project. We might think that extant theories of legal reasoning fail to avoid the pitfall of mere preference, but that rights theories succeed, and vice versa. This possibility is real because American political discourse presupposes that rights exist outside as well as inside the legal system.

Inside and Outside Rights. Rights occupy an ambiguous status in legal discourse, because they can be either rules or reasons for rules.[10] "Congress shall make no law abridging the freedom of speech" is an enacted rule of the legal system, but "protecting freedom of speech" is a reason for adopting a rule or for choosing one interpretation of a rule over another. In this second usage, the right is understood to be something that is outside and preexists legal reasoning.

The outside thing is something that a person has even if the legal order doesn't recognize it or even if "exercising" it is illegal: "I have the right to engage in homosexual intercourse, even if it is forbidden by the sodomy statutes of every government in the universe"; or "Slavery denies the right to personal freedom, which exists in spite of and above the law of slave states."

The Constitution, and state and federal statutes, legalize some highly abstract outside rights, such as the right of free speech in the First Amendment and of property in the Fourteenth. Positive law also legalizes less abstract rights that are understood to derive from more abstract, but not enacted, outside rights. For example, in the nineteenth century, the Supreme Court interpreted the constitutional prohibition of state impairment of the obligation of contracts as legal protection of one species of the more general, but unenacted, category of vested rights.

American courts have also, on occasion, argued that the Constitution protects rights even when it does not explicitly enact them as law. At various points in the nineteenth century, courts did this quite boldly, claiming that the protection of unenumerated outside rights was to be inferred from the "nature of free governments." In the twentieth century, the Supreme Court has seen itself as protecting an unenumerated outside right of privacy whose constitutional (legal) status the Court infers from a variety of more specific provisions (e.g., the Fourth Amendment protection against unreasonable search and seizure).

In classic Liberal political theory, there was an easy way to understand all of this. There were "natural rights," and We the People enacted them into law. After they were enacted, they had two existences: they were still natural, existing independently of any legal regime, but they were also legal. The job of the judiciary could be understood as the job of translation: translating the preexisting natural entity or concept into particular legal rules by examining its implications in practice.

Though the language of natural rights is out of fashion, it is still true that Liberal theory understands *some part* of the system of legal rules as performing the function of protecting outside rights, rights whose "existence" does not depend on legal enactment, against invasion by private and public violence. We don't need, for the moment, to go into the various ways in which laypeople or specialists understand the mode of existence of these extralegal or outside rights. The important point is that judicial (or, for that matter, legislative or administrative) translation of the outside into the legal materials is still a crucial element in the Liberal understanding of a good political order.

Thus we can distinguish three kinds of rights argument: the strictly outside argument about what the existence of some right or rights requires the government (or a private person) to do or not do; the strictly inside argument about what the duty of interpretive fidelity requires judges to do with a body of materials that includes rights understood as positively enacted rules of the legal system; and the form characteristic of constitutional law (and of some private law argument as well), in which the arguer is engaged at the boundary between inside and outside, interpreting an existing outside right that has already been translated into positive law.

Constitutional rights *straddle:* they are both legal rights embedded and formed by legal argumentative practice (legal rules) and entities that "exist" prior to and outside the Constitution. For this reason, an argument from constitutional rights mediates not just between factual judgments and value judgments, but also between legal argument (under a duty of interpretive fidelity) and legislative argument (appealing to the political values of the community). Once again, the word "mediation" means that this form of argument participates in the characteristics of both sides of the dichotomy.

On one side, the argument from constitutional rights is legal because it is based on one of the enacted rules of the legal system (the First Amendment, say); on the other, it is normative or political because it is in the form of an assertion about how an outside right should be translated into law. The advocates and judges doing constitutional rights argument exploit *both* the notion that adjudication proceeds according to a highly determinate, specifically legal method of interpretive fidelity, and the notion that the outside right is a universal, factoid entity from whose existence we can make powerful inferences. Their goal is to make the apparent objectivity of rights theory dovetail perfectly with the apparent objectivity of judicial method.[11] The opponents of a "strictly positivist" position argue the flip side: that appeal to outside rights can and should resolve gaps, conflicts, and ambiguities that arise when the judge tries to ignore the normative sources of law, and so forth. In other words, the positivists celebrate judicial method and denigrate rights theory, and the interpretivists do the opposite. This discussion remains marginal. Most of the time, the ideological intelligentsias that deploy constitutional argument confront each other in the intermediate zone. There, both sides claim enacted constitutional rights *and* the objectivity of judicial method.

RIGHTS IN THE UNIVERSALIZATION PROJECTS
OF IDEOLOGICAL INTELLIGENTSIAS

Rights are a key element in the universalization projects of ideological intelligentsias of all stripes. A universalization project takes an interpretation of the interests of some group, less than the whole polity, and argues that it corresponds to the interests or the ideals of the whole. Rights arguments do this: they restate the interests of the group as characteristics of all people. A gay person's interest in the legalization of homosexual intercourse is restated as the right to sexual autonomy, say. The right here mediates between the interests of the group and the interests of the whole.

When groups are in the process of formation, coming to see themselves as having something in common that is a positive rather than a negative identity, the language of rights provides a flexible vehicle for formulating interests and demands. There is an available paradigm: a group based on an identity, from which we infer a right to do identity-defining things, a right to government support on the same basis as other identity groups, and protection against various kinds of adverse public and private action (a right against discrimination). New groups can enter the discourse of American politics with the expectation that they will at least be understood if they can fit themselves to this template.[12]

Once the interests of the group have been assimilated to the interests of the whole polity by recasting them as rights, the factoid character of rights allows the group to make its claims as claims of reason rather than of mere preference. Because you do or at least ought to agree that everyone has this universal right, and that reasoning from it leads ineluctably to these particular rules, it follows that you are a knave or a fool if you don't go along. To deny the validity of these particular rules makes you *wrong*, rather than just selfish and powerful.

This general Liberal idea is available to all. In other words, both liberal and conservative intelligentsias argue that the group interests they represent should be recognized in law by asserting that the recognition would be an instantiation of some set of outside rights. The proposed legal rules are not "partisan," but rather, represent political beliefs and commitments that transcend the left/right divide. For many conservatives, rent control is unconstitutional. Likewise, the liberal intelligentsia argues that its program is just the vindication of outside rights, enacted in the Constitution, against their mistranslation in wrong legislative, administrative, and judicial decisions.

I argued above that only since the 1970s has the left in general come to rely on rights as the principal basis for universalizing its positions. Before the 1970s, there had always been a live controversy among Marxists hostile to the whole rights formulation, social democratic progressive planners with a universalization project based on savings from eliminating wasteful and chaotic markets, and civil libertarians.

For the conservative ideological intelligentsia, the alternative to rights is efficiency. An efficiency claim has many of the same mediating properties as a rights claim: it is a value judgment that is universal (who can be opposed to making everyone better off according to their own understanding of better-offness?) and factoid (efficiency arguments are nothing if not technical, and they supposedly are empirically based). But whereas this alternative still exists for conservatives, rights now bear the main burden of universalization for both camps.

The Parallel Investments of Ideological Intelligentsias in Legal Reasoning and Rights Discourse. The notion of an "empowerment effect"[13] is helpful in understanding the investment of liberal and conservative intelligentsias in the general idea of a judicial method that will produce "legally correct" results, and also in understanding their more specific investment in judicial review of the constitutionality of legislation. It seems plausible (at least to me) that American political intelligentsias of left and right experience empowerment vis-à-vis legislative majorities through constitutional wishful thinking: the belief that correct judicial interpretations of the Constitution make illegal their opponents' programs, permit the moderate version of their own programs, and check the dangerous tendencies of the masses. People really like to believe that whatever they believe in is validated by the mana of the Judge. Moreover, legal correctness is a weapon equally of the left and the right, so that neither side should see it as "in its favor." Finally, the privileges of the intelligentsias do not seem to depend in any profound way on belief in the nonpolitical character of judicial method.

There is a clear parallel between the role of judicial method and the role of rights. The double mediating effect of rights, between fact and value and between law and politics, allows both camps to feel that they are correct in their rights arguments, just as they are correct in their technical legal arguments. Both claim a whole history of triumph over the other side under the banner of rights. Each recognizes that the other holds some territory, but interprets this as manipulation of legal reasoning, or wrong legal reasoning, to conclusions that violate outside rights.

For both sides, rights are crucial to countermajoritarian security as well as to countermajoritarian reform. The general societal belief in rights, like the parallel belief in legal reasoning, empowers intelligentsias that no longer believe (or never believed) that they represent the "will of the people." For the left in particular, the move to rights rhetoric meant abandoning any claim to represent an overwhelming (white male) working-class majority against a "bourgeoisie" that was by definition a tiny minority and getting smaller all the time.

A final parallel is that rights talk, like legal reasoning, is a discourse — a way of talking about what to do that includes a vocabulary and a whole set of presuppositions about reality. Both presuppose about themselves that they are discourses of necessity, of reason as against mere preference. And it is therefore possible to participate in each cynically or in bad faith.

Cynicism means using rights talk (or legal reasoning) as no more than a way to formulate demands. They may be "righteous" demands, in the sense that one believes strongly that they "ought" to be granted, but the cynic has no belief that the specific language of rights adds something to the language of morality or utility. When one attributes the success of an argument couched in rights language to the other person's good-faith belief in the presuppositions of the discourse, one sees the other as mistaken, as having agreed for a bad reason, however much one rejoices in the success of a good claim.

Bad faith, here and in the case of legal reasoning, means simultaneously affirming and denying *to oneself* the presupposed rationality of the discourse and of the particular demand cast in its terms. It means being conscious of the critique of the whole enterprise, sensing the shiftiness of the sand beneath one's feet, but plowing on "as if" everything were fine. Bad faith can be a stable condition, as I have argued at length elsewhere for the case of legal reasoning.[14] Or it can turn out to be unstable, resolving into loss of faith or into renewed good faith.

LOSS OF FAITH IN LEGAL REASONING

To lose your faith in judicial reasoning means to experience legal argument as "mere rhetoric" (but neither "wrong" nor "meaningless"). The experience of manipulability is pervasive, and it seems obvious that whatever it is that decides the outcome, it is not the correct application of legal reasoning under a duty of interpretive fidelity to the materials. This doesn't mean that legal reasoning never produces closure. It may, but when it does, that experienced fact doesn't establish, for a person who has lost faith, that closure was based on something "out there" to which the reasoning corresponded. It was just an experience and might have been otherwise (had one followed another work path, for example).

As for attempts to demonstrate abstractly that legal reasoning does or could produce closure, the extant examples in law look open either to internal critique or to the critique of partiality by ignoring equally good arguments on the other side. The postfaith minimalist critic finds not that "it can't be done," but only that "it doesn't seem to have been done yet, and I'm not holding my breath."

Loss of faith is a loss, an absence: "Once I believed that the materials and the procedure produced the outcome, but now I experience the procedure as something I *do to* the materials to produce the outcome I want. Sometimes it works and sometimes it doesn't, meaning that sometimes I get the outcome I want and sometimes I don't." Loss of faith is one possible resolution of the tension or cognitive dissonance represented by bad faith. One abandons the strategy of denial of the ideological, or subjective, or political, or just random element in legal reasoning. One lets go of the convention that outcomes are the consequences of "mere" observance of the duty of interpretive fidelity.

The loss of faith in legal reasoning is the across-the-board generalization of a process that has gone on continuously with respect to elements within legal thought at least since Jeremy Bentham's critique of Blackstone. Two examples are the gradual loss of faith in the forms of action and in the characteristic eighteenth- and nineteenth-century legal operation of "implication." When faith is gone, people say things like Holmes's remark: "You can always imply a condition. The question is why do you do it?"[15] Or they write, "Much labor and ingenuity have been expended in the attempt to find some general criterion of legal right and wrong, some general basis of legal liability. But in vain; there is none."[16]

Loss of faith in legal reasoning bears a close analogy to one of the many kinds of experience of loss of faith in God. The atheist who believes that he or she, or "science," has disproved the existence of God is analogous to the maximalist who believes that postmodern critical theory has proved the indeterminacy of legal reasoning. The other kind of maximalist is like the Catholic who becomes a Protestant, rejecting authority while continuing to hold a theology. Loss of faith, by contrast, is not a theory and is not the consequence of a theory.

I think of my own initial faith in legal reasoning as like the religion of eighteenth-century intellectuals who believed that there were good rational reasons to think there was a God, that the existence of a God justified all kinds of hopeful views about the world, and that popular belief in God had greatly beneficial social consequences. But they also had confirmatory religious experiences that were phenomenologically distinct from the experience of rational demonstration.

They engaged in the work of critiquing extant rational demonstrations and in that of constructing new ones, without any sense that their faith was in jeopardy. And they had occasional experiences of doubt without any loss of interest in and commitment to the enterprise of rational demonstration. (This is me in the first year of law school.) Loss of faith meant they woke up one morning in the nineteenth century and realized that they had "stopped believing."

It wasn't that someone had proved to them that God did not exist. They didn't find any extant rational demonstration of this proposition convincing. Nor had they decided that it was impossible to prove that God exists. It was just that they didn't find any extant proof convincing. They might even continue to have experiences like those they had once interpreted as intimations of the Divine. But somehow the combination — the processes of critique and reconstruction of rational demonstrations, along with the process of doubt and reaffirmation — had "ended badly."

It no longer mattered that more work might settle the question rationally, that the idea of a world without God was profoundly depressing, that they might lose their jobs in the clergy if anyone found out what they really felt, or that a generalized loss of belief in God threatened all kinds of terrible social consequences. It didn't even matter that people much smarter than they were pushing rational demonstrations that they hadn't refuted and perhaps wouldn't be able to refute when they tried.

They were in a new position. It was neither a position of certainty nor one of uncertainty. It wasn't certainty because no certainty-inducing rational demonstrations had worked. It wasn't uncertainty because the only possibility left was a surprise: someone might come along and prove that God did or did not exist, and everyone would have to come to grips with that development. In the meantime, there was no subjective state of wondering, no interrogation of the world. The question was "over," or "parked." They were post-God.

I said earlier that loss of faith is neither a theory nor the outcome of a theory. It is an event that may or may not follow critique. For example, in the spring of my first year in law school, I was working on a law review case note. At lunch with a second-year student editor, I waxed eloquent on the doctrinal implications of a paragraph in Chief Justice Warren's majority opinion that indicated, I thought, an important change in the Court's First Amendment theory.

The editor looked at me with concern and said, "I think you may be taking the language a little too seriously." I blushed. It was (unexpectedly, suddenly) obvious to me that the language I had been interrogating was more casual, more a rhetorical turn, less "for real" than I had been thinking. No judicial opinion since has looked the way some opinions looked before this experience.

Working for a law firm during the summer of my second year, I prepared a brief arguing that a threatened hostile takeover of our client would violate the antitrust laws. I was a fervent trust buster and "believed" my argument. The lawyers on the case let me tag along when they visited the Justice Department to urge the Antitrust Division to intervene. Back in New York, in the elevator going up to the office, we ran into another lawyer who told us that a new offer had persuaded our client to go along with the takeover. The lead lawyer said to me: "You know the argument so well, it should be easy to turn it around." Something in my face shifted him from jocular to pensive. "On second thought, we'll get someone else to do it," he said, and patted my arm. Ah, youth!

Nothing was "proved" in either incident, and in each case the person who jolted me was trying, nicely, to induct me into bad faith, not no faith. It would have happened some other time if it hadn't happened then.

Though it is arational, a "leap" in reverse, rather than a "consequence" of critique, loss of faith is nothing like a fully random event. It is a familiar notion that critique may "undermine" or "weaken" faith, preparing without determining the moment at which it is lost. And loss sometimes proceeds by a process like metaphor in poetry. Loss of faith can seem to "spread" like a disease or "jump" like a forest fire.

In the next section, I describe the structural relationship between the critique of legal reasoning and the critique of rights. The idea is not to explain but rather to describe the context within which occurred the migration of loss of faith from one domain to the other.

The Critique of Rights

This part describes a series of contexts for the loss of faith in rights, arranged as a kind of route for the progression of the virus. I begin with the role of rights "inside" legal reasoning, that is, with the way judges argue about the definition and elaboration of rights that are clearly established by positive law. Doubts about this process suggest doubts about the constitutional rights that "straddle" the inside and the outside. And these lead in turn to doubts about popular rights discourse and fancy rights reconstruction projects in political philosophy. I close with an attempt to dispel some common misunderstandings of the nature and implications of rights critique.

FROM THE CRITIQUE OF LEGAL REASONING
TO THE CRITIQUE OF CONSTITUTIONAL RIGHTS
The point of closest contact between legal reasoning and rights talk occurs when lawyers reason about inside rights. This practice is important for rights talk because through it, outside rights are "translated" into the legal order. As we saw in the previous section, this translation is a crucial part of the Liberal program for a good society. Failure in the process of translation — say, a loss of faith in the possibility of doing it while maintaining the double mediation between factual and value judgments and between legal and political discourse — would be a failure for Liberal theory.

But it would pose (has already posed) another danger as well: doubt about the coherence of legal rights reasoning at the business end, so to speak, of the rights continuum threatens to spread "back" to constitutional rights, which "straddle," and thence to fully outside rights. It is just such a progression that I suggest here.

Legal Rights in Legal Reasoning. The critique of legal reasoning operates on inside rights argument in the same way it operates in general. It does not deny that it is "meaningful" to speak of legal rights. For the judge under a duty of interpretive fidelity, legal rules stated in the language of rights are part of the body of materials that "bind" him or her, or that he or she transforms through legal work. Appeals to legal rights, whether constitutional or just mundane common law rights, influence the course of decision, as do appeals to legal rules that are not stated as rights (such as rules about interstate relations) and to precedents or policies (e.g., security of transaction). The appeal to a rule cast in the form of a right, or to a value understood to be represented by a right, may produce the experience of closure: given this legalized right, you can't think of a good reason why the plaintiff shouldn't lose the case.

Participants in ideologized group conflict formulate their demands in rights language and then try to get particular rights legalized (enacted by a legislature, promulgated by an administrative agency, incorporated into judge-made law), both at the particular level (*Miranda* rights) and at the more abstract level (the Equal Rights Amendment). If they succeed, "there is a right to a lawyer during police interrogation," meaning that there is a legal rule requiring a lawyer, one that influences real-world practices as do other rules in the system. In drafting a charter for a limited equity co-op, it makes sense to provide for the "rights" of the cooperators, of the community land trust, and so on.

Although rights arguments have meaning and effect in legal discourse, it is clear that they are open to the same analysis of open texture or indeterminacy as legal argument in general. The crucial point about the critique of legal rights is that in the process of pursuing the general left-wing project of showing the manipulability of legal reasoning, critique flattened the distinction between rights argument and policy argument in general. It did this in two distinct ways. First, when the asserted right deployed in argument is seen as a legal rule, a positive prescription to be interpreted (right to counsel during police interrogation), then we interpret it using the whole range of policy argument. Whatever the right "is" is a function of the open-ended general procedure of legal argument.

Second, when the arguer appeals to a right as a reason for adopting a rule (protect free speech, secure the owner's property rights), minimalist internal critique reduces legal rights reasoning to policy reasoning by showing that it is necessary to balance one side's asserted right against the other side's (protect the right to a nonabusive workplace; tenants' rights). According to the critique, what determines the balance is not a chain of reasoning from a right or even from two rights, but a *third* procedure, one that in fact involves considering open-textured arguments from morality, social welfare, expectations, and institutional competence and administrability. None of this precludes the phenomenon of closure or apparent objectivity of the rule interpretation. It merely undermines its rational basis.

Legal Argument about Rights That Are Legal Rules Reduces to Policy Argument. Judges making legal arguments about interpretive fidelity in common law adjudication and statutory interpretation typically convey that they are dealing with a dense network of rules that have to be followed regardless of their sources and regardless of what the judges think about their rightness or wrongness. The correct interpretation of the materials is a very different question from the question of what would be the best thing to do under the circumstances (the "legislative" question) and from the "philosophical" question of what political morality, or protection of natural rights, say, requires under the circumstances.

In the context of common law or statutory interpretation, rights and rights reasoning are submerged in the argumentative mass that includes precedent, canons of statutory interpretation, institutional competence and administrability arguments, general moral arguments for or against the conduct of parties, utilitarian arguments about how different rule choices will affect the conduct of parties, utilitarian arguments about how different rule choices will affect the conduct of private parties beyond the parties to the case, and arguments about the welfare consequences of those changes. Because the word "right" is generally used synonymously with "a rule legally protecting an interest of a party," there is nothing even slightly odd about casting a judicial opinion in the form "We hold that the plaintiff has a right to x, and the reason is that this will honor precedent, correspond to legislative intent, keep us within our institutional competence, reward morality and punish vice, be easy to administer, and maximize consumer welfare."

The critique of this kind of legal rights reasoning is aimed at the ability of judges to produce convincing, closure-inducing, doubt-eliminating chains of reasoning about particular legal outcomes in the context of interpretive fidelity. The rights are just legal rules, more or less abstract, more or less easy to administer, that we are trying to interpret along with all the other legal materials to justify our outcomes.

Loss of faith in this discourse is loss of faith in the judge/legislator distinction, or in the idea of the objectivity of adjudication. It is the development and extension of the now one-hundred-year-old project of critiquing legal reasoning in general. Of course, it might mean loss of faith in *law*, or in legal authority, as well. But the rights — that is, the legal rules that don't produce closure — might come from anywhere. They might be morally admirable or monstrous; they might be grounded in majority rule, or natural law, or custom, or whatever. In other words, no matter how threatening to *legality*, the critique and loss of faith in legal rights reasoning does not necessarily imply a loss of faith in *normativity* in general or in the use of rights and rights reasoning to decide what we leftists think the law should be.

Nonetheless, it is one part of the context of loss of faith.

Rights Argument within Legal Reasoning Reduces to Balancing and Therefore to Policy. I have been arguing that when by rights we mean legal rights, then rights are legal rules and, like the other rules of the legal system, turn out to be open to strategic work designed to exploit or to generate gaps, conflicts, and ambiguities in particular cases, with the goal of making legal rules that will favorably dispose ideological stakes. The advocates, in the examples above, use social welfare or administrability arguments or whatever in support of their favored interpretation of the legal right. But even when the advocates stick to arguments about the rights of the parties that more or less exactly parallel the rights arguments used in political philosophy, it turns out that they end up with balancing tests that render rights argument indistinguishable from the open-ended policy discourse it was supposed to let us avoid.

The political philosophical discourse of rights uses familiar operations to move from rights generally stated ("Everyone has a right to privacy") to specific outcomes. For example, a right holder can lose because he or she waived the right asserted (he or she can argue back, say, that the waiver was obtained under duress) or forfeited it by misconduct (versus, say, a claim of inevitable accident). For the purpose of critique, the most important of these techniques are those for generating a right that supports what your side wants to do or what your side wants to stop the other side from doing. As Hohfeld showed for property rights, the right your opponent is asserting will often be defined in such a way that you can appeal to the very same right on the other side.[17]

You can also work at constructing a new right by recasting what you want to do as an instance of a more general interest, and then as an instance of an already existing legal right that protects that interest. For example, it was not until the 1930s that labor picketing was reconceptualized as free speech.[18] Or the advocate can claim that a set of precedents previously viewed as protecting several rights actually protect a single interest, which should be legally protected as a new right. The classic example is the generation of the right to privacy, first by Louis Brandeis in the private law context, then by W. O. Douglas in constitutional law.[19]

Another part of the mundane legal practice of rights argument is the critique of your opponent's rights claims. The most basic technique is the internal undoing of a rights argument by showing that it relied on a false deduction, typically on a conceptualist overstatement of what was entailed in the definition of the right. For example, the right to contractual performance does not entail the right to expectation damages.[20]

The upshot, when both sides are well represented, is that the advocates confront the judge with two plausible but contradictory chains of rights reasoning, one proceeding from the plaintiff's right and the other from the defendant's. Yes, the employer has property rights, but the picketers have free-speech rights. Yes, the harasser has free-speech rights, but the harassed has a right to be free of sex discrimination in the workplace. Yes, the landowner has the right to do whatever she wants on her land, but her neighbor has a right to be free from unreasonable interference. And each chain is open to an internal critique.

Sometimes the judge more or less arbitrarily endorses one side over the other; sometimes the judge throws in the towel and balances. The lesson of practice for the doubter is that the question involved cannot be resolved without resort to policy, which in turn makes the resolution open to ideological influence. The critique of legal rights reasoning becomes just a special case of the general critique of policy argument: once it is shown that the case requires a balancing of conflicting rights claims, it is implausible that it is the rights themselves, rather than the "subjective" or "political" commitments of the judges, that are deciding the outcome.

Once again, the prevalent experience, first, of the manipulability of legal rights reasoning and then of its reduction to balancing tests, doesn't preclude instances in which rights reasoning produces the opposite experience of closure. Nor does it show that outside rights don't exist. It is just another context for loss of faith.

Rights Mediate between Law and Policy. The application of the critique to legal reasoning about inside rights suggests that rights do more than mediate, as suggested earlier, between facts and values and between law and politics. *Within legal discourse,* rights arguments are situated midway between merely "technical" or deductive arguments about rule application—appealing to ideas like the plain meaning of words, legislative intent, stare decisis, or the "will of the parties"—and "pure" policy arguments that require the judge to balance the conflicting interests of the parties. Remember that policy arguments are understood to be inevitably present within legal argument, but they are disfavored and marginal in status compared to arguments that appear more consonant with the supposedly objective character of adjudication.

Rights arguments involve something more than the logic of the valid, because they explain and justify rules rather than merely apply them. But they are less "subjective" than pure policy arguments because of their "factoid," half-fact/half-value character. Loss of faith, or the failure of mediation, occurs when we begin to see the techniques of "manipulative" rights argument as potent enough to reduce "every," or at least any particular, rights argument to a question of balancing.

The Proliferation of Balancing Tests Reduces Constitutional Rights Questions to Policy Questions. The second context for loss of faith in rights (the first being the manipulability of rights when viewed as legal rules, just discussed) is the specific history of balancing, or of conflict between rights, in constitutional law. I think the attitude of political lawyers in the United States toward rights has been profoundly influenced by this nationally specific history. As I see it, it has four parts:

1. The legal realist attack, in the 1920s and 1930s, on the rights reasoning by which conservatives had embedded a particular understanding of property rights in constitutional law.[21] The realists argued that because the conservative constitutional rights case against reform statutes neces-

sarily involves mere policy argument, the courts had no specifically legal basis for overruling legislative judgments.

2. The moderate and conservative attack on the liberal attempt, in the 1950s, to embed a particular understanding of freedom of speech and equal protection in constitutional law. Moderates and conservatives argued that because all the courts could do was balance rights against powers, or rights against rights, they had no specifically legal basis for overruling legislative judgments.

3. The liberal success, in the 1950s, 1960s, and early 1970s, in getting the liberal conception of equal protection and identity rights embedded in constitutional law (the victim perspective), followed by an equally successful conservative counterattack, in the 1970s and 1980s, that embedded a contradictory understanding of rights in constitutional law (the perpetrator perspective).

4. The emergence, in the 1970s and 1980s, of contradictory rights claims within the liberal coalition based on different conceptions of identity.

Before I briefly describe each of these contexts, I want to reemphasize that none of them compelled loss of faith. Loss of faith is an event that occurs for some people in one context, and for others in another. Some people lost their faith in constitutional rights reasoning in the 1930s. Others lost their faith in the late 1980s. Many lost faith and then regained it, or lost faith in one kind of rights reasoning but not in another, and so on.

One thing the contexts have in common is that they each presented the problem of how to make abstract rights (property rights, free-speech rights, equality rights, reproductive rights, privacy rights) concrete at the level of rule choice within the legal system. The initial question was: Given that we all agree there is a right of free speech, can a city restrict leafleting on downtown streets? Or: Given that we all agree that there is a right of privacy, can a woman decide without the consent of the father to abort her fetus in the first trimester of pregnancy?

Another thing the contexts have in common is that the inquiry into how to concretize the abstract right occurs in the presence of a countervailing right, or of a power of the legislature presumed to derive from majority will, or from the legislature's duty to protect the rights of parties other than the claimants. This means that there are two opposing concretization projects going on, one from the plaintiff's side and the other from the defendant's. It is always possible that the judge or observer will see these two projects as producing a "draw" or a "stalemate" or a "clash of absolutes."

A final thing the contexts have in common is that the opposing sides in the dispute attacked each other's concretization projects as unsuccessful, on their own terms, in linking the preferred rule to the abstract right. Each side then accused the other of motivated error, that is, of having consciously or unconsciously masked an ideological — a deeply contested — claim about what the law ought to be in a false claim about interpretive fidelity to the body of extant legal materials.

The Liberal Legal Realist Origin of the Critique of Rights. The historiography of balancing in American legal thought is in its infancy.[22] But the idea has well-known legal realist origins. Holmes (not, of course, a liberal, just a hero to liberals) is a convenient starting point. In numerous private law and constitutional decisions, he emphasized that the recognition of rights was a matter of degree: of quantity, not quality.[23] No one got recognition of his or her right to the full extent that might be justified by consideration of its definition in the abstract. Where the right of one party ended and that of the other began had to be determined by looking at the consequences of drawing the line in one place rather than another. The mere recognition and definitional statement of the right (free speech, property) was inadequate because it would seem to justify more for the claiming party than was consistent with equally well-established rights claims of the other side.

This kind of formulation fit the scientistic, antimetaphysical, relativist, pragmatist biases of realism. But it was given a kind of bite that survives the biases by Hohfeld's insight that the word "right" sometimes means a privilege to hurt someone without having to pay and sometimes means a claim to be compensated when hurt. When we talk about property, in particular, we are referring to a collection of rules some of which authorize injury and others of which forbid it. Whenever there is a gap, conflict, or ambiguity in property law, one side can invoke all the rules in the "bundle" that suggest protection, and the other the rules in the bundle that suggest freedom of action.[24]

Learned Hand, who saw himself as a devoted follower of Holmes and Hohfeld, proposed balancing tests in a series of contexts, including the law of unfair competition, antitrust, the definition of negligence, and the definition of free-speech rights threatening to national security.[25] For Hand, as for Holmes and Hohfeld, the move to balancing was initially part of the liberal critical project, because he saw overt judicial balancing as formal acknowledgment that judges decide questions of policy without any methodology that distinguishes them from legislators.

If that is what judges do, there is less basis than there would otherwise be for judges to overrule legislatures. Indeed, if judges can't decide constitutional questions without balancing, one can ask why their balance, their views of policy, should prevail over those of the elected representatives of the people. If balancing means looking in detail at the consequences of drawing the line in one place rather than another, then it would seem that judges are less "institutionally competent" to the task than legislators.[26]

The realist position was that interpretive fidelity just "runs out" in many (not all) cases because they involve conflicts for which there is no resolution other than balancing. In other words, the emergence of balancing was an extension of the basic minimalist critical routine: given the internal critique of extant attempts at determinative legal reasoning, many questions of law can be resolved only by looking at them as questions of policy that will evoke differing responses according to one's ideology.

This extension of the critique did not necessarily produce loss of faith in constitutional rights. The emergence of balancing occurred in an odd and complex context. Balancing was initially liberal because, in private law (right against right), it undermined the claim of judicial objectivity and, in public law (right against power), it undermined the legitimacy of the Supreme Court's protection of property rights against progressive legislation. As such, it was not antirights but only anti–property rights. At the same time that the liberal Court was drawing most clearly the conclusion that questions of economic regulation were so "legislative" that it was inappropriate to interfere, the self-same liberals were gearing up for the defense of human rights, through the *Carolene Products* footnote, *Powell v. Alabama,* "picketing as free speech," and the flag salute cases.[27]

Balancing and the Conservative Critique of Liberal Rights Claims. When the Democrats gained control of the Supreme Court in the New Deal, their legal realist appointees developed a new body of constitutional law doctrine that glorified legislative power. The Supreme Court exploited the gaps, conflicts, and ambiguities of legal rights doctrine, plus the power to overrule its own decisions, to make legal reasoning a principal support of legislative supremacy.[28] The realist critique of adjudication—that it often involves policy choices, which amount to value judgments that are ideologically contested—was an important element in the argument for this turn.

But once the liberals were in control, and fascism and Stalinism emerged as the threat, the realists abandoned the project of internal critique in favor of the more pressing task of managing the new liberal, regulatory, interventionist state. As post-1945 legislatures turned conservative, while liberals retained control of the judiciary, the left intelligentsia went for the adjudicatory empowerment effect. That is, it adopted the position that the federal Constitution enacted a wide range of liberal policy preferences and flatly prohibited a wide range of conservative policy preferences.

One part of this project was to develop the kind of reasoning from individual constitutional rights that liberals had allowed a marginal survival during the period of their attack on constitutionalized property rights. Faced with McCarthyism, police brutality, and conservative gerrymandering, and positively committed to racial justice, the left liberals attacked the jurisprudence of legislative supremacy they themselves had constructed and became civil libertarians with a vengeance.

Another part of the project was to reconstruct the theory of the judicial role, repairing the damage that their parents and grandparents, or they themselves, had done to the mana of the Judge in the process of the storming the robing room. Though some, like Douglas, weren't able to do it with a straight face, the liberal intelligentsia in general followed Herbert Wechsler (neutral principles) or Hugo Black (absolutes), according to taste, in reaffirming the possibility of judicial neutrality and the distinction between law and politics.[29] Here again, balancing was the key.

The initial battle was over the criminalization of the Communist Party. Moderates and conservatives argued that because it was necessary to balance communist free-speech rights against the legislative power to protect national security, and because the balancing process was nothing more than the redoing of the (ideologically charged) policy decision that the legislature had made in passing the statute, the judges should "defer" to the legislature.[30] In short, they used the liberal legal realist critique of judicial activism against the left.

The left liberals answered that the First Amendment was an "absolute," thereby both firmly tying their position to the vindication of individual rights against the state and establishing a basis for nonideological judicial enforcement through adjudication.[31] The conflict played out in a long series of cases. Though the liberals won many of these, "absolutism" did not survive the realist critique.[32] Balancing became a paradigm for constitutional decision in one area after another.

In a second round, the moderates and conservatives critiqued judicial activism in the civil rights era, producing counterrights that had to be balanced against left liberal claims. Wechsler, in his famous article, pointed out that white segregationists were asserting their right of free association with just as much subjective sense of entitlement as the blacks demanding integration. As there was no "neutral principle" by which to decide between the two demands, the judges should have deferred to the legislature.[33] In other words, to assert that the Court should straightforwardly balance in favor of blacks would have been to ask it to usurp legislative power.

The moderates and conservatives also developed another strand of pre–World War II progressive argumentation, that which had favored federal deference to state government regulatory initiatives. Hart and Wechsler's famous casebook, *The Federal Courts in the Federal System,* provided a theory not of states' rights per se but of common interests in the viability of decentralized government.[34] These interests had to be balanced against the rights-based demands of the civil rights movement for intervention against racist Southern government officials and private parties. Once again, the inherently ideological nature of the choice, the necessity of balancing, argued for federal judicial (though not necessarily congressional) deference to state power.

Neither these balancing disputes, nor those in the area of apportionment (right to vote versus states' rights) or regulation of police conduct (suspect's rights versus right of the community to protection from crime), *necessarily* led to loss of faith. Indeed, because the left was usually arguing for a recognized individual constitutional right against a proxy (national security, states' rights, police power) for "rights of the community," it was possible to see each conflict as "good" rights of the individual against "evil" powers of the majority.

Nonetheless, there was something "weakening" or "undermining" about the fact that the liberals were using exactly the rhetoric they had denounced before World War II, about the failure to come up with any alternative to balancing as a methodology for protecting rights, about the very facility they began to feel at inventing new rights (privacy being the most striking case), and about the parallel facility of their opponents at inventing counterrights of one kind or another.[35]

Revalidated Constitutional Rights Reasoning Switches Sides in the 1970s. The violent Southern racist reaction to the civil rights movement, combined with the triumph of the liberals on the Court of the 1960s, had an impact on the critique of rights quite similar to the impact of fascism, Stalinism, and the Roosevelt Court on the realist critique of adjudication. In short, there are no atheists in foxholes.

As I mentioned above, there was a persistent radical 1960s critique of the judiciary as a tool of the Establishment, a critique that fed on every hesitation, compromise, or betrayal by the liberal Supreme Court. It was also grounded in the experiences of local activists, movement lawyers, and legal services lawyers with the arbitrariness or just plain conservatism of local courts of all kinds. But for the liberal ideological intelligentsia, and particularly the legal part of it, these were minor themes compared to the major theme of empowerment through adjudication based on rights claims.

Faith in rights within law fed on the explosion of different popular movements in the 1960s and the 1970s. The "corrosive" effects of the realist critique of conservative property rights and of the conservative critique of 1950s personal rights were internal to the legal intelligentsia. Faith flooded in from outside, at just the moment when liberal lawyers found that their rights arguments had an almost magical effect on the liberal judges with whom they shared the agenda of adjudicatory empowerment.

The dramatic reversal brought about, over fifteen years, by the Burger and Rehnquist Courts changed all this. Conservative judges deployed a new version of rights rhetoric and drew on a new version of conservative white, male, straight, working- and middle-class popular rights culture. The familiar arguments, which had come to seem "correct" in part just because they worked to mobilize the mana of the Judge, stopped persuading. The rights of "victims" gave way to the rights of "perpetrators," perhaps most dramatically in *Bakke* and then across the board.[36] Balancing was everywhere — the left had no alternative — and was everywhere patently an invitation to conservative ideological intervention.

The left in the 1980s was in the position of the right of the 1940s, which had relied for several generations on a rhetoric of property rights that made no careful distinction between natural rights arguments and arguments

based on the Fourteenth Amendment. The right had achieved massive victories in getting the Supreme Court to strike down all kinds of social legislation. In the process, it had woven the natural right to property more and
more tightly together with the constitutional right to property, until the
legal part of the position was much more developed, more coherent, and
more convincing than the "external" part. The left of the 1960s had performed a similar operation with the equal protection clause.

The right in the late 1970s and the 1980s exploited the gaps, conflicts,
and ambiguities in the system of rules, the open texture of the doctrine of
stare decisis, and the semiotic, formulaic, pro/con character of policy argument to cut back and dismantle the liberal victories much as the liberals had
done with the conservative victories of forty years earlier. Of course, it was
possible to interpret this trend, yet again, as no more than the triumph of
vice over virtue. But the demonstration, yet again, of the manipulability of
rights arguments back and forth across the political spectrum provided yet
another context for the loss of faith.

The Internal Disintegration of Left Rights Rhetoric. In the late 1970s
and the 1980s, at the same time that the left legal intelligentsia was constructing its version of the 1960s as a constitutional rights revolution, organizers, activist lawyers, and theorists all began to come up against a kind of
rights-overkill problem. Rights for gays, old people, mentally retarded,
Native Americans, children, mental patients, animals, prison inmates, endangered species, the handicapped, prostitutes, crime victims, people with
AIDS all made sense, if what one meant by each of them was the specific
program of law reform in favor of the group in question. But remember
that the whole point of adopting rights rhetoric was to get beyond or
outside the posture of the mere ideological or interest group demanding
something on policy grounds. The more rights there were, and the more
particularly defined their various classes of bearers, the harder it became to
conceptualize them as universal.

Left thinking evolved in reaction to internal debates about the content of
these "proliferating" rights claims, whether phrased in terms of equality
within the legal order or in terms of substantive rights to freedom of action.
The most striking of the equality debates addressed "equal treatment versus
special treatment" within the feminist legal community. A series of efforts
to use the notion of a right to equal treatment as the basis for a program of
law reform ran up against the classic problem of deciding between formal

and substantive equality as the content of the right. Inasmuch as the debate had an outcome, it seemed to be that rights definition should proceed ad hoc, through something very like balancing.[37]

The equivalent in the black community was the dispute about whether equal protection meant affirmative action in the form of integration or in the form of development of black institutions. In such contexts as schools and housing projects, it seemed that the price of integration would be subjection to unending white racial hostility, acceptance of white social norms, and the loss of black power and opportunity within the integrated settings.[38] At the same time, a black conservative movement began to challenge affirmative action in general, arguing for a definition of the right to equal protection as formal equality.[39]

The substantive branch of identity/rights doctrine has to do with a newly formed identity-based group demanding its rights. The group typically demands lifting of restrictions on its characteristic, identity-defining activities, affirmative governmental support for the group's interests, and the imposition of restrictions on other individuals or groups that are attempting to suppress the newly asserted identity. Thus the left supports the pregnant woman's right to abortion over the right to life of the fetus, and the right to engage in consensual adult homosexual intercourse over the community's right to prohibit what it views as evil conduct.

But then there are splits about whether the woman's right to abort excludes any rights at all for the father, about whether the state should suppress Nazi or Klan neighborhood marches, pornography, and racist and sexist speech on campus. Leftists who combine antistate libertarian commitments with cultural pluralist commitments find themselves constantly balancing freedom-of-action rights against security rights.[40]

Finally, there is the problem of "intersectionality": rights that supposedly flow from a particular group identity may be oppression for subgroups that have a cross-cutting allegiance. For example, black feminists face the nationalist assertion of a black male right to "discipline" black women and of a black community right to freedom from majority or state interference with this practice.[41]

In white feminism, first came the argument that Equal Rights Amendment advocates were denying or attempting to suppress more "traditional" forms of female identity, then that white feminists had defined female identity in essentially white terms, and then that cultural feminists in the antipornography movement were abridging the rights of pro-sex or sex-radical women to read and write erotica. These quarrels were totalized by post-modern feminists under the banner of antiessentialism and given added bite when gay men began to challenge the monolithic cultural feminist construction of male identity.[42]

For some, the project of identifying identities and then defining rights to protect them, in their freedom to engage in defining practices, in claims on public resources, and in protection against discrimination, began to seem a pipe dream. One might lose faith in it as a project, without losing enthusiasm for cultural pluralism or for one's particular list of law reform proposals, just because the process of deciding what the rights were was no different from general policy analysis. The project of identity rights looks uncomfortably like the nineteenth-century project of guaranteeing "everyone's right of freedom of action as long as they don't interfere with the security rights of others," or *sic utere tuo ut alienum non laedas*.

But, once again, there was nothing inevitable about this interpretation of intraleft conflict, any more than there was in the unwinding of nineteenth-century rights faith.

■

Although I have no theory of loss of faith, I would hazard the hypothesis that in the legal context "erosion," "undermining," "unraveling," and "contagion" are likely to be precipitated by the spectacle of reversal: the antirights arguments of the old left used by the new right, the left occupying the exact position of the earlier right. This kind of flip by the two opposing camps undermines belief in the technique in question in a way that criticizing something that is simply analytically incoherent and politically incorrect doesn't. I wonder how abolitionist litigators dealt with their own dramatic shift, from nationalists to states' rights advocates, after the Fugitive Slave Law put the federal government on the side of the South against resisting Northern state governments.

Another hypothesis is that it is undermining to experience the unexpected disintegration of an apparently robust rights discourse within one's own camp. In both the 1950s and the 1980s, a discourse understood unproblematically as a righteous weapon against the wrong thought of enemies suddenly foundered on the inability to convince one's supposed allies that a particular right was good rather than bad.

Does the flattening of constitutional rights argument into policy argument have any relevance to the outside rights that are supposedly "behind" or translated by legal enactment? Yes, because the loss of faith in reasoning about legal rights raises the question of whether one can still have faith in the normative rights project carried on outside legal discourse. If the inside discourse, the translation, is "mere rhetoric," under constant suspicion of ideological partisanship, then isn't that likely to be the case for the "outside," "original" text as well?

The critique shows only that there is often no difference between an argument that you have a constitutional right to x, y, or z, and an argument that on general moral, political, utilitarian, or institutional competence grounds it would be better overall for the legal system to intervene on your side. It does not show that there is no valid procedure for reasoning from rights as prelegal entities to conclusions about what law should be. This was the mode of reasoning of those abolitionists who saw the Constitution as a pro-slavery, hence immoral document. They were antilegalists but in no sense critical of rights.

Moreover, it is still possible to believe that one chooses one's intralegal rhetorical posture by reference to the extra- or prelegal element in constitutional rights discourse. Advocates making constitutional rights arguments can go on believing that the part that is outside, existing prior to the legalization of the right in the Constitution, has a kind of reality quite different from the reality of the right understood as incorporated into positive law and subject to all the mechanisms of legal interpretation.

If you can be correct about the outside right, it isn't so bad to have to give up the objectivity of legal rights reasoning. You can be extremely "legal realist" or even "nihilistic" about law but still believe that correct reasoning from rights solves ethical problems. The point, then, is just to get judges who will manipulate the plastic substance of legal reason to achieve the results that are correct in terms of outside rights.

Or you can believe in the correctness of the outside rights judgments but believe that these judgments are "in the abstract." They may have to be modified "in practice" by the kinds of nonrights considerations typically raised in legal reasoning: utilitarian or institutional competence constraints, for example.[43]

But if the inside/outside divide is breached, and the critical spirit gets applied to the outside rights, there may be trouble. Given the content of the critique of constitutional rights, there is little reason to hope that either fancy theory or lay rights discourse will be able to sustain their extralegal normative claims.

CRITIQUE OF THE LAY DISCOURSE OF RIGHTS

In lay discourse, the word "right" is used in all the ways it is used in constitutional discourse. There is, to begin, a strictly legal positive usage: "Women have no rights in Iran"; "There was no right of free speech in Stalin's Russia." Rights just means rules in force to protect particular interests. But the word is also used in lay legal argument about what the U.S. courts should do about particular statutes or executive actions. The speaker assumes the existence of a "straddling" constitutional right and reasons from it to a conclusion, deploying some version of the standard legal interpretive techniques, including precedent (consistency) and moral, utilitarian, institutional competence and administrability arguments.

Lay discourse also uses rights in self-consciously legislative argument, with the issue no longer interpretive fidelity but rather what people with law-"making" (as opposed to law-interpreting) authority ought to do. Here is an example:

> Civil libertarians shriek about the right to privacy of those infected with AIDS. To me, Kimberly Bergalis had more a right to live than her dentist had to privacy. In the balancing act, there is no contest. But it is important to protect those who test positive with strong antidiscrimination laws.
>
> Those opposed to mandatory testing argue that the risk of patients contracting AIDS from workers is very low, that workers are more likely to contract AIDS from patients. So why not test all patients who are to undergo "invasive" procedures, while at the same time testing health care workers who perform such procedures? Protect everyone, rather than no one.[44]

In this passage, the writer treats rights argument very much as would a lawyer disabused of the sense that "rights are trumps." Rights conflict; they are quantitatively rather than qualitatively powerful; they have to be balanced; how we do the balancing depends on the practical context and on nonrights arguments about things like the degree of harm that will flow from different resolutions of the conflict.

The same presuppositions may underlie statements such as "There is a conflict between privacy rights and free-speech rights"; "The statute gives inadequate recognition to the right of free speech"; "The statute should have recognized a free-speech right"; "We should recognize a right of privacy"; "Our society has a consensus in favor of a right of privacy"; "This is an attempt to cut back the right of privacy"; "We have to find a way to reconcile landlords' rights with tenants' rights."

The justifying role of rights here is ambiguous. The speaker might go on to explain that the reason the statute gave inadequate recognition to free speech was that free speech is an interest more important than the interest in, say, national security, that there were other ways to achieve the national security objective, that the resolution gives courts too much power, and so on. Rights then function as no more than interests (perhaps with an exclamation point). Because the discourse treats rights arguments as no more than policy arguments, they perform no mediating function, produce no transcendence of the fact/value or law/politics divides, as those are commonly presupposed in the discourse.

The same is true of explanations like "We should establish a right of privacy to safeguard people from unreasonable searches" or "to assure a woman control over her reproductive life." Here, the idea is to change a legal rule by inserting a right concept, but the reason given is to change a state of affairs defined otherwise than in terms of violation of the right. If you have lost your faith in the mediating power of legal rights discourse, having come to experience it as no more than a form of ideologically permeable policy talk, then you are not likely to see these forms of lay discourse as any different.

Sometimes laypeople appeal to fully outside rights without employing either positivist legal reasoning or legislative policy argument. The rights claim is intended to be something more than just a claim about what is politically and morally best. The speaker seems to presuppose that it is more "objective" or "absolute" or "conclusive," that it is possible to "be right" about it, to make a "correct" argument, in a way that differentiates it from other kinds of claims: "Banning abortion is wrong because it denies a woman's right to control over her own body"; "Rent control is wrong because it denies the landlord's right to private property."[45]

When challenged, the speaker may quickly turn to defense of the right in the normal legislative way, offering all kinds of arguments as to why a legal decision maker should agree (institutional competence: it should be up to the woman rather than the court to decide; social welfare: back-alley abortions will increase and are an unacceptable cost). When this happens, it reemerges that the right is a "value judgment," supported by a rhetoric, perhaps a rhetoric one finds utterly convincing but without the mediating power promised in the initial formulation.

When the speaker sticks to unadulterated rights talk, the problem is that the assertion is conclusory. The speaker seems unaware that *there is a counterright* that can be asserted in the same tone of voice and that cancels out the first right. I may be missing the existence of a lay rights discourse that avoids this pitfall without slipping into mere balancing. But my own experience has been that the critique of constitutional rights reasoning has spread corrosively from legal to lay discourse.

It is not, not at all, that someone has proved that rights "do not exist" or that they are "nonsense on stilts." It is not a question of proof. It is a question of mediation: of whether one gets any more from rights talk than from social welfare or morality or administrability talk.

FROM THE CRITIQUE OF CONSTITUTIONAL RIGHTS TO RECONSTRUCTIVE PROJECTS IN POLITICAL THEORY

That we don't find convincing rights talk in popular discourse doesn't mean it can't be done convincingly somewhere else. The whole function of fancy theory is to show that it is possible to construct rights arguments, using the most sophisticated philosophical apparatus, that will validate left-wing popular assertions of rights. Here the problem is not that the discourse is conclusory, but that it has the same sophisticated indeterminate quality as legal reasoning, at a less complex and interesting level.

There are an infinite variety of possible nonlegal, purely rights-oriented defenses of statements like "A woman has a right to reproductive freedom and therefore a right to abort her fetus." Without ever straying into obviously contestable utilitarian or institutional competence or "mere value judgment" arguments for the asserted right, fancy theorists can try an indefinite number of strategies to achieve closure or, if not closure, something a lot better than mere political rhetoric.

I would say about this enterprise what I have said elsewhere about the closely analogous, indeed overlapping enterprise of showing how judges can decide cases according to a method of legal reasoning that is not mere policy.[46] On the one hand, as a minimalist, I don't believe it has been shown that it is impossible to do a successful argument from outside rights or even to reconstruct the discourse. On the other hand, the last time I looked into it, it seemed as though critics of each particular rights argument from fancy theory are still managing to show, for one contender after another, that it doesn't quite work on its own terms.[47]

At some point, one just loses the energy to do another internal critique. *You can't prove it can't be done.* Conceded. Therefore, it is possible that the most recent contender is successful. But you don't believe anyone has done it in the past, and don't believe anyone is likely to do it in the future, and it seems like a waste of time to take up each new challenge in turn. In short, the project of reconstructing outside rights through political philosophy is another context for loss of faith.

THINGS THE CRITIQUE OF RIGHTS IS NOT
People sometimes say, "A critique of rights? But if you get rid of rights, then the state could do anything it wanted to you! What about the right of privacy? We wouldn't have any way to object to state intrusion!" They are just missing the point!

In the Western democracies, rights "exist" in the sense that there are legal rules limiting what peole can do to one another and limiting the executive and the legislature. The critique of rights recognizes the reality of rule-making, rule-following, and rule-enforcing behavior. It is about faith in the rational procedures through which legislators, adjudicators, and enforcers elaborate gaps, conflicts, and ambiguities in the "text" of inside or outside rights.

There is nothing in the critique that might suggest a reduction in the rights of citizens vis-à-vis their governments. Having lost one's faith in rights discourse is perfectly consistent with, indeed often associated with, a passionate belief in radical expansion of citizen rights against the state. Moreover, loss of faith is consistent with advocacy of greatly increased tenant rights in dealings with landlords, as well as with the reverse, just as it is consistent with favoring more or less government control over abortion decisions. It is not about the question of what legal rules we should enact to define the limits of conflicting rights claims, but rather about how we should feel about the discourse through which we argue those limits back and forth.

When people want to claim things from the legal system, they put their demands into rights language, as they once put them in religious language.[48] But rights are more than just a language — or we might say that, like any language, rights talk does more and less than translate a clear and constant meaning from one medium to another. Rights talk was the language of the group — the white male bourgeoisie — that cracked open and reconstituted the feudal and then mercantilist orders of Western Europe, and did it in the name of Reason. The mediating power of the language, based on the presupposition of fact/value and law/politics distinctions and on the universal and factoid character of rights, was a part of the armory of this group, along with the street barricade, the newspaper, and the new model family.

Since the bourgeois revolutions, one group after another has defined its struggle for inclusion in the social, economic, and political order as a rational demand for enjoyment of the same rights of freedom and equality that belong to a postulated "normal," "abstract" citizen in a bourgeois democracy. An important part of the struggle between liberals and conservatives in these societies has been over how far to go in incorporating those not included in the initial Liberal formulation of the Rights of Man into the order the revolutions established for a select few.

There has been a connection between rights language and the acquisition by these oppressed groups of an identity in the subjective sense. Rights talk has been connected to daring to claim things on a basis that might previously have been disqualifying, to claiming things *for* blacks, women, gays, or Hispanics, when the feeling before might have been that *because* one was one of these things one was disentitled to make claims. (I think it is as easy to exaggerate as to underplay the role of rights talk — as opposed to religious or moral or just rebellious or even acquisitive discourse — in popular rebellions against oppressive circumstances. And it is not at all clear to me that oppressed groups needed rights talk to know that they were oppressed.)

The critique is not an assertion that these demands for inclusion, for acceptance as equals by the dominant groups in these societies are wrong or misguided. It is certainly not an assertion that they should chasten their rights rhetoric, when it operates effectively, to suit the evolution of belief within a fraction of the white left intelligentsia. But, in its minimalist form, it "applies" to excluded groups as they have defined themselves on the left since the 1960s, as much as it applied to the white male working class of the nineteenth century, to which Marx originally addressed it.

MARX'S CRITIQUE OF RIGHTS

The Marxist origin of the critique of rights lies in the project of showing that the inclusion of the proletariat in the regime of the Liberal Rights of Man did not end illegitimate domination of that class. Its first point was that if, under capitalism, you had all the revolutionary freedoms and strictly equal civil and political rights, you would also have, through the very economic mechanism defined and protected by those rights — the "free market" — exploitation even to the point of death.[49]

Its second point was that rights were by their very structure, their definition as "trumps" against the claims of others, immoral, because they were based on the idea that the invoker of the right can disregard the wishes, over some subject-matter domain, of the people under the duty corresponding to the right. This was Marx's utopian communist critique of Lasallean "equal rights" socialism, quite distinct from the positive analysis of how the property and contract system necessarily worked under capitalist conditions. It was an argument about how to conceptualize a good society. Specifically, it was an antiformalist assertion of the priority of consensus, sharing, and sacrifice over *any* assertion (group or individual) of the legitimacy of ignoring a person affected by one's actions.[50]

Though they are important origins, neither the first nor the second point is implicit in the minimalist internal critique of rights. Marx's necessitarian model of the evolution of capitalism proves vulnerable to the same kind of internal critique that subverts faith in legal reasoning or rights reasoning.[51] As to the second point, the minimalist internal critique and the posture of loss of faith do not suggest an alternative faith that, because human nature is intrinsically "good," we can do without coercion. If the critique suggests anything, it is the constant possibility of undermining or "corroding" *any* faith in the derivation of a utopian scheme from a theory of human nature.

It is an expression of loss of faith in the possibility of conclusively formulating or even of initially deciding on substantive demands through a "logic" or an "analytic" or a "reasoned elaboration" of rights. It is an attack on the claim that rights mediate between fact and value, the rational and the subjective, the political and the legal, law and policy. It is a posture of distance from a particular attitude of some people, some of the time, when they are demanding things from within the liberal order *and* when they are demanding inclusion from a position of exclusion and oppression. The distance comes from loss of faith in the presupposed rational character of the project of rights definition.

There was a third element in Marx's critique. The Liberal constitutional regimes that emerged from the bourgeois revolutions fostered, he argued, a particular kind of false consciousness. He saw Liberalism as based on the fantasy that, by the exercise of universally valid political rights (voting, speech), we participated in a benign collective process of guaranteeing our universally valid private rights (property and contract). It is these rights that define the capitalist mode of production, and their enforcement, their entrenchment in the Liberal constitutions guarantees that real life in "civil society" will operate according to principles of selfishness and exploitation that are the exact opposite of those proclaimed in political theory.[52]

But there is no more a legal logic to Liberal rights than there is an economic logic to capitalism. For this reason, Marx's presentation of the selfishness and exploitation of civil society as necessary consequences of abstract property and contract rights seems seriously wrong. But his psychological analysis of the public/private distinction and of rights consciousness retains its power, at least for me. His notion was that the belief in universal political rights functioned, together with the belief in universal private rights, as a fantasy resolution of our contradictory experience of being, at once, altruistic collective and selfish individual selves. At the same time, the fantasy performed, for the beneficiaries of capitalism, the apologetic function of explaining why they were entitled to the profits they derived from exploiting the propertyless.

I don't think it plausible that rights consciousness, in and of itself, plays either an intrinsically progressive or an intrinsically conservative role in our current politics. But, from my postrights perspective, and with deference to believers, I do think the view of rights as universal and factoid, and so outside or above politics, involves denial of the kind Marx analyzed. As with the denial of the ideological in adjudication, there are many ways to theorize the conflicts that give rise to this particular form of (what seems to me) wishful thinking.[53] And, as with adjudication, psychologizing denial involves suspending dialogue with those for whom the reality of rights is close to tangible.

WHY DO IT?
In part for these reasons, leftists engaged in the rights debate, myself included, often feel that it is dangerous. I don't mean now to critique an argument but to describe an emotion. The discussants may be willing to confront the critique and take in good faith the risk of loss of faith. But isn't

it an experience we should all wish to avoid if that were only possible? To begin with, if "we" lose our belief in rights, we may be disarmed in dealing with our opponents. The notion is that rights rhetoric is or at least once was effective, and we would be giving that up by losing faith in rights.

Of course, it is not an argument in favor of rights that rights rhetoric "works." The critique is not about effectiveness, though possibly useful in understanding effectiveness.[54] One can lose one's faith in an utterly effective rhetoric and keep it in a rhetoric that practically no one seems to find plausible. And it is not a response to the critique of rights rhetoric that everyone uses it, or that our heroes or our parents used it, any more than it is a critique of rights that conservatives used or use them to great effect.

But to explain the sense of danger, one might respond that if "we" lose our faith in rights rhetoric but "they" don't, then they will gain an advantage over us. This is plausible to the extent that the "we" in question derives some measure of power, in confrontation with "them," from the sense of righteousness, of mediation, that rights have historically provided. "Giving up" rights would be like a professional athlete giving up steroids when all his or her competitors were still wedded to them.

If you have *already* lost your faith in rights, the argument has the sound of that in favor of religious faith for the masses, no matter how delusive, on the ground of its beneficial consequences. Yet if we are really talking about effectiveness, it seems merely conjectural.

My own experience has been that some people who lose faith in rights become more politically committed, some become less, and some stay the same. Some switch sides, and some gain rhetorical astuteness in dealing with the good faith, bad faith, or cynical rights arguments of opponents, becoming more powerful rather than less. Many committed leftists, including most of those in the anarcho-Marxist, or Western Marxist, or neo-Marxist anti-Stalinist tradition, today and yesterday, never had faith in rights to begin with. If we are speaking of actual, empirical effects, I think it's hard to make the case one way or another.

Rights are not the "core" or "centerpiece" or "heart" of Liberal legalism, either as an ideology or as a social formation generating a complex mix of happiness and unhappiness, legitimacy and oppression. The prevailing consciousness doesn't have, to my mind, a heart or a core. It is an enormously plastic, loose congeries of ideas, each of which appears from moment to moment to have the force of many army divisions and then no force at all—from Gramscian hegemony to Emily Litella's "Never mind." The critique of rights, even when totally convincing, is a good deal less "effective" than it seems from the position of threatened faith.

But there is an aspect of the sense of danger that I want to acknowledge as rationally grounded. Undermining faith in rights threatens to undermine the unity of the left and its sense of inclusion in "American citizenship." If some of the left have lost faith in rights, and others have not, then those who have will face a constant dilemma, forced to choose between arguing with those who haven't, keeping silent, or engaging in cynical or bad faith manipulation of the discourse within the movement.

Given that the critique is not a solution to any problem of the left, not a panacea or a program, given that the consequences for militancy and commitment are at best uncertain and at worst disastrous, why do it?

Why Do It?

Leftism aims to transform existing social structures on the basis of a critique of their injustice and, specifically, the injustices of racist, capitalist patriarchy. The goal is to replace the system, piece by piece or in medium- or large-size blocs, with a better system. Modernism/postmodernism is a critique of the characteristic forms of rightness of this same culture and aims at liberation from inner and outer experiences of constraint by reason, in the name, not of justice and a new system, but of the dialectic of system and antisystem, mediated by transgressive artifacts that paradoxically reaffirm the "higher" forms of the values they seem to traduce.

Critique is always motivated. The practitioners of the critique of rights have often had mixed motives of the kind I am describing here. One motive is leftist and the other is mpm. Suppose for the moment that one didn't have to worry about the leftist implications: What would be mpm motives for a critique of rights? The answer is that belief in rights and in the determinacy of rights reasoning is an important part of the overall project of bourgeois rightness, or reason, or the production of texts that will compel impersonally.

For the mpm project, the demand for agreement and commitment on the basis of representation with the pretension to objectivity is an enemy. The specific enemies have been the central ethical/theoretical concepts of bourgeois culture, including God, the autonomous individual choosing self, convention morality, the family, manhood and womanhood, the nation-state, humanity. But the central ethical/theoretical concepts of the left have also been targets, including the proletariat, class solidarity, party discipline and socialist realism, and, more recently, sexual and racial identity.

The mpm impulse is to counter or oppose the producers of these artifacts with other artifacts. The transgressive artifacts are supposed to put in question the claims of rightness and, at the same time, induce a set of emotions—irony, despair, ecstasy, and so on—that are crushed or blocked when we are experiencing the text or representation as "right."

If we define the left project as the struggle for a more egalitarian and communitarian society, it is not intrinsically connected to rightness in any particular form. But within the left project it has always been true that rightness has played a central role. Leftism has been a bourgeois cultural project within which many leaders and many followers have believed that they were not just left but also right, in the strong sense of possessing coherent and complete ("totalizing") descriptive and prescriptive analyses of the social order.

Of course, critique has been crucial to the dominant "rightness" faction of leftism—that is, critique as ground-clearing for the erection of new edifices of rightness. In the Marxist tradition, the slogan of the "scientificity" of Marxism was the repository of the impulse to be right. For the non-Marxist left, the slogans of "planning," "rational social policy," and "the public interest" played the same role. But in the United States by the end of the 1970s, with the rise of identity politics, left discourse merged with liberal discourse, and the two ideas of the rights of the oppressed and the constitutional validity of their legal claims superseded all earlier versions of rightness.

Moreover, in the diffuse general culture of the bourgeoisie, the rule of law and rights seem to function as crucial paradigms of rightness for everyone. There has been a kind of concentration of experiences of rightness into the two contrasts of law versus politics and rights versus mere preferences. Finally, in the specialized legal academic culture of the United States, legal discourse in general and rights discourse in particular underwent an aborted or perhaps just compromised, modernist revolution in the 1930s, but after World War II, legal culture as a whole seemed to slide backward into a combination of resurgent formalism with a reified version of policy analysis.

Remember that we are assuming, just for the moment, that it is possible to pursue the mpm project without hurting the left project of change in an egalitarian and communitarian direction. A person with mpm aspirations would "naturally" choose rights and rights reasoning as targets and try to counter or oppose the demand of leftists for agreement and commitment based on correct legal reasoning from the existence of rights. And such a project would have a larger mpm appeal to the extent that the rule of law and rights have become prime vehicles of rightness for the whole society.

The mpm counter to rights and the rule of law looks, at first, like the more traditional mode of left theory, based, say, on the model of alienated powers. It deploys internal critique to loosen the sense of closure or necessity that legal and rights analyses try to generate. But rather than putting a new theory in place, it looks to induce, through the artifactual construction of the critique, the modernist emotions associated with the death of reason: ecstasy, irony, depression, and so forth. It is aimed at the pleasure of shedding Reason's dead skin. All the same, it can be leftist in two senses: when it is carried out by people who see themselves as doing to leftism what mpm artists see themselves as doing to "art," that is, moving it along by attacking its presuppositions and opening it up to what it wants to deny; and when it proposes that the left should confront those with whom it is ideologically engaged through transgressive artifacts as well as (or instead of) rational analysis.

THE PROJECT OF RECONSTRUCTION

It was once the case that the answer to left/mpm was a theory, whether Marxism or Liberalism. That is no longer the case, at least in the academic left. The answer to left/mpm is rather a charge, the charge of "nihilism," a critique of the bad consequences of nihilism, and a project: reconstruction.

Sometimes the author has a specific reconstruction in mind and presents it full blown as the next step after critique, as something to replace what has been critiqued. When this is the case, the only fair response is to critique it in its turn, subscribe to it, or just ignore it. More often, the author proposes *the project of reconstruction* rather than any particular reconstruction. One favors the project not because one has a proposal but because one believes that we ought to have one, or at least be trying to have one, that bad consequences will follow if we fail to develop one, and that there are at least some interesting possibilities, some hopeful avenues, some useful bits and pieces available for the task.

A striking aspect of calls for reconstruction is that the author not uncommonly treats critiques as decisive refutations of previous theories. An important trope is the suggestion that critique is easy, whereas reconstruction is hard, that it is self-indulgently pleasant to go on trashing one thing after another because we all know how to do it, but morally bracing to roll up our sleeves and get down to the less fashionable but in the long run more constructive task of reconstructing.

A second striking aspect is that the same reconstructionist who asserts the validity of prior critiques and claims that they are easy to do is likely to explicitly or implicitly call for reconstructions that will perform just the same function that was performed by the critiqued entities. This is the function of representing social order in a way that would allow us to have assurance that we are right to be left and right to pursue particular strategies in favor of equality and community.

This form of endorsement of critique doesn't problematize the category of theory. Quite the contrary: critique is in the service of ultimate rightness, and the call for reconstruction is an affirmation of faith in theory as a way of rightness. The project of reconstruction (as opposed to any particular proposal) looks, from a left/mpm point of view, like the reification or fetishism of theory, in a mode parallel to the fetishism of God, the market class, law, and rights. Left/mpm, by contrast, is caught up for better or worse in the "viral" progress of critique, and inasmuch as there is a lesson from the progress of the virus it would seem to be to anticipate loss of faith in theory in general and general theory in particular. But I hasten to add once again that losing faith in theory doesn't mean giving up doing theory — it just means giving up the expectation of rightness in the doing.

It will come as no surprise that I don't think I can demonstrate that reconstruction is impossible. But, as usual, I do think something can be said about the rational side of faith. Here, as elsewhere, as in the case of God, legal correctness, and rights, reconstructionists urge us to believe in and strive for reconstruction because there would be many bad consequences of its failure or impossibility, such as that we wouldn't have assurance either in our leftism or in our particular leftist strategies, that we would become totalitarians, and so forth. Although I don't think these are the real issues, I'll address them as best I can.

NIHILISM

Mpm critique, the induction of loss of faith and characteristic associated emotions, seen as a project, negates a particular experience, that of rightness, in favor of another experience. When it comes to "deciding" whether or not to be a leftist, this project has nothing to offer. Because of these commitments, to critique and loss of faith, without commitment to providing other forms of rightness in the place of what it dissolves, it is common to describe it as nihilist. And it is well-known that nihilism is both wrong and of evil tendency.

There is something odd about this argument. It seems to presuppose that we prefer error to enlightenment when enlightenment is at the cost of beliefs that seemed useful when we still believed in them. Why wouldn't we welcome the critique, no matter how left/mpm its ulterior motive, as long as, after hearing it, we were no longer convinced of the truth of our previous view?

Critique doesn't leave us with "nothing," in the sense of making it impossible to decide what to do, say, whether or not to be a leftist, or of making it impossible to figure out enough about how the social order works to choose a strategy of left action within it. Those of us who are not moral realists (believers in the objective truth of moral propositions) are used to committing ourselves to projects and deciding on strategies on the basis of a balancing of conflicting ethical and practical considerations. In the end, we make the leap into commitment or action. That we don't believe we can demonstrate the correctness of our choices doesn't make us nihilists, at least not in our own eyes.

We misunderstand internal critique if we imagine that it might lead to a situation in which we had lost faith in "everything," so that we just wouldn't know what to believe in or do. Critique changes our attitude toward a particular theory (whichever we successfully critique) that generated a particular sentiment of rightness. It leaves us, in the way of tools for working out our commitments and our concrete plans for the future, whatever we had before that theory and its critique. It seems odd to me to suppose that we could ever, conceivably, be without resources of this kind, even if each of us were a veritable Hercules of critical destruction.

Of course, a person might be committed to egalitarianism only because of belief in rights, and in particular rights. The loss of faith in rights in general might lead such a person to abandon egalitarianism in favor of another attitude, say, belief in natural inequality, that seemed more plausible when not countered by a particular belief in rights now undermined by critique. But the causal chain might move in the other direction as well: loss of faith in property rights might permit previously thwarted egalitarian sentiments to flower.

It might be possible to make convincing generalizations about the causal tendency of the left/mpm project of critique, loss of faith, and attendant emotions. After the proposal that the tendency is demoralization, the most popular may be that left/mpm leads to Hitler and Stalin. As I understand this argument, it goes something like this. Stalinism and Nazism represent the powerful, irreducible force of evil in human nature. But they inflicted previously unimaginable suffering, degradation, and destruction, far beyond the normal. They were able to do this because they were nihilist, meaning that they denied the validity of fundamental human rights. Nietzsche's cult of the Superman and the moral relativism of Weimar are responsible.

The mirror image: Stalinism and Nazism represent the powerful, irreducible force of evil in human nature. But they inflicted previously unimaginable suffering, degradation, and destruction, far beyond the normal. They were able to do this because they were totalitarian, meaning that they proclaimed the absolute truth of their theories. Therefore, skepticism is the true antidote to the repetition of the Holocaust and the gulag. Hegel's cult of Absolute Reason and blind obedience to authority are responsible.

It may be possible to combine the theory that the evil of the twentieth century was caused by the denial of reason (nihilism) with the theory that it was caused by excessive commitment to reason (totalitarianism). Perhaps on a higher level true believers are nihilists and vice versa. Or perhaps one should be a true believer in fundamental human rights and a nihilist about racist and Marxist theories.

But from the point of view of loss of faith in reason (which is not an impossibility theory about reason), it seems unlikely that either believing or disbelieving in reason in general or in any particular rational construction has this kind of causal power. It seems more likely that belief and denial of reason can each have many different meanings and combine in an infinite number of ways with idiosyncratic or socially constructed attitudes, sentiments, and dispositions. Belief and denial more likely were constitutive but not controlling elements in many forms of collaboration with and opposition to Nazism and Stalinism, rather than elements with a single intrinsic or inherent tendency.

LEFT/MPM AS AN INTERSECTIONAL PROJECT
Left/mpm artifacts are at the intersection of two projects, one leftist and the other mpm. These are designed to play two dramas on this single stage. One idea is to modernize or postmodernize the leftist project, and the other is to

move the world leftward by doing in right-wing forms of rightness. What this means is that there is strategic behavior within the intersection. The mpm part of left/mpm aims to move the left project along rather than to destroy it: allegiance to mpm is no more "absolute" than allegiance to leftism. In ideological struggle/dialogue with the right, we choose our themes/targets with an eye to converting waverers, and avoid themes/targets that can be predicted to demoralize other leftists (would that we were so powerful) when the mpm payoff is small or nonexistent.

In other words, the left, as I am using the term, is a "site" for particular, outward- and inward-looking ideological encounters and coalitions, rather than a set of principles or a program. It is, for me, a "position" as well, by which I mean that I much prefer to hang with liberals, identity politicians, and post-Marxist radicals — however hostile to mpm — rather than with the varieties of right-wing or centrist/mpm types. But it is no more conceivable, to me, to be left through and through than to be mpm through and through.

Notes

1. I use the word "project" here as a term of art, a term of art that is also a fudge. I mean by it a continuous goal-oriented practical activity based on an analysis of some kind (with a textual and oral tradition), but the goals and the analysis are not necessarily internally coherent or consistent over time. It is a collective effort, but all the players can change over time, and people at any given moment can be part of it without subscribing to or even being interested in anything like all its precepts and practical activities. The situated practice part has as much influence on the theory part as vice versa, but the two never fully conform to one another. It isn't a project unless people see it as such, but the way they see it doesn't exhaust what outsiders can say about it.

2. Making and appreciating artifacts are two paths toward transcendent experience, but they regularly upset the theory of the experience. The analytics, which in modernism are always ex post, are incorporated into the performance by postmodernists who emphasize the omnipresence of repressed or denied "primal forces" or "dangerous supplements" and the plasticity of formal media that presuppose that they are not plastic.

3. Cornel West, "The Struggle for America's Soul," *New York Times Book Review* 15 Sept. 1991, 13.

4. See Gary Peller, "Race Consciousness," *Duke Law Journal* (1990): 758.

5. Mark Tushnet, "An Essay on Rights," *Texas Law Review* 62 (1984): 1363; Peter Gabel, "The Phenomenology of Rights Consciousness and the Pact of the Withdrawn Selves," *Texas Law Review* 62 (1984): 1563; Frances Olsen, "Statutory Rape: A Feminist Critique of Rights Analysis," *Texas Law Review* 63 (1984): 387; Duncan Kennedy, "Critical Labor Law Theory: A Comment," *Industrial Relations Law Journal* 4 (1981):

503; Duncan Kennedy, "The Structure of Blackstone's Commentaries," *Buffalo Law Review* 28 (1979): 205.

6. Louis Schwartz, "With Gun and Camera through Darkest CLS Land," *Stanford Law Review* 36 (1984): 247; Phillip Johnson, "Do You Sincerely Want to Be Radical?" *Stanford Law Review* 36 (1984): 247; Staughton Lynd, "Communal Rights," *Texas Law Review* 62 (1984): 1417; Edward Sparer, "Fundamental Human Rights, Legal Entitlements, and the Social Struggle: A Friendly Critique of the Critical Legal Studies Movement," *Stanford Law Review* 36 (1984): 509; Michael Tigar, "The Right of Property and the Law of Theft," *Texas Law Review* 62 (1984): 1443.

7. See Duncan Kennedy, *A Critique of Adjudication [fin de siècle]* (Cambridge, MA: Harvard University Press, 1997), pt. 3.

8. Martha Minow, "Interpreting Rights: An Essay for Robert Cover," *Yale Law Journal* 96 (1987): 1860; Elizabeth Schneider, "The Dialectic of Rights and Politics: Perspectives from the Women's Movement," *New York University Law Review* 61 (1986): 589.

9. Patricia Williams, *The Alchemy of Race and Rights* (Cambridge, MA: Harvard University Press, 1991); Richard Delgado, "The Ethereal Scholar: Does Critical Legal Studies Have What Minorities Want?" *Harvard Civil Rights–Civil Liberties Law Review* 22 (1987): 301; Kimberlé Crenshaw, "Race, Reform, and Retrenchment: Transformation and Legitimation in Antidiscrimination Law," *Harvard Law Review* 101 (1988): 1331.

10. Kennedy, *A Critique of Adjudication*, 135–40.

11. Since the late eighteenth century, there has been a metadiscussion in constitutional law about the proper role of unenacted outside rights. See *Calder v. Bull,* 3 U.S. (3 Dall.) 386 (1798), and *Loan Association v. Topeka,* 87 U.S. (20 Wall.) 655 (1875). Opponents of judicial reasoning from unenacted outside rights have insisted that there is a clear difference between being outside and being inside, and that judges should concern themselves only with the inside. Outside rights don't "really" exist; even if they exist, they are too much open to ideological controversy; even if they exist and are clear, they are not "law."

12. Minow, "Interpreting Rights"; Schneider, "The Dialectic of Rights and Politics"; Gabel, "Phenomenology."

13. Kennedy, *A Critique of Adjudication*, 224–35.

14. Ibid., 191–212.

15. Oliver Wendell Holmes, "The Path of the Law," in *Collected Legal Papers* (Buffalo, NY: William S. Hein, 1985), 181.

16. Henry Terry, "Legal Duties and Rights," *Yale Law Journal* 12 (1903): 185.

17. Wesley Hohfeld, "Fundamental Conceptions as Applied in Judicial Reasoning," *Yale Law Journal* 26 (1917): 710.

18. Compare *Vegelhan v. Guntner,* 167 Mass. 92, 44 N.E. 1077 (1896), with *Hague v. C.I.O.,* 307 U.S. 496 (1939).

19. Louis Brandeis and Charles Warren, "The Right of Privacy," *Harvard Law Review* 4 (1890): 193; *Griswold v. Conn.,* 381 U.S. 479 (1965).

20. Lon Fuller and William Purdue, "The Reliance Interest in Contract Damages," *Yale*

Law Journal 46 (1936–37): 52, 373. Hohfeld is again the most important originator; see his "Fundamental Conceptions."

21. See William W. Fisher III, Morton J. Horwitz and Thomas Reed, eds., *American Legal Realism* (New York: Oxford University Press, 1993) for a collection of classic texts.

22. But see Alexander Aleinikoff, "Constitutional Law in the Age of Balancing," *Yale Law Journal* 96 (1987): 943.

23. *Pa. Coal v. Mahon*, 260 U.S. 393 (1922); *Hadacheck v. Sebastian*, 233 U.S. 394 (1915). See Thomas Grey, "Holmes and Legal Pragmatism," *Stanford Law Review* 41 (1989): 787, 819–20.

24. Hohfeld, "Fundamental Conceptions."

25. *Cheney v. Doris Silk Co.*, 35 F.2d 279 (2d Cir. 1929); *U.S. v. Aluminum Co. of Am.*, 148 F.2d 416 (2d Cir. 1945); *U.S. v. Carroll Towing Co.*, 159 F.2d 169 (2d Cir. 1947); *Dennis v. U.S.*, 182 F.2d 201 (2d Cir. 1950).

26. Learned Hand, *The Bill of Rights* (Cambridge, MA: Harvard University Press, 1958).

27. *U.S. v. Carolene Products*, 304 U.S. 144, 152–153, n. 4 (1938); *Powell v. Alabama*, 287 U.S. 45 (1932); *Hague v. C.I.O.*, 307 U.S. 496 (1939); *W.Va. v. Barnette*, 319 U.S. 624 (1943).

28. William O. Douglas, "Stare Decisis," *Columbia Law Review* 49 (1949): 735.

29. Herbert Wechsler, "Toward Neutral Principles of Constitutional Law," *Harvard Law Review* 73 (1959); Hugo Black, "The Bill of Rights," *New York University Law Review* 35 (1960): 865.

30. *Dennis v. U.S.*, 341 U.S. 494, 543 (1951) (Frankfurter, J., concurring).

31. See, for example, Alexander Meiklejohn, "The First Amendment Is an Absolute," *Supreme Court Review* (1961): 245.

32. See, for example, Erwin Griswold, "Absolute Is in the Dark," *Utah Law Review* 8 (1963): 167; Paul Freund, *The Supreme Court of the United States* (Cleveland: World Publishers, 1961).

33. Wechsler, "Neutral Principles."

34. Henry Hart and Herbert Wechsler, *The Federal Courts in the Federal System* (Brooklyn: Foundation Press, 1953).

35. Three quite different reactions of this general kind are Robert McCloskey, "Economic Due Process and the Supreme Court: An Exhumation and Reburial," *Supreme Court Review* (1962): 34; Jan Deutsch, "Neutrality, Legitimacy, and the Supreme Court: Some Intersections between Law and Political Theory," *Stanford Law Review* 20 (1968): 169; and John Griffiths, "Ideology in Criminal Procedure, or, A Third 'Model' of the Criminal Process," *Yale Law Journal* 79 (1970): 359.

36. *Regents of the University of California v. Bakke*, 438 U.S. 265 (1978).

37. Ann Freedman, "Sex Equality, Sex Difference, and the Supreme Court," *Yale Law Journal* 92 (1983): 913.

38. Derrick Bell, "Serving Two Masters," *Yale Law Journal* 85 (1976): 470.

39. See the discussion of Thomas Sowell in Crenshaw, "Race, Reform and Retrenchment," 1339–46.

40. Thomas Grey, "Discriminatory Harassment and Free Speech," *Harvard Journal of Law and Public Policy* 14 (1991): 157.

41. Kimberlé Crenshaw, "Mapping the Margins: Identity Politics, Intersectionality, and Violence against Women," *Stanford Law Review* 43 (1991): 1241.

42. Martha Minow, "The Supreme Court, October 1986 Term, Foreword: Justice Engendered," *Harvard Law Review* 101 (1987): 10; Mary Joe Frug, *Post-Modern Legal Feminism* (New York: Routledge, 1992).

43. Even if, for one of these reasons, the realist critique of legal rights reasoning isn't very threatening to the belief that there are universal human rights, it should still be plenty threatening to the idea that identifying them in the abstract will get you away from the kind of "value judgment" that you invented them to avoid. This doesn't seem to have occurred to political philosophers outside law, but it is close to an obsession, in the form of the "countermajoritarian difficulty," of American jurisprudence.

44. Bella English, "Keeping Rights in Perspective," *Boston Globe* 22 July 1991, sect. 2, p. 13.

45. "I can engage in homosexual intercourse because I have a right to sexual freedom"; "I can organize a PAC with corporate contributions because I have a right to free speech"; "Slavery is wrong because it denies the inalienable rights of life, liberty, and property"; "Nondisclaimable strict products liability is wrong because it denies the right of freedom of contract"; "Compulsory membership in a labor union is wrong because it denies the right of free association; the banning of strikes is wrong because it denies the right to strike"; "The banning of the sale of contraceptives is wrong because it violates the right to privacy."

46. Kennedy, *A Critique of Adjudication,* chaps. 4, 5.

47. An exemplary critique of this kind is Jeremy Paul, "Book Review," *Michigan Law Review* 88 (1990): 1622 (review of Jeremy Waldron, *The Right to Private Property*).

48. Minow, "Interpreting Rights"; Schneider, "The Dialectic of Rights and Politics."

49. Karl Marx, *Capital: A Critique of Political Economy*, vol. 1, trans. Ben Fowkes (New York: Vintage Books, 1977).

50. Karl Marx, *Critique of the Gotha Program* (Moscow: Progress Publishers, 1971).

51. Kennedy, *A Critique of Adjudication,* chap. 11.

52. Karl Marx, "On the Jewish Question," in *Writings of the Young Marx on Philosophy and Society,* ed. and trans. Lloyd Easton and Kurt Guddat (Garden City, NY: Anchor, 1967), 216. This essay is full of neo-Hegelian anti-Semitic ideas. I think this is one of those cases where the dross doesn't corrupt the gold. It is also typically "early Marx."

53. See, for example, Gabel, "Phenomenology"; Alan Freeman and Elizabeth Mensch, "The Public-Private Distinction in American Law and Life," *Buffalo Law Review* 36 (1987): 237; Duncan Kennedy and Peter Gabel, "Roll Over Beethoven," *Stanford Law Review* 36 (1984): 1.

54. There are a number of critical analyses of the role of rights rhetoric at different stages of social movements and at different moments in American political history. See Gabel, "Phenomenology," and Alan Hunt, "Rights and Social Movements: Counter-Hegemonic Strategies," *Journal of Law in Society* 17 (1990): 309. They aren't examples of the rights critique, although they sometimes presuppose it.

JUDITH BUTLER

Is Kinship Always Already Heterosexual?

The topic of gay marriage is not the same as that of gay kinship, but it seems that the two become confounded in U.S. popular opinion when we hear not only that marriage is and ought to remain a heterosexual institution and bond but also that kinship does not work, or does not qualify as kinship, unless it assumes a recognizable family form. There are several ways to link these views. One way is to claim that sexuality needs to be organized in the service of reproductive relations, and that marriage, which gives legal status to the family form or, rather, is conceived as that which *should* secure the institution through conferring that legal status, should remain the fulcrum that keeps these institutions leveraging one another.

The challenges to this link are, of course, legion, and they take various forms domestically and internationally. On the one hand, there are various sociological ways of showing that in the United States a number of kinship relations exist and persist that do not conform to the nuclear family model and that draw on biological and nonbiological relations, exceeding the reach of current juridical conceptions, functioning according to nonformalizable rules. If we understand kinship as a set of practices that institutes relationships of various kinds that negotiate the reproduction of life and the demands of death, then kinship practices will be those that emerge to address fundamental forms of human dependency, which may include birth, child rearing, relations of emotional dependency and support, generational ties, illness, dying, and death (to name a few). Kinship is neither a fully autonomous sphere, proclaimed to be distinct from community and friendship — or the regulations of the state — through some definitional fiat, nor is it "over" or "dead" just because, as David Schneider has consequentially argued, it has lost the capacity to be formalized and tracked in the conventional ways that ethnologists in the past have attempted to do.[1]

In recent sociology, conceptions of kinship have become disjoined from the marriage assumption, so that, for example, Carol Stack's now classic study of urban African American kinship, *All Our Kin*, shows how kinship functions well through a network of women, some related through biological ties and some not.[2] The enduring effect of the history of slavery on African American kinship relations has become the focus of new studies by Nathaniel Mackey and Fred Moten, showing how the dispossession of kin relations by slavery offers a continuing legacy of "wounded kinship" in African American life. If, as Saidiya Hartman maintains, "slavery is the ghost in the machine of kinship,"[3] it is because African American kinship has been at once the site of intense state surveillance and pathologization, which leads to the double bind of being subject to normalizing pressures in the context of a continuing social and political delegitimation. As a result, it is not possible to separate questions of kinship from property relations (and conceiving persons as property) and from the fictions of "bloodline" as well as the national and racial interests by which these lines are sustained.

Kath Weston has supplied ethnographic descriptions of lesbian and gay nonmarital kinship relations that emerge outside of heterosexually based family ties and that only partially approximate the family form in some instances.[4] And most recently, anthropologist Cai Hua has offered a dramatic refutation of the Lévi-Straussian view of kinship as a negotiation of a patrilineal line through marriage ties in his recent study of the Na of China, in which neither husbands nor fathers figure prominently in determinations of kinship.[5]

Marriage has also recently been separated from questions of kinship to the extent that gay marriage legislative proposals often exclude rights to adoption or reproductive technologies as one of the assumed entitlements of marriage. These proposals have been offered in Germany and France most recently; in the United States, successful "gay marriage" proposals do not always have a direct impact on family law, especially when they seek as their primary aim to establish "symbolic recognition" for dyadic relations by the state.[6]

The petition for marriage rights seeks to solicit state recognition for nonheterosexual unions, and so configures the state as withholding an entitlement that it really should distribute in a nondiscriminatory way, regardless of sexual orientation. That the state's offer might result in the intensification of normalization is not widely recognized as a problem in the mainstream lesbian and gay movement, typified by the Human Rights Campaign.[7] The normalizing powers of the state are made especially clear, however, when we consider how continuing quandaries about kinship both condition and limit the marriage debates. In some contexts, the symbolic allocation of marriage, or marriage-like arrangements, is preferable to altering the requirements for kinship, for individual or plural rights to bear or adopt children or, legally, to coparent. Variations on kinship that depart from normative, dyadic heterosexually based family forms secured through the marriage vow are figured not only as dangerous for the child, but perilous to the putative natural and cultural laws said to sustain human intelligibility.

As background for this essay, it is probably important to know that the recent debates in France targeted certain U.S. views on the social construction and variability of gender relations as portending a perilous "Americanization" of kinship relations (*filiation*) in France.[8] As a result, this essay seeks to offer a response to this critique, outlined in the third section that follows, not as an effort to defend "Americanization," but to suggest instead that the kinship dilemmas of first world nations often provide allegories for one another of their own worries about the disruptive effects of kinship variability on their own national projects. In turn, I seek here to query the French debate on kinship and marriage to show how the argument in favor of legal alliance can work in tandem with a state normalization of recognizable kinship relations, a condition that extends rights of contract while in no way disrupting the patrilineal assumptions of kinship or the project of the unified nation that it supports.

In what follows, I will consider at least two dimensions of this contemporary predicament in which the state is sought for the recognition it might confer on same-sex couples and countered for the regulatory control on normative kinship that it continues to exercise. The state is not the same state in each of these bids, for we ask for an intervention by the state in the one domain (marriage) only to suffer excessive regulation in another (kinship). Does the turn to marriage make it thus more difficult to argue in favor of the viability of alternative kinship arrangements, for the well-being of the "child" in any number of social forms? Moreover, what happens to the radical project to articulate and support the proliferation of sexual practices outside of marriage and the obligations of kinship? Does the turn to the state signal the end of a radical sexual culture? Does such a prospect become eclipsed as we become increasingly preoccupied with landing the state's desire?

Gay Marriage: Desiring the State's
Desire and the Eclipse of Sexuality

Gay marriage obviously draws on profound and abiding investments not only in the heterosexual couple per se, but in the question of what forms of relationship ought to be legitimated by the state.[9] This crisis of legitimation can be considered from a number of perspectives, but let us consider for the moment the ambivalent gift that legitimation can become. To be legitimated by the state is to enter into the terms of legitimation offered there, and to find that one's public and recognizable sense of personhood is fundamentally dependent on the lexicon of that legitimation. It follows that the delimitation of legitimation will take place only through an exclusion of a certain sort, though not a patently dialectical one. The sphere of legitimate intimate alliance is established through the producing and intensifying regions of illegitimacy. There is, however, a more fundamental occlusion at work here. We misunderstand the sexual field if we consider that the legitimate and the illegitimate appear to exhaust its immanent possibilities. There is, thus, outside the struggle between the legitimate and the illegitimate — which is one that has as its goal the conversion of the illegitimate into the legitimate — a field that is less thinkable, one not figured in light of its ultimate convertibility into legitimacy. This is a field outside the disjunction of illegitimate and legitimate; it is not yet thought as a domain, a sphere, a field; it is not yet either legitimate or illegitimate, has not yet been thought through in the explicit discourse of legitimacy. Indeed, this would be a sexual field that does not have legitimacy as its point of reference, its ultimate desire. The debate over gay marriage takes place through such a logic, for we see the debate break down almost immediately into the question of whether marriage ought to be legitimately extended to homosexuals, and this means that the sexual field is circumscribed in such a way that sexuality is already thought in terms of marriage and marriage is already thought as the purchase on legitimacy.

In the case of gay marriage or of affiliative legal alliances, we see how various sexual practices and relationships that fall outside the purview of the sanctifying law become illegible or, worse, untenable, and new hierarchies emerge in public discourse. These hierarchies not only enforce the distinction between legitimate and illegitimate queer lives, but they produce tacit distinctions among forms of illegitimacy. The stable pair who would marry if only they could are cast as currently illegitimate but eligible for a future legitimacy, whereas the sexual agents who function outside the purview of the marriage bond and its recognized, if illegitimate, alternative form now constitute sexual possibilities that will never be eligible for a translation into legitimacy. These are possibilities that become increasingly disregarded in the sphere of politics as a consequence of the priority that the marriage debate has assumed. This is an illegitimacy whose temporal condition is to be foreclosed from any possible future transformation. It is not only *not yet* legitimate, but it is, we might say, the irrecoverable and irreversible past of legitimacy: *the never will be, the never was.*

Here, a certain normative crisis ensues. On the one hand, it is important to mark how the field of intelligible and speakable sexuality is circumscribed, so that we can see how options outside of marriage are becoming foreclosed as the unthinkable, and how the terms of thinkability are enforced by the narrow debates over who and what will be included in the norm. On the other hand, there is always the possibility of savoring the status of unthinkability, if it is a status, as the most critical, the most radical, the most valuable. As the sexually unrepresentable, such sexual possibilities can figure the sublime within the contemporary field of sexuality, a site of pure resistance, a site unco-opted by normativity. But how does one think politics from such a site of unrepresentability? And lest I am misunderstood here, let me state an equally pressing question: How can one think politics without considering these sites of unrepresentability?

One may wish for another lexicon altogether. The history of sexual progressivism surely recurs time and again to the possibility of a new language and the promise of a new mode of being. In the light of this quandary, one might find oneself wanting to opt out of this whole story, to operate somewhere that is neither legitimate nor illegitimate. But here is where the critical perspective, the one that operates at the limit of the intelligible, also risks being regarded as apolitical. For politics, as it is constituted through this discourse of intelligibility, demands that we take a stand for or against gay marriage; but critical reflection, which is surely part of any seriously normative political philosophy and practice, demands that we ask why and how this has become the question, the question that defines what will and will not qualify as meaningful political discourse here. Why, under present conditions, does the very prospect of "becoming political" depend on our ability to operate within that discursively instituted binary and not to ask, and endeavor not to know, that the sexual field is forcibly constricted through accepting those terms? This dynamic of force is rendered all the more forceful because it grounds the contemporary field of the political, grounds it through the forcible exclusion of that sexual field from the political. And yet, the operation of this force of exclusion is set outside of the domain of contest, as if it were not part of power, as if it were not an item for political reflection. Thus, to become political, to act and speak in ways that are recognizably political, is to rely on a foreclosure of the very political field that is not subject to political scrutiny. Without the critical perspective, we might say, politics relies fundamentally on an unknowingness — and depoliticization — of the very relations of force by which its own field of operation is instituted.

Criticality is thus not a position per se, not a site or a place that might be located within an already delimitable field, although one must, in an obligatory catachresis, speak of sites, of fields, of domains. One critical function is to scrutinize the action of delimitation itself. By recommending that we become critical, that we risk criticality, in thinking about how the sexual field is constituted, I do not mean to suggest that we could or should occupy an atopical elsewhere, undelimited, radically free. The questioning of taken-for-granted conditions becomes possible on occasion; but one cannot get there through a thought experiment, an *epoché*, an act of will. One gets there, as it were, through suffering the dehiscence, the breakup, of the ground itself.

Even within the field of intelligible sexuality, one finds that the binaries that anchor its operations permit for middle zones and hybrid formations, suggesting that the binary relation does not exhaust the field in question. Indeed, there are middle regions, hybrid regions of legitimacy and illegitimacy that have no clear names, and where nomination itself falls into a crisis produced by the variable, sometimes violent boundaries of legitimating practices that come into uneasy and sometimes conflictual contact with one another. These are not precisely places where one can choose to hang out, subject positions one might opt to occupy. These are nonplaces in which one finds oneself in spite of oneself; indeed, these are nonplaces where recognition, including self-recognition, proves precarious if not elusive, in spite of one's best efforts to be a subject in some recognizable sense. They are not sites of enunciation, but shifts in the topography from which a questionably audible claim emerges: the claim of the not-yet-subject and the nearly recognizable.

That there are such regions, and that they are not precisely options, suggests that what troubles the distinction between legitimacy and illegitimacy are social practices, specifically sexual practices, that do not appear immediately coherent in the available lexicon of legitimation. These are sites of uncertain ontology, difficult nomination. If it seems that I am now going to argue that we should all be pursuing and celebrating sites of uncertain ontology and difficult nomination, I actually want to pursue a slightly different point, which is to attend to the foreclosure of the possible that takes place when, from the urgency to stake a political claim, one naturalizes the options that figure most legibly within the sexual field. Attending to this foreclosure, as an act of politics that we unwittingly perform, unwittingly perform time and again, offers the possibility for a different conception of politics, one that attends to its own foreclosures as an effect of its own conscious activism. Yet, one must maintain a double edge in relation to this difficult terrain, for neither the violence of foreclosure that stabilizes the field of activism nor the path of critical paralysis that is entrenched at the level of fundamental reflection will suffice. On the topic of gay marriage, it becomes increasingly important to keep the tension alive between maintaining a critical perspective and making a politically legible claim.

My point here is not to suggest that one must, in relation to gay marriage and kinship debates, remain critical rather than political, as if such a distinction were finally possible or desirable, but only that a politics that incorporates a critical understanding is the only one that can maintain a claim to being self-reflective and nondogmatic. To be political does not merely mean to take a single and enduring "stand." For instance, to say that one is for or against gay marriage is not always easy to do, since it may be that one wants to secure the right for those who wish to make use of it even as one does not want it for oneself, or it may be that one wants to counter the homophobic discourses that have been marshaled against gay marriage, but one does not want to be, therefore, in favor of it. Or it may be that one believes very strongly that marriage is the best way for lesbian and gay people to go and would like to install it as a new norm, a norm for the future. Or it may be that one not only opposes it for oneself, but for everybody, and that the task at hand is to rework and revise the social organization of friendship, sexual contacts, and community to produce non-state-centered forms of support and alliance, because marriage, given its historical weight, becomes an "option" only by extending itself as a norm (and thus foreclosing options), one that also extends property relations and renders the social forms for sexuality more conservative.

For a progressive sexual movement, even one that may want to produce marriage as an option for nonheterosexuals, the proposition that marriage should become the only way to sanction or legitimate sexuality is unacceptably conservative. Even if the question is one not of marriage but of legal contracts, augmenting domestic partnership arrangements as legal contracts, certain questions still follow: Why should it be that marriage or legal contracts become the basis on which health care benefits, for instance, are allocated? Why shouldn't there be ways of organizing health care entitlements such that everyone, regardless of marital status, has access to them? If one argues for marriage as a way of securing those entitlements, then does one not also affirm that entitlements as important as health care ought to remain allocated on the basis of marital status? What does this do to the community of the nonmarried, the single, the divorced, the uninterested, the nonmonogamous, and how does the sexual field become reduced, in its very legibility, once we extend marriage as a norm?[10]

Regardless of one's view on gay marriage, there is clearly a demand on those who work in sexuality studies to respond to many of the most homophobic arguments that have been marshaled against gay marriage proposals. Many of these arguments are not only fueled by homophobic sentiment but often focus on fears about reproductive relations, whether they are natural or "artificial," and what happens to the child, the child, the poor child, martyred figure of an ostensibly selfish or dogged social progressivism? Indeed, the debates on gay marriage and gay kinship, two issues that are often conflated, have become sites of intense displacement for other political fears, fears about technology, about new demographics, and also about the very unity and transmissability of the nation, fears that feminism, in its insistence on child care, has effectively opened up kinship outside the family, opened it to strangers. In the French debates on the PACS (the "pacts of civil solidarity" that constitute an alternative to marriage for any two individuals unrelated by blood, regardless of sexual orientation), the passage of the bill finally depended on proscribing the rights of nonheterosexual couples from adopting children and accessing reproductive technology. The same provision was recently proposed and adopted in Germany as well.[11] In both cases, one can see that the child figures in the debate as a dense site for the transfer and reproduction of culture, where "culture" carries with it implicit norms of racial purity and domination.[12] Indeed, one can see a convergence between the arguments in France that rail against the threat to "culture" posed by the prospect of legally allied gay people having children — and I will suspend for the purposes of this discussion the question of what it means to "have" in this instance — and those taking place on issues of immigration, of what Europe is, and, implicitly and explicitly, of what is truly French, the basis of its culture, which becomes, through an imperial logic, the basis of culture itself, its universal and invariable conditions.

The debates center not only on the questions What is culture? Who should be admitted? and How should the subjects of culture be reproduced? but also on the status of the state and, in particular, its power to confer or withdraw recognition for forms of sexual alliance. Indeed, the argument against gay marriage is always, implicitly or explicitly, an argument about what the state should do, what it should provide, but also what kinds of intimate relations ought to be eligible for state legitimation. What is this desire to keep the state from offering recognition to nonheterosexual partners, and what is the desire to compel the state to offer such recognition? For both sides of the debate, at issue is not only the question of which relations of desire ought to be legitimated by the state, but of who may desire the state, *who may desire the state's desire.*

Indeed, the questions are even more complicated: Whose desire might qualify as a desire for state legitimation? but also Whose desire might qualify *as* the desire of the state? Who may desire the state? And whom may the state desire? Whose desire will be the state's desire? Conversely, and this is just speculation — but perhaps academic work might be regarded as a social site for such speculation — it seems that what one is wanting when one wants "state recognition" for marriage, and what one is not wanting when one wants to limit the scope of that recognition for others, are complex wants. The state becomes the means by which a fantasy becomes literalized: desire and sexuality are ratified, justified, known, publicly instated, imagined as permanent, durable. And, at that very moment, desire and sexuality are dispossessed and displaced, so that what one "is" and what one's relationship "is" are no longer private matters; indeed, ironically, one might say that through marriage, personal desire acquires a certain anonymity and interchangeability, becomes, as it were, publicly mediated and, in that sense, a kind of legitimated public sex. But more than that, marriage compels, at least logically, universal recognition: everyone must let you into the door of the hospital; everyone must honor your claim to grief; everyone will assume your natural rights to a child; everyone will regard your relationship as elevated into eternity. In this way, the desire for universal recognition is a desire to become universal, to become interchangeable in one's universality, to vacate the lonely particularity of the nonratified relation, and, perhaps above all, to gain both place and sanctification in that imagined relation to the state. Place and sanctification: these are surely powerful fantasies, and they take on particular phantasmatic form when we consider the bid for gay marriage. The state can become the site for the recirculation of religious desires, for redemption, for belonging, for eternity. And we might well ask what happens to sexuality when it runs through this particular circuit of fantasy: Is it alleviated of its guilt, its deviance, its discontinuity, its asociality, its spectrality? And if it is alleviated of all that, where precisely do these negativities go? Do they not tend to be projected onto those who have not or will not enter this hallowed domain? And does the projection take the form of judging others morally, of enacting a social abjection and, hence, becoming the occasion to institute a new hierarchy of legitimate and illegitimate sexual arrangement?

The Poor Child and the Fate of the Nation

The proposal in France to institute civil unions (pacts of civil solidarity) as an alternative to marriage sought at once to sidestep marriage and secure legal ties. It ran up against a limit, however, when questions of reproduction and adoption surfaced. Indeed, in France, concerns over reproduction work in tandem with concerns over the reproduction of an identifiably French culture. As suggested above, one can see a certain implicit identification of French culture with universalism, and this has its own consequences for the fantasy of the nation at stake. For understanding this debate, it is important to recognize how, in particular, the figure of the child of non-heterosexual parents becomes a cathected site for anxieties about cultural purity and cultural transmission. In the recent fracas over the PACS, the only way the proposal could pass was by denying rights of joint adoption to individuals in such relations. Indeed, as Eric Fassin and others have argued, it is the alteration of rights of filiation that is most scandalous in the French context, not marriage per se.[13] The life of the contract can be, within a range, extended, but the rights of filiation cannot. In some of the cultural commentary that accompanied this decision to deny adoptive rights to openly gay people, we heard from Sylviane Agacinski, a well-known French philosopher, that it goes against the "symbolic order" to let homosexuals form families.[14] Whatever social forms these are, they are not marriages, and they are not families; indeed, in her view, they are not properly "social" at all, but private. The struggle is in part one over words, over where and how they apply, about their plasticity and their equivocity. But it is more specifically a struggle over whether certain practices of nomination keep in place the presuppositions about the limits of what is humanly recognizable. The argument rests on a certain paradox, however, that would be hard to deny. Because if one does *not* want to recognize certain human relations as part of the humanly recognizable, then one has *already* recognized them, and one seeks to deny what it is one has already, in one way or another, understood. "Recognition" becomes an effort to deny what exists and, hence, becomes the instrument for the refusal of recognition. In this way, it becomes a way of shoring up a normative fantasy of the human over and against dissonant versions of itself. To defend the limits of what is recognizable against that which challenges it is to understand that the norms that govern recognizability have already been challenged. In the United States, we are used to hearing conservative and reactionary polemics against homosexuality as unnatural, but that is not precisely the discourse through which the French polemic proceeds. Agacinski, for instance, does not assume that the family takes a natural form. Rather, the state is constrained in recognizing marriage as heterosexual, in her view, not by nature or natural law, but by something called "the symbolic order" (which corresponds to and ratifies a natural law). It is according to the dictates of this order that the state is obligated to refuse to recognize such relations.

I will lay out Agacinski's view in a moment, not because she is the most vocal opponent to the transformations in kinship that gay marriage might imply, but because some time ago a colleague sent me an editorial Agacinski had written in *Le Monde*, a missive that in some way demanded a response.[15] In her editorial, she identifies a certain American strain of queer and gender theory as the monstrous future for France were these transformations to occur. So let us say, without going into details, that a certain interpellation occurred on the front page of *Le Monde* in which my name figured as a sign of the coming monstrosity. And consider that I am in a quandary here, because my own views are used to caution against a monstrous future that will come to pass if lesbian and gay people are permitted to form state-ratified kinship arrangements. So on one hand there is a demand, in a way, to respond to and rebut these allegations; on the other hand, it seems crucial not to accept the terms in which one's opponent has framed the debate, a debate which, I fear, is no debate at all, but a highly publicized polemic and fear-mongering. My own quandary is not mine alone. Will I, in opposing her, occupy a position in which I argue for state legitimation? Is this what I desire?

On the one hand, it would be easy enough to argue that she is wrong, that the family forms in question are viable social forms, and that the current episteme of intelligibility might be usefully challenged and rearticulated in light of these social forms.[16] After all, her view matches and fortifies those that maintain that legitimate sexual relations take a heterosexual and state-sanctioned form and that work to derealize viable and significant sexual alliances that fail to conform to that model. Of course, there are consequences to this kind of derealization that go beyond hurting someone's feelings or causing offense to a group of people. It means that when you arrive at the hospital to see your lover, you may not. It means that when your lover falls into a coma, you may not assume certain executorial rights. It means that when your lover dies, you may not be permitted to receive the body. It means that when your child is left with you, the nonbiological parent, you may not be able to counter the claims of biological relatives in court and that you lose custody and even access. It means you may not be able to provide health care benefits for one another. These are all very significant forms of disenfranchisement, ones that are made all the worse by the personal effacements that occur in daily life and that invariably take a toll on a relationship. The sense of delegitimation can make it harder to sustain a bond, a bond that is not real anyway, a bond that does not "exist," that never had a chance to exist, that was never meant to exist. If you're not real, it can be hard to sustain yourselves over time. Here is where the absence of state legitimation can emerge in the psyche as a pervasive, if not fatal, sense of self-doubt. And if you've actually lost the lover who was never recognized to be your lover, did you really lose that person? Is this a loss, and can it be publicly grieved? Surely this is something that has become a pervasive problem in the queer community, given the losses from AIDS, the losses of lives and loves that are always in struggle to be recognized as such.

On the other hand, to pursue state legitimation in order to repair these injuries brings with it a host of new problems, if not new heartaches. The failure to secure state recognition for one's intimate arrangements can be experienced only as a form of derealization if the terms of state legitimation are those that maintain hegemonic control over the norms of recognition, in other words, if the state monopolizes the resources of recognition. Are there not other ways of feeling possible, intelligible, even real, apart from the sphere of state recognition? Should there not be other ways? It makes sense that the lesbian and gay movement would turn to the state, given its recent history: the current drive for gay marriage is in some ways a response to AIDS and, in particular, a shamed response, one in which a gay community seeks to disavow its so-called promiscuity, one in which we appear as healthy and normal and capable of sustaining monogamous relations over time. This, of course, brings me back to the question, a question posed poignantly by Michael Warner, of whether the drive to become recognizable within the existing norms of legitimacy requires that we subscribe to a practice that delegitimates those sexual lives structured outside of the bonds of marriage and the presumptions of monogamy.[17] Is this a disavowal that the queer community is willing to make? And with what social consequence? How is it that we give the power of recognition over to the state at the moment we insist that we are unreal and illegitimate without it? Are there other resources by which we might become recognizable or mobilize to challenge the existing regimes within which the terms of recognizability take place?

One can see the terrain of the dilemma here: on the one hand, living without norms of recognition results in significant suffering and forms of disenfranchisement that confound the very distinctions among psychic, cultural, and material consequences. On the other hand, the demand to be recognized, which is a very powerful political demand, can lead to new and invidious forms of social hierarchy, to a precipitous foreclosure of the sexual field, and to new ways of supporting and extending state power, if it does not institute a critical challenge to the very norms of recognition supplied and required by state legitimation. Indeed, in making the bid to the state for recognition, we effectively restrict the domain of what will become recognizable as legitimate sexual arrangements, thus fortifying the state as the source for norms of recognition and eclipsing other possibilities in civil society and cultural life. To demand and receive recognition according to norms that legitimate marriage and delegitimate forms of sexual alliance outside of marriage, or to norms that are articulated in a critical relation to marriage, is to displace the site of delegitimation from one part of the queer community to another or, rather, to transform a collective delegitimation into a selective one. Such a practice is difficult, if not impossible, to reconcile with a radically democratic, sexually progressive movement. What would it mean to exclude from the field of potential legitimation those who are outside of marriage, those who live nonmonogamously, those who live alone, those who are in whatever arrangement they are in that is not the marriage form?

I would add a caveat here: we do not always know what we mean by "the state" when we refer to the kind of "state legitimation" that occurs in marriage. The state is not a simple unity, and its parts and operations are not always coordinated with one another. The state is not reducible to law, and power is not reducible to state power. It would be wrong to understand the state as operating with a single set of interests or to gauge its effects as if they are unilaterally successful. I think the state can also be worked, exploited, and that social policy, which involves the implementation of law to local instances, can very often be the site where law is challenged, thrown to a court to adjudicate, and where new kinship arrangements stand a chance of gaining new legitimacy. Of course, certain propositions remain highly controversial: interracial adoption, adoption by single men, by gay male couples, by parties who are unmarried, by kinship structures in which there are more than two adults in play. So there are reasons to worry about requesting state recognition for intimate alliances and so becoming part of an extension of state power into the socius. But do these reasons outweigh those we might have for seeking recognition and entitlement through entering a legal contract? Contracts work in different ways — and surely differently in the United States and French contexts — to garner state authority and to subject the individuals who enter into contracts to regulatory control. But even if we argue that in France, contracts are conceived as individual entitlements and so less tethered to state control, the very form of individuation is thus sustained by state legitimation, even if, or precisely when, the state appears to be relatively withdrawn from the contractual process itself.

In this way, the norms of the state work very differently in these disparate national contexts. In the United States, the norms of recognition supplied by the state not only often fail to describe or regulate existing social practice, but become the site of articulation for a fantasy of normativity, projecting and delineating an ideological account of kinship, for instance, precisely at the moment when it is undergoing social challenge and dissemination. Thus, it seems that the appeal to the state is at once an appeal to a fantasy already institutionalized by the state, and a leave-taking from existing social complexity in the hope of becoming "socially coherent" at last. What this means as well is that there is a site to which we can turn, understood as the state, that will finally render us coherent, a turn that commits us to the fantasy of state power. Jacqueline Rose persuasively argues that "if the state has meaning only 'partly as something existing,' if it rests on the belief of individuals that it 'exists or should exist,' then it starts to look uncannily like what psychoanalysis would call an 'as if' phenomenon."[18] Its regulations do not always seek to order what exists, but to figure social life in certain imaginary ways. The incommensurability between state stipulation and existing social life means that this gap must be covered over for the state to continue to exercise its authority and to exemplify the kind of coherence that it is expected to confer on its subjects. As Rose reminds us, "It is because the state has become so alien and distant from the people it is meant to represent that, according to Engels, it has to rely, more and more desperately, on the sacredness and inviolability of its own laws."[19]

So there are at least two sides to this coin, and I do not mean to resolve this dilemma in favor of one or the other, but to develop a critical practice that is mindful of both. I want to maintain that legitimation is double-edged: it is crucial that, politically, we lay claim to intelligibility and recognizability; and it is crucial, politically, that we maintain a critical and transformative relation to the norms that govern what will and will not count as an intelligible and recognizable alliance and kinship. This latter would also involve a critical relation to the desire for legitimation as such. It is also crucial that we question the assumption that the state furnish these norms and that we come to think critically about what the state has become during these times or, indeed, how it has become a site for the articulation of a fantasy that seeks to deny or overturn what these times have brought us.

As we return to the French debate, then, it seems important to remember that the debate about laws is at once a debate about what kinds of sexual arrangements and forms of kinship can be admitted to exist or deemed to be possible, and what the limits of imaginability might be. For many who opposed the PACS or who, minimally, voiced skeptical views about it, the very status of culture was called into question by the variability of legitimated sexual alliance. Immigration and gay parenting were figured as challenging the fundamentals of a culture that had already been transformed, but that sought to deny the transformation it had already undergone.[20] To understand this we have to consider how the term "culture" operates, and how, in the French context, the term became invoked in these debates to designate not the culturally variable formations of human life, but the universal conditions for human intelligibility.

Natural, Cultural, State Law

Although Agacinski, the French philosopher, is not a Lacanian and, indeed, hardly a psychoanalyst, we do see in her commentary, which was prominent in the French debate, a certain anthropological belief that is shared by many Lacanian followers and other psychoanalytic practitioners in France and elsewhere.[21] The belief is that culture itself requires that a man and a woman produce a child, and that the child have this dual point of reference for its own initiation into the symbolic order, where the symbolic order consists of a set of rules that order and support our sense of reality and cultural intelligibility.

She writes that gay parenting is both unnatural and a threat to culture, in the sense that sexual difference, which is, in her view, irrefutably biological, gains its significance in the cultural sphere as the foundation of life in procreation: "This foundation (of sexual difference) is generation; this is the difference between the paternal and maternal roles. There must be the masculine and the feminine to give life." Over and against this life-giving heterosexuality at the foundation of culture is the specter of homosexual parenting, a practice that not only departs from nature and from culture, but centers on the dangerous and artificial fabrication of the human and is figured as a kind of violence or destruction. She writes: "It takes a certain 'violence,' if one is homosexual, to want a child [*Il faut une certaine 'violence,' quand on est homosexuel, pour vouloir un enfant*]. . . . I think that there is no absolute right to a child, since the right implies an increasingly artificial fabrication of children. In the interests of the child, one cannot efface its double origin." The "double origin" is its invariable beginning with a man and woman, a man who occupies the place of the father and a woman who occupies the place of the mother. "This mixed origin, which is natural," she writes, "is also a cultural and symbolic foundation."[22]

The argument that there must be a father and a mother as a double point of reference for the child's origin rests on a set of presumptions which resonate with the Lévi-Straussian position in *The Elementary Structures of*

Kinship in 1949. Although Agacinski is not a Lévi-Straussian, her framework nevertheless borrows from a set of structuralist premises about culture that have been revived and redeployed in the context of the present debate. My point is less to hold the views of Lévi-Strauss responsible for the terms of the present debate than to ask what purpose the reanimation of these views serves in the contemporary political horizon, considering that in anthropology, the Lévi-Straussian views promulgated in the late 1940s are not only generally considered surpassed, but are no longer owned in the same form by Lévi-Strauss himself.[23]

For Lévi-Strauss, the Oedipal drama is not to be construed as a developmental moment or phase. It consists instead of a prohibition that is at work in the inception of language, one that works at all times to facilitate the transition from nature to culture for all emerging subjects. Indeed, the bar that prohibits the sexual union with the mother is not arrived at in time, but is, in some sense, *there* as a precondition of individuation, a presumption and support of cultural intelligibility itself. No subject emerges without this bar or prohibition as its condition, and no cultural intelligibility can be claimed without first passing through this founding structure. Indeed, the mother is disallowed because she belongs to the father, so if this prohibition is fundamental, and it is understood, then the father and the mother exist as logically necessary features of the prohibition itself. Now, psychoanalysis will explain that the father and the mother do not have to actually exist, that they can be positions or imaginary figures, but that they do have to figure structurally in some way. Agacinski's point is also ambiguous in this way, but she will insist that they must have existed, and that their existence has to be understood by the child as essential to his or her origin.

To understand how this prohibition becomes foundational to a conception of culture is to follow the way the Oedipal complex in Freud becomes recast as an inaugural structure of language and the subject in Lacan, something I cannot do in this context and probably have done too many times before.[24] What I want to underscore here is the use of Oedipus to establish a certain conception of culture that has rather narrow consequences for both formations of gender and sexual arrangements and that implicitly figures culture as a whole, a unity, one that has a stake in reproducing itself and its singular wholeness through the reproduction of the child. When Agacinski argues, for instance, that for every child to emerge in a nonpsychotic way there must be a father and a mother, she appears at first not to be making the empirical point that a father and a mother must be present and known through all phases of child rearing. She means something more ideal: that there must at least be a psychic point of reference for mother and father and a narrative effort to recuperate the male and female parent, even if one or the other is never present and never known. But if this were guaranteed without the social arrangement of heterosexuality, she would have no reason to oppose lesbian and gay adoption. So it would appear that social arrangements support and maintain the symbolic structure, even as the symbolic structure legitimates the social arrangement. For Agacinski, heterosexual coitus, regardless of the parent or parents who rear the child, is understood as the origin of the child, and that origin will have a symbolic importance.

This symbolic importance of the child's origin in heterosexuality is understood to be essential to culture for the following reason. If the child enters culture through the process of assuming a symbolic position, and if these symbolic positions are differentiated by virtue of Oedipalization, then the child presumably will become gendered on the occasion that he or she takes up a position in relation to parental positions that are prohibited as overt sexual objects for the child. The boy will become a boy to the extent that he recognizes that he cannot have his mother, that he must find a substitute woman for her; the girl will become a girl to the extent that she recognizes she cannot have her mother, substitutes for that loss through identification with the mother, and then recognizes she cannot have the father and substitutes a male object for him. According to this fairly rigid schematic of Oedipalization, gender is achieved through the accomplishment of heterosexual desire. This structure, which is already much more rigidly put forward here, in the effort to reconstruct Agacinski's position, than one would find in Freud (i.e., in either *The Three Essays on the Theory of Sexuality* or *The Ego and the Id*), is then deprived of its status as a developmental phase and asserted as the very means by which an individuated subject within language is established. To become part of culture means to have passed through the gender-differentiating mechanism of this taboo and to accomplish both normative heterosexuality and discrete gender identity at once.

There are many reasons to reject this particular rendition of Oedipalization as the precondition of language and cultural intelligibility. And there are many versions of psychoanalysis that would reject this schema, allowing for various ways of rearticulating the Oedipal, but also limiting its function in relation to the pre-Oedipal. Moreover, some forms of structural anthropology sought to elevate the exchange of women into a precondition of culture, and to identify that mandate for exogamy with the incest taboo operating within the Oedipal drama, but other theories of culture have come to take its place and call that structuralist account into question. Indeed, the failure of structuralism to take into account kinship systems that do not conform to its model was made clear by anthropologists such as David Schneider, Sylvia Yanagisako, Sarah Franklin, Clifford Geertz, and Marilyn Strathern.[25] These theories emphasize modes of exchange different from those presumed by structuralism, and they also call into question the universality of structuralism's claims. Sociologists of kinship such as Judith Stacey and Carol Stack, as well as anthropologist Kath Weston, have also underscored a variety of kin relations that work, and work according to rules that are not always or only traceable to the incest taboo.[26]

So why would the structuralist account of sexual difference, conceived according to the exchange of women, make a "comeback" in the context of the present debates in France? Why would various intellectuals, some of them feminist, proclaim that sexual difference is fundamental not only to culture, but to its transmissibility, and that reproduction must remain the prerogative of heterosexual marriage, and that limits must be set on viable and recognizable forms of nonheterosexual parenting arrangements?

To understand the resurgence of a largely anachronistic structuralism in this context, it is important to consider that the incest taboo functions in Lévi-Strauss not only to secure the exogamous reproduction of children, but also to maintain a unity to the "clan" through compulsory exogamy, as it is articulated through compulsory heterosexuality. The woman from else-where makes sure that the men from here will reproduce their own kind. She secures the reproduction of cultural identity in this way. The ambig-uous "clan" designated a "primitive" group for Lévi-Strauss in 1949, but it comes to function ideologically for the cultural unity of the nation in 1999–2000, in the context of a Europe beset with opening borders and new immigrants. The incest taboo thus comes to function in tandem with a racialist project to reproduce culture and, in the French context, to re-produce the implicit identification of French culture with universality. It is a "law" that works in the service of the "as if," securing a fantasy of the nation that is already, and irreversibly, under siege. In this sense, the invoca-tion of the symbolic law defends against the threat to French cultural purity that has taken place, and is taking place, through new patterns of immigra-tion, increased instances of miscegenation, and the blurring of national boundaries. Indeed, even in Lévi-Strauss, whose earlier theory of clan formation is redescribed in his short text, *Race and History,* we see that the reproducibility of racial identity is linked to the reproduction of culture.[27] Is there a link between the account of the reproduction of culture in Lévi-Strauss's early work and his later reflections on cultural identity and the reproduction of race? Is there a connection between these texts that might help us read the cultural link that takes place in France now between fears about immigration and desires to regulate nonheterosexual kinship? The incest taboo might be seen as working in conjunction with the taboo against miscegenation, especially in the contemporary French context, insofar as the defense of culture that takes place through mandating the family as heterosexual is at once an extension of new forms of European racism. We see something of this link prefigured in Lévi-Strauss, which explains in part why we see the resurrection of his theory in the context of the present debate. When Lévi-Strauss makes the argument that the incest taboo is the basis of culture and that it mandates exogamy, or marriage outside the clan, is "the clan" being read in terms of race or, more specifically, in terms of a racial presupposition of culture that maintains its purity through regulating its transmissibility? Marriage must take place outside the clan. There must be exogamy. But there must also be a limit to exogamy; that is, marriage must be outside the clan, but not outside a certain racial self-understanding or racial commonality. So the incest taboo mandates exogamy, but the taboo against miscegenation limits the exogamy that the incest taboo mandates. Cornered, then, between a compulsory heterosexuality and a prohibited miscegenation, something called culture, saturated with the anxiety and identity of dominant European whiteness, reproduces itself in and as universality itself.

There are, of course, many other ways of contesting the Lévi-Straussian model that have emerged in recent years, and its strange resurgence in the recent political debate will no doubt strike anthropologists as the spectral appearance of an anachronism. Arguments have been made that other kinds of kinship arrangements are possible in a culture. There are also other ways of explaining the ordering practices that kinship sometimes exemplified. These debates, however, remain internal to a study of kinship that assumes the primary place of kinship within a culture, and assumes for the most part that a culture is a unitary and discrete totality. Pierre Clastres made this point most polemically several years ago in the French context, arguing that it is not possible to treat the rules of kinship as supplying the rules of intelligibility for any society, and that culture is not a self-standing notion but must be regarded as fundamentally imbued by power relations, power relations that are not reducible to rules.[28] But if we begin to understand that cultures are not self-standing entities or unities, that the exchanges between them, their very modes of delimiting themselves in distinction constitute their provisional ontology and are, as a result, fraught with power, then we are compelled to rethink the problem of exchange altogether: no longer as the gift of women, which assumes and produces the self-identity of the patrilineal clan, but as a set of potentially unpredictable and contested practices of self-definition that are not reducible to a primary and culture-founding heterosexuality. Indeed, if one were to elaborate on this point, the task would be to take up David Schneider's suggestion that kinship is a kind of *doing,* one that does not reflect a prior structure, but that can only be understood as an enacted practice. This would help us, I believe, move away from the situation in which a hypostatized structure of relations lurks behind any actual social arrangement and permit us to consider how modes of patterned and performative doing bring kinship categories into operation and become the means by which they undergo transformation and displacement.

The hypostatized heterosexuality, construed by some to be symbolic rather than social, and so to operate as a structure that founds the field of kinship itself — and that informs social arrangements no matter how they appear, no matter what they do — has been the basis of the claim that kinship is always already heterosexual. According to its precept, those who enter kinship terms as nonheterosexual will only make sense if they assume the position of Mother or Father. The social variability of kinship has little or no efficacy in rewriting the founding and pervasive symbolic law. The postulate of a founding heterosexuality must also be read as part of the operation of power — and, I would add, fantasy — such that we can begin to ask how the invocation of such a foundation works in the building of a certain fantasy of state and nation. The relations of exchange that constitute culture as a series of transactions or translations are not only or primarily sexual, but they do take sexuality as their issue, as it were, when the question of cultural transmission and reproduction is at stake. I do not mean to say that cultural reproduction takes place solely or exclusively or fundamentally through the child. I mean only to suggest that the figure of the child is one eroticized site in the reproduction of culture, one that implicitly raises the question of whether there will be a sure transmission of culture through heterosexual procreation — not only whether heterosexuality will serve the purposes of transmitting culture faithfully, but whether culture will be defined, in part, as the prerogative of heterosexuality itself.

Indeed, to call this entire theoretical apparatus into question is not only to question the founding norms of heterosexuality, but also to wonder whether "culture" can be talked about at all as a self-sufficient kind of field or terrain. Though I do it, manifesting or symptomatizing a struggle to work through this position in an act of public thinking, I am aware that I am using a term that no longer signifies in the way it once could. It is a placeholder for a past position, one I must use to make that position and its limits clear, but one that I also suspend in the using. The relation between heterosexuality and the unity and, implicitly, the purity of culture is not a functional one. Although we may be tempted to say that heterosexuality secures the reproduction of culture and that patrilineality secures the reproduction of culture in the form of a whole that is reproducible in its identity through time, it is equally true that the conceit of a culture as a self-sustaining and self-replicating totality supports the naturalization of heterosexuality, and that the entirety of the structuralist approach to sexual difference emblematizes this movement to secure heterosexuality through the thematics of culture. But is there a way to break out of this circle whereby heterosexuality institutes monolithic culture and monolithic culture reinstitutes and renaturalizes heterosexuality?

Recent efforts in anthropology no longer situate kinship as the basis of culture, but conceive it as one cultural phenomenon complexly interlinked with other phenomena, cultural, social, political, and economic. Anthropologists Sarah Franklin and Susan McKinnon write, for instance, that in recent studies kinship has become linked to "the political formations of national and transnational identities, the economic movements of labor and capital, the cosmologies of religion, the hierarchies of race, gender, and species taxonomies, and the epistemologies of science, medicine, and technology." As a result, they argue, the very ethnographic study of kinship has changed such that it now "include[s] topics such as diasporic cultures, the dynamics of global political economy, or changes occurring in the contexts of biotechnology and biomedicine."[29] Indeed, in the French debate, Eric Fassin argues that one must understand the invocation of the "symbolic order" that links marriage to filiation in a necessary and foundational way as a compensatory response to the historical breakup of marriage as a hegemonic institution, the name for which in French is *démariage*.[30] In this sense, the opposition to the PACS is an effort to make the state sustain a certain fantasy of marriage and nation whose hegemony is already, and irreversibly, challenged at the level of social practice.

Similarly, Franklin and McKinnon understand kinship to be a site where certain displacements are already at work, where anxieties about bio-technology and transnational migrations become focused and disavowed. This seems clearly at work in Agacinski's position in at least two ways: the fear she bespeaks about the "Americanization" of sexual and gender rela-tions in France attests to a desire to keep those relations organized in a specifically French form, and the appeal to the universality of the symbolic order is, of course, a trope of the French effort to identify its own national-ist project with a universalist one. Similarly, her fear that lesbians and gay men will start to fabricate human beings, exaggerating the biotechnology of reproduction, suggests that these "unnatural" practices will eventuate in a wholesale social engineering of the human, linking, once again, homo-sexuality with the potential resurgence of fascism. One might well wonder what technological forces at work in the global economy, or indeed, what consequences of the human genome project raise these kinds of anxieties in contemporary cultural life, but it seems a displacement, if not a hallucina-tion, to identify the source of this social threat, if it is a threat, with lesbians who excavate sperm from dry ice on a cold winter day in Iowa when one of them is ovulating.

Franklin and McKinnon write that kinship is "no longer conceptualized as grounded in a singular and fixed idea of 'natural' relation, but is seen to be self-consciously assembled from a multiplicity of possible bits and pieces."[31] It would seem crucial, then, to understand the assembling opera-tion they describe in light of the thesis that kinship is itself a kind of doing, a practice that enacts that assemblage of significations as it takes place. But with such a definition in place, can kinship be definitively separated from other communal and affiliative practices? Kinship loses its specificity as an object once it becomes characterized loosely as modes of enduring relation-ship. Obviously, not all kinship relations last, but whatever relations qual-ify for kinship enter into a norm or a convention that has some durability, and that norm acquires its durability through being reinstated time and again. Thus, a norm does not have to be static to last; in fact, it *cannot* be static if it is to last. These are relations that are prone to naturalization and that are disrupted repeatedly by the impossibility of settling the relation between nature and culture; moreover, in Franklin and McKinnon's terms, kinship is one way for signifying the origin of culture. I would put it this way: the story of kinship, as we have it from Lévi-Strauss, is an allegory for the origin of culture and a symptom of the process of naturalization itself, one that takes place, brilliantly, insidiously, in the name of culture itself. Thus, one might add that debates about the distinction between nature and culture, which are clearly heightened when the distinctions between animal, human, machine, hybrid, and cyborg are no longer settled, become figured at the site of kinship, for even a theory of kinship that is radically culturalist frames itself against a discredited "nature" and so remains in a constitutive and definitional relation to that which it claims to transcend.

One can see how quickly kinship loses its specificity in terms of the global economy, for instance, when one considers the politics of international adoption and donor insemination. For new "families" where relations of filiation are not based on biology are sometimes conditioned by innovations in biotechnology or international commodity relations and the trade in children. And now there is the question of control over genetic resources, conceived of as a new set of property relations to be negotiated by legislation and court decisions. But there are clearly salutary consequences, as well, of the breakdown of the symbolic order, as it were, since kinship ties that bind persons to one another may well be no more or less than the intensification of community ties, may or may not be based on enduring or exclusive sexual relations, may well consist of ex-lovers, nonlovers, friends, community members. In this sense, then, the relations of kinship arrive at boundaries that call into question the distinguishability of kinship from community, or that call for a different conception of friendship. These constitute a "breakdown" of traditional kinship that not only displaces the central place of biological and sexual relations from its definition, but gives sexuality a domain separate from that of kinship, allowing as well for the durable tie to be thought outside of the conjugal frame and opening kinship to a set of community ties that are irreducible to family.

Psychoanalytic Narrative, Normative Discourse, and Critique

Unfortunately, the important work in what might be called postkinship studies in anthropology has not been matched by similarly innovative work in psychoanalysis, and the latter sometimes still relies on presumptive heterosexual kinship to theorize the sexual formation of the subject. Whereas several scholars in anthropology have not only opened up the meaning and possible forms of kinship, but have called into question whether kinship is always the defining moment of culture, this opening has not been matched by an equally well-known body of scholarship in psychoanalysis, although there is some important work there, for instance, that of Ken Corbett.[32] Indeed, if we call into question the postulate by which Oedipalization, conceived in rigid terms, becomes the condition for culture itself, how do we then return to psychoanalysis once this delinkage has taken place? If Oedipus is not the sine qua non of culture, that does not mean there is no place for Oedipus. It simply means that the complex that goes by that name may take a variety of cultural forms and that it will no longer be able to function as a normative condition of culture itself. Oedipus may or may not function universally, but even those who claim that it does would have to find out in what ways it figures, and would not be able to maintain that it always figures in the same way. For it to be a universal — and I confess to being an agnostic on this point — in no way confirms the thesis that it is the condition of culture: that thesis purports to know that Oedipus always functions in the same way, namely, as a condition of culture itself. But if Oedipus is interpreted broadly, as a name for the triangularity of desire, then the salient questions become: What forms does that triangularity take? Must it presume heterosexuality? And what happens when we begin to understand Oedipus outside of the exchange of women and the presumption of heterosexual exchange?

Psychoanalysis does not need to be associated exclusively with the reactionary moment in which culture is understood to be based on an irrefutable heterosexuality. Indeed, there are so many questions that psychoanalysis might pursue in order to help understand the psychic life of those who live outside of normative kinship or in some mix of normative and "non-": What is the fantasy of homosexual love that the child unconsciously adopts in gay families? How do children who are displaced from original families or born through implantation or donor insemination understand their origins? What cultural narratives are at their disposal, and what particular interpretations do they give to these conditions? Must the story that the child tells, a story that will no doubt be subject to many retellings, about his or her origin conform to a single story about how the human comes into being? Or will we find the human emerging through narrative structures that are not reducible to one story, the story of a capitalized Culture itself? How must we revise our understanding of the need for a narrative understanding of self that a child may have that includes a consideration of how those narratives are revised and interrupted in time? And how do we begin to understand what forms of gender differentiation take place for the child when heterosexuality is not the presumption of Oedipalization?

Indeed, this is the occasion not only for psychoanalysis to rethink its own uncritically accepted notions of culture, but for new kinship and sexual arrangements to compel a rethinking of culture itself. Indeed, when the relations that bind are no longer traced to heterosexual procreation, the very homology between nature and culture that philosophers such as Agacinski support tends to become undermined. Indeed, they do not stay static in her own work, for if it is the symbolic order that mandates heterosexual origins, and the symbolic is understood to legitimate social relations, why would she worry about putatively illegitimate social relations? She assumes that the latter have the power to undermine the symbolic, suggesting that the symbolic does not precede the social and, finally, has no independence from it.

It seems clear that when psychoanalytic practitioners make public claims about the psychotic or dangerous status of gay families, they are wielding public discourse in ways that need to be strongly countered. The Lacanians do not have a monopoly on such claims. In an interview with Jacqueline Rose, the well-known Kleinian practitioner Hanna Segal reiterates her view that "homosexuality is an attack on the parental couple," "a developmental arrest," and she expresses outrage over a situation in which two lesbians raise a boy. She adds that she considers "the adult homosexual structure to be pathological."[33] When asked at a public presentation in October 1998 whether she approved of two lesbians raising a boy, she answered flatly "No." To respond directly to Segal, as many people have, with an insistence on the normalcy of lesbian and gay families is to accept that the debate should center on the distinction between normal and pathological: whether she is wrong to think of homosexuality, for instance, as pathological, whether it ought rightly be said to be normal. But whether we seek entrance to the halls of normalcy or, indeed, reverse the discourse, to applaud our "pathology" (i.e., as the only "sane" position within homophobic culture) we have not called the defining framework into question. And once we enter that framework, we are to some degree defined by its terms, which means that we are *as* defined by those terms when we seek to establish ourselves within the boundaries of normality as we are when we assume the impermeability of those boundaries and position ourselves as its permanent outside. After all, even Agacinski knows how to make use of the claim that lesbians and gays are "inherently" subversive when she claims that they should *not* be given the right to marry because homosexuality is, by definition, "outside institutions and fixed models."[34]

We may think that double-edged thinking will lead us only to political paralysis, but consider the more serious consequences that follow from taking a single stand in such debates. If we engage the terms these debates supply, we ratify the frame at the moment in which we take our stand. This signals a certain paralysis in the face of exercising power to change the terms by which such topics are rendered thinkable. Indeed, a more radical social transformation is precisely at stake when we refuse, for instance, to allow kinship to become reducible to "family," or when we refuse to allow the field of sexuality to become gauged against the marriage form. For as surely as rights to marriage and to adoption and, indeed, to reproductive technology ought to be secured for individuals and alliances outside the marriage frame, it would constitute a drastic curtailment of progressive sexual politics to allow marriage and family, or even kinship, to mark the exclusive parameters within which sexual life is thought. That the sexual field has become foreclosed through such debates on whether we might marry or conceive or raise children makes clear that either answer, that is, both the "yes" and the "no," work in the service of circumscribing reality in precipitous ways. If we decide that these are the decisive issues, and know which side we are on, then we have accepted an epistemological field structured by a fundamental loss, one that we can no longer name enough even to grieve. The life of sexuality, kinship, and community that becomes unthinkable within the terms of these norms constitutes the lost horizon of radical sexual politics, and we find our way "politically" in the wake of the ungrievable.

Notes

1. See David Schneider's *A Critique of the Study of Kinship* (Ann Arbor: University of Michigan Press, 1984) for an important analysis of how the approach to studying kinship has been fatally undermined by inappropriate assumptions about heterosexuality and the marriage bond brought to ethnographic description. See also Schneider, *American Kinship: A Cultural Account,* 2d ed. (Chicago: University of Chicago Press, 1980). For a continuation of this critique, especially as it relates to the presuppositional status of the marriage bond in kinship systems, see John Borneman's critical review of contemporary feminist kinship studies in "Until Death Do Us Part: Marriage/Death in Anthropological Discourse," *American Ethnologist* 23.2 (May 1996): 215–35.

2. Carol Stack, *All Our Kin: Strategies for Survival in a Black Community* (New York: Harper and Row, 1974).

3. Saidiya Hartman, in conversation, spring 2001.

4. Kath Weston, *Families We Choose: Lesbians, Gays, Kinship* (New York: Columbia University Press, 1991).

5. In a blurb for Cai Hua's *A Society without Fathers or Husbands: The Na of China,* trans. Asti Hustvedt (New York: Zone, 2001), Lévi-Strauss notes that Hua has discovered a society in which the role of fathers "is denied or belittled," thus suggesting that the role may still be at work but disavowed by those who practice kinship there. This interpretation effectively diminishes the challenge of the text, which argues that kinship is organized along nonpaternal lines.

6. I gather that recent domestic partnership legislation in the United States, as in California, does offer explicit provisions for parental rights shared equally by the couple, though many proposals explicitly seek to separate the recognition of domestic partnerships from rights of joint parenting.

7. See Michael Warner, *The Trouble with Normal: Sex, Politics, and the Ethics of Queer Life* (New York: Free Press, 1999).

8. For a full consideration of Franco-American cultural relations with respect to gender and sexuality, see the following work by Eric Fassin which, in many ways, has formed a background for my own views on this subject: " 'Good Cop, Bad Cop': The American Model and Countermodel in French Liberal Rhetoric since the 1980s," unpublished essay; " 'Good to Think': The American Reference in French Discourses of Immigration and Ethnicity," in *Multicultural Questions,* ed. Christian Joppke and Steven Lukes (London: Oxford University Press, 1999), 222–41; "Le Savant, l'expert et le politique: La famille des sociologues," *Genèses* 32 (Oct. 1998); "Same Sex, Different Politics: Comparing and Contrasting 'Gay Marriage' Debates in France and the United States," unpublished essay; "The Purloined Gender: American Feminism in a French Mirror," *French Historical Studies* 22.1 (winter 1999): 113–39.

9. In 1999, the state of California passed the Knight initiative, which mandated that marriage be a contract entered into exclusively by a man and a woman. It passed with 63 percent of the voting public in its favor.

10. See Sylviane Agacinski, "Questions autour de la filiation," interview with Eric Lamien and Michel Feher, *Ex æquo* (July 1998): 22–24. For an excellent rejoinder, see Michel Feher, "Quelques Réflexions sur 'Politiques des Sexes,' " *Ex æquo* (July 1998): 24–25.

11. In Germany, the Eingetragene Lebenspartnerschaft legislation that recently passed (August 2001) stipulates clearly that the two individuals entering into this alliance are gay, and that the law obligates them to a long-term relationship of support and responsibility. The law thus obligates two individuals, understood to be gay, to an approximation of the social form of marriage. Whereas the French PACS simply extends the right of contract to any two individuals who wish to enter it in order to share or bequeath property, the German arrangement requires, in neo-Hegelian fashion, that the contract reflect a specific way of life, recognizably marital, worthy of recognition by the state. See Deutscher Buundestag, 14. Wahlperiode, *Drucksache 14/5627*, 20 March 2001.

12. Lauren Berlant, *The Queen of America Goes to Washington City: Essays on Sex and Citizenship* (Durham, NC: Duke University Press, 1997), argues persuasively that "in the reactionary culture of imperiled privilege, the nation's value is figured not on behalf of an actually existing and laboring adult, but of a future American, both incipient and pre-historical: especially invested with this hope are the American fetus and the American child" (5).

13. Fassin, "Same Sex."

14. Agacinski, "Questions," 23.

15. Sylviane Agacinski, "Contre l'effacement des sexes," *Le Monde* 6 Feb. 1999.

16. This argument forms the center of my objection to Lacanian arguments against the viability of same-sex marriages and in favor of heteronormative family in *Antigone's Claim: Kinship between Life and Death*, the Wellek Library Lectures (New York: Columbia University Press, 2000) (see especially 68–73). For a further argument against Jacques-Alain Miller's and other forms of Lacanian skepticism toward same-sex unions, see my "Competing Universalities," in *Contingency, Hegemony, and Universality: Contemporary Dialogues on the Left,* ed. Judith Butler, Ernesto Laclau, and Slavoj Žižek (London: Verso, 2000), 136–81.

17. Michael Warner, "Beyond Gay Marriage," in this volume.

18. Jacqueline Rose, *States of Fantasy* (Oxford: Clarendon, 1996), 8–9.

19. Ibid., 10.

20. See Catherine Raissiguier, "Bodily Metaphors, Material Exclusions: The Sexual and Racial Politics of Domestic Partnerships in France," in *Violence and the Body,* ed. Arturo Aldama (New York: New York University Press, 2002).

21. The Lévi-Straussian position has been even more adamantly defended by Françoise Héritier. For her most vehement opposition to the PACS, see "Entretien," *La Croix,* Nov. 1998, where she remarks that "aucune societé n'admet de parenté homosexuelle." See also *Masculin/Féminin: La pensée de la difference* (Paris: Odile Jacob, 1996) and *L'Exercise de la parenté* (Paris: Gallimard, 1981).

22. Agacinski, "Questions," 23; my translation.

23. Lévi-Strauss made his own contribution to the debate, making clear that his views of over fifty years ago do not coincide with his present positions, and suggesting that the theory of exchange does not have to be tied to sexual difference but must always have a formal and specific expression. See Claude Lévi-Strauss, *The Elementary Structures of Kinship,* rev. ed., ed. Rodney Needham, trans. James Harle Bell, John Richard von Sturmer, and Rodney Needham (Boston: Beacon, 1969), and "Postface," special issue on "Question de Parenté," *L'Homme,* nos. 154–55 (Apr.–Sept. 2000): 713–20.

24. See Butler, "Competing Universalities."

25. Schneider, *Critique* and *American Kinship;* Sylvia Yanagisako, *Gender and Kinship: Essays Toward a United Analysis* (Stanford University Press, 1987); Sarah Franklin and

Susan McKinnon, "New Directions in Kinship Study: A Core Concept Revisited," *Current Anthropology* (forthcoming), and Franklin and McKinnon, eds., *Relative Values: Reconfiguring Kinship Studies* (Durham, NC: Duke University Press, forthcoming); Marilyn Strathern, *The Gender of the Gift: Problems with Women and Problems with Society in Melanesia* (Berkeley: University of California Press, 1988) and *Reproducing the Future: Anthropology, Kinship, and the New Reproductive Technologies* (New York: Routledge, 1992).

26. Judith Stacey, *In the Name of the Family: Rethinking Family Values in the Postmodern Age* (Boston: Beacon Press, 1996) and *Brave New Families: Stories of Domestic Upheaval in Late 20th Century America* (Berkeley: University of California Press, 1998); Stack, *All Our Kin;* Weston, *Families.*

27. See Lévi-Strauss's discussion of "ethnocentrism" in *Race et histoire* (Paris: Denoël, 1987), 19–26.

28. See Pierre Clastres, *Society against the State: Essays in Political Anthropology,* trans. Robert Hurley (New York: Zone, 1987); *Archeology of Violence,* trans. Jeanine Herman (New York: Semiotext(e), 1994).

29. Franklin and McKinnon, "New Directions," 17. See also Franklin and McKinnon, *Relative Values.*

30. Fassin, "Same Sex."

31. Franklin and McKinnon, "New Directions," 14.

32. Ken Corbett, "Nontraditional Family Romance: Normative Logic, Family Reverie, and the Primal Scene," unpublished essay.

33. Hanna Segal, "Hanna Segal Interviewed by Jacqueline Rose," *Women: A Cultural Review* 1.2 (Nov. 1990): 210, 211, 210. Segal remarks, "An analyst, worth his salt, knows about illness from the *inside.* He doesn't feel 'you are a pervert unlike me' — he feels: 'I know a bit how you came to that point, I've been there, am partly there still.' If he believes in God, he would say: 'there but for the grace of God go I.' " And then a bit later: "You could argue rightly that heterosexual relationships can be as, or more, perverse or narcissistic. But it's not inbuilt in them. Heterosexuality can be more or less narcissistic, it can be very disturbed or not so. In homosexuality it's inbuilt" (212).

34. Agacinski, "Questions," 24.

MICHAEL WARNER

Beyond Gay Marriage

In 1996, debating the so-called Defense of Marriage Act in the House of Representatives, Henry Hyde delivered what he thought was a clinching argument against same-sex marriage: "People don't think that the traditional marriage ought to be demeaned or trivialized by same-sex unions." Congressman Barney Frank quickly seized on what seemed a careless phrase. "How does it demean your marriage? If other people are immoral, how does it demean your marriage?" Hyde, who was later forced to admit an adulterous affair even as he came to head the Republican prosecution in the Clinton impeachment, could not manage much of an answer. "It demeans the institution," he said, lamely. "My marriage was never demeaned. The institution of marriage is trivialized by same-sex marriage."[1]

The thing that makes Hyde's remark wrong—not just illogical or pompous—is that it becomes a program not for his own sexuality but for someone else's. He doesn't just want his marriage to be holy; he wants it to be holy *at the expense of someone else's*. To see gay marriage as "demeaning" is, in his view, a way of seeing "traditional marriage" as more significant. Barney Frank and other marriage advocates have only to expose such thinking to the ridicule it deserves in order to point up its injustice.

But the invidiousness of Hyde's remark is a feature of marriage, not just straight marriage. Marriage sanctifies some couples at the expense of others. It is selective legitimacy. This is a necessary implication of the institution, and not just the result of bad motives or the high-toned non sequiturs of Henry Hyde. To a couple that gets married, marriage just looks ennobling, as it does to Hyde. But stand outside it for a second and you see the implication: if you don't have it, you and your relations are less worthy. Without this corollary effect, marriage would not be able to endow anybody's life with significance. The ennobling and the demeaning go together. Marriage does one only by virtue of the other. Marriage, in short, discriminates.

That is one reason why same-sex marriage provokes such powerful outbursts of homophobic feeling in many straight people, when they could just as easily view marriage as the ultimate conformity of gay people to their own norms. They want marriage to remain a privilege, a mark that they are special. Often, they are willing to grant all or nearly all the benefits of marriage to gay people, as long as they don't have to give up the word *marriage*. They need some token, however magical, of superiority. But what about the gay people who want marriage? Would they not in turn derive their sense of pride from the invidious and shaming distinction between the married and the unmarried?

It must be admitted from the outset that there is something unfashionable, and perhaps untimely, about any discussion of marriage as a goal in gay politics. One is apt to feel like the unmannerly wedding guest, gossiping about divorce at the rehearsal dinner. At this point the only people arguing against gay marriage, it seems, are those homophobic dinosaurs—like Hyde, and Senator Jesse Helms, and the feminist philosopher Jean Bethke Elshtain—who still think that marriage is about procreation, or that same-sex marriage somehow threatens to "tear apart America's moral fabric," as Helms put it on the Senate floor. Pope John Paul II is reported to have claimed that same-sex marriage "is a serious threat to the future of the family and society itself." If the arguments against gay marriage are as silly and phobic as this, then naturally, marrying will seem to strike deep against bigotry. What purpose could be served by a skeptical discussion of marriage now, given the nature of the opposition?[2]

None at all, says Evan Wolfson, director of the Marriage Project at the Lambda Legal Defense and Education Fund. Wolfson argues that in the wake of *Baehr v. Lewin,* the Hawai'i Supreme Court decision that appeared to pave the way for gay marriage, we should "end, or at least suspend, the intra-community debate over whether to seek marriage. The ship has sailed."[3] He cites the need for a united front against the wave of homophobic state and national initiatives designed to wed marriage indissolubly to heterosexuality. As he also points out, there is ample room for foolishness or hubris when intellectuals ask, at this date, whether gay marriage is a worthy political cause. The decision is no longer up to us. The legal system of the United States has its own momentum. The last thing the courts are likely to care about is whether marriage is a good idea from a queer point of view.

There is a kernel of truth in this. One has only to pop the question — For or against gay marriage? — to find oneself at once irrelevant to a process that is no longer a debate, blinded by the urgent temporality of the headline, and suckered into a phony plebiscite. But on this, as on so much else, it may be the courts that will prove to have the narrow view. Within the context that Wolfson takes for granted, dissent is indeed almost unheard. Since the 1993 March on Washington, marriage has come to dominate the political imagination of the national gay movement in the United States. To read the pages of *The Advocate* or *Out* is to receive the impression that gay people hardly care about anything else, other than entertainment. I have no doubt that a large constituency has been formed around this belief. But the commitment is not universally shared, to put it mildly. Gay men, lesbians, and many other unmarried people on the street are just as likely to be made slightly sick by the topic, or perhaps to shrug it off as yet another example of that weird foreign language that people speak in the media world of politics, policy, and punditry.

No one was more surprised by the rise of the gay marriage issue than many veterans of earlier forms of gay activism. To them, marriage seems both less urgent and less agreed-upon than such issues as HIV and health care, AIDS prevention, the repeal of sodomy laws, antigay violence, job discrimination, immigration, media coverage, military antigay policy, sex inequality, and the saturation of everyday life by heterosexual privilege. Before the election of Bill Clinton in 1992, marriage was scarcely a visible blip on the horizon of queer politics; Paula Ettelbrick and Tom Stoddard's 1989 debate on the issue seemed, at the time, simply theoretical. Many gay activists abroad are equally baffled by the focus on marriage in the United States. To them, at least, it is hardly up to Americans to "suspend the intra-community debate." Both within the United States and abroad, people have tried or discussed an immense array of other options, from common law marriage and domestic partnership to the disentangling of health and other benefits from matrimony, to the Scandinavian model of a second-tier marriage (identical to straight marriage except for parenting rights), to the French model of legal concubinage, to the newer package of reforms known in France as the *pacte civil de solidarité* (PACS), a "civil solidarity pact" that in its original version would have bestowed benefits on households of all kinds, including cohabiting siblings. Given this variety of alternatives, it may well strike many as odd that the question has suddenly been reduced to this: same-sex marriage, pro and con.

The time is ripe to reconsider the issue. The campaign for marriage, never a broad-based movement among gay and lesbian activists, depended for its success on the courts. It was launched by a relatively small number of lawyers, not by a consensus among activists. It remains a project of litigation, though now with the support of the major lesbian and gay organizations. But the campaign has come up dry. After initial success with the Supreme Court of Hawai'i in *Baehr v. Lewin,* advocates of same-sex marriage had reason to be optimistic. The tactic of legal advocacy apparently had worked. But outside the courtroom, the homophobic backlash was building. First, the so-called Defense of Marriage Act was passed by Congress and signed by President Clinton. Then, in November 1998, a statewide referendum in Hawai'i neutralized the *Baehr* decision by allowing the legislature to amend the constitution so as to restrict marriage to heterosexual couples. A similar measure passed in Alaska. Moreover, the Hawai'i vote was not even close. Though advocates of same-sex marriage had predicted an even battle, the final vote was nearly 70 percent to 30.

Are these merely stumbles in the progress of history? States are codifying restrictions on marriage that had merely been tacit custom before, making new obstacles to marriage reform for the future. Powerful antigay forces have been mobilized around the issue. If reform of marriage was the goal, the tactics of legal advocacy have not worked, and in some ways have made the problem worse. And if a reconsideration of the tactics seems to have been forced by this turn of events, it is also reasonable to reconsider the long-term strategic goal, since debate over the ultimate goal of reform was cut short by the turn to legal advocacy in the first place. "The ship has sailed," Wolfson confidently declared; but now that the ship has run aground, we might ask whether it was headed in the right direction.

How did the shift in an American national agenda come about? What will its consequences be? For whom would marriage be a victory? What would the value of gay marriage be, for example, to sexual dissidents who are not marrying couples? It is at least possible that the worst consequences would fall on those who did not recognize the question of gay marriage as an "intra-community debate" at all, but considered it something foisted on them by fundamentally alien organizations. (It is no accident that the organizations promoting marriage are defined primarily as advocates for lesbian and gay identity rather than for nonnormative sexual cultures.) Where does the politics of gay marriage lead? What kind of marriage are we talking about, and how might its place in the larger context of state regulations about sexuality be changed? Behind the question of gay marriage as it is posed in the United States, these fundamental questions are not being aired. But they are the questions that count. We cannot wait until American courts settle the marriage issue before addressing them, not least because the way they are answered will play a large part in determining the meaning and consequences of marriage.

Marriage: Why Not?

Marriage became the dominant issue in lesbian and gay politics in the 1990s, but not before. If marriage is so fundamental to a program of rights, why did gay men and lesbians resist it over the twenty-five-year period of their most defiant activism? The issue was raised at the beginning: in 1970, riding a burst of radical enthusiasm after Stonewall, the Reverend Troy Perry officiated a ceremony for two lesbians. Under California law at the time, common law marriage could be formalized by a church ceremony after a couple had lived together for two years. (California law said nothing about the sexes of the couple.) The two women had lived together for just over two years and so demanded (unsuccessfully, it turned out) that California recognize theirs as an already established common law marriage. The same year, a gay male couple in Minnesota made national headlines by applying for a marriage license. One of the men, Jack Baker, wrote a lengthy rationale for what they had done. He emphasized that marriage was "used by the legal system as a distribution mechanism for many rights and privileges" and that as long as the culture considered marriage a right, it was necessary to demand it: "When any minority allows itself to be denied a right that is given to others, it is allowing itself to be relegated to a second-rate position."[4] The mere posing of the issue was a jolt. It made the heterosexuality of marriage visible, to many people, for the first time. It drew attention to the exclusions entailed by marriage, through provisions for inheritance, wrongful death actions, tax rates, and the like. And it advanced a claim of equality that had undeniable appeal. Baker's claims seemed scandalous to the straight press. But they sparked animated discussions of theory and strategy within the groups that had organized in the wake of Stonewall.

Despite the strength of Baker's reasons, and despite the potent theatrical appeal of the issue, gay and lesbian groups did not pursue marriage as a central part of their strategy over the next twenty years. Why not? Was it simply a matter of lesbian resistance derived from the feminist critique of marriage? Were gay men just too busy snorting poppers at the baths? Was American culture simply "not ready" for gay marriage? These are the stories now being told by the advocates of same-sex marriage, back in the headlines after more than a quarter century. But we should not discount other explanations. There were, I think, strong and articulate reasons why the gay movement for decades refused to pursue the path on which it is now hell-bent. They lay at the heart of an ethical vision of queer politics, and centered on the need to resist the state regulation of sexuality. Queer thought both before and after Stonewall rested on these principles:

- It called attention to the mythology by which marriage is idealized.
- It recognized the diversity of sexual and intimate relations as worthy of respect and protection.
- Indeed, it cultivated unprecedented kinds of commonality, intimacy, and public life.
- It resisted any attempt to make the norms of straight culture into the standards by which queer life should be measured.
- It especially resisted the notion that the state should be allowed to accord legitimacy to some kinds of consensual sex but not others, or to confer respectability on some people's sexuality but not others'.
- It insisted that much of what was taken to be morality, respectability, or decorum was, in practice, a way of regulating sexual pleasures and relations.
- It taught that any self-esteem worth having must not be purchased by a disavowal of sex; it must include esteem for one's sexual relations and pleasures, no matter how despised by others.
- It made itself alert to the invidiousness of any institution, such as marriage, that is designed both to reward those inside it and to discipline

those outside it: adulterers, prostitutes, divorcees, the promiscuous, single people, unwed parents, those below the age of consent — in short, all those who become, for the purposes of marriage law, queer.

– It insisted that any vision of sexual justice begin by considering the unrecognized dignity of these outcasts, the ways of living they represent, and the hierarchies of abjection that make them secondary, invisible, or deviant.

– It became alert on principle to the danger that those same hierarchies would continue to structure the thought of the gay and lesbian movement itself — whether through "internalized homophobia," in-group hostility, or simply the perspective unconsciously embedded in so much of our thought and perception.

– It tried to correct for the tendency of U.S. debates to ignore other societies, on whom they nevertheless have an impact.

These insights and principles are so basic that they found expression equally in the work of academic theorists and untutored activists. They made up the ethical vision I encountered in the writings of 1970s gay activists when I was first coming out; the same vision later served as the basis for much of the AIDS activist movement. Because of these basic commitments, when gay and lesbian organizations did include the expansion of marriage in their vision of change after Stonewall, they usually contextualized it as part of more sweeping changes designed to ensure that single people and nonstandard households, and not just same-sex couples, would benefit. In 1972, for example, the National Coalition of Gay Organizations called for the "repeal of all legislative provisions that restrict the sex or number of persons entering into a marriage unit and extension of legal benefits of marriage to all persons who cohabit regardless of sex or numbers." They also demanded "elimination of tax inequities victimizing single persons and same-sex couples."[5] This may not have been a focused, detailed reform program, but it showed an insistence that the demands of couples be accompanied by those of the unmarried and of nonstandard households.

Those who now advocate gay marriage have not shown how doing so is consistent with this tradition. They have induced widespread amnesia about it. It is possible, at least in theory, to imagine a politics in which sex-neutral marriage is seen as a step toward the more fundamental goals of sexual justice: not just formal equality before the law, based on a procedural bar to discrimination, but a substantive justice that would target sexual domination, making possible a democratic cultivation of alternative sexualities. (This kind of question was explicitly ruled out of consideration by the *Baehr* court.) But the advocates of gay marriage have not made this case. Many, indeed, have made the opposite case: that pursuing marriage means abandoning the historical principles of the queer movement as an antiquated "liberationism." For writers such as Andrew Sullivan, Gabriel Rotello, Michelangelo Signorile, Jonathan Rauch, and Bruce Bawer, this is part of the appeal of marriage. Others argue, either ingenuously or disingenuously, that marriage has nothing to do with these historical commitments, that it is not a question of social change or cultural politics at all but a neutral matter on which each individual must decide. This is the official or semiofficial position of the major national gay and lesbian organizations: the National Gay and Lesbian Task Force, the Human Rights Campaign, and Lambda Legal Defense. Either way, the crucial founding insights behind several decades' worth of gay and lesbian politics are now being forgotten. If the campaign for marriage requires such a massive repudiation of queer culture's best insights on intimate relations, sex, and the politics of stigma, then the campaign is doing more harm than marriage could ever be worth.

Marriage without Cost

A blandly benign position on marriage has become the creed of the major national gay organizations and is fast becoming entrenched as the new common sense. It is best expressed by Kerry Lobel, executive director of the National Gay and Lesbian Task Force, in a press release announcing support for gay marriage: "Marriage is an important personal choice and a basic human right. Whether gay people decide to get married or not, it should be our choice." This line of thinking was established by the late Tom Stoddard, who worked hard to launch both the gay marriage and military service campaigns. He wrote in *Out/Look* in 1989 that the fundamental issue "is not the desirability of marriage, but rather the desirability of the *right* to marry." Activists, in Stoddard's view, were obliged to work for as many options as possible for gay people, even if they disliked marriage in its currently sanctioned form.

A conception of activism as enlarging the life options of gay men and lesbians has a manifest appeal. And it is undeniable that many gays and lesbians want to marry. But this way of thinking says nothing about whether pursuing legal marriage is a good political strategy, about the ethical question of what marrying does, about state regulation, or about the normativity of marriage. Is marrying something you do privately, as a personal choice or an expression of taste, with no consequences for those who do not marry?

That would be true only if marriage were somehow thought to lack the very privileged relation to legitimacy that makes people desire it in the first place, or if the meaning of marriage could somehow be specified without reference to the state. As long as people marry, the state will continue to regulate the sexual lives of those who do not marry. It will continue to refuse to recognize our intimate relations, including cohabiting partnerships, as having the same rights or validity as a married couple. It will criminalize our consensual sex. It will stipulate at what age and in what kind of space we can have sex. It will send the police to harass sex workers and cruisers. It will restrict our access to sexually explicit materials. All this and more the state will justify because these sexual relations take place outside of marriage. In the modern era, marriage has become the central legitimating institution by which the state regulates and permeates people's most intimate lives; it is the zone of privacy outside of which sex is unprotected. In this context, to speak of marriage as merely one choice among others is at best naïve. It might be more accurately called active mystification.

The idea that marriage is simply a choice, a right that can be exercised privately without cost to others, dazzles by its simplicity. To most Americans it seems unthinkable that one might argue with it. And that is the key to its success, because it makes us forget the history of principled critique of marriage in queer politics. The same might be said of the other dominant argument for marriage: that it is just about love.

Many gay men and lesbians in America, echoing the language of Lobel, Stoddard, and Wolfson, seem to think that considerations of social consequence and institutional change are beside the point. They believe that marrying has nothing to do with the unmarried, nor with the state regulation of sex, nor with changing cultural norms. They seem to think that marriage is a long-term relationship of commitment between two people who love each other—end of story. "Whatever the history," Wolfson writes, "today marriage is first and foremost about a loving union between two people who enter into a relationship of emotional and financial commit-

ment and interdependence, two people who seek to make a public statement about their relationship, sanctioned by the state, the community at
large, and, for some, their religious community."[6]

This definition plays well to the kind of pious common sense that people
nod along with as long as their everyday knowledge of sex and status is
suspended. It is an exceedingly odd definition for Wolfson to offer in what
is generally a tightly reasoned theoretical essay. A shrewd lawyer, he might
be expected to know that love is not necessary for legally sanctioned marriage, and vice versa. One can be married without love, just as one can love
without marrying. Nor is the purpose of legal marriage "to make a public
statement." You can make a public statement with any kind of ceremony,
or by talking to people, or by circulating a queerzine. A legal marriage, on
the other hand, might well be private or even secret. The *Baehr* court,
which Wolfson celebrates, is more frank in its definition: "Marriage is a
state-conferred legal partnership status." Wolfson mentions the sanction of
the state only as a kind of amplifying power for the public statement of
marriage, as though the state's role in marriage were nothing more. His
definition works hard to mystify the institution. But it is typical of what
passes for common sense.

Many gay men and lesbians who now say that they want marriage seem
to focus on the way it confers, in their view, respectability and public
acceptance. Often, they do not even mention the extensive slate of legally
enforceable benefits, entitlements, and obligations that come with marriage. To them, marriage is a statement. For example, writer Barbara Cox
asks: "How could a feminist, out, radical lesbian like myself get married a
year ago last April?" (Of course, it turns out that she has not gotten "married" in the legal sense; she means that she has had a private ceremony.)
"My ceremony was an expression of the incredible love and respect that I
have found with my partner. My ceremony came from a need to speak of
that love and respect openly to those who participate in my world."[7] In this
way the state disappears when gay men and lesbians think about marriage.
They assimilate it to the model of *coming out*. It is driven by expressive
need. It speaks a self-validating truth, credible because it is "incredible." It
is without invidious distinction or harmful consequence to others. It transforms the surrounding world, making what Cox calls a "radical claim."
Even though people think that marriage gives them validation, legitimacy,
and recognition, they somehow think that it does so without invalidating,
delegitimating, or stigmatizing other relations, needs, and desires.

Such naïveté is all the more striking because Cox writes as a legal theorist. Such is the world-canceling force of love that Cox can imagine the government as merely the most general audience for her private relations — another guest at the ceremony. Although she argues for legally sanctioned marriage, the transition from private ceremony to public regulation appears seamless to her. Ceremonies can do many laudable things, especially in making concrete the social worlds that queers make for themselves. They are a kind of public. But as a way of thinking about legal marriage this notion of pure love, like so much else in contemporary U.S. politics, is an image of sentimental privacy. Love, it says, is beyond criticism and beyond the judgments of the law. Where law adjudicates conflict and competing claims, love speaks an inner truth, in a space where there is no conflict, no politics. It is the human heart, not ideology. Its intentions are pure. It has no unconscious.

I would argue that any politics based on such a sentimental rhetoric of privacy is not only a false idealization of love and coupling; it is an increasingly powerful way of distracting citizens from the real, conflicted, and unequal conditions governing their lives, and it serves to reinforce the privilege of those who already find it easiest to imagine their lives as private. Then, too, the transcendent self-evidence of love leads people to think that any question of the ethical problems of marrying must be crass or, at best, secondary. If their unmarried friends ever express resentment about marital privilege, the married can always absolve themselves of their participation in marriage by appealing to the self-validating nature of their love — which, strictly speaking, should have rendered marriage unnecessary.

But there is a further irony in the appeal to love as an argument for marriage. Love, as Cox describes it, is deeply antinomian: a revolt against law. Like Hester Prynne in Hawthorne's *The Scarlet Letter*, Barbara Cox is saying to her critics, What we did had a consecretion of its own. (Unlike Hester, though, she thinks that it should therefore be consecrated by law.) Love is self-validating. This claim for her love allows Cox to say that no one has a right to judge her and her lover. She directs this rebuke to gay critics of marriage, but it also extends to the fifty states, which, by sanctioning heterosexual marriage, are felt to pass judgments of illegitimacy on gay love. The appeal for legal marriage, in this way, is *also* a form of resistance to the legal character of marriage. That is why Cox can think of it as "radical," and why mass solemnizations such as the one at the 1987 March on Washington do have at least some of the flavor of queer protests. Nothing shows the tensions and contradictions of our historical moment more clearly than the way the upsurge of sentiment about marriage among gay people gives voice to an antinomian protest — in the very act of demanding marriage.

In the antinomian tradition, love is more than a noble virtue among others and more than a mass of disorderly and errant desire: it is a determinate negation of legality. Christopher Hill traces this idea back at least to the fifteenth century, when religious reformers known as the Lollards denied the necessity of church marriage. While the American Puritans concluded that marriage should be a purely secular matter left to magistrates, other reformers such as George Fox (whose followers came to be known as Quakers) questioned the validity of the institution outright: "The right joining in marriage is the work of the Lord only," he wrote, "and not the priest's or magistrate's for it is God's ordinance and not man's. . . . Friends marry none; it is the Lord's work, and we are but witnesses."[8] After the Restoration, as government grew to be a more active participant in marriage, making marriage more and more a legal institution of the nation-state rather than a customary network of kinship, the appeal of love's rebelliousness in the face of spreading regulation intensified. The legality of the modern state changed the background conditions of love.

In the early nineteenth century, the poet John Clare was able to describe an unsolemnized relationship as "Not felon-like law-bound, but wedded in desires."[9] By 1852 the American physician M. Edgeworth Lazarus could write a treatise whose title says it all: *Love vs. Marriage*. In post-Romantic culture especially, the antinomian and world-canceling moment has even become necessary to validate love as love. That is why nearly all the great love stories have not been stories of marriages, but stories of extramarital or illegitimate love: Hester and Arthur, Tristan and Isolde, Catherine and Heathcliff, *The Bridges of Madison County, Titanic*. Occasionally a politics has been built on the basis of the antinomian strand. "We don't need no piece of paper from the city hall keeping us tied and true, no," sang the oft-married-and-divorced Joni Mitchell in 1971. But this politics has proven to be fragile, largely because it was built on the self-validating claims of the couple form, rather than on a recognition of other relations, intimacies, or sexualities.

After all, those stories of extramarital and illegitimate love may have prepared some people to do without that piece of paper from the city hall, but they have hardly brought the legal institution of marriage to an end. Most people who thrill to the spectacle of young unwed lovers revolting against the horrors of an arranged marriage in *Titanic* do not imagine that marriage itself — arranged or not — might be dropped in the ocean as lightly as that diamond necklace. Why not? Why is the institution so resilient, even though so many have come to recognize that you can have a perfectly legitimate love without that piece of paper from the city hall? Is love any less valid because it has not been certified by the government? Most Americans would offer an instinctive and vigorous answer: no. But then why does anyone imagine that love is an argument for marriage?

One reason may be that the couple form is sentimentalized by the internalization of a witness, as when Cox speaks of her "incredible love" and "a need to speak of that love." One admires one's being-in-love. (As Robert Gluck writes in the opening sentence of *Jack the Modernist*, "You're not a lover till you blab about it.")[10] Just as easily as the mass audience is permitted to sigh, weep, and throb during the lovers' most intimate moments, so also the state in its generality can embody the witnessing of that private consecration. When Wolfson speaks of making a "public statement," it does not seem surprising that the state is there, *sanctioning* it. One simply doesn't inquire into what it means for the state to sanction a statement. The state can piggyback on sentimentality in this way, making itself the silent partner and constitutive witness to what people imagine as their most private and authentic emotion.

The culture of marriage, in fact, thrives on stories of revolt against it. This has been true ever since the Enlightenment, when marriage ceased to be understood as an alliance of families forged to preserve estates. The modern legal machinery of marriage is powered, paradoxically, by the love-couple's ability to transcend law. The state merely certifies a love that is beyond law; but by doing so, it justifies its existence as keeper of the law.

No other form of intimacy or sexuality has this power to couple with the state. One could make an antinomian claim to validity on behalf of, say, a blow job in a tearoom. Especially if the blow job expressed a stigmatized, forbidden, and oppressed sexuality, the pleasure of its realization might be intensified by a sense of the wrongness of the law that banned it, as that law embodied an unjust social order and a lifetime of oppressive experience — all swept aside in the discovery, through pleasure, that the desire to reject that social order was shared with another. People in any nonnormative intimate or consensual sexual situation may in this way feel that they have turned the law under foot. It might seem in such moments that whether the emotion or the pleasure results in shared property or common respectability has no bearing on its authenticity. But outside the tearoom such claims would fall flat, lacking any reverberation in the carefully tuned wind chimes of sentimental couplehood. Whatever we value in a tearoom, or whatever we sentimentalize there, we don't sentimentalize it in a way that requires the state to be our solemn witness. The language of the love-couple is different. It wants recognition. It wants to rule.

Evan Wolfson draws on the powerful hidden resource of self-validating love when he argues that we have no right to question lesbians and gay men who want marriage. He believes that their desires must be valid just because they are desires: "The suggestion that lesbians and gay men who want equal marriage rights do not know what is best for them as gay people is not uncommon in the intra-community arguments against pursuing marriage. In the charge that the demand for equal marriage rights is insufficiently radical or liberationist, a contemnable desire to 'mimic' or 'emulate' the non-gay world, or a sell-out of less 'assimilationist' or less 'privileged' gay people, there is an inescapable whiff of imputed false consciousness. However, given the diversity and number of women and men within our communities who strongly want the equal right to marry, the imputation seems wrong, as well as unfair."[11] Wolfson is right, I think, to reject the idea that gays and lesbians who want to marry are simply imitating straights. That is a naïve view of how norms work. He is also right to say that the argument against marriage has too often been put in these terms. But there is also a will to naïveté in the implication that false consciousness cannot exist. What kind of reasoning would tell us that something could not be false consciousness because it was widely shared? Isn't that the idea? False consciousness is an undeniable force throughout history. From age to age, serfs have revered their masters, young men have marched gaily off to be slaughtered on behalf of deities and nations, and wives have lovingly obeyed patriarchal husbands. Why should gay people be immune to similar mistakes about their interests? It would not be surprising if they adhered to alien interests even on sober reflection. Marriage, after all, is a concrete personal benefit imbued with intense affect and nearly universal legitimacy. The alternative, a world capacious enough in its recognition of households to be free from such invidious regulatory institutions altogether, can easily seem abstract, even unimaginable. These options are not equally weighed, for the simple reason that marriage has a taken-for-grantedness and an apparently natural emotional force that prevent anything resembling rational choice.

Wolfson seems to assume that whatever passes as common sense must be right; people in numbers are never mistaken; their actions never have consequences that they themselves do not foresee; and they never act in a context the full ramifications of which remain unconscious to them. When he asks, rhetorically, "Does everyone who gets married, from Ruth Bader Ginsburg to Catherine [*sic*] MacKinnon, endorse every retrograde aspect of marriage?" he implies that the meaning of an act lies in the actor's motive.[12] This assumption, characteristically American, obscures the issue. Whether an individual is right or wrong in choosing to marry, whether he or she is sincere or not, acting in false consciousness or not, or *intends* all of the consequences of marrying has little to do with the ramifications of the act.

People might marry for all kinds of reasons. They might want to stick it in the face of the straights. They might want access to health care. They might want a public armature for their own will to sustain a relationship of care. They might have chosen with eyes wide open to embrace a world in which a coupling supported by shared property is the only sign of real belonging and the only publicly recognized context for intimacy. They might simply not trust the relationship to last without third-party assurances. They might think that marriage will relieve their fears of getting old, fat, or undesirable. They might marry for no better reason than that marrying is what one does. Or they might want in-laws. Richard Posner worries, rather extravagantly, that a gay man would marry a succession of AIDS patients in order to collect the life insurance.[13] It's likely enough that people will have many motives, and that most will be marked by ambivalence. That's life.

Claudia Card illustrates well the difficulties posed by marriage for queers with nonstandard intimacies:

> My partner of the past decade is not a domestic partner. She and I form some kind of fairly common social unit which, so far as I know, remains nameless. Along with such namelessness goes a certain invisibility. . . . We do not share a domicile (she has her house; I have mine). Nor do we form an economic unit (she pays her bills; I pay mine). Although we certainly have fun together, our relationship is not based simply on fun. We share the sorts of mundane details of daily living that [Richard] Mohr finds constitutive of marriage (often in her house, often in mine). We know a whole lot about each other's lives that the neighbors and our other friends will never know. In times of trouble, we are each other's

first line of defense, and in times of need, we are each other's main support. Still, we are not married. Nor do we yearn to marry. Yet if marrying became an option that would legitimate behavior otherwise illegitimate and make available to us social securities that will no doubt become even more important to us as we age, we and many others like us might be pushed into marriage. Marrying under such conditions is not a totally free choice.[14]

This account reminds us that lived intimacies seldom take the form imposed by marriage. It also shows that people are likely to encounter in marriage a mix of constraints, and that the meaning of marriage is only partly what they themselves bring to it.

Because the institution of marriage is itself one of the constraints on people's intimate lives, to judge the worthiness of the institution is not to condemn the people in it. But it does mean that marrying should be considered an ethical problem. It is a public institution, not a private relation, and its meaning and consequences extend far beyond what a marrying couple could intend. The ethical meaning of marrying cannot be simplified to a question of pure motives, conscious choice, or transcendent love. Its ramifications reach as far as the legal force and cultural normativity of the institution. That is a heavy ethical burden to take on, and feminists such as Card have long shown courage in addressing it. No wonder people are so grateful to Wolfson, Lobel, and others who are willing to dismiss the ethics of marriage in such a radical and shallow way.

It is undeniable that the restriction of marriage to heterosexual couples is a potent form of discrimination, regulation, and stigma. But to combat that inequality requires us to think beyond the mere inclusion of gay couples, and to recognize that marrying has consequences for the unmarried. Those consequences can be treated, roughly, under the following headings:

- The menu of privileges and prohibitions, incentives and disincentives, directly tied to marriage by the state
- The material incentives and disincentives tied to marriage in civil society
- The matrix of state regulations of sexuality of which marriage is the linchpin
- The broader cultural normativity of marital status

Each of these should be challenged, not celebrated, as a condition of same-sex marriage.

The strategic question facing the lawyers is this: Should we try to extend benefits and recognition even further beyond conventional marriage, uncoupling them from marital status and making them available to individuals, households, and intimate relations? Or should we claim for ourselves the status of marriage and thereby restrict entitlements and recognition to it? But *it is not the decision that is posed to individual lesbians and gay men in the form of a choice to marry.* A poll of gay men and lesbians does not address this issue. We have good reason to be alarmed, given the potential for majoritarianism, when apologists such as Wolfson appeal to a silent majority that favors marriage. You need not argue that gays who marry have chosen to sell out less assimilationist or privileged queers to believe that the effect would be to reinforce the material privileges and cultural normativity of marriage. Individual choices to marry are not only rewarded with material benefits and normative recognition, but made from the limited slate of socially supported alternatives. Because the desire to marry is an aspect of the normativity of marriage, it cannot be said to validate the norm, any more than the desire to buy a Coke validates capitalism. Buying commodities sustains the culture of commodities whether the buyers like it or not. That is the power of a system. Just so, marrying consolidates and sustains the normativity of marriage. And it does so despite what may be the best intentions of those who marry.

Wolfson's view of marriage as simply a personal choice, like Cox's and like Lobel's, is wholly inadequate to evaluate the strategy of pursuing legal marriage because it neglects marriage's legal and cultural consequences for others — those who resist marriage, as well as those who are drawn to it for a mix of reasons not of their own making. Whether they like it or not, married people have countless privileges, some that define marriage and some that ought to have nothing to do with it. They are taken more seriously than unmarried people; they are more likely to be invited to dinner parties, offered jobs, and elected to public office. In short, they have status. It is therefore hard to credit Wolfson's blunt assertion that the marriage issue is not about "the pros and cons of a way of life."

A more honest argument for gay marriage is made by those who know very well that to marry has consequences beyond oneself. Jonathan Rauch, for instance, has no truck with the illusion of choice or innocent diversity: "If marriage is to work," he writes, "it cannot be merely a 'lifestyle option.' It must be privileged. That is, it must be understood to be better, on average, than other ways of living. Not mandatory, not good where everything else is bad, but better: a general norm, rather than a personal taste."[15] Similarly, Gabriel Rotello, in a cover story for *The Nation* excerpted from his book *Sexual Ecology,* argues that gay marriage would be a system of rewards and punishments designed to steer gay men into monogamy and away from sex with other partners. "Marriage would provide status to those who married and implicitly penalize those who did not," he writes. Rotello at least acknowledges the normalizing intent of his argument about marriage. Most gay advocates of marriage, he notes, "are generally careful not to make the case for marriage, but simply for the *right* to marriage. This is undoubtedly good politics, since many if not most of the major gay and lesbian organizations that have signed on to the fight for same-sex marriage would instantly sign off at any suggestion that they were actually encouraging gay men and lesbians to marry."[16]

Hardly anyone else has the guts to embrace the politics of shame quite so openly in arguments for gay marriage. But it is generally implicit. William Eskridge at times pretends that marriage is a noninvidious recognition of gay lives, but the subtitle of his book, *From Sexual Liberty to Civilized Commitment,* reveals that it is rather a state-sanctioned program for normalizing gay sexuality.[17] (One reviewer noted that Eskridge's title bespeaks "the puritanical impulse to make bachelorhood equivalent to moral lassitude, where all sexual expression outside wedlock is morally tainted.")[18] When leading gay legal theorists dismiss gay sexuality as mere liberty, uncivilized and uncommitted, it is no wonder that so many gay men and lesbians feel either indifferent to or assaulted by this campaign allegedly waged on their behalf.

But Eskridge and others like him are not content to pass private moral judgment on unmarried queers. They see marriage as an engine for social change and the state as the proper instrument of moral judgment. These deep assumptions about the social welfare and the state's role are almost never challenged in the current debate. Even liberal writers, such as the editors of the *New York Times,* typically endorse the idea that the state's business is "to foster stable, long-term" coupling.[19] But this kind of social engineering is questionable. It brings the machinery of administration to bear on the realm of pleasures and intimate relations, aiming to stifle variety among ways of living. It authorizes the state to make one form of life, *already normative,* even more privileged. The state's administrative penetration into contemporary life may have numbed us to the deep coerciveness in this way of thinking. We take it for granted. Yet it is blind majoritarianism, armed not only with an impressive battery of prohibitions and punishments, but with an equally impressive battery of economistic incentives and disincentives, all designed to manipulate not just the economic choices of the populace, but people's substantive and normative vision of the good life.

The ability to imagine and cultivate forms of the good life that do not conform to the dominant pattern would seem to be at least as fundamental as any putative "right to marry." If so, then the role of the state should be to protect *against* the abuses of majoritarianism. The claim that the state has an interest in fostering long-term coupling is profoundly antidemocratic. When the state imposes a majoritarian view of the good life, it cannot claim to act on the basis of a neutral consideration of the possibilities; it acts to prevent such consideration. Andrew Sullivan, for one, makes the antidemocratic impulse clear:

> There are very few social incentives of the kind conservatives like for homosexuals *not* to be depraved: there's little social or familial support, no institution to encourage fidelity or monogamy, precious little religious or moral outreach to guide homosexuals into more virtuous living. This is not to say that homosexuals are not responsible for their actions, merely that in a large part of homosexual subculture there is much a conservative would predict, when human beings are abandoned with extremely few social incentives for good or socially responsible behavior. But the proper conservative response to this is surely not to infer that this behavior is inevitable, or to use it as a reason to deter others from engaging in a responsible homosexual existence, if that is what they want; but rather to construct social institutions and guidelines to modify and change that behavior for the better.[20]

Marriage, in short, would make for good gays: the kind who would not challenge the norms of straight culture, who would not flaunt sexuality, and who would not insist on living differently from ordinary folk. These behavioristic arguments for gay marriage are mostly aimed at modifying the sexual culture of gay men. Left and right, advocates of gay marriage assume that marriage as a social institution is, in the words of Bishop John Shelby Spong, "marked by integrity and caring and . . . filled with grace and beauty"; that it will modify "behavior"; and that a culture of "gay bars, pornography, and one-night stands" is desperately in need of virtue.[21] This idealization of marriage is typical of those who are excluded from it:

priests, gays, adolescents. It shows an extraordinarily willful blindness. As one observer notes: "To presume that morality follows on marriage is to ignore centuries of evidence that each is very much possible without the other."[22] Worse, it is predicated on the homophobic equation of "gay bars, pornography, and one-night stands" with immorality — the very equation against which the gay movement came into being. If the conservative arguments *against* gay marriage reduce to almost nothing but homophobia, these arguments in favor of it are powered by homophobic assumptions as well.

It may be more precise to call these arguments antiqueer rather than homophobic, and as a way of commandeering the resources and agenda of gay politics, that's what they are. Yet the image of the Good Gay is never invoked without its shadow in mind: the Bad Queer, the kind who has sex, who talks about it, and who builds with other queers a way of life that ordinary folk do not understand or control. Marriage could hardly produce in reality the Good Gays who are pictured in this rhetoric: gays who marry will be as likely to divorce, cheat, and abuse each other as anyone else. The more likely effect is much uglier, because any politics that makes full social membership conditional on the proprieties of the marital form is ultimately a way to pave over the collective world that lesbians and gays have made. From the homophile movement until recently, gay activism understood itself as an attempt to stave off the pathologization of gay life — by the police, by the McCarthy inquest, by psychologists and psychiatrists, by politicians, by health and sanitation departments. Now we are faced with activists who see the normalization of queer life precisely as their role.

So it seems as though there are two ways to argue for gay marriage: embrace the politics of shame outright, allowing married gay couples to be relieved of stigma in order to make its coercive effects felt by the unmarried; or simply deny that the legal institution of marriage has any connection to the politics of shame at all. It is of course possible, given the dissociative consciousness that prevails in American culture on the topic of sex, to believe both that marriage is a private choice without normative consequences *and* that it would make the queers behave themselves. It is equally possible, apparently, to believe both that marriage is just a neutral choice and that it is a crazy idea. ("Mad vow disease," Kate Clinton calls it.) Many gay activists who currently toe the party line — that marriage is simply a personal choice — privately oppose it. But they feel uncomfortable publicly criticizing those who want to marry. Because no one is publicly voicing any opposition, the party line seems a safe way out. It also frees activists in the national identity organizations from having to recognize any connection between the gay marriage debates and the growing crackdown on all queerer forms of sexual culture in the United States. Apologists for gay marriage, such as Rotello and Sullivan, can make that connection explicit again and again; yet the gay organizations have not entertained the possibility of such a connection long enough to take a stand against it. Too many activists see marriage only as a way of overcoming the stigma on identity and are willing to ignore — or even celebrate — the way it reinforces all of the other damaging hierarchies of shame around sex.

What Is Marriage?

I have argued here that the *debate* over gay marriage has been regressive. But is that true of gay marriage necessarily? That depends in part on what kind of marriage we are talking about. The first thing to get over, in thinking about the possibility of a better politics and ethics of marriage, is the idea that marriage just is what it is. People mean very different things by marriage, and not simply because they are confused. If we begin by recognizing that it is a package rather than a single thing, it might be easier to imagine redefining it.

It is always tempting to believe that marrying is simply something that two people do. Marriage, however, is never a private contract between two persons. It always involves the recognition of a third party — and not just a voluntary or neutral recognition, but an *enforceable* recognition. We speak of entitlements when the third party is the state, and of status when the third party is others generally. Either way, marital benefits are vast.

Let us begin with the menu of privileges directly tied by the state to marriage. Marriage is nothing if not a program for privilege. "Marriage," as Posner notes in *Sex and Reason,* "is a status rich in entitlements."[23] The Supreme Court of Hawai'i, in *Baehr v. Lewin,* handily lists some of those entitlements:

1. a variety of state income tax advantages, including deductions, credits, rates, exemptions, and estimates;
2. public assistance from and exemptions relating to the Department of Human Services;
3. control, division, acquisition, and disposition of community property;

4. rights relating to dower, curtesy, and inheritance;

5. rights to notice, protection, benefits, and inheritance under the Uniform Probate Code;

6. award of child custody and support payments in divorce proceedings;

7. the right to spousal support;

8. the right to enter into premarital agreements;

9. the right to change of name;

10. the right to file a nonsupport action;

11. post-divorce rights relating to support and property division;

12. the benefit of the spousal privilege and confidential marital communications;

13. the benefit of the exemption or real property from attachment or execution;

14. the right to bring a wrongful death action.

To these state entitlements would have to be added others, such as next-of-kin privileges in hospital visitation, medical decision making, and burial. There are also federal entitlements, including federal tax advantages and immigration and naturalization benefits, as well as local ones such as rent control benefits, already available to domestic partners in some cases. Even this list of state-guaranteed benefits, or rights, doesn't touch on the benefits that can be collected in civil society in the form of kin groups, discounts on and joint applications for services, memberships, and insurance policies — not to mention trousseaux and the power to make all your friends and relations fly hundreds of miles to see you, wear expensive costumes, and buy you housewares from Bloomingdale's.

Most of these benefits could be extended to other kinds of households and intimate relations. Very few have a necessary relation to a couple or intimate pair — perhaps, logically enough, only those having to do with divorce. All the others could be thought of in different ways. Many, such as health care and tax equality, are social justice issues, and should be extended to single people. Why should being in a couple be necessary for health benefits? But for many in the United States, it is. Health care is uppermost in the minds of many couples who apply for domestic partnership where it exists, and it is the issue that gives an edge of urgency to marriage. But think about the implication: that we happily leave single people uninsured. A just health care system would remove this distinctive privilege from marriage.

Other benefits, such as those having to do with property sharing, are specific to households rather than romantic couples and could be broadened to cover all cohabiting arrangements (ex-lovers, relatives, long-term intimate friends, etc.). This is one of the most interesting features of PACS; it is a status giving legal recognition to living arrangements rather than regulating sex. It allows people to share property, inherit, and provide mutual care, whatever their emotional or sexual relation.

Still other benefits, such as immigration rights, parenting rights, rights to bring wrongful death actions, and even the prohibition against spousal testimony in court, seem to be attached to powerful intimate commitments; but these need not be thought of as marriages. Such benefits could be extended to domestic partners, nondomestic partners of the kind described by Claudia Card, legal concubinage, or common law relations. In Australia, for instance, immigration policy already treats all unmarried couples alike, whether gay or straight, under the "interdependency" category of the country's visa regulations. Even in the United States, a country not known for enlightened immigration policy, it was possible to win special consideration for intimate partners until 1996. Then Congress made it impossible for judges to waive deportation on humanitarian grounds, even in the case of partners who shared mortgages, businesses, or children. The painful separations that result from this policy testify vividly to the costs of marriage for those excluded from it. But gay marriage is not the only solution, nor necessarily the best one. Even if marriage were now allowed by a state, the Defense of Marriage Act prevents its extension to federal benefits such as immigration. It would be better if the right to intimate association were recognized and interdependencies valued in any form, not just the married couple.

Similarly, child custody could be linked to relations of care rather than to marriage. Gay and lesbian parenting arrangements very often involve three adults, rather than two, a situation that is denied by the attachment of parenting rights to marriage. Courts in some states have already made strides toward redefining family to reflect the reality of people's relationships. Why reverse that trend by linking everything to marriage?

The only kind of benefit that is necessarily linked to marriage is divorce. But even here, a number of different legal statuses could be made available to people, with different means of dissolution. This remains one of the principal differences between concubinage and marriage in French law, for example, and there is no reason why domestic partnership might not eventually be expanded to cover the same benefits as marriage, for both gay and straight couples, while allowing for less bureaucratically encumbered dissolutions.

Marriage, in other words, is defined partly by the bundling of various privileges and statuses as a single package. The argument for gay marriage no doubt appeals to many people because it is a shortcut to equalizing these practical social advantages. But the unmodulated demand for same-sex marriage fails to challenge the bundling of privileges that have no necessary connection one to another, or to marriage. Indeed, if successful, the demand for same-sex marriage would leave that bundling further entrenched in law. Squeezing gay couples into the legal sorting machine would only confirm the relevance of spousal status, and would leave unmarried queers looking more deviant before a legal system that could claim broader legitimacy.

Interestingly, the gay marriage debate almost never turns on specific benefits or entitlements. As the lawyer David Chambers notes, in the only extensive review of the legal entailments I have seen, "Whatever the context of the debate, most speakers are transfixed by the *symbolism* of legal recognition."[24] Argument turns on the status conferred informally by marriage, on the function of marriage in altering "behavior," and on the real or imagined social purpose of marriage. This is an odd fact considering that the past several decades have seen many efforts to detach state entitlements such as spousal support from marital status, for straight and gay couples alike, and that these efforts have created new possibilities (e.g., palimony). Extending benefits as an issue of justice, apart from marriage, reduces the element of privilege in marriage, as many conservatives fear. That strategy has enjoyed considerable success in the Scandinavian social democracies. But the United States seems headed down the opposite path, given the revived popularity of marriage among straight couples and the generally conservative turn of the culture.

For example, the Family and Medical Leave Act of 1993 provides for leaves to care for spouses, children, and parents but, as Chambers points out, "makes no provision of any kind for friends, lovers, or unmarried partners."[25] A congressional commission on immigration policy, meanwhile, has widened the gap between the treatment of noncitizen spouses and the treatment of all other noncitizen relatives and partners. Republican reforms in the tax code are designed to provide further incentives to marry. Citing such developments, Chambers contends that gay couples will benefit from marriage. My argument here runs counter to Chambers's, but I find his evidence more useful to mine than to his own. Chambers shows that gay couples would gain many benefits from spousal status. No one doubts that. But it does not follow that those benefits should be restricted to spouses, or that they should be bundled together, or that their acquisition by spouses would be either beneficial or neutral to unmarried queers. Chambers's review is admirably broad and detailed, but it does not show that same-sex marriage would be the appropriate solution to all the exclusions he documents. Rather, it shows, in case after case after case, that such areas of law as probate, custody, and immigration need far more sweeping reforms than same-sex marriage. Pursuing same-sex marriage as a strategy fails to address the privilege of spousal status that is the core of the problem. The conservative trend of shoring up this privilege is mirrored, wittingly or unwittingly, by the decision of U.S. advocates of gay marriage to subordinate an entire bundle of entitlements to the status of marriage.

Apart from the question of what benefits exactly we mean by "marriage," there is the more fundamental question about what the state's role in marriage is or should be. Government now plays a much more direct role in marriage than it has for most of Western civilization's history. In the anthropological literature, the main debate about marriage is whether its primary function in nonmodern society is to establish alliances between men, or lines of descent. But in modern societies, marriage has less and less to do with either of these aspects of kinship systems. The powerful dynamic tension in premodern societies between marriage and the moiety system — in which your spouse is socially foreign to you, a representative of all that is opposite to your own kin — is lost and, for most moderns, unimaginable. In-laws are less and less material. Bastardy laws, where they remain on the books, seldom have an effect. People reckon family and descent through households, affinity, and blood rather than through the symbolic exchanges of ritual marriage. Some early modern features of marriage, such as publishing the banns, have all but vanished. Others, like the fertility ritual of flinging rice, survive only in vestigial form. Still others, like giving away the bride, probably retain more significance than anyone would like to admit. But as these world-orienting horizons of kinship and exogamy systems have receded, the state as mediator has loomed up in their place.

In the contemporary United States, unlike most times and places in world history, state certification is a constitutive event, not a secondary acknowledgment of a previously established relationship. Some people naïvely imagine that a marriage license is essential to marriage. But the

marriage license is a modern invention. (Its history, as far as I know, remains unwritten.) Even the widespread use of parish registers to formalize
marriages does not go back much before the eighteenth century. Until then,
common law marriage was the rule, not the exception. (In America it is
currently recognized, even for heterosexual couples, in only one-fourth of
the states.) Richard Mohr points to the importance of this fact, arguing that
the best model for the legitimation of same-sex households would be common law marriage: "In a common-law arrangement, the marriage is at
some point, as the need arises, culturally and legally acknowledged in retrospect as having existed all along. It is important to remember that as matter
of law, the standard requirement of living together seven years is entirely
evidentiary and not at all constitutive of the relation as a marriage. . . .
Indeed, that immigration fraud through marriage licenses is even conceptually possible is a tacit recognition that marriage *simpliciter* is marriage
as a lived arrangement, while legally certified marriage is and should be
viewed as epiphenomenal or derivative — and not vice versa."[26] To Mohr,
this is an argument for common law marriage. In my view, common law
marriage still suffers from many of the same limitations that other kinds of
marriage do. But the distinction Mohr makes here is important, because it
dramatizes how the state's constitutive role is simply taken for granted
when we ask only whether we want "marriage." Countless systems of
marriage have had nothing to do with a state fetish or with the regulatory
force of law. Most of the options are not open to us. But others, more or less
live, might be open if we did not think that the question was simply same-
sex marriage, pro or con.

In a way, the common law tradition seems to be what writers such as
Cox and Wolfson have in mind when they treat the state as if it merely
recognized a marital relationship that the partners had created by themselves. This tradition harks back to a time not only before parish registers
and marriage licenses, but before vice cops, income taxes, social security,
and the rest of what we now call "the state." If American culture were
better at recognizing what Mohr calls "marriage as a form of living and
repository of norms independent of law,"[27] and if state recognition were
more widely understood as deriving from that form of living rather than as
authorizing it, it might be easier to push the state to recognize single parents
and other nonstandard households, interdependencies, and intimacies that
do not take the form of shared property. In fact, all of these arrangements
have gained status during the twentieth century. In respect to the family,

real estate, and employment, for example, the state has taken many small steps toward recognizing households and relationships that it once did not. The current drive for gay marriage appeals to gay people partly because of that trend. People conclude, reasonably, that the state should be forced to recognize same-sex households as well.

But the drive for gay marriage also threatens to reverse the trend, because it restores the constitutive role of state certification. Gay couples don't just want households, benefits, and recognition. They want marriage licenses. They want the stipulative language of law rewritten, and then enforced. Certainly *Baehr* has triggered a trend toward a more active and constitutive role for statutory law in controlling the evolution of marital practice. This trend comes at a time when the state recognition of nonstandard households is being rolled back in the United States and is increasingly targeted by a neoconservative program of restricting divorce, punishing adultery, stigmatizing illegitimacy, and raising tax incentives for marriage. The campaign for marriage may be more in synchrony with that program than its advocates intend.

Despite the *Baehr* decision, there is no sign that the strategy of demanding the package currently defined as marriage is working. In fact, like the rest of the "mainstream" program of gay politics — so often justified in the name of pragmatic realism — it seems to lead backwards. The reaction to it further codified the distinctness of spousal status and its bundling. In Hawai'i, the *Baehr* decision has not resulted in marriage for anybody. It has resulted in a number of new homophobic initiatives, including the referendum that allowed the state legislature to codify the heterosexuality of marriage. It has also given rise to a politically brokered compromise whereby, to win moderate and liberal support for the referendum, the state passed a new domestic partner bill. It is the most sweeping domestic partner legislation in the country. It might therefore seem to be a progressive gain. But there is a catch to it, in addition to its having been a sop to buy off critics of marriage: domestic partnership under the new law is available only to those who are not allowed to marry. For heterosexuals, in other words, it eliminates an alternative to conventional marriage. There have been two results: a sharper commitment by the state to the privilege of spousal status, and a sharper distinction among couples on the basis of sexual identity. The first result, in my view, has been wrongly embraced by gay advocates. The second is the unintended consequence of their efforts.

The legal system is not likely to produce a clear verdict of the kind that its champions imagine. Given the spectacular political reaction against the campaign for same-sex marriage in Hawai'i and Alaska, the outcome has been a definitive, homophobic repudiation of gay marriage for some time. Should the gay organizations win similar battles in Vermont, California, and elsewhere, the future will likely hold a long and complex series of state-by-state struggles over federal policy, the "full faith and credit" clause of the Constitution, and other limitations on the meaning of marriage.

Perhaps these are temporary setbacks leading to the eventual victory for same-sex marriage. And perhaps marriage, with all its flaws, might itself be a step toward further progress. How can we decide what the future is likely to hold? Marriage takes place in different registers, cuts across contexts. And, as we have seen, it can even express protest against itself. Who, then, is to say what its ultimate significance will be? The question is a real one; the situation is one of profound historical dynamism. But we cannot take for granted that marriage will result in progress on the package of privileges, prohibitions, incentives, and regulations that marriage represents.

Beyond Gay Marriage

Where does this leave us? Not at the altar, to be sure. In the straight press, and often in the gay press, the marriage issue is presented as the final frontier in the antagonism between gays and straights. Most queer people I know, however, do not see it that way. The marriage issue, defined as "same-sex marriage, pro or con," seems to most of us a lose-lose proposition for queers. The most disturbing aspect of the debate, to my mind, is that its framing has created a widening gap in the United States between the national lesbian and gay movement and queers. In addition to the arguments I have made here against the strategy of pursuing legal marriage as it is, we face a serious issue that threatens only to get worse: the campaign for gay marriage is not so much a campaign for marriage as a campaign about the constituency and vocabulary of the gay and lesbian public. The normalizing interpretation of marriage is increasingly established as the self-understanding of the national gay public. Whether marriage is normalizing or not for the individuals who marry, the debate about marriage has done much to normalize the gay movement, and thus the context in which marriage becomes a meaningful option.

Apologists for marriage often say that it would give the gay movement new power to demand further reforms. What they do not take into account, besides the deep and nearly inaccessible power of the institutions and norms of marriage, is the change that the campaign is likely to bring in the movement itself — as its enemies are repositioned, its battles redefined, its new leaders and spokespersons identified, and as millions of dollars of scarce resources are poured into fights that most of us would never have chosen. In fact, as the campaign is not likely to result in same-sex marriage, despite the claims of its triumphal prophets, the most significant dimension of the marriage struggle may turn out to be these internal effects.

The burden now lies on the advocates of marriage, especially the national gay organizations, to explain what they intend to do about the invidious consequences, intended or unintended, of their policy. Is it possible to have a politics in which marriage could be seen as one step to a larger goal, and in which its own discriminatory effects could be confronted rather than simply ignored? I can at least imagine a principled response to this challenge that would include ending the discriminatory ban on same-sex marriage. But it would not be a program that said simply that marriage is a right or a choice. It would have to say that marriage is a desirable goal only insofar as we can also extend health care, tax reform, rights of intimate association extending to immigration, recognition for joint parenting, and other entitlements currently yoked to marital status. It would have to say that marriage is desirable only insofar as we can eliminate adultery laws and other status-discriminatory regulations for sexuality. It might well also involve making available other statuses, such as expanded domestic partnership, concubinage, or something like PACS for property-sharing households, all available both to straight and gay people alike. Above all, a program for change should be accountable to the queer ethos, responsive to the lived arrangements of queer life, and articulated in queer publics.

In the meantime, the triumphalist narrative — according to which we have emerged from the long night of marginalization into the full glory of our rights, our acceptance, our integration, and our normalcy — goes almost unchallenged. Queer theory cannot counteract this narrative by insisting that we are inevitably, permanently queer. To do so is to give up the struggle for the self-understanding not only of individual queers — who may be persuaded despite their best instincts and the evidence of their daily lives that their sense of world alienation is their private moral failing rather than a feature of dominant ideology — but also of the gay world's media and publics, which increasingly understand themselves as belonging to a market niche rather than to a counterpublic. Queer counterpublics still exist and have not lost their vitality. But they have become increasingly isolated, as their connection with the national organizations, magazines, and publics has eroded. What will matter more and more is the world-making activity of queer life that neither takes queerness to be inevitable nor understands itself from the false vantage of "society." Because love, privacy, and the couple form obscure this effort, even the most generous estimate of the politics of marriage puts new pressure on keeping the world-making project in view. And because sexual culture and nonnormative intimacies are so commonly the practices of this world making, any argument for gay marriage requires an intensified concern for what is thrown into its shadow.

Notes

1. The exchange of May 30, 1996, is reproduced in Andrew Sullivan, ed., *Same-Sex Marriage: Pro and Con* (New York: Vintage, 1997), 225–26.

2. Jesse Helms's speech on the Senate floor in favor of the Defense of Marriage Act is printed in Robert M. Baird and Stuart E. Rosenbaum, eds., *Same-Sex Marriage: The Moral and Legal Debate* (Amherst, MA: Prometheus Books, 1997), 22. Jean Bethke Elshtain's "Against Gay Marriage" appeared in *Commonweal*, October 22, 1991, and is reprinted in Sullivan, *Same-Sex Marriage,* 57–60. Pope John Paul II is quoted in the *New York Times,* "Pope Deplores Gay Marriage," 23 Feb. 1994.

3. Evan Wolfson, "Crossing the Threshold: Equal Marriage Rights for Lesbians and Gay Men, and the Intra-Community Critique," *New York University Review of Law and Social Change* 21 (1994): 611. See also Evan Wolfson, "Why We Should Fight for the Freedom to Marry," *Journal of Gay, Lesbian, and Bisexual Identity* 1 (Jan. 1996).

4. Jack Baker, quoted in Don Teal, *The Gay Militants* (New York: Stein and Day, 1971), 284.

5. National Coalition of Gay Organizations, quoted in William Eskridge, *The Case for Same-Sex Marriage: From Sexual Liberty to Civilized Commitment* (New York: Free Press, 1995), 54.

6. Wolfson, "Crossing the Threshold," 479.

7. Barbara Cox, "A (Personal) Essay on Same-Sex Marriage," in Robert Baird and Stuart Rosenbaum, *Same-Sex Marriage: The Moral and Legal Debate* (Amherst, NY: Prometheus, 1997), 27–29.

8. Quoted in Christopher Hill, *Liberty Against the Law: Some Seventeenth-Century Controversies* (London: Penguin, 1997), 201.

9. Quoted in Hill, *Liberty Against the Law,* 203.

10. Robert Gluck, *Jack the Modernist* (New York: Gay Press of New York, 1985), 3.

11. Wolfson, "Crossing the Threshold," 585.

12. Ibid., 602.

13. Richard Posner, *Sex and Reason* (Cambridge: Harvard University Press, 1992), quoted in Sullivan, *Same-Sex Marriage,* 185–89.

14. Claudia Card, "Against Marriage and Motherhood," *Hypatia* 11.3 (1996): 7.

15. Jonathan Rauch, "For Better or Worse?" *New Republic,* May 6, 1996.

16. Gabriel Rotello, "Creating a New Gay Culture: Balancing Fidelity and Freedom," *The Nation,* April 21, 1997, 11–16.

17. Eskridge, *The Case for Same-Sex Marriage.*

18. Fenton Johnson, "Wedded to an Illusion: Do Gays and Lesbians Really Want the Freedom to Marry?" *Harper's,* November 1996, 4.

19. "The Freedom to Marry," *New York Times,* April 7, 1996.

20. Andrew Sullivan, *Virtually Normal: An Argument About Homosexuality* (New York: Knopf, 1995), 107.

21. John Shelby Spong, "Blessing Gay and Lesbian Commitments," in Sullivan, *Same-Sex Marriage,* 79–80.

22. Johnson, "Wedded to an Illusion," 47.

23. Posner, *Sex and Reason,* quoted in Sullivan, *Same-Sex Marriage,* 209.

24. David Chambers, "What If? The Legal Consequences of Marriage and the Legal Needs of Lesbian and Gay Male Couples," *Michigan Law Review* 95 (1996): 450.

25. Ibid., 459.

26. Richard Mohr, "The Case for Same-Sex Marriage," *Notre Dame Journal of Law, Ethics, and Public Policy* 9 (1995), reprinted in Baird and Rosenbaum, *Same-Sex Marriage,* 94.

27. Ibid., 91.

KATHERINE M. FRANKE

Putting Sex to Work

When I was living in New Haven a number of years ago, a miracle happened that drew people by the thousands to witness evidence of the Divine. A crucifix had been found to appear in the body of an oak tree in the middle of Worchester Square. I went — after all, how often do you get to see that kind of thing? Not surprisingly, at first I couldn't see anything but the usual trunk and limbs of a tree. Yet a believer took the time to show me what was *really* there, something that my untrained eye could not at first see: the cross on which Jesus Christ had been crucified. Well, maybe there was something there.[1]

To the believers, the shape of the oak tree was evidence of something that was really there: a corporeal manifestation of an omnipresent Divine Being. For them, once you've seen the crucifix, you really can't not see it, you can't un-see it.

For most people, sex is like the Divine Being: it is an obscure and powerful domain that reveals itself in expected and unexpected places, and that is immediately visible to the trained eye. Indeed, once you see it, it's hard to look away. Like the tree in Worchester Square, the human body is an "inscribed surface"[2] that is discursively marked in such a way that renders certain body parts and particular behaviors essentially sexual.

What are we seeing when we recognize something as sexual? How do we know what makes a practice sexual in nature? That is, how do we distinguish a practice that is fundamentally sexual from one that is not? I ask these questions in order to beg two more normative questions: Why do we do so, and what happens to what we "know" once we have done so? My curiosity derives from a concern that to call something sexual is at once to say too much and not enough about the meaning of a practice so named.

When men in a workplace make life intolerable for their female co-workers by calling them sexual names, putting up pictures of naked women, and touching their breasts and behinds, their conduct — unwelcome conduct of a sexual nature — is legally described as sexual harassment. When a group of male police officers viciously assault a man in their custody by shoving a toilet plunger up his anus, those cops are charged with aggravated sexual abuse. When an adult male forces a ten-year-old boy to fellate him, this man is arrested for having sexually molested a minor. These offenses receive special legal regulation by our civil and criminal laws as sexual misconduct. Yet the use of excessive violence when placing handcuffs on a suspect, the aggressive use of choke holds, or chaining a stranger to a pipe in the basement — whatever crimes these are, they are not sex crimes.

By focusing, often exclusively, on what we regard to be the sexual aspect of conduct of this kind, we tend to ignore or eclipse the ways in which sex operates "as an especially dense transfer point for relations of power"[3] — often gender-, race-, or sexual orientation–based power. For a complex set of reasons, we almost intuitively label some behavior as sexual; take workplace sexual harassment, for instance. Yet, if pressed, most people would not be able to either identify or defend a set of criteria they apply in such nominalist moments. To uncover a satisfactory and stable definition of sex is, to borrow an expression from Abraham Lincoln, like undertaking to shovel fleas: "You take up a shovelful, but before you can dump them anywhere they are gone."[4] It is the initial regulatory move, the marking of behavior as fundamentally sexual, that I want to interrogate. If it is in fact true that "there is not some ahistorical *Stoff* of sexuality, some sexual charge that can be simply added to a social relationship to 'sexualize' it in a constant and predictable direction, or that splits off from it unchanged,"[5] then it is worth asking what we are doing and what we are missing when we assume that such *Stoff* exists.

The questions I ask directly here are ones I first considered in my earlier work on sexual harassment. In "What's Wrong with Sexual Harassment?" I explored how workplace sexual harassment could be a species of sex discrimination. I criticized both courts and commentators who identified the wrong of sexual harassment to lie in the sexual nature of the conduct.

Rather, I argued, sexual harassment must be understood as a technology of sexism, that is, as a tool or instrument of gender regulation which feminizes women as sexual objects and masculinizes men as sexual subjects.[6]

In this essay, I push these insights about the use of sex as a technology of sexism one step further by probing two more fundamental questions: first, why certain practices get labeled as sexual, and second, what flows from their being so designated. I explore the ostensibly denotative practice of naming particular behavior as primarily sexual in nature by examining two contexts in which the label "sexual," understood as erotic, occludes the way sex mediates other social relations of power. In each setting, I argue that we make a grave mistake when we interpret certain behavior as primarily erotic in nature. This mistake, I argue, is amplified in the legal treatment of these practices as sex crimes, or sexual offenses. First I look to ritualized practices in the Highlands of Papua New Guinea, where boys as young as seven are forced to fellate older men for a period of up to eight years as part of the process of becoming a man. At first impression, most nonnative interpreters of ritualized man-boy fellatio conclude, without hesitation, that this conduct is fundamentally erotic in nature — how can it not be so? In fact, Western anthropological readings of these practices first described them as sodomy, and today the behavior is most commonly referred to as ritualized or institutionalized homosexuality.[7] I provide an alternative reading of the ritualized semen practices of the Sambia that illustrates the way ingestion of semen is undertaken primarily in the service of teaching and reinforcing the cultural power and supremacy of both men and masculinity, while at the same time teaching and reinforcing the cultural subordinancy and inferiority of women and femininity. In this regard, semen practices play a role in Sambia culture similar to that played by workplace sexual harassment in ours.

Next I examine the assault of Abner Louima, a black man who was attacked by white New York City police officers in August 1997. Louima sustained serious injuries after several police officers severely beat him, then forced the wooden handle of a toilet plunger into his rectum, and then removed it and forced the soiled handle into Louima's mouth. The sexual nature of the police conduct animated much of the outrage expressed by the public, the press, and legal authorities in the weeks following the assault. Prosecutors initially charged the white police officers arrested in connection with the assault of Louima with sex crimes.[8] Two aspects of this case are worthy of examination. First, why should we consider this assault a sex crime? Second, by reading the assault as primarily sexual, important insights about the way sex is used as an instrument of gender- and race-based humiliation and injury are elided or at least minimized.

Do these examples instruct that we best desexualize crimes like rape and forced sex with children? There are compelling arguments in favor of such a reformation of the laws regulating behavior traditionally treated as sex crimes. Indeed, Michel Foucault made such an argument in the mid-1970s. Surely, the problems that inhere in the project of differentiating sexual assault from a punch in the face suggest that one should give serious consideration to the position that "there is no difference, in principle, between sticking one's fist into someone's face or one's penis into their sex."[9] Ultimately, however, I reject such a wholesale move given that the material experience of sexual assault by its victims instructs that "they cannot afford to jump into the realm of the ideal and pretend that . . . sex (the genitals) is the same as other parts of the body."[10] Rather, I suggest a solution more retail in nature drawn from the experience of the prosecution of sex-related violence by the International Criminal Tribunal for the Former Yugoslavia. The Tribunal has exercised jurisdiction over the individual and mass rapes and sexual assaults of women and men in the former Yugoslavia as violations of international humanitarian law. Due in part to the provisions of international law within the enforcement authority of the Tribunal, as well as to the way sex-related violence was used to torture, humiliate, and degrade civilians in Bosnia, the Tribunal has chosen not to focus exclusively on the sexual nature of these crimes. Instead, it treats sex-related violence as the *actus reus* of torture, genocide, and crimes against humanity. Thus, the Tribunal prosecutors have the ability, on a case-by-case basis, to fashion their arguments in a way that highlights the gendered nature of these crimes, where appropriate, without perpetuating the essentialization of certain body parts and human behaviors as fundamentally sexual. In this way, the prosecutor has resisted the pull to characterize the wrong of these violent acts as predominantly sexual in nature, but rather, has demonstrated how sex can be used as a tool in the service of race-, ethnicity-, or religion-based war crimes.

Through these examples, I hope to illustrate the productivity of sex, that is, how sex gets put to work in the service of myriad power relations. Sometimes sex is used to satisfy erotic desire. Sometimes sex accomplishes reproduction. Sometimes it does both. But, as Robin West recently pointed out to me in conversations about this topic, "much reproductive hetero-sex

is non-erotic." Sometimes sex pays the rent. Sometimes it sells cars, ciga-
rettes, alcohol, or vacations in Mexico. Sometimes sex is used to subordinate, or has the effect of subordinating, another person on the basis of
gender or race, or both.

To understand sex as a fundamentally erotic drive, and as a "natural
given which power tries to hold in check [e.g., the prosecution of sex
crimes], or as an obscure domain which knowledge tries gradually to uncover"[11] (e.g., anthropological discoveries of primitive homosexuality), is
to risk two grave errors. First, once something is classified as sexual we
understand its meaning primarily in erotic terms and lose sight of the ways
sex is easily deployed as an instrumentality of multiple relations of power.
Second, we are likely to understand the erotic to be present in too few
human behaviors insofar as we deny or ignore the role of the erotic in
behavior less susceptible to being read as "sexual."

Seminal/Sexual Practices

In *Guardians of the Flutes,* anthropologist Gilbert Herdt provided an initial
monograph of what he terms "ritualized homosexuality" among the Sambia, a tribe in the Eastern Highlands of Papua New Guinea.[12] For the
Sambia, the process of becoming a man is not one that may be left to
nature, as is the case with girls, but must be accomplished by the ritualized
intervention of culture. Thus, beginning at around age seven, boys com-
mence a process of ritualized masculinization that is completed only when
a young man fathers a child. This process begins with a series of ritualized
practices designed to purge the polluting and feminizing effects of contact with women from the male body. Herdt terms these "egestive rites"
designed to "remove internal, essentially 'foreign' material believed acquired through intimate, prolonged contact with one's mother (and other
females)."[13]

Boys are first required to undergo cane-swallowing, whereby canes are
forced down their throats so as to induce vomiting and defecation, thereby
purging food belonging to the mother from the male body — a necessary
prerequisite for masculinization.[14] Second, nose bleeding is undertaken to
remove the pollution of menstrual blood remaining in the male body. Stiff,
sharp grasses are thrust into the boy's nose until blood flows, thereby re-
moving the "bad blood" from his body. It is a matter of "urgent concern
that the mother's contaminated blood be removed from boys; otherwise

male biological development is impeded." Men alone conduct these rituals, keeping them hidden from women in the community; to effectuate this, the boys are sworn to secrecy.[15]

Next follow the "ingestive rites"; this is where all the attention is paid by those intrigued by the practices of this culture. "The most important early ingestive rite of all," according to Herdt, is that of fellatio. Sambia men believe that without the daily ingestion of semen, a boy's body will not mature into that of a man, and he may likely wither and die. Thus, "repeated inseminations create a pool of maleness: the boy, it is believed, gradually acquires a reservoir of sperm inside his semen organ. . . . The semen organ changes from being dry and hard to fleshy, moist, and then firm. . . . Semen gradually transforms the initiate's body too. It internally strengthens his bones and builds muscles." According to these beliefs, boys must avoid all interaction with women, including their mothers, and must fellate older men on a daily basis until they reach adolescence, about the age of fifteen, at which time they switch roles and are fellated by younger boys.[16] These bachelors, as Herdt calls them, are fellated by initiates until the woman they marry begins menstruation. At that point, Sambia culture dictates that they cease same-sex seminal practices and engage only in heterosexual coitus. Again, males closely hold these ingestive rites secret; indeed, the men threaten the boys with death should they reveal any of this information to women.[17]

Thus you have what Herdt describes as "ritualized homosexuality." Herdt is careful not to describe the Sambia as homosexual.[18] In fact, it is the distinction between homosexual practices and homosexual identity that constitutes the central conundrum of Sambia culture for Herdt. How is it that "seven-to-ten-year-old Sambia boys are taken from their mothers when first initiated into the male cult, and thereafter experience the most powerful and seductive homosexual fellatio activities," yet "they emerge as competent, exclusively heterosexual adults, not homosexuals"? The boys "experience [ritualized fellatio] as pleasurable and erotically exciting. Yet, in spite of this formidable background, the final outcome is exclusive heterosexuality." It is precisely because "homosexual behavior" among the Sambia men can be explained neither by genetic determinism nor social learning theory that Herdt finds the Sambia so fascinating.[19] According to what theory of sexual identity acquisition can "normal" adult heterosexuality evolve out of ritualized childhood same-sex sex?

Initial accounts of Sambia culture by Western anthropologists simply failed to mention the same-sex seminal practices described above.[20] Herdt, among other anthropologists, attributed this omission to a larger refusal in anthropology to regard sexuality as a legitimate subject of ethnographic inquiry.[21] In Papua New Guinea, this oversight quickly yielded to revulsion and condemnation by Western anthropologists, accompanied by aggressive efforts by missionaries to dissuade the locals from such perversion.[22] Indeed, many of the practices Herdt observed in his early fieldwork no longer persist in Sambia culture.[23] Herdt, however, was one of the first Western observers to encounter the Sambia practices and declare: Look, homosexuality. Hallelujah, we are everywhere! Thus, with *The Guardians of the Flutes,* his edited collections, and subsequent writings on the Sambia,[24] Herdt has "established a framework for the study of homosexualities cross-culturally."[25] Through the scientific lens of anthropology, Herdt has, therefore, undertaken the task of shedding light on the "obscure domain" of the homo-sex drive in New Guinea.

From virtually all vantage points, commentators have interpreted Sambia semen practices as both erotic and homosexual, that is, as homo-erotic.[26] How can one deny the sexual nature of fellatio? Or the homoerotic nature of fellatio between men? It is this way of knowing these practices that I want to contest. From the perspective of the fellated, fellatio involves arousal, penile erection, ejaculation — surely this practice is about the bachelors "getting off." Herdt's fieldwork documents the fact that the bachelors truly enjoy and seek out sex with boys.[27] Similarly, the boys seem to enjoy, to varying degrees, their "erotic relationships" with the bachelors. For this reason, Herdt is willing to characterize some of these unions as "lover relationships."[28]

Herdt finds Sambia culture an interesting subject of ethnographic study because of its exotic manifestation of the erotic; others would, no doubt, be aghast at the way adult men sexually exploit young boys. The ritualized nature of the practice merely compounds the sexual violation. Just as I have cautioned against understanding workplace sexual harassment as a fundamentally sexual activity,[29] so too there is danger in interpreting Sambia semen practices as fundamentally erotic. Deborah Elliston has argued that "to identify the man-boy 'homosexual' practices as 'ritualized homosexuality' imputes a Western model of sexuality to these Melanesian practices, one that relies on Western ideas about gender, erotics, and personhood, and that ultimately obscures the meanings that hold for these practices in Melanesia."[30]

Among the interesting questions to be posed in analyzing semen practices among the Sambia are those regarding the purpose of these practices. Is the fellatio undertaken in the service of satisfying individual erotic desire, or in the service of advancing broader cultural norms that have, no doubt, a sexual component? Herdt poses this question, and ultimately determines to maintain the centrality of the erotic in his interpretation of Sambia initiation rituals. He expresses concern about ethnographies that tend to "ignore, dismiss, trivialize, or even invalidate the actor's homoerotic meanings and desires." He is determined not to "deodorize the erotic and peripheralize the homoerotic ontology."[31] Herdt is not alone in this concern. Gerald Creed, while expressing some criticisms with respect to Herdt's interpretations of Sambia culture, echoes a commitment to keep a focus on the erotic: "The actual physical and erotic aspects of homosexuality . . . are often overlooked when it is treated as institutionalized behavior. Institutionalized homosexuality is still sex and it may still serve a pleasurable function. Analyses that neglect this fact are incomplete."[32]

It is exactly this "homoerotic ontology" that concerns me. Why should we assume that the central meaning of Sambia initiation practices is sexual, that is, erotic? To ask this question thoughtfully requires the category "sexual" to be broken down into constitutive parts. To describe the semen practices as homoerotic, as Herdt and Creed insist, is to collapse several important concepts that deserve disaggregation. For Herdt, one must understand the male erection as the product of arousal, and arousal must be defined in erotic terms.[33] Yet men can become aroused such that they achieve penile erections for a spectrum of reasons independent of an erotic response to another person or situation.[34] It has been well documented that men can have erections associated with non-sexual fear, sleep, full bladders, violence, and power.[35] Alfred Kinsey observed that, for boys, erection and ejaculation are easily induced by "non-sexual" sources such as carnival rides, fast bicycle rides, sitting in warm sand, setting a field afire, war motion pictures, being chased by police, hearing the national anthem, and, my personal favorite, seeing one's name in print. Kinsey concluded, however, that by the late teens males have been conditioned to respond primarily to "direct physical stimulation of the genitalia, or to psychic situations that are specifically sexual."[36] Notwithstanding this general conditioning, "a romantic context is not a necessary condition for sexual arousal, in either men or women."[37]

Therefore, there is reason to question interpretive strategies that tend to

essentialize certain bodily responses, such as the male erection, as fundamentally erotic or romantic in nature. To the extent that "Herdt posits a
tautologous ordering of eroticism that makes penile erection contingent on
a kind of arousal that is by definition erotic,"[38] he is making just this
mistake in interpreting Sambia culture.

Similarly, I want to resist the inclination to essentialize certain practices
as undertaken principally to satisfy erotic desire. Of course, this issue arises
in what I have described elsewhere as "the ongoing intramural debate within feminism about whether rape should be understood as a crime of violence or sex."[39] Rather than consider the question of sex and power in
relation to rape in antinomous terms, consider the following examples. In
ancient Rome, when a husband caught another man in bed with his wife, it
was acceptable punishment for the husband and/or his male slaves to orally
or anally rape the male offender.[40] So too, oral and anal rape were used as a
punishment in medieval Persia for various crimes.[41] Although it is possible
that the person administering the punishment in these circumstances derived some erotic satisfaction from these practices, to characterize them as
fundamentally erotic in nature is to radically pervert their meaning. Of
course, I don't mean to imply that practices of this kind are subject to
"correct" interpretations, because they do not possess meaning independent of interpretation. However, I do think some interpretations better
reflect the ways the practices are understood by the participants, the significance they hold in the cultures in which they take place, and the unique
ways sex can be a powerful tool to inflict myriad forms of harm.[42]

Thus, I want to challenge the inclination to declare man-boy fellatio in
Melanesia a principally homoerotic practice. Rather, I prefer that we understand these activities not as homoerotic or homosexual, but as *homosocial*. Like Eve Kosofsky Sedgwick, I believe that the descriptor homosocial
provides better purchase on the relation between and among men in Sambia society. Rather than reduce that relation to the erotic, to describe it as
homosocial leaves room for the role of the erotic while recognizing the
"range of ways in which sexuality functions as a signifier"[43] for and instrument in the enforcement of power relations. The work that sex does can be
and often is at once symbolic and material, productive and reproductive,
pleasurable and dangerous. Close examination of the Sambia male initiation rituals reveals that semen practices function symbolically, metonymically, and literally in the transmission of an ideology of gendered power.

Rather than evidencing the expression of man-boy love or desire, ritu-

alized semen practices among the Sambia must be understood relative to
their location in larger gender norms in their society. Sambia culture is
fundamentallly sexually polarized and sexually segregated.[44] Strict divisions of labor and ritual taboos regulating physical contact between the
sexes are in evidence throughout the culture. From the time when boys are
first isolated from all women at about seven years old, they are taught to
disparage women as dangerous creatures whose body fluids can pollute
men and deplete their masculine substance. Women are frequently referred
to as "dirty polluters," and men engage in purification rites after coitus,
such as nose bleeding, to rid their bodies of female contamination.[45] So
dangerous is the threat of pollution from women that public and private
spaces are strictly sex-segregated.[46] During the initiation process, men
teach boys the reality of the threat that women pose to both maleness and
masculinity.

Accompanying the notions of female danger for Sambia are concomi-
tant beliefs about the tremendous material and symbolic power and value
of semen. According to Herdt and Stoller, "semen is the most precious
human fluid . . . more precious than even mother's milk." Semen is related
to human reproduction and growth in several ways. First, men orally in-
seminate their wives prior to conception, believing that the semen prepares
the wife's body for making babies, as well as for lactation when the semen is
converted into milk. After oral insemination, the couple engages in repeated vaginal insemination, depositing semen into the woman's womb,
where it is transformed into a fetus. Multiple inseminations are necessary
for this evolution to come off because the creation of a baby requires a
critical mass of semen.[47]

Semen is also necessary for human growth. Thus, "initial growth for
every fetus occurs through semen accumulation." Babies grow from the
ingestion of breast milk; the Sambia believe women's breasts transform
semen into milk. After weaning, young girls continue to grow on their own
due to the presence of female blood in their systems. Growth in boys,
however, requires daily ingestion of semen in order to develop their skin,
bones, and male features.[48]

Thus, the Sambia is a highly sex-stratified culture in which men are
superior to and vilify women and in which men exclusively possess the
elixir necessary for human reproduction and growth. In light of the central
role that semen plays in the Sambia gender-based belief system, it would be
careless to understand the transmission of semen, either between males or

between males and females, solely or even primarily as an erotic practice. Given that fellatio between men and boys is explicitly undertaken to effect the transformation of boys from a feminized to a masculinized state, and is part of a larger indoctrination process whereby the boys learn of and internalize gender norms premised on male superiority, the integrity of an interpretation of these practices that understands them as primarily erotic in nature is quite questionable. In effect, semen practices are both the lubricant that facilitates and the glue that adheres the representational ideal of male superiority and female inferiority.

In his later writings on the Sambia, Herdt reflects a sensitivity to the critique that he has made the most grave of ethnographic errors—the imposition of his own notions of sexual identity on his subjects: "But what is it—attraction to the boy, excess libido, power, exhibitionism, fantasies of nurturance, and so on—that arouses the adult male? And is his younger partner also aroused? Should we represent the nature of these desires as homoerotic, not homosexual—that is, as a form of desire and not just of social conformity to a sex role?" Yet even here, in interrogating the "meaning" of same-sex semen practices among the Sambia, Herdt's gaze remains transfixed by what he regards as the brute fact of homoerotic arousal. Again, he rejects any interpretation that "peripheralizes the homoerotic ontology."[49]

To be fair, Herdt does acknowledge the role that "ritualized homosexuality" plays in the masculinization of boys as they become initiated into "the whole male sexual culture."[50] But he fails to see the indispensable relation masculinity bears to misogyny and gender hierarchy within Sambia culture. Herdt's insistent focus on Sambia homoeroticism denies him the opportunity to appreciate the degree to which notions of the superiority of men and the inferiority of women are mutually constitutive within the Sambia culture. Deborah Elliston describes these practices as "traumatic lessons in social hierarchy for the initiates. . . . Ritual teachings about men's and women's differences inculcate among men a generalized suspicion and fear of women while simultaneously exalting men's abilities and supremacy; together these teachings instantiate a gender hierarchy."[51] To represent their man-boy semen practices as being only about male sexuality or only about men elides the systemic nature of sex and gender norms as regulatory ideals among Sambia men and women.

Rather than homo*sexual* in nature, Sambia man-boy semen practices are better understood as homo*social*. Sedgwick would term them the product of male homosocial desire rather than male homosexuality.[52] The drape of male homosociality extends beyond the domain of the erotic to other bonds and norms of social identity that regulate inherited privilege, patriarchal power structures, and the enduring inequality of power between women and between men. Lauren Berlant made a similar observation in her reading of Nella Larson's *Passing,* a story about the intimate and intense interactions of two light-skinned women of African descent.[53] Berlant resisted a reading of the text that characterized it as "a classically closeted narrative, half-concealing the erotics between Clare and Irene." Rather, according to Berlant, "there may be a difference between wanting someone sexually and wanting someone's body." For the women in Larson's story, and for the Sambia boys, perhaps the best way to understand their desire for a more privileged person of the same sex is as "a desire to occupy, to experience the privileges of [the other's] body, not to love or make love to her [or him], but rather to wear her [or his] way of wearing her [or his] body, like a prosthesis, or a fetish."[54] The concealed erotics that mediate the race-envy in *Passing* are made literal among the Sambia: the swallowing of semen is necessary for the boy to become a man, for the initiates to occupy adult male bodies. Thus the homosocial as a frame accommodates both the erotic and the gender-generative significance of the Sambia ritualized semen practices. To label the desire underlying the semen practices homosocial rather than homosexual is to situate desire within these interlocking social bonds in such a way that the erotic does not eclipse other relations of power.

Herdt observes the Sambia and represents the same-sex semen practices as fundamentally homoerotic, thereby neglecting the role these practices play in both the creation and maintenance of male supremacy in Sambia culture. If it is true across cultures that "the body requires incessant ritual work to be maintained in its sociocultural form,"[55] then we must acknowledge the ways sexual practices produce not only sexual identity, but corporal and social identity as well: "the sutures of [social identity] become most visible under the disassembling eye of an alternative narrative, ideological as that narrative may itself be."[56] Thus, the man-boy semen practices of the Sambia, while astonishing at first, provide an instructive opportunity to challenge the inclination to essentialize certain practices as erotic. I turn next to a less exotic, although no less astonishing, incident that further illustrates the danger in essentializing certain behavior as sexual/erotic. The Sambia and the assault of Abner Louima both illustrate how the classification of practices as sexual holds the danger of obfuscating how sex "*both* epitomizes *and* itself influences broader social relations of power."[57]

Anal/Sexual Practices

On the night of August 9, 1997, Abner Louima was leaving the Rendez-Vous, a nightclub in Brooklyn popular among Haitian immigrants in New York, when the police arrived to break up a fight that had broken out between club patrons.[58] "The white cops started with some racial stuff," Louima later reported. "They said, 'Why do you people come to this country if you can't speak English?' They called us niggers."[59] One police officer believed Louima had knocked him down during the altercation.[60] The officer later declared, "No one jumps me and gets away with it."[61] Officers pushed Louima to the ground, handcuffed him, and delivered him to the 70th Precinct — beating him severely on the way. Louima was charged with disorderly conduct, obstructing governmental administration, and resisting arrest.[62]

Once at the stationhouse officers strip-searched Louima in a public area, and with his pants down,[63] took him into the men's room, where they brutally assaulted him:

> My pants were down at my ankles, in full view of the other cops. They walked me over to the bathroom and closed the door. There were two cops. One said, "You niggers have to learn to respect police officers." The other one said, "If you yell or make any noise, I will kill you." Then one held me and the other one stuck the [wooden handle of a toilet] plunger up my behind. He pulled it out and shoved it in my mouth, broke my teeth and said, "That's your s —— t, nigger." Later, when they called the ambulance, the cop told me, "If you ever tell anyone . . . I will kill you and your family."[64]

Louima was then taken to a jail cell, and only after other prisoners complained that he was bleeding did the police call for an ambulance.[65] Louima required surgery to repair a pierced lower intestine and a torn bladder.[66] He remained in the hospital for two months recovering from the injuries he sustained from the police officers at the 70th Precinct.[67]

It took a short while for the media to learn of this vicious assault, yet once they did the headlines screamed: *Police Sodomize Suspect; Suspect Claims Police Raped Him with Plunger; Officer Accused of Sexually Brutalizing*

Suspect Arrested.[68] Members of the Haitian community marched in protest against this outrageous form of police brutality, waving toilet plungers and carrying signs declaring the cops to be "Criminals," "Perverts," "Rapists."[69] A retired transit police officer who attended the march exclaimed: "That's a foul and sordid act they performed on that man."[70] Mayor Giuliani exclaimed that the attack inside the 70th Precinct station was "personally repulsive to him" and that the cops charged with the assault were "perverted."[71] Immediately after the assault, several police officers who were associated with Justin Volpe, one of the officers charged with assaulting Louima, claimed that the Rendez-Vous was a gay club and that Louima's injuries stemmed from violent anal sex he had engaged in while at the club.[72] When the two police officers arrested in connection with the assault appeared for their arraignment, courthouse protesters taunted the cops by calling them "faggots."[73] The district attorney charged the officers with aggravated sexual abuse and first-degree assault, both class B felonies for which they could receive a maximum sentence of twenty-four years.[74] Only later was the indictment amended to include aggravated harassment, a racial bias crime for which the maximum sentence is, interestingly enough, only four years.[75]

It was precisely the sexual aspect of this assault that provoked journalists to grant Louima the moniker "America's most famous victim of police brutality since Rodney King."[76] Sure, the police get carried away from time to time, shoot at fleeing suspects when deadly force isn't called for, choke a suspect to death with a choke hold, or even rape female prostitutes in a brothel they had raided.[77] But, as *Village Voice* journalist Richard Goldstein observed, "None of these documented cases arouse the outrage of this 'barbaric' act, which . . . is only supposed to happen in the Third World. *Here in the land of the free, when it comes to police brutality, we draw the line at raping a man.*"[78]

That this crime is heinous cannot be denied, but is it best characterized as a sex crime? What exactly was sexual about this assault? As Goldstein asked: "What's sex got to do with it?" Virtually every report of the case mentions early in the article that Louima is married and has children, and nightly news broadcasts regularly showed pictures of Louima and his family in the days following the assault.[79] What is more, the assailants were portrayed by the media as healthy heterosexuals.

So why call it a sex crime? The easy answer is tautological: the allegations fit the description of crimes so labeled.[80] But what is a sex crime?

There are several ways to differentiate a sexual assault from an assault *simpliciter:* (1) it is motivated by the erotic desire of the perpetrator; (2) it involves contact with the perpetrator's or the victim's sexual body parts (e.g., vagina, breasts, or penis) or involves acts that are typically regarded as sexual (e.g., kissing, fellatio, sexual intercourse); or (3) it is experienced as sexual by the victim.

The New York Penal Law defines criminal sexual offenses to be rape, sodomy, sexual misconduct, sexual abuse, aggravated sexual abuse, and course of sexual conduct against a child.[81] Two of these crimes explicitly anchor the crime's sexual nature, in whole or in part, in the satisfaction of sexual desire: criminal sexual abuse and course of sexual conduct against a child. The Penal Law defines criminal sexual abuse as *sexual contact* with another person by force or when the person is incapable of granting consent. Course of conduct against a child is committed when, among other things, a person engages in aggravated *sexual contact* with a child less than eleven years old. As a foundation for these two violations, the Penal Law defines "sexual contact" as "any touching of the sexual or other intimate parts of a person not married to the actor *for the purpose of gratifying sexual desire of either party.*"[82]

But because the satisfaction of sexual desire must be accomplished by touching sexual or intimate parts, it must be those parts that make this conduct a sex crime. Yet what are sexual or other intimate parts? Courts have found the chest, the upper leg, the leg, the mouth, and the navel to be "sexual or intimate parts" for purposes of the criminal sexual abuse statute.[83] Further, it has been established that " 'intimate parts' is much broader than the term 'sexual parts' " and that "intimacy . . . must be viewed within the context in which the contact takes place. . . . A body part which might be intimate in one context, might not be intimate in another."[84] So really, any body part could be considered a sexual or intimate body part depending on the context. It appears that it is the perpetrator's erotic desire that sexualizes the body part, thus making contact with that body part a sex crime.

But it cannot be the perpetrator's desire that sets some crimes apart as sex crimes. Sexual misconduct, rape, sodomy, and aggravated sexual abuse are all premised on penetration of the vagina, rectum, or mouth.[85] The satisfaction of sexual desire is irrelevant to these crimes. So, at least for purposes of the criminal law, these body parts are essentially sexual, thus rendering crimes involving them, ipso facto, sex crimes.

The Sex Offender Registration Act, New York's version of "Megan's Law," provides a salient example of the power of law to label or mark certain behavior as sexual exogenously.[86] In New York, persons who have been convicted of rape, sodomy, sexual abuse, aggravated sexual abuse, incest, sexual performance by a child, unlawful imprisonment, or kidnapping of a person under seventeen years old are subject to the notification and registration provisions of the New York Sex Offender Registration Act.[87] The last two categories, unlawful imprisonment and kidnapping of a person under seventeen years old, in no way require the crime to have been sexual in nature, yet the law labels persons convicted of these crimes sex offenders.[88] What is more, parents of the person imprisoned or kidnapped are specifically exempt from the notification law[89] — the presumption being that no parent would kidnap or imprison his or her own child for sexual reasons. This is, of course, a demonstrably false premise.

This brief tour through the New York Penal Law illustrates that those behaviors labeled sex crimes bear, at best, a family resemblance to one another. The answer to the question What makes something a sex crime? is not revealed in the positive law itself. Instead, a complex set of interpretive moves is required to ascribe a sexual nature to the behavior. Some of the symbolic work is done endogenously by one or both of the parties involved, and some of it is done exogenously by those who act as public interpreters of the behavior: prosecutors, judges, and juries. But in all cases, that which makes the crime sexual "is a discursive formation . . . not a fact or property of the body."[90]

So what rendered the assault of Abner Louima a sex crime? Of course, the penetration of his rectum. But why? Surely we would not want to ground the sexual nature of the crime in the erotic pleasure, latent or otherwise, that the officers received from performing this act. Louima certainly did not experience this assault as erotic. Nor would we want to say that the violent insertion of a wooden handle in a person's rectum is intrinsically a sexual act, or that all acts involving a rectum are to be so construed.

Nevertheless, most people would want to say that there was something particularly wrong with this assault that distinguishes it from an equally violent punch in the face or a kick in the ribs. Justin Volpe, the police officer charged with principal responsibility for Louima's injuries, was quoted as having said to other cops on the night of the assault: "I had to break a man."[91] In this comment lies the key for understanding the power and the wrong of the assault on Louima. I suggest that the power of the assault principally lies not in its sexual nature, *simpliciter,* but in the unique way that it humiliated Louima as a black man. For white men, particularly white police officers, to assault a black man anally is one of the most powerful ways to assault black masculinity. Tragically, Louima is not the first man to experience this kind of assault. At least six black men, all immigrants, have complained that a white police officer abducted them, took them to an isolated place in Queens, and anally raped them at gunpoint. The victims and witnesses report that the cop threatened them with death if they spoke to the authorities about these assaults.[92] What distinguished Louima's assault from other incidents of police violence was not that it was sexual, but that the police officers got caught.

A preoccupation with the supposedly sexual nature of these assaults deflects attention away from the gender- and race-based nature of this crime. Here we have an example of what is commonly thought to be a sexual act being used as an instrument of gender- and race-based terror.[93] One cannot understand the meaning of this conduct without taking into account its gender- and race-based significance. To view it as primarily sexual is to make the same mistake as that made by Herdt in Melanesia: it is to essentialize certain conduct and body parts as sexual, and to occlude the ways in which "the sexual" can be deployed as the instrumentality by which other forms of power and supremacy are cultivated. After all, the Louima incident began with a police officer telling him, "You niggers have to learn to respect police officers."[94]

What is more, hyper-sexualizing the Louima assault carries the additional danger of normalizing other violent police practices because they aren't sexually barbaric. Recall Richard Goldstein's observation: "When it comes to police brutality, we draw the line at raping a man." Other nonsexual forms of police violence may be regrettable, but many may view this behavior as a kind of police-based droit du seigneur.[95] In fact, it may well be the case, as Goldstein argues, that there is a kind of sadist satisfaction that accompanies the use of handcuffs, choke holds, or other excessive methods of police restraint, such as hog-tying suspects. To regard the Louima assault as the exception, where perverted cops acted completely beyond the pale, "prevents us from imagining that cops who specialize in [violent] tactics might find them exciting."[96] To over-eroticize the treatment of Louima carries the danger of under-eroticizing police tactics that do not involve penetration of a "sexual or intimate body part." After all, if, as Kinsey suggested, young men can get aroused by being chased by police, why shouldn't police get aroused when running after suspects? Recent misconduct charges filed against a police officer in Seattle lay bare the erotic potential of routine police practices.[97]

Which, of course, prompts the most fundamental of questions: Is it the sexual/erotic nature of any of these practices that makes them wrong? For the most part, I think not. It seems to me that these incidents should be analyzed to uncover the way the sexual/erotic operates as a particularly efficient and dangerous conduit with which to exercise power. Thus, to say that the Louima assault was sexual is at once to say too much and not enough about it. As Ana Ortiz has explained so eloquently, this simple construction of the injury of Louima's assault occludes the particularly gendered and raced salience of anal penetration for a Caribbean black man.[98] "They have always taken us for this frail and vulnerable community," said Tatiana Wah, a Haitian activist who was one of the organizers of the march protesting the police assault of Louima.[99] The anal assault of Louima, performed not in private, but in front of an audience of white cops on their turf, effectively enacted the perceived frailness and vulnerability of Haitian men.

How best to avoid the erasure of racial- or gender-based subordination by and through the invocation of the sexual? In the section that follows, I consider the desexualization of sodomy, rape, and other assaults labeled sex crimes.

The Desexualization of Violence

Beginning with *The History of Sexuality,* Michel Foucault developed a theory of the discursive truth of sex and, for present purposes, a critical analysis of the means by which certain forms of knowledge-based power are deployed such that sexuality gets anchored in certain parts of the body.[100] The examples I provide above from the New York Penal Law illustrate quite well Foucault's point: the Penal Law does not merely pick out the set of practices that are truly sexual in nature, but rather, certain body parts or practices become sexual by virtue of their regulation by law. As a result, different parts of the body become attached to different fields of knowledge: when we interrogate practices involving the genitals we are, by definition, learning something sexual.

Shortly after the publication of *The History of Sexuality,* Foucault entered into a set of discussions with feminists about rape.[101] Given his concerns about the dangers of punishing sexuality, Foucault poses the question: "What should be said about rape?" In these conversations, he urges the position that "when one punishes rape one should be punishing physical violence and nothing but that. . . . It may be regarded as an act of violence, possibly more serious, but of the same type, as that of punching someone in the face."[102] Well, Foucault is unequivocally weighing in on the violence side of the sex versus violence debate among feminists about the meaning of rape.[103]

In response to the women who objected to his insistence on desexualizing rape, Foucault reveals his true concern. By making rape a "sex" crime, we are once again anchoring sexuality in certain parts of the body, and in so doing, "the body is discursively marked [thereby] construct[ing] certain parts of the body as more important than others."[104] By bestowing this "special" status on parts of the body marked sexual, "sexuality as such, in the body, has a preponderant place, the sexual organ isn't like a hand, hair, or a nose. It therefore has to be protected, surrounded, invested in any case with legislation that isn't that pertaining to the rest of the body."[105]

Many feminists would respond: So what's wrong with that? Sexual assaults *are* different. Foucault's concern derives from the way the deployment of sex in this fashion occludes the way power operates on the body, "ordering it as it studies, organizing its movements as it observes, categorizing as it probes. In this way, power, or power/knowledge, produces our understanding of the body."[106] Thus, for Foucault, sex is not a thing we have or do, but is instead a regulatory ideal. Judith Butler expresses a similar interest in the ways "sex" "produces the bodies it governs" and in so doing, produces bodies that matter, and bodies that don't.[107] Wendy Brown pushes these Foucauldian insights in yet another direction, illuminating the danger of a rights-based politics that is built on the naturalization of identity which is, in fact, the result of a regulatory ideal: "disciplinary productions of identity may become the site of rights struggles that naturalize and thus entrench the powers of which those identities are the effects."[108]

It is the regulatory power of sex that Foucault seeks to interrupt by questioning the need to treat rape differently from a punch in the face. To his mind, we stand to gain much and lose little by punishing the physical violence of rape "without bringing in the fact that sexuality was involved."[109]

For the most part, I find myself in agreement with Foucault's theoretical point, yet I think Monique Plaza is right when she argues that women, in particular, cannot afford the jump into the realm of the ideal.[110] Although in principle, there is much to Foucault's suggestion that we treat rape and "non-sexual" assault as crimes of violence, to recommend such a change in the positive laws at this moment means that rape victims will bear the transition costs of this representational reform. That is, rape victims will continue to experience rape as an assault to their sexual body during the period in which the withdrawal of regulation by sex crime laws transforms the way we know the body.

To reconcile the tension between the damage done by laws that perpetuate "the sexual" as a regulatory ideal, and the cost to rape victims of demanding that the law not recognize a sexual aspect to their injury, I now turn to what I regard as an example of a compromise position: the recognition of sex-based violence as a violation of international humanitarian law.

Rape and Torture

Between 1991 and 1995 an inter-ethnic, inter-religious war devastated the country that had been known as Yugoslavia. Rape and sexual assault have always been a part of war, but what happened "in Bosnia and Herzegovina to Muslim and Croatian women seems unprecedented in the history of war crimes. Women [were] raped by Serbian soldiers in an organized and systematic way, as a planned crime to destroy a whole Muslim population, to destroy a society's cultural, traditional and religious integrity."[111] Serbian soldiers were not the only ones accused of using rape and other sexual assault as an instrument of war in the former Yugoslavia. Muslim and Croat soldiers as well have been found to have engaged in sex-based atrocities in manners similar to those used by the Serbs.[112] Never has this seemingly inevitable aspect of war been granted the degree of international attention and consternation as have the atrocities committed in the former Yugoslavia. In what came to be called euphemistically ethnic cleansing, Serbs established camps that were "set up for the purpose of rape [of Bosnian Muslim women] . . . to impregnate the women." Furthermore, they detained pregnant women until abortion was no longer an option.[113] A UN commission characterized this pattern of rape as "part of a policy of 'ethnic cleansing.' "[114] Although mass executions of civilians also characterized the inhumanity that lay at the core of this conflict, it was clear that both women and men were victims of sexual assault, as sex-related violence became "a weapon of war" in ways never seen before.[115]

In response to enormous pressure placed on the United Nations from its member states as well as from international media, in May 1993 the UN Security Council established the International Tribunal for the Prosecution of Persons Responsible for Serious Violations of International Humanitarian Law Committed in the Territory of the Former Yugoslavia since 1991 (ICTY or the "Tribunal") with the "power to prosecute persons responsible for serious violations of international humanitarian law committed in the territory of the former Yugoslavia since 1991." Pursuant to the Statute of the International Tribunal, the Tribunal has authority to prosecute individuals who have committed, among other things, (1) Grave Breaches of the Geneva Conventions of 1949, (2) Violations of the Customs of War, (3) genocide, and (4) Crimes Against Humanity. The Tribunal Statute specifically enumerates rape as a Crime Against Humanity when committed in armed conflict and directed against any civilian population. In his report elaborating the specific grounds for Tribunal jurisdiction, the secretary-general set forth that Crimes Against Humanity include "torture or rape, committed as part of a widespread or systematic attack against any civilian population on national, political, ethnic, racial or religious grounds." Specifically, the secretary-general declared that "in the conflict in the territory of the former Yugoslavia, such inhumane acts have taken the form of so-called 'ethnic cleansing' and widespread and systematic rape and other forms of sexual assault, including forced prostitution."[116] Thus, in this Tribunal, rape and sexual assault were for the first time to be prosecuted as serious violations of international humanitarian law.[117]

Since its creation in 1993, the Tribunal has investigated and prosecuted extreme forms of human cruelty and brutality, some of which were sexual in nature. In interesting ways, the manner in which sexual violence is characterized by the Tribunal, as well as the particular provisions of international human rights law that it has invoked to prosecute sex-based violence, have evolved over this period. The changes occurring within the Tribunal in this regard reflect an increasingly sophisticated approach to the role that sex can play in the degradation, humiliation, torture, and great suffering experienced by the victims of this horrible war.

In May 1992, Serb forces were alleged to have rounded up and sent to the Omarska Prison Camp roughly three thousand Muslims and Croats, in particular intellectuals, professionals, and political leaders. Of these prisoners, approximately forty were women. Conditions in Omarska were horrible, and soldiers subjected many civilians "inside and outside the camps to a campaign of terror which included killings, torture, sexual assaults, and other physical and psychological abuse." In February 1995, the Tribunal prosecutor issued two separate indictments, the Meakic indictment and the Tadic indictment, in connection with atrocities committed by Serbian forces against Croat Muslims at Omarska. Both indictments, commonly referred to as the Omarska indictments, contained allegations of sexual violence — in the Meakic case primarily by men against women, and in the Tadic case by men against both women and men.[118] The allegations of rape and sexual violence in both cases are absolutely horrifying, yet, as was typical for indictments filed early in the Tribunal's tenure, the prosecutor's juridical treatment of these atrocities differed depending on the sex of the victim.

In the Meakic indictment, the prosecutor charged Serbian soldiers with a number of violations of international humanitarian law. Among them were charges that, between May and December 1992, Serbian soldiers had repeatedly raped female prisoners at Omarska. Croatian women were forcibly removed from their beds at night, taken to a room downstairs, thrown on a table or on the floor, and repeatedly raped, night after night.[119] Young women between the ages of twelve and nineteen were the most vulnerable. A prisoner with medical training who was assigned to treat and counsel many of the rape victims testified before the Tribunal:

> The very act of rape, in my opinion — I spoke to these people, I observed their reactions — it had a terrible effect on them. They could, perhaps, explain it to themselves when somebody steals something from them, or even beatings or even some killings. Somehow they sort of accepted it in some way, but when the rapes started they lost all hope. Until then they had hope that this war could pass, that everything would quiet down. When the rapes started, everybody lost hope, everybody in the camp, men and women. There was such fear, horrible.[120]

For this conduct, the Prosecutor charged Serbian soldiers with, among other things, Grave Breaches of the Geneva Convention of 1949 under Article 2(c) of the Tribunal Statute (willfully causing great suffering or serious injury to body or health), Violations of the Laws or Customs of War under Article 3 of the Tribunal Statute, and Crimes Against Humanity under Article 5(g) (rape). Contrast this construction of the nature of the injury with the charges filed in connection with the torture of men at the Omarska camp. According to the indictment, Serb soldiers fatally beat male prisoners for using Muslim expressions, stripped male prisoners to their underwear, kicked them in the testicles, and beat them in the ribs until they became unconscious. Soldiers ordered other prisoners to drink water like animals from puddles on the ground and later discharged a fire extinguisher into the mouths of those prisoners. Like the prosecutions involving female victims, the prosecutor charged offending soldiers with grave breaches under Article 2(c) (willfully causing great suffering or serious injury to body or health), and Violations of the Law or Customs of War under Article 3. But instead of charging a violation of Article 5(g) (rape), the prosecutor alleged a Crime Against Humanity for "other inhumane acts" under Article 5(i).[121]

Thus, the torture and humiliation of female prisoners by raping them was prosecuted as "willfully causing great suffering or serious injury to body or health" and rape, but the torture and humiliation of male prisoners, even when it involved the genitals, was prosecuted as "willfully causing great suffering or serious injury to body or health" and the residual category for "other inhumane acts." This differential is even greater exemplified by the indictment in the Tadic case.

The Tadic prosecution relates to the well-publicized atrocities committed against Muslim Croats at Omarska. As in the Meakic indictment, the Tadic indictment includes allegations of sexual and non-sexual violence against civilian prisoners in the camp. Just as in the Meakic indictment, in the allegations relating to the rape of a woman "F" at Omarska, the defendant is charged with committing a Crime Against Humanity under Article 5(g) (rape) of the Tribunal Statute.[122] However, the charges associated with sexual violence involving men exemplifies a different approach. The Tribunal found that the defendants beat a male prisoner named Harambasic, after which they ordered two male prisoners to lick his buttocks and suck his penis, and then to bite his testicles. As stated by the Tribunal:

> Meanwhile a group of men in uniform stood around the inspection pit watching and shouting to bite harder. . . . Witness H was threatened with a knife that both his eyes would be cut out if he did not hold Fikret Harambasic's mouth closed to prevent him from screaming; G was then made to lie between the naked Fikret Harambasic's legs and, while the

latter struggled, hit and bit his genitals. G then bit off one of Fikret Harambasic's testicles and spat it out and was told he was free to leave. . . . Harambasic has not been seen or heard of since.[123]

For this conduct, the prosecutor charged Tadic with a Grave Breach under Article 2(b) (torture or inhuman treatment), a Violation of the Laws or Customs of War under Article 3 (cruel treatment), and a Crime Against Humanity under Article 5(i) (other inhumane acts) of the Tribunal Statute. Although the presiding judge at turns referred to the above-described conduct as a sexual assault and sexual mutilation, Tadic was not charged with violating Article 5(g) of the Statute (rape), even though the conduct included forced fellatio and other sex-based violence.[124]

Five months after issuing the indictments in the Tadic and Meakic cases, the Tribunal issued five more indictments, three of which contained allegations of sex-related violence.[125] These indictments evidence an evolution in the form in which the prosecutor's office drafted its pleadings, as well as a shift in the substantive manner in which atrocities involving rape, forced sex, and other forms of sex-related torture were prosecuted. These changes better represent, to my mind, the complex ways in which sex figured in the torture, humiliation, and inhumane treatment of both women and men in the war in the former Yugoslavia. What is more, the approach now used by the prosecutor's office in dealing with sex-related violence, shaped in no small part by the work of Tribunal advisor for gender-related issues Patricia Sellers,[126] provides a helpful model as an alternative to the more essentializing and static ways in which the New York Penal Law, for instance, categorizes certain behavior as a sex crime.

Although sex-related atrocities make up a significant part of the prosecutor's docket, they are not prosecuted as sex crimes per se, but instead as the *actus reus* of other crimes, such as Crimes Against Humanity, Grave Breaches, Genocide, or Violations of the Laws and Customs of War. This mode of charging these crimes, together with the Tribunal's Rules of Procedure and Evidence that reflect a sensitivity to the unique issues that arise in the prosecution of sex-related violence,[127] make for a juridical structure that at once acknowledges the way sex operates as "an especially dense transfer point for relations of power"[128] without over-sexualizing rape and other sexual violence.

In the indictments issued in July 1995, the prosecutor's office for the first time adopted the use of headings within which various counts were organized, such as, "Genocide," "Killing of [X]," "Torture of [Y]," "Beatings of [Z]," and "Sexual Assault."[129] These headings represent not only a change in form, but an evolution in the substantive manner in which the Tribunal prosecuted sex-based violence. The Brcko indictment, for instance, charged that Ranko Cesic forced two brothers at gunpoint "to beat each other and perform sexual acts on each other in the presence of others, causing them great humiliation and degradation." For this conduct, the prosecutor charged Cesic with a violation of Article 2(b) (inhuman treatment), Article 3 (humiliating and degrading treatment) and Article 5(g) (rape, which includes other forms of sexual assault) of the Tribunal Statute.[130] Two important changes are worth noting in this indictment. First, Crimes Against Humanity as set forth in Article 5(g) was interpreted for the first time to include not only rape but also "other forms of sexual assault." Second, the sexual assault of a man by a man was determined to constitute a sexual assault within the meaning of Article 5(g) rather than a generalized inhumane act under Article 5(i).[131]

In a separate indictment issued in July 1995, in connection with atrocities committed in the town of Bosanski Samac, Serbian soldiers were charged with forcing two male prisoners "to perform sexual acts upon each other in the presence of several other prisoners and guards." For these allegations the Tribunal indicted the accused under the same violations of humanitarian law as the Brcko defendants: among other things, Crimes Against Humanity under Article 5(g) (rape, which includes other forms of sexual assault).[132]

In two indictments issued in 1996, the prosecutor developed an even more refined approach to the prosecution of conduct that included some degree of sex-related violence. Continuing the use of subject headings in the indictments, in March 1996, the prosecutor issued an indictment in connection with atrocities committed in a camp in the village of Celebici.[133] One allegation charges that Hazim Delic, the commander of the Celebici camp, submitted a female prisoner to repeated forcible sexual intercourse, sometimes in public and other times by more than one rapist. In a separate allegation, he was charged with raping another female prisoner during her first interrogation, and then every few days for the next six weeks. For these actions, Delic was charged with a Grave Breach under Article 2(b) (torture), and Violations of the Laws and Customs of War under Article (3) (torture and cruel treatment). This is the first time that the ICTY prosecutor characterized sex-related violence against either a man or a woman as torture, not rape.[134]

Further, the Tribunal issued an indictment in June 1996 in which rape, sexual enslavement, and other forms of sexual assault made up the central focus of the charges. In the Foca indictment, the Tribunal described how, between April and July 1992, soldiers detained young and adult Muslim women of the town of Foca in houses, athletic fields, the local high school, detention centers, apartments, and houses. Both individuals and groups of Serbian soldiers systematically raped, tortured, and humiliated these women.[135] On several occasions, the soldiers told women, while raping them, that they would give birth to Serbian babies, and in one case, that her body "would be found in five different countries if she told anyone that he had raped her." In addition, the indictment describes how many Muslim women were enslaved in houses and apartments converted into "rape camps,"[136] and were subjected to rape and other sexual assaults continually. These women were also forced to perform domestic duties for the Serbian soldiers such as cooking, laundry, and cleaning, and were bought and sold by Serbian and Montenegrin soldiers.

The prosecutor indicted eight Serbs for these crimes. Where women were alleged to have been raped and tortured individually rather than in "rape camps," the prosecutor placed the allegations under the heading "Torture and Rape" and charged the defendants with Grave Breaches under Article 2(b) (torture), Violations of the Laws or Customs of War under Article 3 (torture), and Crimes Against Humanity under Article 5(f) (torture) and 5(g) (rape). Allegations of rape, with no additional allegations of actual or threatened violence, such as cutting or biting, appeared under the heading "Rape," and the defendants were charged only with a Crime Against Humanity under Article 5(g) (rape), but not with a Grave Breach (torture). Finally, allegations involving "rape camps" appeared under the heading "Enslavement and Rape," and the prosecutor charged the defendants with Crimes Against Humanity under Article 5(c) (enslavement) and 5(g) (rape), Grave Breach under Article 2(b) (inhumane treatment), and Violations of the Laws and Customs of War under Article 3 (outrages to personal dignity). Why this conduct was not characterized as torture is curious. Similarly puzzling is the prosecutor's decision in the Foca indictment to abandon the descriptions of acts charged under Article 5(g) as "rape, which includes other forms of sexual assault."

Finally, in the Kovacevic indictment, the prosecutor charged two Serbian officials with Genocide in connection with the torture of Muslim men and women in the towns of Prijedor and Banja Luka.[137] Although the indictment enumerated the rape and torture of women and girls by subordinates of the named defendants, they were not charged with rape under Article 5(g), but rather with Genocide under Articles 4 and 7. The indictment was later amended to charge the defendants with Crimes Against Humanity, Violations of the Laws or Customs of War, and Grave Breaches. In this case, rapes and other forms of sexual assault constituted the predicate acts of Genocide, but not a substantive violation of international humanitarian law.

Thus, over time, the manner in which the ICTY prosecutor's office framed sex-related violence has shifted. At the outset, the prosecutor interpreted sex-related violence to amount to a Grave Breach, a Violation of the Laws and Customs of War, and a Crime Against Humanity. However, violence suffered by women was pled as rape under the Statute's Crimes Against Humanity provisions, whereas sex-related violence suffered by men was prosecuted under the provision reaching other inhumane acts. After a period of time, rape, a crime specifically enumerated as a Crime Against Humanity in the Statute, was interpreted broadly to mean sexual assault, "an 'umbrella phrase' that refers to . . . forcible sexual penetration, indecent assault, enforced prostitution, sexual mutilation, forced impregnation, and forced maternity."[138] Thus, charges now brought under Article 5(g) are frequently described as "rape which includes other forms of sexual assault." This expanded term has been applied to the rape of women as well as to men who were forced to perform sex acts, whether forced sexual intercourse or forced fellatio.

What is more, the ICTY prosecutor has come to regard sex-related violence as not only a sexual assault under Article 5(g), but as a form of torture and genocide — whether committed against men or women. "This is done by prosecuting sexual assaults not as enumerated crimes in and of themselves (such as under Article 5(g)), but rather as elements, usually the actus reus, of the crimes."[139] Thus, borrowing the definition from other conventions on torture, the ICTY prosecutor defines torture, in relevant part, as "any act by which severe pain or suffering, whether physical or mental, is inflicted on a person for such purposes as . . . punishing him for an act that he or a third person has committed or is suspected of having committed, or intimidating or coercing him or a third person, or for any reason based on discrimination of any kind."[140]

Sexual assault is therefore regarded as an element of the crime of torture—as an act by which severe pain and suffering, whether physical or mental, is inflicted on a person for a prohibited purpose. This view mirrors that of the UN Special Rapporteur on torture, who called rape "an especially traumatic form of torture."[141] Thus, evidence of rape or other sexual assault "only partially satisfies the elements of torture . . . which in turn only partially satisfies the elements required to establish a grave breach."[142] The evolution in the manner in which sex-related violence is charged before the ICTY has culminated in two judgments issued by the Tribunal's Trial Chamber in cases involving charges of rape and other forms of sexual assault. In the Celebici case, three military officials, two Muslims and a Croat, were convicted of having committed a number of war crimes, including rape of female prisoners, placing burning fuses around the genital areas of male prisoners, and forcing brothers to perform fellatio on one another. In the Furundzija case, the Trial Chamber convicted the defendant of aiding and abetting the rape and sexual assault of a female prisoner by a soldier in Furundzija's command while he looked on and did nothing.[143]

In both of these cases, the judges were careful to thoroughly discuss the manner in which sexual assaults, including rape, were used as a form of torture. To make a claim of torture, the prosecutor must show the intentional infliction of severe physical or mental pain or suffering undertaken for a prohibited purpose. According to the Celebici panel, "It is difficult to envisage circumstances in which rape . . . could be considered as occurring for a purpose that does not, in some way, involve punishment, coercion, discrimination or intimidation."[144] With regard to the specific sexual assaults with which the defendants were charged, the panel concluded that "the violence suffered by [a female prisoner] in the form of rape, was inflicted upon her by Delic because she is a woman. [T]his represents a form of discrimination which constitutes a prohibited purpose for the offence of torture."[145] Similarly, the Furundzija panel concluded that the prosecutor had proved that the rape of the female prisoner was a form of torture because they inflicted this form of severe physical and mental suffering to obtain information from her during an interrogation. It is worth noting that the man who raped the victim in the Furundzija case had warned another soldier "not to hit her as he had 'other methods' for women, methods which he then put to use."[146] Thus, the Furundzija panel could have concluded that the rapes and other sexual assault of the female prisoner were conducted for a discriminatory purpose as well as for the purpose of extracting information.

This shift to treating sex-related violence, including rape, as torture under Article 2(b) pertaining to Grave Breaches is a position that Professor Rhonda Copelon has urged to the prosecutor both directly in correspondence and indirectly in her scholarly publications. Her reasoning for doing so is threefold. First, Copelon argues, it is most appropriate to classify rape and other sexual assault as a Grave Breach because "under the Geneva Conventions, the most serious war crimes are designated as 'grave breaches.'" Second, to prove a grave breach, one need not show that the conduct was systematic or took place on a mass scale; "one act of rape is punishable," just as one act of murder or torture would be. Finally, crimes classified as Grave Breaches are conferred universal jurisdiction, thereby providing authority for the prosecution of such crimes before an international tribunal.[147] Thus, Copelon and others urge the prosecution of rape and other sex-related crimes as a form of torture in order to remove any ambiguity as to the seriousness of the offense.[148] The prosecutor and the Trial Chambers have adopted this strategy not as a matter of amendment of the Statute, but as a matter of interpretation: the Grave Breach provisions of Article 2(b) pertaining to torture have now been interpreted by the Trial Chamber to include the rape of women in the Lasva River Valley and at Celebici.

What the ICTY prosecutor has devised, in effect, is a strategy to evaluate on a case-by-case basis what role sex-related violence plays in the context of violations of international humanitarian law, insofar as it "shock[s] the conscience of humankind to such a degree [that it has] an international effect."[149] Rather than rely on special laws that isolate rape and/or sexual assault as a privileged kind of injury, the Tribunal's prosecutor and judges have chosen to tailor the construction of these crimes to the way sex-related violence figured in the physical or mental destruction of a people or person. Where sex-related violence takes place on a mass scale or is the subject of orchestrated policy, it is appropriately prosecuted as a Crime Against Humanity, which requires a showing that the accused's actions were part of a widespread or systematic attack against a civilian population.[150] Where it operates as part of a campaign to destroy a national, ethnic, racial, or religious group, it should be prosecuted as Genocide.[151] Yet, as ICTY Judge

Elizabeth Odio Benito observed, "It will be difficult to compile sufficient evidence to prosecute persons individually responsible for . . . crimes against humanity or genocide."[152] Thus the Tribunal can and should invoke its Statute's provisions relating to Grave Breaches and Violations of the Laws and Customs of War in cases involving sex-related violence as well.

All of these formulations are clearly preferable to the treatment of rape as a spoil of war, as a crime of passion or lust, or as a crime against honor, modesty, or dignity, as international humanitarian law has in the past.[153] Although it is true that rape and other sex-related violence was undertaken in the former Yugoslavia systematically as part of a campaign of ethnic- and religious-based persecution,[154] it was also undertaken as part of a systematic campaign of gender-based persecution. International human-itarian law has begun to recognize the significance of gender-based persecu-tion insofar as rape has been treated as a form of sex discrimination within the context of torture prosecutions. The ICTY Trial Chambers construction of rape as torture made a tremendous step beyond the view that "rape and other sexual assaults have often been labeled as 'private,' thus precluding them from being punished under national or international law."[155]

The same interpretative advance must be undertaken with respect to the meaning of Crimes Against Humanity: "The women victims and survivors in Bosnia are being subjected to crimes against humanity based on *both* ethnicity and religion, and gender. It is critical to recognize both and to acknowledge that the intersection of ethnic and gender violence has its own particular characteristics."[156] Thus, persecution based on gender must be recognized as its own class of crimes against humanity. It is important to be clear, however, that to do so is a quite different interpretive strategy from focusing on the role of sex in war.

The ICTY has for the first time treated sex-related violence as a serious, and often grave, breach of international humanitarian law, while avoiding the mistake of essentializing sexual conduct as a special kind of injury that deserves to be "protected, surrounded, invested"[157] with a unique legal response. The Tribunal's Rules of Procedure and Evidence reflect a sen-sitivity to the particularities of sex-related violence with respect to the corroboration of sexual assault victims' testimony, evidence of prior sexual conduct, and complexity of the notion of consent.[158] Indeed, the Trial Chamber rested its conviction in the Celebici case on the uncorroborated testimony of the rape victim. Thus, the prosecution of sex-related violence before this Tribunal stands a good chance of being done in a way that recognizes how sex was used as a weapon of war, yet avoids many of Foucault's concerns with respect to the ways sex is legally inscribed on the body. At the same time, this method of prosecution remains sensitive to particular meanings of sex-related violence for the people who suffered it, as well as for the larger culture in the former Yugoslavia.

Conclusion

Of course, all cultures sexualize different body parts and behaviors in myriad ways. In a sense, I am urging a reverse sociology of the erotic. Rather than study the ways fingers, toes, lips, ears, penises, vaginas, or anuses become eroticized across cultures, I am concerned with the way body parts and practices, once sexualized, cannot escape a signification process by which contact with those body parts and the enactment of those practices are always already and exclusively understood to be sexual. In this sense, I want to question whether the sexual is a satisfactory lens of analysis by which to understand the meaning of interpersonal practices such as sexual harassment, seminal practices in Melanesia, the assault of Abner Louima, or sex-related violence in the former Yugoslavia.

In the Tadic case, the Tribunal found that Suada Ramica, a Muslim woman who was three to four months pregnant as a result of being raped by a Serbian soldier in a camp, was "taken to the Prijedor police station by a Serb policeman with whom she was acquainted through work. On the way he cursed at her, using ethnically derogatory terms and told her that Muslims should all be killed because they 'do not want to be controlled by Serbian authorities.' When she arrived at the police station she saw two Muslim men whom she knew, covered in blood. She was taken to a prison cell which was covered in blood and . . . raped again and beaten."[159] This evidence supported a finding by the Tribunal that Tadic was guilty of religious persecution: a Crime Against Humanity. This evidence sounds eerily similar to Abner Louima's recount of the conduct and comments of the police officers who verbally and physically assaulted him on the night of August 19, 1997. Recall that the white police officers are accused of saying:

"You niggers have to learn to respect police officers." The other one said, "If you yell or make any noise, I will kill you." Then one held me and the other one stuck the [wooden handle of a toilet] plunger up my behind.

He pulled it out and shoved it in my mouth, broke my teeth and said, "That's your s——t, nigger." Later, when they called the ambulance, the cop told me, "If you ever tell anyone . . . I will kill you and your family."[160]

If what Sauda Ramic experienced was sexual violence in the service of religious persecution, surely what Abner Louima suffered was sexual violence as a form of recial persecution. In both cases, the victims suffered a form of gender-based violence as well. Hopefully, international humanitarian law will one day recognize gender-based crimes as being on a par with crimes that are racial, religious, ethnic, or political in nature. But in either case, it would be a mistake to reduce the wrong of the atrocities they suffered to the fact that they were sexual. So too, when observers object to the ritualized semen practices of the Sambia because they amount to intergenerational sex, we lost sight of the power those practices have to teach boys important gender-based lessons. In all these cases, it is paramount that we keep our focus on how sex is put to work to construct men, masculinity, and nations, and to destroy women, men, and a people.

Notes

1. The Blessed Virgin Mary seems to appear all the time in Queens, New York. In fact, there are ads in the subway announcing a phone number you can call, for only $1.50 a minute, to receive information about the most recent sightings of the BVM. I have always wondered: Why Queens of all places? Carol Rose recently answered the question for me: lots of Catholics, of course.

2. Michel Foucault, *Language, Counter-Memory, Practice: Selected Essays and Interviews*, ed. Donald F. Bouchard, trans. Donald F. Bouchard and Sherry Simon (Ithaca, NY: Cornell University Press, 1977), 148.

3. Michel Foucault, *The History of Sexuality,* trans. Robert Hurley (New York: Vintage Books, 1990), 103.

4. David Herbert Donald, *Lincoln* (New York: Touchstone, 1995), 389.

5. Eve Kosofsky Sedgwick, *Between Men: English Literature and Male Homosocial Desire* (New York: Columbia University Press, 1985), 6.

6. See Katherine M. Franke, "What's Wrong with Sexual Harassment?" *Stanford Law Review* 49 (1997): 691, 730–47, 762–72.

7. See, e.g., F. E. Williams, *Papuans of the Trans-Fly* (Oxford: The Clarendon Press, 1936), 158; Gilbert H. Herdt, *Guardians of the Flutes* (New York: McGraw-Hill, 1981): (1); Gilbert H. Herdt, "Ritualized Homosexual Behavior in the Male Cults of Melanesia, 1862–1983: An Introduction," in *Ritualized Homosexuality in Melanesia*, ed. Gilbert H.

Herdt (Berkeley: University of California Press, 1984); Gerald W. Creed, "Sexual Subordination: Institutionalized Homosexuality and Social Control in Melanesia," *Ethnology* 23 (1984): 157, 158. Herdt asks, for instance, "Why should a society of manly warriors believe that a boy must be orally inseminated to become masculine? What happens when this conviction is implemented through prolonged ritualized homosexuality?"

8. E.g., Merrill Goozner, "NYC Cut in Crime Has a Brutish Side," *Chicago Tribune* 16 Aug. 1997.

9. Michel Foucault, *Politics, Philosophy, Culture: Interviews and Other Writings 1977–1984*, ed. Lawrence D. Kritzman, trans. Alan Sheridan et al. (New York: Routledge, 1988), 200.

10. Vikki Bell, "Beyond the 'Thorny Question': Feminism, Foucault and the Desexualisation of Rape," *International Journal of the Sociology of Law* 19 (1991): 83, 89.

11. Foucault, *The History of Sexuality*, 105.

12. Herdt provides the name Sambia as a pseudonym for the tribe's true name to "protect the identities of those who trusted [him] and to guard the community's ritual cult, which still remains a secretive way of life in the strict sense of the term. Sambia men explicitly stipulated that no part of [his] original material be allowed to circulate within Papua New Guinea" (*Guardians of the Flutes*, xvi).

13. Ibid., 204–5, 223. Herdt summarized the Sambia beliefs as follows: "Femininity is thought to be an inherent development in a girl's continuous association with her mother. Masculinity, on the other hand, is not an intrinsic result of maleness; it is an achievement distinct from the mere endowment of male genitals. Masculine reproductive maturity must be artificially induced, by means of strict adherence to ritual techniques" (160).

14. Ibid., 224. Herdt observes that cane-swallowing was abandoned sometime around 1964 because it was too painful (223 n. 29).

15. Ibid., 224–26, 262–65.

16. "Ingestive rites" involve the practice of swallowing and absorbing substances believed essential in effectuating masculine growth (ibid., 227, 232, 234, 236, 252); See also 281–82, noting an interim stage when boys approaching puberty take an active role in motivating younger boys to join them as fellators.

17. Ibid., 233, 252.

18. Ibid., 3 n. 2: "It is crucial that we distinguish from the start between homosexual *identity* and *behavior*."

19. Ibid., 2–3, 8.

20. See Herdt, *Ritualized Homosexual Behavior*, 2, citing a number of early Melanesian studies that ignored same-sex seminal practices.

21. See ibid., 3, recognizing that, as of 1984, "sex remains one of the 'taboo' subjects in anthropology"; Kath Weston, "Lesbian/Gay Studies in the House of Anthropology," *Annual Review of Anthropology* 22 (1993): 339: "Throughout the first half of the century, most allusions by anthropologists to homosexual behavior remained as veiled in ambiguity and as couched in judgment as were references to homosexuality in the dominant discourse of the surrounding society." Herdt attributed three additional factors to this failure: (1) a lack of data; (2) "the tendency for writers still to view homosexual behavior as universally deviant, unnatural, or perverse"; and (3) the use of authorities viewing only heterosexuality as "normal" (Herdt, *Ritualized Homosexual Behavior,* 3).

22. See Gilbert Herdt, "Representations of Homosexuality: An Essay on Cultural Ontology and Historical Comparison, Part II," *Journal of the History of Sexuality* 1 (1991): 603, 607, addressing the negative response of white missionaries, government officers, and Western agents to the "boy-inseminating man."

23. See ibid., 607–8. One must wonder how Herdt's published work may have contributed to the extinction of the very practices he set out to document.

24. Herdt, *Ritualized Homosexuality in Melanesia* (collection of articles addressing same-sex sexual practices in different societies in the South Pacific region); Gilbert Herdt, ed., *Rituals of Manhood: Male Initiation in Papua New Guinea* (Berkeley: University of California Press, 1982), analyzing male maturation rites in Papua New Guinea; Gilbert Herdt, *Same Sex, Different Cultures: Gays and Lesbians across Cultures* (Boulder: Westview Press, 1997), 81–88, 112–23.

25. Deborah A. Elliston, "Erotic Anthropology: 'Ritualized Homosexuality' in Melanesia and Beyond," *American Ethnologist* 22 (1995): 848.

26. See, e.g., Herdt, "Representations of Homosexuality," 606–7.

27. Herdt observes: "[M]en are not simply biding time by fooling around with initiates. Boys were their first erotic partners. For this reason, and other personality factors, bachelors are sometimes passionately fond of particular boys" (*Guardians of the Flutes,* 288).

28. See ibid., 282, 319; Herdt, "Representations of Homosexuality," 611, discussing the protections and bonds that may develop between bachelors and boys.

29. See Franke, "What's Wrong," 729–47.

30. Elliston, "Erotic Anthropology," 849.

31. See Herdt, "Representations of Homosexuality," 603: "Do boy-inseminating relationships, one must wonder, express erotic desire?" Herdt recognizes and rejects two interpretative trends that largely dismiss the erotic nature of Melanesian homosexuality. The first trend treats such practices as "purely customary ritual practice" (607).

32. Creed, "Sexual Subordination," 160.

33. See Herdt, "Representations of Homosexuality," 613: "It is a necessary redundancy to say that without sexual excitement—as signified by erections in the inspirer and bawdy enthusiasm in the inspired boy—these social practices would not only lie beyond the erotic but, more elementarily, would not exist."

34. As noted by Thorkil Vanggaard, *Phallós: A Symbol and Its History in the Male World,* trans. Thorkil Vanggaard (New York: International Universities Press, 1972), 102: "It appears, then, that emotions and impulses other than erotic ones may cause erection and genital activity in men; just as, in the baboon, mounting and penetrating to show superiority, or sitting on guard with legs apart and penis threateningly exposed show erection of an asexual origin. . . . The same will probably have been the case with the Bronze Age people of Scandinavia — or of northern Italy for that matter — since they equated phallic power with the power of the spear, the sword and the axe, as we can see from their petroglyphs."

35. See, e.g., Ron Langevin, *Sexual Strands: Understanding and Treating Sexual Anomalies in Men* (Hillsdale, N.J.: L. Erlbaum Associates, 1983) 8; Joost Dekker and Walter Everaerd, "Psychological Determinants of Sexual Arousal: A Review," *Behavior RES and Therapy* 27 (1989): 353, 361.

36. Alfred C. Kinsey et al., *Sexual Behavior in the Human Male* (Philadelphia: W.B. Saunders Co., 1948): 164–65.

37. Dekker and Everaerd, "Psychological Determinants," 361.

38. Elliston, "Erotic Anthropology," 854.

39. Franke, "What's Wrong," 740.

40. See Amy Richlin, *The Garden of Priapus: Sexuality and Aggression in Roman Humor,* rev. ed. (Oxford: Oxford University Press, 1992), 215, 256.

41. See Vanggaard, *Phallós:* " 'A favourite Persian punishment for strangers caught in the Harem or Gynæceum is to strip and throw them and expose them to the embraces of the grooms and Negro slaves' " (101, quoting Richard Burton, "Thousand Nights and a Night," *Terminal Essay* X [1885]: 235).

42. As Foucault noted, "Sexuality is not the most intractable element in power relations, but rather one of those endowed with the greatest instrumentality: useful for the greatest number of maneuvers and capable of serving as a point of support, as a linchpin, for the most varied strategies" (*The History of Sexuality,* 103).

43. Sedgwick recognizes that aspects of the Sambia culture fit within her "homosocial continuum." *Between Men,* 7; see also 5.

44. One clear example of this polarization is found in the many spatial segregations evidenced by the Sambia culture. The male "clubhouse," site of many of the masculinization rites, is off-limits to women (see Herdt, *Guardians of the Flutes,* 74–75). Similarly, female "menstrual huts" are strictly avoided by men (75). This spatial segregation operates in many other areas, including domiciles and footpaths (75–76).

45. See ibid., 28–29, 162, 244–45; Herdt, *Same Sex, Different Cultures,* 113.

46. Herdt observed that, in the Sambia culture, "Men hold that women may pollute them by simply 'stepping over'. . . , above, or beside them, or by touching persons, food, or possessions. During their menstrual periods women leave their houses and retire to the menstrual hut, which is situated slightly below the hamlet. Men and initiates completely avoid the area of the hut. Likewise, women must not walk near the men's clubhouse or look inside" (*Guardians of the Flutes,* 75). Domestic arrangements are also organized around the danger of male pollution by women. On entering a house, women immediately must squat near the doorway, thereby reducing the possibility of transferring their polluting fluids to men in the house (75–76).

47. Gilbert Herdt and Robert J. Stoller, *Intimate Communications: Erotics and the Study of Culture* (New York: Columbia University Press, 1990): 60, 62, 63. Interestingly, more semen is necessary to make a girl than a boy.

48. Ibid., 65, 62.

49. Herdt, "Representations of Homosexuality," 605–6, 607.

50. Herdt, *Same Sex, Different Cultures,* 121.

51. Elliston, "Erotic Anthropology," 855.

52. Sedgwick posits that: " 'Male homosocial desire' is intended to mark both discrimina-
tions and paradoxes. 'Homosocial desire,' to begin with, is a kind of oxymoron. 'Homosocial' is a word occasionally used in history and the social sciences, where it describes
social bonds between persons of the same sex; it is a neologism, obviously formed by
analogy with 'homosexual,' and just as obviously meant to be distinguished from 'homosexual.' In fact, it is applied to such activities as 'male bonding,' which may, as in our
society, be characterized by intense homophobia, fear and hatred of homosexuality. To
draw the 'homosocial' back into the orbit of 'desire,' of the potentially erotic, then, is to
hypothesize the potential unbrokenness of a continuum between homosocial and homosexual" (*Between Men,* 1).

53. Nella Larson, "Passing," in *Quicksand and Passing,* ed. Deborah E. McDowell (New
Brunswick, N.J.: Rutgers University Press, 1986) 135, 149–61.

54. Lauren Berlant, "National Brands/National Body: Imitation of Life," in *Comparative
American Identities: Race, Sex, and Nationality in the Modern Text,* ed. Hortense J.
Spillers (New York: Routledge, 1991), 110, 111.

55. T. O. Beildelman, *The Cool Knife: Imagery of Gender, Sexuality, and Moral Education
in Kaguru Initiation Ritual* (Washington, D.C.: Smithsonian Institute Press, 1997), 244.

56. Sedgwick, *Between Men,* 15.

57. Ibid., 13.

58. E.g., Goozner, "NYC Cut in Crime," 1.

59. Mike McAlary, "The Frightful Whisperings from a Coney Island Hospital Bed," *New
York Daily News* 13 Aug. 1997, 2, quoting Abner Louima as Louima lay in his hospital
bed four days after the attack.

60. See Richard Goldstein, "What's Sex Got to Do with It? The Assault of Abner Louima
May Have Been Attempted Murder. But It Was Also Rape," *Village Voice* 2 Sept. 1997,
57; Tom Hays, "Haitian's Beating May Have Been Case of Mistaken Identity, Punch,"
Arizona Republic 22 Aug. 1997, A11, reporting that witnesses claimed another individual, not Louima, threw the punch against Officer Volpe.

61. "Report: Officer Boasted after Attack," UPI 19 Aug. 1997, available in Lexis, Nexis
Library, UPI File, reporting the alleged statement of Justin Volpe, New York City police
officer.

62. One report stated that "the officers became furious when he protested his arrest, twice
stopping the patrol car to beat him with their fists." McAlary, "Frightful Whisperings," 2;
see also David Kocieniewski, "Injured Man Says Brooklyn Officers Tortured Him in Custody," *New York Times* 13 Aug. 1997, B1.

63. Louima recounted the incident to a newspaper: " 'The cops pulled down my pants in
front of the desk sergeant.' . . . 'They marched you naked across the precinct?' 'Yes.'
'There were other cops around?' 'Yes. There was the sergeant and other cops. They saw.'

'And they said nothing?' 'I kept screaming, "Why? Why?" All the cops heard me, but said nothing.' 'What they said to me I'll never forget. In public, one says, "You niggers have to learn how to respect police officers." ' " (Mike McAlary, "Victim and City Deeply Scarred," *New York Daily News* 14 Aug. 1997, 4).

64. McAlary, "Frightful Whisperings," 2.

65. Kocieniewski, "Injured Man," B1.

66. Tom Hayes, "Officer Accused of Sexually Brutalizing Suspect Arrested," AP 13 Aug. 1997, 1 (as reproduced by a number of newspapers).

67. See "Louima Starts on a Long Road Back," *Newsday* 12 Oct. 1997, A39.

68. J. Zamgba Browne, "Police Sodomize Suspect: The Tale of Torture at 70th Precinct," *New York Amsterdam News* 20 Aug. 1997, 1; "Suspect Claims Police Raped Him with Plunger," *Salt Lake Tribune* 14 Aug. 1997, A13. Hayes, "Officer Accused," 1; see also "New York Officer Surrenders in Sexual Assault on Immigrant," *Los Angeles Times* 14 Aug. 1997, A18; "Cop Surrenders on Sexual Brutality Charges," *San Diego Union & Tribune* 14 Aug. 1997, A12.

69. See Vinette K. Pryce, "A Week of Outrage, Pain and Celebration," *New York Amsterdam News* 10 Sept. 1997, 1, containing a photograph of a protester at a march holding a sign saying "Criminals, Perverts, Rapists."

70. Charles Baillou, "Marchers Blast Police Barbarism at City Hall," *New York Amsterdam News* 10 Sept. 1997, 8.

71. David Firestone, "Giuliani's Quandary: Mayor Who Linked Name to Police Success Is Now Facing a Very Ugly Police Failure," *New York Times* 15 Aug. 1997, A1. The press reported that, during the assault of Louima at the 70th Precinct, one of the officers said: "This is Giuliani time, not Dinkins time" (Eleanor Randolph, "In Police Abuse Case, Giuliani's Balance Tested," *Los Angeles Times* 16 Aug. 1997, A1). But see Carolina Gonzalez and Bill Hutchinson, "Sharpton Promises He'll Defend Louima," *New York Daily News* 19 Jan. 1998, 8, reporting that Louima was then unsure of whether the officer actually made this statement. Mayor Giuliani provided a quite interesting response to reports of the officer's alleged comment: "The remark is as perverted as the alleged act" (in Randolph, A1).

72. John Sullivan, "New Charges Filed in Police Brutality Case," *New York Times* 22 Aug. 1997, B3.

73. Goldstein, "What's Sex Got to Do with It," 57.

74. See Goozner, "New York Cut in Crime," 1; see also New York Penal Law § 120.10 (McKinney 1998) (first degree assault); New York Penal Law § 130.70 (first degree aggravated sexual abuse).

75. See "2 NYC Officers Get New Charge in Haitian's Beating," *Boston Globe* 9 Sept. 1997, A8; see also New York Penal Law § 240.31 (first degree aggravated harassment).

76. Mike McAlary, "Home Sweet Heartache: Love Alone Won't Aid Louima in Brooklyn," *New York Daily News* 10 Oct. 1997, 3.

77. A New York City commission report provides two examples of police overzealousness: "One officer from a Brooklyn North precinct told us how he and his colleagues once threw a bucket of ammonia in the face of an individual detained in a precinct holding pen. Another cooperating officer told us how he and his colleagues threw garbage and then boiling water on a person hiding from them in a dumbwaiter shaft" (City of New York, Commission to Investigate Allegations of Police Corruption and the Anti-Corruption Procedures of the Police Department, *Commission Report* [1997], 47; hereafter *Mollen Report*). Also see Amnesty International, United States of America, *Police Brutality and Excessive Force in the New York City Police Department* (1996), 26, 37–54.

78. Goldstein, "What's Sex Got to Do with It," 57; emphasis added.

79. See, e.g., Charles Baillou, "Angry Haitians March at the 70th Precinct in Brooklyn," *New York Amsterdam News* 27 Aug. 1997, 1; "The Blue Wall, Police Brutality and Police Silence," *Nightline*, ABC, 22 Aug. 1997.

80. See, e.g., n. 81 below, providing the New York Penal Law's definition of first degree aggravated sexual abuse.

81. See New York Penal Law §§ 130.00–.85 (McKinney 1998 and Supp. 1998; listing New York's sex offenses). The New York Penal Law defines sexual misconduct as:

1. Being a male, he engages in sexual intercourse with a female without her consent; or

2. He engages in deviate sexual intercourse with another person without the latter's consent; or

3. He engages in sexual conduct with an animal or a dead human body. (§130.20)

"Deviate sexual intercourse" is defined as "sexual conduct between persons not married to each other consisting of contact between the penis and the anus, the mouth and penis, or the mouth and the vulva" (§130.00(2)). First degree sexual abuse occurs when:

[A person] subjects another person to sexual contact:

1. By forcible compulsion; or

2. When the other person is incapable of consent by reason of being physically helpless; or

3. When the other person is less than eleven years old. (§130.65)

First degree aggravated sexual abuse occurs when:

[A person] inserts a foreign object in the vagina, urethra, penis or rectum of another person causing physical injury to such person:

(a) By forcible compulsion; or

(b) When the other person is incapable of consent by reason of being physically helpless; or

(c) When the other person is less than eleven years old. (§130.70(1))

First degree course of sexual conduct against a child occurs when, "over a period of time not less than three months in duration, [a person] engages in two or more acts of sexual conduct, which includes at least one act of sexual intercourse, deviate sexual intercourse or aggravated sexual contact, with a child less than eleven years old" (§130.75; see also §130.80, second degree course of sexual conduct against a child).

82. New York Penal Law §130.00 (3); emphasis added. In its entirety, "sexual contact" means: "Any touching of the sexual or other intimate parts of a person not married to the actor for the purpose of gratifying sexual desire of either party. It includes the touching of the actor by the victim, as well as the touching of the victim by the actor, whether directly or through clothing."

83. See *People v. Cammarere,* 611 N.Y.S.2d 682, 684 (App. Div. 1984); *People v. Gray,* 607 N.Y.S.2d 828, 829 (App. Div. 1994); *People v. Graydon,* 492 N.Y.S.2d 903, 904 (Crim. Ct. 1985); *People v. Rondon,* 579 N.Y.S.2d 319, 320–21 (Crim. Ct. 1992); *People v. Rivera,* 525 N.Y.S.2d 118, 119 (Sup. Ct. 1988); *People v. Belfrom,* 475 N.Y.S.2d 978, 980 (Sup. Ct. 1984).

84. *Rivera* at 119.

85. The New York Penal Law provides as follows. Sexual intercourse, defined as "its ordinary meaning and occur[ing] upon any penetration, however slight," New York Penal Law §130.00(1)) (McKinney 1998), is a necessary element of sexual misconduct (§130.20), rape (§130.35), and sodomy (§130.50). Aggravated sexual assault requires "insert[ion] of a foreign object in the vagina, urethra, penis, or rectum of another person" (§130.70).

86. New York Corrections Law §§168–168-v (McKinney Supp. 1998); New Jersey Statutes Annotated §§2C:7-1 to -11 (West 1995, 1998).

87. New York law requires the registration of "sex offenders" (New York Corrections Law §168-b). The statute defines sex offender as a person convicted of certain enumerated offenses; see §168-a(1), referencing the offenses listed in §168-1(2), (3). These enumerated offenses consist of those crimes listed in the text accompanying this note.

88. Under the New York Penal Law, unlawful imprisonment in the second degree occurs when "a person . . . restrains another person" (§135.05). First degree unlawful imprisonment must meet this definition plus "expose the [victim] to a risk of serious physical injury" (§135.10). Kidnapping in the second degree occurs when "a person . . . abducts another person" (§135.20). First degree kidnapping must meet this definition plus include one of a number of other circumstances, including death, intent to extract a ransom, or restraint for more than twelve hours with intent to "inflict physical injury upon him or violate or abuse him sexually" (§135.25).

89. New York Penal Law §135.15 (unlawful imprisonment); §135.30 (kidnapping).

90. Bell, "Beyond the Thorny Question," 86 (attributing this argument to Michel Foucault).

91. See Goldstein, "What's Sex Got to Do with It," 57.

92. Earl Caldwell, "Police Sodomy in Queens: The Column the *Daily News* Killed," *New York Amsterdam News* 27 Aug. 1997, 12. The "black" newspapers in New York reported these incidents at great length, but none of the "white" papers have mentioned them. See Earl Caldwell, "Earl Caldwell to the *Daily News* . . . 'I warned you. You fired me,'" *New York Amsterdam News* 27 Aug. 1997, 1: "The major papers seemed to have a blackout of the story. The *Daily News* had published nothing. The *New York Times* had published no story either."

93. In a characteristically laconic passage in *Beloved,* Toni Morrison depicts the acrid humiliation suffered by African American men on a chain gang who are forced each morning by white male guards to put on their own chains, kneel down in a row and fellate the guards on demand. See Toni Morrison, *Beloved* (New York: Knopf, 1987), 107–8. I read this passage not to be principally about the expropriation of sex from African American men, but rather about the routine ways sexual practices were used to degrade these prisoners.

94. See McAlary, "Frightful Whisperings," 2, quoting Louima's recollection of an officer's statement just prior to the insertion of a plunger into Louima's anus.

95. Droit du seigneur, or "right of the lord," historically referred to "a supposed legal or customary right at the time of a marriage whereby a feudal lord had sexual relations with a vasal's bride on her wedding night" (*Webster's Third New International Dictionary* [1993], 633).

96. Goldstein, "What's Sex Got to Do with It," 57.

97. After flirting with a female bartender while on his break, a male police officer followed her when she drove home from work, pulled her over, and teasingly said, "Now you know what it's gonna be like to be arrested. . . . He then took her out of the car, handcuffed her, grabbed her hair and pulled her head back and began to fondle her sexually" (Ronald K. Fitten, "County Officer Faces Charges of Misconduct," *Seattle Times* 24 Oct. 1998, A7).

98. See Ana Ortiz, "Remarks at the InterSEXionality Symposium," University of Denver College of Law, 6 Feb. 1998 (transcript on file with *Denver University Law Review*).

99. Richard Goldstein and Jean Jean Pierre, "Day of Outrage," *Village Voice* 9 Sept. 1997, 44, quoting Tatiana Wah.

100. See Foucault, *The History of Sexuality,* 57–63. "Is 'sex' really the anchorage point that supports the manifestations of sexuality, or is it not rather a complex idea that was formed inside the deployment of sexuality?" (152).

101. See Foucault, *Politics,* 200–204; Bell, "Beyond the Thorny Question," 84–87.

102. Foucault, *Politics,* 200–201. Foucault sets up the discussion with the provocative declaration that "in any case, sexuality can in no circumstances be the object of punishment."

103. See, e.g., Franke, "What's Wrong," 740–44, discussing the debate among feminists concerning the proper meaning of rape: as a crime of violence or sex.

104. Bell, "Beyond the Thorny Question," 92.

105. Foucault, *Politics*, 201–202.

106. Bell, "Beyond the Thorny Question," 87.

107. Judith Butler, *Bodies That Matter: On the Discursive Limits of "Sex"* (New York: Routledge, 1993), 1. In addressing Foucault's "regulatory ideal," Butler notes: "sex not only functions as a norm, but is part of a regulatory practice . . . whose regulatory force is made clear as a kind of productive power, the power to produce—demarcate, circulate, differentiate—the bodies it controls."

108. Wendy Brown, *States of Injury: Power and Freedom in Late Modernity* (Princeton University Press, 1995), 120.

109. Foucault, *Politics,* 202.

110. Monique Plaza, "Our Costs and Their Benefits," *M/F: A Feminist Journal* (1980): 28, 35.

111. Slavenka Drakulic, "Rape after Rape after Rape," *New York Times* 13 Dec. 1992, sect. 4, p. 17.

112. See *Prosecutor v. Delalic et al.,* Judgment, Case No. IT-96-21-T (ICTY 16 Nov. 1998); hereafter, Celebici Judgment. At the time of this writing, seventy-eight suspects had been indicted by the tribunal. The majority of those charged with committing war crimes were Bosnian Serbs, and most of the tens of thousands of victims of the 1991–1995 war were Croats and Muslims. However, "most of those indicted who have surrendered or been arrested are Muslims or Croats; the tribunal's two convictions to date involved a Bosnian Serb and a Croat, and one Bosnian Serb has confessed." See Charles Trueheart, "Bosnian Muslims, Croat Convicted of Atrocities against Serbs," *Washington Post* 17 Nov. 1998, A34.

113. *Final Report of the Commission of Experts Established Pursuant to Security Council Resolution 780,* 49th Sess., ¶248, UN Doc. S/1994/674 (1994); hereafter, *Final Report.*

114. The *Final Report* identified five patterns of rape, of which the rape camp for the purposes of ethnic cleansing was one (¶¶244–45). Four other patterns were recognized: (1) rapes occurring in conjunction with looting and intimidation; (2) rapes occurring in conjunction with fighting in the area; (3) rapes at detention facilities; and (4) rapes at detention facilities established for the "sole purpose of sexually entertaining soldiers" (¶¶245–47, 249). One Muslim woman was told that "she would give birth to a chetnik boy who would kill Muslims when he grew up" (¶249).

115. "Rape Becomes a Weapon of War," *New York Times* 10 Jan. 1993, sect. 4, p. 4.

116. *Report of the Secretary-General Pursuant to Paragraph 2 of Security Council Resolution 808* (1993), UN SCOR, 48th Sess., Annex, art. 1, p. 36, UN Doc. S25704 (1993), reprinted in *ILM* 32 (1993): 1163, 1192, available at ⟨http://www.un.org/icty/basic/i-bencon.htm⟩ (visited 2 Sept. 1998); hereafter *Tribunal Statute* (setting forth the Statute of the International Tribunal in the annex), adopted by S.C.Res. 827, UN SCOR, 48th Sess., 3217th mtg., p. 2, UN Doc. S/RES/827 (1993). See also *Tribunal Statute,* art. 2, 36; art. 3, 37; art. 4, 37; art. 5, 38; art. 5(g), 38; ¶48. Many documents from the International Criminal Tribunal for the Former Yugoslavia, including the indictments and opinions discussed here, are available from the ICTY homepage: ⟨http://www.un.org/icty/⟩ (visited 11 July 2002).

117. See Justice Richard Goldstone, "The United Nations' War Crimes Tribunals: An Assessment," *Connecticut Journal of International Law* 12 (1997): 227, 231: "The ICTY is setting an important precedent in respect to gender-related crimes because it is the first time that systematic mass rape is ever being charged and prosecuted as a war crime"; Jennifer Green et al., "Affecting the Rules for the Prosecution of Rape and Other Gender-Based Violence before the International Criminal Tribunal for the Former Yugoslavia: A Feminist Proposal and Critique," *Hastings Women's Law Journal* 5 (1994): 171, 173, n.5. The International Criminal Tribunal for Rwanda, a sister UN war crimes tribunal to the ICTY, has undertaken prosecution of similarly heinous sex-based atrocities committed in 1994 during the ethnic war in Rwanda. On September 2, 1998, the Rwanda War Crimes Tribunal issued a final judgment in which it determined that Jean-Paul Akayesu, a Hutu official, was guilty of nine counts of genocide and crimes against humanity for having incited the rape and sexual assault of Tutsi women. See *Prosecutor v. Jean-Paul Akayesu,* Judgment, Case No. ICTR-96-4-T (ICTY 2 Sept. 1998), available at ⟨http://www.un.org/icty/English/judgements/akayesu.html⟩ (last visited 11 July 2002).

118. See *Prosecutor v. Meakic,* Indictment, Case No. IT-95-4, ¶1 (ICTY 13 Feb. 1995), reprinted in *ILM* 34 (1995): 1013, 1014 (hereafter Meakic Indictment); *Prosecutor v. Tadic,* Second Amended Indictment, Case No. IT-94-1-T, ¶2.3 (ICTY 14 Dec. 1995), reprinted in *ILM* 36 (1995): 908, 915; *Prosecutor v. Tadic,* Opinion and Judgment, Case No. IT-94-1-T, ¶377 (ICTY 7 May 1997), excerpts reprinted in *ILM* 36 (1997): 908 (excerpting ¶¶1–12, 557–765 of the Opinion and ¶¶1–14 of the Separate and Dissenting Opinion of Judge McDonald Regarding the Applicability of Article 2 of the Statute; hereafter Tadic Opinion); *Prosecutor v. Tadic,* Initial Indictment, Case No. IT-94-1-T (ICTY 13 Feb. 1995), reprinted in *ILM* 35 (1995): 1011, 1028. The Tadic Initial Indictment was amended twice. See *Prosecutor v. Tadic,* First Amended Indictment, Case No. IT-94-1-T (ICTY 1 Sept. 1995); Tadic Second Amended Indictment; see also Tadic Opinion, ¶36; Meakic Indictment, ¶¶2.6, 22.1, 25.1, 26.1, 30.1; Tadic Initial Indictment, ¶¶4.1, 5.1. The charges associated with ¶4.1 were ultimately withdrawn at trial (see Tadic Opinion, ¶37). Given the posture of the following argument, subsequent citations will be to the initial indictment with pertinent alterations provided when necessary.

119. Meakic Indictment, ¶¶22.1–22.16, 25.1–25.4, 26.1–26.4, 30.1–30.4; see also Tadic Opinion, ¶165: "Women who were held at Omarska were routinely called out of their rooms at night and raped. One witness testified that she was taken out five times and raped and after each rape she was beaten."

120. Tadic Opinion, ¶175.

121. Meakic Indictment, ¶¶27.1, 29.1, 31.1, 29.2, 31.2, 29.4, 31.4. Article 5(i), crimes against humanity, authorizes prosecution for "other inhumane acts." See Tribunal Statute, art. 5(i), 38.

122. Compare Tadic Initial Indictment, ¶¶4.1–.4 (charging violations of Article 2(c) [willfully causing great suffering], Article 3, and Article 5(g) [rape]), with Meakic Indictment, ¶¶22.1–.4 (charging the same violations). The Amended Tadic indictments substituted a violation of Article 2(b) (inhuman treatment) for the initial Article 2(c) (willfully causing great suffering) charge of the Tadic Initial Indictment. See Tadic Second Amended Indictment, ¶5, count 2. The charges associated with this rape of a woman were eventually dropped at trial. See Tadic Opinion, ¶37 (noting the withdrawal of the charges associated with ¶5 of the Second Amended Indictment, which corresponds to ¶4.1 of the initial indictment).

123. Tadic Opinion, ¶206. See also Tadic Initial Indictment, ¶5.1; Tadic Second Amended Indictment, ¶6.

124. Tadic Initial Indictment, ¶¶5.29, 5.32, 5.21, 5.24, 5.31, 5.34. In the amended indictments, Tadic was charged with, among other things, violations of Article 2(b) (torture or inhuman treatment), Article 2(c) (willfully causing great suffering or serious injury to body and health), Article 3 (cruel treatment), and Article 5(i) (inhumane acts). See Tadic Second Amended Indictment, ¶6, counts 8–11. Tadic was eventually found guilty of violating Articles 3 and 5(i) of the Tribunal Statute, but the Tribunal found the evidence did not overcome the reasonable doubt standard for the Article 2 charges. See Tadic Opinion, ¶¶237, 719–30, 222, 231, 45, 231.

125. See *Prosecutor v. Karadzic,* Case No. IT-95-5 (ICTY 25 July 1995); *Prosecutor v. Martic,* Case No. IT-95-11 (ICTY 25 July 1995); *Prosecutor v. Sikirica,* Indictment, Case No. IT-95-8, ¶19 (ICTY 21 July 1995; hereafter Karaterm Indictment); *Prosecutor v. Kiljkovic,* Indictment, Case No. IT-95-9, ¶31 (ICTY 21 July 1995; hereafter Bosanski Samac Indictment); *Prosecutor v. Jelisic,* Indictment, Case No. IT-95-10 (ICTY 21 July 1995; hereafter Brcko Initial Indictment), amended by *Prosecutor v. Jelisic,* Amended Indictment, Case No. IT-95-10-PT (ICTY 3 Mar. 1998; hereafter Brcko First Amended Indictment) and *Prosecutor v. Jelisic,* Second Amended Indictment, IT-95-10-PT (ICTY 19 Oct. 1998). See also Karaterm Indictment, ¶¶19, 20 (forcing victims to engage in fellatio); Bosanski Samac Indictment, ¶33 (forcing two brothers to "perform sexual acts on each other").

126. Formerly Legal Advisor for Gender-Related Crimes at the International Criminal Tribunals for the Former Yugoslavia and Rwanda, and at the time of this writing ICTY prosecutor at The Hague.

127. See *International Tribunal for the Prosecution of Persons Responsible for Serious Violations of International Humanitarian Law Committed in the Territory of the Former Yugoslavia since 1991: Rules of Procedure and Evidence 96,* UN Doc. IT/32/REV. 13 (1998), reprinted in *ILM* 33 (1994): 484, 535, available at ⟨http://www.un.org/icty/basic/rpe/rev13e.htm⟩ (visited 11 July 2002); hereafter *Tribunal Rules of Procedure.* Rule 96, "Evidence in Cases of Sexual Assault," states:

In cases of sexual assault:

(i) no corroboration of the victim's testimony shall be required;

(ii) consent shall not be allowed as a defence if the victim

(a) has been subjected to or threatened with or has had reason to fear violence, duress, detention or psychological oppression, or

(b) reasonably believed that if the victim did not submit, another might be so subjected, threatened or put in fear;

(iii) before evidence of the victim's consent is admitted, the accused shall satisfy the Trial Chamber in camera that the evidence is relevant and credible;

(iv) prior sexual conduct of the victim shall not be admitted in evidence.

128. Foucault, *The History of Sexuality,* 103.

129. See, e.g., Brcko Indictment.

130. Brcko Indictment, ¶33, counts 50–52. The Amended Indictment, issued March 3, 1998, eliminated the Article 2(b) charge. See Brcko Amended Indictment, ¶32, counts 34–35.

131. The reform of indictment policy evidenced in the Brcko Indictment, however, was not consistently implemented by the prosecutor's office. Compare Brcko Initial Indictment (charging violation of Article 5(g) [rape, which includes other forms of sexual assault] when defendants allegedly forced two brothers to perform sexual acts on each other), with Tadic Initial Indictment, ¶¶5.1, 5.31, 5.34 (charging violation of Article 5(i) [other inhuman acts] when defendants forced two individuals to "lick [a victim's] buttocks and genitals and then to sexually mutilate [the victim]"). In another indictment issued the same day as the Brcko Indictment, the prosecutor charged several Serbian soldiers with forcing a man to engage in "degrading, humiliating and/or painful acts, such as lying on broken glass, repeatedly jumping from a truck, and engaging in fellatio" (Karaterm Indictment, ¶19). For this conduct, the defendants were charged with committing great suffering under Article 2(c), cruel treatment under Article 3, and inhumane acts under Article 5(i), but not rape or sexual assault under Article 5(g). See Karaterm Indictment, ¶¶19.2.1–2.3. Male soldiers were similarly charged in a separate count for forcing a male prisoner to run while carrying a heavy machine gun and to engage in fellatio (Karaterm Indictment, ¶20). The Karaterm Indictment did not contain the subject headings contained in the Brcko and other indictments issued in July 1995.

132. Like the Brcko defendants, the Bosanski Samac defendants were charged with a grave breach under Article 2(b) (inhuman treatment), violation of the laws or customs of war under Article 3 (humiliating and degrading treatment), and a crime against humanity under Article 5(g) (rape, which includes other forms of sexual assault). See Bosanski Samac Indictment, ¶31, counts 36–38.

133. *Prosecutor v. Delalic,* Indictment, Case No. IT-96-21 (ICTY 21 Mar. 1996); hereafter Celebici Indictment.

134. It is very possible that the prosecutor did not include a charge of crime against humanity under Article 5(g) (rape) because she felt that she did not have sufficient evidence to prove that the rapes were committed as part of a widespread or systematic attack against a civilian population on national, political, ethnic, racial, or religious grounds.

135. *Prosecutor v. Gagovic,* Indictment, Case No. IT-96-23 (ICTY 26 June 1995); hereafter Foca Indictment. One victim was gang-raped for three hours by at least fifteen men, then sexually abused in "all possible ways," including having a soldier threaten to cut off her breast with a knife (Foca Indictment, ¶9.10). Another victim was gang-raped by at least eight men, during which time one man bit her nipples to the point of bleeding, and then another squeezed and pinched her breasts while he raped her. She then lost consciousness from the pain (¶9.11). While one other victim was being raped by a male soldier, the soldier threatened to cut off her arms and legs and take her to church to be baptized (¶9.15).

136. For the use of the term, see Amnesty International, *Bosnia-Herzegovina: Rapes and Sexual Abuse by the Armed Forces* (New York: Amnesty International, 1993), 10–12; Roy Gutman, "Rape Camps: Evidence Serb Leaders in Bosnia Okd Attacks," *Newsday* 19 Apr. 1993, 5; Maggie O'Kane, "Bosnia Crisis: Forgotten Women of Serb Rape

Camps," *Guardian* 19 Dec. 1992, 9; Tom Post, "A Pattern of Rape," *Newsweek* 4 Jan. 1993, 32.

137. *Prosecutor v. Drljaca,* Initial Indictment, Case No. IT-97-24-1 (ICTY 13 Mar. 1997; hereafter Kovacevic Initial Indictment; naming Drljaca and Kovacevic as defendants), amended by *Prosecutor v. Kovacevic,* Amended Indictment, Case No. IT-97-24-I (ICTY 28 Jan. 1998), hereafter Kovacevic Amended Indictment.

138. Patricia Viseur Sellers and Kaoru Okuizumi, "Intentional Prosecution of Sexual Assaults," *Transnational Law and Contemporary Problems* 7 (1997): 45, 51; see also Tribunal Rules of Procedure, Rule 96 (use of "sexual assault" in Rule 96, as opposed to "rape," indicates Tribunal's intent to interpret Article 5(g) broadly).

139. Sellers and Okuizumi, "Intentional Prosecution," 57–58.

140. *Convention against Torture and Other Cruel, Inhuman, or Degrading Treatment or Punishment,* art. 1, G.A. Res. 39/46, UN GAOR 3d Comm., 39th Sess., Supp. No. 51, p. 197, UN Doc. A/39/51 (1984); see C. P. M. Cleiren and M. E. M. Tijssen, "Rape and Other Forms of Sexual Assault in the Armed Conflict in the Former Yugoslavia: Legal, Procedural, and Evidentiary Issues," *Criminal Law Forum* 5 (1994): 471, 492.

141. *Question of the Human Rights of All Persons Subjected to Any Form of Detention or Imprisonment, in Particular: Torture and Other Cruel, Inhuman or Degrading Treatment or Punishment. Report of the Special Rapporteur, Mr. Nigel S. Rodley, Submitted Pursuant to Commission on Human Rights Resolution 1992/32,* UN ESCOR, 50th Sess., ¶19, UN Doc. E/CN.4/1995/34. The 1949 Geneva Conventions, which now constitute the core rules of the international humanitarian law applicable in international armed conflicts, do not enumerate rape as a grave breach. See Geneva Convention Relative to the Protection of Civilian Persons in Time of War of August 12, 1949, art. 147, 6 UST 3516, 75 UNTS 287, 388 (hereafter Geneva Convention), including "wilful killing, torture or inhuman treatment . . . wilfully causing great suffering or serious injury to body or health" as grave breaches. However, the International Commission of the Red Cross and the U.S. State Department have declared that grave breach under Article 147 (relating to "torture or inhumane treatment") encompasses rape. See Simon Chesterman, "Never Again . . . and Again: Law, Order, and the Gender of War Crimes in Bosnia and Beyond," *Yale Journal of International Law* 22 (1997): 299, 331, n. 199, citing Theodor Meron, Editorial Comment, "Rape as a Crime under International Humanitarian Law," *American Journal of International Law* 87 (1993): 424, 426–67, quoting International Commission of the Red Cross, Aide-Memoire (3 Dec. 1992); *Final Report,* ¶105.

142. Sellers and Okuizumi, "Intentional Prosecution," 62. The Trial Chamber has determined that the elements of torture in an armed conflict require that torture:

> (i) consists of the infliction, by act or omission, of severe pain or suffering, whether physical or mental; in addition
>
> (ii) this act or omission must be intentional;
>
> (iii) it must aim at obtaining information or a confession, or at punishing, intimidating, humiliating or coercing the victim or a third person, or at discriminating, on any ground, against the victim or a third person;

(iv) it must be linked to an armed conflict;

(v) at least one of the persons involved in the torture process must be a public official or must at any rate act in a non-private capacity, e.g. as a de facto organ of a State or any other authority-wielding entity. (*Prosecutor v. Furundzija,* Judgment, Case No. IT-95-17/1-PT, ¶162 [ICTY 10 Dec. 1998]; hereafter Furundzija Indictment)

See also *Prosecutor v. Tadic,* Prosecutor's Pre-Trial Brief, Case No. IT-94-1-T (ICTY 10 Apr. 1995). To prove a grave breach, the prosecutor must show (1) that the act was undertaken during "armed conflicts of an international character," and (2) that the victim was a person "regarded as 'protected,' in particular civilians in the hands of a party to a conflict of which they are not nationals" (Tadic Opinion, ¶559).

143. Furundzija Judgment, ¶¶264–75. The man accused of assaulting the female victim in this case was charged with "rubb[ing] his knife on the inner thighs of [the victim] and threaten[ing] to cut out her private parts if she did not tell the truth in answer to the interrogation" (¶264). Subsequently, she was vaginally, anally, and orally raped by the same man as part of the interrogation while Furundzija watched and interrogated her as well as other prisoners (¶¶266–67).

144. Celebici Judgment, ¶495.

145. Celebici Judgment, ¶941.

146. Furundzija Judgment, ¶¶267, 87 (footnote omitted).

147. See Rhonda Copelon, "Surfacing Gender: Re-Engraving Crimes against Women in Humanitarian Law," *Hastings Women's Law Journal* 5 (1994): 243, 253–54, n.46 (describing communications between Copelon and the chief prosecutor of the ICTY), and 248–57 (arguing for the prosecution of rape as a Grave Breach under Article 2(b) of the Tribunal Statute [torture]); see also 249, 250.

148. See, e.g., Chesterman, "Never Again," 327; Copelon, "Surfacing Gender," 248–57; Madeline Morris, "By Force of Arms: Rape, War, and Military Culture," *Duke Law Journal* 45 (1996): 651, 685 n. 108; Amy E. Ray, "The Shame of It: Gender-Based Terrorism in the Former Yugoslavia and the Failure of International Human Rights Law to Comprehend the Injuries," *American University Law Review* 29 (1997): 793, 818.

149. Goldstone, "The United Nations' War Crimes Tribunals," 228.

150. See Tadic Opinion, ¶626; Sellers and Okuizumi, "Intentional Prosecution," 57 n. 47; Elizabeth Odio Benito, "Rape and Other Sexual Assaults as War Crimes Prohibited by International Humanitarian Law," 8 Mar. 1998, 22 (unpublished manuscript, on file with author).

151. See Kovacevic Initial Indictment, ¶¶9–16; Tribunal Statute, art. 4, 37.

152. Benito, "Rape," 12.

153. See Geneva Convention, art. 27, 61 UST, 3516 (declaring that women "shall be especially protected against any attack on their honour, in particular against rape, enforced prostitution, or any form of indecent assault"); Copelon, "Surfacing Gender," 249.

154. See *Further Promotion and Encouragement of Human Rights and Fundamental Freedoms, Including the Question of the Programme and Methods of Work of the Com-*

mission, UN Commission on Human Rights, 50th Sess., Agenda Item 11(a), ¶268, UN Doc. E/CN.4/1995/42 (1994).

155. Celebici Judgment, ¶471.

156. Copelon, "Surfacing Gender," 261.

157. Foucault, *Politics,* 202.

158. Tribunal Rules of Procedure, Rule 96 (providing strict rules for the admission of testimony and limiting the defense of consent in cases of sexual assault); see n. 127 above (providing the full text of Rule 96). The Celebici defendants were convicted.

159. Tadic Opinion, ¶470.

160. McAlary, "Frightful Whisperings," 2.

DRUCILLA CORNELL

Dismembered Selves and Wandering Wombs

The question of women's right to abortion has been one of the most divisive issues in this country's history. The clash has not only taken place in words. Abortion clinics have been burned to the ground. Doctors who have performed abortions have been murdered. These violent acts are said to be justified in the name of the potential lives of the unborn children. The specter of murdered fetuses is conjured up with the intent to expose feminists who defend the right to abortion as heartless narcissists, if not downright killers.

Yet under our constitutional schema, fetuses are not recognized as legal persons and, therefore, abortion is not legally murder. Nor is there any moral or religious agreement as to when life begins.[1] Ironically, all the killings of adults in the abortion debate—and certainly everyone would recognize adults as "alive"—has been done by the so-called right-to-lifers. It would seem that it is the extremists in the right-to-life movement, not those who defend the right to abortion, who are the heartless killers. But is there any truth to the charge that feminists who demand the right to abortion are indifferent to the fate of fetuses?

There is a basic assumption made by the right-to-lifers that must be closely examined that allows them to answer that question in the affirmative. They assume that the demand for the right to abortion and the concern for fetuses are antithetical. Explicitly or implicitly, this assumption demands a vision of the pregnant mother and her fetus that artificially separates the two. Without this view of the pregnant woman and the fetus, it would be obvious that the "life" of the fetus was inseparable from the physical and mental well-being of the woman of whose body *it is a part*.

Clearly, there are means for expressing the need to reduce unwanted pregnancies and the desire to ensure the welfare of the fetus and the pregnant woman that are affirmative rather than negative, that are not simply attempts to outlaw or limit women's access to abortion. Sex education, prenatal care, and emotional support groups immediately come to mind. It is only if one makes the assumption that the only way to "save" a fetus is to regulate women that one would turn the concern for the life of the fetus — which is *inseparable* from the health of the mother — into a crusade against the right to abortion.

Let us also not forget that, if the projections are right, over half of the fetuses that will be born in the next fifty years will be female, beings who, as a matter of right, should be able to demand no less than the legal guarantee of their equivalent chance to become a person. In the name of these imaginary female children, we are called on to struggle for the right to abortion as part of what it means to guarantee equality through the generations. Clearly, our living daughters — actual and symbolic — demand no less of us than that we proclaim our right as women to have legally protected the equivalent chance to be a person. The "us" to which I refer are women of my generation, in the "second wave" of feminism, who remember what we endured, growing up without the right to abortion. There is solace, at least for this feminist mother, in the paradoxical demand that the reproductive rights we did not have be established as the legacy of equality we should have inherited. Without the protection of the right to abortion, there can be no meaningful equality for women.

How can I make this claim? My argument will proceed as follows: first, I argue that the right to abortion should be treated as the right to equivalent "bodily integrity."[2] Understood under the rubric of bodily integrity, the wrong in denying a right to abortion is not a wrong to the "self," but a wrong that prevents the achievement of the minimum conditions of individuation necessary for any meaningful concept of selfhood. I provide a psychoanalytic account of how individuation demands the projection and the recognition by others of bodily integrity.

Second, I argue that because the conditions of individuation are social and symbolic, the right to bodily integrity cannot be understood as a right to privacy, if that right is understood as a right to be left alone.[3] Thus, it is not enough for the state to refrain from actively blocking women's "choice" to have abortions. The right to bodily integrity, dependent as it is on social and symbolic recognition, demands the establishment of conditions in which safe abortions are available to women of every race, class, and nationality. I place the word "choice" in quotation marks because the word itself trivializes how basic the right to abortion is to women's individuation. Moreover, it should be obvious that no woman *chooses* to have an unwanted pregnancy. If we could control our bodies, "our selves," then we would not need state intervention to ensure conditions for safe abortions. The rhetoric of choice and control assumes the much criticized dualistic conception of the subject as the king who reigns over the body. Distancing ourselves from the conception of individuality as a preexisting core or substance demands both a different political rhetoric and a redefinition of the content of the right to abortion itself.

The demand for new rhetoric also inheres in the effort to symbolize the feminine within sexual difference, a difference that is necessarily erased by a conception of the subject as being above sex. This erasure underlies the difficulty in liberal jurisprudence of conceptualizing abortion as a right: such a right cannot be separated from some notion of ourselves as embodied and sexuate beings.[4] Even so, we need to be very careful in how we conceive of the embodied self. The courts have too often relied on the "reality" of the womb as a preexisting natural difference in order to defeat equality claims under the equal protection doctrine.[5] We must find a way to resymbolize feminine sexual difference in the law so that such a resymbolization is not incompatible with claims of equality.

To do so, we first need an account of how bodies come to matter. As Judith Butler shows us, the word "matter" has a double meaning.[6] Bodies matter; that is, they materialize and take on reality while also carrying an implicit normative assessment. Bodies matter, in other words, through a process by which they come to have both symbolic and ethical significance. The feminine "sex" is, in this sense, a symbolic reality inseparable from an implicit evaluation of the worth of that body. As we will see, the difficulty in defending abortion through an appeal to equality has been the devaluation of the feminine sex, not the mere fact of the difference itself.

If we assume the equivalent value of the feminine sex as we are called on to do by the demands of the Kantian "as if," which, in my interpretation, demands that each of us be valued by the law as worthy of personhood, then there can be no *reasonable* justification for denying a woman's right to bodily integrity. It is only on the basis of some account of women's lesser worth that one could allow the state to regulate our bodies. Of course, one could argue that bodily integrity is not necessary for individuation. I hope to convince the reader that bodily integrity does indeed play an integral part in establishing individuation. That, however, is a different argument. If it is accepted that bodily integrity is necessary, then women cannot hope to achieve individuation without it. Thus, they are cut off from the equivalent chance to become a person.

There is another potential argument against my position. Reproductive capacity is not an essential aspect of bodily integrity, and therefore being divested of the right to determine whether to have a baby is not a legal act that undermines that right. But, in reality, it is difficult to think of an aspect of bodily integrity more central to a woman's ability to project herself as whole over time. This is a proposition that I defend in the course of this essay.

What does it mean that the state is allowed to regulate women's bodies? It means that we are not treated as inviolable. Indeed, the opposite is the case. We are treated as violable because we are the sex with the capacity to give life. This capacity, in other words, is used to justify our treatment as lesser beings, not truly worthy of personhood. My argument is simple: this treatment of women as lesser beings fundamentally violates the demands of an egalitarian legal system. The conclusion that necessarily follows from this argument is that concern for fetuses and pregnant women cannot be expressed by outlawing, or even limiting, the right to abortion. If a woman's personhood is truly to be respected by the law, then she must also be the ultimate source of both the decision to abort and the meaning given to that decision. It is the woman, not the state, that should have the narrative power over her decision. The narrative power is as important for her personhood as the decision itself because the chance to become a person is dependent on the imagined projection of one's self as whole.

Note, however, that my argument is universal. Pregnancy, and the potential to become pregnant, is a condition unique to women and incomparable to any male capacity or ability. The ability to bring forth human life is an extraordinary power, and part of the demand for the reevaluation of the feminine sex is that it should be recognized as such. But my argument for abortion demands only that we be treated as worthy of personhood with the right to bodily integrity. Thus, our sexual difference can be recognized in that it is women who need the right to abortion for their bodily integrity, without turning that recognition into a demand for protection. The right to bodily integrity must be differentially allotted to women to include their unique capacity to get pregnant as part of what it means to equivalently evaluate our sex as worthy of personhood.

Because I strongly defend abortion as a matter of right, I disagree with Ronald Dworkin's attempt to take abortion out of the sphere of rights and interests and address it under the rubric of the sanctity of life.[7] Ultimately, I disagree with Dworkin's defense of the metric of disrespect of the intrinsic value of life as he uses this measure in the context of abortion to provide a sliding scale for morally better and morally worse abortions. To develop my response to Dworkin, I return to the analysis of how bodies come to matter.

Dworkin claims that some restrictions on what he calls "procreative autonomy" have to be justified out of respect for the sanctity of life.[8] Dworkin's defense of this argument is that the language of entitlement is simply inadequate to address the concern for life expressed both by those who insist on the right to abortion and those who demand that abortion be outlawed. He correctly insists that feminists who demand the right of abortion are also expressing a concern for life in that they understand life not just as a brute existence but as what in my analysis is explained as the chance to become a person. My response is that women need the language of entitlement to claim the equivalent evaluation of our sex and with it our chance to become persons. Our reproductive capacity has been used, throughout human history, to justify treatment of us as less than persons. As feminists, we have to demand an end to the history that has degraded our sex as less than worthy of personhood. But does that mean that as feminists we do not care for life, including the lives of fetuses and pregnant women? The answer is absolutely not.

My argument is that we cannot legally recognize the sanctity of life by denying women the right to abortion or treating them as if they were not capable of understanding and giving meaning to their decisions to abort. There are many other ways to express the concern for future life consistent with seeing the fetus as part of a woman's body. Nor am I giving abortion any inherent meaning. I am only too well aware of how tragic an experience abortion can be for some women. My only argument is that we should allow each woman to come to terms, in her own way, with her decision to abort. Simply put, once we understand abortion as a right of bodily integrity, we can begin to understand both how devastating it is for a woman to be denied that right and, correspondingly, how essential its protection is if women are to achieve minimum conditions of individuation.

The Social and Symbolic Conditions for
Bodily Integration and Individuation

My account of how and why individuation is an extremely fragile achievement, one made possible only by spinning out a meaning for and image of a coherent self from a pregiven web of social ties, symbolic relations, and primordial identifications, is based on the writings of Jacques Lacan. Lacan relied on an interpretation of Sigmund Freud's notion of the bodily ego. I believe my presentation of Lacan's theory of how an infant comes to perceive himself or herself as a coherent whole or self is compatible with divergent psychoanalytic perspectives. It is not, however, compatible with positions advanced in political and legal philosophy that fail to give full weight to the social and symbolic constitution of the self. This is why my own account has a certain affinity with communitarianism and its critique of a version of radical individualism.

The Lacanian account allows us to understand just how fragile the achievement of individuation is, and how easily it can be undermined, if not altogether destroyed, by either a physical or symbolic assault on the projection of bodily integrity. The denial of the right to abortion should be understood as a serious symbolic assault on a woman's sense of self precisely because it thwarts the projection of bodily integration and places the woman's body in the hands and imaginings of others who would deny her coherence by separating her womb from her self.[9] But before we can fully understand why the denial of the right to abortion can and should be understood as a symbolic dismemberment of a woman's body, we need to explore Lacan's explanation of the constitution of selfhood.

For Lacan, there is an impressive singularity that distinguishes human beings from other primates: their reaction on seeing their mirror image. Between the ages of six and eighteen months, human infants display jubilation at the recognition of their mirror image. Lacan refers to this period as the mirror stage. In comparison, chimpanzees, for example, lose interest in an image of themselves as soon as they realize it is just an image and not another chimpanzee. The jubilation, according to Lacan, lies in the infant's first experience of perceiving itself as a whole. This perception of wholeness occurs when the infant is, in reality, in a state of complete helplessness. Thus, the image functions both as a projection and an anticipation of what the infant might become but is not now.

This disjuncture between the reality of helplessness and the projection of a unified self is an effect of our premature birth such that our perceptual apparatus is much more advanced than our motor functions. In other words, during the mirror stage — which, I would argue, is not a stage in the traditional sense, because one never completes it — the infant can perceive what it cannot produce. The infant obviously cannot provide himself or herself with a mirror image so that the experience can be evoked repeatedly. Thus, the infant is completely dependent on others to have the experience repeated and its projected identity and bodily integrity confirmed. In this way, the sight of another human being, including the infant's actual image in a mirror or in the eyes of the mother or primary caretaker, is crucial for shaping identity. This other, who, in turn, both appears as whole and confirms the infant in its projected and anticipated coherence by mirroring him or her as a self, becomes the matrix of a sense of continuity and coherence that the child's present state of bodily disorganization would belie.

It is only through this mirroring process that the infant comes to have an identity. The body's coherence depends on the future anteriority of the projection in that what has yet to be is imagined as already given. The infant, then, does not recognize a self that is already "there" in the mirror. Instead, the self is constituted in and through the mirroring process as other to its reality of bodily disorganization, and by having itself mirrored by others as a whole.

The power that mirroring has over the infant is not, then, the recognition of similarity in the mirror, a "Wow, that looks like me" reaction to the image; rather it is the *anticipated* motor unity associated with bodily integration. Thus, it is not the exact image, but the reflection of bodily integrity that does not match the infant's own body that *matters*. In this sense, there is always a moment of fictionality, of imagined anticipation, in and through which the ego is constituted.

The sense of self-identity is internalized in the adult and continues to involve the projection of bodily integrity and its recognition by others. Our "body," then, is never really our own. The idea that we own our body is a fantasy that imagines as completed that which always remains in the future anterior. Therefore, to protect "ourselves" from threats to our bodily integrity we have to protect the future into which we project our unity and have our bodily integrity respected by others. To reduce the self to just "some body" is to rob it of this future anterior. This is the meaning of my earlier statement that the mirror stage is not really a stage at all because the self never completes it. As I understand it, the mirror stage is never simply overcome in a "higher" stage of development; it is a turning point through which the self must always come around, again and again, to guard continuously against social and symbolic forces that lead to dismemberment, disintegration, and total destruction of the self.

I want to turn briefly to Lacan's critique of ego psychology. Lacan's notion is that the ego is caught in a vicious circle. This Lacanian circle of egoism is destructive, first because it forever turns in on itself and is fated to be repeated and, second, because in the projection of autoreflection, the Other on whom this illusion is dependent is erased. This moment of erasure is itself erased by a defensive posturing that reduces the Other to a mirror — an object that plays no active role in the constitution of the ego — and which, therefore, cannot threaten the ego's imagined self-sufficiency by distorting or denying the truth of its ego's projected image of itself as self-constituted. Lacan explicitly connects what he calls "the era of the ego" with the objectification of women as mirrors who, as mirror objects of confirmation for men, must not be allowed to ascend to the position of subjects.[10]

It would be impossible here to answer fully the question "who comes after the ego" or even what "after" could mean thought outside of linear temporality. But I can at least articulate "the beginning" of that other subject. I believe this must be done in a context that assumes the recognition of the alterity of the future from which the self has been constituted and on which, through a projection, it depends for its survival as a self and not just as "some body." The feminist legal reform program I advocate depends on no less than the symbolic recognition of this specifically egoistic form of misrecognition, particularly as it erases the mother and reduces women to objects that confirm the masculine ego as existing only "for itself." The egoism that finds its value only in its narcissistic investment, in its illusion of being for itself, is not only vicious, it is false. I am using the language of the Kantian moral critique of egoism deliberately.[11] The Kantian critique emphasizes that if people have value only for themselves, they are necessarily of a lesser order of worth because their worth is only narcissistic, and, thus, a person is only instrumentally valuable rather than valuable in itself. In the Kantian tradition, the "in itself" implies impersonal valuation of the person as a person. The legal system, if it is to be just, recognizes the inviolability that inheres in this impersonal evaluation that has already been given.

I believe my psychoanalytic account is consistent with the rejection of the evaluation of persons based on narcissistic ego investment. As I have already argued, pure narcissistic ego-confirmation is both impossible and based on an unethical erasure of the Other.[12] A more interesting point is to be made, however, by asking the question, Can the value of a person just be "there" in itself? In psychoanalytic terms, such value, in the most primordial sense of even achieving a sense of oneself as a self, is always bestowed by the Other. The mystery of impersonal evaluation of the person "in itself" can be solved only if we remember the time frame of the heteroreflection that gave personhood to the infant in order to be valued as a self "in itself." This time frame is that of the future anterior, in which the self is always coming to be through the confirmation of the projection of what he or she has been given to be by Others.

If we take this time frame together with the role of the Other in constituting the person, we can begin to think of a legal system as a symbolic Other, a system that does not merely recognize but constitutes and confirms who is to be valued, who is to *matter.* Moreover, if the legal system as a symbolic Other is also understood to operate through the future anterior, then its operations are transitive in that they constitute what is recognized. Such an understanding of the legal system as "active," as a symbolic Other, validates a feminist claim for legal reform. It allows for a fuller appreciation of how the denial of legal and social symbolization can be so significant to whoever is confirmed as a self, and, in that sense, guarantees what I have called the minimum conditions of individuation.

This conception also allows us to remove rights from their so-called basis in what has come to be called negative freedom, which traditionally has been defined as freedom from state intervention for already free persons. But, because the self depends on the Other for the achievement of individuation, if the state recognizes and confirms whoever is recognized as a constituted person, then there can never be any simple negative freedom for persons. This move away from a pure conception of negative freedom is important in redefining the right to abortion to include conditions for safe abortions. Thus, the removal of state intervention from a woman's choice or right to privacy is not the only definition of abortion as a right, and defending a right to abortion need not be so restricted.

Let me now summarize before moving to a discussion of the precise wrong to women in the denial of the right to abortion, and of my argument for reconceiving the content of such a right. This analysis begins with a rejection of the current viability analysis that has been used to curtail significantly the right to abortion.[13] First, the projection and confirmation of one's bodily integrity remains fundamental to the most basic sense of self. The body is socially conceptualized at the very moment we imagine "it" as ours. This "body" is thus distinguished from the undifferentiated thereness, or what Charles Peirce called "Secondness," of the undifferentiated "matter" that subtends the imagined body.[14] Second, I believe the state and the legal system should themselves be understood as symbolic Others that confirm and constitute who is established as a person. It is only from within such a psychoanalytic framework that we can see how Other-dependent the sense of self is, and why the time frame of its constitution through the future anterior demands the protection of the future self's anticipated continuity and bodily integrity. Without the protection of the future of anticipation, the self cannot project its own continuity. The denial of the right to abortion makes such an anticipation of future wholeness impossible for women. What is at stake in this loss are the conditions for even a primordial sense of self (the critical significance of which I do not want to deny).

The Significance of Projection and Anticipation in the Context of Abortion

My intent is to rearticulate the wrong of the denial of the right to abortion by redefining it as an equivalent right and justifying its protection under the rubric of equality. I do so by showing how both the fragility of a coherent selfhood and the time frame of anticipation necessary for the projection of bodily integrity demand that we rethink this wrong. The ability to internalize the projection of bodily integrity so that one experiences oneself as whole is central to a conception of selfhood. Our embodiment makes this very projected sense of unity all too easy to lose. Throughout our lives, the disjuncture between what we have come to think of as mind and body is always latent, and we depend on its remaining so. In a case of physical assault, one's sense of projected unity is completely shattered. Physical violence imposes a horrifying dualism of self. In a violent assault we are reduced to "some body": as other to our body. The representation of the body as apart, as "made up" out of parts, is described by Elaine Scarry in her discussion of torture:

But the relation between body and voice that for the prisoner begins in opposition (the pain is so real that "the question" is unreal, insignificant) and that goes on to become an identification (the question, like the pain, is a way of wounding; the pain, like the question, is a vehicle of self-betrayal) ultimately ends in opposition once more. For what the process of torture does is to split the human being in two, to make emphatic the ever present but, except in the extremity of sickness and death, only latent distinction between a self and a body, between a "me" and "my body." The "self" or "me," which is experienced on the one hand as more private, more essentially at the center, and on the other hand as participating across the bridge of the body in the world, is "embodied" in the voice, in language. The goal of the torturer is to make the one, the body, emphatically and crushingly *present* by destroying it, and to make the other, the voice, *absent* by destroying it.[15]

The self-betrayal of which Scarry speaks here is the betrayal of answering the torturer's questions "against one's will." I want to take Scarry's insight into just how shattering it is to have the factitiousness of the integrated body and the self's coherence so brutally exposed and place it into the context of abortion.

Bodily integrity always remains imaginary. But there is no self without this imaginary projection. Scarry makes this point when she insists that violent assaults on the body always imply an attack on the conditions under which the self has been constituted and thus through which it could be reconstituted. Rendering abortion illegal undermines the entitlement to a self at a time when it is most needed to protect the necessary projection that there is a self that is still "there" and, more specifically, that the womb is part of that self, not apart from it. Wombs do not wander except in the wild imagination of some men who have come up with very colorful stories of what a womb "is."[16] To separate the woman from her womb or to reduce her to it is to deny her the conditions of selfhood that depend on the ability to project bodily integrity.

The denial of the right to abortion enforces the kind of splitting that inevitably and continuously undermines a woman's sense of self. Her womb and body are no longer hers to imagine. They have been turned over to the imagination of others, and those imaginings are then allowed to reign over her body as law. The wrong in denial of the right to abortion is often thought to be that the woman is forced to turn over her body to the fetus as an invader. The wrong as I reconceive it involves a woman, at a crucial moment, having her body turned over to the minds of men.

Judith Jarvis Thompson's essay on abortion provides an example of the first argument.[17] She argues that we do not, under our law or moral institutions, believe that any person should be forced to rescue another person. To draw out the implications of this position, Thompson uses the analogy of a person being hooked up to a very talented, dialysis-needy violinist in order to save the artist's life; the violinist's accomplishments and value to society are clearly established. She argues that even in this situation, we would not impose a duty to rescue. If we would not impose such a duty in that case, why would we contradict our law and moral institutions by insisting that women should be required to rescue fetuses whose lives have yet to begin? But Thompson's argument itself portrays an imagined projection of the relationship between the fetus and the mother, and one that I believe should not be allowed to hold sway over our own imaginings, because the portrayal does not adequately envision the uniqueness of the condition of pregnancy. This failure is inseparable from the subsumption of feminine sexual difference within the so-called human in which pregnancy is analogized with a relationship between two already independent persons. This formulation, in other words, assumes that the womb and the fetus are other to the woman rather than a part of her body. Such an assumption implies a "view" of the woman's body and her "sex," and a conception of the meaning of pregnancy, that cannot be separated from imagined projections that erase the specificity of feminine sexual difference.

Any analogy of a fetus to an already autonomous being rests on the erasure of the woman; it reduces her to a mere environment for the fetus. This vision of the woman is connected necessarily to one's view of the fetus, because the fetus can be seen as a person only if the woman is erased or reduced to an environment. Once the woman is put back into the picture, the pregnancy is no longer like any of the conditions to which it is analogized, because, as I have already argued, it is unique. Thus, I agree with George Fletcher when he argues:

> The point is, rather, that any attempt to draw an analogy to abortion will be imperfect and deceptive. . . . The relationship between the fetus and its carrying mother is not like that between the dialysis-needy musician and a stranger with good kidneys. Nor is it like any other ingenious hypothetical cases that Johann Kis poses in an attempt to elicit our

moral intuitions about killing and letting die. The fetus is not like a pedestrian whom a driver hits (when her brakes fail) in order to avoid hitting two others. Nor is it like the drowning boy whom a swimmer may save or not. Nor is it like a man overboard in a shipwreck whom we keep out of the over-filled lifeboat. These other standard characters make up the pantheon of moral philosophy as it has been plied at least since Carneades imagined the problem of two shipwrecked sailors fighting for the same plank to avoid drowning.[18]

All of these examples involve cases of individuals who are clearly human beings. Fletcher's insight is to argue that whatever the fetus is, it is not a fully developed human being, and therefore, analogies such as the one Thompson uses to other justified or excused killings cannot hold. Abortion, then, is not killing, in any traditional sense and cannot be adequately discussed under that rubric. As a result, Fletcher concludes that we need another framework to adequately analyze abortion. I agree with him, and it is obviously my intention to provide such an alternative framework.

My addition here, however, is that the erasure of the uniqueness of the fetus that Fletcher emphasizes cannot be separated from the erasure of the uniqueness of the condition of pregnancy, which in turn cannot be separated from the failure of our legal system to symbolize and reimagine the specificity of the feminine within sexual difference. More sharply put, the status of the fetus comes into question once the uniqueness of pregnancy as a condition different from all others is recognized, and thus turns on how the woman and her "sex" is viewed. The construction of the womb as a container, as an environment for the fetus, is just that: a construction, an imaginary projection that gives meaning to what cannot actually be seen. Here we have an extraordinarily clear example how a woman's "sex" is constructed. To imagine a womb as a container is to imagine "it," not to know "it" in its truth. But for purposes of trying to provide an adequate framework to defend abortion as a right, we also need to "see" just how divergent constructions of the woman's sex and particularly of her womb will necessarily affect how the fetus is understood and how abortion will be viewed. If we think of the womb as a part of the woman, if her body is respected as opaque, as bound, if the woman's "insides" cannot be forcibly "exposed" as an outside, then the idea that the woman and her body can be rendered transparent is denied. This view of the woman as a container for the fetus reduces her "sex" to a maternal function.

Reducing a woman to the maternal function in the crude form of designating her "sex" as a container explicitly denies her the right of bodily integrity and thus the conditions of selfhood in which a woman can project the meaning of her own "insides" as "hers." What is a woman under this fantasy of her "sex"? She is *a what,* a thing, a container, an environment, not *a who,* a self. We do not need to be essentialists to argue that the feminine "sex" is both more than and other to this reduction of her "sex" to a container.

To summarize, the way a fetus and the woman are "seen" (and I put "seen" in quotation marks to remind us again of my argument that one does not see a woman directly but imagines her through projections of the significance or lack of same of her sex) is right at the heart of the abortion debate. This is a classic example of precisely why a feminist program of legal reform and the rearticulation of rights cannot proceed without the reimagining and the resymbolization of the feminine within sexual difference that takes back "our selves" from the masculine imaginary.

Men and women create themselves by projecting the body as integrated, as being one's "own." The body matters as a psychic object, and its reality always has a phantasmatical dimension. Bodily integrity is actualized through the externalized fantasy one has of one's body, although this externalized idea of one's body as one's "own" can be effectively undermined. Any experience of illness graphically teaches us that lesson. But it is precisely the very fragility of bodily integrity that makes its protection so crucial. To deny women the conditions in which they can project bodily integrity by turning their bodies over to the projections of others is to deny them a basic condition of selfhood.

There are innumerable pre-*Roe* accounts of how the fear of unwanted pregnancies and illegal abortions haunted women's sense of themselves long before the women themselves actually became pregnant. As part of that generation, I remember the horrific stories of knitting needles, back-alley washrooms, lives lost, and long-lasting damage to the women's reproductive capacity. "Sex" was haunted by the specter and the fear of what an unwanted pregnancy would mean for the woman when abortion was illegal. At stake in the imposition of this specter is the serious undermining of women's ability to project their own bodily integrity over time. This undermining has serious implications because it becomes internalized as the inability to imagine oneself as whole. The very constitution of selfhood cannot be separated from the protection of the future projection of the woman's self as a whole body. The threat takes effect before any woman actually has to face an unwanted pregnancy. Here we have an important example of how the symbolization of a woman's "sex" has a constitutive effect on what we have come to think of as selfhood. Not only is a woman's individuality not just given, it is limited in its very definition by certain symbolizations of her "sex" in the law. This reduces her to those definitions. To deny a woman the right to abortion is to make her body not "hers" at the same time that it reduces her to her "sex," limitedly defined as maternal function. Such restrictive symbolizations deny a woman her imaginary domain.

The Rearticulation of the Right to Abortion

Abortion should be protected as a right necessary for the establishment of the minimum conditions of individuation for women, which must include the protection of the individual's projection of bodily integrity. I stress the word "individual" here to reiterate my argument that what the feminine within sexual difference "is" has been defined by the masculine imaginary and then resymbolized in law so that women are not representable as fully individuated beings with their own imaginary. The move from the objectification of the feminine within sexual difference as a "what," as a container for a fetus in the case of abortion, to a "who," a sexuate being with her own imaginary, is precisely what my own rearticulation of the right to abortion seeks to effectuate.

The right to abortion should not be understood as the right to choose an abortion, but as the right to realize the legitimacy of the individual woman's projections of her own bodily integrity, consistent with her imagination of herself at the time that she chooses to terminate her pregnancy. Once the right is rearticulated in this manner, we can provide an alternative analysis that completely rejects the conclusion of *Webster v. Reproductive Health Services,* in which the Court stated that it is consistent with the right to abortion to allow states to enjoin public facilities and employees from providing abortions because such an injunction purportedly does not place a governmental obstacle in the way of the right defined abstractly as "the right to choose."[19] The right to abortion, as I define it, would also reject the denial of Medicaid coverage for abortions which was similarly defended as no impediment to "the right to choose."

We can further reject the "undue burden" analysis set forth in *Planned*

Parenthood of Southeastern Pennsylvania v. Casey in which the Court upheld a series of state restrictions on the exercise of the right to abortion. My rearticulation of the right is consistent with the imaginary dimension of the projection of bodily integrity. Once we understand that the right to abortion is essential to bodily integrity and individuation, we can see that what is at stake in the states' efforts to regulate abortion is the woman's right to be insulated from state imposition of the views of others on her own imaginary. States have argued that their programs regulating abortion are intended to inform women of the seriousness of the act terminating pregnancy. Such efforts deny the woman's status as a fully individuated human being, capable of acting and of giving meaning to that action without help from the state. It is not only an issue of *who* can make the ultimate decision, as Justices Souter, Kennedy, and O'Connor argue in their opinion in *Casey,* which attempts to justify the legitimacy of certain of the provisions of the Abortion Control Act passed in Pennsylvania in 1982 to regulate abortion. It is also *how* that decision may be exercised. The protection of *how* is essential for the establishment of respect for women as fully individuated sexuate beings with their own imaginary and, therefore, their own understanding of what it means to end a pregnancy.

This rearticulation is transitive in that it hopes to promote the bringing into "being" of what has been both explicitly and implicitly denied as "true": the equivalent value of the feminine within sexual difference. This denial is particularly evident in court cases that have denied the validity of women's equality claims in the supposed name of recognizing a difference that is just "there" in its meaning prior to the evaluation. The debate over whether women should have the right to abortion as well as how that right is to be articulated forces us to face the fact that how a woman's body matters is inseparable from how "it" is symbolized and whether "it" is evaluated as of equivalent value to the masculine body.[20] The reevaluation of the feminine within sexual difference as of equivalent value inevitably changes how a woman's body is thought to matter in the senses of both material reality and significance.

Privacy versus Equality Rethought

In *Roe v. Wade,* the Supreme Court first recognized the right of privacy to include the right to choose abortion as a limited right in which the state's interest in regulating abortion would gain ever greater legitimacy as the pregnancy approached birth. The Court argued against the appellant and some amici that the woman's right to abortion could not be absolute, even though it would take a compelling state interest to justify regulation, and even though there was much rhetoric in earlier privacy cases that the right of privacy was absolute in the sense that a state absolutely could not interfere with certain zones of personal life. From the outset of its analysis, the *Roe* Court realized the difficulty of defining a right of privacy that would not be absolute in the above sense, yet that would recognize how crucial the right to abortion was for women. The Court sought a compromise position through its viability analysis. To quote the majority opinion:

> Appellant's arguments that Texas either has no valid interest at all in regulating the abortion decision, or no interest strong enough to support any limitation upon the woman's sole determination, are unpersuasive. As noted above, a State may properly assert important interests in safeguarding health, in maintaining medical standards, and in protecting potential life. At some point in pregnancy, these respective interests become compelling enough to sustain regulation of the factors that govern the abortion decision. The privacy right involved, therefore, cannot be said to be absolute.[21]

The Court's use of the phrase "at some point in pregnancy" meant that a specific point had to be located and fixed. But the Court had difficulty making this determination once they rejected protection of the fetus as a person for purposes of the Fourteenth Amendment. The state's compelling interest thus could not be justified as protecting the rights of the fetus as against those of "the mother." If the state was not concerned with protecting the fetus per se, then where exactly did its interest lie? The Court attempted to develop a compromise by finding a substantial increase in the state's interest as the fetus reached viability. Use of the word "viability" simultaneously allowed the Court to recognize that one cannot meaningfully speak of persons until the fetus is outside the mother's body, while recognizing that there is a point in pregnancy when the fetus could live outside the mother's body. It was at this point that the fetus's definition as a part of the mother no longer seemed to weigh in favor of the mother as primary decision maker. The point at which the fetus could be realized as a person took on normative significance for the Justices who signed the majority opinion. But even once they had justified why what they called viability should have normative significance enough to change the weight given to the state's interest in regulating abortion, they still had the difficulty of deciding when viability actually took place. The key was when the fetus could live outside the mother's body with the important qualification "with artificial aid." The best definition they could derive once they had added the qualification "with artificial aid" included a spread: "Viability is usually placed at about seven months (28 weeks) but may occur earlier, even at 24 weeks."[22]

Thus, the point at which the state's interest seemed to gain greater weight was left unclear. Yet clarity was desperately needed for the framework of the decision, because viability was supposed to serve as a crucial point in the Court's argument, which stated that the right to abortion could not be absolute even though the fetus was not a person for the purposes of the Fourteenth Amendment. Once the right was defined as not absolute and the state's compelling interest left imprecise, the possibility of justifying ever greater restrictions on the right to abortion was left open.

This possibility has now been actualized in post-*Roe* decisions.[23] The line of post-*Roe* cases with ever more elaborate and restricted readings of *Roe* makes it easy to forget the connection the Court at least tried to draw, admittedly with much waffling, between their viability analysis and the argument against making the right to abortion absolute. Prior to the viability analysis, the trimester division of the pregnancy could be interpreted to mean that until then the state had no compelling interest to justify the regulation of abortion. Blackmun's separation in *Roe* of viability and the trimester division should be noted here. The trimester approach allowed Blackmun to indicate, first, when the right to abortion could be rendered absolute (i.e., in the first trimester), and second, when concern for the woman's health would allow greater regulation of the abortion facilities provided for her. Greater regulation of facilities in the second trimester was to be allowed. The second trimester begins before viability, at least for the purpose of regulating health facilities in which women can have abortions. Viability, on the other hand, was used to analyze when the state's interest in protecting the fetus could be separated from the mother's. Viability and the trimester division have often been read in post-*Roe* decisions as if both analyses were solely addressed to concern for the fetus. But Blackmun used the trimester division to focus on women's health. He has consistently interpreted *Roe* this way in his passionate dissents in post-*Roe* decisions.

The Court's uneasiness and uncertainty in the enunciation of the right to abortion has made *Roe* famous for the equivocation of its language and an easy target for its critics. I suggest that this uncertainty cannot be separated from the Court's recognition of the uniqueness of pregnancy, which seemingly made such a right an unlikely candidate for the privacy rubric as they did not see fit to define the right as absolute.[24]

But the Court itself argues that because pregnancy and abortion involve a fetus and because the latter is a medical procedure, they cannot be understood as private, at least in terms of the space in which abortion must take place if it is to be conducted safely.[25] One must differentiate the "situation" of abortion from the "situations" confronted in the other privacy decisions:

> The pregnant woman cannot be isolated in her privacy. She carries an embryo and, later, a fetus, if one accepts the medical definitions of the developing young in the human uterus. See Dorland's Medical Dictionary 478–479, 547 (24th edition 1965). The situation therefore is inherently different from marital intimacy, or bedroom possession of obscene material, or marriage, or procreation, or education, with which Eisenstadt and Griswold, Stanley, Loving, Skinner, and Peirce and Meyer were respectively concerned. As we have intimated above, it is reasonable and appropriate for a state to decide that at some point in time another interest, that of the health of the mother or that of the potential for human life, becomes significantly involved. The woman's right is no longer sole and any right of privacy she possesses must be measured accordingly.[26]

In the first trimester the "public" nature of the abortion led the Court to include only the doctor in the process of decision. Because later cases have rarely mentioned the significance of women's health in justifying certain restrictions on abortions, I quote *Roe* again in support of the proposition that there was a sincere concern for the need to regulate later abortion in the name of providing women with safe facilities. Again quoting the majority opinion:

> In respect to the State's important and legitimate interest in the health of the mother, the compelling point, in the light of present medical knowledge, is at approximately the end of the first trimester. This is so because of the now established medical fact, referred to above at 149, that until the end of the first trimester mortality in abortion may be less than

mortality in normal childbirth. It follows that, from and after this point, a State may regulate the abortion procedure to the extent that the regulation reasonably relates to the protection and preservation of maternal health. Examples of permissible state regulation in this area are requirements as to the qualifications of the person who is to perform the abortion; as to the licensure of that person; as to the facility in which the procedure is to be performed, that is, whether it must be a hospital or may be a clinic or some other place of less than hospital status; as to the licensing of the facility and the like.[27]

Blackmun has taken his concern for women's health expressed in *Roe* into all of his dissents in post-*Roe* decisions.[28] At the same time he has tried to separate the legitimacy of the kinds of restrictions listed above in the second trimester from the restrictions that have nothing to do with the woman's health but have to do with the state's imposition of specific interpretations of the meaning of abortion in all stages of pregnancy. In his dissent in *Webster,* Blackmun appealed to the concern for women's health and the need to provide public facilities for abortion explicitly expressed in *Roe.* Unfortunately, this distinction in terms of the kinds of restrictions allowed in the arena of abortion has not been maintained. Instead, the language about the state interest has been stressed and reinterpreted at the same time that the viability standard has been rejected. In her dissent in *Akron v. Akron Center for Reproductive Health,* which clearly influenced the analytical framework of Souter, Kennedy, and O'Connor in *Casey,* Justice O'Connor explicitly rejected the use in *Roe* of viability to determine the point at which the state could claim that it had a compelling interest in the regulation of abortion: "The choice of viability as the point at which the state interest in potential life becomes compelling is no less arbitrary than choosing any point before viability or any point afterward. Accordingly, I believe that the State's interest in protecting potential human life exists throughout pregnancy."[29]

I will return shortly to why there is a point "after" viability that is surely not arbitrary in the determination of when the state's interest in protecting a baby separately from its mother could become compelling. For now, I want only to emphasize again that *Roe* itself did not just define the state's interest in protecting potential life, but was also concerned with the health of the woman in the second trimester. The woman has completely dropped out of the picture as a source of concern in the post-*Roe* cases. I strongly argue that the distinction between different kinds of restrictions, such as concern with proper facilities for later-date abortions, and imposition of particular views of women's bodies and their sexuality by state agencies who wish to discourage abortion, should be maintained. The former I justify, the latter I reject in accordance with the rearticulation of the right I have already offered. But first, we need to return to the dilemma recognized in *Roe* that it is very difficult to justify the right to abortion under the privacy rubric because a "pregnant woman is not alone in her privacy." Therefore, any adequate analysis of the right to abortion must enunciate exactly in which ways the state must both "keep its hands on" and "keep its hands off" in the protection of the right to abortion.

One can try also to expand the right to include a positive concept of liberty, as Justice Douglas did in his concurring opinion in *Roe*. But even the expanded definition, which emphasizes choice "in the basic decisions of one's life respecting marriage, divorce, procreation, contraception, and the education and upbringing of one's children," does not recognize the full significance of the reality "that a pregnant woman is not alone in her privacy." In the third dimension of what Douglas refers to as the right of privacy and liberty established in the privacy precedents, he emphasizes "the freedom to care for one's health and person, freedom from bodily constraint or compulsion, freedom to walk, stroll or loaf."[30] The first prong of this third dimension comes very close to what I have called the right of bodily integrity. The problem with Douglas's analysis in the context of abortion is twofold. First, his view of the privacy and liberty rights elaborated in the line of precedents beginning with *Griswold v. Connecticut* does not recognize fully the dependency on the provision of public facilities in the area of health.[31] We need to provide certain conditions in order to have, as the *Roe* decision reads, the "freedom to care for one's health and person." This first limitation brings us to the underlying philosophical problem. Douglas's conception of autonomy rests on the view of the self as pregiven, in its autonomy, because the self is from the beginning "in-itself." Of course, Justice Douglas would not have put it that way. But his conception of the self reflects a philosophical conception of the person that underlies much of liberal jurisprudence and which I criticized for failing to come to terms with the full legal significance of the self as a fragile and continuing process of internalization of a projected self-image that has been recognized by others in its coherence and bodily integrity. That the self depends on others for its constitution demands that we confront the social and legal conditions under which individuation can be achieved and, in the case of those sexuate beings who have been symbolically engendered as women, that we also confront the conditions for their equivalent chance to become persons.

The shift in the conception of the self demands that we think of what Douglas has called the "right to liberty" within a more overarching conception of equality. I have advocated that the view of equality is best understood as equality of well-being and capability because such a view is consistent with the philosophical and psychoanalytic critique of the pregiven self that I defend. As I have already argued, this view of the subject rests on a profound erasure of sexual difference and the complex social and symbolic network in which the engendering of the subject takes place so that what is masculine comes to stand in for the human. This erasure becomes particularly important because the right to abortion cannot be adequately articulated without confronting sexual difference and how it has been symbolized or erased in law.

Yet it is also the inevitable confrontation with sexual difference that has led some feminists to conclude that one cannot recognize pregnancy as a unique condition and still demand equality.[32] It was perhaps inevitable that the so-called divide between the difference approach and the equality approach became very heated in the area of pregnancy. This debate, however, actually created this divide because it operated on a view of equality that reflected the idea that persons before the law could be equal only if they purportedly were already in fact equal, that is, shared identical or analogous properties.[33] Thus, the search began to find ways to argue that pregnancy was analogous to some engendered condition in men. The analogies never seemed to work. The underlying problem was that the measure for equality that was being used was modeled on the masculine subject in the guise of the person. To show their equality women had to show that they were identical to men at least in those properties relevant for the challenged classification. When it came to pregnancy, such a showing seemed impossible to make. In a now infamous Supreme Court decision, *Geduldig v. Aiello,* Rehnquist, writing for the Court, rejected a challenge to an insurance policy that covered male-correlated disorders but not pregnancy because under his analysis the refusal of coverage was due to a real difference that insurance companies could rationally take into account, particularly as it only operated to disadvantage pregnant women and not all women. Rehnquist argued:

Normal pregnancy is an objectively identifiable physical condition with unique characteristics. Absent a showing that distinctions involving pregnancy are mere pre-texts designed to effect an invidious discrimination against the members of one sex or the other, law-makers are constitutionally free to include or exclude pregnancy from the coverage of legislation such as this on any reasonable basis, just as with respect to any other physical condition.[34]

The argument was not only that there was no invidious discrimination — a term of art that, at least currently, has been interpreted so as not to include the unconscious motivation that would lead law makers to devalue the feminine within sexual difference — but also that pregnancy was a unique physical condition that differentiated women from men. But the problem in *Geduldig* did not stem in any way from the condition per se, but from the evaluation of the insurance companies that did not find it worth covering. The problem was with the valuation, not with the purported difference. This is a classic example of how the devaluation of the feminine is attributed to "nature," to a natural difference. But nature does not make evaluations, human beings do.

In her thoughtful article "Reasoning from the Body," Reva Siegel argued that the decisions about abortion reinforce social judgments about women's roles and therefore that the Court should proceed under an equality analysis.[35] Her argument insists that the Court focus its analysis on the social organization of reproduction and reject physiological naturalism, which it has used to justify denying women's equality claims, particularly in the area of reproduction. I agree with Siegel that we should examine the way reproductive regulation is grounded in gender-based judgments about the proper role of women. But I would also insist that a closer reading of the cases reinforces my point that it is impossible to separate so-called facts about feminine sexual difference from the symbolizations that make it matter. The problem with the Court's analysis is not that it has reasoned from the body, but that it has instead proceeded from an unconscious set of imaginary projections about the significance of women's "sex." This significance is not just social in the sense of "outside" the body itself, but instead should be understood as the symbolic inscription that marks bodily difference as to the way such difference will be viewed. *Geduldig* and the other cases in which the Court argued from the body return us to the importance of Butler's argument that there is a crucial connection between the two senses of matter that must be noted — and indeed have been noted in both the classical Greek and Latin definitions — in any analysis of the body and, in particular, regarding the "matter" of sexual difference:

> To speak within these classical contexts of bodies that matter is not an idle pun, for to be material means to materialize, where the principle of materialization is precisely what "matters" about that body, its intelligibility. In this sense, to know the significance of something is to know how and why it matters, where "to matter" means at once "to materialize" and "to mean."[36]

It is not, then, just that the Court reasoned from the body, but that it reasoned from a body already marked in its difference through its symbolic devaluation. The problem was not that difference was not actually recognized, but that it was recognized as not being of equivalent value. In *Geduldig*, equivalent value meant equally worthy of being covered under the insurance program. This case is a classic example of how pregnancy is symbolized as a difference from men precisely so it can be devalued. But this measurement of pregnancy makes sense only within a relational concept of difference that takes men as the measure. To argue that pregnancy is a unique condition does not at all mean that it has to be devalued in its differential worth. Indeed, the very use of the word unique denies that there is a basis for comparison on the so-called immediate physical level of the body. I use the words "so-called" here to remind the reader of my argument that the "sexed" body is always engendered in a symbolic web of meaning, it is never just given. Feminine sexual difference is erased if it is reduced to a relational concept of difference.

Simone de Beauvoir argued this point when she insisted that a woman is defined as man's other and that as so defined she will be always evaluated as both inferior and not individuated.[37] But Beauvoir could see no way to symbolize the difference of the feminine except within a relational conception of difference. For her, equal recognition of women demanded the repudiation of their "sex," including its manifestation in pregnancy. The project of reimagining and symbolizing the feminine within sexual difference has to reject the relational concept of difference in which the feminine is devalued, at the same time that it must reject the alternative of neutralizing sex difference in an asexual notion of the human. This project, then, has nothing to do with either the analysis represented in *Geduldig* nor with the differences approach that tries to find women's difference in any appeal to so-called physical reality, including the reality of the body. At its heart is the reevaluation of the feminine so that it can matter as other than its reduction to matter.

If women matter only as the maternal function, then they matter only as matter, as a condition of the flesh, not as persons. The recognition of pregnancy as a unique condition that must be both valued and symbolized in its uniqueness and in the power of the gift of birth must not reduce the definition of woman to her reproductive capacity. The question of how abortion is defined as a right can play an important role in the resymbolization of pregnancy in a way that would neither deny the power of maternity nor define a woman only through her reproductive capacity. The denial of the right to abortion reinforces effectively the identification of women with the maternal function. Thus, an equality analysis need not, as Mary Poovey has suggested, "make reproductive capacity *the* defining characteristic of every woman."[38] It is the denial or restriction of abortion, not an equality analysis, that imposes that definition.

The Specific Justification of the Rearticulation of the Right to Abortion

My equality analysis does not rest on any direct comparison of women with men, but rather on an analysis of the minimum conditions for all sexuate beings to achieve individuation. The project also demands that women be valued as beings who can constantly contest and reevaluate their own self-images in an endless process of re-creation. Crucial to the specifically feminist aspect of this program is a corresponding recognition of the way the feminine has either been erased altogether, reduced to a unique physical condition (the maternal function), or been symbolized only within a relational concept of difference. But the goal of this recognition is not the affirmation of a system of gender binarism that tries to encompass the feminine within a pregiven hierarchy. Instead, we call for equal valuation of the feminine within sexual difference, knowing that this equality cannot exist within a system of hierarchy in which the feminine is devalued or simply erased in its specificity, a specificity that, in the most profound sense, cannot now be known but only reimagined and resymbolized.

The reasoning of *Roe* faltered because the majority opinion clearly recognized the dilemma it was confronting in abortion, which, on the one hand, involved the need for public facilities and the social and symbolic evaluation of the fetus, and thus seemed to undermine the privacy analysis, and, on the other hand, involved a condition unique to women, which then seemed to undermine the equality analysis. The Court recognized the dilemma but could not solve it precisely because under the traditional conceptions of liberty and equality it cannot be solved. Thus, as I have argued, we need a framework that explicitly seeks to reevaluate the feminine within sexual difference within the definition of the right of abortion itself, and then justifies the right as necessary to achievement of the minimum conditions of individuation. Under this understanding of equality the justification of the right to abortion would proceed as follows.

First, pregnancy is a unique condition and one that should be valued so as not to create a barrier to women's equality, as in *Geduldig*. But even if pregnancy is valued, a woman must not be reduced to this physical capacity because such a definition identifies her with a function rather than as a self who projects and continuously reimagines herself and the meaning of her embodiment. Pregnancy may be a unique condition, but there is also a shared need for all human beings to project a self-image of bodily integrity. This projection includes the protection of some control over the divide between what is inside the body and out, and over what is to be publicly exposed, in order that even the most primordial sense of self may be retained. Thus, it makes perfect sense to argue that if this protection of bodily integrity is necessary to secure minimum conditions of individuation for all sexuate beings, then women a fortiori must not be denied these conditions because to do so would not mark them as unequal. To mark them would reduce them to a function that is then commanded for the use of others, for the use of the anonymous other of the state that imposes its own meaning on a woman's reproductive capacity. This imposition denies women their personhood, pure and simple.

Second, the right to abortion may be justified not, as I have argued, as an "abstract right to choose," but as a fundamental condition of one's ability to imagine — and to project into the future — one's bodily integrity. Because abortion does involve the need for access to some kind of medical facility, the state may not prevent women from being able to live out their own self-image by making it either well-nigh impossible or unsafe for them to actually have abortions. The image necessary for personhood is that of coherence and self-control. If one were truly in control of one's body, then the problem of unwanted pregnancy would solve itself. What is being protected is not any actual power to control, but the need to retain some image of coherence in spite of the loss of actual control that threatens a return to a raw, fragmentary experience of the body. It is at the point when one is most fragile concerning this most basic sense of projected coherence that one needs to have one's self-image respected the most. Some forms of bodily integrity do not demand access to public facilities to be lived out. We can walk down the street and loaf around without needing access to a public facility. If the state in practice denies access, demands delays, or imposes its own meaning against the woman's own self-image and understanding of her action, then it effectively undermines her sense of selfhood at the moment when it is most fragile. By engaging in such practices the state denies women minimum conditions for their individuation, turning their bodies over to the imaginations and symbolizations of others. Because a crucial aspect of the right to project one's self as a coherent whole is control over what is exposed to the public, the woman must be allowed to make the final decision of when and how the fetus is to be taken out of her body. The fetus is like no other being precisely because it exists inside the body of the woman. Justice O'Connor is right that, given constant change in technology, viability is at best arbitrary. It is not arbitrary, however, to argue that there is a point of distinction between when a fetus is in the woman's body and when it is born and thus outside by the process of birth. At this latter point only does the state's right in protecting a potential self outweigh the woman's decision to terminate her pregnancy. What is at stake here is the woman's most basic sense of self. The utilitarian argument, such as the one made by Judge Posner that a woman's loss is less at the point of viability and the state's loss greater if the pregnancy is terminated at this stage, does not hold. Posner remarks, "The killing of the fetus is peculiarly gratuitous if the fetus has developed to the stage where the mother is no longer required to devote her body to nurturing it. What does she lose if the fetus is extracted and allowed to live rather than killed?"[39]

The answer is that she loses her most basic sense of self. The argument that the woman has the right to get rid of the fetus at the point of viability — but not to prevent the state from trying to keep it alive — is to take away from the woman her right to keep a baby, her baby, from happening. She is forced to give birth and be a mother. I agree with Barbara Katz Rothman that once we put the woman back in the picture and allow her bodily integrity to count, abortion would be understood as keeping a baby from being born.[40] The woman who has a fetus removed from her which is then kept alive by the state has not been allowed to exercise this right. As I have discussed before, a crucial component of the projection of bodily integrity is the protection of control over what is "inside" from what is forced "out." To force the woman to have the baby denies her that protection. That is also why this loss cannot be calculated. It is a loss of the self, rather than a loss to the self. Simply put, to deny women the right to have an abortion is to deny them equal protection of the minimum conditions of individuation.

Does this mean that there should be no regulations on abortion? My answer is no, because I take very seriously the concern for women's health expressed in *Roe v. Wade*. On this basis, the state must be allowed to pass regulations to ensure basic conditions for safe abortions in second and third trimesters. Does this mean that I have no concern with the other state interest protected in *Roe*, the state's interest in fetal life? I recognize the importance of the concern. Nevertheless, I disagree sharply that the legal result of this concern should be the state's attempt to protect the fetus against the mother. I have argued already that to make sense of this legal conclusion one must imply both a view of the woman and a vision of the woman's body, in which her womb is understood as a container and not as an intrinsic part of herself. If, rather, both the womb and the fetus are envisioned as a part of the woman, then it is logical to argue that concern for the health of the fetus cannot and should not be separated from concern for the health of the woman.

How and Why Abortion on Demand Should Be Defended as a Right

We now need to turn to the critique that some feminists have made of treating abortion as a right. To examine the reasons behind this critique I use the example of India. Feminists in India have been forced to ask the following question: Can we restate the right to abortion in the case of women who abort female fetuses? Nivedita Menon has explicitly discussed the difficulty of making a distinction between disabled fetuses and female fetuses in delineating exceptions to a prohibition on abortion. Some feminists in India have argued that the solution to this practice would be either to restrict use of the amniocentesis test, or at least to restrict communication about the "sex" of the baby, so that such information would not become part of the decision to abort. Menon argues, however, that the specific practice of aborting female fetuses should be understood as an aspect of the devaluation of bodies inherent in the perpetuation of a hierarchy that evaluates how bodies matter:

The issue of the morality of aborting handicapped foetuses (for the detection of which feminists in India continue to endorse amniocentesis) takes us to another level of complexity. Once it is accepted that there can be a hierarchy of human beings, classified by reference to physical characteristics, and that it is legitimate to withhold "rights" to be born from those who are at low levels of the hierarchy, then this reasoning can be extended to other categories, whether females, "inferior" races, or any other.

One feminist response to this dilemma is to argue that since women would have to look after handicapped children they should have the option not to look after them. It hardly bears repeating that the identical argument may be made about female children: because the social pressure to bear male children falls entirely on the woman, she should have the right to abort a female foetus.[41]

As a result, limiting access to information about the "sex" of the fetus hardly seems to solve the problem if it stems from the perpetuation of a hierarchy that determines which bodies matter. Menon also argues forcefully against relinquishing control over the amniocentesis test to the state. She is concerned that attempts to limit directly the right to abortion will be made, as some feminists have already done, using "right to life" arguments on behalf of female fetuses. Menon notes correctly that such arguments could be used against the right to abortion itself. She notes further that the right to abortion has never been as controversial as in the West because the state has successfully promoted population control. It is important to note here that the example of India obviously implicates a much wider discussion of the question of developmental economics, and of the program sponsored by the government to control population growth as crucial to such development programs. Amartya Sen has forcibly argued that such development programs must be based on a notion of entitlement if they are to achieve any kind of equality for women.[42] Further, Sen has argued that questions of entitlement are inevitably implicated in how basic development decisions are made. It is precisely India's development program, which has included a program of population control, that has made the right of abortion much less controversial in the Indian context. Because feminists in India have understood the kind of argument made by Sen to be crucial to development programs (i.e., that entitlement will play a major role in the achievement of equality), they have been both advanced and subtle in their thinking about the question of rights as it plays out in a broad sphere of social life. Due to the experience with the debate over questions of entitlement and development, the Indian example can help feminists in the United States reexamine their own elaboration of the right of abortion.

For Menon, this dilemma of locating a limitation on the right to abortion to subvert the abortion of female fetuses while still maintaining the overall right to abortion raises an even more basic problem about the very definition of "rights." Menon critiques the feminist analysis that situates the body in the realm of privacy, and that then justifies protection of the right to abortion as the right to be free from state intervention in that realm. For Menon, the "body" clearly has a public dimension. I agree that the body always has a public dimension, in the sense that how the body matters cannot be separated from the symbolic order that signifies, and thus gives meaning to, bodies. I do not believe that we can ever simply "own" our bodies, and that the very idea that we do own them is a fantasy. But this sense of one's body as one's own is a necessary projection for any sense of self. This position cannot, in itself, solve the dilemma in India.

The addition that must be made is that the right to abortion must be viewed in the greater context of a legal reform that would systematically challenge devaluation of the feminine within sexual difference and, as a crucial aspect of this devaluation, the reduction of our "sex" to the maternal function. Menon argues that "a feminist manifesto on 'equality of conditions for reproductive choice' would have to recognize the materiality of cultural and ideological practices which constitute 'bodies' and 'rights,' and even 'women.' " She then adds that "this materiality cannot be tackled by law but a counter practice of ideology."[43] But if one understands law as one of the important systems of cultural symbolization, then law, and more particularly rights, should not be dismissed. Certainly the masculine white Western definition of rights must also be challenged, as it cannot provide a coherent defense of the right to abortion. Traditional justifications for rights are then hardly justifiable as universal, because they have been based on a very particular and inaccurate conception of the subject and of the self. Recognition of this particularity does not demand that we switch to a cultural relativist conception of rights, for what is crucial for feminists is the revaluation of the feminine within sexual difference, which has been degraded by the gender hierarchy. For example, Sharon Hom argues:

> For Chinese women, the relativist concept of rights is also problematic. By uncritically contextualizing a rights claim within the cultural and

developmental goals of the country, women have no conceptual basis for challenging the legitimacy of the existing culture itself. The recent attention paid to abuses inflicted by "traditional practices" is illustrative of the beginning of a serious international effort to grapple with the political and methodological issues raised by this problem. In the Chinese context, female infanticide and preference for sons are clearly traditional (and modern) practices of Chinese culture.[44]

Indeed, one problem inherent in the justification of abortion in India was that its definition was relativized to the development goals of that country, without the explicit recognition of women's equal entitlement as subjects of rights. Women were effectively valued as replacement mothers. Implicit in the plan was the evaluation that the number of mothers should not be reduced or increased. Menon does not argue that "rights talk" should be completely forsaken or simply relativized to context; rather, she warns us that rights do not exist as simple and self-evident facts, given to beings understood as atomized individuals. I agree that selves do not exist other than through symbolic formation and social constructions. But once the right of bodily integrity is recast, part of a feminist struggle is to protect the feminine imaginary, to allow us to take "our selves" back from the masculine imaginary as it has been symbolized in law. This symbolization devalues Woman as the not-man, and therefore defines her not as the subject of rights, but as an object of exchange. The governmental proposal that encourages women to replace themselves as mothers should be understood to reflect this imaginary which recognizes the prime value of women through the maternal function. It is the effect of the plan in its reinforcement of the devaluation of the feminine within sexual difference that Menon addresses in her argument.

Of course, the explicit practice of aborting female fetuses is a horrifying example of this devaluation. But if we seriously contemplate protecting a woman's own imagining of the meaning of her abortion, then it would seem that we must include the woman who imagines her female fetus as so devalued that she would rather it were not born. It is also arguable that such practices in law reflect the systematic denial of the equivalent value of the feminine within sexual difference, that is, that the woman who imagines her female fetus as being of lesser value than a male fetus does so because the feminine imaginary and the symbolization of the value of the feminine within sexual difference has almost been foreclosed.

What does it mean to allow abortion on the basis of sex under the protection of the rubric of the right to abortion if it denies equivalent value to the feminine within sexual difference? My preferred solution is to criticize all exceptions to antiabortion laws that turn on the perpetuation of hierarchies that evaluate whose body is to matter. This solution does mean that in a choice between protecting the right to abortion on demand and legally restricting the right in order to curb the practice of aborting female fetuses as a violation of the equivalent value of the feminine "sex," I would choose the former. This is, in part, because the resymbolization of women as subjects of rights is for me one prong of the overall challenge to the devaluation of the feminine within sexual difference.

Gender hierarchy systematically denies women their status as subjects of rights.[45] As we have seen in the context of the United States, the regulation of abortion reduces women to objects, denies their "sex" as the maternal function, and further forecloses the play of the feminine imaginary by trying to define the meaning of abortion for the woman. The question becomes: How do we adopt or create a discourse that enhances what Hom has called women's "subject possibilities" and what I have explained as the equivalent right to become a person?[46] To develop a discourse of the would-be female person, whose imaginary can be symbolized in its own specificity, irreducible to that of the Other by which the man measures himself, necessarily has a utopian dimension, for it is precisely this position of the subject as woman that cannot be confirmed in a masculine symbolic. It is no coincidence that the projection of woman as a subject of rights challenges the traditional discourse of rights that has kept women captive in a patriarchal system of law that reflects and perpetuates the gender hierarchy in which women are governed as violable objects only because of their sex. The promise of the recognition of woman as a subject of rights is a promise of an imagined future, in which sexual difference might be articulated as other than its definition within the gender hierarchy, with its limited binarism on whose basis the normalization of heterosexuality is justified. It is that promise that must be expressed in the rearticulation of rights. The discourse in which such a promise can be expressed must also be created. Such a discourse, then, does not rest on the so-called universalist premises that turn us toward the past of gender, national, and racist hierarchy that disguises the particularity of the Western man. As we imagine women reimagining themselves, our captivity by a discourse that has told us what we are as women is also challenged. Recognizing the right to abortion challenges the discourse that legitimizes our social status as objects to be manipulated, because it insists that it is women who must be empowered to define and reimagine what maternity means to them.

Notes

1. For an excellent discussion on the history of the debate on when life begins, see, generally, Ronald Dworkin, *Life's Dominion: An Argument about Abortion, Euthanasia, and Individual Freedom* (New York: Knopf, 1993).

2. My explanation of bodily integrity seeks to encompass the concept of the process of integration.

3. The original analysis of the common law right to privacy was presented by Samuel Warren and Louis D. Brandeis in "The Right to Privacy," *Harvard Law Review* 4 (1890): 193. Warren and Brandeis advocated the protection of the "inviolate personality" of each person. Justice Brandeis set forth the basis for the modern right when he recognized a right to protection of one's private life from government intrusion. He called it "the right to be left alone — the most comprehensive of rights and the most valued by civilized man." See *Olmstead v. U.S.*, 277 U.S. 438, 478 (1928) (Brandeis, J., dissenting).

4. Luce Irigaray writes that as living, sexuate beings, our identities cannot be constructed without conditions of respect for difference and equality of rights to bring out such differences. Limited sexual choice denies us the most fundamental recognition of our differences and, therefore, the potential for the attainment of equality of rights. See Luce Irigaray, "How to Define Sexuate Rights?" in *The Irigaray Reader,* ed. Margaret Whitford, trans. David Macey (Oxford: Basil Blackwell, 1991), and Luce Irigaray, *Je, tu, nous: Toward a Culture of Difference,* trans. Alison Martin (New York: Routledge, Chapman and Hall, 1993).

5. The Supreme Court has repeatedly upheld the regulation of reproductive freedom against equal protection challenges. In *Geduldig v. Aiello,* 417 U.S. 484 (1974), the Court held that state regulation of pregnancy is not sex-based because such regulation does not categorically distinguish the class of women from the class of men. However, in *Michael M. v. Superior Court,* 450 U.S. 464 (1981), the Court suggested that state regulation of pregnancy by its nature cannot discriminate on the basis of sex for such regulation pertains to a real and categorical difference between genders.

6. See Judith Butler, *Bodies That Matter: On the Discursive Limits of "Sex"* (New York: Routledge, 1993), 1–56.

7. Dworkin, *Life's Dominion,* 68–101.

8. Ibid., 48.

9. I am using the word "self" here to indicate what Lacan means by ego identity in the mirror stage. Jacques Lacan, *Écrits: A Selection,* trans. Alan Sheridan (New York: Norton, 1977), 1–7.

10. For a discussion of Lacan and the mirror stage, see Teresa Brennan, *The Interpreta-*

tion of the Flesh: Freud and Femininity (New York: Routledge, Chapman and Hall, 1992), 70–71, 114.

11. See Thomas Nagel, *The Value of Inviolability* (1992, unpublished manuscript on file with author, N.Y.U. Law School), for an excellent and succinct discussion of the significance of this distinction in Kantian morality and more specifically how it relates to the value of inviolability.

12. See Drucilla Cornell, *The Philosophy of the Limit* (New York: Routledge, 1992).

13. *Planned Parenthood of Eastern Pennsylvania v. Casey,* 112 S.Ct. 2791 (1992).

14. See Charles Peirce, *The Collected Papers of Charles Sanders Peirce,* vols. 1, 2, ed. Charles Hartshorne and Paul Weiss (Cambridge, MA: The Belknap Press of Harvard University Press, 1960), particularly vol. 1, bk. 3, chaps. 5 and 6.

15. Elaine Scarry, *The Body in Pain* (New York: Oxford University Press, 1985), 48–49.

16. Ibid., 186–204, 282.

17. Judith Jarvis Thompson, "A Defense of Abortion," *Philosophy and Public Affairs* 1.1 (fall 1971).

18. See George Fletcher, "Reflections on Abortion" (unpublished manuscript on file with the author, Columbia University School of Law).

19. *Webster v. Reproductive Health Services,* 492 U.S. 490 (1989).

20. See Butler, *Bodies That Matter,* 32.

21. *Roe v. Wade,* 410 U.S. (1973) 153–54.

22. Ibid., 160.

23. See *Casey,* 112 S.Ct. at 2791. Most post-*Roe* decisions define the issue of abortion rights as a battle between the fetus's rights and the woman's rights. *Casey,* however, has left the pregnant woman out of the picture entirely, instead focusing on the husband's right to notification.

24. One way out of this dilemma is to define the right to abortion as absolute in order to make its definition consistent with a strong interpretation of what the right of privacy entails. See Jed Rubenfeld, "The Right of Privacy," *Harvard Law Review* 102 (1989): 737, for a powerful argument for this solution to defending abortion under the right to privacy.

25. It is difficult to define abortion as a completely private issue, considering that it is a surgical procedure that must take place in a public facility. Even RU486, a nonsurgical method of abortion, requires medical supervision, and thus cannot be considered completely private.

26. *Roe,* 410 U.S. at 158.

27. Ibid., 162–63.

28. In *Rust v. Sullivan,* 111 S.Ct. 1759 (1991), the Court considered the constitutionality of a physician's "gag rule" concerning the option of abortion. Justice Blackmun's dissent pointed out that the effect of the gag rule is that a physician's advice is often "wholly unrelated to the [pregnant woman's] situation" (1788).

In *Ohio v. Akron,* 497 U.S. 502 (1990), parental notification laws were considered.

Blackmun's concern was that the notification requirement would cause up to a twenty-two-day delay in the procurement of an abortion. He criticized the majority, writing that "the Court ignores the fact that the medical risks surrounding abortion increase as pregnancy advances and that such delay might push a woman into her second trimester, where the medical risks, economic costs, and state regulation increase dramatically" (520–21).

Relying on the District Court findings in *Webster v. Reproductive Health Services*, 492 U.S. 490 (1989), Justice Blackmun criticized mandatory viability and lung maturity testing because the procedure has "no medical justification [and] imposes significant additional health risks on both the pregnant woman and the fetus" (543–44). He further noted:

> [If women are forced to carry unwanted pregnancies to term,] hundreds of thousands of women, in desperation, would defy the law, and place their health and safety in the unclean and unsympathetic hands of back-alley abortionists, or they would attempt to perform abortions upon themselves, with disastrous results. Every year, many women, especially poor and minority women, would die or suffer debilitating physical trauma, all in the name of enforced morality or religious dictates or lack of compassion, as it may be. (557–58)

Planned Parenthood, Kansas City v. Ashcroft, 450 U.S. 398 (1989), the Court considered a statute that mandated that postviability abortions may not take place unless a second physician is in attendance to care for the fetus after it is discharged. The statute applied even where, in light of the abortion method used, it was completely impossible that a live child could be born. Blackmun wrote, "By requiring the attendance of a second physician even where the resulting delay may be harmful to the health of the pregnant woman, the statute fails to make clear that the woman's life and health must always prevail over the fetus' life and health when the two are in conflict" (499–500).

29. *Akron v. Akron Center for Reproductive Health*, 462 U.S. 416 (1983) at 460.

30. *Roe*, 410 U.S. at 209–19.

31. *Griswold v. Connecticut*, 381 U.S. 479 (1965).

32. See Wendy Williams, "The Equality Crisis: Some Reflections on Culture, Courts, and Feminism," in *Feminist Legal Theory*, ed. Katharine T. Bartlett and Rosanne Kennedy (Boulder, CO: Westview Press, 1991); Zillah Eisenstein, *Feminism and Sexual Equality: Crisis in Liberal America* (New York: Monthly Review Press, 1984).

33. See *Geduldig v. Aiello*, 417 U.S. 484 (1974), and *Michael M. v. Superior Court*, 450 U.S. 464 (1981), as examples of cases in which the Court has held that state regulation of pregnancy is not sex-based regulation and thus does not violate the Equal Protection Clause.

34. *Geduldig v. Aiello*, 417 U.S. 484 (1974).

35. Reva Siegel, "Reasoning from the Body: A Historical Perspective on Abortion Regulation and Questions of Equal Protection," *Stanford Law Review* 44 (1992): 261.

36. Butler, *Bodies That Matter,* 32.

37. See Simone de Beauvoir, *The Second Sex,* trans. H. M. Parshley (New York: Knopf, 1974).

38. Mary Poovey, "The Abortion Question and the Death of Man," in *Feminists Theorize the Political,* ed. Judith Butler and Joan W. Scott (New York: Routledge, 1992), 241.

39. Richard Posner, *Sex and Reason* (Cambridge, MA: Harvard University Press, 1992).

40. Barbara Katz Rothman, *Recreating Motherhood: Ideology and Technology in a Patriarchal Society* (New York: Norton, 1989).

41. See Nivedita Menon, "Abortion and the Law: Questions for Feminism," *Canadian Journal of Women and the Law* 6 (1993): 115.

42. See Amartya Sen, "Well-Being, Agency and Freedom," *Philosophy and Public Affairs* 19 (Apr. 1985), and "Equality of What?" in *Choice, Welfare and Measurement* (Cambridge, MA: MIT Press, 1982). See also Isaiah Berlin, *Four Essays on Liberty* (London: Oxford University Press, 1969).

43. Menon, "Abortion and the Law," 118.

44. Sharon Hom, "Female Infanticide in China: The Human Rights Specter and Thoughts toward (An)Other Vision," *Columbia Human Rights Law Review* 23 (1992): 292.

45. Drucilla Cornell, "The Philosophy of the Limit: Systems Theory and Feminist Legal Reform," in *Deconstruction and the Possibility of Justice,* ed. Drucilla Cornell, Michel Rosenfeld, David Carlson (New York: Routledge, Chapman and Hall, 1992), 68–91.

46. Hom, "Female Infanticide in China," 249–314.

DAVID KENNEDY

When Renewal Repeats:
Thinking against the Box

This essay was originally the conclusion to a longer study of renewal and criticism in the discipline of international law in the United States in the twentieth century. That study developed two ideas about what might be thought of as the "politics" of a professional discipline — here, international lawyers — involved in governance. These ideas served in turn as background for this effort to understand how one might intervene "critically" in the field as a progressive intellectual without being either hemmed in by the limits of the professional vocabulary or consigned to play the role of outsider or gadfly. How one might, as the title suggests, "think against the box" in a profession that had long since routinized the practices of criticism and disciplinary renewal.

The first idea about the politics of a professional discipline: the forms of expertise that constitute the vocabulary of the discipline might have biases or blind spots that could affect the distributional consequences of the discipline's governance activities. And might do so even when this sort of bias or blindness is self-consciously denied and avoided in the discipline's everyday work generating and defending the various institutions, doctrines, and policy ideas that make up the profession's most direct contribution to global governance. Although there might be a scrupulous disciplinary practice of political evenhandedness, or of disengagement from politics, or of engagement with only the most benign universal humanism, the modes of expertise within which these disinterested denials and benign disengagements were propounded might nevertheless themselves introduce a bias.

This idea required a rather lengthy elaboration of what constituted the field's "vocabulary": the stock of problems, solutions, terms of justification, explanation, and criticism that made up the expertise of international lawyers. It turned out that international lawyers had returned for more than a century to a small stock of simple polarized arguments about what international law was and could be. Disagreements about how to draw the line between these recurring argumentative pairs constituted the bulk of the profession's actual work in thinking about how international life should be organized. The terms of these disagreements were rearranged from one generation to the next, but the discipline's continuity was marked in their repetition. My project was to see whether this entire range of arguments left some things unsaid or biased the discipline's work in one or another political direction.

A great deal of the material produced by the discipline turned out to be denunciations of the weaknesses, biases, and blind spots of either the field as a whole or the international legal arguments and institutional proposals advanced by other people in the field. This disciplinary practice of self-criticism and renewal returned the field repeatedly to the same stylized arguments — but in the process it cleansed the discipline's vocabulary of overt signs of bias or blindness. Although the international law discipline has certainly been "captured" by one or another political position, ideological commitment, doctrinal or methodological idea in one or another time and place, the broad history of the field is of a systematic effort to avoid precisely this type of fixity. Like many contemporary governance disciplines, the field of international law is pragmatic, open, flexible, reasonable, moderate, cosmopolitan, expert, disengaged, balanced, and absolutely not dogmatic. Of two or more minds on just about everything.

This made it extremely difficult to sustain the intuition with which I began the project: that the discipline encouraged those who deployed its expertise to see some things and not others, and to contribute to global governance in ways that favored the interests of some and not others. And yet there were also, as it turned out, some commitments — to ideas like the distinction between public and private law and the distinction between government and the market — that were shared across the range of positions about which the field has self-consciously been preoccupied and that might, in some cases, introduce a bias or blind spot into the governance work of the profession. The preoccupation with a set of recurring arguments about which we would have to conclude that the discipline, taken as a whole and over time, was ambivalent might in some senses have reinforced both this tendency to bias and inattention to it. In this sense, we might locate the politics of a discipline in the vocabulary it speaks. We might say that international lawyers, whatever their own political affiliations and professional sensibility, were being politically spoken by their shared expertise.

The second idea about disciplinary politics explored in the original study was sociological rather than rhetorical. Although a common vocabulary does structure the exercise of expertise and may blind or bias outcomes, this vocabulary is extremely plastic. It can be torqued in dozens (although not hundreds) of different shapes. The political and personal projects of particular international lawyers — their intellectual commitments and aversions, their professional affiliations and disaffiliations, their wills to power and to submission — are also important elements in generating the "politics" of the discipline and in accounting for the shape the field's vocabulary took at different times. The second half of the earlier study developed a typology for thinking about these sorts of sociological factors and explored the intersection between the semiotic possibilities of the vocabulary and the projects of particular waves of international lawyers over time.

My idea was to understand the current state of play in the field as both a consequence of the very human political, intellectual, and professional projects of specific international lawyers, and as movements within a shared professional vocabulary. Understanding the politics of the field requires a sense for the blind spots and biases of this vocabulary as they intersect with the available range of actual social, personal, and professional projects. It was after developing this model that I turned, in the last part of the study, included here, to an interpretation of the international legal profession during the heyday of the Clinton administration's foreign policy. This provides the background for an account of my own effort to intervene in the profession as a teacher and a scholar during that period, aiming to expand its political range and counteract its bias and blindness by offering an experience of "thinking against the box" of its established vocabulary.

International Law Today:
Anxiety and the Search for a New Consensus

The end of the cold war roughly coincided with the end of a stable professional consensus among American international lawyers about what international law was and could become. From the early 1980s, the field has been home to much ideological, methodological, and political debate — as well as much anxiety about what precisely international law could and should aspire to achieve. In the early Clinton years, a loose group of American international lawyers began a bid to establish a new consensus in the field that would support and accompany a return to power for international law and international lawyers within the American foreign policy establishment. By the last years of the Clinton presidency, this set of ideas and these professionals had largely established themselves as a new common sense. There were, and remain, criticisms, from the right and the left, but dominance of the field lay within their grasp.

Many of the reform ideas advanced as part of this broad project to renew the field were undoubtedly good ideas: more use of national judiciaries rather than foreign ministries to interpret and enforce international norms, emphasis on the role of nongovernmental organizations rather than intergovernmental bureaucracies to build a more cooperative and legally sanctioned international order, more insistent international support for democratic forces and voices at all levels of society rather than deference to national sovereign autonomy, increased attention to human rights enforcement, a new willingness to acknowledge the problems caused by failed states and governments, an embrace of the new global market as a potential force for stability and law, replacement of the aspiration for quasi-federal "world government" with a more flexible insistence on the necessity of "good governance."

Although presented as recipes for broad reform of the field and of the world, many of the most compelling of these proposals restated and rearranged themes long present in the discipline — but saying so neither criticizes nor validates them. That this new mainstream had found a novel arrangement of ideas in the professional lexicon that could reposition the profession more successfully within the broader American foreign policy establishment is testimony to their ingenuity and intuitive grasp of the politics of their time. My worry about this wave of disciplinary renewal and consolidation has been another: that the urge to consolidate a new consensus about what law and governance can be at the international level will reinforce the field's long-standing biases and blind spots and miss the opportunity presented by this period of anxiety and contestation to probe more deeply into the politics of the profession. To understand the politics of the discipline, its distributional legacy and potential, we need a more basic understanding of the assumptions common to both these new ideas and the projects they seek to displace, as well as the patterns of commitment, affiliation, and ambition within which these debates are occurring and this bid for a new consensus has been launched.

The most significant projects, affiliations, and commitments moving the international law profession at the moment are generational and political. Both are easy stories to sketch. The generational account picks up as the long engagement between my own generation, now in our forties, and our predecessors, now in their sixties and seventies, ends. From the late 1950s until the mid-1980s, the field of international law in the United States had been arranged as a gentlemanly disputation between a "Yale School" committed to "policy" and a realist focus on national interest, and a more dominant internationalist mainstream or "Columbia School" more committed to the use of legal norms to build a more collective and cosmopolitan international community. The displacement of this Yale-Columbia axis by the axis of support for and opposition to the proposed consensus — which is variously associated with the words "transnationalism," "legal process," and "liberalism" — is an event in the development of ideas that took fifteen years to achieve, from the mid-1980s to the end of the Clinton administration.

People in the field recognize it also easily as a generational phenomenon. The 1960–1989 generation was an extremely coherent one that entered the field early in the Kennedy administration and only began to lose its grip after the elections of Reagan and Thatcher. Since the end of the cold war they have retreated with remarkable generosity and grace or have reinterpreted themselves as allies of the new generational consensus. The leaders in the field are now largely my contemporaries, whose formative experiences in the field came after the disappointments of 1968 and Vietnam. At the same time, the field is expanding rapidly, and a much larger and potentially more diverse generation is coming on the scene, bringing new recruits and new critical voices. The disciplinary success of the transnational–legal process–liberals remains tenuous.

Generational change within a field is rarely smooth. A field can be dominated by people who understand themselves to be part of one generation for thirty or more years, and they can quite suddenly be displaced by another group who might differ in age among themselves by as much as twenty years, but still see themselves as a single generation. In American international law, this has been extremely pronounced, providing an opportunity to examine how a generation coalesces, announces itself, and displaces its predecessors. The presence of a potential third generation offers the opportunity to think about something equally complex: what strategic possibilities are open to an age cohort that is not yet formed either as junior members of my middle generation as it comes into power or as the avant-garde of the generation that will displace us. To put it starkly, "new thinking" for today's students can mean either submission to a proposed disciplinary common sense just being consolidated, or a far more uncertain effort to think beyond where my own generation has gone before we have even gotten there.

If we are to place this generational story in a social and political context, we might start with the observation that for international law in the United States the 1990s were like the 1950s. There are certainly contextual similarities: long economic expansion, newly unchallenged global role, a period of national cultural retrenchment, reaffirmation of conventional "family values" against the periodic cycles of modernist sexual and political openings. International lawyers again find themselves defending the machinery of multilateralism against a conventional isolationism translated by hegemony into a unilateral internationalism. We find again a displacement of public law aspirations by the priorities of free trade economic expansion on one side, and a creeping tendency to idiosyncratic humanitarian interventions on the other. It is not surprising that we find leading international lawyers today returning also to the ideas and practices of the 1950s: antiformalism, legal process, transnationalism, universal humanism, embrace of international relations, postwar liberal triumphalism, worry about the viability of humanism in a divided and decolonizing world, talk about a liberal world public order, defense of the universal in human rights. For international law, the 1950s were also a time of disciplinary doubt, of postwar anxiety about the viability of collective security, multilateralism, even international law itself, in the new world of "totalitarianism," "ideology," and the cold war. The 1950s saw deep methodological division in the field as scholars trained in the world of cultural modernism, sociological jurisprudence, functionalism, and legal realism struggled to reinvent their field on these new terms in new conditions — people like Hans Morgenthau, Pitman Potter, Josef Kunz, Leo Gross, Hans Kelsen, Myres McDougal, and Philip Jessup.

It was only in the 1960s that a methodological and political consensus settled on the field, the internationalist liberalism of people like Richard

Falk, Louis Henkin, Oscar Schachter, Tom Franck, Louis Sohn, and Abe Chayes, who consolidated a new mainstream way of thinking against the backdrop of the Yale policy alternative. In a way, the old public international law simply shipwrecked on the rocks of legal realism and policy science, and all the standard disciplinary debates about what international law was and could be that had been dominant before the 1950s were swept away. After 1960 it was routine to assert that all those who had come before had missed the most significant political developments: superpower convergence, decolonization, the emergence of development as a central substantive issue, the existence of cosmopolitan space between the superpowers. The field had been in urgent need of renewal, and suffered from an unhealthy methodological extremism when the practical problems of a newly interdependent world called out for an eclectic *via media*. The discipline's marginal status discouraged dissident voices in the field, even as it established a practice of professional dissidence. A call for new ideas in 1959 would have had many takers, all proposing one or another version of the liberal humanism that would then dominate the field for a generation. Their program would have rekindled the modernist and cosmopolitan recipes of the 1920s, enthusiasm about international administration, a chastened collective security, a critique of sovereignty, an embrace of political science, of expertise, a call for renewal.

The new generation that followed hitched their wagons to the foreign policy of the Kennedy era and to an American-style liberalism with an internationalist and cosmopolitan perspective at first promised by Kennedy's New Frontier, then by Hammarskjöld's revitalized United Nations. The disciplinary hegemony of the Hammarskjöld liberals in the field of public international law was surprisingly complete and long-lasting. It also had an enormous echo outside the United States, in many ways more than here at home for generations of young lawyers from the third world, as well as our industrialized allies and colonies, looking for a safe space between socialism and embrace of the American empire. As the liberal consensus on American internationalism dissipated, the field became increasingly marginal, isolated from both the cosmopolitanism of Republican free traders and the increasingly interventionist cold war liberalism of the Democratic Party, in Vietnam and elsewhere. Their commitment to the formal rules necessary to criticize the American hegemon or build a regime of coexistence with the Soviet Union isolated them further from American legal scholars in other fields eagerly embracing the world of "policy." There was

Ford, there were spurts of energy in the Carter years around human rights and the law of the sea, and then came Thatcher and Reagan and Bush.

By the time Clinton was elected, the field had again broken apart, its consensus dissipated — exactly as the isolationist consensus of American international lawyers before the Second World War collapsed after 1941 — and for more than ten years we have been in a period of contestation and disciplinary anxiety. The context in which my disciplinary colleagues urge renewal of the field is one in which international lawyers have fallen far from power. For most in my generation, this is a problem, not an opportunity. The central project common to the new mainstream throughout the last decade has been an urgent effort to permit international lawyers to return to a position of authority within the American political establishment that they have not had in almost a century. The leaders of the field are no longer content to criticize power: they are anxious to exercise it. New ideas are thought necessary if the field is to give international lawyers a workable set of myths and methods to imagine themselves into the same social frame as the governing establishment of the Clinton presidency.

In this sense, the leading "new" scholars of my generation are to the Clinton era of renewed, if chastened, Democratic Party foreign policy what the Hammarskjöld generation was to the Kennedy and Johnson administrations. Their shared political project is the defense and development of a benignly hegemonic foreign policy of humanitarian interventions. They share with the Clintonites a way of thinking about markets and human rights, share with Clinton's World Bank appointees a skepticism about neoliberalism, an earnest faith in modest interventionist development policy, and so forth. They seek a more humane, if only marginally more open, immigration, refugee, and asylum policy. Inside American legal culture, they are internationalist about the foreign relations law of the United States, favoring an expanded federal authority in foreign affairs and an increased role for international law in U.S. courts, even as they favor chaining the State Department to law when it acts abroad. Thus they favor decentralization of judicial adherence to international law and the use of national, or even local, courts to enforce human rights norms. Anyone and everyone should try Pinochet, for example. But they do not favor decentralization of American executive power in the foreign affairs field — allowing Massachusetts to use its purchasing power to sanction Burma, for example — at least whenever the Democratic Party finds itself in control of the national administration.

There are differences within the group, of course, about this or that intervention, the viability of a criminal court, and so on, but everyone wants U.S. courts to pay more attention to the International Court of Justice, wants the United States to "use" the institutions of multilateral dispute resolution more sincerely and more often. This is not the party of Buchanan or Helms or Perot or Nader — and also not of Rockefeller or Bush Republicanism. It is certainly not the party of Reagan, with his belligerence on cold war interventions, bilateral or unilateral enthusiasms, his obsession with the Contras, and all that. For international lawyers to be players in today's political climate, the leaders of my generation concur that the discipline must dump the rule piety and policy skepticism inherited from the Columbia School. A dose of political science would obviously be a good idea, and the transnational–legal process–liberalism school has embraced a strand of the political science academy whose vocabulary converges with their own, worrying about "governance," "regimes," "global management," and so forth. After all, recent Secretaries of State and National Security Advisors have been political scientists or Wall Street attorneys, but none have been international lawyers. These people are skeptical of human rights dogma — far too unrealistic and formal — but extremely supportive of the human rights ethic, process, procedures, machinery, just as they are empathetic about culture and poverty and other humanist commitments and enthusiastic about all sorts of efforts to dialogue and understand. Unlike some Catholic figures in the field, however, raison d'état rather than social justice is their first commitment. But it is a soft, embedded, humane raison d'état.

The transnational–legal process–liberalism school recognizes that the real players behind globalization are economists or international economic law specialists, and understand that an appreciation for economics alongside political science wouldn't hurt. Still, they tend to be people who share the common idea in the broader liberal intelligentsia that economics is in some sense bloodless, or has a tin ear for ethics. As members of the governing establishment, they certainly support free trade, but these are not neoliberals of the Washington consensus. They are modest interventionists, interested in tempering free trade with appropriate regulations, sympathetic to the concerns raised by nongovernmental organizations (a new term for labor unions) about the social impact of trade. And so on.

What we have is a generational cohort proposing a new synthesis, animated by a set of overlapping political projects that they are pursuing vigorously. It is not difficult to identify among those promoting the new consensus international lawyers with more specific commitments and affiliations. There are people who want to promote international economic law as a field, want to affiliate with law teachers in other, "tougher" fields, want to reinterpret international economic law as a somewhat public or constitutional legal order, amenable to at least some socially responsible regulatory initiatives. Being seen as a person who knows about economics or who consorts with law and economics scholars might well advance such a project. Similarly, there are people who want to redeem public international law as a possible partner in managing American foreign policy. To make it a worthy participant in statecraft, they feel they must demonstrate a certain hard-boiled understanding of power, and a rapprochement with the political scientists who have staffed the Democratic Party foreign policy establishment might be a good strategy.

This generational cohort of international law professionals has sought out allies among those sharing one or another of their intellectual commitments—to interdisciplinarity in general, to the importance of economics and political science—among international lawyers and among those in neighboring fields who have felt international law had somehow gone astray, needed a cold hard look, a reengagement with policy science. They have cultivated friends among those of their elders who chafed most under the dominance of the old mainstream consensus. They have found support among those drawn to their intellectual and professional style, their hip sensibility and apparent political with-it-ness. They have mobilized institutional resources in universities, law firms, government. They have worked to mobilize professionals in a number of subdisciplines to generate operational examples of their general ideas: environmental law, refugee affairs, arms control. They have written broad-scale reinterpretations of the field's most basic doctrines and institutions: judicial review, the power of the Security Council, the role of courts, the function of international institutions. They have sought out and supported mentees and followers, have appealed to the desires of others in the field for energetic leadership. They have presented their suggestions for doctrinal and institutional reforms to one another's practitioner-beings in the hope of confirming adoption. All this is quite normal. Had they not done so we might have wondered about the usefulness of their ideas or the depth of their professional commitment and competence.

This emerging professional consensus has been criticized in numerous ways, by people within and without the field, by international lawyers from the United States and elsewhere. Critics have made efforts to mobilize constituencies in opposition, just as the transnational–legal process–liberalism proponents have sought to do on their own behalf. Some of this opposition comes from people proposing other ideas to reorganize the field, some from people opposing one or another of the pet projects of the transnational–legal process–liberalism cohort. Some comes from the left and some from the right. Those who make these criticisms are working within the disciplinary vocabulary, but they generally take a somewhat stricter attitude about the formality of entitlements and the autonomy of national traditions. They are also professionals with projects and commitments and aversions of their own. In my own view, much criticism of the new mainstream international lawyers is both too sweeping and too wedded to the discipline's own vocabulary. Efforts to identify the dark side of disciplinary common sense and its capture by groups are important, but seem unlikely to be accomplished by a silver bullet. This new mainstream will not be defeated by a good argument, nor even a showing that its main ideas are tainted by historical or contemporary association with bad political actors. Rather, opposition requires an ongoing performance and counterdemonstration, an effort to uncover and make visible the blind spots and political projects firmed up in the more neutral vocabulary of disciplinary renewal and pragmatic persuasion.

As a result, my own hope has been that as the field rushes to embrace a new consensus, there will remain some who will keep doubt alive. While this new consensus has slowly emerged, generating and shaping its opposition, it has been my project to open a space within the field for a range of critical initiatives and alternative voices: to seek alliances, affiliations, power, to permit the development of ideas that did not fit into the available disciplinary lexicon. I have not tried to develop an all-points criticism of transnational–legal process–liberalism, any more than of the disciplinary vocabulary within which it has been articulated. Nor have I proposed an alternative. Many ideas in the new consensus might be worth pursuing further in one or another context. My project has been to sidestep these preoccupations to focus instead on the disciplinary vocabulary as a whole, on its blind spots and biases, and on its intersection with the sociological projects of the profession at particular times and places.

I have come to this project myself partly by following the energy of an intuition: that in some way the international legal profession has often made less likely the very things it claims to care most about, that the professional discipline is part of the problem, and that the established professional argumentative practice in the field repeatedly places its speaker in a posture of bad faith — overestimating small differences and overpromoting broad arguments about which one is also professionally ambivalent. This is an intuition, I'm afraid, that applies equally to those of my generational cohorts now proposing a new political and intellectual synthesis for the discipline, as well as to their most notable opponents.

Unfortunately, this remains, after close to twenty years of collaborative work, a very unworked-out intuition and a comparatively unsuccessful project. We have started to figure out how the discipline participates in keeping a terribly unjust international order up and running, even as it seeks with great passion to be a voice for humanitarian reform, even as it renews itself constantly to be more effective. But we are just getting started. The difficulty is not only an intellectual one, however. Transforming the discipline, just like reinforcing it, is a project that requires the mobilization of affinities, the building of groups, the staging of controversy, and the announcement of opposition and seductive appeals of recognition, engagement, play. Thinking against the box the field has built for itself is a performance in a particular context, a project of affiliation and disaffiliation, commitment and aversion, dominance and submission. On that score, I can offer some experiences that have stretched across the period from the collapse of one disciplinary common sense in the internationalist disappointments of the Carter and Reagan years to the consolidation of another in the last years of the Clinton era.

Critical Performativity: The Situation and the Audience for Extravernacular Disciplinary Projects

A professional vocabulary for criticism and innovation is the backbone of an international lawyer's expertise. This vocabulary has limitations: a recurring experience of overstatement, an extreme plasticity, a range of blind spots and biases. Deploying this vocabulary seems conducive to a kind of professional sectarianism, the repeating narcissism of small differences. Still, it offers a form of ritualized combat, through which all sorts of projects and groups compete with one another, legitimate and delegitimate one another, the parties speaking with various degrees of sincerity. This presents a problem for those who have the intuition that the field's quotidian practices of criticism and renewal do not go far enough in some way, that they may repeat and reinforce disciplinary blindnesses and biases.

My own search for "new thinking" in the field of international law arose from just this sort of intuition. It arose at a time of disciplinary self-doubt, when the accumulation of criticisms within the field seemed to overwhelm self-confidence in the profession's capacity to reform and rebuild itself. I felt a strong identification with the field of international law, with the promise and premise of international governance, with the perils of and possibilities for cosmopolitan rationalism. But I wanted to think outside the professional lexicon, and I wanted to build the institutional and social conditions that could make doing so possible and enjoyable. This desire faced an immediate obstacle in the quite normal tendency of a discipline either to interpolate frame breakers back into the disciplinary vocabulary or place them outside the field. I wanted to be in the field, but I wanted to develop and make known an intuition about the field's limits and dark side that seemed impossible to speak in the disciplinary vocabulary.

I have always had a hard time explaining that I meant this effort as a project within the field but outside the field's lexicon, that I was motivated both by the search for something new, for novelty, the excitement of fashion innovation, and by the impulse to criticize the field for shortcomings that could best be framed in earnestly ethical and political terms, that I meant it as something pleasurable and was quite serious, that I was probably on-the-left but that vernacular left-wing projects seemed as much a part of the problem as the solution, that my project was an intellectual one but that I felt this meant it was also a project in the domain of social power and institutional politics.

Perhaps most frustrating has been navigating the disciplinary demand for usefulness. It is conventional to distinguish new thinking that leads somewhere, that helps the field, that is linked to useful reform, and new thinking that does not — that is, depending on who is speaking, more daring or irresponsible, or theoretical, or perhaps simply "more radical." It is certainly true, in a discipline where practically everyone calls for "new thinking," that some people will seem to do so with a shorter-term reform horizon, will question less of the existing field, will harness their criticisms more directly to concrete reforms. Other people will see it as an act of brave disaffiliation to refuse all this, to place rather more of the discipline under question, to forgo the demand for immediate reformist suggestions. This can be an important distinction to be sure, but throughout the discipline's history, and even in my own life, it is often very difficult to untangle these threads. If your project is to step outside the disciplinary vocabulary for reform, however, or if you neglect to orient your work to the imaginary practitioner-being, then you will be understood to be "more radical," not useful — or useful only if you succeed in becoming a generational innovator who reorients the field's lexicon for usefulness.

Being interpreted in this way places you in an odd double bind. Either you must want to remake the field's entire vocabulary, and will be judged not immediately, but pretty soon, on your ability to be accepted by everyone's practitioner-being as a new establishment in the field, or you are somewhere on the fringes of the field, perhaps even over the edge someplace. You will be thought "critical," and not in the sense that everyone else in the field is constantly criticizing one another's proposals. They are criticizing things in the real world, or at least on behalf of or for an imaginary audience of the real world. If you are not speaking that language, you must be in some place other than the real world, and you must be criticizing them. As a colleague of mine once said, "I analyze the real world and you analyze me." This, of course, was itself meant as a criticism, of me, in the real world, just as it imagined my interlocutor somewhere outside the real world, a scholar, a proposer, someone who might influence practitioner-beings, but not an actor with a project.

Conventionally, criticism and reform within the field's vocabulary are thought more than compatible; they seem to be phases in the great cycle of progress: open things up, then reform. But this doesn't happen in a strictly linear way. It's much more mixed up than that, and people in the field are often criticizing and proposing at the same time. At any one time, some people will focus more on criticism, others on renewal. A discipline might go through periods in which many participants agree that the project should be one or the other, in which critics get all the evil parts, say, while modest reformers keep inheriting the kingdom. In international law, the uneasy interaction between these two related impulses has long been a central drama. When international lawyers frame the field as stuck, they call out the critical troops. When it seems they know already what the problems are, they figure the discipline as ripe for movement forward to reform. When I have looked for "new thinking," or thinking "outside" the field's current vernacular, or thinking against the field's current political effects, it can seem that I'm simply endorsing the excessive by-product of the field's own commitment to reform, the distracting work of people who don't know when to stop.

I have never thought the distinction between critics and reformers was very helpful. Everyone is doing both. The distinction I have been interested in is between people operating within the disciplinary lexicon and people pursuing projects of criticism and reform outside it. But this way of stating the distinction is also misleading, for the boundaries of the field's self-conscious vernacular are porous. Once a blind spot or bias in the field's background assumptions has been identified, argument about it can easily become part of the field's routine vocabulary. And if we focus on political effects, it is very hard to tell when argument within the field's terms will be more effective than efforts to unblock the profession's background assumptions. We just don't have a good metric for identifying things that are "really" critical or effective or progressive or reforming or whatever. These are matters of contestation and desire, decided as much by audience reaction as by the script or the players. Creating the performative effect of having been critical, or innovative, or reforming is an alchemy of the professional situation, the projects and affinities of other actors, the seductive powers of the performer, the narrative desires of the audience, and more. Sometimes the most banal or commonplace observation generates all the heat of critical insight; at others, the most outspoken criticism reinforces the routines of the status quo.

In international law, moreover, the conventional debate between reformers and critics has never been a very balanced one. In a simple sense, it is only natural that individual international lawyers will often feel *other people's* ideas are stuck and need critique, but that they know, themselves, which way to go forward. Critique has a pretty short life in a progress narrative: who would want to invest in the background-looking techniques of ground clearing when the alternative is getting on with building a new society? It seems almost perverse not to see that at any particular moment it is better to look forward than back. We might say, as a rule of thumb, that for the energetic center of the discipline's mainstream, it always appears that the moment for critique has just passed and the moment for renewal is just dawning, just as, for those with a more critical impulse, more ground clearing will always seem necessary.

Even, perhaps especially, at moments of great disciplinary anxiety and self-doubt — American international law 1975–1989 — it can feel obvious that we know what is wrong and yearn always already for reconstruction.

As a result, it can be risky to volunteer for the role of critic when many others in the field have already cast themselves as reformers. International lawyers often feel that rejecting the critic for the reformer would *itself* be progress. Much of the literature self-consciously situates itself forward of critique in the urgent task of reorienting, restructuring, rebuilding, redirecting the field. Although the field has passed through periods of both bold enthusiasm and more anxious introspection, for a century it has been broadly accepted in the field's mainstream that *right now,* whenever that is, is not the time for criticism — that was last year. We know what the problems are, it is time to move toward solving them. By this posture — forward of criticism, toward renewal — the field guarantees its progressivity by arousing, and then renouncing, its own critical energy. Or by embracing, and then marginalizing, those who indulge too long the critical impulse.

It is very difficult to explain that one wants to involve people in intellectual work *without* rushing to renew or rebuild the discipline. At least not right away. It is not surprising that new thinking so often means a reconfiguration of the field's existing projects, or a shift in emphasis among enduring commitments. Although always a bit out of step with the establishment — viewing matters from a more rational and cosmopolitan point of view — international law has never been a radical spot, either intellectually or politically. The field's mainstream was rather quick to reject socialism, anarchism, Marxism, even anticolonialism in its most innovative and most challenging phase, and it has been very hesitant in absorbing the waves of intellectual innovation that have swept across the American legal academy in this century. Whereas American international lawyers have often criticized American foreign policy, enough to be largely left out of foreign policy making, they have rarely been in the vanguard of opposition. From Wilson forward, the discipline has offered a safe and modest platform for criticizing government action. If we think about internationally oriented third world intellectuals with innovative or critical energy, international law has provided a quite secure platform from which to criticize the "West" or "American hegemony" or the "global market," without embracing democratic socialism or any other alternative that might have political consequences at home. The exceptions, of course, would be various human rights campaigns, most notably perhaps the anti-apartheid struggle, but here again, we rarely find international lawyers in the vanguard. We find them translating political initiatives into long-term, often procedural language with which to instruct what they imagine to be an international establishment mistaken about its true interests.

Indeed, the key disciplinary contribution has been refracting these political and intellectual sympathies through the lens of a rational, cosmopolitan sensibility. This viewpoint *is* an original intellectual and political accomplishment. The repeated practice of criticism and renewal has produced a voice that performs the virtues of *speaking to power from a high place*. This is a very seductive voice. Speaking it requires that one manage one's interest in criticism and reform to place oneself ever so slightly forward of common sense, that one be, in a word, *savvy*. Savvy is the voice of the very best newspaper editorials. Taking on the field's vocabulary will mean forgoing the pleasures and powers of sounding savvy. And all I have to offer is the intuition, and from time to time the experience, that there are other pleasures and other powers.

In this sense, the international law profession is more than a professional lexicon, it is also this voice and viewpoint, and a whole bunch of people pursuing projects with and against one another. It never seemed to me that the discipline could be renewed by an idea, that one could write a great criticism of some doctrine and people would simply stop using it, that one could articulate the limitations of the professional lexicon and people would stop speaking it. And anyway, that would be a very lonesome project. The field builds itself, renews itself, pursues its vision and enforces its biases as a performance for an audience, as a project among people. My idea is that a project of criticism/reform that wants to step outside that vernacular would have to do the same: articulate a voice and viewpoint, a sensibility, style, or character more than a plan or proposal.

For a start, this means developing a strategy about the audience and the situation. It might be just my personality, but it has always seemed clear to me that my own project would likely have little resonance among either senior figures in the field or those of my own generational cohort most concerned about strengthening international law's role in the establishment. Perhaps if my project had been to renew the international legal vocabulary so that the discipline could return to power the situation would be different. Of course, the elder figures most wedded to the earlier particular arrangement of schools — at Yale, at Columbia — still might not have been interested. But senior figures who were a bit offside that debate, who were on the lookout for new energy, who yearned for someone to promise the return of their disciplinary vocabulary to the national intelligentsia's lexicon of savvy thinking could be expected to be supportive. And it would not be that difficult to forge an age cohort alliance: this is the new thinking we need if this discipline is going to get us back to power. Something like this seems to have been part of the situation and strategy for the transnational–legal process–liberals as they sought to reorient the field after the cold war.

I have always assumed that the better audience for my own project would be younger people and people outside the power struggles of the international law discipline with the rest of the American foreign policy establishment, in other disciplines, in other countries. Of course, people in the established field have been terribly important, as friends, as mentors, offering encouragement, training, criticism. And you can't have any project about the field unless you can get and maintain a foothold somewhere in it, and for that you must appeal also to people older and more established than yourself. And for all the discipline's mechanisms of, well, discipline, it can also be a porous and welcoming place, open to being entertained and even energized by a project that seems provocative or new.

Still, I have written and taught primarily to appeal to people not yet committed to the discipline's vocabulary and mission. This can be a pretty tough audience too, of course. Let us imagine law students who come to international legal studies with critical energy and reformist enthusiasm. It is difficult to compete with the promise of becoming savvy. Sometimes people who just know they already *are* savvy can become intrigued by the idea of adding something a bit exotic to their repertoire. And sometimes people who fear they never will be savvy, geeks and those who feel like outsiders at the party for various reasons, can be attracted to a project that seems to arrange status in different ways. Some people get interested if there seems to be buzz around the project, the teaching, the group. Some people come with political projects of their own and seek to make an alliance; people opposed to one or another project associated with the field might think they could learn more about criticism or find a sympathetic intellectual and social milieu for their own efforts. What I don't imagine is that there are lots of students out there reading and comparing different "approaches" to international law and deciding which one makes the most sense intellectually. But there might be some.

In pitching an extravernacular project to this audience, you need to have some sense for the sources of their interest and their resistance. Although most students begin rather skeptical even of the existence of international law—as law, as a profession, as a possible lifestyle, as a solution to the world's ills—they do quickly become quite savvy about foreign policy, about law, about the possibilities for international governance. For most, criticism remains a rusty tool, harnessed to enthusiasm for the reform of the day. It is often startling how fluently they already speak the voice of the jaded but hopeful professional. Of course, law students are already rather well assimilated to the professional establishment and its status quo culture of modest reform. Learning about international law may simply provide a new terrain for displaying a well-developed posture. But young lawyers and scholars are also drawn into the discipline's project, come to share its will to power as their own. Energy to do something for international society— make peace, strengthen the global market, promote development, and so forth—is somehow harnessed to work both *for* the discipline and *on* the discipline, improving international law, procedures, governance, institutions, norms, that they might then make or simply *be* a contribution to the international community. There may remain skepticism about international law's power, but the idea that the discipline itself might be part of the problem gets lost. Alongside the critical impulse and the cautious skepticism arises an intense desire for international law to exist and a fealty to the project of its renewal.

At least in the United States, for many young lawyers and law students, taking up international law, even at its most conventional, is already a gesture of both professional rebellion and personal renewal. It isn't clear what the career options are in international law. It is clear that the political and professional posture of the field is somewhat offside the mainstream of the legal profession. Young international lawyers in the United States often feel they are rejecting, or toying with rejecting, or hoping for an escape from more conventional legal specializations. They know that they are embracing marginalization in some way; they have to explain having chosen international law to their parents, to their peers, and to themselves. They might explain it as a moral and political commitment—to better global governance, world peace, human rights—or as a reflection of their diagnosis of the future: things are becoming more global.

It is not *all* rebellion, of course. These young people also hope or expect that their choice will be redeemed by experience, that in the future everything will be international. There might be something chic in being a cosmopolitan internationalist, jetting around, seeing the big picture. There might somewhere be a spiffy career as well. But it is also not corporate or intellectual property or commercial law. As a result, just becoming an international lawyer can feel like the expression of a broadly critical impulse. By comparison, all the rest of law seems too parochial or insufficiently humanitarian. At least in the United States, the field has been associated with pacifism, with critique of the American empire, with the progressive movement, with the left, with law as an instrument of social change, as well as with an insistently pluralist and cosmopolitan attitude toward the national political and legal culture. The mainstream players in the field announce themselves as "the left" in the national political culture, suggesting that if you are critical of *their* vocabulary you must be pretty wacky indeed. This places demands on the field, demands that the field live up to personal and professional choices that have already been or, more likely, are in the process of being made. These demands are familiar from other self-consciously humanitarian professional disciplines: poverty law, public interest law, increasingly all fields of public law.

It is not surprising that, having chosen a marginal discipline to express a humanitarian commitment or more general critical impulse, one is defensive about anything that would challenge the identity of the discipline. But the motive to build the field is stronger still. One is attracted to international law because it promises a professional domain that will institutionalize or routinize one's critical or humanitarian impulse as a professional practice. The discipline's routine practices become themselves signs of humanitarianism or cosmopolitanism. This demand for a routinization of professional virtue places the discipline in a difficult spot. Surely the current modes of practice only rarely offer this opportunity. The field is marginal, misunderstood, a sideshow to both the parochialism of national law and the vagaries of international politics. Something will have to change. To promise an establishment practice that sets itself against both national elites and the world of diplomacy, international law has its work cut out for it.

But the mainstream discipline has a pretty good strategy for filling this bill. International lawyers constantly reiterate — to one another, to themselves, to anyone who will listen — a belief in historical progress toward internationalism. They are also committed to the idea that in a global world, the broadly liberal, cosmopolitan, and rationalist sensibility they embody is and will be a virtue. This commitment lies so deep that to argue it explicitly, as has been tried from time to time, comes across as vaguely vulgar and unnecessary. To ensure that the field will be ready when the world gets international, to be sure that its practice will rightly express a cosmopolitanism appropriate to that future world, to be sure its commitments will be recognized and embraced once the establishment understands the direction of history, all those in the field must meanwhile — and this is the crucial step — work nonstop to align the field with progress. If the field is virtue's future, work on its updating can only be a sign of grace. And so the good work of the field becomes work on the good field, paddling out, aligning the board, adjusting our weight, watching the water, waiting for the wave.

As a result, the classroom situation is not neutral. It is against something (the field up to now), it is for something (reforming international law), and it is waiting for something (the historical progress of internationalization). There is certainly a critical element here: whatever has kept the field marginal in the past must be rejected, and urgently. But there is a limit to this impulse: the point is to support international law and get it back into the mainstream to become, as the world progresses, ever more the voice of the international establishment or "community."

At least since the late nineteenth century, many international lawyers have experienced international law as both a commitment and a modest transgression, and this posture has become something of a professional identity. It is in this sense that to be an international lawyer is less to know a canon of cases or treaties than to have mastered the exhibition of a particular fantasy about one's progressive role among the governing elites. One has the tools, talents, and habits of *appearing as* one who tells the establishment where its real or long-term interests lie, speaking to power, not exactly as truth, but as the view from a point high above national pettiness, subjectivism, parochialism, offering a cosmopolitan and rational analytic standpoint as an ongoing professional practice. On offer are not simply ideas and expertise, but also an identity and a project. The field's promise turns into a program and a practice: for both students and senior figures, expressing and reaffirming the professional identity of international lawyers normally fulfills (and exhausts) both critical and renewal impulses. In some way, it would be progress if more people in government and out viewed matters as international lawyers do.

There is no doubt that this impulse to affirm their professional identity by renewing the field sometimes makes international lawyers willing to risk and challenge the broader establishment, as it sometimes makes them creative in their approach to practical problems. Affirming the international lawyer's position, viewing the elites from a higher, more cosmopolitan and rationalist point of view, speaking to them from this great height, can be a challenging political intervention. But more often it makes the field timid, careful to preserve its own (now marginal) status in the name of a future boldness.

How this plays depends in part on the distribution of projects and powers in the field at a given moment. Near the end of a period of consolidation, a discipline can look stuck, can have trouble promising the pleasures and powers of savvy thought. A student with an extravernacular project looks out at a relatively unified field of ideas stretching from those just a few years older through to those nearing retirement. When I started in international law in 1980 there were few people in their twenties, thirties, or forties working in the discipline, and things had been intellectually stable for quite a time. In such a situation, new thinking is not that difficult to get going; often, many of the field's own familiar tropes have lain long dormant and need only be revived. There was also a lot of new thinking lying around in neighboring legal fields that had not yet been imported. For someone with the project of disciplinary renewal, a certain kind of will to power and the project of opening the field to criticism for, say, apologetic participation in an unjust status quo, it was not that difficult to figure out what to do.

The situation now is quite different, after more than a decade of anxious disputation. The lions of the early 1960s are still there, alongside the anxious, critical, and unsettled voices of the past decade. But there is also the Clinton cohort, riding into leadership in the field on the strength of their proposals for renewal. Each proposal has its idiosyncracies, but there is a broad sense that it is time to move forward from disciplinary doubt and disputation into a new consensus for a new millennium. There are already several dozen partially worked out renewal projects on the table, each of which needs help. These new ideas exert the intoxicating pull of affiliation with and submission to very well-established voices claiming to represent possibilities for statecraft and professional leadership.

We might look at the situation from the point of view of law students who have become interested in international law as a field of study and potential career option. They face a set of strategic choices. Some calls for renewal, of course, will blow over. But some of these new vocabularies will stick, and some of the current leadership's reform ideas will be implemented. International law might well migrate from administration to adjudication, from litigation to alternative dispute resolution, from multilateral standard setting to tradable permits. In a way, the field demands that young international lawyers select among the various renewalist projects on offer. Renewalists of my generation all need the energy of today's enthusiastic students to ride their ideas across the track from new thinking to established wisdom. Will the field be renewed by economics or political science? By adjudication or alternative dispute settlement? By trade law or human rights? In an important sense, today's students will decide.

They will decide in part by their career choices. Most renewal projects associate themselves with a career trajectory, the making-real-as-a-project of their intellectual appeal to practitioner-beings. If transnational adjudication is the thing, one should work for a nongovernmental organization bringing human rights cases in U.S. courts. If economic law is the thing, one should work for a firm in Washington advising interest groups on the use of trade law, the world's new "constitution," to expand or contract social regulation. If political science is the thing, one should do a joint degree, and work in the foreign relations establishment on projects of global "governance," building a multilateral "regime" as a multilevel game, and so forth. In many ways, the test of a new way of thinking about international law is precisely whether it theorizes an emerging practice, bringing the field in from the cold of marginalization to implementation in a now-really-for-the-first-time internationalized establishment. Those ideas that turn out to describe emerging professional practices, either because they predicted correctly or because they helped influence the emergence of the practice, are more successful academically. By building careers in the sector identified by one or another renewalist theory, they both confirm and help extend the theory. As a result, the siren call of academics in the discipline is strong. Sign up now to ride the latest wave — you can both build a new establishment and then run it.

Precisely because the debate about "new thinking" in international law has placement consequences, however, our students will want to proceed cautiously here. Students of international law, like other law students, learn a lot in the effort to select a career path and find a job. There are lots of strategic issues, not unlike those that face practicing lawyers across their career. Which fields of law are hot? Will they still be hot in five, ten, twenty years? Which way is the practice moving: larger or smaller firms, regional or national or global practices, one-stop-shopping or niche markets? You don't want to become an antitrust specialist because it will offer interesting ways to think about public regulation of the market just before they stop enforcing the antitrust rules for ten years or stop seeing it as an arena of public regulation. Similarly for litigation or environmental law or land-use planning. When I was in law school, the chic alternative to firm practice was management consulting; ten years before it had been government, ten years later it was investment banking. Then Internet startups and stock options. But for how long? Imagine you had settled into the field of security studies with all its terrifically sophisticated vocabulary about throw weights and elaborately modeled computer games in 1985, just before the end of the cold war would push the silo counters firmly to the margin. Or perhaps gone off to bring law to the developing world in 1965, shortly before disillusionment with the American empire and with the potential impact of liberal law on economic development dried up all the grant money.

In international law, it is not simply a matter of selecting a domain of practice with staying power. If one goes into international law as a commitment, signing up for a collective project to build a better international governance structure, the viability of the commitment will depend a great deal on what happens to the sector one selects. The experience of a career — the buzz, if you like — will vary dramatically depending on where one is working. Imagine you had gone enthusiastically to the United Nations Secretariat in 1963, full of excitement for changing the world and riding the wave. Downer. Well, looked at now, will Amnesty International or Greenpeace be part of a broad project of disciplinary renewal in five years? Is CNN a better bet than the State Department? Citibank better than the World Bank? Will the daily work in human rights advocacy continue to feel connected to a broader aspiration to transform international society, or will it become a narrow specialty? We might think here of poverty law, refugee law, or legal services over the past thirty years: the career is still there, but the buzz has altogether changed.

A similar thing happens at the level of ideas. Much of the professional work of international lawyers in the United States participates in a polemic about and in favor of international law. Selecting among the renewalist options on offer is not merely to select a domain of practice, it is also to select a polemical style that will become part of one's professional identity. Will you be the sort of international lawyer who is always trying to get norms adopted, or trying to work loosely with whatever principles seem to be lying about? Either way you will connect better with some people in your office and less well with others. It is quite common in practice environments for people to feel bonded to one another because they share an implicit understanding about what is hot and what is not. Imagine a human rights organization that has participated in one multinational UN conference cycle after another: suddenly a few people get hired who "know" that it's not worth it to codify another generation of human rights, what everyone should now be doing is litigating in domestic courts.

As students shop among the renewal proposals now on offer in the discipline, there is some danger that they will become stuck between generations, acolytes of ideas that now seem new but that will be pushed from fashion five or ten years from now. Of course, this might not happen; these might also be the students who push some of us a few years out off the stage. There is no reason to think my generation is entitled to a long run at the top, and there seems to be lots of loose and exciting energy in the field just at the moment among people under thirty. In a way, the dissensus among those thirty to fifty has its up side; it may be a while before consensus settles. There is already a right wing in the field that simply ignores the new center. They may all soon be gone; each of their proposals might fizzle for want of resonance with the establishment of the young, and today's students would get a shot at dominance rather than submission. But that might not be their project in the first place.

My own hope is that as today's students select among proposals and projects on offer in the field, they will also be interested in keeping a spark and energy alive to think beyond the discipline's current frame. That has been my own project: to draw out the dissensus a bit further, to slow the emergence of a new disciplinary middle way. Of course, whether that makes me a traitor to my age cohort or just another guy with a proposal, I leave to the audience. I should say, though, that drawing out the dissensus, exploring the edges and difficulties, hanging on to the ambivalence of the post–cold war moment does not translate directly into a mode of practice. It is certainly a project in the academy, but beyond that, what I have in mind is a kind of professional project that we would have to make up as we go. I thought I would conclude with some reflections on my efforts to launch and sustain an extravernacular project in the field, to make known the dark side of the box.

One Project to Make New Thinking and Make It Known:
New Approaches to International Law

Looking back on my own extravernacular efforts, it is hard to know whether to foreground the development of "new thinking" or to situate my own project in a world of commitments, aversions, affiliations, and wills to power. One could probably tell the story either way. In my own mind, it probably had phases in which I would have described it more as one or the other. What I can remember is that as I began teaching and writing, I tried to set aside the discipline's normal assumptions about what international law is and is for: that international law is a set of broadly universal norms governing relations among states rather than the professional practices and culture of particular people in specific contexts, that the discipline's goal is to strengthen "international law" against the forces of "politics" or "national interest," that international law is basically a good thing and that there should be more of it, that the discipline's central intellectual challenge will always and forever be to square respect for sovereign autonomy with a governable international community, that international lawyers function best as technocratic handmaidens to statecraft.

Perhaps, I imagined, we have lots of law and not enough politics; perhaps international law and the "international community" do as much harm as good; perhaps another question — about identity or cultural difference, or inequality, or social justice — could be placed front and center; perhaps international law could be better understood in cultural or intellectual terms, as a professional disciplinary project for its own sake, disconnected from the giving of advice to statespeople. These were not "new insights" about what international law should be about in the next millennium; rather, they were possible thought experiments, efforts to set traditional issues aside and see what we see. If it turned out that answering the field's central questions did, in some way, keep generating the same answers in wave after wave of "new thinking," it seemed better simply to leave these questions for the moment, to struggle for an attitude of agnosticism about all the issues that defined the poles between which the field had traditionally oscillated.

I don't want to underestimate the counterintuitive quality of the thought experiment, nor to propose it as a recipe. I tried to perform the posture, in teaching, in writing, in practice, of being an international lawyer, but not being at all preoccupied with the field's classic debates or doctrinal choices. Rather than inaugurate a sect within the field by presenting my own modest doctrinal or institutional readjustments as signs of a broad disciplinary renewal, such as by vowing to end the field's attachments to "sovereign autonomy" or "legal form," I experimented with escaping the oscillation between these classic alternatives. I tried to do this by running the arguments insistently, eagerly, in both directions at once and by foregrounding or drawing out the professional ambivalences in my audience. Often, this produced only befuddlement, I must admit. More critical friends scoffed at my insistence on the posture of being *in* the field, rather than in some larger, longer, more fashionable and erudite tradition of criticism. Many in the field thought it an oddly unhelpful performance, strangely uninterested in responding to the pressing needs for reform and disciplinary engagement. But sometimes it did work, as far as I could tell, to open up the idea of a space for collaboration in the field that might at least promise to look beyond the discipline's conventional preoccupations.

If I think back to the moment in the late 1970s or early 1980s when I began this project, there was always a question about its "politics." We need to remember a time when Reagan had momentum and Carter didn't, when the left, both in and outside the academy, seemed split between a tired and assimilated establishment and a world of sectarian identity projects, when the effort to purge critical legal studies from the American legal academy was in full and successful swing. It was strategy, it was personality, it was commitment, but I felt far more comfortable launching a project for "new thinking" than one for a revitalized "critical" or "leftist" practice in the field. At the level of strategy, I thought there would be more young people intellectually open to the idea that the existing disciplinary lexicon was preposterous than to the idea that it was evil or status quo. At that time, the earnest projects of the identitarian left seemed as rooted in a misguided disciplinary vocabulary as those of their adversaries.

This may all be different now, when the energy in the field lies with a resurgent and Clinton-inspired center-left. Perhaps an extravernacular project would be more successful now presenting itself as a more critical and potent outsider-left. People in the field, the mainstream, the identity mavens, all have metabolized the idea that their vocabulary is preposterous, but not that it is less useful than it claims, that it might even be counterproductive. In the 1980s, the reverse seemed more the case: people had gotten used to the idea that the field was useless, but they didn't think it was preposterous.

In any event, I focused on the plasticity and hyperbole of the vocabulary, even though that put off possible allies interested in more immediate political payoff. I should probably acknowledge that although left-liberal statespeople everywhere could probably be helped in their practice by better international law arguments, doctrines, and institutions, this has never been my first concern. I have never been opposed to trying to offer some, but in my experience, there are always lots of people stepping into that breach. We do not need to worry that the left-liberal establishment won't be able to think up good arguments for its hold, however tenuous, on state power. I think we are more in need of inreach than outreach: of looking at our discipline as a practice, as an intellectual project, with its own will to power, its own cultural contribution. Like any good dose of history, such an effort might help us avoid mistaking ideology for insight.

My intuition has always been that broad constitutional changes, changes in emphasis among the discipline's many ambivalent and contradictory ideas about how international governance ought to be achieved, seem like ways of *not* seeing, or of apologizing for other enduring injustices and systemic incapacities. At the same time, shared assumptions and commitments that lie just beneath the surface of the professional common sense and that seem implicated in these injustices are frustratingly difficult to bring to the forefront of the discipline's attention. It seems obvious to me, for example, that the most important work of perpetuating and normalizing the astonishing distributional inequities of our current world is done by the spatial division of the world's political cultures and economies into local and national units and by the conceptual separation of a political public law, which operates nationally, from an apolitical private law that operates internationally. We now think it obvious that poverty is a local problem, while wealthy people live more and more globally. But although these spatial and conceptual boundaries are legal productions, they are simply off the map of the discipline's concerns. I have spent most of my own disciplinary energy trying to figure out how the repeating practice of disciplinary renewal might entrench rather than eliminate background ideas like this.

Unfortunately, I don't think we yet have a very good idea about how this happens or how to avoid it. Why *are* spatial and conceptual ideas of this sort off the agenda when people speak of little else than rearranging space, "globalizing," ending sovereignty, and so forth? It is a real puzzle. It has something to do with colonialism, something to do with the distinction between public and private law, something to do with attitudes about cultural difference and geography, something to do with images of the natural differences between law and politics. It seems bound up with the difference between procedural and substantive matters in national and international law. We could perhaps date it: to nineteenth-century territorialization? To colonial expansion in the seventeenth century? To twentieth-century efforts to unbundle sovereignty, rights, and personality, if only ever partially? It has something to do with the ideology of "development" and "participation" and assumptions about what is a fact and what is more plastic, political, or legal. There are some good projects picking away at these problems, but this whole line of inquiry remains speculative, partial, groping.

Perhaps as a consequence of the very preliminary nature of the inquiry, this line of work has not produced anything like a program for action or disciplinary renewal. I don't think I, or to my knowledge anyone else, has discovered a list of methodological errors or political mistakes, on the order of "too much sovereignty" or "too much formalism" or "not enough political science" or "too few women" or "too few third world nationals" at the drawing board, which cleanly account for the difficulties I am worried about, and whose elimination or reversal could therefore easily inspire a program of action. As a result, I am thrown back on the idea that we need to keep thinking before we rush to reform the field along any general line, not for any philosophical reason, and certainly not because I am not interested in reform, but because I haven't yet seen any critical work that has produced so clean a line or direction.

When I started out in international law with this sort of impulse in the early 1980s I was more or less on my own in the field. There were lots of generous folks among the senior figures who were receptive to a young person with energy, but my most important intellectual and professional support came from people who were pursuing similar projects in other fields. As I was trying to figure out how to think about international law, my most helpful intellectual interlocutors were mentors associated with critical legal studies who were completely outside the field, as well as my age cohort of assistant professors who were pursuing projects of criticism and renewal in other fields — contract law, trade law, family law. We read things together, tried to understand the lines of analysis that had been developed around the critical legal studies movement and the intellectual work of people in other fields who we had heard had an impulse that might turn out to be similar to our own. We differed in our attitudes about our work: some of us were more interested in reform than others, some more convinced of the plausibility of our own field's available modes of analysis than others. As I remember it, none of us was sure how our own particular projects related to modes of criticism already present in our fields. Would we end up uncovering a recipe for reform, or would our work put the field's reform terrain under question in some broader way? We weren't sure, but some of us were more optimistic one way or the other.

As we tanked up intellectually for work in our various disciplines, our reading was not particularly systematic. The process was, at least in my experience, extremely interactive: a group of people learning together how to express our own intellectual, political, or libidinal impulses. In this sort of a project, the work of a "significant" intellectual — say, Foucault or Derrida — who was in vogue at the time was often helpful, and we puzzled together about numerous then-famous theoretical texts. But it turned out that texts written by our mentors and by one another were equally, often even more useful in terms of epiphanies per paragraph. As were conversations. The first people I met in international law who were at all interested in this project were students. Some had long been interested in international law but were somehow dissatisfied with the modes of renewal and analysis on offer. They had at least a vague intuition that if something stronger or more "radical" was out there, they would be interested. Others were far more sophisticated about critical methods and far more widely read in theoretical matters than I, and were willing to become interested in international law if the field could be made to seem a worthy terrain for development of their intellectual muscles.

In the early 1980s I met Martti Koskenniemi at a conference in Geneva; he was the first international lawyer I met who seemed interested in the project I was trying to pursue. We exchanged manuscripts and began a friendship. Soon thereafter I met Philip Allott, like Martti a person with significant experience in his foreign ministry, an established international lawyer, and a European at that, who seemed to have an analogous project. Someone told me I might like a book by Tony Carty called *The Decay of International Law* and I read it. Günter Frankenberg spent a year at Harvard teaching comparative law in the early 1980s and became a close friend. We began discussing our frustrations with the way foreign law study was undertaken. My old law school colleague Joel Paul began teaching international economic law, and we started talking about his critical intuitions in that field. We read Dan Tarullo's work together. And so it went, for the better part of a decade, while I got tenure, experimented with practice in the field of various sorts, dabbled in the neighboring fields of European Community law and international trade.

I had a couple of exceptionally good groups of students, and several went on to careers in the field. I began a long collaboration with Nathaniel Berman, Karen Engle, Ileana Porras, Annelise Riles, Leo Specht, and others. During this period other people were developing a strong feminist approach to international law, and our paths kept crossing. Several people I knew, including some, like Hilary Charlesworth, whom I had met as students, were also interested in launching a broad feminist reexamination of the field. There were lots of overlaps between what my friends and I were doing and what mainstream feminists in the field were doing, but also lots of points of difference, and we had lots of discussions and arguments. Karen Engle's work on international human rights became something of a canonical intersection among these groups, as did Hilary's work and later that of Karen Knop. Fred Snyder and Lew Sargentich, then in charge of the somewhat moribund International Graduate Program at Harvard, had the idea that foreign students could form a far more cohesive and intellectually engaged cohort of colleagues and we began thinking about how that could be brought about. Throughout this period, as I was writing about the intellectual history of the field and seeking to capture the discipline's mainstream consciousness, I was very much helped by the support and encouragement of people in the field like Tom Franck and Louis Sohn, who made my representations of the discipline's thought more plausible by their example and careful criticism.

It is a weird experience to write critically about a field from within its voice, and I tried to write in a bunch of different styles that I cobbled together by imitating articles I liked. It took experimenting to have a sense of what would come across too strong, what would be too weak to be provocative. Lots of things I wrote fell flat, never got read, or succeeded only in offending people. After lots of rejections from all the major law journals, I stopped submitting manuscripts to them and simply published wherever I met someone sympathetic or could get solicited to write by promising to speak at a symposium or conference. Getting tenure had taken its toll, and the original community that had sustained my effort unraveled. Getting a plausible tone in an academic or professional talk, managing to sound engaged yet be heard as somehow critical, simply being comprehensible, figuring out who the audience might be, was and remains a real challenge. I found myself increasingly writing and speaking for an imaginary younger person in the back of the room, a person who might turn out to have a critical impulse of his or her own, rather than for senior colleagues. In 1989 I left the academy to practice with Cleary, Gottlieb,

Steen and Hamilton in Brussels. My commitments to academic work had always competed with the desire to do something more hands-on and I had gotten interested in the law of the European Community on a sabbatical in Brussels five years earlier. I really enjoyed the teamwork and intensity of practice and let the critical project lie dormant for a time.

Nevertheless, by the time I returned to the academy there were probably a dozen law teachers and international lawyers beginning their careers who felt, to one degree or another, that they had a project in common with one another, and also with me. I don't think that any of us had a clear grasp of one another's work. I would say it was more that we recognized one another as people who had as a project mounting a more thoroughgoing criticism of the field of international law than we had seen. By early in the Clinton years, the situation had changed considerably. I suddenly had responsibility for a large number of foreign graduate students at Harvard, and some of them seemed, as Fred Snyder had predicted, more interested in developing critical and innovative intellectual work than most American law students at the time. In all this, the importance of leading intellectual institutions, their intellectual capital, reputation, resources, in the development of something that can seem "new" or critical is hard to ignore. The whole experience would have been quite different had I not been fortunate early on career-wise.

As it turned out, I suddenly had a fantastically energetic new group of friends in the graduate program, led by Jorge Esquirol and Athena Mutua. Of course, most of our work had nothing to do with a critical intellectual project; we were trying to improve the foreign program, to raise the status, profile, and quality of foreign legal education within Harvard. Most of the students and most of our program initiatives were oriented to other student and faculty constituencies. But I also got the chance to work with a number of advanced students from all over the place who were interested in new thinking and who formed something of an intellectual community with one another, a community that reminded me of the group with whom I had worked in the first years of my career with other young assistant professors. They read a range of then-fashionable theory together, puzzled over one another's texts, learned from one another's projects. I began to organize my own international law course around the work of my friends and students, offering their work as a continual counterpoint to more conventional materials in the course. By the early 1990s there was enough work to offer a wide range of quite different critical vantage points on many, if not yet most, of the conventional doctrinal topics. A wide enough body of scholarly work (with lots of cross-citations) had been published to provide the basis for the network of friends-sharing-a-project to be noticed by people who were not part of the conversation.

Not all the recognition was favorable, of course, or even particularly related to the actual content of the work. Mainstream authors tended to assimilate us all to whatever they imagined "critical legal studies" or "feminism" to have been in other legal fields. We were variously thought to be policy types or Marxists or Grotian eclectics; people repeatedly would interpret our work as if it had set out to respond to the field's enduring questions in the available lexicon. In a way these were generous readings — at least we were being interpreted *into* the field — although readers were often frustrated at what seemed our obscurantism in stating what, as it turned out, was always already old hat. And sometimes we were also read as simply off point, interested in something that was not international law, unhelpful as it was in pointing the way to immediate reform. Most puzzling, we were all understood to be saying the same thing, when even we often couldn't see what our work had in common. The first people who produced broad and critical analyses of our work were often students, including my own, seeking their own way in the field by recapitulating and rejecting what they understood to be our project. In an odd twist, it was these dismissive essays that first got the group recognition. I took the opportunity of some lectures in Greece to try writing a more sympathetic introduction to the work produced to that point, but my text ended up being way too dense to be useful.

Once the group came to be recognized as a group, and had received critical notice, my relation with new students and colleagues shifted. At least some students came to my courses already thinking of me as somehow different or critical or just "new." For some students, of course, this is seductive, although sometimes this enthusiasm substitutes for any real engagement and the student ends up thinking one stands for whatever he or she came in thinking of as "critical." More often, this sort of identification makes students wary, suspicious that everything one says is part of a "line," that they are not really learning the field, that the teacher will not validate their own reform enthusiasm. I shifted my own teaching quite starkly to read classic materials in the field as carefully as possible, hoping to make it unmistakable that we were learning and exploring the consciousness of mainstream international law. I began taking numerous votes in the class and teaching from the sensibility of the class majority, while foregrounding their own ambivalences. Critical recognition and reaction also made students who were, for one reason or another, skeptical about the field easier to recognize and engage.

As I became known to embody something "new," opportunities to speak and write increased. I began looking for younger colleagues and students who seemed to respond to the vague idea that "we could do something different," could go beyond the range of particular reforms now on display. There was a sort of implicit deal in my relations with these people as I came to know them: I would tell them what I knew about existing modes of critique in the field and they would share their own intuitions about how these critiques might be extended or where we might look for promising critical or reform ideas. Students or colleagues in other places often had an idea about some new vein of theoretical material that could be mined or brought to the discussion a new political or disciplinary preoccupation.

As it turned out, people who came into the project in the early 1990s differed a great deal from one another. Some were interested in pursuing theoretical critiques rooted in one or another branch of social theory they had studied. One person wanted to apply "autopoesis" to international law, another had been influenced by Lacan, another by Baudrillard, still another by Bourdieu, another by Spivak and Bhabha. Some were interested in expressing a critical impulse within and about adjacent fields, particularly comparative law and international economic law. Some were interested in developing criticisms of modes of analysis they had become familiar with in other fields: law and economics, law and society. A large number became interested in the group to see if we could help them understand and express the disaffection they felt with other public interest–oriented internationalist fields. We had a large number of people who had lost faith in the "human rights" field, which by the early 1990s had in many ways lost its initial luster.

Perhaps the largest group of people who came into the milieu to express dissatisfaction with international law did so to express or understand their own experience as outsiders to the mainstream of the profession. Many of these people were intellectuals from the third world, who were far more identified with international law than were American students; it was already a real profession for them, as well as an important identity in their own local establishment. At the same time, many were also frustrated by the difficulty "third world voices" had in articulating criticisms that did not fold easily back into the standard modes of modest reform. They were sometimes willing to work on developing new ways of understanding and criticizing the tradition from the inside, while encouraging the broader group to focus more attention on the exclusions and biases of the international law tradition.

Some foreign students were more interested in the ways their own local legal cultures were understood, both at home and abroad, through the disciplines of comparative law and area studies. There were often students from the Middle East or Asia or Latin America frustrated by the available traditions of area studies in the United States. I began to learn from them about the similarities and differences between the disciplinary limitations of comparative and international law. Others were women frustrated by the limitations of a "women's rights" approach in expressing their feminism within international law. The now expanding milieu was appealing, I think, to people who came with critical projects of their own and who were open to the idea that the humanitarian promises and practices of mainstream international law might not exhaust their critical or progressive ambitions. And some people were attracted to the milieu simply because it seemed like something was happening, like there was buzz, perhaps like that which was remembered or imagined to have been part of earlier moments of intellectual innovation and change in law associated with critical legal studies or the early moments of the law and society movement. We picked up the occasional person interested in legal theory with no prior interest in international law. Some people frustrated with the normalization of critical race theory, or hoping to launch a more active network of critical legal scholars interested in Latina/Latino affairs, or interested in generating a queer theory alternative to the mainstream gay and lesbian rights movement came to meetings and began influencing the group.

In short, the group was anything but homogeneous. There were deep national differences: the East Asian types influenced by postcolonial theory, the American human rights types straddling the line between reform and critique, the African scholars interested in renewing third world legal studies, influenced by third world nationalist and socialist traditions of criticism. The particular political projects of participants also differed, from becoming an organic third world intellectual, to doing something concrete to improve the situation of women in development, to opposing neoliberal trade policy in the name of expanded labor rights. There were all the classic tensions between African men and East Asian women, between Latin

Americans and Asians, and so forth. And of course, all this was overlaid by numerous interpersonal struggles for recognition, affiliation, domination, of students by teachers and teachers by students, of competition among mentees and mentors. Sometimes these different projects could be kept in conversation, but sometimes they couldn't. People got discouraged or angry or felt betrayed or used and left, carrying on their projects elsewhere or simply becoming demobilized.

While we were working to sort out these differences, the field of international law also changed. The broad consensus that had stabilized the field in the United States from the early 1960s had begun to break down. There were now other people of my generation who had also been working in the mid- to late 1980s to renew the field along lots of different lines. And there had been the dramatic changes of 1989, ending the cold war. My generational cohort shared a commitment to the field and a sense that the field had lost its way. Although our interest in international law had kept us somewhat distant from the methodological disputes that had divided American legal education in the 1980s, we had come through our legal education and our early professional development in law at a time when legal thought was divided methodologically and politically. It was not surprising that we would end up reflecting the range of theoretical and political commitments fashionable in legal education more generally — from critical legal studies, through left-liberalism, law and society, legal process, the interdisciplinary policy analysis of specialized fields that emerged from international business transactions, through to public choice theory and law and economics. Most renewalists of my generation did not share my own critical impulse and were more interested than I in the field's conventional problems, doctrinal and institutional choices. But suddenly the project I had been pursuing with friends and colleagues was one "new thinking" effort among many. Moreover, while we had been preoccupied with our own internal discussions, a completely alternative group of disciplinary outsiders had emerged among younger international law teachers who were more traditionally leftist and progressive, more enthusiastic about human rights, and more linked to American identitarian movements and methodologies.

By the mid-1990s, I found myself less the apostle of all things new than a positioned polemicist. I was associated with a particular intellectual project, a self-conscious effort to build a collective intellectual project of disciplinary criticism and renewal, which I called, I hesitate to say, New Approaches to International Law, or NAIL. I called it "new approaches" to suggest a big tent, interested in the widest range of innovative energy without predetermining where it would lead. I also wanted to differentiate the group from critical legal studies, which had accumulated a lot of baggage by then. For many young scholars and students, critical legal studies seemed at once passé and dangerous, too politicized, too much associated with a "line" of some sort. The NAIL was not a movement of ideas or the working out of a general disciplinary problem, but a specific effort by a group of legal academics in particular institutions to encourage one another's work, hold conferences, write more and differently, get to know people they would not otherwise have met, experiment with new methods and ideas. We did not start with an insight or a disciplinary program, although we all came to think about international law as a legal intelligentsia with its own cultural politics and will to power rather than as a pragmatic handmaiden to governance.

In the 1990s, there were a series of academic meetings: at the European Law Research Center at Harvard held in Essex, Massachusetts, in October 1993; at Northeastern University in October 1994 (organized by Karl Klare); at the University of Connecticut in April 1995 (organized by Joel Paul); at the University of Wisconsin in June 1996 (organized by David Trubek and his Global Studies Research Program); at Utah College of Law in October 1996 (organized by Karen Engle, Mitch Lasser, Ileana Porras, and Tony Anghie). There were meetings abroad as well: at ONATI in Spain in June 1994 at the European University Institute in Florence in July 1993; at the International Institute for Peace in Vienna in 1993 (organized by Leo Specht); at the Real Colegio Complutense in Madrid in 1992 (organized by Enrique Alonso); at the University of Athens in May 1994 (organized by Iannis Drossos)—when people associated with the group had institutional resources to hold a meeting. During the years that I was director of the Graduate Program at Harvard Law School, some of the conferences and workshops organized by Harvard students brought NAIL-related academics together in Cambridge. We held an international feminism workshop (organized by Stella Rozanski), a postcolonial group (initiated by Tony Anghie), a meeting on private law theory and on progressive uses of law and economics (organized by Duncan Kennedy), a conference on third world approaches to international law (organized by James Gathii), and a conference bringing critical race theory, law and development, and postcolonial theory into discussion with one another (organized by Robert Chu).

Along the way a number of us tried a variety of typical academic initiatives to keep people talking with one another, to bring new people into the group, to provide an outlet for people's work: producing a symposium issue for a law journal, doing a collection of essays as a book, publishing a bibliography of people's ongoing work, keeping a mailing list of those who had come to meetings or were interested in staying in touch. This institutionalized effort lasted about ten years, depending on how one counts, beginning in the late 1980s. In the spring of 1998, we celebrated the end of this institutional project at a conference in Cambridge which we called "Fin de NAIL: A Celebration." Of course, one can't simply decree a network of people and a set of ideas to an end. There remain lots of echoes and side projects and successor groups active in many places. But I had lost some battles, my own institutional effort ended, and I sought to retire the moniker NAIL. There was some disagreement about drawing this phase of the effort to a close. My successor in the Harvard Graduate Program often asked me why I was ending it. Some combination of lost institutional resources and an intuition that this particular formula had run out its string, that the factoid NAIL was about to overtake whatever interesting work we were doing.

The numbers were always quite small. By 1998, I would say something like 500 people had come to one or another NAIL-related event, we had about 350 people on a mailing list, there were perhaps 20 people with professorships, about half of those in the United States, who put organizational energy into the project. There may have been as many as 50 younger scholars working on dissertations or beginning an academic career who were interested, at least vaguely, in NAIL-related work. About 200 came to the 1998 Fin de NAIL celebration. The number of people who helped organize this activity was also pretty small; perhaps a dozen or two over the lifetime of the project were central to the events. Since the NAIL project finished, a large number of its participants have extended our collaboration in other contexts: in the American Society of International Law, in the Helsinki Summer Program for International Lawyers, in a range of smaller reading groups and workshops. From time to time I have brought together people who participated in the project in small reading groups to critique one another's work, as well as to put together smaller conferences around more specific themes: the role of antiformalism in legal thought, the relationship between ideas about structural bias in law and ideas about identity.

Intellectually, the project was always rather diffuse. I was interested in public international law, others were interested in women's rights, in nationalism, in social theory, in colonial history. The NAIL offered an opportunity for cross-training, for those interested in feminism to learn about the economics of development policy and vice versa. For me, the most surprising, pleasurable, ambitious, even crazy aspect of the NAIL was the range of intellectual themes and disciplinary subsects brought to the party at various points. And of course, each constituency had to struggle with its own divisions and differences. Early on quite deep differences emerged between the Europeans and Americans in the group: the Europeans more devoted to the field of international law, the Americans more interdisciplinary; the Europeans more rigorous in their theoretical thinking, the Americans more interested in a sprawling network of questions related to constituency groups and identity politics. Those most interested in public international law were often European and male, preoccupied with historical studies and philosophical inquiry, although some were women frustrated with the tradition of human rights activism or developing a broader feminist critique of the field as a whole. There was a shared project — escaping the hypocritical and utopian lethargy of the pre-1989 field, or the neoliberal triumphalism of the post–cold war discipline — but there was no shared set of ideas or commitments or critiques.

Although some of us were friends, there were lots of people in the group who didn't particularly get on. Many of the public international law scholars who worked with the NAIL had taken my course at Harvard or elsewhere, but many had not. And it was not all public international lawyers by any means. Those most interested in international economic law were more technocratic in orientation, interested in trade liberalization and harmonization, often in the European Union context. Some were focused on strengthening public policy capacity in particular areas: labor standards, environmental protection, immigration. There were specialists in media or telecom, scholars interested in economic development, in private law theory, in comparative law. Many of these were people who had no preexisting interest in international law per se; they came to the group through study of local government, welfare policy, critical legal studies, or because they were friends with someone or had heard it was a fun scene. Linking public and private law in a common project meant that lots of public international law people had to learn about international economic law and vice versa. Private law people had to get over their phobia of politics and public law people had to get over their policy, math, and economics phobias. There were also a number of people who were not particularly interested in either international law or trade policy, who were focused on identity issues: third world nationalists, postidentity diasporic intellectuals, third world nationals frustrated by the limitations of the human rights establishment, activists and literary theorists, queer theorists, not to mention men and women. A great deal of what went on under the heading of New Approaches to International Law was simply the working out of differences among all these constituencies.

There always seemed to be some disconnection between how I experienced the NAIL from the inside and how it was understood by the broader discipline. I was constantly being asked to write a brief summary of what NAIL people thought or to describe "the NAIL point of view" on something. The heterogeneity and yearly changes in the preoccupations of the group as one after another group of people placed their own concerns at the center of our activity would have made this difficult in any event. But it was also always difficult to explain why we didn't fit easily into the existing range of "schools of thought" about international law, to explain how one might foreground a different range of issues and questions. Efforts, like this one, to explain the effort in human rather than pragmatic terms always risk being dismissed as self-indulgent or not serious. As the group came to be known, moreover, it was difficult to avoid its acting as a sort of ink blot onto which people could project whatever they imagined the most salient critical issues to be.

For example, in the early years after the end of the cold war, people interested in international affairs at my own institution often seemed polarized, with the NAIL label somehow implicated in broad divisions between those who were generally optimistic about American hegemony and the emerging neoliberal consensus among international economic and humanitarian institutions and those who were more pessimistic about America's role in the world, between those who embraced political science and those more comfortable with cultural studies or economics, between those committed to liberal universalism and those more interested in the third world or in cultural identity, even between those who were women and those who were men. These are all important differences, to be sure, just as the difference between those who thought judges overstated the determinacy of law and those who thought critics overstated its indeterminacy was once a marker for the difference between mainstream and critical postures in the

American legal academy. But one can easily overstate differences of this sort, just as one can overstate the difference within the discipline between criticism and reform. There was always far more political and methodological agreement, crossover, and confusion than such a neat polarization suggests. Indeed, these differences initially had little to do with the preoccupations of the NAIL. And yet, as the foreign and American student body became more polarized along these lines, I found myself cast as opposition to neoliberal hegemony, and my colleagues in the international law field who seemed outside or hostile to the NAIL efforts were understood to be far more optimistic defenders of American neoliberal hegemony than they were. After some time, people drawn to the project by the set of polarized images went on to place the critique of neoliberal economic and political internationalism squarely on the group's agenda.

I was often aware that people who had not been involved with the group (and, in fairness, some who had) described it as a "cult" or "clique" or, more kindly, a "school of thought" united by a set of ideas or ideological commitments, or by fealty to a group of charismatic fanatics. It won't be surprising to hear that I didn't experience it this way. From the inside, I was constantly struck by the difficulty of keeping so many disparate marbles from rolling off the table, at the resistance within the group to learning from one another, at the difficulty of getting anyone in the circuit to restate anyone else's idea clearly. Of course I did try, with differing degrees of success, to influence others in the group to work on things I was interested in and pursue lines of inquiry I thought promising. And I also wanted to submit to the group's discipline, as an alternative audience and as a source for new ideas or avenues of inquiry.

I think the effort to see activities like the NAIL as cults is quite similar to the tendency by mainstream eclectics to think of schools of thought in terms of adherence to a set of propositions or methodologies, or by secular people to speak about religious groups as all "believing" in this or that. If your own project is to insist on the ecumenical, pluralistic, and rational openness of the mainstream or establishment, then it will be difficult to think of yourself as part of a "school" or "group" or "religion" and easy to think of those who are setting aside the mainstream preoccupations as unencumbered by differences of opinion or commitments to pluralism and rationality. In my own experience, however, it's just not so. Not for religion, not for international law, and not for the NAIL. Indeed, in my own experience, the disciplining effects of mainstream insistence on preserving broad unresolvable debates while inflating modest doctrinal or institutional differences into matters of deep principle are themselves intensely sectarian.

Indeed, the group was filled with projects of intellectual affiliation and disaffiliation, as well as dominance and submission. Most of our events were structured as encounters between quite different tendencies: American critical race scholars, postcolonial theorists and people interested in developmental economics, or feminists and third world men interested in human rights, or Arabs and Israelis interested in progressive law and modernization, and so on. These discussions always seemed to me in danger of collapsing, as Latin Americans and Africans or South Asians and Arabs suddenly found it inconceivable to be part of the same endeavor. The Europeans and Americans, those with and without an affinity to critical legal studies, women and men, third world men and first world women were always in danger of refusing to engage. I don't think we ever figured out much of an intellectual basis for alliance among these different constituencies, other than the idea that one should "attend" to the interests of other constituencies who might be part of one's audience. Various of these constituencies connected with one another at different times, in partnership, in charismatic association, in opposition, in symbiotic arrangements of authority and submission. But if I look back on the NAIL for methodological tips about getting the spark of critical energy to light, I would probably point first to this obsessive effort with cross-training and building a broader imaginary audience for people. A large part of what was going on was encouraging people to imagine that one might write for this weird and diverse group of people rather than for those within one's preexisting specialty or affinity group.

But it is true that we sought to make some ideas known that were not known, to articulate a criticism of the disciplinary lexicon as a whole, and to link its blind spots to bias in the world. We had things in common, overlapping projects of political or intellectual commitment. For all the difficulty of our internal alliances and the diversity of people who became interested in the NAIL, there was also, at least some of the time for some people, the experience of being part of an undifferentiated ego mass, of sharing something — a commitment, a project, an experience — with a large group of others in a way otherwise unavailable in one's experience of either a professional context or disciplinary identity.

My guess is that the basis for this feeling was more a sensibility than a set of ideas. One could probably name a sort of canon of works that many people in the NAIL would have heard about or read: Koskenniemi's *From Apology to Utopia,* Berman's piece on international law and cultural modernism, my own "Spring Break," Lama Abu-Odeh's piece on the veil, Duncan Kennedy's "Hale and Foucault" and *Critique of Adjudication,* Knop's "Re/statements," Anghie's piece on Vitoria and colonialism, Danielsen and Engle's *After Identity.* There were undoubtedly others as well, but I'm not sure very many people in the group could state very clearly the arguments of even the "canonical" texts. Nevertheless, we did develop a group vocabulary, which changed over time. For the last NAIL conference I wrote down a list of slogans in an effort to capture some of that vocabulary, to remember what words we had used to generate the feeling of being outside the disciplinary vernacular. When I read them out there was laughter at their routinization into slogans, some cheering at favorite propositions. Here is the list, many items of which are in tension with one another:

- Write history against the progress narrative.
- The politics of international private law.
- Law as culture.
- Not interdisciplinarity but counterdisciplinarity.
- There is more than one market.
- Economics is multiple (subslogans: institutionalism, path dependence, unstable equilibrium).
- Link internal and external critiques.
- Down with proceduralization, with process, with participation.
- Be skeptical about the sites of liberal political engagement, about human rights, about the new "civil society."
- Engage the new "civil society," support new social movements, seek postdevelopment strategies.
- Identities are important. *After Identity.*
- Identities are hybrids and constructs and projections.
- Celebrate intersectionality/the first world in the third, the third world in the first.
- Read liberalism symptomatically, its doctrines and institutions the surface face of a desire.
- Be alert for the will to power.
- Embrace the dark side — of modernism, of law, of liberalism.
- Ambivalence Rules: perilous, pervasive, personal, political ambivalence.

Whenever the ideas that move a group get codified, they quickly seem stable. This list seems somehow flat to me now, but not because I've given up on these ideas. Quite the contrary: they each are embedded in bits of work and still are worth thinking about. We certainly didn't exhaust their application or interpretation in the field. But a voracious critical energy often does devour its best ideas, outrun its own slogans. As energy like that which animated the NAIL goes on in other ways, these forms disappear. If I think about people whose work vibrates with critical energy today, some are elaborating these ideas, others have reached elsewhere, working on the comparative legacy of antiformalism, on the renewal of law and development, on the interface between human rights and development policy, on the legal culture of Latin American identity, on connections between critical space theory in local and global settings. The story moves on. Perhaps the NAIL goes on as well.

What did it all add up to? There were, in the end, lots of paradoxes about the NAIL. It was an eclectic project, a project of difficult alliances and unfinished dialogues, of growth by cross-training and interdisciplinarity. For some people it provided the satisfying experience of being part of an undifferentiated ego mass; for others this always left a bitter taste. It was a committed intellectual project. The work was there; we had some ideas about questions that might be explored, projects that might replace the field's canonical inquiries and ambivalences. Some of the work was better than the people who produced it, better than the group that inspired it, and some was a lot worse. I'm not a very reliable witness on that.

But as I've said, I don't think about "new thinking" as a set of methods or ideas or propositions. For me new thinking is a performance. I imagine that when dancers and choreographers think about their work, it must be interesting to look at videos, to study choreographic notation, to find recognition in empathetic reviews, but dance remains somehow inexorably a performance. It happened, and people who came, who danced, who choreographed, who played had an experience that would otherwise not have been available to them. When I think of the NAIL, I think of it as a performance artwork. There was a sensibility, there were moments of intellectual engagement when people felt the presence of innovation, when the bonds of conventional wisdom relaxed, when the discipline suddenly looked altogether different. Some people wrote things up, and taught things, and did things in the world afterwards, but to my mind these are largely dead things. At the Fin de NAIL celebration many participants knelt down to hammer a finishing nail into a charred and fur-bedecked chunk of wood Günter Frankenberg had brought along. It was a disturbing ritual, and the relic remains an arresting mark of our endeavor together.

As one participant, I found in the NAIL a place where the spirit of new thinking lived for awhile for some people. There will be others. This book might be one. There is certainly a kind of empty feeling sometimes when the dancing stops, a nostalgia for favorite moments on tour when the production folds. But performances are also affirmations: that dramatic things are possible, that people do get together, that affiliation is possible, that projects can find their way to expression, that quotidian practices don't exhaust the possible. Of course, performance art doesn't just happen either. We can think about how to stimulate and support initiatives that might be animated by this sort of spirit. It might have something to do with decoupling critique from reform, with setting aside the discipline's template of institutional, doctrinal, and theoretical alternatives. It might have something to do with the anger and distance and hope people outside the field can bring to its central operations when given the opportunity. It might have to do with intellectual cross-training in the discipline's margins. And also with friendship and mentoring, with the mutual pleasures of commitment and aversion, domination and submission.

The animation for my own choreography has been the ambitious idea that terribly important questions — about society, poverty, governance, and also about ourselves as professionals — are not being attended to by the mainstream intelligentsia and that we can aspire to address them. Not simply as a form of cultural politics, not as back-office work for the party in opposition, but also not simply as creative play. I have in mind a shared sense that description matters, that things are terribly misrepresented, and that correcting, changing, influencing what is understood, what is seen, what can be asked can be a matter of passion and politics. I've noticed that you can sometimes ignite someone's creative impulse by providing a terrain that is not quite fully assimilated to the establishment or the mainstream, that provides a safe hint of ongoing opposition and possibility. Something terrific can happen when people who share this sense find ways of telling one another, of touching, itching, expressing the animus within. My own experience is that people — doctoral students, young lawyers — sometimes really turn on the gas if they see plausible professional life outside the mainstream, if they become convinced that intellectual work can be more than assimilation, credentialization, or work on the self.

This is probably not a project for everyone in the audience. It exploits a kind of division in the professional world sometimes marked by subtle and ephemeral questions of style and starting point and sensibility that are hard to describe. It might divide people who think things are basically legitimate from those who do not. Or those who believe in the unconscious and those who do not. Or "people of the body" and "people of the mind." Or those with a critical impulse and those with a more conventional will to rule. Those who are interested in genealogies of inequality and desire and those more interested in systemic restatement and renewal. Or those who begin intuitively and those who find rationalist modes of understanding and explanation largely satisfying. Those who are comfortable with ambivalence and those who are not, those with modernist and those with premodern sensibilities. I am not sure any of these distinctions would stand up under much scrutiny. But for me, "new thinking" is less a matter of new methods or ideas or programs than a lived experience that can split the audience along lines like these.

Such a common intellectual project also takes (and needs) institutional shape: as a series of conferences, a bibliography, an intervention in particular institutional and professional settings. It takes shape with all the anxieties of influence, contamination, exclusion, suffocation that attend collective work. These sorts of institutional settings are pretty ephemeral; the project attracts hostility and misdescription, the initiative passes to others, there are the routine professional coups d'état and disagreements. Someone with critical energy has some institutional resources — a journal, a class, a program, publishing space — and tries something. And the form can become rigid, a factoid one cannot escape, prisoner of imposed misdescriptions. The resulting institutional changes can really shock the project. Losing a slice of bureaucratic power here or there can change who is involved. Initiatives just getting going can collapse, people who seemed well-established can lose the incentive or space to connect with one another. Without a base camp, the initiative can flounder. I am sure a lot of this went on as the NAIL initiative and my association with the Harvard Graduate Program ended.

The sensibility I have in mind can also shed the skin of these forms, can move to another institutional frame and intellectual question. It is worth celebrating moments when this sort of thing comes together, and I am very proud of all that went on in the NAIL in this last incarnation. But I do not think we got to the end of the effort to figure out what the discipline should do. I can say that on our best nights, we performed what the discipline can be. There will be other performances, projects, parties. Perhaps some new NAIL will emerge. If I hear of anything, I will be sure to let you know and hope to see you there. And if you find yourself with an exciting project of criticism and innovation or if you see the light on far off down some road and think something great might be going on, call me. I've got my dancing shoes polished, and I'd love to come along.

Note

I would like to thank Nathaniel Berman, David Charny, Dan Danielsen, Karen Engle, Janet Halley, Duncan Kennedy, Martti Koskenniemi, Alejandro Lorite, and Hani Sayed for conversations about this essay.

WENDY BROWN

Suffering the Paradoxes of Rights

It is hard to acknowledge that liberal individualism is a violating enablement.
— Gayatri Chakravorty Spivak, *Outside in the Teaching Machine*

This essay does not take a stand for or against rights, but rather, seeks
to map some of the conundrums of rights for articulating and redressing
women's inequality and subordination in liberal constitutional regimes.
The essay responds to the question posed by the organizer of an American
Philosophical Association session as that session's title: What is the value of
rights language for women? An impossible question in many ways, especially when it is uninflected by historical, political, or cultural specificity, I
nevertheless took it as an opportunity to consider, at a very general level,
the difficult relation between select contemporary feminist ambitions and
rights discourse in the United States. There is a certain political immediacy
to the study of this relation, given the transposition of venue from the
streets to the courtroom of many social movements over the past two decades. If much of the struggle against male dominance, homophobic practices, and racism now dwells irretrievably in the field of rights claims and
counterclaims, what are the perils and possibilities of this dwelling?

■

Speaking for the disenfranchised in loose cross-cultural fashion, Gayatri
Spivak depicts liberalism (and other modernist emancipatory formations)
as "that which we cannot not want."[1] This from a Derridean Marxist
postcolonial feminist critic keenly aware of what liberalism cannot deliver,

what its hidden cruelties are, what unemancipatory relations of power it conceals in its sunny formulations of freedom and equality. Indeed, Spivak's grammar suggests a condition of constraint in the production of our desire so radical that it perhaps even turns that desire against itself, foreclosing our hopes in a language we can neither escape nor wield on our own behalf. Patricia Williams refigures this condition of entrapment as one that might be negotiated through dramatic catachresis. Forcing rights out of their usual ruses of abstraction that mystifies and universalism that excludes, she insists that we procure them for "slaves . . . trees . . . cows . . . history . . . rivers and rocks . . . all of society's objects and untouchables."[2] Albeit in a very different register, Drucilla Cornell argues in parallel with Williams, insisting that women's right to "minimum conditions of individuation," and in particular to an imaginary domain in which a future anterior is not beyond women's grasp, is the surest way to finesse the trade-off between liberty and equality that liberal rights discourse is generally thought to force.[3] Yet even in Williams's and Cornell's critical yet ultimately utopian rapprochements with rights discourse, there is a tacit confession that recalls Spivak's own weary recognition of the historical limits of our political imagination. If we are constrained to need and want rights, do they inevitably shape as well as claim our desire without gratifying it?

Given the still precarious and fraught conditions of women's existence in a world ordered by a relentless construction and exploitation of sexual difference as subordination, certainly rights *appear* as that which we cannot not want. Our relative reproductive unfreedom; our sexual violability and objectification; the highly exploitable character of much of our paid and unpaid labor; our vulnerability to losing our children, means of subsistence, and social standing when we resist compulsory heterosexuality — all of these require redress if we are not only to survive in this world but amass the strength and standing to create a more just one. And the panoply of rights women have acquired in this century — to vote, work, and divorce; to keep our children when we deviate from sexual norms; to not be sexually harassed at work and school; to have equal access to jobs and be paid equal sums for the work we do side by side with men; to prosecute sexual violence without putting our own sexual lives on trial; to decide whether, when, and how we will have children; to be free of violence in our homes — these are things we cannot not want. And if these acquisitions remain tenuous and partial, then surely procuring and pressing our rights to them can only abet the process of making them more certain possessions.

Yet this very list of our historical woes and their minimal redress over the past century through a proliferation of rights for women also recalls that rights almost always serve as a mitigation — but not a resolution — of subordinating powers. Although rights may attenuate the subordination and violation to which women are vulnerable in a masculinist social, political, and economic regime, they vanquish neither the regime nor its mechanisms of reproduction. They do not eliminate male dominance even as they soften some of its effects. Such softening is not itself a problem: if violence is upon you, almost any means of reducing it is of value. The problem surfaces in the question of when and whether rights for women are formulated in such a way as to enable the escape of the subordinated from the site of that violation, and when and whether they build a fence around us at that site, regulating rather than challenging the conditions within. And the paradox within this problem is this: the more highly specified rights are as rights for women, the more likely they are to build that fence insofar as they are more likely to encode a definition of women premised on our subordination in the transhistorical discourse of liberal jurisprudence. Yet the opposite is also true, albeit for different reasons. As Catharine MacKinnon has rightly insisted, the more gender-neutral or gender-blind a particular right (or any law or public policy) is, the more likely it is to enhance the privilege of men and eclipse the needs of the women as subordinates.[4] Cheryl Harris and Neil Gotanda have made similar claims about race and the "color-blind" Constitution.[5]

The first part of the paradox might be understood as the problem that Foucault painted most masterfully in his formulation of the regulatory powers of identity and of rights based on identity. To have a right *as* a woman is not to be free of being designated and subordinated by gender. Rather, though it may entail some protection from the most immobilizing features of that designation, it reinscribes the designation as it protects us, and thus enables our further regulation through that designation. Rights ranging from the right to abort unwanted pregnancies to the right to litigate sexual harassment have presented this dilemma: we are interpellated *as* women when we exercise these rights, not only by the law but by all the agencies, clinics, employers, political discourses, mass media, and more that are triggered by our exercise of such rights. The regulatory dimension of identity-based rights emerges to the extent that rights are never deployed "freely," but always within a discursive, hence normative context, precisely the context in which "woman" (and any other identity category) is iterated and reiterated.

The second paradox is the one illuminated by Marxist and neo-Marxist critiques of liberalism: in inegalitarian orders, rights differentially empower different social groups, depending on their ability to enact the power that a right potentially entails. This is not to say that generically distributed rights offer nothing to those in the lower strata of such orders — First Amendment rights offer something to all — but that, as countless critics have pointed out, the more social resources and the less social vulnerability one brings to the exercise of a right, the more power that exercise will reap, whether the right at issue is sexual freedom, private property, speech, or abortion. And still another conundrum of rights comes into play here. To the extent that rights such as private property rights are exercised not only against the state but against one another in economic arrangements in which some gain at the expense of others, universally distributed rights function not only as power but as deprivation: the right to private property is a vehicle for the accumulation of wealth through the production of another's poverty. Some in feminist jurisprudence and critical race theory argue that free speech functions in similar fashion: hate speech against historically subordinated peoples and pornographic male speech is said to enact the silence of its subjects. Antiabortion activists have argued that women's right to abort limits the fetus's right to its future as a person, and advocates of gun control have argued that an absolutist reading of the Second Amendment compromises the safety of all citizens. The point is that even as rights that are gender-specific entrench the regulation of women through the regulative norms of femininity, rights that are neutral and universal potentially entrench the subordinated status of women by augmenting the power of the already powerful. The paradox, then, is that rights that entail some specification of our suffering, injury, or inequality lock us into the identity defined by our subordination, and rights that eschew this specificity not only sustain the invisibility of our subordination but potentially even enhance it.

There are still other variations on this dilemma. Consider the manner in which feminist legal reformers often appear pinned between a tendency, on the one hand, to inscribe in the law the experience and discursive truths of *some* women which are then held to represent all women, and, on the other hand, to render gender so abstractly that the particulars of what constitutes women's inequality and women's violation remain unarticulated and unaddressed. This is a recurring problem not only in the political and legal debates concerning pornography, where it has been extensively rehearsed, but in sexual harassment law and numerous corners of divorce and custody law. What understanding of the interconstitutive powers of gender and sexuality is lost when sex discrimination (as sex harassment) is cast as something that women can do to men? On the other hand, what presumption about women's inherent subordination through sexuality is presumed if sexual harassment is understood as a site of gender discrimination only for women? What do women lose — in economic standing and custody claims — when we are treated as equals in divorce courts, and yet what possibility of becoming equals — of sharing responsibility for child rearing with men and of having equal potential for earning power — is forfeited if we are not treated as equals in this setting? Similarly, if some women experience pornography as a violation and others maintain that it is sexual prudishness, shaming, and regulation that constitute their unfreedom, what does it mean to encode one or the other perspective as a right in the name of advancing women's equality? Hate speech legislation has presented a parallel dilemma: whereas Mari Matsuda insists that hateful racist speech is "shattering" and "restricts its victims in their personal freedom" and Charles R. Lawrence III claims it is equivalent to "receiving a slap in the face," Henry Louis Gates and others claim a different experience of racial invective and fear its legal restriction more than its circulation.[6] In the pornography dilemma and the hate speech dilemma, two related problems emerge: first, how to restrict hateful speech or pornography in the name of equality and through civil rights discourse without, on the one hand, inscribing certain victims of hatred as its permanent victims (i.e., as permanently hatable) and without, on the other hand, making all persons equally viable as victims of such speech, thereby forfeiting a political analysis that recognizes the specific function of hateful epithet in sustaining the subordination of historically subordinated peoples. In other words, how can rights be procured that free particular subjects of the harms that porn, hate speech, and a history of discrimination are said to produce without reifying the identities that these harms themselves produce? Second, how to navigate the difficulty of differences within marked groups: this woman feels oppressed while that one feels liberated by pornography; this black person is shattered, that one almost indifferent to racial invective; one gay man is devastated by homophobic slurs, another speaks them.

A second, related dilemma is that rights procured specifically for women tend to reinscribe heterosexuality as defining both what women are and what constitutes women's vulnerability and violability. This problem emerges whenever it seems that "woman's difference" must be addressed. Indeed, gender tends to be treated as synonymous with heterosexuality in the law, not only because most "gender issues" are framed in terms of heterosexual women, but also because sex and sexuality are treated as two different bases of discrimination. The framing of reproductive freedom primarily in terms of accidental and unwanted pregnancy — the need for abortion — represents the first problem; conventional codes of nondiscrimination, in which gender and sexual preference are distinct and unrelated items in a list, represent the second. Of course, legal reformers working on behalf of gay and lesbian rights have actively sought reforms in laws pertaining to childbearing, adoption, and custody by homosexual parents, and have struggled as well to make visible homophobic harassment in schools and workplaces, but this only reaffirms the extent to which these issues, defined as gay and lesbian issues, are understood as separate from the project of securing *women's* rights. The problem here is not just that heterosexuality continues to be naturalized and normalized by these moves while other sexualities are marginalized, but that the extent to which the category woman is itself produced through heterosexual norms remains completely untouched by this approach. In sum, the process by which women become women, by which both woman as signifier and woman as effect of gender power is produced and sustained, is eschewed and thereby reinforced by the heteronormativity of most women's rights projects. Put more generally, the rights that women bear and exercise as women tend to consolidate the regulative norms of gender and thus function at odds with challenging those norms.

This problem emerged in a complex way in the case heard in 1997 by the Supreme Court on same-sex sexual harassment, in which a man claimed that he was repeatedly subjected to sexual harassment on the all-male offshore oil rig where he worked. The plaintiff in *Oncale v. Sundowner Offshore Services* argued that same-sex harassment ought to constitute discrimination, whereas the defense argued that a man harassing another man could not constitute gender discrimination, either because there was no gender difference between the parties or because there was no way to establish that the victim had been harassed *because* of his gender. (If there had been women on the oil rig where the harassment occurred, the defense argued, perhaps the putative harasser would have treated the women in the same way.)[7] The questions raised by this argument, indeed by the Supreme Court Justices themselves, are many: Does gender discrimination transpire only when women and men are treated differently, even if both can be sexually humiliated or subordinated? Is there no sexual harassment, or simply no gender discrimination when one humiliates both women and men? Does sexual harassment, defined as gender discrimination, not exist if it is equally deployed against both women and men by a single agent (i.e., are bisexuals inherently incapable of committing the act of sexual harassment)? Does sexual harassment as currently defined in the law then depend on the sexual orientation of the putative harasser? The confusions in this case suggest, among other things, a disadvantage in the move to cast sexual harassment as gender discrimination if gender discrimination is something that can happen to anyone and be perpetrated by anyone. (This disadvantage does not mitigate but does complicate the fact that the *Meritor* [1986] case, which established sexual harassment as gender discrimination, involved a critical feminist recognition about the relationship between women's subordination and sexual harassment.) These confusions also reveal the extent to which classification of sexual harassment as gender discrimination tacitly defines gender heterosexually. More broadly, they reveal the extent to which sexuality and gender have been folded together in the rights designed to protect women from injuries sustained on the basis of heterosexually defined gender. That is, they reveal the extent to which the basis of the injury, the heterosexual designation of women, is reinscribed in the formulation of rights promising redress.

I want to make brief mention of two other paradoxes in the framing of feminist aims in terms of rights. The first pertains to the problem of the compound production of subjects, theorized most prominently in the legal arena by Kimberlé Crenshaw as the matter of "intersectionality" in black women's experience of racial and gender subjection; the second pertains to the problem of conflating acts with identity, theorized most prominently by Janet Halley as a dilemma for gay rights advocates working against sodomy laws.[8]

Crenshaw argues persuasively that to the extent that black women cannot have the social perils of their blackness, and hence their existence as black women, addressed within the terms of gender discrimination, gender functions as a category purified of *all* inflection by race, and hence as a tacitly white category. Historically, the fiction that gender is produced and regulated autonomously, independently of other modalities of social power, has been one of the most severe impediments to the development of a racially inclusive feminism, a feminism that does not require an analytic or political distinction between feminism and the experiences of women of color. Yet within civil rights law, it is nearly impossible to feature subjects marked by more than one form of social power (race, gender, age, sexual orientation, disability) at a time. Not only must plaintiffs choose a single basis on which discrimination occurred, but the widely divergent modalities of power through which racialized, gendered, and other dimensions of subject production (and injury) are achieved means that even well-intentioned critical legal scholars tend to focus on one form of social power at a time, or at best, sequentially.[9]

Here is the central paradox constitutive of this problem. On the one hand, various markings in subjects are created through very different *kinds* of powers, not just different powers. That is, subjects of gender, class, nationality, race, sexuality, and so forth are created through different histories, different mechanisms and sites of power, different discursive formations, different regulatory schemes. Thus, theories that articulate the workings of social class, or the making of race, or the reproduction of gender are not likely to be apt for mapping the mechanisms of sexuality as a form of social power. On the other hand, we are not fabricated as subjects in discrete units by these various powers: they do not operate on and through us independently, or linearly, or cumulatively, and they cannot be radically extricated from one another in any particular historical formation. Insofar as subject construction does not transpire along discrete lines of nationality, race, sexuality, gender, caste, class, and so forth, these powers of subject formation are thus not separable in subjects themselves. As many feminist, postcolonial, queer, and critical race theorists have noted in recent years, it is impossible to pull the race out of gender, or the gender out of sexuality, or the colonialism out of caste out of masculinity out of sexuality. Moreover, to treat these various modalities of subject formation as simply additive or even intersectional is to elide the way subjects are brought into being through subjectifying discourses, the way that we are not simply oppressed but produced through these discourses, a production that does not occur in additive, intersectional, or overlapping parts but through complex and often fragmented histories in which multiple social powers are regulated through and against one another.

Law and critical legal theory bring this problem — that distinctive models of power are required for grasping various kinds of subject production, yet subject construction itself does not transpire in accordance with any of these models — into sharp relief. Bracketing the sphere of formal and relatively abstract antidiscrimination law, where discrimination on the basis of a laundry list of identity attributes and personal beliefs is prohibited, it is rare to find the injuries of racism, sexism, homophobia, and poverty harbored in the same corners of the law. They are rarely recognized or regulated through the same legal categories and are rarely redressed through the same legal strategies. Consequently, legal theorists concerned with these respective identity categories not only turn to different dimensions of the law depending on the identity category with which they are concerned, but they often figure the law itself in quite incommensurate ways.[10]

Now, given these kinds of variations, it is unsurprising that concern with securing certain legal terrain does not simply differ, but often works at cross-purposes for differently marked identities. Privacy, for example, is for many feminists a site that depoliticizes many of the constituent activities and injuries of women: reproduction, domestic assault, incest, unremunerated household labor, and compulsory emotional and sexual service to men. Yet for those concerned with sexual freedom, with welfare rights for the poor, and with the rights to bodily integrity historically denied racially subjugated peoples, privacy generally appears unambiguously valuable. Indeed, the absence of a universal right to privacy was the ground for invading Hardwick's bedroom in *Bowers v. Hardwick* (1986). This absence is also the legal basis on which surprise visits by social workers to enforce the "man in the house rule" for welfare recipients were tolerated for so many decades. Like rights themselves, depending on the function of privacy in the powers that make the subject, and depending on the particular dimension of marked identity that is at issue, privacy will be seen variously to advance or deter emancipation, to cloak inequality or procure equality.

If the powers producing and situating socially subordinated subjects occur in radically different modalities, which themselves contain different histories and technologies, touch different surfaces and depths, form different bodies and psyches, it is little wonder that it has been so difficult for politically progressive legal reformers to work on more than one kind of marked identity at once. And it has made it nearly impossible to theorize a socially stigmatized legal subject that is not single and monolithic. We appear not only in the law but in courts and public policy either as (undifferentiated) women, or as economically deprived, or as lesbians, or as racially stigmatized, but never as the complex, compound, and internally diverse subjects that we are. This feature of rights discourse impedes the politically nuanced, socially inclusive project to which feminism has aspired in the past decade.

Janet Halley's reflections on the figure of sodomy reveal a different dimension of the troubling way rights discourse not only reinforces the fiction of a monolithic subject but potentially regulates us through that monolith. In "Reasoning about Sodomy: Act and Identity in and after *Bowers v. Hardwick*," Halley explores the way the remarkably mobile and unstable signifier sodomy stabilizes homosexual identity through a routine conflation, by homophobes and homophiles alike, of sexual act with sexual identity. Although sodomy's technical definition (any form of oral-genital or anal-genital sexuality) itself undoes the linguistically achieved opposition between homosexuality and heterosexuality precisely by undoing the presumed singularity of the sex acts that take place on either side of the divide, the equation of sodomy with homosexuality (again, in both anti- and pro-gay discourses) resurrects the binary opposition between homo- and heterosexuality. Halley calls for exploiting the instability of the term, for dissociating act and identity, in part to establish more effective coalitions among those targeted by sexually repressive legislation, in part to expose the discursive mechanics of what she calls "heterosexual superordination."[11] To the extent that heterosexuals engage in sodomitical acts yet are immune from their stigma (and criminality) when sodomy operates as a metonym for homosexuality, homosexuals appear to be prosecuted not for the kind of sex they are having but for being associated with a kind of sex that heterosexuality disavows in order to mark its distance from homosexuality. The point for thinking about rights is not only that gay rights activists ignore at their peril the way the act-identity conflation works against them, but that rights in this context must be understood as shoring up a fictional identity, an identity premised on the fictional singularity of sexual acts that privileges while masking the privilege of heterosexuals.

What happens if we think about gender along the lines that Halley has mapped? To what extent is male identity as well as male superordination consolidated through the ontological disavowal of certain activities, vulnerabilities, and labors and their displacement onto women? If gender itself is the effect of the naturalized sexual division of almost everything in the human world, then rights oriented toward women's specific suffering in this division may have the effect of reinforcing the fiction of gender identity and entrenching the masculinist disavowal of putatively female experiences or labors, from sexual assault to maternity. More generally, to the extent that rights consolidate the fiction of the sovereign individual generally, and of the naturalized identities of particular individuals, they consolidate that which the historically subordinated both need access to—sovereign individuality, which we cannot not want—and need to challenge insofar as the terms of that individuality are predicated on a humanism that routinely conceals its gendered, racial, and sexual norms. That which we cannot not want is also that which ensnares us in the terms of our domination.

■

It would appear that a provisional answer to the question of the value of rights language for women is that it is deeply paradoxical: rights secure our standing as individuals even as they obscure the treacherous ways that standing is achieved and regulated; they must be specific and concrete to reveal and redress women's subordination, yet potentially entrench our subordination through that specificity; they promise increased individual sovereignty at the price of intensifying the fiction of sovereign subjects; they emancipate us to pursue other political ends while subordinating those political ends to liberal discourse; they move in a transhistorical register while emerging from historically specific conditions; they promise to redress our suffering as women but only by fracturing that suffering—and us—into discrete components, a fracturing that further violates lives already violated by the imbrication of racial, class, sexual, and gendered power.

Paradox is certainly not an impossible political condition, but it is a demanding and frequently unsatisfying one. Its master theorist in the Western tradition is Jean-Jacques Rousseau, whose thought stands historically as both incitement to and constraint on radical political aims. The constraint is generally attributed to his own penchant for paradox; indeed, Rousseau's aporias may be one of the reasons paradox has such a bad political reputation. But if Rousseau insisted that men must be forced to be free, and that the development of human culture is inevitably accompanied by a descent into unfreedom, inequality, and alienation, how much is the paradoxical nature of these claims the consequence of the discourse of progress, freedom, and human perfectibility into which he was speaking, and which he was also seeking to displace with an alternative discourse? In other words, to what extent can political paradox be read not as truth or confusion about certain political conditions, but as the constraints imposed by those conditions on the truths that may be uttered?

Paradox may be distinguished from contradiction or tension through its emphasis on irresolvability: multiple yet incommensurable truths, or truth and its negation in a single proposition, or truths that undo even as they require each other. But paradox also signifies a doctrine or opinion that challenges received authority, goes against the doxa. In *Only Paradoxes to Offer*, a study of nineteenth-century French feminists, Joan Wallach Scott parlays this definition into a political formation: "Those who put into circulation a set of truths that challenge but don't displace orthodox beliefs create a situation that loosely matches the technical definition of paradox."[12] Scott then suggests that the paradoxical utterances and strategies of the feminists she studied emerged as a consequence of arguing on behalf of women's rights, and of women's standing as individuals, in a discursive context in which both individuals and rights were relentlessly identified with masculinity. Thus, feminists were arguing for something that could not be procured without simultaneously demanding a transformation in the nature of what they were arguing for, namely, the "rights of man" for women. This rendered paradox the structuring rather than contingent condition of their political claims.

Scott's insight into nineteenth-century French feminism may be of help in understanding our own circumstances. First, the problem she identifies persists into the present, namely, that women's struggle for rights occurs in the context of a specifically masculinist discourse of rights, a discourse that presumes an ontologically autonomous, self-sufficient, unencumbered subject.[13] Women both require access to the existence of this fictional subject and are systematically excluded from it by the gendered terms of liberalism, thereby making our deployment of rights paradoxical. Second, moving beyond Scott's focus, even as invocations of rights for a particular subject (e.g., women) on a particular issue (e.g., sexuality) in a particular domain (e.g., marriage), all of which have been historically excluded from the purview of rights, may work to politicize the standing of those subjects, issues, or domains, rights in liberalism also tend to depoliticize the conditions they articulate.[14] Rights function to articulate a need, a condition of lack or injury, that cannot be fully redressed or transformed by rights, yet within existing political discourse can be signified in no other way. Thus rights for the systematically subordinated tend to rewrite injuries, inequalities, and impediments to freedom that are consequent to social stratification as matters of individual violations and rarely articulate or address the conditions producing or fomenting that violation. Yet the absence of rights in these domains leaves fully intact these same conditions.

If these are the conditions under which rights emerge as paradoxical for women, as simultaneously politically essential and politically regressive, what are the possibilities for working these paradoxes in politically efficacious fashion? Unlike contradictions, which can be exploited, or mystification, which can be exposed, or disavowal, which can be forced into confrontation with itself, or even despair, which can be negated, the politics of paradox is very difficult to negotiate. Paradox appears endlessly self-canceling, as a political condition of achievements perpetually undercut, a predicament of discourse in which every truth is crossed by a countertruth, and hence a state in which political strategizing itself is paralyzed.

Yet, it is telling that the language carrying the fatality of paradox occurs in the temporality of a progressive historiography: precisely the language Marx used in evaluating rights when he argued that "political emancipation certainly represents a great progress . . . not the final form of human emancipation . . . but the final form . . . *within* the framework of the prevailing social order."[15] Might the political potential of paradox appear greater when it is situated in a nonprogressive historiography, one in which, rather than linear or even dialectical transformation, strategies of displacement, confoundment, and disruption are operative? How might paradox gain political richness when it is understood as affirming the impossibility of justice in the present and as articulating the conditions and contours of justice in the future? How might attention to paradox help formulate a political struggle for rights in which they are conceived neither as instruments nor as ends, but as articulating through their instantiation what equality and freedom might consist in that exceeds them? In other words, how might the paradoxical elements of the struggle for rights in an emancipatory context articulate a field of justice beyond "that which we cannot not want"? And what form of rights claims have the temerity to sacrifice an absolutist or naturalized status in order to carry this possibility?

Notes

1. Gayatri Chakravorty Spivak, *Outside in the Teaching Machine* (New York: Routledge, 1993), 45–46.

2. Patricia Williams, *The Alchemy of Race and Rights* (Cambridge, MA: Harvard University Press, 1991), 165.

3. Drucilla A. Cornell, *The Imaginary Domain* (New York: Routledge, 1995).

4. Catharine MacKinnon, *Feminism Unmodified* (Cambridge, MA: Harvard University Press, 1987), 73.

5. Cheryl Harris, "Whiteness as Property," and Neil Gotanda, "A Critique of 'Our Constitution Is Color Blind,'" in *Critical Race Theory: The Key Writings That Formed the Movement,* ed. Kimberlé Crenshaw, Neil Gotanda, et al. (New York: New Press, 1995).

6. Mari Matsuda, Charles R. Lawrence III, et al., *Words That Wound: Critical Race Theory, Assaultive Speech, and the First Amendment* (Boulder, CO: Westview Press, 1993), 24, 68; Henry Louis Gates, "Truth or Consequences: Putting Limits on Limits," ACLS Occasional Paper 22, p. 19.

7. "Court Weighs Same-Sex Harassment," *New York Times* 4 Dec. 1997, A21. It is worth noting that the argument by the defense attorney that gender discrimination cannot be proven because there were no women on the oil rig where the harassment occurred tacitly cloaks the homosexual overtures of the accused by drawing on the trope of the sexually frustrated heterosexual prison inmate. Lacking available women to have sex with, this reasoning suggests, men will turn to or on one another, but this does not equate with homosexual desire. That this argument has enough salience to be advanced before the Supreme Court Justices, when it is unimaginable as a defense in the more conventional scene of a man harassing a female employee, further suggests both the impossibility and the necessity of conceiving gender and sexual discrimination simultaneously if gender justice is to be pursued.

8. Kimberlé Crenshaw, "Demarginalizing the Intersection of Race and Sex," *University of Chicago Legal Forum* 129 (1989), and "Mapping the Margins: Intersectionality, Identity Politics, and Violence against Women of Color," in Crenshaw, Gotanda, et al., *Critical Race Theory;* Janet Halley, "Reasoning about Sodomy: Act and Identity in and after *Bowers v. Hardwick,*" *Virginia Law Review* 79.7 (1993).

9. A handful of critical legal scholars escape this categorization, but, probably by their own accounts, none do so with complete success. See the work on race, gender, and sexuality in A. I. Wing, ed., *Critical Race Feminism: A Reader* (New York: New York University Press, 1977), especially Angela Harris's reprinted essay, "Race and Essentialism in Feminist Legal Theory." See also Cornell, *The Imaginary Domain,* which attends to gender and sexuality inside a single analytic frame.

10. For a fuller development of this argument, see Wendy Brown, "The Impossibility of Women's Studies," *differences* 9.3 (1997).

11. Halley, "Reasoning about Sodomy," 1770–71.

12. Joan Wallach Scott, *Only Paradoxes to Offer* (Cambridge, MA: Harvard University Press, 1996), 5–6.

13. The masculinism of liberalism generally, and rights discourse in particular, is something I discuss at length in "Liberalism's Family Values," chapter 6 of *States of Injury: Power and Freedom in Late Modernity* (Princeton, NJ: Princeton University Press, 1995).

14. I have pursued this argument at length in "Rights and Losses," chapter 5 of *States of Injury.* This is the paradox articulated as a troubling contradiction by Marx in "On the Jewish Question" in his recognition that civil and political rights for the disenfranchised both articulate that disenfranchisement and trivialize it as a simple failure of universality to realize itself. However, this paradox is also cast as a certain form of political possibility by Judith Butler in her argument that "the temporalized map of universality's future" is a kind of "double-speaking" by those who, "with no authorization to speak within and as the universal, nevertheless lay claim to the term." She argues: "One who is excluded from the universal, and yet belongs to it nevertheless, speaks from a split situation of being at once authorized and deauthorized. . . . Speaking and exposing the alterity within the norm (the alterity without which the norm would not 'know itself') exposes the failure of the norm to effect the universal reach for which it stands, exposes what we might underscore as *the promising ambivalence of the norm*" (*Excitable Speech: A Politics of the Performative* [New York: Routledge, 1997], 91).

15. Karl Marx, "On the Jewish Question," in *The Marx-Engels Reader,* 2d ed., ed. R. Tucker (New York: Norton, 1978), 35.

Lauren Berlant is Professor of English and Director of the Center for Gender Studies at the University of Chicago. She is the author of *The Anatomy of National Fantasy: Hawthorne, Utopia, and Everyday Life* (1991); *The Queen of America Goes to Washington City: Essays on Sex and Citizenship* (1997); and has edited *Intimacy* (2000); and, with Lisa Duggan, *Our Monica, Ourselves: Clinton, Scandal, and Affairs of State* (2001).

Wendy Brown is Professor of Political Science and Women's Studies at the University of California, Berkeley. Her most recent books are *States of Injury: Power and Freedom in Late Modernity* (1995) and *Politics Out of History* (2001). She is currently completing a study entitled "Retreat from Justice: A Critique of Tolerance in the Age of Identity."

Judith Butler is Maxine Elliot Professor in Rhetoric and Comparative Literature at the University of California at Berkeley. She is the author of several books, including *Bodies That Matter: On the Discursive Limits of "Sex"* (1993), *The Psychic Life of Power: Theories in Subjection* (1997), and *Antigone's Claim: Kinship Between Life and Death* (2000).

Drucilla Cornell is Professor of Political Science and Senior Scholar in Women's Studies at Rutgers University. She is the author of numerous works of political philosophy and feminist theory, including *At the Heart of Freedom: Feminism, Sex, and Equality* (1998), *Just Cause: Freedom, Iden-*

tity, and Rights (2000), and *Between Women and Generations: Legacies of Dignity* (2002).

Richard T. Ford is Professor of Law at Stanford Law School. His publications include "Law's Territory (A History of Jurisdiction)" 97 *Michigan Law Review* (1995) and "The Boundaries of Race" 107 *Harvard Law Review* (1994). He is coeditor of the *Legal Geographies Reader: Law, Power, and Space* (with Nicholas Blomley and David Delaney) (2000) and of the textbook, *Local Government Law, 3rd Edition* (with Gerald Frug and David Barron) (2001).

Katherine Franke is a Professor of Law and Codirector of the Center for the Study of Law and Culture at Columbia University. Her articles include "Theorizing Yes: An Essay on Feminism, Law & Desire," 101 *Columbia Law Review* (2001); "The Uses of History in Struggles for Racial Justice: Colonizing the Past and Managing Memory" 47 *UCLA Law Review* (2000); "Becoming A Citizen: Post-Bellum Regulation of African American Marriage" 11 *Yale Journal of Law & the Humanities* (1999); and "What's Wrong with Sexual Harassment?" 49 *Stanford Law Review* (1997).

Janet Halley is Professor of Law at Harvard Law School. She is the author of *Don't: A Reader's Guide to Military Anti-Gay Policy* (Duke University Press, 1989); "Recognition, Rights, Regulation, Normalization: Rhetorics of Justification in the Same-Sex Marriage Debate," in *Legal Recognition of Same-Sex Partnerships,* ed. Robert Wintemute and Mads Andenas (2001); and "Like-Race Arguments," in *What's Left of Theory?* ed. Judith Butler, John Guillory and Kendall Thomas (2001).

Mark Kelman is William Nelson Cromwell Professor of Law at Stanford Law School. He has written a good deal about how distinct conceptions of the dictates of the antidiscrimination norm might translate into distinct legal practices in a host of areas. He is the author of "Market Discrimination and Groups" 53 *Stanford Law Review* (2001) and *Strategy or Principle?* (1999).

David Kennedy is Henry Shattuck Professor of Law at Harvard Law School. He has practiced law with various international institutions, including the United Nations, the Commission of the European Union, and the firm of Cleary, Gottlieb, Steen, and Hamilton. He is founder of the New Approaches to International Law project and the author of "Spring Break," 63 *Texas Law Review* (1985); "The International Human Rights Movement: Part of the Problem?" 3 *European Human Rights Law Review* (2001); and "The Politics and Methods of Comparative Law," forthcoming in *Comparative Legal Studies: Traditions and Transitions* (2002).

Duncan Kennedy is Carter Professor of General Jurisprudence at Harvard Law School. He writes on legal theory, private law, housing, and law and development. He is the author of *Sexy Dressing etc.* (1993), and *A Critique of Adjudication [fin de siècle]* (1997).

Gillian Lester is Professor of Law at UCLA School of Law. She teaches Contracts and Employment Law. Her recent publications include "Unemployment Insurance and Wealth Redistribution" 49 *UCLA Law Review* (2001); "Restrictive Covenants, Employee Training, and the Limits of Transaction Cost Analysis" 76 *Indiana Law Journal* (2001); and "Careers and Contingency" 51 *Stanford Law Review* (1998).

Michael Warner is Professor of English at Rutgers University. His most recent works include *Publics and Counterpublics* (Zone 2002), *The Trouble with Normal: Sex, Politics, and the Ethics of Queer Life* (1999), and *American Sermons: The Pilgrims to Martin Luther King* (1999). He is also the author of *The Letters of the Republic: Publication and the Public Sphere in Eighteenth-Century America* (1990) and the editor of *Fear of a Queer Planet: Queer Politics and Social Theory* (1993). His essays and journalism have appeared in *The Village Voice, VLS, The Nation, The Advocate, POZ,* and *In These Times.*

INDEX

Abortion, 19, 30, 110, 117–21, 337–72

Abortion Control Act, 352

Abu-Odeh, Lama, 415

Ackerman, Bruce, 180

Action, 105, 138. *See also* Politics

ACT-UP, 10

Adoption: gay and lesbian, 13–15, 236, 242, 246; law, 13–14. *See also* Kinship; Parenting

Adultery, 114

Affirmative action, 3, 16, 27, 29–30, 45–49, 207. *See also* Discrimination, race

Agacinski, Sylviane, 239–40, 244–46, 251, 255

Akron v. Akron Center for Reproductive Health, 356

Allott, Philip, 402

American Civil Liberties Union, 180

American Medical Association, 120

American Philosophical Association, 420

Americans with Disabilities Act, 146

Amnesty International, 396

Anghie, Antony, 415

Antidiscrimination, 139–51. *See also* Discrimination

Antipornography, 86–87, 124. *See also* Pornography

Appiah, Anthony, 67

Assimilation: discourse of 40–42, 50–52. *See also* Integration

Atheism, 191. *See also* God

Austin, Regina, 57–60

Autonomy, 357

Baehr v. Lewin, 260, 262, 266, 268, 279, 285

Baker, Jack, 263–64

Bakke, 45–49, 205

Bakke, Alan, 9, 45

Baudrillard, Jean, 406

Bawer, Bruce, 266

Benito, Elizabeth Odio, 319

Benjamin, Jessica, 100

Bentham, Jeremy, 191

Berlant, Lauren, 18, 34, 301

Beverly Hills Cop, 51

Bhabha, Homi, 406

Bid Whist and Tonk, 49–50

Bilingualism, 54

Biopower, 11

Biotechnology, 251

Birth control, 114

Black, Hugo, 116, 203

Blackmun, Harry A., 118, 354, 356

Blackstone, Sir William, 191

Bloom, Alan, 142

Body, 94, 308, 320; integrity of, 338–41, 342–56, 361–64, 367; reduced to its reproductive function, 349–51, 361; sexual signification of, 293, 320

Bourdieu, Pierre, 406

Bowers v. Hardwick, 78–79 n.22, 119, 124, 428, 429

Brandeis, Louis, 198

Bratton, William, 41

Bridges of Madison County, The, 270

Brown, Wendy, 30, 34, 126–27, 308

Burger Court, 205

Burke, Edmund (Burkean conservatives), 138, 141, 143, 153, 154

Bush, George, Sr., 380, 381

Butler, Judith, 28, 35, 308, 339, 359

Buxton, Lee, 114

Califia, Pat, 97

Capitalism, 7, 105–6, 125, 136, 151, 181–82, 275

Card, Claudia, 273–74, 281

Carter, Jimmy, 380, 384, 399

Carty, Tony, 402

Censorship, 22

Cesic, Ranko, 314

Chambers, Crystal, 57–60

Chambers, David, 282–83

Chambers v. Omaha Girls Club, 57–60

"Chicago School," 137

Children: and kinship, 236–37; and the transmission of culture, 237, 238, 248–49

Citizenship, 107–9, 110, 113, 119, 218

Civil rights, 8, 10, 41, 163; movement, 8, 43, 75, 205

Civil Rights Act, 38, 62, 65, 140

Civil Rights Initiative (1998), 9

Clare, John, 270

Class, 7, 40; -based politics, 181

Clastres, Pierre, 248

Cleaver, Eldridge, 181

Clinton, Bill, 183, 259, 261, 262, 375, 376, 377, 380, 384, 394, 399, 404

Collective bargaining, 9

Colonization, 10

"Columbia School," 377, 381

Communist Party, 203

Connerly, Ward, 9

Consciousness, 105, 106

Consciousness raising, 84

Consumer market, 12

Copelon, Rhonda, 318

Corbett, Ken, 253

Cornell, Drucilla, 30, 34, 41, 180, 421

Cosmopolitanism, 16, 389, 392

Cover, Robert, 50

Cox, Barbara, 268, 269, 271, 275, 284

Creed, Gerald, 297

Crenshaw, Kimberlé, 61, 426

Critical legal studies, 178–227, 401, 405, 409

Critical race theory, 184, 407

Critique, 25–33, 75, 178–79, 216–23, 233–35, 386–88, 391, 404–7; as affirmative practice, 28; and community, 31; and crisis, 25; and Enlightenment, 25; and genealogy, 26; immanent, 26, 222; and loss of faith, 193–94; as negative practice, 25, 222; and the political, 234; and politics, 3, 4, 28–33, 235, 386; and reconstruction, 212–13, 220–21, 388, 401; and the "relief effect," 28–29, 31, 32; of subject, 2. *See also* Left Critique

Cultural preservation, 14–16

Cultural reproduction, 247–50

Culture: heteronormitivity of, 244, 248,

250; racial, 40–41, 49–52, 56–60, 65–68; and identity, 70–74; women's, 87–89, 93
Cynicism, 111, 112

Danielsen, Dan, 415
de Beauvoir, Simone, 360
Deconstruction, 26
Defense of Marriage Act, 29, 259, 262, 281
Delic, Hazim, 214
Department of Youth Services, 13, 14
Derrida, Jacques, 26, 180, 402, 420
Desire, 232, 237–38
Difference: cultural, 41, 52; and disability, 156; politics of, 38–76, 358; preservation of, 44–45; racial, 41, 42; relational versus sexual, 361; sexual, 339, 340, 348, 349, 352–61, 362, 367–68, 421
Disability: and education, 18, 134–77
Discrimination, 64–65, 72–75; heterosexual assumption of sex, 101; race, 9, 16–17, 38–44, 45, 53–55, 57–60, 74–75, 180; sex, 80–103, 424, 426; state's role in combating, 137. *See also* Antidiscrimination
Douglas, William O., 115, 116, 198, 203, 357, 358
Du Bois, W. E. B., 43
Dworkin, Andrea, 86–87
Dworkin, Ronald, 180, 341

Economics, 381
Education: and disability, 18, 134–77; special, 134–77
Educational Testing Service, 65
Eisenstadt v. Baird, 118
Elliston, Deborah, 296, 300
Elshtain, Jean Bethke, 260
Engels, Friedrich, 243
Engle, Karen, 415

Enlightenment, the, 25, 26, 85, 141, 271
Epstein, Richard, 140
Equal Employment Opportunity Commission (EEOC), 142, 144
Equal protection, 182
Equal Rights Amendment, 195, 207
Equality, 352–61, 362; formal versus substantive, 6, 107; liberal defense of, 6
Eskridge, William, 276
Essentialism, 39–40
Ethnic studies, 47
Ettelbrick, Paula, 261

False consciousness, 66, 272
Family and Medical Leave Act of 1993, 282
Fassin, Eric, 238, 250
Feminine, the, 348, 359–61, 367. *See also* Difference, sexual
Feminism, 20–23, 81–93, 124, 184, 407; cultural, 87–93; debates within, 207–8; nineteenth-century French, 431; and pornography, 20–23; second-wave, 20, 23; and sexual subordination, 81, 82–93, 101–2; socialist, 81; structural, 82–87, 90–93
Ferrill v. The Parker Group, 40–41
Firestone, Shulamith, 181
Flagg, Barbara, 41, 54–55
Fletcher, George, 348–49
Flynt, Larry, 22
Food and Drug Administration, 10
Ford, Richard T., 17, 18, 31, 34, 35
Foucault, Michel, 11, 13, 26, 34, 293, 307–9, 320, 402, 422
Fox, George, 270
Frank, Barney, 259
Franke, Katherine, 30, 34, 35
Frankenberg, Gunther, 402
Frankfurt School, 25, 26
Franklin, Sarah, 247, 250–51
Freedom Summer, 8

Freedom, 113; libertarian defense of, 6; negative, 345; reproductive, 425
Freud, Sigmund, 111, 245, 246, 342
Fugitive Slave Law, 208

Gabel, Peter, 183
Gandhi, Mahatma, 182
Gates, Henry Louis, 424
"Gay gene," 24
Geduldig v. Aiello, 358, 359, 360
Geertz, Clifford, 247
Gender, 82–84, 90; performance of, 95–96
Geneva Convention of 1949, 310, 311
German idealism, 26
Gilligan, Carol, 180
Ginsburg, Ruth Bader, 273
Gluck, Robert, 271
God, 76, 218, 221; loss of faith in, 35, 191–93
Goldberg, Arthur J., 114, 116
Goldstein, Richard, 303, 306
Gotanda, Neil, 422
Gramsci, Antonio, 217
Griggs v. Duke Power Co., 141, 142, 144
Griswold v. Connecticut, 113–18, 120, 121, 127, 357
Griswold, Esther, 114
Guiliani, Rudolf, 303

Habermas, Jürgen, 180
Halley, Janet, 29, 31, 35, 78–79 n.22, 426, 429
Hammarskjold, Dag, 379, 380
Hand, Learned, 116, 201, 202
Harambasic, Fikret, 312
Harlan, John M., 114, 116
Harris, Cheryl, 422
Hart, Henry, 204
Hartman, Saidiya, 230
Hate speech, 3, 19, 23, 124, 423, 424
Hawthorne, Nathaniel, 269

Hegel, G. W. F., 25, 223
Heidegger, Martin, 25
Helms, Jesse, 260, 381
Herdt, Gilbert, 294–302, 306
Hill, Anita, 56–57
Hill, Christopher, 270
Hitler, Adolf, 223
Hohfeld, Wesley, 198, 201, 202
Hollywood, 110
Holmes, Oliver Wendell, 191, 201, 202
Hom, Sharon, 366, 368
Homophobia, 81, 92, 236, 260, 261, 262, 285
Homosexuality: ritualized, 293, 295; versus homoeroticism, 91–92, 296; versus homosociality, 300–301. *See also* Homosociality
Homosexual panic, 81, 94, 96, 98–99
Homosociality, 298, 325 n.52. *See also* Homosexuality
Hua, Cai, 92, 230
Human Rights Campaign, 231, 266
Humanism, 42, 43
Hyde, Henry, 259, 260

Identity, 7, 46, 53, 49, 64, 105, 122–23, 188, 214, 343; politics, 107, 126–28, 181–82, 207–8; sexual, 78–79 n.22, 295–98, 429
Ideology, 127
Immigration, 247
Individualism, 5, 39, 59; critique of, 342
Individualized Educational Plan (IEP), 134, 158
Individuals with Disabilities Education Act (IDEA), 134–35, 157–61
Individuation, 342–56, 361–64
Injury, 2, 19, 86, 90
Integration, 40–42, 52. *See also* Assimilation
International Criminal Tribunal for the Former Yugoslavia, 293, 310–20

International law, 31, 373–419
Irigaray, Luce, 369 n.4

Jencks, Christopher, 153
John Paul II, Pope, 260
Johnson, Alex, 49, 50
Johnson, Lyndon B., 8, 380
Justice, 13, 17, 27; distributive, 3, 8; for-
   mal versus substantive, 266; and left cri-
   tique, 6; liberal formulations of, 5;
   racial, 8, 41, 75–76

Kant, Immanuel, 25, 26, 339, 344
Kelman, Mark, 18, 34
Kennedy, Anthony, 352, 356
Kennedy, David, 31, 34, 35
Kennedy, Duncan, 9, 34, 35, 415
Kennedy, John F., 377, 379, 380
King, Martin Luther, Jr., 8, 182
King, Rodney, 303
Kinsey, Alfred, 297, 306
Kinship, 229–30; gay, 13–15, 229–58;
   Lévi-Strauss on, 252; and the reproduc-
   tion of culture, 244–52; the state in,
   231. See also Adoption; Parenting
Klein, Melanie, 254
Knight Initiative, 29
Koskenniemi, Martii, 402, 415

Labor: politics of, 9; child, 109, 110, 128
   n.2; women's, 148–49
Lacan, Jacques, 244, 245, 254, 342–46, 406
Lambda Legal Defense and Education
   Fund, 260, 266
Larson, Nella, 301
Lasalle, Ferdinand, 215
Law, 1, 3, 6–8, 11, 13–16, 19, 24, 68–70,
   366; antidiscrimination, 428; and culture, 13; and desire, 123; and discretionary standards, 14; and employment
   discrimination, 139; feminist, 86, 89,
   423–24; as instrument, 9, 24; limita-

tions of, 19–20, 75, 127; nihilism of,
   and pain, 124, 209; redemptive notion
   of, 107; reform, 1, 4, 15; and utopia,
   121. See also Legalism
Lawrence, Charles R., III, 424
Lazarus, M. Edgeworth, 270
Left critique, 4, 5–7. See also Critique
Left Hegelianism: Marx's critique of, 4–5,
   7–11, 23, 27
Left legalism, 4–5, 7–11, 23. See also
   Legalism
Left multiculturalism, 10, 136, 137, 147–
   52, 156–61. See also Multiculturalism
Legal Defense Fund, 180
Legalism, 1–37, 159–60; and critique, 19;
   and disability, 160; governance, 10, 21;
   invisibility of, 11–12; liberal, 4–11, 17–
   18, 201–4, 217; and normalization,
   13–14, 17; and politics, 19–25; regula-
   tory capacities of, 11–16. See also Left
   legalism; Law
Legal realism, 19, 63–65, 199–202, 205,
   209
Legal reasoning, 194–99; loss of faith in,
   191–94
Legal Services Corporation, 180
Lester, Gillian, 18, 34
Lévi-Strauss, Claude, 230, 244–55
Liberalism, 5–7, 9, 186, 194, 215–16,
   220, 420–21, 430, 431; Marxist and
   neo-Marxist critique of, 423
Lincoln, Abraham, 91
Litela, Emily, 217
Lobel, Kerry, 266, 267, 274, 275
Lorde, Audre, 52
Louima, Abner, 292, 301, 302–7, 320–21
Loving v. Virginia, 42

Mackey, Nathaniel, 230
MacKinnon, Catharine, 22, 23, 81, 82–
   87, 88–93, 101, 120, 273, 422
Malcolm X, 38, 39

March on Washington: 1964, 8; 1987, 261; 1993, 269

Marcuse, Herbert, 183

Marriage, 17, 229–31, 232–38, 260, 268, 270, 277, 284; common-law, 284–85; entitlements, 240, 279–83; as legitimated public sex, 237; and normalization, 267, 286; as a mode of state regulation, 232, 267; regulation of, 17; and the rhetoric of privacy, 269; same-sex, 17, 229–68, 258–89; and sexuality, 232–33; the state in, 231. *See also* Kinship

Marx, Karl, 25, 26, 27, 81, 183, 184, 189, 214–16, 217, 219, 223, 420, 432

Marxism, 219, 220

Masculinity, 90

Masculinization, 294–95

Matsuda, Mari, 121, 424

McCarthyism, 203, 278

McKinnon, Susan, 250–51

Meagan's Law, 305

Melancholy, 129 n.5

Michelman, Frank, 180

Minow, Frank, 180

Minow, Martha, 180

Miranda rights, 195

Misrecognition, 53, 55. *See also* Recognition

Mohr, Richard, 284

Montgomery bus boycott, 8

Moten, Fred, 230

Mourning, 106–7, 127, 129 n.5

Moynihan Report, 51

Murphy, Eddie, 51

Multiculturalism, 44–49. *See also* Left multiculturalism

NAACP v. Alabama, 115

Nathanson, Bernard, 109

National Abortion Rights Action League (NARAL), 109–10

National Coalition of Gay Organizations, 265

National Gay and Lesbian Task Force, 266

Nationalism, 31, 109, 238–52; versus cosmopolitanism, 377

National Labor Relations Act, 9

National Lawyers Guild, 180

New Approaches to International Law (NAIL), 35, 397–419

New Deal, 202

New Left, 181

Nietzsche, Freidrich, 26, 120, 126, 223

Nihilism, 220, 221–23; of law, 209

1960s, 181–83

O'Connor, Sandra Day, 117, 121, 352, 356, 363

Oedipal complex, 245–48, 253–54

Olsen, Frances, 183

Oncale v. Sundowner Offshore Services, Inc., 80, 82, 90–99, 425

Oncale, Joseph, 90, 91, 93–98

Ortiz, Ana, 307

Pacts of Civil Solidarity (PACS), 236, 238, 243, 251, 262, 281, 287

Pain, 105–12; as ideology, 127; presumed objectivity of, 111; subject of, 122–28; women's, 117

Paradox: politics of, 430–32; rights as, 422–27, 430–32

Parenting, 13–15; and cultural transmission, 238; gay, 13–15, 238–44. *See also* Adoption; Kinship

Passing, 301

Patterson, Orlando, 56–57

Pennsylvania Abortion Control Act, 118

Perea, Juan, 41, 53–54, 65–67

Perry, Reverend Troy, 263

Perspectivism, 84–86, 122

Pierce, Charles, 346

Planned Parenthood of Southeastern

Pennsylvania v. Casey, 105, 117, 118, 121, 351–52

Plato, 36 n.8

Plaza, Monique, 308

Pleasure, 32–33

Pluralism: cultural, 207–8

Police brutality, 302–7

Politics, 19–25, 121–28, 223, 235–36, 255, 266–67; and critique, 4, 28–33, 235, 386; feminist, 20–23; and the intellectual, 33

Poovey, Mary, 361

Pornography, 20–21, 23, 423. *See also* Antipornography

Posner, Richard, 273, 279, 363

Postcolonial theory, 407, 420

Postmodernism, 2, 178, 218–21, 223–24

Poststructuralism, 7

Powell v. Alabama, 202

Powell, Lewis F., 45, 46

Power, 298, 300–302, 305–7, 321

Pregnancy, 350, 362

Privacy, 22, 112–21, 338, 345, 352–61, 362, 428; marital, 114–17

Progress, 392–93

Psychoanalysis, 245–46, 252–54, 342–46

Public education, 154–57

Public: versus private, 64. *See also* Privacy; Publicity

Publicity, 64, 118

Queer theory, 35, 82, 93–103, 286–88, 407

Racism, 16–17, 29, 38–79, 124, 153, 180, 302–7, 426–27. *See also* Discrimination, race

Radin, Margaret, 180

Ramica, Suada, 320, 321

Rape, 83–86, 88, 308–9. *See also* Sexual violence

Rauch, Jonathan, 266, 275

Rawls, John, 180

Reagan, Ronald, 183, 377, 380, 381, 384, 399

Reason, 220, 214, 223

Recognition, 239–43; politics of, 52–60, 64

Redistribution, 8, 137–39; and antidiscrimination, 139, 145, 163

Rehnquist, William H., 358

Rehnquist Court, 205

Renee Rogers, et al. v. American Airlines, Inc., 38–41

"Repressive tolerance, 183

Rights, 6, 9, 61–62, 86, 179–81, 184–90, 196–99, 202, 210–12, 216–18, 353, 421, 423, 428–29; abortion, 366; balancing claims of, 199–202, 207; civil, 8, 10, 41, 163; critique of, 178–227, 420–34; cultural, 41, 53–55, 60–70; cynicism of, 190; and disability, 160; of the fetus, 110; as a form of state power, 61–65; formal and substantive, 18; Foucault's critique of, 422–23; and identity, 188, 422–23; in projects of ideological intelligentsia, 188–91; and left legalism, 7; loss of faith in, 184, 194, 197, 213, 216–18; marriage, 230; Marxist critique of, 183, 189, 215–16, 423; natural, 186; paradoxes of, 9, 422–27; postmodernist critique of, 218–20; and the production of subjectivity, 18; reproductive, 341; as social control, 61; voting, 8; for women, 368, 420, 424–25, 432

Roe v. Wade, 117–21, 350, 352, 353, 354, 355, 356, 357, 361, 364

Rogers, Renee, 39, 49

Roosevelt Court, 205

Rorty, Richard, 180

Rose, Jacqueline, 243, 254

Rotello, Gabriel, 266, 276, 279

Rousseau, Jean-Jacques, 430

Ruscha, Ed, 42

Scalia, Antonin, 80, 92, 97, 101, 118, 119

Scarry, Elaine, 124, 129 n.8, 346–47

Schneider, David, 230, 247, 249

Schultz, Vicki, 82–87

Scott, Joan Wallach, 431

Sedgwick, Eve Kosofsky, 298, 300, 325 n.52

Segal, Hanna, 254

Segregation, 9

Sellers, Patricia, 313

Sen, Amartya, 365

Sentimentality: and subaltern pain, 107; politics of, 107–9, 111–12

Separatism, 10–11, 43

Sex, 82–84, 88; as a technology of sexism, 91; in the service of power, 293

Sex crime, 303–7

Sex harassment, 3, 20, 23–24, 29, 80–103; as discrimination, 424, 426; same-sex, 80–103, 425

Sex Offender Registration Act, 305

Sexuality, 21, 22, 81–90, 91, 92, 96–97; versus eroticism, 91; as a form of power, 82–87; hybridity of, 234; regulation of, 112–13

Sexual liberation, 3

Sexual violence, 307–20

Siegal, Reva, 359

Signorile, Michelangelo, 266

Snyder, Fred, 403, 404

Socrates, 36–37 n.8

Sodomy, 78–79 n.22, 429

Souter, David H., 352, 356

Spivak, Gayatri, 114, 406, 420–21

Spong, Bishop John Shelby, 277

Stacey, Judith, 247

Stack, Carol, 230, 247

Stalinism, 183, 203, 205, 223

Stare decisis, 117, 119, 206

State, the, 6, 7, 231, 242; and legitimation, 232, 235, 242–43; men's interests expressed in, 85; as micropower, 13; and

normalization, 14, 231; versus private action, 65; and the production of subjectivity, 7; as site of religious desire, 238

Stoddard, Tom, 261, 266, 267

Stoller, Robert J., 299

Stonewall, 35, 263, 264, 265

Strathern, Marilyn, 247

Structuralism, 245–48, 250

Student Nonviolent Coordinating Committee (SNCC), 8

Subjectivity, 7; production of, 427–29; utopian/traumatized, 111, 124, 127

Suffering, 2, 32–33, 156

Sullivan, Andrew, 266, 277, 279

Tarullo, Dan, 402

Taylor, Charles, 52, 60

Thatcher, Margaret, 377, 380

Thomas, Clarence: sexual harassment hearings, 56–57

Thomas, Kendall, 124–25

Thompson, Judith Jarvis, 348, 349

Thoreau, Henry David, 63

Titanic, 270, 271

Title VII, 39, 41, 49, 54, 65, 80, 98, 140, 143

Torture, 309–20, 346–47. *See also* Sexual violence; Violence

Trans-Nationale, The, 106

Trauma: politics of, 110–12, 121–26

Tushnet, Mark, 183

Tyson, Cicely, 38

United Nations, 379, 396

U.S. Congress, 8, 62, 154, 185, 262

U.S. Constitution, 38, 183, 186, 187, 189, 203, 209, 286; Bill of Rights, 116; Eighth Amendment, 125; Fifth Amendment, 115; First Amendment, 62, 115, 186, 187, 193, 353, 354, 423; First

Amendment doctrine, 202, 203; Fourteenth Amendment, 45, 114, 115, 186, 206; Fourth Amendment, 115; Ninth Amendment, 115; Thirteenth Amendment, 38
U.S. House of Representatives, 259
U.S. Supreme Court, 17, 42, 80, 92, 186, 202, 205, 206, 358
U.S. v. Carolene Products, 202

Vietnam War, 377, 379
Violence: desexualization of, 307–9. *See also* Sexual violence
Volpe, Justin, 303, 305

Wah, Tatiana, 307
Wallerstein, Immanuel, 49
Warner, Michael, 17, 35, 241
Warren, Earl, 193

Webster v. Reproductive Health Services, 351, 356
Wechsler, Herbert, 203, 204
West, Cornel, 181
West, Robin, 123, 293
Weston, Kath, 230, 247
Will to knowledge, 30
Will to power, 15, 393–94, 400
Williams, Patricia, 61, 117, 180, 421
Wilson, Woodrow, 388
Wizard of Oz, The, 113
Wolfson, Evan, 260, 261, 267, 268, 271, 272, 273, 274, 275, 284
Women's movement. *See* Feminism

"Yale School," 377
Yanagisako, Sylvia, 247

Zoning and Planning Commission, 87

Wendy Brown is Professor of Political Science and Women's
Studies at the University of California, Berkeley.

Janet Halley is Professor of Law at Harvard University.

Library of Congress Cataloging-in-Publication Data
Left legalism/left critique / edited by Wendy Brown and Janet Halley.
p. cm.   Includes index.
ISBN 0-8223-2975-1 (cloth : alk. paper)
ISBN 0-8223-2968-9 (pbk. : alk. paper)
1. Law — United States — Philosophy. 2. New Left — United States.
3. Critical legal studies. I. Brown, Wendy. II. Halley, Janet E.
KF380 .L44 2002   340.1 — dc21   2002006794